The Transformation
of Wall Street

By Joel Seligman

The
Transformation
of Wall Street

A History of the
Securities and Exchange Commission
and Modern Corporate Finance

by Joel Seligman

HOUGHTON MIFFLIN COMPANY · BOSTON

1982

Library of Congress Cataloging in Publication Data

Seligman, Joel.
    The transformation of Wall Street.

    Includes bibliographical references and index.
    1. United States. Securities and Exchange Commission
— History. 2. Corporations — United States — Finance —
History. I. Title.
HG4910.S4   353.0082'58'06   82-2901
ISBN 0-395-31329-5   AACR2

Printed in the United States of America

V 10 9 8 7 6 5 4 3 2 1

*For Harvey J. Goldschmid
and for Mary*

Government regulatory agencies are often referred to as "independent" agencies, but this cannot be taken at face value by anyone who has ever had any experience in Washington. In fact, government regulatory agencies are stepchildren whose custody is contested by both Congress and the Executive, but without much affection from either one . . . Without the cooperation of both Congress and the Executive, little constructive can be achieved. To reemphasize the point, an agency is literally helpless if either branch is uninterested or unwilling to lend support.

— WILLIAM CARY

Contents

Preface and Acknowledgments

THIS IS A HISTORY of the Securities and Exchange Commission and its relationship to corporate finance covering the period from the 1929–1932 stock market crash, which led to the agency's creation in 1934, to the end of the Nixon-Ford presidential administration early in 1977. Certain issues, such as the SEC's efforts to facilitate the establishment of a national securities market system, have been updated to the spring of 1981. A few recent developments, including the initiation of securities options markets, the municipal bond disclosure debate, and efforts to improve financial auditing, are not treated in this history. Insufficient time has passed for a historical analysis of these developments. Although I have attempted to write a comprehensive history of the leading developments in securities regulation during the 1929–1977 period, I was not unmindful of the existing literature. Because securities fraud litigation, the corporate disclosure process, and exemptions from the securities law have received extensive treatment in the technical literature (see, for example, Louis Loss, *Securities Regulation*), they are discussed less extensively in this book than they otherwise would have been. Similarly, certain recent events like the corporate questionable payment cases, the bankruptcy of the Penn Central Railroad, and the "big" fraud cases of the late 1960s and early 1970s have been so well described in both the technical and the popular literature that I chose not to emphasize them in this work. By contrast, issues concerning the structure of the securities markets have received relatively less attention in both the technical and popular literature. These issues are emphasized in the concluding chapters of this history.

During the last half-century, this nation's system of corporate finance has been fundamentally transformed. Long gone are the days when new securities sales were dominated by private investment banks, such as J. P. Morgan and Company, when references to "bear raids" or stock market "pools" daily appeared in the nation's press, when the New York Stock Exchange fairly could be described as a "private club," when Senate hearings riveted the nation's attention with revelations of fraudulent Peruvian bond sales, "preferred" stockholder lists, bribed journalists who "touted" securities, or stock price manipulation. Gone too are the public utility holding companies, the least justifiable corporate structure to evolve during the 1920s' "bull" market, "blank" corporate proxies, and the time when securities fraud usually was irremediable because of the deficiencies of state corporate law. In the past decade, fixed minimum commission rates, a way of life on the New York Stock Exchange since 1792, have been abolished. Efforts today are under way to supplant, partially or fully, the hardwood floors of this nation's securities exchanges with an electronically linked national securities market system.

The principal actor in this transformation of corporate finance has been the Securities and Exchange Commission. During and immediately after the New Deal period, the SEC earned the reputation as one of the most ably administered federal regulatory agencies, principally because of the competence of the Commission's staff, the agency's role in restoring confidence in the safety of securities investment in the 1935–1937 period, the SEC's 1937–1938 reorganization of the New York Stock Exchange's governance, and the Commission's enforcement of the geographic integration and corporate simplification provisions of the Public Utility Holding Company Act.

The SEC's performance after World War II, by contrast, has been frequently criticized. Although the quality of the Commission's staff and its enforcement and corporate disclosure programs generally continued to receive high marks, the SEC's caution in challenging the New York Stock Exchange's fixed commission rates and anticompetitive rules early in the 1970s was severely criticized by Congress, the Justice Department, and independent commentators. Throughout the decade, the SEC similarly was criticized for the slow pace with which it facilitated the creation of a competitive national market system and its oversight of accounting-standard-setting and corporate governance.

In writing a history of the Securities and Exchange Commission, I have sought to explain the determinants of Commission policy, both during the SEC's highly regarded New Deal period and during the post—World War II period, when the quality of the agency's performance was more erratic. A primary purpose of "independent" regulatory agencies like the SEC is to allow an experienced and expert staff to resolve specific, highly technical regulatory problems. Throughout much of the Commission's history, the value of its staff's expertise has been limited by the mediocrity of presidential Commission appointments and inadequate budgets. The performance of the SEC also has been influenced by other more subtle political factors. Many of the SEC's most highly criticized recent decisions concerning commission rates, the structure of the securities markets, and mutual fund sales practices may, in part, be traced to the agency's failure to apply the theory of economic competition implicit in the federal antitrust laws to the securities industry, or to articulate a persuasive alternative economic theory. Other recent decisions of the SEC, notably those concerning accounting-standard-setting and corporate governance, seem to have been influenced by the breadth of the SEC's mandate. Like all other political actors, the SEC has had to select programs to emphasize. In part, because of the vagueness of the relevant enabling statutes, accounting-standard-setting and corporate governance consistently have been relegated to the bottom of the SEC's list of priorities. Moreover, even among those programs that the SEC has chosen to concentrate on, historical analysis can illuminate the interconnectedness of decisions in a manner that more narrowly focused analyses often do not. An accurate appreciation of how decisions at an agency such as the SEC are made must take into account a constellation of political considerations. One must study not only the agency's enabling statutes, but also the policy preferences of its leadership, its relations with the White House, Congress, other federal agencies, and affected industries, as well as its immediate priorities, the competence and determination of the staff members concerned, and so on.

Few have suggested seriously that the SEC has been a "captive" of the industries it regulates. Quite simply, such a suggestion cannot be sustained by a reasonable reading of the Commission's history. A historical study of the politics of SEC-industry relations does make plain that the "capture" theory and its many variants, like the agency "life-stage" theory, are of relatively little use in explaining how any particular SEC decision actually was made. Such theories typically begin with the unarticulated premise that all firms and trade associations in an industry have identical aims. In fact, much of the power of an agency such as the SEC is derived from the divisions within the industries it regulates. Accurately perceived, the SEC did not directly "reorganize" the New York Stock Exchange in 1937–1938. The Commission enabled a reform faction within the Exchange to do so. The capture and kindred theories also tend to underestimate the political force of well-prepared agency studies, the idealism of agency staffs, the differences for an agency among proceeding by litigation, a rule, or legislation, and the political pressures on an agency exerted by Congress, other federal agencies, and the press. Only when agency decisions are studied in a broad political and historical context are the complexity, and the reality, of how an agency functions likely to be accurately perceived.

Besides providing a vehicle for the analysis of the prevailing rules that regulate corporate finance, a history of the SEC has a second utility. Somewhat fortuitously, Felix Frankfurter and James Landis, two of the individuals who helped draft the SEC's initial enabling statutes, were among the leading theorists of the administrative process during the New Deal. A study of their actions in helping establish the SEC is also a study of the theory of federal agencies in general. Today much thought is given to the desirability of "deregulation." It is an appropriate time to recall how the administrative agencies became a "fourth branch" of American government, what they were expected to accomplish, and how they functioned during a period when they were regarded by their proponents as a panacea.

By studying the theory of the administrative agencies and a case history of one influential commission, this book, I believe, suggests the extent to which both the New Deal's confidence in the regulatory agencies and the recent hostility to them was not wholly warranted. The routine work of the federal government and the solution of certain largely technical problems generally will continue to be administered by government agencies, because Congress, the Judiciary, and the states lack sufficient time, expertise, or jurisdiction to perform these functions equally well. But the way we view the appropriate functions of the agencies will change over time and may grow more sophisticated. The history of the SEC, for example, well illustrates that certain regulatory problems, such as the restructuring of the public utility holding company industry, were better addressed by a significant one-time agency action than through ongoing administrative regulation. The history also illustrates the frequently inadequate role that the White House and Congress have played in overseeing the administrative agencies. Too often appointments of SEC commissioners have been made by the President as a form of political reward, with little regard for competence of the appointees to perform the job, and have been whisked through Senate confirmation hearings. For sustained periods, Congress has ignored serious problems in the securities or accounting profession that the SEC handled poorly. At the same time, the SEC frequently has experienced great difficulties in re-examining long-standing policies or changing policy directions. As the debate concerning federal regulation evolves, concern is increasingly likely to shift from the general question of whether deregulation is wise or unwise to a more specific concern. Given the perceived necessity of particular federal agencies, how can these agencies be administered most efficiently? Ultimately the appropriate inquiry is not whether federal regulation as a general matter is a good or bad thing, but, rather, how those federal agencies perceived as necessary can be structured to work most effectively.

* * *

I wish to express my gratitude to the Securities and Exchange Commission, during the chairmanship of Harold Williams, for giving me unrestricted access to the *SEC Minutes* during the period 1934–1969 and to some four hundred containers and volumes of papers assembled by SEC chairmen who served between 1934 and 1969. By studying the commissioner and staff correspondence and memoranda in these files, I was aided in understanding the process by which SEC decisions were made during the SEC's first thirty-five years. I also am grateful to the Williams Commission for allowing me access to several specific categories of documents from the 1969–1977 period. At all times, Chairman Williams and his fellow commissioners, Philip Loomis, John Evans, Irving Pollack, Roberta Karmel, and Stephen Friedman, treated the claims of history with sympathy and consideration. A similar spirit of consideration was exhibited by the Commission's General Counsel, Ralph Ferrara, his associate, Theodore Bloch, Division of Corporation Finance Chief Counsel Jeffrey Steele, Office of Chief Accountant Chief Counsel Linda Griggs, and Office of Public Affairs Director Andrew Rothman. I owe a special debt of gratitude to the SEC's Secretary, George Fitzsimmons, his associate, Shirley Hollis, and the Administrator of SEC Records, Nathan Harrison, for their many considerations in facilitating my use of Commission documents.

I also studied several other collections of unpublished papers. Specifically, I wish to acknowledge my gratitude to those who permitted me to use the Franklin Delano Roosevelt Papers, Hyde Park, New York; the Carter Glass Papers, the University of Virginia; the Felix Frankfurter Papers, Harvard Law School and the Library of Congress; the James Landis Papers, Harvard Law School and the

Library of Congress; the Huston Thompson Papers, Library of Congress; the William O. Douglas Papers, the Library of Congress; the Jerome Frank Papers, Yale University; Professor Louis Loss's Papers held at Harvard Law School; certain papers of SEC Chairman Edward Gadsby held by his family in Boston, Massachusetts; certain SEC-related papers in the John F. Kennedy Library in Boston, Massachusetts; and certain papers of SEC Chairman Manuel Cohen held by the law firm of Wilmer, Cutler & Pickering, Washington, D.C. I also am grateful to Columbia University's Oral History Collection for granting permission to quote material from "The Reminiscences of James M. Landis" (copyright 1975 by the Trustees of Columbia University in the City of New York), "The Reminiscences of Chester Lane" (copyright 1972), "The Reminiscences of Jerome Frank" (copyright 1975), and "The Reminiscences of James Warburg" (copyright 1980).

In preparing this history, I interviewed numerous past and present SEC officials. I would particularly like to express my gratitude to: J. Sinclair Armstrong, Andrew Barr, John Burton, William Cary, Milton Cohen, Donald Cook, Ralph Demmler, Meyer Eisenberg, John Evans, Lloyd Feller, Gene Finn, Arthur Fleischer, Abe Fortas, Roger Foster, Milton Freeman, Harry Heller, Edward Herlihy, Milton Katz, Leonard Leiman, Theodore Levine, Philip Loomis, Louis Loss, Barbara Lucas, Arthur Mathews, Robert Millonzi, Robert O'Brien, Ira Pearce, Irving Pollack, Sheldon Rappaport, David Ratner, Eugene Rotberg, Ralph Saul, David Silver, Richard Smith, A. A. Sommer, Stanley Sporkin, Raymond Vernon, Walter Werner, Francis Wheat, Jack Whitney, Harold Williams, and Byron Woodside.

I am thankful to those who criticized part or all of this manuscript: John Burton, William Cary, Milton Cohen, Ralph Demmler, John Evans, Gene Finn, Abe Fortas, Tamar Frankel, Harvey Goldschmid, Leonard Leiman, Theodore Levine, Aaron Levy, John Liftin, James Lorie, Louis Loss, Thomas McCraw, Arthur Mathews, Robert O'Brien, Hugh Owens, Irving Pollack, Sheldon Rappaport, David Ratner, Sidney Robbins, David Silver, A. A. Sommer, Stanley Sporkin, Raymond Vernon, Walter Werner, Francis Wheat, and Jack Whitney. Obviously none of these individuals is responsible for the contents of this book. But all furthered my understanding of the SEC's history, and for this they have my gratitude.

I wish to express my heartfelt gratitude to several associates and friends at Northeastern University Law School in Boston, Massachusetts. I especially am grateful to Dean Michael Meltsner for his invaluable aid in arranging for me to have the time and practical support to research and write this book. Both the law school and the Northeastern University Research and Scholarship Development Fund generously helped fund my research. Ms. Barbara Iredell, the law school's Executive Assistant, solved innumerable practical problems. My secretary, Corinne Lewis, was unflagging in her good spirits and moral support as the burden of typing this history and associated correspondence mounted. Corinne was aided in the typing of the final manuscript by several equally good-spirited souls, including Rita Laffey, Sheryl Lawrence, Dawn Soares, and Evelyn Wiley. Several students helped me research this book. I am particularly grateful to Diane Nigrosh, Jean Grumet, and Dan Becker. I also am grateful to the many Northeastern University Law School faculty members, administrators, and students who encouraged me during the four years I worked on the book. I feel very fortunate to have had their kind words and concern.

Finally, I wish to express my greatest gratitude to Ellen Joseph, my editor at Houghton Mifflin. From the time I wrote the initial outline of this book to the moment I completed the last word of the final draft, I was aided by Ellen's unstinting support, patience, and editorial judgment.

— JOEL SELIGMAN

The
Transformation
of Wall Street

1

After the Crash

As protection against financial illusion or insanity, memory is far better than law. When the memory of the 1929 disaster failed, law and regulation no longer sufficed. For protecting people from the cupidity of others and their own, history is highly utilitarian. It sustains memory and memory serves the same purpose as the SEC and, on the record, is far more effective.

— JOHN KENNETH GALBRAITH
The Great Crash

THE SECURITIES AND EXCHANGE COMMISSION was created at the conclusion of the Senate Banking and Currency Committee's 1932–1934 investigation of stock exchange practices, usually called the Pecora Hearings, in recognition of the decisive role played by the committee's counsel, Ferdinand Pecora.[1] Between September 1, 1929, and July 1, 1932, the value of all stocks listed on the New York Stock Exchange shrank from a total of nearly $90 billion to just under $16 billion — a loss of 83 percent. In a comparable period, bonds listed on the New York Stock Exchange declined from a value of $49 billion to $31 billion. "The annals of finance," the Senate Banking Committee would write, "present no counterpart to this enormous decline in security prices." Nor did these figures, staggering as they were, fully gauge the extent of the 1929–1932 stock market crash. During the post–World War I decade, approximately $50 billion of new securities were sold in the United States. Approximately half or $25 billion would prove near or totally valueless. Leading "blue chip" securities, including General Electric, Sears, Roebuck, and U.S. Steel common stock, would lose over 90 percent of their value between selected dates in 1929 and 1932.[2]

Formally, the purpose of Pecora's stock exchange hearings was to determine why these staggering decreases in security values had occurred and to propose legislation to prevent another stock market crash. The Pecora hearings also had an obvious political purpose. During the preceding twelve years, a majority of the country's voters had supported the laissez-faire economic policies suggested by Calvin Coolidge's often-quoted remark "This is a business country . . . and it wants a business government."

The revelations of the Pecora hearings were intended to diminish that faith in the nation's financial institutions. No other explanation can account for the attention lavished by Pecora on such matters as the salary levels and income tax returns of the financiers who appeared before him. Such data were virtually irrelevant to an investigation of the causes of the stock market crash. But in the political context in which the Senate Banking Committee functioned, such data seemed essential. In spite of the severity of the stock market crash, effective securities legislation might not have been enacted had Pecora's revelations not galvanized broad public support for direct federal regulation of the stock markets. President Roosevelt, personally, would attribute to the Pecora hearings a decisive role in making possible the legislation of the First Hundred Days of his administration. In retrospect, it is plain that the combination of the stock market crash and the Pecora hearings' revelations were instrumental in transforming national political sentiment from a laissez-faire ideology symbolized by the views of President Coolidge to a regulatory-reform ideology associated with Roosevelt's New Deal.

This political transition began nearly five years before the SEC was created. Throughout the first eight years of the 1920s, prices on the New York Stock Exchange had approximately doubled. This was an impressive increase, but not markedly out of line with corporate profits, which rose over 80 percent during the decade. It was only during the final year of the Coolidge administration that the market began to exhibit a manic quality. In an eighteen-month period, commencing in March 1928, the value of shares listed on the securities markets nearly doubled again.

In September 1929 the great bull market began to come undone. It was a crash unique in financial history. When the mania in overseas investments and joint stock companies crashed in London in 1720, it burst with a suddenness that forever afterward caused it to be known as the South Sea Bubble. The same had been true of the 1719 Mississippi Bubble in France, and the collapse of the Florida land boom in 1926. But matters were different in the stock markets in 1929. "When the crash finally came," financial historian John Brooks wrote almost lyrically, "it came with a kind of surrealistic slowness — so gradually that, on the one hand, it was possible to live through a good part of it without realizing that it was happening, and, on the other hand, it was possible to believe one had experienced and survived it when in fact it had no more than just begun."

The decline accelerated in October. Substantial losses occurred on Friday, October 18, Saturday, October 19, and Monday, October 21. The market advanced Tuesday, but on Wednesday, October 23, *The New York Times* Average lost a breathtaking eighteen points. In less than a week, the average surrendered thirty of its 291 points.

On October 24, a bankers' pool organized by J. P. Morgan and Company's Thomas Lamont purchased $20 to $30 million worth of securities to stabilize the market. But within a few days share prices again collapsed. Losses on Monday, October 28, far exceeded those previously recorded. The *Times* Average fell twenty-nine points; individual securities like General Electric lost as many as fifty points. This time bankers' support did not materialize. On Tuesday, the 29th, the *Times* Average fell another twenty-four points. In the eight weeks after Labor Day, the average fell 111 points (36 percent), nearly as much as it had gained in the preceding eighteen months. In all, the two-month loss on the New York Stock Exchange totaled $18 billion. And the price collapse had, in fact, just begun.[3]

From the White House Herbert Hoover anxiously regarded the 1929 crash. As early as 1925, Hoover had been concerned about "the growing tide of speculation." On a few occasions while he was Secretary of Commerce, Hoover had complained to President Coolidge about the Federal Reserve Board's "easy money policies."[4]

But at the time, Hoover did not care to press such views too firmly. Calvin Coolidge had achieved his substantial popularity not by criticizing the booming economy, but by identifying himself with it. Hoover campaigned for President in 1928 as the candidate who would sustain "Coolidge prosperity." Praising Coolidge for "introducing a new basis in government relation with business," Hoover maintained that for prosperity to last, "a continuation of the policies of the Republican Party is fundamentally necessary."[5] Once elected, Hoover symbolized his association with Coolidge's economic views by reappointing, as Secretary of the Treasury, Andrew Mellon, the Coolidge administration's most visible link to the business community.

And yet, Hoover's economic views were never as doctrinaire as those of Coolidge or Mellon. Denounce "bureaucraticizing of business" he might, but Hoover also insisted that the American economy "is no system of laissez faire."[6] To prevent credit inflation from jeopardizing industrial employment and farm prices, Hoover, in theory, endorsed limited federal intervention.

It was only in practice that he hesitated. Twice in February 1929 the Federal Reserve Board cautioned member banks against borrowing money "for the purpose of making speculative loans," statements that President-elect Hoover supported. Hoover was appalled when President Coolidge, just a few days before leaving office, had helped undermine the board's tentative efforts at "moral suasion" by assuring the country that stocks were "cheap at current prices."[7]

Two days after his March 4 inaugural, Hoover urged the Federal Reserve Board to reduce credit for speculative purposes.[8] The Federal Reserve Board began meeting daily in Washington. On March 23, the board held an unprecedented Saturday meeting, but still did not issue a policy statement. The following Monday, the market jolted sharply downward. By Tuesday, March 26, the Fed's silence alone seemed to be dampening the "speculative fever." Not only did prices again plummet, but a then-unprecedented eight million shares changed hands on the New York Stock Exchange.[9]

But the Fed's influence, moral or otherwise, was short-lived. On March 26, Charles E. Mitchell, chairman of the National City Bank, in flat defiance of the board's February warnings, announced that the National City Bank would borrow money from New York's Federal Reserve Bank to prevent liquidation of margin loans.[10]

The Federal Reserve Board and Hoover backed down. Throughout the summer of 1929, share prices soared by nearly 25 percent; brokers' loans increased at a rate of $400 million per month. Neither Hoover nor the board intervened.[11]

A similar ambivalence characterized Hoover's response to the October stock market crash. By then, Hoover feared an "inevitable collapse which will bring the greatest calamities upon our farmers, our workers, and legitimate business."[12] But Hoover's initial response was to join Charles E. Mitchell, Thomas Lamont, John D. Rockefeller, and other business leaders in reassuring the country. On October 25 Hoover informed the press, "The fundamental business of the country, that is, production and distribution, is on a sound and prosperous basis."[13] Beginning on November 21, Hoover assembled conferences of industrial leaders to urge "voluntary" action to maintain employment and wages.[14] In his *Memoirs*, Hoover would attribute his reluctance to propose direct action concerning the securities markets to a deep split among his advisers. Secretary of the Treasury Mellon and others advocated the traditional laissez-faire formula: let the slump liquidate itself. Even a panic was not, in Mellon's view, altogether a bad thing. "It will," Hoover recalled the Secretary explain, "purge the rottenness out of the system. High costs of living and high living will come down. People will work harder, live a more moral life. Values will be adjusted and enterprising people will pick up the wreck from less competent people."[15] What gave Mellon's argument particular force was Hoover's awareness that it reflected the intellectual belief of many Republicans. Hardhearted as Hoover may have found the Treasury Secretary's advice, he was well aware of the political risk of attacking the financiers who helped lead his party.

There were additional reasons for Hoover to urge volunteerism. For most of the next three years, he remained convinced that there was "doubtful constitutional authority . . . [for] Federal regulation of the sale of securities," and that, in any event, "the primary responsibility for initiation of official action lay on Governor Franklin Roosevelt of New York."[16]

The Democratic minority in Congress did not share Hoover's reluctance either to criticize the financial community or to propose regulation of the securities markets. Having seen the Republicans prevail in 1928 by claiming responsibility for "general prosperity," Democratic Party spokesmen claimed that the incumbent administration was equally responsible for the market collapse. On November 1, 1929, Senator Joseph T. Robinson, the Democrats' minority leader, issued a statement to the press:

> If the foundation of the belief of ruined investors was faith in the strong position of American industry, it is also true that the prophets and high priests of American prosperity, represented by no less personalities than a former President of the United States, the Secretary of the Treasury, and the former Secretary of Commerce, now President, contributed, by unduly and repeated optimistic statements, to the creation of enthusiastic, if not frenzied adventures in stocks.[17]

Within ten weeks of the October stock market crash, six members of Congress introduced bills to regulate corporate financial statements, margin loans, or short sales of securities.[18]

The Democratic Party's criticisms were soon muted. In December 1929 and the first four months of 1930, the stock market experienced a modest, though sustained, advance, recovering by April 1930 about one half of what had been lost in October and November of 1929.[19]

Hoover claimed that the "systematic, voluntary measures of co-operation with business" he instituted "have re-established confidence." At first, Hoover's tone was tentative. In his December 1929 State of the Union Address, he suggested that it might, nonetheless, be desirable for Congress to "consider the revision of some portions of the banking law."[20] But as "the Little Bull Market" galloped on, Hoover became more emphatic. In mid-February, he indicated to the press that the preliminary shock of the collapse had abated.[21] By March he was predicting that the worst effects of the crash on unemployment would be over within sixty days.[22] Addressing the United States Chamber of Commerce on May 1, Hoover engaged in what he termed "some moderate optimism," stating, "We are not through the difficulties of our situation [but] I am convinced we have passed the worst and with continued effort we shall rapidly recover."[23] On May 28 Hoover was reported to have said that he believed business conditions would be normal by fall.[24]

These were Hoover's most often quoted statements on the stock market crash and the economic depression. Not only did they give rise to the erroneous belief that he said, "Prosperity is just around the corner"; they tightened the public's association between Hoover's policies and responsibility for the economy's health.

In June 1930, the market began another long slide. The proximate cause was Hoover's signing of the Smoot-Hawley tariff bill, but the endurance of the decline, virtually unabated for the next twenty-five months, suggests that the impact of declining productivity was a more significant factor.[25]

This time the reaction of the Democrats in Congress was a serious threat to Hoover. Congressional elections were only four months away. The flurry of bills introduced were not just the hastily drawn creations of relatively obscure junior members.[26] Leading the critics was the senator whose voice mattered most on financial issues, Virginia's Carter Glass. A lifelong conservative, Glass generally opposed "centralized" federal power. But the senator's conservatism permitted one consistent exception. By the time of the crash, Senator Glass had built his career around the application of federal controls against the New York City "money crowd."

Soon after his election to the House of Representatives in 1902, Glass had been assigned to the Banking and Currency Committee. Although nearly totally ignorant of economics, Glass drove himself to master the subject by reading at night with such determination that he was eventually recognized as one of the leading congressional authorities in the field.

In 1913, President Wilson requested that Glass prepare legislation to reform the nation's banking system. Although Glass initially preferred a private, decentralized system of banks, he effectively lobbied for Wilson's conception of an independent Federal Reserve Board that could directly control currency and member banks. Thereafter, Glass took a proprietary interest in the Federal Reserve system he had "fathered." After briefly serving as Wilson's Secretary of the Treasury in 1919, Glass was appointed to the Senate in 1920. By 1927, he had grown so concerned about "stock market gamblers" borrowing money from reserve banks with which to speculate on securities, he began publicly advocating a tax of 5 percent on sales of stock held less than sixty days. The following year he charged that "the Federal Reserve system [was being] grossly misused." In one magazine article, Glass wrote that if the "country's resources" continue to be employed "in gambling in stocks and bonds, without regard to the need for money in legitimate industry . . . the people of the United States may find it necessary to overhaul the whole conduct of the Federal Reserve system . . ." With the roaring twenties nearing their apex, the crusty voice of Carter Glass was largely ignored. But in the spring of 1929, Glass modestly embarrassed the Hoover administration by charging that the Federal Reserve Board should have rebuked Charles E. Mitchell for defying the board when the banker announced that the National City Bank would lend investors margin money.[27]

The stock market crash restored Glass to a position of prominence on financial issues. Although he was neither chairman nor the ranking Democrat on the Senate Banking Committee, he was the committee's most influential member. In December 1929 Hoover had attempted to persuade Glass to join him in urging that a "joint commission" be established "to study our whole financial system." Glass refused, and Hoover acknowledged uneasiness at being opposed by "the dominant Senate voice on banking."[28]

In June 1930 Glass again attacked Republican financial policies. The assault was important not just because of the senator's reputation. Glass was the first national politician effectively to move beyond the vague charge that Hoover's excessive optimism had contributed to the crash to an enumeration of some of the causes of the debacle. Predictably, Glass introduced a banking bill "to prevent the undue diversion of funds into speculative operations."[29]

However, the senator's more publicized challenge concerned foreign bonds. Under President Harding, the State Department had adopted a procedure requiring American banks to clear loans to foreign countries with the department. The bankers soon found it to their advantage to do so. After receiving State Department clearance, the banks could advertise the department's approval when selling foreign bonds in the United States. On June 16, Glass secured Senate endorsement of a resolution requesting "the Secretary of State . . . to inform the Senate upon what authorization of law . . . does the State Department base its right either to approve or disapprove investment securities offered for sale in the money markets of the United States." Glass had known about the procedure for close to three years. But now, with newspapers regularly reporting foreign bonds near default, he firmly reiterated his protest "against another dangerous centralization of power in the Federal Government, and particularly against usurpation of a power with which the Executive Government is not legally clothed, and which, exercised without responsibility . . . may easily be frightfully prostituted in various ways."[30]

Secretary of State Henry L. Stimson attempted to mollify Glass by characterizing the procedure as an "informal scrutiny" permissible because of the "voluntary cooperation of American investment bankers" and the President's constitutional authority respecting foreign affairs.[31] Glass immediately labeled Stimson's contention that the State Department did not approve loans "an affront to the intelligence" of the Senate, and secured passage of a second resolution advising the department to "desist from the dangerous practice of involving the United States Government in any responsibility of whatever nature, either by approval or disapproval, for foreign investment loans floated in this country."[32]

As the 1930 congressional elections neared, Hoover felt a growing sense of exasperation. The market continued to fall; his earlier optimistic predictions about business conditions were being quoted by Democratic congressional candidates with devastating irony. Soon after the market declined in October 1930, the White House confirmed that President Hoover had entertained New York Stock Exchange president Richard Whitney at a "secret" dinner on October 12. According to the White House, the two had been consulting on methods to curb "bear raids" for some time.[33]

Hoover's belated effort "to do something" about the securities market had no appreciable effect on the 1930 election. For the first time since 1919, the Democrats won control of the House and came within one vote of controlling the Senate. By the time the Seventy-second Congress officially convened thirteen months later, in December 1931, Hoover's "voluntary" approach to the securities markets was no longer credible.

But the President continued to side with the faction within his administration that advocated Mellon's laissez-faire approach. Bitterly, Hoover would recall in his *Memoirs* his statement to Whitney "that I preferred to let American institutions and the states govern themselves, and that the Exchange had full power under its charter to control its own members and to prevent it from being used for manipulation against the public interest. Mr. Whitney made profuse promises, but did nothing."[34] In fact, the Exchange did call for daily reports on short sales* in May 1931 after a number of newspaper accounts "reported" that bear raiders were selling short to depress the market.[35] For a few days after the Bank of England suspended gold payments, in September 1931, the Exchange banned short sales altogether. But the ban was soon lifted.[36] And on October 16, 1931, in a nationally broadcast address from Hartford, Connecticut, Whitney insisted that short-selling was "essential to an open market for securities." "Every man" he said, "who has sold short is . . . a potential buyer of securities, and this is a source of great stability to a market, because experience shows that when prices suddenly decline the short sellers purchase stock in order to discharge their loans."[37]

Whitney's Hartford address fed a vengeful mood in Congress. In the first three days of the Seventy-second Congress alone, ten separate bills to regulate securities markets were introduced.[38] Most of these bills were intended to regulate short-selling. Senator Arthur Capper introduced two bills, one of which would have imposed a 25 percent tax on all short-sale profits, the second of which declared that "short sales . . . exert a vicious influence and produce abnormal and disturbing declines of prices that are not responsive to actual supply and demand."[39] Not to be outdone, Senator Smith W. Brookhart proposed a bill to imprison each investor who sold stock short.[40]

More significant to Hoover than the number of bills introduced was the growing impatience of the Republicans in Congress. Two months before the session convened, Senator James E. Watson, the

---

* Usually an investor purchases stock and later sells it, earning a profit if the sales price of the security exceeds the purchase price. A short sale reverses the chronology. The investor who believes the market price of a security will decline sells the stock first, borrows shares from a broker to deliver to the purchaser, and profits if the price of the share does, in fact, decline, by purchasing shares at a lower price to return to the lending broker.

Republican floor leader, publicly warned the President that a resolution to investigate the stock markets was all but certain to be adopted in the Senate.[41] Hoover made no public response. When Congress convened, the Progressive Republicans — acknowledged by Hoover to hold the balance of power in the Senate — led the clamor for securities law reform. Early in the session, Hiram Johnson sought approval for a Finance Committee investigation of foreign bonds. The aging Progressive was a long-time foe of both Herbert Hoover and international bankers,[42] but his determination personally to supervise an examination of "the terms and conditions" of all foreign debt securities sold in the United States was a striking illustration of the new political climate. Within a day the Senate approved Johnson's enabling resolution.[43] Hearings began on December 18.

For fifteen hearing days, Johnson led the Finance Committee's investigation. Told was a story he would later characterize as "at once grotesque and tragic."[44] Between 1923 and 1930 American investors had purchased close to $6.3 billion of foreign bonds.[45] (This equaled approximately 10 percent of new security sales in the United States during those years.)[46] Then, in rapid order, the collapse of the world economy had led to substantial depreciation in over 90 percent of all foreign bonds sold in the United States. By December 1931, the aggregate market price for fourteen Latin American nations' bonds was 26 percent of their face value. Peruvian bonds were selling at less than 7 percent of their par value.[47]

Johnson's hearing focused on the role of the American investment banks that distributed these securities. By the late 1920s, investment banks issuing foreign bonds were earning commissions as high as 14 percent.[48] These commission rates, unusually high for bonds, prompted an intense competition among the investment banks. Reversing the historic rule that the borrowing nation contact the underwriting house, by the late 1920s as many as twenty investment banks were sending representatives to a South American capital to solicit the opportunity to make a loan.[49] On occasion, the bankers' methods were less than scrupulous. The J. & W. Seligman* firm paid the son of the president of Peru $415,000 for his aid in securing for it the right to sell Peruvian bonds.[50] The Chase National Bank hired the Cuban president's son-in-law to manage its Havana office.[51] Virtually every witness questioned on the point agreed that such "commissions" were "quite customary . . . particularly in South American loans."[52]

* The author is not related to any member of the firm.

What particularly outraged Senator Johnson, as it had earlier galled Carter Glass, was the role of the United States government in foreign bond sales. In spite of Senator Glass's resolution, the State Department continued to clear foreign bonds. Pressed hard by Senators Johnson and Edward P. Costigan, Assistant Secretary of State Francis White conceded that the department's practice in many cases led the public to assume that "the security is ample and the investment is a good one," even though the department would not object to a loan if it knew the loan "was absolutely rotten."[53]

Early in February 1932, Andrew Mellon resigned as Secretary of the Treasury and left for London to become Ambassador to the Court of St. James. This was a clear signal that Hoover's ambivalence toward federal regulatory programs (as distinguished from subsidy programs, such as the Reconstruction Finance Corporation) was being resolved in favor of intervention. Mellon had a favorite formula to describe his laissez-faire approach: "Liquidate labor, liquidate stocks, liquidate the farmers, liquidate real estate." By 1932, there was very little of the economy left to liquidate. One fourth of the labor force was unemployed. Industrial productivity was down to half its 1929 rate. So was national income. Aggregate share prices were slipping toward values equal to less than one-fifth their high prices of but thirty-four months before. New securities issues had nearly ceased. While investors had purchased $9.4 billion worth of new corporate issues in 1929, only $644 million would be sold in 1932. Already the giant Insull utilities pyramid had fallen. The Morgan-backed Van Sweringen railroad system was wobbling. Shares in the Transamerica Corporation (which owned the Bank of America) would sell as low as 2⅛ in 1932. There had been no more inveterate optimist in the business community than U.S. Steel's Charles Schwab, but by early 1932 even his faith was shaken. "I'm afraid, every man is afraid," Schwab was quoted as saying. "I don't know, we don't know, whether values we have are going to be real next month or not."[54]

In January 1932, Hoover met with directors of the New York Stock Exchange. This time no "pleasant dinner" was reported. Hoover demanded that the Exchange take immediate action against pool operators and bear raiders. He offered Whitney "curative amendments" that had been formulated by "responsible members of the Exchange." With evident disgust the former President later would recall, "The directors repeatedly promised they would adopt these amendments, but made only minor changes." On February 16, Hoover again met with Whitney. The President was uncharacteristically blunt. Unless the New York Stock Exchange effected substantial reforms, Hoover would ask Congress to investigate the Exchange "with a view to Federal control legislation."[55]

The following day the stock exchange adopted a new rule requiring brokers to secure written permission from clients before lending their shares to short-sellers. Although a few brokers predicted that the new rule might reduce short sales by as much as 50 percent, most commentators in Congress and the financial press disagreed. *Business Week* labeled the rule a "grandiose gesture" by the Exchange to satisfy the President and thwart congressional action. The rule's endurance, suggested the magazine, "will depend upon the political need for a burnt offering." *Wall Street Journal* columnist Thomas Woodlock questioned whether it would have much effect even if it did last. Richard Whitney, testifying at House Judiciary Committee hearings on short-selling, on February 24 all but implied that the rule was meaningless: "I do not believe in the last analysis that it will prevent stocks being available for loaning purposes."[56]

Hoover's patience had run out. At a press conference on February 19 Hoover sharply warned "the managers of the Exchange that they should take adequate measures to protect investors from artificial depression of the price of securities for speculative profit. Individuals who use the facilities of the Exchange for such purposes are not contributing to recovery of the United States."[57] When "the managers of the Exchange" did not respond, Hoover summoned Frederick Walcott and Peter Norbeck, Republican members of the Senate Banking Committee, to a highly publicized meeting at the White House. Walcott, a former investment banker, had served as Hoover's assistant in the U.S. Food Administration during World War I and was one of Hoover's closest personal friends, besides being an ally in Congress.[58] Norbeck, the chairman of the committee, apparently was invited only as a courtesy. During the meeting, Hoover repeated rumors he had received concerning "vicious pools . . . in which corporation and even bank directors were manipulating their own stocks." He asked Walcott to take charge of an investigation of stock exchange practices.[59]

Although Hoover insisted in his *Memoirs* that he meant the investigation to be undertaken "with a view to legislation," this is doubtful. The beleaguered President still believed federal control of the stock exchange might be unconstitutional. In several public statements, Senator Walcott emphasized that the purpose of the hearings should be to call "some of the outstanding bear raiders" to testify and that the hearings should then adjourn. It may be reasonably inferred that Hoover wanted to pressure Whitney to adopt effective stock exchange reforms and to demonstrate to voters early in an election year that leading Democrats like national party chairman John J. Raskob and Bernard Baruch had contributed to the recent share price decline.[60]

Regardless of his motives, it soon became apparent that neither Hoover nor Walcott could control the Senate Banking Committee. In committee sessions beginning on February 28, Walcott lobbied for a resolution limited to a study of recent bear-raiding, informing the press: "I hope this will not result in Federal legislation. We have no legislative plans."[61] There was little support for so limited an investigation. On March 3, Republican senators Norbeck, James P. Couzens, and John G. Townsend, aided by the Democrats on the Banking Committee, voted in favor of a resolution calling for "a thorough and complete investigation" of stock exchange practices to conclude with a report "and recommendations for the necessary remedial legislation . . . as soon as practicable." The following day the full Senate authorized the "thorough and complete" investigation of the stock exchanges, voting an allocation of $50,000, an extraordinarily large sum in that day, especially considering that Congress was expected to remain in session for only three more months.[62]

Hoover again vacillated. Although his influence in Congress had been reduced, the moral authority of the presidency remained such that but a single word from the White House would have initiated the stock exchange hearings. For five weeks Hoover remained silent, and the Senate Banking Committee repeatedly postponed the stock exchange inquiry in favor of previously scheduled hearings on Carter Glass's revised banking bill.[63]

A surge in short sales early in April finally moved Hoover to act. Learning of a rumor that a massive bear raid was planned for Saturday, April 9, the President summoned Walcott to the White House on April 7.[64] Walcott scheduled an emergency meeting of the Senate Banking Committee the following day. Within hours the committee unexpectedly subpoenaed New York Stock Exchange president Whitney to appear the following Monday as the first witness at the stock exchange inquiry.[65]

Ultimately the Senate Banking Committee's stock exchange hearings would transform American capitalism. They would be directly responsible for the Securities and Banking Acts of 1933, the Securities Exchange Act of 1934, and the creation of the Securities and Exchange Commission. But the hearings began like a Keystone Kops comedy.

Peter Norbeck was the dominant figure in the stock exchange inquiry for the first nine months. The South Dakotan characterized himself as a "Theodore Roosevelt Republican." John T. Flynn, both a political radical and a leading financial journalist of the day, more colorfully styled the senator "one of those Prairie Republicans — half Democrat, half other ingredients — but less than one-half of one percent Republican." Party labels were not particularly relevant. The former well-driller was an unabashed sectionalist and champion of farm-relief legislation. Norbeck's most visible achievement as senator would be helping to secure funds for the carving of the monument on Mount Rushmore.

By his own admission, Peter Norbeck was not qualified to be chairman of the Banking Committee. He knew little about finance. He had been named to the committee in 1921 in an attempt to give it greater geographic balance. At least once he tried to resign. However, in 1926, when unexpected election results made him the ranking Republican member, Norbeck feared he would suffer too great a loss of prestige if he did not accept the chairmanship of the influential committee. Besides, he observed, "as an authority on banking and currency he was the ablest well-driller in Congress."

Soon after his elevation to the chairmanship, Norbeck all but officially delegated full control of banking legislation to Carter Glass. When the depression heightened the importance of the Banking Committee's work, Norbeck acknowledged being flabbergasted by the pleas, suggestions, and criticisms he received. "I really begin to think," he wrote an acquaintance, "I am fortunate in the fact that part of the stuff goes over my head. I do not understand it all. If I did, maybe I wouldn't sleep."

Whatever Norbeck's technical limitations as chairman, he brought to the Senate Banking Committee as clear an anti–Wall Street bias as a prairie Progressive could muster. Flynn would go so far as to write, "It was Norbeck, big, honest, calm, filled with common sense, who made this an investigation of Wall Street, who kept doggedly at the probe . . . and who, more than any other man, gave to the investigation its tone, its character, and direction."[66]

Such an encomium could come only in retrospect. It was nearly impossible to find anything in the senator's performance to praise at the start of the hearings. When the Banking Committee unexpectedly voted on April 8 to begin hearings the following Monday, Norbeck was in Chicago. He had yet to name a counsel for the stock exchange probe. Just four days before, he had informed the press that, in deference to the Glass banking bill, the stock exchange inquiry had been indefinitely postponed.[67]

On being informed of the Banking Committee's hurried action — taken, Norbeck would write, "without my knowledge or consent"

— Norbeck rushed back to Washington, convinced that Hoover and Walcott had executed a "well-laid scheme" to name a Wall Street attorney as chief investigator and through him limit the scope of the hearings. If Norbeck's suspicion was correct, he returned too late. Walcott's nominee, Claude Branch, an attorney from Providence, Rhode Island, already had been appointed temporary counsel.

The stock exchange hearings officially began on Monday, April 11, 1932. For the first two days they were a near-total disaster. A smooth, haughty Richard Whitney was the lead-off witness. The self-confident stock exchange president dazzled the five hundred or so reporters and spectators jammed into the modestly proportioned committee room. Suavely he denied knowledge of a bear raid scheduled for the previous Saturday. Indeed, Whitney testified, "constant investigations have shown . . . bear raids [do] not exist." Nor did short-selling have much effect on market prices, accounting as it did for less than 5 percent of all stock exchange transactions. If they wanted culprits to blame for the exaggerated price movements of the great bull market and succeeding crash, Whitney suggested they look at "the high-powered political agents of prosperity," who misled the country into a "state of mind that . . . thought poverty was about to be abolished in our country forever." With Norbeck playing a passive role as chairman, and Claude Branch interjecting only vague queries about aggregate short-sale statistics, the hearings deteriorated into uncoordinated posturing by the obviously unprepared senators. Growing weary of listening to Senator John J. Blaine thunder at Whitney for failing to recall Herbert Hoover's view on stock speculation published in the *London Mining Journal* of May 1912, and Iowa's Brookhart belligerently lecture Whitney for his ignorance of commodity prices, Senator Glass tartly observed, "Mr. Whitney, I am beginning to wonder what we are here for." One member of the committee termed the sum total of information gathered during the first two days as "nothing at all."[68]

Norbeck labored to revitalize the hearings. At the conclusion of the second hearing day, he began easing out Claude Branch in favor of Branch's assistant, William Gray, a Philadelphia trial attorney with a reputation as a forceful cross-examiner. When the hearings resumed on April 18, the determined Gray attempted to show that short-selling artificially depressed the market. But Gray had no investigative base to draw on. When he argued that Whitney's view of short-selling was "opposed . . . by a great many intelligent, clear-thinking people, who know as much as can be known . . . about market conditions," the stock exchange president stated flatly, "Mr. Gray, I have never denied that intelligent people might not have a different opinion than I; but in this I would say they are wrong."

Usually Whitney did not concede even that much. Throughout protracted testimony on April 18 and again on the 21st, he denied that stock exchange members spread false rumors to depress the market, denied that large operators traded under fictitious names, and at one point all but denied that he knew what a pool operation was. Gray's questioning proved so ineffective that Whitney could barely conceal his amusement. When the counsel asked Whitney on the fourth hearing day, "Would you like to get home tonight?" Whitney replied, "I do not particularly care, Mr. Gray. I will say that I am very happy here in Washington."[69]

Whitney's testimony discouraged several senators on the Banking Committee. Having initially expected hard evidence of "a giant bear raid," they saw instead the sophisticated Whitney easily deflect accusations based on rumor, gossip, or unsubstantiated suspicion. One Democratic senator termed the whole inquiry a joke. Hoover's confidant, Walcott, backpedaled. "I am not sure now that short sales depress the market," he informed reporters. Even Norbeck had to admit that the committee had been proceeding with "pretty punk" information.[70]

But Norbeck remained determined to investigate the "deplorable" practices of the securities industry.[71] After a stormy committee session on April 20, the South Dakotan angrily stalked out of the committee room. "We are going to carry this investigation through to the end," he shouted to waiting reporters.[72] Five days later, Norbeck announced that a new steering group would direct the inquiry. The group included Chairman Norbeck, ranking Democrats Duncan Fletcher and Carter Glass, and Progressive Republican James Couzens. Conspicuously omitted was Frederick Walcott.[73]

The stock exchange hearings effectively began on April 26. After two days of entertaining but uncorroborated testimony from such notorious Wall Street traders as Ben "Sell 'em" Smith and Matthew Brush (who explained with Runyonesque logic that "nobody is in Wall Street for their health"),[74] Norbeck promised "sensational disclosures" at the following day's session. Rumors swirled that Fiorello La Guardia would be a "surprise witness" and that the congressman recently had received documents so inflammatory that he had them placed under guard at police headquarters.

The next morning, La Guardia arrived accompanied by a squad of uniformed policemen and two plainclothes policemen carrying a heavy brown trunk. From the trunk, La Guardia produced canceled checks and news clippings showing that, over a ten-year period, publicist A. Newton Plummer had received $286,279 for planting favorable news stories to boost the prices of sixty-one separate stocks. Among other beneficiaries of Plummer's payments were reporters for *The New York Times*, the *Wall Street Journal*, the *New York Herald Tribune*, the *New York Evening Post*, and the *New York Evening Mail*. In return, these reporters had published as fact articles written by Plummer, such as ones stating that Superior Oil's production has increased "approximately 200 percent since the first of the year" and Indian Motorcycle "orders [were] 65 percent ahead of business a year ago." "Shocking as these facts may seem," La Guardia told the senators, "I believe that the same sordid story could be told about nearly every stock in which there has been a pool and in which there have been efforts to shoot up the price."[75] Norbeck enthusiastically concurred: "I believe Mr. Plummer was a piker compared to what will be shown later."[76] La Guardia did not know. Nor did Norbeck. But the sensation generated by the "La Guardia ballyhoo story" — even Richard Whitney could not deny a canceled check — gave Norbeck the confidence to adjourn the hearings temporarily while Gray tracked down further evidence.[77]

The Senate Banking Committee resumed the hearings in mid-May. Over the next month Gray conducted a wide-ranging investigation of market manipulations. Among other revelations, Gray showed a pool organized by the firm of M. J. Meehan and Company had generated profits equal to nearly $5 million by trading Radio Corporation of America stock during one week in March 1929. Profit participants included Mrs. David Sarnoff, the wife of RCA's chief executive officer, John J. Raskob, and Mrs. M. J. Meehan.[78] Gray also demonstrated that film magnate Harry Warner saved $9.25 million by selling Warner Brothers stock prior to the elimination of dividend payments, then repurchasing the securities after the price dropped.[79] David Lion, a publicist, it was disclosed, had earned at least $2 million from thirty pool operations.[80] And Fox Film's William Fox caused his corporation to take ownership of 210,300 shares of company stock after the October 1929 crash reduced their value by $3.3 million, but personally claimed the loss on his New York State income tax return.[81]

These revelations were widely reported by the nation's press, but Gray's scattershot approach led to serious evidentiary gaps. For example, Gray was unable to corroborate his suspicions that the RCA pool had been aided by planted news stories and "wash sales"* or to

---

* A wash sale is a transaction in which shares of stock are bought and sold by the same person or pool of persons to create the appearance of activity in the stock. Since an increase in trading volume may have the effect of increasing stock prices by luring

prove the effect of David Lion's publicity on share prices or even that the publicity was fraudulent. Even more surprising was Gray's failure to subpoena Michael Meehan, with the result that this key potential witness sailed to Europe "for several months" the night before he was scheduled to testify. On another occasion, Gray angered Democrats on the committee by calling John J. Raskob to testify about short sales in General Motors stock. When Gray was unable to establish that the Democratic Party national chairman had sold any stock short, Senator Glass and others charged Gray with a political motivation.[82]

By mid-June, senatorial attention again was waning. Norbeck barely was able to persuade a majority of the Banking Committee members to seek $50,000 in additional funds to continue the stock exchange inquiry until March 3, 1933, when the Seventy-second Congress would adjourn. The Senate Audit Committee reported the resolution with a recommendation for a $25,000 appropriation. Norbeck fought hard for the full appropriation, emphasizing that "the recovery of evaded income tax will offset the expense 100 times." With the testimony of William Fox still drawing newspaper comments, Norbeck succeeded.[83]

But when the hearings adjourned on June 24, it was unclear whether they would be resumed. The Banking Committee voted to discontinue the services of William Gray and his investigators.[84] Temporarily, Norbeck assigned supervision of evidence-gathering to James E. Stewart, a friend from South Dakota.[85] The senator instructed Stewart to hold down expenses and avoid political controversy.

For like Finley Peter Dunne's proverbial Supreme Court, Peter Norbeck was watching "the iliction results." Had Herbert Hoover been re-elected, the stock exchange hearings might not have been resumed. After Walcott lost control of the Banking Committee hearings, Hoover distanced himself from the inquiry. The Republican platform, adopted on June 1, 1932, contained not a word about stock exchanges. Hoover virtually ignored the issue in his re-election campaign. In the final week of the campaign, Hoover again made explicit his earlier view that securities reform was primarily a state matter. Responding to Roosevelt's charges that he had allowed the country to be flooded with bogus foreign bonds, Hoover stated, "The Governor does not inform the American people that there is no

---

new investors to trade in the security, wash sales were considered fraudulent long before the Senate Banking Committee investigation, but were seldom detected or penalized by stock exchange officials.

Federal law of regulation of the sale of securities and that there is doubtful constitutional authority for such a law; that most of those bonds are issued from New York State, which has such authority; and that the Governor has done nothing to reform that evil, if it be one."[86]

By contrast, Franklin Roosevelt assumed a commanding position among those advocating federal securities legislation. His presidential nomination acceptance speech was best remembered for its famous peroration: "I pledge you, I pledge myself to a new deal for the American people." But the address was devoted to the "dry subject of finance." "In a comprehensive planning for the reconstruction of the great credit groups," Roosevelt said, "I list an important place for that prize statement of principle in the platform here adopted calling for the letting in of the light of day on issues of securities, foreign and domestic, which are offered for sale to the investing public. * [87]

Seven weeks later in a key campaign address in Columbus, Ohio, Roosevelt charged Hoover with responsibility for "encouraging a vast speculative boom." "Much of our troubles," claimed Roosevelt, "came from what [Hoover] described as a 'new basis in government relation with business' . . . The administration lined up with the stock market." When the market broke, Hoover's administration "attempted to minimize the crash . . . it erroneously charged the cause to other Nations . . . it delayed relief; it forgot reform." For his part, Roosevelt pledged himself to a comprehensive program of securities law reform. "First . . . to inspire truth telling, I propose that every effort be made to prevent the issue of manufactured and unnecessary securities of all kinds which are brought out merely for the purpose of enriching those who handled their sale to the public." Second, he proposed federal regulation of securities exchanges and holding companies that sell securities in interstate commerce. Third, he urged the complete divorce of investment and commercial banking. And finally, the candidate recommended prevention of Federal Reserve funds from being used for speculative enterprises. Periodically throughout the campaign, Roosevelt returned to the

---

* The platform called for "regulation to the full extent of federal power of holding companies which sell securities in interstate commerce . . . and Exchanges in securities," "the divorce of the investment banking business from commercial banks," and "protection of the investing public by requiring to be filed with the government and carried in advertisements of all offerings of foreign and domestic stocks and bonds true information as to bonuses, commisssions, principal invested, and interests of the sellers." A related provision, inspired by Carter Glass, "condemn[ed] the usurpation of power by the State Department in assuming to pass upon foreign securities offered by international bankers as a result of which billions of dollars in questionable bonds have been sold to the public upon the implied approval of the Federal Government."[88]

issue of securities law reform, scorning "the reckless promoter, the Ishmael or Insull whose hand is against every man's."[89] A center-piece of his address on public utilities was the call for "full public-ity" in securities sales. Repeatedly Roosevelt admonished, "Let in the light!"[90]

Nine days after Roosevelt's election, Norbeck announced plans to resume the stock exchange hearings, beginning with an investiga-tion of the President-elect's bête noire, Samuel Insull.[91] A deter-mined search was launched to find a new special counsel. Norbeck offered the post to Harold Ickes, Samuel Untermyer, and Samuel Seabury (who recently had conducted an investigation of corruption in Mayor Jimmy Walker's administration in New York City).[92] Each declined. Norbeck then hired Irving Ben Cooper, one of Seabury's associates.[93] The flamboyant Cooper promptly announced to the press that he had engaged seven assistants and established a new headquarters for the probe in New York City. Privately he de-manded that Norbeck sign five hundred blank subpoenas. Norbeck refused, noting that the inquiry had issued only twenty-seven sub-poenas to date. When a Banking Committee staff member arrived at Cooper's New York City headquarters to act as liaison, Cooper re-signed, declaring that Norbeck might want someone to "sit on the lid," but that he had no intention of being associated with anything but a "genuine" investigation.[94]

Norbeck then made his final contribution to securities law re-form. After consultation with Senator Fletcher, the senior Demo-crat on the Banking Committee, Norbeck hired Ferdinand Pecora to be the committee's counsel.[95] Born in Nicosia, Sicily, in 1882, Pecora had immigrated to New York City at the age of four. There his family lived in a cold water flat. As a schoolboy, Pecora worked a milk route in the morning and a paper route in the afternoon. Never-theless, he graduated as valedictorian of his public school class. The future "hellhound of Wall Street" briefly applied himself to the pursuit of the Episcopal ministry, before a factory injury incapaci-tated his shoemaker father, requiring him to leave college and help support his family. His career in the law began when, at the age of fifteen, Pecora became a junior clerk in a one-man law office diago-nally across the street from J. P. Morgan and Company. Five years later Pecora started part-time study at New York Law School. After graduating in 1906, Pecora served as a managing clerk in several firms before passing the bar in 1911.

He entered public life via local politics. In 1912, Pecora joined Theodore Roosevelt's National Progressive Party. An astute district leader, Pecora became vice president of the Bull Moose Party in New

York State. Impressed with Woodrow Wilson's policies, Pecora switched his allegiance to the Democrats in 1916. The following year, the mayor of New York City rewarded Pecora's campaign efforts with a position in the office of New York City's district attorney.

There, Pecora thrived. District Attorney Joab H. Banton, who named Pecora his chief assistant in 1922, later credited Pecora with successful prosecution of over 150 fraudulent securities salesmen, and with the conviction of corrupt politicians in the city's Health Department and the Office of Comptroller of the State of New York. In a 1933 telegram to Senator Norbeck, Banton praised Pecora as "the best-qualified lawyer" in the country to lead the Banking Committee's investigation. Bainbridge Colby, Secretary of State under Wilson, after declining the counsel position himself, recommended Pecora to Senator Fletcher as "the most brilliant cross-examiner in New York."

Pecora was undeniably among the most theatrical. A compact, swarthy man with curling black and gray hair, he punctuated his courtroom appearances with the vigorous jabbing of a stubby finger. During the stock exchange hearings, Pecora's manner alternately could be genial, courtly, mocking, or belligerent. It was always relentless. (So relentless, in fact, that a startled J. P. Morgan, Jr., later would protest that Pecora pursued him as if he were "a horse thief.") He was given to intellectual excesses as well. A wholesale subscriber to the Brandeis bigness-is-badness thesis, he often treated Wall Street witnesses as if they had something to hide.

By early 1933, Pecora's public career had been stymied. Having failed to win the Democratic Party's nomination for district attorney in 1930, he was forced into private practice. Always politically ambitious,* when Norbeck offered the $3000-a-year counsel post on January 24, 1933, Pecora accepted without hesitation.[96]

Still smarting over Cooper's resignation, Norbeck pledged that Pecora would "have all the authority necessary to make a comprehensive investigation."[97] Pecora moved swiftly. Hastily adding a small team of attorneys and accountants to the Banking Committee's permanent staff,[98] the new special counsel issued his first subpoena within a week.

Hearings resumed on February 15 with the long-delayed examination of the Insull public utility empire. Before its collapse, the Insull

---

* Later in 1933, Pecora ran unsuccessfully for district attorney on an anti-Tammany Democratic ticket while simultaneously directing the stock exchange hearings. In 1950, he again ran unsuccessfully as the Democratic nominee for mayor of New York City.

group of utility companies had been the third largest utility group in the country, producing approximately 10 percent of the nation's total electrical power. The local level of the system comprised over a hundred gas, electricity, and transportation firms scattered throughout thirty states. These operating companies were largely administered through five holding companies, in each of which the Insull family owned a minority controlling interest. When Cyrus Eaton, the Cleveland financier, in 1927 began purchasing large blocks of Insull holding company securities, Insull reacted defensively by forming two super-holding companies "to perpetuate," a press release explained, "the existing management of the Insull group of securities."

The collapse of the stock markets in September 1931 toppled the heavily indebted Insull system. Newspapers claimed that the fall of the $3 billion empire was "the biggest business failure in the history of the world." Insull's personal fortune of over $150 million also vanished. An early advocate of "customer ownership," Insull took down with him 600,000 shareholders and 500,000 bondholders. On learning in October 1932 that he was about to be indicted in federal court on charges of mail fraud,* Insull fled to Greece.

Pecora's three-day inquiry focused on the securities sales that accompanied the formation of the final two super-holding companies, Insull Utility Investment and the Corporation Security Company. Documentary evidence demonstrated that, besides thwarting Eaton, Insull, in the words of his most sympathetic biographer, "was not entirely immune to the intoxification" of wealth. The Insull Utility Investment Corporation had been organized with three million shares of common stock in December 1928. Of these, 750,000 shares were sold to the Insull family at $7.54 per share. By a January 17, 1929, agreement, the Insull family had the option to purchase 200,000 more shares at $15 per share; Samuel Insull personally agreed to buy an additional 250,000 shares at a price of $12 per share. That same day, trading commenced in the common stock on the Chicago Stock Exchange with an opening price of $30 per share. The reorganization gave the Insull family an immediate $24.4 million paper profit merely for trading their shares in the next lower rung of holding companies for Insull Utility common stock. The second day, Insull Utility stock reached $40 a share. On August 2, 1929, it reached a peak price of $149 (or a highly intoxicating paper profit for Insull of $166 million).

---

* Insull subsequently returned to the United States and was acquitted of these charges, as well as charges of violating the federal bankruptcy laws and a state indictment for embezzlement.

By comparing Insull Corporation annual reports with Insull Corporation federal tax returns, Pecora was able to suggest that at least part of this remarkable accretion could not be attributed to the great bull market. The Insull Utility Investment Company 1930 annual report to shareholders, for example, indicated a $10.3 million profit. The same year's tax return reported a $6.5 million loss. Allied efforts "to protect the market" in Insull securities were undertaken by the Halsey Stuart investment bank, then the nation's largest dealer in corporate bonds. The Halsey Stuart firm organized two trading syndicates to maintain designated market prices during the initial issuance of securities in Insull's super-holding companies without disclosing its own investment in Insull securities (which at one point would have yielded a profit of more than $36 million). By fragmenting operations in over a hundred separate corporations, Insull, in addition, induced virtually every major bank in Illinois, including one managed by Charles Dawes, a former Vice President of the United States, to exceed the state's 15 percent limit on the amount of loan money that a bank could advance to any single borrower.[99]

Four days after Pecora completed taking testimony from Halsey Stuart, he began an examination of the National City Bank that would make his a household name. The National City Bank only recently had been surpassed as the largest bank in the country by the Chase National. Charles E. Mitchell was the bank's president and chairman of the board. To a far greater degree than J. P. Morgan, Jr., whose reputation was largely, and undeservedly, derived from his father, Mitchell was the representative banker of his generation. In the preceding two decades, he had helped fundamentally transform commercial banking.

Before Mitchell, commercial banks generally limited themselves to the familiar functions of receiving deposits and making loans to home-buyers or business firms. Commercial banks rarely invested their funds in stocks or corporate bonds, or originated or underwrote new issues of securities. These riskier, though potentially more profitable, investment banking practices were left to "private" investment houses, such as J. P. Morgan and Company or Kuhn, Loeb. Such restraint not only reflected the historic conservatism of commercial bankers; it was required by state and national laws, which prohibited banks from engaging in "nonbanking" (meaning noncommercial banking) functions.[100]

In 1911, the National City Bank became one of the first commercial banks to circumvent these restrictions. The bank's senior executives incorporated the National City *Company*, a securities investment firm, which, under the general incorporation law of New York State, was permitted to engage in almost any business but commercial banking. Technically, the new securities affiliate was an entirely separate institution. But as Frederick Lewis Allen drolly observed, to consider an affiliated firm like the National City Company independent was "a masterpiece of legal humor." All of the National City Company's $10 million in start-up capital was advanced by the National City Bank, which declared a special 40 percent dividend and persuaded the bank's shareholders to invest "their money" in the new firm. The shareholders also agreed that they would not exercise voting rights in the new company, but by a "trust agreement" permanently vested voting control in three senior officers of the National City Bank. Shareholders could not even sell their nonvoting shares in the National City Company without simultaneously selling their shares in the bank. The nonvoting shares in the company were printed on the reverse side of the stock certificates of the bank, "physically as well as legally indivisible," Ferdinand Pecora would write. The bank and the company were "like one body with two heads."

Sharply questioned by President William Taft's Department of Justice, the National City Company remained a relatively small operation until 1916, when Charles E. Mitchell accepted its presidency. In thirteen years Mitchell boosted a four-person office into the largest investment house in the country, complete with nineteen hundred employees, sixty-nine branch offices, a private wire stretching 11,300 miles, its own engineers, accountants, bookkeepers, policemen, and annual securities sales averaging over $1.5 billion per year. To accomplish this, Mitchell simply ignored time-honored banking practices. "Instead of waiting for investors to come," an admiring business executive wrote, "he took young men and women, gave them a course of training on the sale of securities, and sent them out to *find* the investors. Such methods, pursued with such vigor and on such a scale were revolutionary." To lure investors, the National City Company advertised extensively in national magazines, had its salesmen selling bonds door to door like Fuller brushes or Hoover vacuum cleaners or clerking in brightly lit downtown securities offices. "To keep the salesmen on their toes," Mitchell's headquarters sent out a daily stream of demands, pep talks, and inducements known as "flashes." The most welcome flashes offered cash prizes to the salesmen who earned the most points selling a list of hard-to-move securities. When sales lagged, Mitchell displayed a harsher side. "I should hate to think," he once telegraphed, "there is any man in our sales crowd who would confess to his inability to sell at least some of any issue of either bonds or preferred stock that we think good enough to offer. In fact, this would be an impossible situation and in the interest of all concerned, one which we would not permit to continue."

Sales rarely lagged. Mitchell astutely had foreseen as early as June 1917 that the World War I Liberty Bond drives would result in "the development of a large, new army of investors in this country." So esteemed was Mitchell's leadership that in 1921 the National City Company president was also made president of the considerably larger National City Bank; in 1929, he became the bank's chairman as well. He was, by then, one of the nation's most influential bankers. Even as scornful a critic as Edmund Wilson would concede, "He was the banker of bankers, the salesman of salesmen, the genius of the New Economic Era." A more coveted judgment was that of the advertising pioneer Bruce Barton. Nearly every social historian of the 1920s has paused to ridicule Barton's 1924 best seller, *The Man Nobody Knows*, in which Barton acclaimed Jesus of Nazareth as "the founder of modern business." ("He picked up twelve men from the bottom ranks of business and forged them into an organization that conquered the world.") What is most intriguing about Barton's tract is that many of the virtues he attributed to Christ — personal magnetism, blazing conviction, power to pick men, patience, humility, and faith in good advertising — he had attributed to Mitchell the previous year in a magazine article, "Is There Anything Here That Other Men Couldn't Do?"[101]

Pecora prepared to interrogate Mitchell by studying National City minute books for the years 1924–1929. They apparently were extraordinarily revealing. On February 21, the seemingly indomitable Mitchell strode into the Banking Committee's hearing room flanked by a retinue of senior associates. Ten days later, Pecora would spy Mitchell walking to Union Station alone, carrying his own grip, a discomfited and beaten man.

The banker's fall occurred with astonishing quickness. Pecora commenced his examination by focusing on Mitchell's remuneration. The president and each of several vice presidents of the National City Company received an annual base salary of $25,000. But the investment company's executives also shared in a management fund. After 80 percent of the company's net profits were set aside as retained earnings, senior executives were given 20 percent of annual profits. Twice a year the executives themselves voted on how to distribute the management fund — with Mitchell regularly receiving about one third of the pay-out both from the investment affiliate and from a similar fund administered by the National City Bank. In

1927, Charles E. Mitchell's portion of the investment company's fund was $529,230 and his share from the bank was $527,000, or a total of $1,056,230. In 1928, his pay-out from the two funds came to $1,316,634,14; in 1929, approximately, $1,108,000.[102] When the October 1929 crash eliminated the possibility of profit-sharing during the latter half of that year, National City established a "morale loan fund" for officers who might have been overextended in the securities markets. Without interest or collateral, $2 million was loaned to about a hundred National City Bank and National City Company officers. Only 5 percent had been repaid by the end of February 1933.[103] Additionally, Mitchell and National City senior executives periodically also were allowed to purchase new securities issues at bargain prices. For example, when Boeing Airplane's common stock was first sold on the New York Curb Exchange at $57 in November 1928, National City executives held 45,000 shares, which they had earlier purchased privately for $30 per share.[104] At a time when a concerted effort was being made to reduce the salary of $1600 a year paid to many federal employees, Mitchell's remuneration seemed astronomical.*

But the least expected revelation was saved for the late afternoon of the first day's testimony. After persistent questioning by Pecora and Senator Brookhart, Mitchell conceded that in 1929 he had sold 18,300 shares of National City stock to a relative (later revealed to be his wife) to establish a loss of $2,872,305.50 "for tax purposes."[106] Since Mitchell later repurchased all 18,300 shares at the initial sale price even though the market price was considerably lower, it was widely assumed that the banker had violated federal income tax laws. Within three days, George Medalie, the United States Attorney for New York City, publicly launched an investigation of the transaction.[107] Mitchell resigned from all National City positions on February 26.[108]

The investigation of the bank continued. It was Pecora's thesis that National City's extravagant incentive salary arrangements had encouraged bank officers to engage in unsound security-selling and unsound banking practices.[109] The counsel now turned to what Mitchell had labeled the "production" side of National City Company operations, that is, "the manufacture of long-term credits."

---

* Mitchell defended his remuneration in a subsequent shareholder suit, arguing with characteristic bravado: "Unless the man of energy and perhaps ability can see within the organization for which he is working a point that he can possibly reach that has great material benefit attached to it, I say unless he can see that his work is going to be somewhat . . . dulled."[105]

Fourteen months before, Senator Johnson had won headlines for revealing that the J. & W. Seligman investment house had bribed the son of the Peruvian president to secure the right to sell the country's bonds in the United States. The Seligman house had turned to the National City Company for help in marketing the bonds. By cross-examining several National City officers, Pecora adduced the background of the company's participation in the sale of $90 million worth of Peruvian bonds, which at one point in 1933 would sell for less than 5 percent of their offering price.

As early as 1921, National City Company had contemplated "merchandising" Peruvian securities. However, a preliminary investigation by a company representative had discouraged National City from doing so. "The condition of Government finances is positively distressing," the investigator had found. "Treasury obligations are almost impossible to collect. Government officials and employees are months in arrears in their salaries, and as one business man expressed it, the Government treasury is 'flat on its back and gasping for breath.' " Subsequent reports over a six-year period warned that "the moral risk was not satisfactory" and "the internal debt of Peru has not yet been placed on a satisfactory footing." "Peru," cabled Victor Schoepperle, National City's Latin American financing expert, in 1923, "has been careless in the fulfillment of contractual obligations . . . the *London Times,* in its issue of March 30, 1922, alluded to Peru's 'frequent unobservance of her undertakings to the Peruvian Corporation, her broken pledges over the Chimbote concession, and her flagrant disregard of guarantees given to the North Western Railway." In 1925, Schoepperle summarized for National City officials Peru's long history of bond defaults.

Yet in March 1927, the National City Company joined the Seligman investment house and others to sponsor a $15 million Peruvian bond issue. When the bond issue was quickly absorbed by the public, National City telegraphed its Latin American representatives for updated reports. The replies were uniformly unfavorable. In July 1927, the overseas manager of the National City Bank wrote Mitchell: "As I see it, there are two factors that will long retard the economic importance of Peru. First, its population of 5,500,000 is largely Indian, two-thirds of whom reside east of the Andes, and a majority consume almost no manufactured products. Second, its principal sources of wealth, the mines and oil wells, are nearly all foreign-owned, and excepting for wages and taxes, no part of the value of their production remains in the country." The manager pointedly added, "The country's political situation is equally uncertain." Six months later, National City received another report that "the balance of international payments is unfavorable to Peru"; in March 1928, "the whole taxation system is a hodge-podge." The manager of the Lima branch of the bank concluded a September 1928 cablegram: "We have assumed (a) no further national loan can be safely issued and (b) integrity Republic's finances threatened until floating debt problem solved." The National City Company nonetheless cosponsored a December 1927 $50 million Peruvian bond issue, and a $25 million bond distribution in October 1928.

In none of the prospectuses that accompanied the three bond issues did the bank describe Peru's bad debt record or the other adverse economic information on file. Instead, National City printed a disclaimer at the bottom of the first page: "The above statements are based on information received partly by cable from official and other sources. While not guaranteed, we believe them to be reliable, but they are in no event to be construed as representations by us." By the time of the Senate Banking Committee hearings in February 1933, investors had lost nearly $75 million on Peruvian bonds; Pecora showed that the bankers' initial commissions had been worth $4.5 million.[110]

In 1927, with the great bull market beginning its final manic phase, National City abandoned a long-held policy and commenced selling common stock to the public for the first time, including common stock in the National City Bank. Under the national banking law, it was illegal for a national bank to purchase its own stock. To minimize the possibility of speculation in bank securities, the law forbade banks even from lending money when their own stock was used as collateral. The National City Bank's investment affiliate persistently evaded these strictures. In 1928, the company began the sale of bank stock worth $650 million. Just before the sales campaign, the investment affiliate purchased a worthless $25 million National City Bank loan to Cuban sugar firms, with a resultant improvement in the bank's financial statements. To establish what Flash No. 3873 called "working control of this market," the bank's stock was removed from the New York Stock Exchange and traded on the more volatile over-the-counter market. There, by making purchases for its own account as frequently as every three or four minutes in quantities as vast as 30,000 to 40,000 shares a day, the company helped push up the bank's stock price from $785 in January 1928 to the equivalent of $2925 ($585 per share after a five-for-one split) in 1929. At the same time as the company manipulated the bank's stock price, company salesmen were offered special bonuses for hawking the stock. National City Company securities customers were encouraged to sell other securities and switch to the bank's stock. In February 1929, prospective purchasers were offered the opportunity to purchase bank stock for $5.00 below the rapidly rising market price. After the October 1929 crash, the bank's stock price fell from its peak of nearly $3000 to just over $100.[111]

The nine days of hearings devoted to Mitchell and National City concluded with the revelation that the company had "lent" $10,020 to John Ramsey, general manager of the Port Authority of New York, before receiving the right to sell $66 million worth of Port Authority bonds. The "loan," never repaid, was charged off as an expense of the bond issue. National City officers were unable to find a note giving evidence of the loan, although a senior vice president testified that such a note had existed for the uncollateralized cash advance.[112]

The National City hearings were conducted against the backdrop of the "bank holiday" crisis. With depositors nearing panic, as state after state ordered banks to close their doors, Mitchell in particular, and New York City bankers in general, became the objects of a near-hysterical public rage. Surveying press response at the conclusion of the National City hearings, the *Literary Digest* recorded an unforgiving mood: "Apologies, even resignations, do not satisfy listening editors." The mood in Congress rivaled that of the editors. "The best way to restore confidence in our banks," argued Senator Burton Wheeler, "is to take these crooked presidents out of the banks and treat them the same as they treated Al Capone when Capone avoided payment of his tax." Carter Glass more than agreed. Reported the gentleman from Virginia, "One banker in my state attempted to marry a white woman and they lynched him."[113]

By contrast to the generally conciliatory attitude Franklin Roosevelt exhibited toward manufacturers in the first months of his presidency, in his inaugural address he implied that the bankers were responsible for the depression. Barely had the new President finished reassuring the country that "the only thing we have to fear is fear itself," when he launched into a slashing denunciation of the financial sector: "Practices of the unscrupulous money changers stand indicted in the court of public opinion, rejected by the hearts and minds of men . . . The money changers have fled from their high seats in the temple of our civilization. We may now restore that temple to the ancient truths."[114]

Roosevelt's first days in the White House were dominated by the bank holiday crisis. Although the crisis concerned commercial banking, Roosevelt used the occasion of his first fireside chat, on March 12, to suggest that investment banking practices like those employed by Mitchell had caused the banks to close.

> We had a bad banking situation. Some of our bankers had shown themselves either incompetent or dishonest in their handling of the people's funds. They had used the money entrusted to them in speculations and unwise loans. This was, of course, not true in the vast majority of our banks, but it was true in enough of them to shock the people for a time into a sense of insecurity and to put them into a frame of mind where they did not differentiate, but seemed to assume that the acts of comparative few had tainted them all.[115]

The following day, Roosevelt met with Duncan Fletcher, the new chairman of the Senate Banking Committee, and urged him to broaden the inquiry to include "all of the ramifications of bad banking so that the government will be able to guard against their continuance and prevent their return."[116] Roosevelt also publicly requested Attorney General Homer Cummings to prosecute vigorously any violations of law revealed by the Banking Committee's inquiry.[117] Cummings personally conferred with United States Attorney Medalie.[118] In late March, Charles E. Mitchell was indicted by a federal grand jury for willfully evading the payment of $573,312.81 in income taxes in 1929.[119]

By mid-March, Roosevelt had established himself as political patron of the Pecora hearings. Wary of the unpredictable Carter Glass — who declined his offer to become Secretary of the Treasury — Roosevelt persuaded Duncan Fletcher to remain on the Banking Committee as its chairman, rather than use his seniority rights to claim the chairmanship of the Commerce Committee.[120] The seventy-five-year-old Floridian was so soft-spoken, his voice was barely audible during the Banking Committee hearings. Often during the hearings, he appeared to doze in his chair. But Fletcher, a party loyalist, had actively campaigned for Franklin Roosevelt. A proverbially hard worker, Fletcher had, since 1908, favored regulation of the "gambling sharks and rascals in Wall Street."[121] Soon after his inaugural, Roosevelt privately began meeting with Pecora as well. At Roosevelt's suggestion, Pecora and Fletcher agreed to make J. P. Morgan and Company the next target of the investigation.[122]

Unlike Mitchell and the National City Bank, the House of Morgan opposed Pecora's requests for evidence. John W. Davis, the 1924 Democratic Party nominee for President, who served as attorney to Morgan, assumed that Pecora meant to conduct a "witch hunt."[123] This sentiment no doubt was reinforced when Pecora demanded a meeting with Morgan in the unfurnished "shabby-looking office" his staff rented in uptown Manhattan, because Pecora professed to be "too busy" to meet Morgan in the banker's famous "house on the corner," as Morgan had requested.[124] After examining the stock exchange practices enabling resolution, Davis counseled Morgan and his associates against permitting Pecora to examine the company's financial records. "I stated distinctly," Davis wrote, that the inquiry "was not directed to the investigation of investment bankers as such but to their dealings in securities."[125] Following a March 22 meeting with Pecora, Morgan representatives refused to answer seven of twenty-three questions formally submitted by the Senate counsel.[126] At Senator Fletcher's direction, Pecora returned to Washington, D.C., and drafted a new enabling resolution, which authorized the Banking Committee "to make a thorough and complete investigation of the operation by any person, firm, copartnership, company, association, corporation, or other entity of the business of banking, financing, and extending credit."[127] Without a word of debate, Congress adopted the resolution on April 4.[128]

The public investigation of the House of Morgan began on May 23. Days before, a special bank of telegraph lines was installed in the Senate Office Building so that reporters could wire intermittent reports. Because the noise of spectators inside and outside the Senate Banking Committee room repeatedly disrupted the hearings, the investigation was moved to the cavernous Senate Caucus Room.[129] Klieg lights were installed in the Caucus Room's chandeliers to aid photographers. For twelve hearing days, newspapers gave the testimony front-page coverage, many printing it verbatim. "So completely," reported *The New Republic*, "has the Senate probe into the great House of Morgan blanketed all other issues on the Washington stage that it is impossible at this time to arouse interest in any other topic." News sources generally tinted their coverage in purple. *Time* magazine characterized the House of Morgan as "the greatest and most legendary private business of modern times." *Business Week* termed "Morgan & Co. . . . unique in the magnitude of its operations and in the world prestige it enjoys." The *Richmond Times-Dispatch*, like many daily newspapers, seemed unable to contain its awe: "J. Pierpont Morgan, the twentieth-century embodiment of Croesus, Lorenzo the Magnificent, Rothschild; the lordly Mr. Morgan, financier and patron of arts; the unreachable Mr. Morgan, with his impregnable castle at Broad and Wall Streets and his private army of armed guards; the austere Mr. Morgan, to whose presence only the mighty are admitted, in a committee-room and upon his bare brow the gaze of the 'peepul.' Truly an extraordinary event!"[130]

Although J. P. Morgan, Jr., dominated the attention of news report-

ers, the real target of Pecora's probe was the firm built by his father.*
J. P. Morgan and Company was the nation's leading private bank.
Compared to commercial banks like the Chase or National City,
Morgan and Company was a minuscule operation. As late as 1933,
"the house on the corner" included only twenty partners. Drexel
and Company, an allied company in Philadelphia, added but four
partners to that number. Yet the firm's reputation for financial acu-
men persisted for two decades after the elder Morgan's death. These
twenty-four partners held 126 directorships and trusteeships in
eighty-nine firms with well over $20 billion in total resources. Fifty-
two corporations, including American Telephone and Telegraph,
Standard Oil of New Jersey, General Motors, Du Pont, and U.S.
Steel, each maintained an average daily deposit of over $1 million
for at least one of the years 1927 to 1932. Eighty-three other firms
maintained an average daily balance of at least $100,000 each, vest-
ing Morgan and Company with over half a billion dollars of monies
to invest at the end of 1927. Most significantly, between January
1919 and May 1933, Morgan and Company had helped offer $6 bil-
lion in new securities.

This enormous sum was sold without the high-pressure sales efforts that characterized more aggressive firms, such as Mitchell's
National City Company. Morgan and Company did not employ
salesmen. To maintain its status as a private bank totally exempt
from state or federal regulation, it did not advertise even to the
extent of placing a sign on the outer door of its Wall Street office.[132]
The firm's success, Morgan argued in an uncompromising opening
statement[133] written for him by John W. Davis,[134] was the result of
"the respect and esteem of the community." The private banker was
"a national asset and not a national danger," because he was subject
to a code of professional ethics so exacting that "we have never been
satisfied with simply keeping within the law." Echoing his father's
celebrated argument to the 1912 Pujo Committee that commercial
credit was based on "character," not on "money or property," the
younger Morgan insisted: "As to the theory that [a private

---

* The personal reputation of J. P. Morgan, Jr., was highly exaggerated. At sixty-five,
the tall, avuncular Morgan was a pleasant, shy man, obviously ill at ease in public.
Far from being Lorenzo the Magnificent, "Jack" Morgan had succeeded his scowling,
imperious father like a dull prince following the reign of an empire-building king.
Although Morgan and Company's articles of copartnership specified that his decisions "shall be final," since his father's death in 1913 the younger Morgan generally
had deferred to the business judgment of more able partners, such as Henry Davison
and Thomas Lamont.[131]

banker] may become too powerful, it must be remembered that any power which he has comes, not from the possession of large means, but from the confidence of the people in his character and credit, and that that power, having no force to back it, would disappear at once if people thought that the character had changed or the credit had diminished."

It was Morgan and Company's reputation as a "national asset" that Pecora challenged in the stock exchange hearings. Five years later Pecora would write, "In truth, the investigation of the Morgan firm elicited no such glaring abuses" as he uncovered in his investigation of "other great banking institutions and personalities."[135] But the fact that the name J. P. Morgan was, as *The New York Times* put it, "a magic one in American finance" caused the Morgan revelations to be the most influential of the stock exchange hearings.

As with Mitchell, Pecora began the Morgan hearings with a probe of income taxes. The revelation that the partners in the House of Morgan paid only $48,000 in income taxes in 1930 and none at all in 1931 and 1932 was treated by the press as the most sensational disclosure of the Morgan hearings. Even newspapers sympathetic to Morgan, like *The New York Times*, printed front-page headlines proclaiming, MORGAN PAID NO INCOME TAX FOR THE YEARS 1931 AND 1932 or TAX "EVASION" BY MORGAN IN LEGAL STOCK DEALINGS IS NOW HUNTED BY PECORA. But there was a crucial difference between the income tax disclosures about Morgan and the disclosures about Mitchell. J. P. Morgan, Jr., had violated no laws. Between 1917 and 1929, Morgan partners had paid over $57 million in income taxes, largely on their stock market profits. When the market plummeted, the Morgan partners reported no taxable income in 1931 and 1932, since their stock market losses exceeded all other taxable income. In fact, the net worth of Morgan and Company and Drexel and Company fell 55 percent between 1929 and 1931, declining from $119 million to $53 million. Pecora's scornful probe of the Morgan tax returns established that the firm, by delaying the admission of new partner S. Parker Gilbert until January 2, 1931, had been able to claim a capital loss of $21 million for 1931, which, under the existing tax laws, could be carried over until 1933. Had Gilbert been admitted in 1930, the tax loss could have been extended only until 1932. A subsequent examination by Internal Revenue agents found no illegality in this practice. As the *New York Evening Post* reported: "It is not criminality. Mr. Pecora only makes it seem so." At best, Pecora was able to show that Thomas S. Lamont, the son of Morgan and Company's managing partner, and himself a junior partner in the firm, illegally evaded paying income taxes by a paper "sale" of securities to his wife on December 30, 1930, and her "resale" of the securities to him three months later. But the younger Lamont evaded the Internal Revenue Code for no one but himself. Pecora's calculated blurring of the distinction between illegal tax evasion and permissible tax avoidance was devious, justifying on this one issue John Brooks's assertion that the "righteous tribune of the people was one-quarter demagogic inquisitor."[136]

Nearly as widely publicized as the Morgan tax returns was the disclosure, the next day, of Morgan and Company's "preferred lists." During securities distributions for at least five firms, Morgan and Company had offered stock to firm members and influential individuals at cost or nearly at cost shortly before the security was expected to be traded on a public securities market at a substantially higher figure. This allowed the investors on the preferred list almost immediately to dispose of the security with a sure profit. In June 1927, for example, J. P. Morgan and Company acquired 400,000 shares of Johns-Manville common stock for $47.50, 344,000 shares of which later were resold to a private list at cost, and 56,000 sold at $57.50. The week the offerings were made to the individuals on the preferred lists, market quotations for Johns-Manville fluctuated between $78 and $84. On January 28, 1929, J. P. Morgan and Company purchased 1.25 million shares of common stock from Alleghany Corporation. During the next weeks, the Morgan firm privately sold 575,000 of these shares to a preferred list at the purchase price of $20 per share. At the same time, the stock was being traded on the New York Stock Exchange on a "when-issued" basis at prices ranging from $33 to $37 per share. Later in 1929, 723,000 shares in Standard Brands were sold to a favored list at the original cost of $32 per share. Within five days, Standard Brands shares were publicly traded at $44.

Those on the lists who were not members of J. P. Morgan and Company were people who seemed to have the ability to benefit the firm. There were a striking number of prominent political figures, led by former President Calvin Coolidge, Wilson's Secretary of War, Newton D. Baker, and Senator William McAdoo, Wilson's Secretary of the Treasury, who to his embarrassment was serving on the Senate Banking Committee investigating Morgan and Company. Also listed were Franklin Roosevelt's current Secretary of the Treasury, William Woodin, who had received his shares when he was president of the American Car and Foundry Company, former Republican National Committee chairman Charles D. Hilles, and Democratic national chairman John J. Raskob. Other influential public figures listed included Silas Strawn, former president of both the U.S. Chamber of Commerce and the American Bar Association, John C. Martin, general manager of the *New York Evening Post*, Democratic Party adviser Bernard Baruch, and attorney Owen Roberts, who since had been elevated to the United States Supreme Court. E. H. H. Simmons and Richard Whitney,* while president and vice president of the New York Stock Exchange, had been favored. So had fellow bankers Charles E. Mitchell, Albert Wiggin, and George Baker, and the officers of dozens of the nation's largest firms, beginning with the chief executive officers of the very largest: Alfred P. Sloan of General Motors, Walter Teagle of Standard Oil, Myron C. Taylor of U.S. Steel, Owen D. Young of General Electric, and Walter Gifford of American Telephone and Telegraph.

Morgan and Company partner George Whitney vehemently denied that any quid pro quo was expected of anyone on a preferred list, prompting an astonished Senator Couzens to exclaim, "I never heard of anybody quite so altruistic in my life before." One letter offering shares did state, "There are no strings tied to this stock, so you can sell it whenever you wish." But it was difficult to accept such disclaimers at face value. At least one recipient of preferred shares, John J. Raskob, accompanied his return check with a note to George Whitney, stating, "I appreciate deeply the many courtesies shown me by you and your partners, and sincerely hope the future holds opportunities for me to reciprocate." Albert Wiggin, chairman of the Chase National Bank, would testify that when he received the opportunity to buy 10,000 shares of Alleghany Corporation at $20 while the shares were publicly traded at $35, "I assumed it was a favor and I was very glad to take it." At the very least, Morgan and Company's private security sales seem to have been employed to create a hospitable political and business climate for its banking operations. Even if the preferred lists accomplished no more than that, their existence fortified the belief that most investors entered the marketplace at a disadvantage.[137]

It was a sobering reflection of the limited ability of a congressional inquiry to educate the public about a technical subject that the most serious case built against the House of Morgan received considerably less press attention than the preferred lists. The crux of Pecora's presentation was that late in the 1920s, Morgan and Company, too, had surrendered its traditional austere standards and

---

* Richard Whitney was the brother of Morgan partner George Whitney. A few other recipients of the share offerings were family relations, notably Charles Lindbergh, son-in-law of firm member Dwight Morrow.

helped organize three giant holding companies whose primary function was to increase promoters' profits. Most significant was the
evidence Pecora developed over the course of several hearing days
concerning the United Corporation. Before January 1929, Morgan
and Company owned substantial blocks of stock in the United Gas
Improvement Company, the Public Service Corporation of New
Jersey, and the Mohawk Hudson Power Corporation, three gas and
electricity firms whose operations were centered in New York and
New Jersey. Each was a holding company; the United Gas Company, for example, owned stock in sixty separate local operating
companies. Such local or regional part-holding and part-operating
utility firms often had been defended as contributing to the most
efficient generation of power in a local market.

Early in 1929, however, J. P. Morgan and Company joined with
Bonbright and Company to create the United Corporation, which
ultimately held shares in public utility holding and operating companies in localities as widely dispersed as Connecticut, Illinois, Mississippi, Georgia, and France. Even Morgan and Company's George
Whitney was able to identify but one "useful public purpose . . .
served by the incorporation of the United Corporation": the opportunity for investors to diversify their holdings in public utility
firms.

Pecora belittled that purpose. Persistent questions contrasted the
opportunities accorded the Morgan and Bonbright firms and favored
individuals on Morgan's United Corporation preferred list with the
opportunities offered the public investor. United Corporation's initial capital structure had been formed in January 1929, when Morgan and Company traded its utility corporation shares and a small
quantity of cash for 600,000 preferred shares, 800,000 common
shares, and 714,200 perpetual option warrants issued by United.
United also sold 400,000 shares of common stock and one million
option warrants both to the Morgan and Bonbright firms in return
for $10 million in cash investment from each. Theoretically, the
aggregate market value of United's preferred and common stock
should have equaled approximately the value of the shares United
held in other firms plus United's other assets. But the 2,714,200
perpetual option warrants gave the Morgan and Bonbright firms the
chance to buy up to that many common shares at the option price of
$27.50 at any time in the future. In effect, the options placed a
ceiling on how much of the common stock's price appreciation the
two investment firms had to share with other United Corporation
shareholders. Any time the common stock price exceeded $27.50,
the investment banks could have exercised their warrants, obtain-

ing an instant profit equal to the difference between the market price and option price for the stock, and reducing the proportion of earnings and assets available for each common share.

Pecora documented that the combination of the frenzied 1929 stock market and public confidence in the "magic" Morgan name had swiftly elevated the United common stock from an initial market price just over $25 to a price of $73 at one point in 1929. By selling some of its United preferred stock, common stock, and option warrants, Morgan and Company was able to realize over $19 million in profits by 1933, including profits of $8.5 million on the sale of 200,000 option warrants between June and September 1929. Had Morgan and Company sold all 1,714,200 warrants during that period its profit could have been approximately $80 million, or a greater than 100 percent profit for the transfer of $61 million of stock and $10 million in cash to the holding company. Similarly, had the Morgan and Bonbright firms exercised all of their option warrants, the value of United Corporation's outstanding common shares would have been reduced by approximately 25 percent.[138]

Public reaction to the Morgan hearings was almost as condemnatory as that to the Charles E. Mitchell and National City Company revelations. Although the failure of the Morgan partners to pay income taxes and their use of the preferred lists won the greatest attention from journalists, the most serious editorial judgment was that the House of Morgan had forfeited its right to remain unregulated. "Why It Hurts" *The New York Times* titled an editorial as sorrowful as if it were describing the fall of the House of Thebes: "Here was a firm of bankers, perhaps the most famous and powerful in the whole world, which was certainly under no necessity of practicing the small arts of petty traders. Yet it failed under a test of its pride and prestige. By a mistake which had with the years swollen into a grievous fault, it sacrificed something intangible, imponderable, that had to do with the very highest repute." Walter Lippmann termed "the system of favoritism to insiders . . . a system which can be explained but cannot be defended." He called on Washington to "reduce the sheer power of so much privately directed money." Though guilty of "no crude crime against the law," the House of Morgan, according to the *New York World-Telegram*, was guilty of "the far deeper, more dangerous offense of what Lord Bryce well calls 'The submarine warfare which wealth can wage.' The country, the tone of its business, finance, and government, the whole capitalistic structure will be better, safer, and more stable when this long-standing notion of wealth's high prerogatives and immunities has gone finally into the discard." "No banking is private," *Business Week* insisted flatly. William Allen White summed up the hearings in his *Emporia Gazette*: "If the turmoil in the courts and in the Congressional committees stops, changes, or modifies the great thimble-rigging game of Wall Street, the depression of the last four years will have been worth all it cost."[139]

The public response to the Morgan hearings was directly responsible for the passage of the Banking Act of 1933, which, among other things, required private banks to limit themselves either to receiving deposits or to providing investment services. Roosevelt had offered the bill only lukewarm support. Treasury Secretary Woodin favored delaying its adoption. But on the third day of the Morgan hearings, the Senate unexpectedly enacted the bill by a voice vote. The House soon followed suit.[140]

The hearings also galvanized support for a new $100,000 appropriation for Pecora's investigation.[141] But the most enthusiastic appreciation of Pecora's work came from the Executive Branch. On May 27, President Roosevelt signed into law the Securities Act of 1933, the most important consequence to that date of the stock exchange hearings. With a sideward glance toward Capitol Hill, Roosevelt stated:

> The new law will also safeguard against the abuses of high-pressure salesmanship in security flotations. It will require full disclosure of all the private interests on the part of those who seek to sell securities to the public. The Act is thus intended to correct some of the evils which have been so glaringly revealed in the private exploitation of the public's money.[142]

2

Frankfurter's Turn

Finance is a means for assuring the flow of capital. Historically, it has also been a means for guiding that flow. In the first use, it is a mechanism in aid of the industrial system as we know it. In the second, it is a power controlling it . . . The next few years will probably determine whether the elements of power or control now tied to finance remain in the hands of the financial group or whether they pass, measurably, into the hands of the community. That finance has been serviceable, few dispassionate observers would deny. That its power and its control have been the wisest method of developing the community, is in serious doubt. That this power and this control should continue to dominate our national life has become extremely questionable. This, in brief, is the significance of the almost revolutionary movement athwart American long-term finance at present.

> — ADOLF BERLE
> *"High Finance: Master or Servant" (1933)*[1]

THE SECURITIES ACT of 1933 was a conservative response to the economic crisis known as the depression. Yet much more than the depression or the preceding stock market crash, it was the Pecora hearings that influenced the character of the 1933 Securities Act and of the Securities and Exchange Commission later created to enforce it. As with the Pecora investigation, a primary enduring mission of the SEC has been to compel disclosure of data by firms involved in the securities markets, indirectly inducing these firms to avoid illegal or embarrassing activities. After nearly fifty years of the Commission's "disclosure philosophy," this policy has become so well established, it is generally regarded as the appropriate or inevitable method of regulating corporate finance. Only by returning to the historical moment when the 1933 Securities Act was fashioned can one fully appreciate how modest the disclosure philosophy was in aim, how comparatively little effect on the economy it was intended to have, and how fortuitous were critical aspects of its adoption.

Each of Roosevelt's principal 1932 presidential campaign advisers favored the creation of a very different type of federal agency to direct the flow of new investment in private industry. Raymond Moley, chief of the presidential campaign "brains trust," was an admirer of the regulatory approach urged by Charles Van Hise, University of Wisconsin president, in his celebrated 1912 book, *Concentration and Control.* Agreeing with Van Hise that the growth of large corporations was inevitable, Moley disparaged any attempt to "atomize" big business because it would threaten "America's greatest contribution to a higher standard of living for the body of its citizenry — the development of mass production." Instead, Moley recommended a turning away "from the nostalgic philosophy of the trust busters" toward the development of federal "controls to stimulate and stabilize economic activity." At the same time, Moley was convinced that Roosevelt's financial policies would have to shore up business confidence in order to stimulate private investment.[2] In retrospect, Moley would term the 1933 Securities Act "a grave mistake" that had "only a negative effect upon recovery," since it lacked the support of the investment banking community it regulated.[3] After Moley left the Roosevelt administration, in December 1933, he wrote an editorial proposing "an NRA for finance" as a means to establish both "supervised self-government in finance [and] a harmonious relationship" among all participants in the financial sector.[4]

Economist Rexford Tugwell, Moley's colleague at Columbia University and a fellow brains truster, agreed with Moley that "we were . . . a long way on the road to a system of monopolies . . . we should allow it to evolve and should manage it publicly, rather than go back to a more primitive state where no social management existed." In Tugwell's view, the depression had been caused, in part, by the misallocation of capital. Overexpansion of plant facilities had raised prices, but there was no corresponding increase in consumer purchasing power. Where industries had as much as twice the plant, machinery, materials, and men needed for current production, Tugwell regarded the need for a "system of planning" as all but self-evident:

> If there were a system of planning, which allocated to specific industries capital sufficient to produce an amount of goods which would be taken by consumers at the price possible with capacity production, and no more, prices could be lower than they are at present. The surplus investment capital could then be assigned to other industries, and because less of each individual's income was required to buy good number 1, he could buy more of number 2, 3, and so on.

After Roosevelt's nomination, Tugwell presented him with a "proposal for an Economic Council" to provide "integrated industrial planning." Tugwell explained, "The average of demand must be gauged in advance by experts, co-ordinated production programs must be based on them, and it must be made certain that the amount of goods flowing into the markets is proportional to the purchasing power of consumers." Tugwell recommended that the federal Economic Council comprise "economists and representatives from industry." A chief function of the council would be to "encourage or discourage the flow of capital into various industries."[5]

Similarly, Adolf Berle, a Columbia University Law School professor and the brains truster with the greatest technical familiarity with corporate finance, urged Roosevelt in May 1932 to establish a federal board that would "exact full information about securities sold" and would also "exercise a real control over undue expansion of groups of credit instruments, where issue of these reached a point threatening the safety of the financial structure."[6]

Roosevelt disagreed. He approached the problem of securities regulation with the instincts of a progressive politician in the Wilson and Brandeis tradition, rather than of an economist concerned with the larger questions of capital allocation and economic recovery.[7] Rarely did Roosevelt speak about the stock market without invoking the title of Louis Brandeis's celebrated study, *Other People's Money*.[8] Like Brandeis, Roosevelt viewed the need to reform securities sales practices primarily as stemming from the self-interest of investment bankers, particularly the House of Morgan. Like Brandeis, Roosevelt believed the moral delicts of the bankers would be curbed when fully exposed to public scrutiny. Frequently Roosevelt's speeches paraphrased the first sentences of Chapter 5 of the Brandeis book, which was appropriately titled "What Publicity

Can Do": "Publicity is justly commended as a remedy for social and industrial diseases. Sunlight is said to be the best of disinfectants; electric light the most efficient policeman."

Roosevelt committed himself to the long-held populist and progressive goal of superseding lax state corporation laws with more stringent federal standards. His securities policy was an attempt to remedy the weaknesses in the four bodies of state and private rules then in effect, which cumulatively failed to minimize fraud or unfairness in the initial sale of corporate securities.

Most fundamental of the rules Roosevelt sought to supersede were the state corporation laws. No business corporation could begin operations until it filed a certificate of incorporation obliging it to operate subject to a state's corporation laws. Originally the state corporate statutes had been restrictive, limiting, among other things, the amount of capital a business firm could raise. But an anomaly in the United States Constitution permitted a business firm to incorporate in any state, regardless of where the firm actually did business. By the turn of the twentieth century, "chartermongering" states like New Jersey, Delaware, and Nevada had stimulated a "race for the bottom" by removing the restrictive features of their corporate statutes in order to induce out-of-state firms to incorporate within their increasingly hospitable borders. In return, the chartermongering states received from each firm an annual franchise tax. In Delaware, where chartermongering was elevated to a fiscal science, corporate franchise taxes and related fees averaged 31 percent of the state's total revenues from 1913 to 1934. Delaware's corporate fees might have been even higher but for the fact that other states emulated the most obviously attractive features of Delaware's statute in an effort to swell their tax returns.[9]

Throughout the nineteenth century, corporate securities sales had been rigidly supervised by state corporate laws. Each shareholder was required to contribute not less than a stated amount — called a par value — for shares. Stock not paid for by the minimum contribution could not legally be issued. Although the par value originally was intended to protect creditors by ensuring that a firm would not run up bills before raising sufficient capital to pay them, it protected shareholders as well by guaranteeing that "every stockholder in a corporation is entitled to insist that every other stockholder shall contribute his ratable part of the company's capital."[10]

Demonstrably, the requirement that a firm could sell its shares at no less than par value could be most inconvenient if the value of a firm's assets declined and the firm needed to raise additional capital. Firms soon took to employing a loophole implicit in the corporate statutes by selling "low par" stock with a stated capital as low as a penny and most of the price paid for a share denominated as "surplus." The practice received legislative blessing in 1912, when New York became the first state to authorize "no par" stock. The practical consequence of both low par and no par shares was that a board of directors no longer bound by the requirement of selling all shares at a stated par value price now had discretion to raise or lower the sales price of corporate shares.[11]

The concept that each shareholder must contribute his "ratable part of the company's capital" also was challenged by the facility with which directors could issue stock in exchange for property or services, rather than for cash. Crucial amendments to state corporate statutes gave color of law to the issuance of "watered" stock (or stock valued at more than the property exchanged for it). By the 1920s the acts typically stated, "The judgment of directors as to the value of property purchased shall be conclusive."

Occasionally stock-watering was effectively challenged by a shareholders' fraud suit.[12] But by the 1920s, the ability of the judiciary to protect noncontrolling shareholders from management self-favoritism had been outrun by a series of statutory innovations that allowed corporate insiders to achieve profits from securities distributions without risking a fraud suit. Many of these enactments came into being as the result of 1927 and 1929 amendments to the Delaware General Corporation Law.

Prominent was a 1927 amendment that permitted Delaware corporations to waive the better than century-old protection accorded shareholders by their "pre-emptive rights." By judicial decisions dating back as far as 1807, the original shareholders in a corporation had been guaranteed the right to subscribe to each additional issue of shares proportional to their initial holdings. This ensured for the shareholders who had assumed the original risk of the enterprise the power to maintain their proportional rights to corporate profits as a firm expanded. Without these shareholders' pre-emptive rights, a board of directors could add to its existing power to issue stock at any price deemed appropriate the power to issue new shares to whomever it chose.[13]

As the Morgan-backed United Corporation illustrated, similar results could be achieved by the issuance of stock options or stock purchase warrants, either of which permitted a corporation to distribute rights to buy corporate stock at a designated price regardless of how high above the option price the stock's market price rose. Stock option warrants first received legislative sanction in March 1929, when the Delaware General Assembly amended Section 14 of its General Corporation Law.[14] Alternatively, under Section 13 of the revised Delaware General Corporation Law a corporation could issue so-called blank stock, whose "voting powers, designations, preferences, and relative, participating, optional or other rights" could be fixed by a board of directors after original subscribers had purchased their shares.[15] Adolf Berle scathingly concluded in 1930 that the effect of these and kindred corporate law devices could accord corporate management "the power of confiscation": "By using them, or a combination of them, appropriately, the profits of the enterprise and also in a considerable measure the underlying assets may be shifted from one group of stockholders to another."[16]

As early as 1911 the failure of lax state corporation statutes to prevent securities fraud gave rise to the first significant legislative response when Kansas enacted the first well-known state securities law, popularly known as a "blue sky" law, since it was intended to check stock swindlers so barefaced they "would sell building lots in the blue sky." It is one of the more improbable ironies of corporate law that the man who initially popularized securities regulation in the United States was not a sophisticated reform attorney like Louis Brandeis or Felix Frankfurter, but, rather, a retired grocer and sometime populist politician named J. N. Dolley.

Appointed bank commissioner in 1910, Dolley organized a special department to investigate securities offered for sale in Kansas. His action was in response to a wave of recent land, mining, and insurance company stock frauds. Dolley asserted that firms selling securities should be subject to "the very strictest of supervision. Why should the bank be regulated and supervised any more so than the stock selling company?" he wrote. "History and statistics show that losses through banks are but a drop in the bucket compared with the money which is lost through investment in worthless stocks and bonds." So prodded, the Kansas legislature in 1911 enacted a sweeping securities licensing statute. By its terms, no "investment company" could sell securities in Kansas until it filed a description of its operations with the bank commissioner and received a permit. The bank commissioner was given broad discretion not to grant a permit if he found any aspect of a company's business to be "unfair, unjust, inequitable, or oppressive to any class of contributors, or if he decides from his examination of its affairs that said investment company is not solvent and does not intend to do a fair and honest business, and in his judgment does not promise a fair return on the stocks, bonds or other securities by it offered for sale."

Dolley broadly advertised the law's "wonderful results," estimating, in one often-quoted statement, that the act in its first year of operation had saved the citizens of Kansas "at least six million dollars" and that fewer than a hundred of the fourteen to fifteen hundred companies investigated by his Banking Department had been granted a permit. Each of these claims was a fantastic exaggeration. A painstaking 1913 report by Thomas Mulvey, Canada's Undersecretary of State, found, on the basis of an examination of Dolley's own records, no substantive basis for Dolley's estimate that Kansas citizens had been saved at least $6 million, and that, through May 1913, only sixty-two firms had been refused a permit.

At the time, Mulvey's sobering appraisal was ignored. Within two years after the Kansas blue sky act had been adopted, twenty-three states enacted securities regulation statutes, all but six of which were either identical with the Kansas law or modeled on it.[17] After the Kansas-type blue sky law was held to be constitutional by the United States Supreme Court in 1917,[18] the movement swept the country. By 1933, every state except Nevada had adopted a securities law.[19]

Rarely have statutes enacted with such fanfare and general support subsequently been so universally deprecated. In the brutal glare that followed the stock market crash, it was apparent to virtually all commentators and congressional witnesses on the subject that the blue sky laws never really had a chance to succeed. As early as 1915, the Investment Bankers Association had reported to its members that they could "ignore" all blue sky laws by making offerings across state lines through the mails. Unscrupulous securities promoters soon adopted the technique. A 1933 Department of Commerce study found, "The most effective and widely used method of evading the provision of State blue sky laws consists in operating across State lines." Robert E. Healy, chief counsel to the Federal Trade Commission, testified before Congress that same year that over 90 percent of the securities sold in Pennsylvania were sold through the mails.[20]

Nor were purely intrastate securities sales much better policed. Effective lobbying, principally by the Investment Bankers Association, had riddled most state blue sky laws with exemptions.[21] Typically, an act might exempt the securities of all corporations listed on a stock exchange and all securities issued by a public utility subject to the regulation of a federal or state agency. The more porous statutes also exempted the securities of all firms incorporated intrastate, bank corporations, insurance companies, investment companies, cooperative associations, building and loan associations, business trusts, as well as issues "guaranteed by friendly foreign govern-

ments," mortgage bonds and notes secured by property within the
state, short-term commercial paper, "isolated" securities transactions, one-year debentures, and a myriad of other types of securities
or transactions.[22]

Only eight states appropriated sufficient funds to support securities commissions that could work full time investigating suspected
frauds and prosecuting violators. In forty states, administration of
the blue sky act was "a football of politics" as the chairman of the
Conference on Prevention of Fraudulent Transactions in Securities
put it in 1931. Enforcement responsibilities were assigned to un-
specialized attorneys working for state officials as disparate as the
railroad commission or the state auditor. When political administrations changed, responsibility for blue sky enforcement frequently
also was reassigned.[23]

Even in New York, which was widely regarded as having the most
effective blue sky agency, enforcement was inadequate. In 1932, the
attorney general's Bureau of Securities employed more than a hundred men, secured injunctions against 1522 persons and firms, and
instituted 146 criminal prosecutions. At approximately the same
time, officials of the New York Stock Exchange estimated that of
the billion dollars or so of fraudulent securities annually sold in the
United States, about half were sold in New York State.[24]

A somewhat more effective system of securities regulation was
administered by the New York Stock Exchange stock-listing committee. Before a security could be offered for sale on the Exchange,
the corporate issuer had to file an application describing in detail the
firm's capital structure, history, liabilities, properties, financial
statements over the past five years, and officers. The firm had to
forward, along with the application, copies of its charter, by-laws,
leases, franchises, relevant director and shareholder resolutions, an
opinion of an independent legal counsel as to the legality of the
corporate organization and the immediate securities issuance, and a
copy of a report of a qualified engineer describing the actual physical
condition of properties at a recent date.[25] Not only were the stock
exchange listing requirements far more precise than any found in
the blue sky laws; they more closely resembled the standards subsequently adopted in Schedule A of the 1933 Securities Act than those
found in the English Companies Act, which proponents of the federal Securities Act usually identified as their model.[26] Even the
most unrelenting critics of corporate finance lauded the Exchange's
listing requirements. Harvard's Professor William Z. Ripley, for example, declaimed unequivocally in his influential 1927 work, *Main
Street and Wall Street*, "Beyond peradventure of doubt the New

York Stock Exchange is today the leading influence in the promotion of adequate corporate disclosure."[27] Similarly, Adolf Berle believed that "the most forward-looking steps in finance taken during the 1925–1929 boom were not taken by government, but by that most maligned institution, the New York Stock Exchange."[28]

Nonetheless, the New York Stock Exchange's listing requirements proved little more effective than the blue sky laws. Being purely voluntary standards, they could be avoided by any corporation that chose to register as an "unlisted" security on the New York Curb Exchange (which in 1953 was renamed the American Stock Exchange) or any of the other seventeen securities exchanges which permitted securities to be traded on an "unlisted" basis.*[29]

Nor did the New York Stock Exchange scrupulously enforce its listing requirements. As the number of new stock applications approved increased to 300 in 1926, 571 in 1928, and 759 in the first nine months of 1929, responsibility for enforcing the requirements remained with the eight Exchange members who composed the Listing Committee and a small investigative staff. Testifying at the Pecora hearings, Frank Altschul, chairman of the Exchange's Committee on Stock List, conceded that the NYSE ceased making any independent investigation of an application for the listing of additional stock by a firm whose stock was previously listed unless there appeared patently suspicious matter in the listing application. Pressing the point, Pecora demonstrated that in at least one instance the Stock List Committee did not respond when an application *did* include patently suspicious matter. When Ivar Kreuger's Kreuger and Toll Company in 1929 applied to list a thirty-year debenture, reserving the right to substitute new pledged securities for those listed as collateral on the application, Altschul and the Stock List Committee were aware that no American firm had ever been accorded so sweeping a substitution privilege. The Stock List Committee did not make an independent investigation of Kreuger and Toll, nor did it consult an attorney as to the legality of the substitution provision. When Ivar Kreuger subsequently replaced the French debentures serving as collateral with less valuable Yugoslavian ones, Altschul could only testify that the New York Stock Exchange had been "deceived."[30]

---

*An "unlisted" security was one about which the corporate issuer had supplied no information whatever, but which had been admitted to trading on an exchange on the application of a member of that exchange, who usually forwarded a pro forma description of the company based on data appearing in a statistical manual like *Moody's*. Although the New York Curb Exchange was the second largest in the country, as of November 1933, 82 percent of all securities there traded were on an unlisted basis.

Further contributing to the deficiencies of state corporation statutes, blue sky laws, and the New York Stock Exchange listing requirements was the primitiveness of accounting standards. Along
with the Exchange's efforts to upgrade its listing requirements in
the 1920s and early 1930s there had been a similar effort to upgrade
corporate annual and periodic reporting to shareholders. In 1923,
over 30 percent of the firms listed on the New York Stock Exchange
were not subject to an agreement to provide shareholders with
either annual or quarterly financial statements, and only 242 of the
957 listed firms provided both annual and quarterly financial reports. But a decade later all 1157 firms listed on the Exchange provided at least annual financial reports, and over 60 percent provided
quarterly reports as well.[31] Also, by 1933 at least 85 percent of the
firms listed on the New York Stock Exchange were periodically
audited by independent certified public accountants.[32]

The rapidity with which periodic audited financial statements
became commonplace masked the continuing unreliability of financial reporting. Through 1933 no government or private agency effectively defined generally accepted accounting principles. Instead, individual corporate managements retained broad discretion to choose
among alternative accounting principles.[33] On occasion this discretion was employed to create an exaggerated impression of a firm's
worth. Federal Trade Commission attorneys testified before Congress in 1933 that public utilities investigated by the FTC had "written up" assets by more than $1 billion by substituting an estimated
appraisal or reproduction value for the preferred method of recording
the assets' original cost on the firm's balance sheet.[34] A firm's periodic income statements could be similarly misleading. M. B.
Hoxsey, executive assistant to the New York Stock Exchange's
Stock List Committee, complained in a 1930 speech that the consolidated income statement commonly employed by holding companies often obscured as much as it revealed. In one instance "a
certain very large corporation formerly published consolidated
statements including only its wholly owned subsidiaries. These
statements apparently justified the dividends which were regularly
paid." Subsequent examination by the Exchange, however, showed
that "the company's proportion of the current losses of the uncon-
solidated [partially owned] subsidiaries had for years been larger
than the total profits of the rest of the system as shown by the
consolidated statements."[35] At the very least, commonly employed
accounting practices did not provide investors with a reliable tool
with which to compare the worth and performance of different
firms. Through 1933 there were several commonly employed

methods of recording inventory value or depreciating the value of perishable assets.[36] Any period's earnings could be swollen by a firm's selling a corporate asset, since the distinction between operating income and other income was not regularly made.[37] In some states, dividends could be paid out of invested capital when a firm was not earning profits.[38] A 1929 survey of 580 leading firms actively traded on the New York Stock Exchange found that only 323 reported gross income.[39] Until a uniform system of financial accounting could be imposed on comparable firms, the policy aim of meaningful corporate disclosure quite simply could not be realized.

Only once had the federal government regulated corporate securities sales. In April 1918, Congress authorized the wartime Capital Issues Committee "to investigate, pass upon, and determine" whether each securities sale of more than $100,000 was "compatible with the national interest." The committee's authority was voluntary, not compulsory. Its purpose was to direct the flow of capital toward "essential uses" by disapproving securities issuances that interfered with the government's wartime use of credit, labor, and materials. Although the committee functioned for only six months, it reviewed over three thousand applications, disapproving $917,133,000 of proposed securities.

But in two final reports, the Capital Issues Committee emphasized its limitations. "In the absence of specific power either to compel submission to its jurisdiction or to enforce its findings," the committee reported, it was "unable to deal effectively with many enterprises whose promoters or managers remained deaf to every appeal to their patriotism. This situation permitted the continuance of a considerable traffic in worthless or fraudulent securities," which the committee "conservatively" estimated to equal $500 million annually and predicted would soon rise as investors exchanged Liberty Bonds for more speculative securities. Accordingly, the Capital Issues Committee was "unanimously of the opinion that federal supervision of security issues, here undertaken for the first time, should be continued by some public agency, preferably by one of the government departments, in such a form as to check the traffic in doubtful securities, while imposing no undue restrictions upon the financing of legitimate industry."[40]

President Wilson soon also recommended the adoption of a federal securities act "to prevent the fraudulent methods of promotion by which our people are annually fleeced of many millions of hard-earned money."[41] Numerous securities bills were introduced in Congress between 1919 and 1927,[42] the most important of which was first offered by Congressman Edward Dennison in December

1920. The Dennison bill would have plugged the largest loophole in the enforcement of state blue sky laws by making it illegal for any person to use the mails or any of the facilities of interstate commerce to sell securities in any state until there had been compliance with the formalities of that state's blue sky law. Although there was some doubt as to whether a federal statute whose sole purpose was to aid in the enforcement of state laws was constitutional, Dennison briefly won the grudging support of the Investment Bankers Association by agreeing to exempt a wide range of securities transactions. After being favorably reported out by the House Commerce Committee, the bill was passed almost unanimously by the House of Representatives. But in the Senate the Dennison bill was referred to the Judiciary Committee, which never reported out the measure to the full Senate.[43] With the death of the Dennison bill, the opportunity for a Wilson-inspired federal securities act temporarily also died. It was this Brandeis-Wilson approach to corporate law that Roosevelt revitalized in his 1932 presidential campaign.

The process of transforming Roosevelt's securities policy into a bill began within hours of Roosevelt's election. On November 9, 1932, Roosevelt received a telegram from Huston Thompson requesting a conference to discuss an "outline to cover platform pledge regarding sale of securities and holding companies."[44] Thompson, a Western populist transformed into a Wilsonian Democrat, had been much affected by Brandeis's arguments for local government and small-scale industry when he had served in the Wilson administration as an Assistant Attorney General and a commissioner of the Federal Trade Commission. From 1920 to 1921 and again from 1923 to 1924 he had been the FTC's chairman. While at the FTC, Thompson had publicly supported the efforts of the Capital Issues Committee to prevent, as he wrote, a "speculative orgy in 'wild cat' investments." When the Capital Issues Committee disbanded, Thompson directed an FTC securities fraud program, although he came to believe it had doubtful legal authority.

"As I see it," Thompson had written in a magazine article much influenced by Other People's Money, "the solution must be effected through a system of publicity which shall protect the public by informing the investors as to the securities to be sold by giving the prospective purchaser a full opportunity to be enlightened and then leaving to him the responsibility of purchase."[45] Thompson personally had written the 1932 Democratic Party platform plank calling for control of the sale of securities and had urged Roosevelt to deliver campaign speeches both on securities sales and holding companies.[46] In 1933, at the age of fifty-eight, Thompson was a courtly, distinguished-looking man of considerable presence, not unaware that Louis Howe, Roosevelt's political mentor, and Progressive Senator George Norris were encouraging the President-elect to nominate Thompson as his Attorney General.[47] Roosevelt met with Thompson, whose abilities as a courtroom attorney Roosevelt admired, and Thompson soon forwarded a memorandum outlining his approach to securities, holding companies, and amendments to the antitrust laws.[48]

Soon after the election Raymond Moley and Adolf Berle also urged Roosevelt to carry out swiftly the promises implicit in his Columbus, Ohio, campaign speech by recommending to Congress both a bill concerning the federal regulation of security issues and perhaps a federal incorporation act. Moley considered the securities regulation bill, in particular, "a 'must' of the first order."[49] In December, shortly after Moley had settled into his new role as supervisor of the formulation of Roosevelt's legislative program,[50] Roosevelt authorized Moley to elicit from Samuel Untermyer suggestions regarding regulation of the stock exchanges and securities issues.

At seventy-four, Untermyer was the grand old man of the corporate reform movement. His crusading service as counsel to the 1912 Pujo investigation of the "money trust" had won him Moley's regard as a "colorful, voluble John the Baptist preparing the way for the solemnities of Wilson, Brandeis, and Glass." The celebrated money trust investigation had been instrumental in persuading Congress to enact the Federal Reserve Act, increasing public sentiment for state adoption of blue sky laws, and much else. But Untermyer's 1914 proposal to regulate the securities exchanges and vest the Post Office with power to supervise the interstate sale of securities not registered under a blue sky law had not received the endorsement of President Wilson or Congress. For close to twenty years, Untermyer had continued to study and speak out on the need for stock exchange regulation and was the outside expert most frequently quoted by *The New York Times* on the revelations of the Pecora investigation. Moley, a recent acquaintance, was hardly alone in believing that Untermyer "had more knowledge and more constructive ideas about [stock market] reform than anyone else."[51] After an exchange of letters in late December, Moley asked Untermyer to prepare a securities bill, suggesting that Adolf Berle and economist Charles Taussig work with him.

Moley was soon disappointed. In mid-January 1933, Untermyer forwarded a bill "to prevent the use of the mails and of the telegraph and telephone in furtherance of fraudulent and harmful transactions on stock exchanges." As convinced in 1933 as he had been in 1914 that the only method to guarantee the constitutionality of the bill was to grant enforcement powers to the Post Office, Untermyer formulated his bill to give the Postmaster General sweeping powers to issue regulations and prohibitions concerning transactions on the stock exchanges, new securities issuances, periodic corporate financial statements, and the membership of the stock exchanges.[52] Moley's first impression was horror. "The Post Office Department was essentially a service organization," he later wrote. "The idea of sticking an immense regulatory machine into it horrified my sense of the administrative and legal proprieties." Although Untermyer adamantly disagreed with Moley's belief about the Post Office, Moley concluded "that Untermyer could nevertheless be of vital assistance in the drafting of the precise kind of bill desired."[53]

Roosevelt shared Moley's doubt that empowering the Post Office to supervise such matters as a uniform system of accounting would be wise. According to one subsequent news account, Roosevelt also was annoyed with Untermyer for leaking a self-serving story to a New York City newspaper just before a scheduled meeting with Roosevelt.[54] But the factor that finally persuaded Roosevelt to shelve the Untermyer bill was the unique opportunity rapidly to enact legislation created by the favorable public and congressional response to his handling of the bank crisis just after his inauguration on March 4. Roosevelt's entire legislative program was accelerated. After making the previously unplanned decision to keep Congress in session, Roosevelt indicated to Moley on March 18 that among his legislative priorities for the first session of the Seventy-third Congress would be "regulation of corporations," by which he meant a securities bill.[55] From about that date onward, Roosevelt was determined to draft and quickly submit to Congress a securities bill that could be voted on while he still enjoyed the extraordinary political support generated by the bank crisis. Without initially informing Moley, Roosevelt began discussing alternative securities proposals with two other drafting teams.

Shortly after taking office on March 4, Roosevelt had directed his Attorney General, Homer Cummings, and his Secretary of Commerce, Daniel Roper, to work with Huston Thompson in preparing another draft of the securities bill. Roper assigned two staff attorneys, Walter Miller, chief of the Commerce Department's Foreign Service Division, and Ollie Butler, also of the Foreign Service Division, to assist Thompson. Apparently Thompson, Miller, and Butler

were well aware of Roosevelt's self-imposed deadline. After studying blue sky laws and earlier federal proposals, the three hurriedly
assembled a draft of a bill that combined features of several of these
precedents, as well as provisions modeled on the English Companies
Act. Thompson then consulted with Justice Brandeis and officials of
the Federal Reserve Board and Interstate Commerce Commission
before presenting his draft to Roosevelt, Moley, and Roper on
March 19.[56]

Roosevelt almost immediately indicated to Thompson that the
draft was acceptable.[57] On March 23, the press was informed that a
securities bill prepared under the supervision of Commerce Secretary Roper and Attorney General Cummings would soon be introduced.[58] At Moley's insistence, Roosevelt attempted to mollify the
deeply wounded Untermyer. Thompson called on Untermyer on
March 26 and attempted to convince "the old maestro" that there
was no conflict between his bill and Untermyer's, which Roosevelt
had come to view as a securities exchange measure that could be
introduced later.[59] At a subsequent "reconciliation" meeting that
day, attended by Roosevelt, Moley, Cummings, Roper, Taussig, and
others, Roosevelt delivered much the same message.[60] Untermyer
was unappeased; responsibility for preparing the separate securities exchange bill was reassigned to Secretary Roper. At the
"reconciliation" meeting, Roosevelt also indicated to Thompson
that he wanted Thompson's securities bill reduced in length and a
paragraph empowering the Federal Trade Commission to refuse the
registration of foreign securities eliminated entirely. These revisions were completed by March 28.[61]

Roosevelt submitted Thompson's bill to both Houses of Congress
the following day. In an accompanying message, which borrowed
heavily from Brandeis's *Other People's Money*, a final report of the
Capital Issues Committee and the 1932 Democratic Party platform,
Roosevelt emphasized:

> The Federal Government cannot and should not take any action
> which might be construed as approving or guaranteeing that newly
> issued securities are sound in the sense that their value will be main-
> tained or that the properties which they represent will earn profit.
>
> There is, however, an obligation upon us to insist that every issue of
> new securities to be sold in interstate commerce shall be accom-
> panied by full publicity and information, and that no essentially im-
> portant element attending the issue shall be concealed from the buy-
> ing public.
>
> This proposal adds to the ancient rule of caveat emptor the further

doctrine: "Let the seller also beware." It puts the burden of telling the whole truth on the seller. It should give impetus to honest dealing in securities and thereby bring back public confidence.[62]

The initial public and congressional response was almost universally favorable. The *Times* predicted that the bill "would be on its way to the statute books by the latter part of next week."[63] The *Wall Street Journal* concluded a hasty analysis of the bill by stating: "The measure is in the main so right in its basic provisions . . . the country will insist upon its passage."[64] Unexpected support came from the perennially conservative *Barron's* magazine, which charitably allowed that the authors had "admirably restrained themselves."[65]

As originally submitted to Congress, Thompson's draft empowered the Federal Trade Commission to investigate and prosecute fraudulent securities sales. With respect to corporate security issuances made by firms with $100,000 or more of a capital stock, except for securities sold by common carriers or public utilities already supervised by the federal government and other limited exemptions, no sale or offer to sell a security would be lawful until a registration statement was filed with the FTC. Unlike Dolley's Kansas blue sky law and its numerous progeny, Thompson's draft stipulated that securities sales could commence immediately, without the commission's prior approval. Consistent with the Democratic Party platform and Roosevelt's March 29 message, Section 10 of Thompson's bill emphasized that no action of the FTC lawfully could be represented to be approval of a security.

However, the commission was vested with powers to revoke the registration of any security whose issuer "has been or is about to engage in fraudulent transactions . . . is not conducting its business in accordance with law . . . is in any other way dishonest," or whose business is "in unsound condition or insolvent." It also could revoke a security's registration when "the enterprise or business of the issuer . . . is not based upon sound principles, and . . . the revocation is in the interest of the public welfare." In an accompanying statement, Thompson wrote of this provision that it did "not attempt to prevent investment in speculative projects, inasmuch as many of the industrial developments in the country began as speculations. An effort is made, however, to draft the law in such a manner that prospective investors are enabled to know the extent of the speculative features and have reasonable knowledge concerning the chances of success or failure."

If any statement in a registration statement was false in any material respect, the civil liabilities section of Thompson's bill gave a purchaser the right to rescind the transaction and receive all of the purchase price back from the promoters, issuers, principal officers, and directors who were required to sign the registration statement before a security could be offered for sale.

In addition, the FTC was given unlimited power to investigate the sale of all securities, including those otherwise exempt from the act, if it suspected that any firm or promoter was willfully attempting to defraud a purchaser, and to forward any evidence uncovered to the Justice Department for criminal prosecution.

The bill also adopted the theory of Congressman Dennison's 1920 proposal that the federal government should have the power to prosecute any firm that offered for sale across state lines securities that would have been illegal if offered on a purely intrastate basis without complying with a state blue sky law.[66]

In the House of Representatives, Thompson's bill was claimed by Commerce Committee chairman Sam Rayburn. This was fortunate for Roosevelt. Rayburn was just beginning his most effective years in Congress. In the next three years he would be the member of the House of Representatives most responsible for the enactment of the SEC's three basic enabling laws. Although by inclination Rayburn was a conservative cut-the-federal-budget-and-don't-interfere-with-the private-economy Southern Democrat, once branded by the AFL "the workingman's enemy," his intense loyalty to Roosevelt and his populist suspicion of Wall Street soon led Rayburn to consider himself "a helluva New Dealer." Besides being one of the ablest legislative tacticians ever to serve in Congress, Rayburn had some technical familiarity with securities law as a result of an eight-year campaign, ultimately successful in 1920, to subject railroad stocks and bonds to the regulation of the Interstate Commerce Commission.[67]

Like Roosevelt, Rayburn was convinced of the strategic advantage of moving for rapid enactment of a securities bill. Hearings began on March 31, with only two days of testimony scheduled.[68] Initially, Rayburn invited no opposition witnesses to appear. Thompson, Miller, and Butler led off the hearings by urging that the combination of an estimated $25 billion worth of "undesirable or worthless" securities sold between 1919 and 1932 and the failure of blue sky laws to be enforced across state lines made adoption of a federal securities bill imperative.[69] Almost immediately, however, Thompson's bill was subjected to a buzz saw of criticism, first from the congressmen on the Commerce Committee, then from the opposition witnesses

Rayburn reluctantly allowed to testify.[70] Most harshly criticized were the provisions permitting the FTC to revoke any security it found "not based upon sound principles" and the section subjecting directors to strict liability to any securities purchaser for an indefinite period of time for any material misstatement of fact in the registration statement. The latter provision was considered so broad by Investment Bankers Association counsel William Breed that he warned it could "open up more litigation by crooked and unprincipled people than any legislation you could pass." Also criticized were the provisions about fraud in the resale of securities after the securities were first issued, the section empowering the FTC to enforce blue sky laws, and the failure to exempt short-term bank loans, commonly called commercial paper.[71] By the early afternoon of the second hearing day, Chairman Rayburn was openly skeptical of the wisdom of so severe a bill. Specifically quoting Section 6(f) of the proposed bill, which empowered the FTC to revoke securities "not based upon sound priniciples," Rayburn stated to witness Ollie Butler:

> Now, we have passed a lot of laws since we met here on the 5th of March, but I do not think we have given anybody that much power yet . . . Do you believe that an administrative officer of the Government ought to be given that much power, as a general principle — to pass upon whether or not a man's business is based on sound principles? It is mighty easy when you go to write a statute, if you want to delegate absolute authority; you can write that in a very short statute; but the question that this committee has got to determine is whether or not you want to give anybody that kind of authority.[72]

By April 4, the day before the House hearings concluded, Rayburn was convinced that the Thompson bill was too stringent and would have to be thoroughly revised or replaced. That day, Rayburn called on Raymond Moley and through him swiftly won President Roosevelt's agreement to alter drastically Thompson's bill.[73]

Roosevelt acquiesced to Rayburn's view that the bill was too far-reaching, because the only substantive feature of the legislation he felt strongly about was the basic disclosure principle, and Rayburn persuaded him that so stringent a bill might prove unnecessarily divisive. The point is significant, because when Roosevelt agreed to bring in his third drafting team in four weeks, he was not merely seeking — as Moley suggests in his *Memoirs*[74] — draftsmen who could hone the technical provisions of the bill, but, rather, draftsmen who could produce a bill conservative enough to be rapidly enacted.[75] In the interest of speed, Roosevelt was willing to compromise considerably his securities proposal. In deference to Sam Rayburn's sentiments about Thompson's bill, he did so.

* * *

Among the papers of Felix Frankfurter, there is an intriguing letter dated March 23, 1933, written by Frankfurter to a younger colleague at Harvard Law School, James Landis, in which Frankfurter described "specifically what we ought to achieve in this legislation for truth-telling and the disclosure of financial self-interest" and then proceeded to enumerate the need to publicize bankers' "commissions or profits . . . when issuing securities," underwriters' commissions or profits, and any other contract or agreement by which "secret underwriting profit" might be secured. He concluded: "I still think we ought also to cover the mischief of peddling securities from door to door or over the telephone, as was so widely practiced prior to 1929. I think the English Companies Act furnishes a model for the legislation that ought to be attempted."[76] On the face of it, there is no direct indication in the letter that Roosevelt earlier had contacted Frankfurter and asked him to begin studying securities law, but this is a plausible, if not probable, inference. The previous day Frankfurter had recommended to Moley that Bernard Flexner, a former general counsel to one of Samuel Insull's utility firms, was "particularly qualified to help in perfecting [the securities] bill."[77] Considering the number of occasions Roosevelt, as governor of New York, had consulted Frankfurter on legislation and the number of times in the future, as President, he would do so, it seems likely that on or just before March 22, when Roosevelt decided to shelve Untermyer's bill and move swiftly for the adoption of Thompson's proposal, he also asked Frankfurter to familiarize himself with the problems of drafting a securities bill. Roosevelt often employed more than one drafting team, and with the Securities Act he was particularly determined to move swiftly.

What is certain is that on April 4, when Rayburn communicated his unhappiness with Thompson's draft to Moley, Moley contacted Frankfurter.[78] Within hours, Frankfurter wired back: "Three of us will arrive at the Carlton Friday morning."[79] From the time of that telegram onward, Frankfurter was the man Roosevelt and Moley relied on to supervise the drafting and enactment of a securities bill. Long after the legislation was on the statute books, the Harvard Law professor would retain Roosevelt's near-total confidence in matters concerning securities law reform. Frankfurter would help select the draftsmen of the SEC's three basic statutes, the FTC officials who enforced the Securities Act during its first year, most of the original

SEC commissioners, and many of the Commission's top staff appointees. It would be Frankfurter's ideas, more than the simpler slogans of Louis Brandeis, that would dominate the Commission during the New Deal.

Felix Frankfurter, as Raymond Moley later would explain to Huston Thompson, "was . . . in the eyes of the administration the leading lawyer of this country."[80] Such encomiums are nearly always suspect, but there was considerable evidence that Roosevelt so regarded Frankfurter. During Roosevelt's two terms as governor of New York, Frankfurter periodically visited Albany or Hyde Park and was a frequent correspondent. An admiring Roosevelt observed to a close associate, "Felix has more ideas per minute than any man of my acquaintance. He has a brilliant mind, but it clicks so fast it makes my head fairly spin. I find him tremendously interesting and stimulating." Frankfurter was Roosevelt's initial choice to be Solicitor General, a position that Roosevelt urged Frankfurter to accept explicitly because "I can't put you on the Supreme Court from the Harvard Law School." Frankfurter stunned Roosevelt by declining, but Frankfurter believed, and arguably demonstrated, "that I can do much more to be of use to you by staying in Cambridge than by becoming Solicitor General." Roosevelt chided Frankfurter for being "an independent pig" ("How," the President asked, "can I find anybody with just your qualifications to appear on behalf of the government before the Supreme Court?"), but never wavered in his determination to nominate Frankfurter to the highest Court, a nomination ultimately telephoned to Cambridge early in 1939.[81]

Although Frankfurter was best known to the public as the journalist-defender of Sacco and Vanzetti, his primary academic interest was administrative law. An intimate of Brandeis, he was not unmoved by the Justice's Jeffersonian arguments for local government and deconcentrated industry. But Frankfurter's thought was too empirical and too questioning to allow him fully to accept any easy political formula. As he wrote Moley in 1935, "I am right, am I not, in saying that neither you nor I are doctrinaire either about the curse of bigness or the blessings of littleness. Like most things that matter in the world, it's a question of more or less, of degree, of when is big too big, and is little too little."[82] In Frankfurter's unromantic reckoning, the advent of modern industry made inevitable the growth of government bureaus and a diminution of the role of the courts as the basic arbiter of private rights. Prefacing one of the first administrative law casebooks in 1932, he characterized this transformation as "the distinctive development of our era":

Governmental regulation of banking, insurance, public utilities, industry, finance, immigration, the professions, health and morals, in short, the inevitable response of government to the needs of modern society, is building up a body of enactments not written by legislatures and of adjudications not made by courts, and only to a limited degree subject to their revisions. These powers are lodged in vast congeries of agencies. We are in the midst of a process, still largely unconscious and unscientific, of adjusting the play of these powers to the traditional system of Anglo-American law and courts.[83]

In retrospect, it is obvious that the emergence of "vast congeries of agencies" is the most fundamental transformation to have occurred in twentieth-century American governance. Indeed, today it is a commonplace to assume that most routine Executive Branch decisions in a modern democracy will be made by its "fourth branch," the administrative agencies. Precisely because Franklin Roosevelt ushered into existence an "alphabet" of regulatory bureaus, political scientists usually identify him as the pivotal figure in the development of the modern federal government.

But in 1933, Felix Frankfurter was one of a comparatively few scholars who were thinking seriously about how the administrative agencies themselves should be administered. With the 1933 Securities Act, Frankfurter had his first opportunity to apply his approach to government-by-administrative-agency at the federal level. In time, his views would become a form of conventional wisdom, broadly influencing several of the regulatory agencies spawned by the New Deal.

Frankfurter's approach to the agencies was premised on his skepticism that Congress by legislative enactment could effectively administer the structure or behavior of a modern economy. The greatest experiment in congressional management of the economy had been the 1890 Sherman Antitrust Act,[84] whose grandiloquent generalities — among them, "every contract, combination in the form of trust or otherwise, or conspiracy, in restraint of trade . . . is hereby declared to be illegal" — had been limited by judicial decisions culminating in the Supreme Court's 1911 "rule of reason" opinion in the *Standard Oil* case.[85] Three years later, Congress had enacted the more specific Clayton Antitrust Act,[86] but that statute, too, initially had fared poorly, as the courts identified significant loopholes that the Congress, even when aided by attorneys as talented as Brandeis, had proven incapable of fully anticipating.

On the other hand, Frankfurter was even more skeptical of the wisdom of nearly unlimited delegations of power to administrative agencies along the lines proposed by Tugwell. An authority on constitutional law, Frankfurter had strong grounds for believing that too broad a grant would be unconstitutional, a belief confirmed in 1935 when the National Recovery Administration Act was so ruled. But his thought was dominated by an even more fundamental consideration. Rule by experts simply could not survive without popular support.

> The expert [Frankfurter insisted] should be on tap, but not on top . . . In a democracy, politics is a process of popular education — the task of adjusting the conflicting interests of diverse groups in the community, and bending the hostility and suspicion and ignorance engendered by group interests toward a comprehension of mutual understanding. For these ends, *expertise* is indispensable. But politicians must enlist popular support for the technical means by which alone social policies can be realized.[87]

Moreover, years of experience as a federal official in the Taft and Wilson administrations had convinced Frankfurter that there was no certainty that democratically elected American Presidents would consistently appoint talented regulators. As he later wrote in a letter to William Douglas, he had ceased to be "a hot Hamiltonian."[88]

The problem of administrative law was to persuade Congress to adopt laws that both particularized substantive legal goals so specifically that these ends could survive hostile or indifferent interpretation by the courts or political appointees and were sufficiently flexible in means that a creative agency could adjust to changed or newly discovered circumstances. The success of Frankfurter's approach to administrative governance was dependent on the creation of a new class of expert administrators. As Frankfurter wrote in a related context in 1924, "Everything is subordinate to personnel, for personnel determines the governing atmosphere and understanding from which all questions of administrative organization take shape."[89] By 1930, this instinct had grown into a theory memorialized in Frankfurter's book *The Public and Its Government:*

> The staples of contemporary politics — the organization of industry, the course of public utilities, the well-being of agriculture, the mastery of crime and disease — are deeply enmeshed in intricate and technical facts, and must be extricated from presupposition and partisanship. Such matters require systematic effort to contract the area of conflict and passion and widen the area of accredited knowledge as the basis of action.[90]

"There are some things we can no longer afford," Frankfurter would write in 1934. "Above all we can no longer afford to do without a highly trained, disinterested governmental personnel. What this Administration has had to do is to create something like the English Civil Service overnight."[91] Like John Stuart Mill, Frankfurter came to believe that "mediocrity ought not to be engaged in the affairs of State."[92] "The greatest immediate need," Frankfurter would write Walter Lippmann while lobbying for the 1933 Securities Act, is "qualified men for key jobs."[93]

By April 7, when he arrived in Washington to meet with Roosevelt and Moley, Frankfurter had selected three younger associates, James M. Landis, Benjamin V. Cohen, and Thomas G. Corcoran, to help draft the Securities Act. In time, each of the three would achieve political prominence in his own right, but in the spring of 1933, Landis, Cohen, and Corcoran still were considered Frankfurter's aides, sympathetically referred to as "Felix's boys," occasionally derided as "Frankfurter's little hot dogs."

Of the three, the most prominent in a history of the SEC was Landis. Landis was Frankfurter's protégé. The son of a Presbyterian missionary, Landis was born and lived until the age of thirteen in Japan. After working his way through Cicero, Horace, and solid geometry under the tutelage of a knuckle cracking pedant, Landis "ran out of schooling" and was shipped to the United States for further education. Here, his intellectual prowess was readily apparent: he graduated first in his high school class, was "first group" in every subject at Princeton but German, and received such high marks at the Harvard Law School that Dean Roscoe Pound would have to remind journalists that Landis "wasn't the brightest student at Harvard since Mr. Justice Brandeis, as has been said," but had merely led all students in the class of 1924.

A decisive moment in Landis's career occurred in his second year at Harvard Law School, when he met Frankfurter. Frankfurter championed him, making it possible for Landis to spend a fourth year as a special fellow in Cambridge, where the two began collaborating on articles, then sending him to Washington to serve a year as a clerk to Justice Brandeis. In 1926, at the age of twenty-seven, Landis began teaching at Harvard Law School as an assistant professor. His advance thereafter, even Dean Pound would concede, was "meteoric, almost unheard of." Two years later, Landis co-authored with Frankfurter *The Business of the Supreme Court* and became the youngest full professor in the law school's history and the school's first professor of legislation. As with his mentor, Frankfurter, Landis's academic interests included administrative and public utilities law. He also made a detailed investigation of state blue sky laws, which was why Frankfurter turned to him to help draft the 1933 Securities Act.[94]

In time, Landis would be responsible for the most memorable articulation of Frankfurter's view of government-by-administrative-agency. In 1938, responding to criticism that the independent administrative agencies had become "a headless fourth branch of the government, a haphazard deposit of irresponsible agencies and uncoordinated powers," Landis would defend the administrative process as "the most significant development in legal history in the last century," essential because of "the inadequacy of a simple tripartite form of government to deal with modern problems." In Landis's view, only the administrative agencies could "provide for the efficient functioning of the economic processes of the state." Legislation was "forced to represent compromise," and often "does so by the use of vague phraseology." The Judiciary had a broad general jurisdiction, depriving it of the ability "to maintain a long-time uninterrupted interest in a relatively narrow and carefully defined area of economic and social activity." Neither branch could regulate industry as effectively as the administrators of an agency with a specific function.

As Landis put it: "With the rise of regulation, the need for expertness became dominant; for the art of regulating an industry requires knowledge of the details of its operations, ability to shift requirements as the condition of the industry may dictate." Disparaging legislation that attempted to prescribe in too great detail "the conditions of administrative action" and administrators who took "the legislative approach" of reading "a governing statute with the hope of finding limitations upon authority," Landis argued that the appropriate relationship of the democratic legislature to the expert agency was to define the agency's area of expertise and recite the appropriate problems for it to solve, leaving it broad discretion as to means. Exceeding even Frankfurter's faith in administrative experts, Landis would recommend in his seminal work, *The Administrative Process*, greater insulation of the agency from court review and an increase in the sanctions agencies could enforce. He would urge that the "singleness" of an agency's function would lead to "a professionalism of spirit" that would justify its greater independence.[95]

Cohen, at the age of thirty-nine, was the eldest of the three men Frankfurter brought to Washington. Although he later would secure William Douglas's judgment as "the best and most intelligent man in the New Deal," Cohen's shyness camouflaged his exceptional legal talents. Impressed with Cohen's intelligence, Frankfurter considered him "perhaps the most brilliant graduate of the Chicago Law

School, one of the most brilliant doctors we [meaning the Harvard Law School] ever had."[96]

The more personable Corcoran also had been a Frankfurter favorite while at Harvard Law School. Not only had he co-authored articles with Frankfurter, but he had assimilated Frankfurter's view of the decisive significance of agency staffing. Five years later, at his apogee in the Roosevelt administration, he would state that his highest ambition was to be Civil Service Commissioner. Already by the spring of 1933 he was operating out of an attorney's office in the Reconstruction Finance Corporation as "a sort of Washington general manager for Frankfurter," wrote Raymond Moley, "demoniacally attempting to staff the entire federal government," in the view of journalists Joseph Alsop and Robert Kintner. Like Cohen, Corcoran had had considerable experience as a corporate attorney in a New York City law firm before gravitating to Washington in 1932.[97] But Frankfurter had sought out the thirty-three-year-old Corcoran primarily to help lobby for the securities bill that Landis and Cohen would draft. Although Cohen and Corcoran would become such close friends that the phrase "drafted by Cohen and Corcoran" would be a New Deal standard, there was little love lost between the two of them and Landis. Both would bridle at what they perceived to be Landis's emotional immaturity, Cohen frequently complaining to Frankfurter of Landis's "temperamental inability to consult with others"; Corcoran labeling Landis "an easily flattered man."[98]

Rayburn, a touch awed that so famous an academic as Frankfurter was selected by Roosevelt to supervise the preparation of a new securities bill, quickly gave the nod for Landis and Cohen to set to work.[99] Both agreed with Frankfurter that the English Companies Act should constitute the basis of their draft. Working feverishly, Landis and Cohen were able to assemble a new bill within two days. The core of the Securities Act of 1933, Landis would recall twenty-five years later, is "to be found in that hurried draft of ours":

> Our draft remained true to the conception voiced by the President in his message of March 29, 1933, to the Congress, namely, that its requirements should be limited to full and fair disclosure of the nature of the security being offered and that there should be no authority to pass upon the investment quality of the security . . . We also provided for the passage of a period of time before a registration statement could become effective, giving the Commission power during that period to issue a stop-order because of misrepresentation or inadequacy of disclosure . . . This device of a waiting period, then completely

novel, in our opinion would accomplish several things. It would slow up the procedure of selling securities and the consequent pressures that the underwriters could exert upon their selling group or other dealers to take sight unseen an allotment of the issue. It would give an opportunity for the financial world to acquaint itself with the basic data underlying a security issue and through that acquaintance to circulate among the buying public as well as independent dealers some intimation of its quality.[100]

Frankfurter formally presented the draft to Sam Rayburn at an all-day special meeting of the House Commerce Committee on Monday, April 10.[101] In deference to Huston Thompson, Frankfurter and his draftsmen characterized the new bill as "perfecting amendments" to Thompson's draft.[102] After a subsequent executive session with the Commerce Committee and Felix Frankfurter, Rayburn emerged to inform Landis and Cohen that the committee had been convinced "this was a bill that was worth working on."

From Cambridge, Frankfurter supervised Landis and Cohen as they worked with Middleton Beaman, chief draftsman of the House of Representatives, to hone the bill. The process soon proved exasperating. "For two days," Landis recalled, "Beaman wouldn't allow you to put a pencil to paper. He wanted you to know just exactly what you wanted to do before you started writing." In retrospect, Landis would appreciate the patience of the veteran draftsman, but at the time, Landis, Cohen, and Corcoran suspected "that this delay bore symptoms of sinister Wall Street plotting."[103] Cohen had even more difficult problems working with Landis, who brusquely attempted to write the entire bill himself and often lost his temper with Cohen. In particular, Landis fought with Cohen about the wisdom of including a detailed schedule of data to be disclosed by each firm before it sold securities to the public.

In Landis's view it was preferable to give the Federal Trade Commission general power to issue regulations concerning the data to be disclosed and allow the commission the opportunity to develop administrative expertise before issuing the regulations. Cohen argued that Landis's formula ran too high a risk of ineffectual regulation. But Cohen was overruled by Beaman, who was eager to eliminate from the draft any material not essential to the bill's structure. Frustrated, Cohen telephoned Frankfurter to complain that it was "impossible" to work with Landis and that he intended to quit. Frankfurter forcefully intervened. On April 14 he telegraphed Roosevelt that the omission of specific data to be disclosed would "raise needless questions of constitutionality as to delegation of legislative power," invite frustration of the bill's purposes by hostile judicial interpretation, and "jeopardize effective enforcement because of the enormous discretion it leaves to Commission . . . thereby [inviting] laxity, favoritism, and indifference."[104]

Roosevelt was convinced, and on April 17, Frankfurter wrote to express "my warmest thanks for your personal intervention with Rayburn on the Securities bill. It came at a crucial moment and was decisive."[105] At approximately the same time, Frankfurter telegraphed Cohen that he was "indispensable and . . . must not leave till ship is in port," simultaneously writing Moley to ask that he "somehow find a few minutes to send for Ben Cohen alone [and] make him feel he is coordinate with Landis, who in his intensity has not been wholly wise in his relations with Ben."[106]

By April 21, Landis and Cohen had completed a revised draft. The hard-won schedule of items to be disclosed remained and had been somewhat expanded. Significantly, the FTC was to be given the power to define accounting concepts used in preparation of registration statements. Pivotal matters, such as the act's distinction between regulated "public offerings" versus unregulated "private offerings" and a definition of fraud, had reached polished form. Rayburn was impressed, and later that day wrote Frankfurter of his belief that "we are going . . . to get out a good, workable bill."[107]

Earlier, Rayburn had named a Commerce Committee Subcommittee to supervise preparation of the new securities bill. Rayburn insisted that railroad securities — subject to regulation under the congressman's 1920 amendment to the Interstate Commerce Act — be added to the list of exempted securities. Municipal securities also were exempted, Landis explained in a letter thirty years later, because "the mayors of our various cities rose up en masse when we tried to bring the issuance of municipal securities under the 1933 Act."[108] But Rayburn dissuaded the subcommittee from adopting other significant changes. Nor did Rayburn facilitate opportunities for Wall Street to oppose the bill. Virtually until the day the bill was presented to the full Commerce Committee, Rayburn effectively forbade subcommittee members from discussing its contents with journalists. No public subcommittee hearings were held. Only after Moley repeatedly insisted did Rayburn agree that the subcommittee would hold a private meeting to consider the objections of leading corporate lawyers John Foster Dulles, Arthur H. Dean, and Alexander I. Henderson. Dulles, leading the group, insinuated that Rayburn was sponsoring legislation that would undermine the financial system. Rayburn, incensed, retorted that all that was being demanded was that capitalism live up to its pretensions. Later, privately, "in very obscene language," Rayburn rhetorically asked Landis "what these people were doing there? Why didn't they know what they were talking about?" The more low-keyed Dean and Henderson also failed in attempts to persuade the subcommittee to soften the civil liability provision and eliminate the thirty-day waiting period.[109]

Although local commercial banks had some success in broadening the exemptions under the Securities Act, the Wall Street investment banking community and the New York Stock Exchange were almost entirely ineffective in their lobbying efforts. To reverse a popular saying of the day, the period of the First Hundred Days of the Roosevelt administration was that rare time when money talked and nobody listened. Rayburn, after twelve years in the Washington of Harding, Coolidge, and Hoover, was fully aware of the period's uniqueness. Like Roosevelt, he was animated by a conviction that the moment could not last, that he had to move swiftly or it might be too late.

After further technical refinements, Rayburn formally introduced the Landis-Cohen draft on May 3.[110] The full Commerce Committee modestly added to the list of exemptions securities issued by state banks, then reported out the bill to the House on May 4.[111] The following day Rayburn moved that the entire House enact the measure. After securing a special rule limiting debate to five hours and prohibiting all amendments except those "offered by direction of the Committee on Interstate and Foreign Commerce" (meaning those acceptable to Rayburn), Rayburn introduced the bill, drawing applause at the conclusion of an otherwise closely reasoned address when he draped the Securities Act in the flag, claiming it to be a mechanism to restore confidence in American institutions and avoid "the evils that attend socialism, bolshevism, and communism."

The ensuing House debate was an anticlimax. There was almost no discussion of the provisions of the bill itself. Although a few members of Congress bridled at Rayburn's gag order, far more were inclined to accept Congressman Arthur H. Greenwood's conclusion: "I have never read a bill that appeared to be more carefully drawn . . . This bill should not be mutilated or garbled by amendments that have not been thought out." Shortly before 5:00 P.M., the House of Representatives unanimously adopted the Landis-Cohen bill on a voice vote.[112] Even Rayburn seemed a little startled by how easily it had been pushed through, gleefully saying to Cohen, who had sat with him during the final debate, that he "did not know whether the bill passed so readily because it was so damned good or so damned incomprehensible."[113]

Cohen's pleasure could only have been short-lived. In the Senate, the Landis-Cohen bill was in serious trouble. Duncan Fletcher, chairman of the Senate Banking Committee, did not share Rayburn's anxieties about Thompson's securities bill. During the course of eight hearing days, early in April, Thompson had shown considerable flexibility, agreeing to remove the controversial revocation section, eliminating the provision empowering the federal government to enforce state blue sky laws, limiting the bill to prospective applications, exempting commercial paper, and expanding the items to be disclosed[114] — changes cumulatively so fundamental that Fletcher later would inform his Senate colleagues that "there are not a great many differences" between the revised Thompson draft and the House-backed Landis-Cohen bill.[115] In fact, the differences that did remain were significant. Thompson's bill was considerably sketchier in detail, imposed strict liability on persons signing a registration statement "false or deceptive in any material respect," did not include a waiting period between the time a firm registered a security with the FTC and was allowed to sell the security to the public, and was ambiguous in its characterization of many items that needed to be disclosed.[116] Obviously moved by Pecora's revelations before the Banking Committee, Fletcher seemed all but unwilling to consider Wall Street objections to Thompson's bill, at one point snapping at the bill's most articulate opponent, Arthur Dean, "We do not want to spend our time hearing criticism of the bill, with people picking it to pieces here and there and getting nowhere."[117] On another occasion, Fletcher denounced the president of the Chamber of Commerce for urging investment bankers to oppose the bill, stating, "It was not to be expected that a measure, such as the Federal Securities bill . . . designed to protect the public from the financial racketeering of certain classes of so-called investment bankers could be enacted without arousing the most determined opposition on the part of that profession which has mulcted the people of some $50 billion during the past ten years."[118]

As Thompson's bill progressed toward Senate Banking Committee approval in late April, Frankfurter made an unsuccessful attempt to have it withdrawn. Using Banking Committee member Senator James Byrnes as an intermediary, Frankfurter attempted to convince Fletcher of the Thompson bill's deficiencies. Byrnes failed, and the Banking Committee officially reported out the bill on April 27.[119] Privately, Moley blamed Rayburn for "not nursing

Fletcher more carefully."[120] Frankfurter may have had similar thoughts about the overworked Moley, who during the preceding three weeks had virtually washed his hands of the Securities bill except for his often-expressed insistence that Frankfurter's draftsmen consult with Arthur Dean and Alexander Henderson.[121]

Thereafter, Frankfurter assumed a much more active role in lobbying on behalf of his disciples' bill. On April 28 he wired Moley an analysis of the Thompson draft, beginning, "Detailed consideration of Senate securities bill proves that in essential aspects it is partly innocuous and partly unconstitutional."[122] With Roosevelt's approval, Moley showed Frankfurter's telegram to Senate majority leader Joseph T. Robinson and impressed on Robinson Roosevelt's preference for Frankfurter's bill.[123] Robinson, keenly aware of Senator Fletcher's possessive sentiments concerning securities legislation, agreed to attempt to delay Senate enactment of the Thompson bill until after the House had voted on the Landis-Cohen bill, then work to substitute the House bill in Conference Committee. On April 29, Robinson wired Frankfurter to supply a memorandum detailing the inadequacies of Thompson's bill.[124] Frankfurter soon did so, and dispatched Corcoran to lobby Senator Costigan of the Banking Committee, among others.[125]

With little debate, the Senate enacted the revised Thompson bill on May 8,[126] three days after the House had adopted the Landis-Cohen bill. Unexpectedly, however, Senator Johnson successfully appended to the bill a Title II. Johnson's amendment required the Federal Trade Commission to name twelve persons to be directors of a Corporation of Foreign Security Holders, which would be empowered to negotiate on behalf of American investors the collection of funds from foreign governments whose bonds were in default. Title II, though a well-meaning attempt to protect the holders of foreign bonds whose colossal losses had been dramatized by Senator Johnson's earlier hearings, further complictated the enactment process. The idea of a Corporation of Foreign Security Holders negotiating with foreign governments was anathema to the State Department, which vehemently complained that such a quasi-official body could only "complicate and confuse . . . the Department's work."[127] Yet the Johnson proposal had been approved by the entire United States Senate and was a measure about which Senator Johnson felt intensely. For Roosevelt to oppose Title II in deference to the State Department might have prevented the Conference Committee from agreeing on a bill. Roosevelt met with Johnson and attempted to negotiate a compromise: "the Bond Holders' Committee should not in any shape, manner, or form be given powers which would directly or by implication overlap or conflict with the executive or congressional authority. There must be no possibility of involving the government nor must there be anything which would lead either our own American bond holders or foreign debtors to assume that this committee speaks for the government."[128]

While the State Department and Senator Johnson squabbled, Majority Leader Robinson performed the delicate task of reconciling Senator Fletcher to the adoption of the Landis-Cohen draft. By May 9, Robinson could write Frankfurter that the conferees would have "a free hand in working out what form the legislation finally shall take. I have acquainted the conferees with the fact that in many respects the House Bill is preferable to the Senate Bill."[129]

The decisive Conference Committee sessions began on May 15. Fletcher led the five-man Senate contingent, which included Carter Glass and Hiram Johnson. Rayburn led the five members from the House. Also attending were Landis, Cohen, and Beaman as technical experts for the House, and Ollie Butler and Walter Miller, co-authors of Thompson's bill, as advisers to the Senate. Fletcher graciously accepted the inevitable, and suggested that the younger Rayburn act as Conference Committee chairman. As a practical matter this ensured that the Landis-Cohen draft would be the basis of the committee's negotiation. But the word "from on high" had not been passed on to Butler and Miller, who fought tenaciously for the provisions of the Thompson bill throughout the first day's session, until Frankfurter and Moley succeeded in muzzling them on May 16. The irritability of Butler and Miller was exceeded by that of Senator Glass, who unexpectedly burst into a tirade after scanning the bill, because he erroneously assumed the securities bill conflicted with his proposed Banking Act. Only after being reassured by Landis and Cohen that the House bill systematically excluded from its operations all securities issued by state or nationally chartered banks was the Virginian mollified. Hastily thumbing the bill for any further reference to banks, he growled an additional warning, then departed from the Conference Committee, never to return.

Because meetings of conference committees are the penultimate step in the enactment process, when legislators are particularly eager to reach a mutually satisfactory compromise, they often result in the weakening of regulatory measures. Precisely this occurred in the securities bill conference. Members of both Houses' negotiating teams agreed to compromise and make the bill less stringent in order to ensure rapid passage. For the Senate conferees, this primarily meant surrendering their more severe civil liability. For the House, it meant agreeing to shorten the waiting period from thirty days to twenty and surrendering the provision (originally proposed in the Thompson bill) empowering the federal government to enforce the state blue sky laws when securities were sold across state lines. The final compromise was made by Senator Johnson. On the fifth day of the conference he accepted a resolution of his battle with the State Department, whereby Title II's Corporation of Foreign Security Holders would go into effect only by a subsequent proclamation of the President.* [130]

As enacted, the 1933 Securities Act involved a modest grant of regulatory power to the Federal Trade Commission. The act was more remarkable, considering the sentiments of the day, for the powers it did not grant than for the limited powers it did. The heart of the act was the detailed list of data in Schedule A that an issuer of securities had to disclose in the registration statement filed with the FTC and in prospectuses available to investors before it offered securities to the public. Schedule A attempted to do more than give an investor detailed financial records of the issuer; it called for disclosure of information about the firm's business, need for capital, officers, and the costs of the securities issuance. In discouraging fraud or unfairness, the act was most likely to be effective. A subsequent *Columbia Law Review* study, for example, demonstrated that virtually every undisclosed aspect of the option warrants issued by J. P. Morgan in connection with the United Corporation would have been revealed by Schedule A. [132] Securities issuers were required to wait twenty days after filing a registration statement to allow the FTC to study its contents. If the commission found the registration statement "on its face incomplete or inaccurate in any material respect," it could seek a stop order barring public sale of the securities. A corporation's board of directors, principal executive, financial or accounting officers, outside accountants, engineers or appraisers who certified a part of the registration statement, and the firm's underwriters (investment bankers) could be held liable for any untrue statement or omission of a material fact in the registration statement after it became effective unless they could prove they had acted with due diligence.

The act, however, did not invest the FTC with power to pass on the quality of securities issued, and did not attempt to direct capital to those industries where it was most needed. It gave the commission no authority to enforce state blue sky laws even for issues that were exempt from the filing provisions of the federal Securities Act.

---

* Roosevelt never did issue the proclamation, but supported instead the formation of a private Foreign Bond Holders Protective Council, incorporated in December 1933, to perform similar functions. [131]

It totally exempted all securities already issued, all securities issued intrastate, all securities issued by the United States, any state, or political subdivision of a state, all securities issued or guaranteed by national or state banks, building and loan associations, or similar institutions, securities issued by railroads, insurance annuity contracts, securities to be repaid in less than nine months, and, if the FTC saw fit, securities issuances of less than $100,000.

No one better understood the modest nature of the statute than Felix Frankfurter. "The new Federal Securities Act," he explained in an August 1933 *Fortune* magazine article, "is a belated and conservative attempt to curb the recurrence of old abuses which, through failure of adequate legislation, had attained disastrous proportions." It was "a modest first installment of legislative controls to assure commerce and industry a continuous flow of their necessary capital . . . strong insofar as publicity is potent; it is weak insofar as publicity is not enough." Yet Frankfurter discerned more in his creation than a federal blue sky law. The act's greater import was the opportunity it offered for a modern administrative agency to evolve. Far more significant than the detailed Schedule A was the little-discussed residual authority granted to the FTC to evolve uniform accounting standards; it was this power, more than any other part of the act, that Frankfurter calculated would "have far-reaching beneficial effects on American corporate practices."[133]

Virtually from the date of its legislation, the Securities Act was controversial. Initially it was assailed by disappointed reformers. As early as April 26, *The New Republic*'s T.R.B. informed his readers, "The bankers rewrote the bill."[134] This was arrant nonsense, but no more sweeping in its condemnation than Moley's privately held opinion that the act "had been hurried through with inadequate debate,"[135] or Berle's published condescension that the act "leaves unsolved the major questions."[136] Sharing this view was William O. Douglas, then a young Yale law professor, who, like Berle, was one of the nation's leading authorities on corporate finance. Doubtful that most investors had "the time, money, or intelligence to assimilate the mass of information in the registration statement," he characterized the Securities Act as "wholly secondary in any thoroughgoing and comprehensive program for social control in this field":

> There is no machinery provided for obtaining subsequent reliable information either in the form of annual reports or otherwise . . . there is nothing in the Act which controls the power of the self-perpetuating management group which has risen to a position of dominance in our industrial organization. There is nothing in the Act which purports to deal with the protection of the rights of minorities. There is nothing

which concerns the problem of capital structure, its soundness or unsoundness. There is nothing that deals with the problem of mobilizing the flow of capital to various productive channels. And, finally, there is nothing which deals with the fundamental problem of the increment of power and profit inherent in our present forms of organization.

Later, Douglas would express himself very differently, but in 1933 he spoke for many corporate law reformers when he criticized the Securities Act as "a nineteenth-century piece of legislation" since it did not "perfect a plan for control of our present forms of organization."[137]

The hostility of the business community to the Securities Act, especially its civil liability provision, was every bit as intense as that of the frustrated reformers. But in May 1933, Wall Street and business in general were on the defensive, daily embarrassed by the Pecora investigation's revelations. Only later would the New York Stock Exchange, investment banks, and corporate spokesmen effectively respond; and when they did, their collective discontent would become a maelstrom of criticism, eventually requiring even the compromise Securities Act Roosevelt endorsed to be further pruned. At issue, basically, was the political question of who should regulate the economy, or, as Berle wrote, whether high finance would be master or servant. The securities legislation of 1933 was a modest act, but it constituted, the first effective regulation of corporate finance. It was as much in bitterness at being regulated at all, as because of the details of the Securities Act, that Wall Street soon rebelled.

3

"A Perfect Institution"

MR. WIGGIN.   *I think it was a God-given market.*
MR. PECORA.   *What is that?*
MR. WIGGIN.   *I think it was a God-given market.*
SENATOR ADAMS.   *Are you sure as to the source?*

"A PERFECT INSTITUTION," Richard Whitney called it.[1] In November 1937, SEC chairman William O. Douglas would offer a less sanguine opinion, implying that it was a "private club" with "elements of a casino."[2] However characterized, there was no real dispute that the New York Stock Exchange was the primary object of the Securities Exchange Act of 1934, and in that year the Exchange was forced to compromise some of its independence as a result of one of the most bruising lobbying struggles ever waged in Washington.

On Wall Street, it was known simply as "the Exchange." By 1932, there were at least thirty-three other organized securities exchanges in the country; in addition, thousands of unlisted stock and bond issues were traded in unorganized over-the-counter markets. But the New York Stock Exchange alone accounted for as much as three fourths of all listed securities transactions, and in the period between 1928 and 1933 over 90 percent of securities brokerage commissions were received by its members. With a few exceptions, the securities of the nation's largest publicly owned firms were listed there.[3]

Technically, the New York Stock Exchange was an unincorporated association whose 1375 members had paid as much as

$625,000 for the privileges of membership.[4] But the Exchange was effectively governed by a loose alliance of floor members called specialists and floor traders. In a quite literal sense, the NYSE revolved around its three hundred or so specialists. Their function was "to make a market" in a particular stock by serving as sub-brokers through whom other brokers could buy and sell securities and as dealers who themselves would buy or sell stock for their own accounts when other investors would not. Often floor brokers were able to execute orders to buy or sell securities at the market price by trading with other floor brokers "in the crowd." When, however, floor brokers were not requested to execute orders at the market price but, instead, were presented with orders to buy or sell when a security price ascended or descended to a given price, these future orders typically would be entered into the specialist's "book" and executed when the market reached the designated price. This central role made the specialist highly controversial. Throughout the Pecora hearings, allegations were made repeatedly that specialists used their pivotal position to orchestrate pool operations or exploited their knowledge of the specialist books in trading for their own accounts.[5]

Closely allied with the specialists in Exchange politics were the floor traders, approximately 170 members who traded solely for their own accounts, rather than serving as brokers executing orders for others. Since floor traders were vulnerable to the charge that they performed no socially useful function, they drew even heavier criticism from the New Deal reformers than did the specialists. Thomas Corcoran, for example, testified:

> They take no chances. They take no position against the market. They simply follow the market the way sea birds follow a ship, following the trend and picking up what they can on the way. They sense the market and follow the pools, whether the market is long or short . . . They serve no purpose, in the long run, to make the market any better for the investor on the outside, but rather because they are quick and on the inside, they help to accentuate the swings of pools. They are naturally pool operators.[6]

By contrast, the majority of Exchange members who were floor brokers, or members of the broker-dealer firms that had direct contact with the public, exerted comparatively less influence on Exchange politics in 1933. The floor brokers' function was largely ministerial — to execute purchase and sell orders wired to them by customers' men located in the broker-dealer firm offices throughout the country. Since the Exchange's broker-dealer firm members were not physically present on the Exchange floor, they usually deferred to the leadership of the specialists and floor traders. During the initial years of the SEC, a schism would develop in Exchange politics. A sustained decline in trading volume would move leading broker-dealer firm members including Edward A. Pierce and Paul Shields to challenge the specialists' and floor traders' dominance of the Exchange. Although nearly all specialists and floor traders opposed the SEC for fear that the agency might seek the abolition of their rights to trade for their own accounts, the Pierce-Shields faction of broker-dealer house members supported many Commission reforms as means to restore the reputation of the Exchange. This, they assumed, would in time increase trading volume.[7]

Throughout the 1933–1934 battle over the securities exchange bill, however, the New York Stock Exchange's membership remained almost entirely unified in opposition to the New Deal's stock exchange proposals. President Richard Whitney reflected the uncompromising opposition to federal regulation characteristic both of the Exchange's floor members and of private investment banks, such as J. P. Morgan and Company, for whom his brother worked and for whom Whitney's own firm, Richard Whitney and Company, served as a bond broker.

In lectures, radio broadcasts, and congressional testimony Whitney's message was consistent: "The Exchange by maintaining . . . a free and open market for securities, rendered a great service to the Nation." The New York Stock Exchange should not be made "a goat" for the depression. Like the financiers he represented, Whitney's distrust of Washington was instinctive; his was a near-certain conviction that government regulation could only be crude, vengeful, and ultimately destructive.[8]

The political significance of Roosevelt's First Hundred Days, however, was not lost on Whitney. On March 29, 1933, Roosevelt had introduced his securities bill, which, with the public outrage at Charles Mitchell and the National City Bank at its zenith, was widely expected to be enacted shortly. In his message, Roosevelt had implied that he would soon introduce a bill to supervise the stock exchanges as well. Whitney was realistic enough to appreciate that if Roosevelt actually had a bill ready, this too might be rapidly enacted. He immediately requested an opportunity to visit the White House and on April 5 met with Roosevelt and attempted to strike a compromise with the New Deal. Whitney conceded that "the vast majority of the members of the Exchange are anxious to put the security business on a higher plane than it has ever been before" and volunteered a number of modest actions the Exchange could initiate to prevent members from engaging in more than one type of securities business, such as prohibiting private bankers from employing salesmen.

But Whitney's larger message was plain: the New York Stock Exchange was firmly opposed to any federal statute; it should be allowed to clean its own house. Roosevelt, equally firm, gave Whitney no reason to believe that he would refrain from offering a statute, but Whitney pressed ahead with a campaign "to cooperate" with the new administration.[9] Early in August, the Exchange adopted a series of new rules, requiring customers to maintain a specified minimum balance in margin accounts, requiring weekly reports from stock pools, syndicates, and joint trading accounts, and encouraging brokerage firms to pay customers' men a minimum cash salary as a method of reducing their incentive to engage in high-pressure sales tactics.[10]

It was unlikely that Roosevelt was much impressed by these actions either. Like Herbert Hoover, Roosevelt accepted the conventional wisdom that "unregulated speculation in securities . . . [was] one of the most important contributing factors in the artificial and unwarranted 'boom' which had so much to do with the terrible conditions in the years following 1929." Unlike Hoover, Roosevelt favored legislation to prevent "the use of the exchanges for purely speculative operations," principally by setting brokers' margin loan requirements "so high that speculation . . . will of necessity be drastically curtailed," prevent "insofar as possible manipulation of prices to the detriment of actual investors," and give "the government . . . definite powers of supervision over exchanges [so] that the government itself will be able to correct abuses which may arise in the future."[11] Even though the Democratic Party platform had called for such a law, however, there were political reasons, principally related to divisions within his administration, for Roosevelt not to press his administration during the balance of the First Hundred Days legislative session, or for months afterward, to prepare a stock exchange bill.

With the conclusion of the J. P. Morgan hearings in June 1933, the momentum for stock exchange legislation perceptibly slowed. Then, in late June, a jury found Charles Mitchell "not guilty" of income tax evasion — a setback to the New Deal so totally unexpected that Attorney General Homer Cummings felt compelled to acknowledge publicly "Nevertheless, I still believe in the jury system."[12] After the Pecora hearings recessed in July for the summer, Wall Street's long-dampened opposition to the 1933 Securities Act began to be expressed vehemently.

In August, corporate attorney Arthur Dean, the most articulate opponent of the Securities Act, published a slashing attack in *Fortune*, anticipating that the law would be "drastically amended at the next session" because of its complexity and severe civil liability sections, which were such "as to render financing exceedingly difficult, if not actually impossible, in the case of corporations with extensive interests." Dean predicted dire results from the Securities Act: it alone might "seriously retard economic recovery . . . result in unemployment because corporations may be forced to make drastic economies and to suspend the payment of dividends in order to obtain necessary working capital," make it difficult for "new and speculative corporations [to obtain] long-term capital," increase the cost of selling securities to all corporations, and discourage underwriters from helping issue securities, thus forcing "American corporations to go abroad for capital." "With the purposes of the Act," Dean concluded, "the writer is in full sympathy, but it seems hardly necessary to burn down the house to exterminate vermin."[13] Dean's call to amend the 1933 Securities Act was roundly echoed. Frank Gordon, president of the Investment Bankers Association, soon won unanimous support from the association for a resolution seeking "redefinition" of the act "so as to make it possible for responsible enterprises to meet their requirements for new capital and to cooperate with the recovery program."[14] Privately, R. C. Leffingwell, a J. P. Morgan partner, warned Roosevelt: "Your recovery program is in eminent peril from threatened defaults or forced extensions of corporate bonds, and the resulting destruction of confidence and credit . . . I think that a remedy can be found without in the slightest degree imperiling the liberal reforms which you have initiated."[15]

Publicly, Roosevelt adamantly opposed any significant amendments to the act. At an October 18 press conference, he scornfully insisted:

> There is a very definite drive being made by certain elements to have the Securities Act modified or repealed. They would much rather have it repealed. They would much rather have the old, free use that they had before — being able to sell watered stocks to you and me. Well, they are not going to have that right anymore . . . There will be mighty few changes, if any, in the Securities Act this winter.

Six weeks later, he responded to a reporter's query, "Has it been definitely determined to amend the Securities Act?" by airily observing, "No. I don't know where you people get all those silly stories."[16] Roosevelt was able to ignore the Wall Street campaign against the Securities Act because of the stunning revelations of the Pecora hearings in the autumn of 1933, including evidence that Albert Wiggin, president of the Chase National Bank, then the nation's largest bank, had formed six private corporations that had earned over $10 million between 1928 and 1932, by, among other transactions, receiving a cut from the Chase Securities Corporation's investment and pool operations and by short-selling stock in the Chase National Bank itself during the 1929 stock market crash.[17]

But a far more influential lobby to amend the Securities Act developed within the Roosevelt administration. Before the year was out, Lewis Douglas, Roosevelt's Director of the Budget, Secretary of the Treasury William Woodin, National Recovery Administration head Hugh Johnson, top officials of the Commerce Department, and Secretary of Agriculture Henry A. Wallace would urge Roosevelt to amend the act. The intra-administration opposition began with the conservative Budget Director Douglas, whom Thomas Corcoran considered "instinctively hostile" to the securities law. Prior to a September 8 Cabinet meeting, Douglas circulated a memorandum prepared by Paul Mazur, an economist for Lehman Brothers, that criticized the Act as standing in the way of "needed long-term financing."[18] Agriculture Secretary Wallace wrote to Roosevelt that he agreed with Mazur "about the necessity for amending the Securities bill." Although he would endorse the act in its full rigor if the economy were functioning as well as it had in 1924 or 1929, Wallace wrote, "I am really fearful of its influence at the present time."[19] At about the same time the Federal Reserve Board's Federal Advisory Committee adopted a resolution calling for amendment of the Securities Act to facilitate securities flotation.[20] By November, Secretary of the Treasury Woodin[21] and NRA Administrator Hugh Johnson[22] also were urging modification.

Senator Fletcher, Congressman Rayburn, Felix Frankfurter, and James Landis sharply defended the securities law. The counsel of Frankfurter and Landis was particularly influential. After the passage of the Securities Act, Roosevelt continued to rely on Frankfurter as his senior adviser on securities law, regularly consulting him on appointments of FTC commissioners and staff to enforce the act, and directing the White House staff to solicit Frankfurter's approval of the commission's first regulations and registration forms interpreting the securities law.[23] As early as July 6, Frankfurter warned Roosevelt of "the fray that is ahead." He wrote, "There are still too many in 'the Street' who think that . . . the 'green goods business' . . . will flourish as of old. It is hard for some folk to realize that new social and economic standards ever come into play."[24] When leading financiers and corporate attorneys assailed the act in August and September, Frankfurter wrote to Roosevelt again: "There is no question but that leading bankers and the big law firms are trying to create a bankers' strike," employing the act as an "opportunity publicly to oppose the New Deal."[25] In a separate letter to Henry Stimson, once his political mentor, Frankfurter bitterly claimed:

> The leading financial law firms who have been systematically carrying on a campaign against this Act have been seeking — now that they and their financial clients have come out of their storm cellar of fear — not to improve but to chloroform the Act. They evidently assume that the public is unaware of the sources of the issues that represent the baldest abuses of fiduciary responsibility and of the lawyers who, to their fat profit, "passed" on these issues.[26]

When Frankfurter late in September boarded the M.V. *Britannic* to sail to England and a year of teaching at Oxford, the main burden of the act's defense was assumed by his protégé James Landis. Landis's reputation in Washington had been secured by his work in drafting the 1933 Securities Act. As the act neared adoption, Sam Rayburn had written Frankfurter, as if addressing a proud father, "What I think of the character and great ability of Mr. Landis. I have not known a man for the same length of time for whom I have a higher personal regard and for whose character and ability I have more unstinted admiration."[27] Rayburn's high opinion of Landis was shared by others in official Washington.

About a week after the Securities Act was signed, Landis received an emergency call in Cambridge, requesting him to return as a consultant to the Federal Trade Commission to help set up a special division to enforce the act. Then in October, when a vacancy unexpectedly developed on the FTC, Roosevelt named the Harvard Law School professor an FTC commissioner, after Landis received strong endorsements from FTC chairman Charles March, departing commissioner Ray Stevens, as well as Frankfurter.[28] Landis soon was convinced that the drive to amend the Securities Act had been led by New York City investment banks and by Hugh Johnson and Lewis Douglas.[29] In late October, Landis made a spirited defense of the act in an address to the New York State Society of Certified Public Accountants. Castigating "the attack of selfish and short-sighted interests," Landis asserted that "if half of the energy that has been expended in fulminating against the Act and propagandizing for amendments were enlisted in the effort to advise the Commission in the wise exercise of its powers, the government and issuers, bankers, lawyers, and accountants would be far nearer a solution of their problems."[30]

Characteristically, Roosevelt attempted to conciliate the warring administration factions by initiating two studies of the effect of the act on capital formation. Neither effort succeeded, but out of the failure grew a renewed impetus for a stock exchange bill. The first study was initiated late in October, after Henry Bruere,[31] a friend of Roosevelt and president of the Bronx Bank, who was acting as an adviser on credit issues, wrote the President: "There seems to be an honest belief that the liability and certain other provisions of the Securities Act in its present form has actually prevented or limited and will prevent and limit the natural flow of capital into industry." He attached to his memorandum a list of six instances provided by William Breed, counsel to the Investment Bankers Association, "where financing is said to have been prevented by provisions of the Securities Act."[32] Roosevelt urged Bruere "to get working on the problem of possible revision" by meeting with a committee including Landis, his fellow FTC commissioner George Mathews, and Breed, but Roosevelt insisted that "this should be done quietly," since he "wished to take his position after further consideration of matured recommendations from the Committee."[33]

A general conference was held on November 14, attended not only by Bruere, Landis, Mathews, and Breed, but also by such conservative administration figures as Lewis Douglas and Assistant Secretary of Commerce John Dickinson, a former Sullivan and Cromwell attorney. No consensus was reached. But four days later Bruere reported to Roosevelt, "I strongly feel that the severe liability provisions of the Act constitute a serious obstacle to business recovery." He urged that the liability provisions be redrawn to limit damages to those directly caused by an untrue statement or omission and only when an investor had relied on the falsehood.[34] Douglas and Dickinson generally concurred — as did the Commerce Department Business Advisory Committee a few days later.[35] Roosevelt forwarded Bruere's report to Landis for comment.[36]

At approximately the same time that Roosevelt requested Henry Bruere study possible revisions of the 1933 Securities Act, he also asked Commerce Secretary Daniel Roper to revitalize his interagency stock exchange study group. But Roosevelt's charge to Roper was considerably broader and more formal than his request of Bruere. The Secretary of Commerce was expected to investigate claims that the 1933 Securities Act obstructed new securities sales, and was also to return with recommendations for a securities exchange bill.

The choice of Roper was telling. In the early months of the New Deal, the Secretary of Commerce self-consciously had attempted to play a role as a bridge between the generally conservative business community and the reform elements of the Roosevelt administration. To improve business–New Deal "cooperation," in June 1933 Roper had established the Business Advisory and Planning Council, which included such industrial and financial stalwarts as A T & T's Walter Gifford and investment banker Averell Harriman.[37] Roper viewed the problem of stock market regulation as another opportunity to minimize the differences between Wall Street and Washington. But it was an opportunity Roper badly bungled. Soon after Roosevelt asked him to revise Samuel Untermyer's stock exchange bill in the spring of 1933, Roper had requested Assistant Commerce Secretary Dickinson to study the bill.[38]

No revision was completed before Congress adjourned, and during the summer Dickinson seemed content to let the project drop. Then in early October, after Roosevelt again asked Roper to study the securities laws, Roper once more turned to Dickinson.[39] Dickinson, a former corporate attorney unsympathetic to securities law reform, invited James Landis and Adolf Berle to join a committee Dickinson stacked against reform by adding his former Sullivan and Cromwell partner Arthur Dean and a conservative Washington attorney, Henry Richardson.

Dickinson, Dean, and Richardson strongly favored amending the act. In time, Roper would forward to Roosevelt recommendations of the majority of the Dickinson Committee that liability under the act be limited to the amounts caused by an untrue statement or omission, that most underwriters be exempt from liability, and that courts have the power to assess both costs and a $500 penalty on the losing party in securities law litigation to discourage bad-faith litigation.[40]

By November, it was also clear that the majority of the Dickinson Committee favored as well a limited stock exchange bill. Early that month, Landis had presented to the committee what he considered the "irreducible minima" of a stock exchange bill: a requirement of periodic publicly filed corporate reports; public reports of stock transactions of directors, principal officers, and the corporation itself when it was dealing in its own stock; "police regulation" of specialists, brokerage houses, customers' men, pool operations, short-selling, and fraudulent "washed" sales or matched orders; regulation of over-the-counter transactions; and "any other proposals necessary to give effectiveness to any of the above."[41] Rather than requesting Landis to prepare a draft statute, Dickinson had turned to Henry Richardson, who, on November 16, 1933, had circulated the outline of a much different bill. "The general idea of the draft here presented," Richardson explained, "is that the bill is to be drawn on the theory that insofar as possible each exchange will discipline its own members and conduct its own affairs." The heart of Richardson's proposal was the recommendation that each securities exchange's rules be approved by a seven-member security exchange commission, which would include two representatives of the general investing public, two members of stock or commodities exchanges, one representative from industry, one representative from agriculture, and a chairman who would be a member of the Federal Reserve Bank of New York.[42]

Shortly after Landis had received Bruere's recommendation to amend the 1933 Securities Act and Richardson's proposal for an industry-dominated stock exchange bill, he requested a meeting with President Roosevelt.[43] This may have been the decisive meeting in the history of the 1934 Securities Exchange Act. Landis, in effect, was seeking Roosevelt's encouragement to develop proposals for a stock exchange bill outside the President's official committee. Roosevelt, by this time, was aware that conciliatory efforts within his administration would fail and that he would soon have to side with one of the contending factions.

On the same day as the Dickinson Committee met with Richard Whitney to hear his view on stock market reform,[44] Landis forwarded to Roosevelt a blistering memorandum defending the Securities Act. Taking issue with the argument that the dearth of new private security issues could be attributed to the act, Landis argued that "an examination of situations where the Act is alleged to have caused the non-flotation of an issue brings forcibly to the forefront the recognition that so many factors are responsible for this non-flotation that isolation of the fear of the Act is impossible." However, even when the FTC had "intimated its willingness to relax registration requirements on refunding issues wherever that can be done," no firm had registered with the commission. Instead, corporate attorneys, especially William Breed, had lobbied for "changes" that, though "seemingly innocuous, may open wide opportunities for evasion." For example, Landis asserted that the frequent suggestion that recovery under the act be limited to situations where an investor directly "relied" on a falsehood might fully subvert the act, since the act did not, and Landis believed constitutionally could not, compel securities dealers to deliver to each investor a copy of the firm's registration statement or prospectus. Similarly, limitation of damages to those directly "caused" by a false statement or omission might make it nearly impossible for investors to prove damages. Without the stringent civil liability sections, Landis asserted, the FTC would not have been able to compel firms attempting to sell securities to the public to acknowledge "such facts as the pendency of damaging litigation" or the existence of "outstanding liabilities, misleading accounting practices . . . and the like."

In Landis's view, the tactics of the opponents of the act "created a situation where the only safe course seems to be that of remaining adamant on the Securities Act. Not only would there be the danger of appearing not to be able to withstand the pressure of financial interests," but if Roosevelt agreed to amend the act in the face of a bankers' strike, "the 'strike' may very well be continued until further modifications again take place." It would be better, Landis suggested, for Roosevelt to support amendments that would "strengthen" the 1933 Securities Act by extending "the principles of registration and publicity to the solicitation of proxies from stockholders," requiring "periodic certified financial reports from corporations," "eliminating exemptions" under the 1933 act, "licensing of security dealers," and legislating "minimum requirements for the issuance of any securities."[45]

Roosevelt, aware of Fletcher's and Rayburn's strong support of the act, sided with Landis. Early in December Roosevelt twice denied that he would support any changes in the Securities Act that could weaken the law.[46] At nearly the same time, Landis released a public letter to Senator Fletcher, claiming that the 1933 act had kept hundreds of millions of dollars of worthless securities off the market.[47] Privately, Landis directed an FTC associate, I. N. P. Stokes, to continue previously initiated efforts to draft a securities exchange bill that would place the securities exchanges under FTC control.[48] Roosevelt informed Raymond Moley "of his intention to get securities-exchange legislation through the coming [congressional] session." Moley was asked to contact Benjamin Cohen and Thomas Corcoran and ask that they also begin drafting a stock exchange measure.[49] Cohen earlier had begun working with Pecora's staff on a bill after Duncan Fletcher publicly had expressed his belief that the government would soon exercise rigid supervision of stock exchanges.[50] Another young attorney, Telford Taylor, then joined Stokes in drawing up drafts of a stock exchange bill; these were reviewed by both Landis and Cohen. By mid-January, Stokes and Taylor were collaborating on a revised draft bill, which, on January

23, was circulated for comment to Senator Fletcher and his Banking Committee counsel, Ferdinand Pecora.[51]

Significantly complicating the reformers' efforts was the Dickinson Committee. By January 23 its report, "Stock Exchange Regulation," had been forwarded to the White House. Roosevelt, attempting to play down the importance of the report, transmitted it to Senator Fletcher with a public letter stating, "I shall leave with you and your associates the matter of the construction of the legislation," but this was a caveat virtually no one appreciated when the report was publicly released on January 27. News accounts universally assumed that the report was meant to embody Roosevelt's recommendations for stock exchange reform, an impression buttressed by the fact that both Landis and Berle had signed the report, indicating "general accord" with its contents.

The Dickinson report recommended that a new federal stock exchange authority or new division of the Federal Trade Commission be empowered to license securities exchanges, but that the federal agency should be "constituted as to place responsibility to the fullest extent possible on the private bodies now handling the work of the securities exchanges" and should include "a representative of the stock exchanges." The report then listed several powers it recommended that the stock exchange authority *not* exercise. Among other things, the committee said that it was "not . . . desirable to require the licensing of individual brokers [since] there is a distinct danger that such a system would break down the controls exercised by the stock exchanges"; it was not feasible to regulate "unorganized" or over-the-counter securities markets, because this would entail "building up a Federal policing agency on such a scale as to be impracticable"; it was not appropriate to give the new stock exchange authority power to limit margin loans beyond the opportunity "to consult" with the district Federal Reserve banks, "which should be empowered to prescribe margin requirements"; and short sales should not be "curbed," since they acted "as a stabilizing influence on the downside of the market." Even in those substantive areas where the Pecora hearings most clearly had demonstrated a need for regulation, the Dickinson Report temporized. The problems associated with stock market pools, specialists, and the non-segregation of brokerage from underwriting and dealing firms were all recognized as serious concerns. But Dickinson's report insisted that additional studies should be conducted before any prohibitory rules were established. Only with respect to a few matters, like fraudulent "matched orders" and the need for periodic corporate reporting, did Dickinson's committee unequivocally recommend immediate regulation.[52]

Senator Fletcher, his colleague on the Banking Committee, Senator Couzens, and Pecora and his staff were appalled by the Dickinson Report. Pecora soon let it be known that he personally favored a bill that severely restricted short-selling pools, and margin-trading.[53] By February 1, the latest Stokes-Taylor draft had been delivered to Benjamin Cohen for a final rewrite. Pecora instructed Cohen to toughen the draft by establishing fixed margin requirements, segregating brokers from dealers, and flatly outlawing all pools, wash sales, matched orders, and short sales. Landis was uncomfortable with so rigid an approach. He had been sympathetic to the Dickinson Report's recommendation of further study of several stock exchange controversies. But Cohen, in part influenced by the view that a reform bill should initially seek far broader reforms than Congress was likely to enact so that the bill's proponents would have room to compromise, incorporated most of Pecora's stringent prohibitions.[54]

On February 9, two weeks after the Dickinson Report had been submitted, Roosevelt sent a message to Congress formally recommending the enactment of legislation to regulate the securities exchanges.[55] In deference to the serious divisions within his administration, Roosevelt did not publicly endorse Cohen's final revision.[56] But his frequent subsequent public and private comments that he would not be satisfied with a bill unless it had "teeth in it" left little doubt about his personal preference.[57]

Simultaneously with Roosevelt's message, Senator Fletcher and Congressman Rayburn introduced Cohen's stock exchange proposal, thereafter called the Fletcher-Rayburn bill.[58] The breadth and severity of the Fletcher-Rayburn bill startled both official Washington and Wall Street. *The New York Times*, for example, reflected the view of many with its pejorative headline DRASTIC STOCK MARKET BILL.[59]

The proposed law primarily was addressed to the regulation of securities exchanges.[60] Each securities exchange was required to register with the FTC, which was given the power to approve or disapprove exchange rules and regulations. The bill itself, however, proscribed nine specific types of market manipulation, including the carrying out of wash sales or matched orders or otherwise creating a "false and misleading appearance of active trading" in a security, or disseminating false or misleading information to influence investors to buy or sell a particular security.

Section 6 of the bill forbade brokers to lend investors margin credit equal to more than 80 percent of the lowest price of a security during the preceding three years or 40 percent of current prices. The Federal Trade Commission could mandate more severe loan limits if "appropriate in the public interest or for the protection of investors." These provisions were consonant with the conviction of Roosevelt and the draftsmen that "the two real causes of trouble in the stock market are speculation with borrowed money, that is, on margin, and lack of adequate publicity." The vesting of the FTC with discretion to impose even more severe loan limits reflected the New Dealers' doubts that the Federal Reserve Board possessed sufficient political independence from the New York financial community to regulate adequately margin limits.

Section 10 of the bill proposed to revolutionize stock exchange membership. Floor traders were to be abolished. Explained Corcoran, "The only interest the public has in a stock exchange is that it should be a place where the outside public can buy and sell its stocks. There is no public interest to be served by giving an inside seat to a small group of men who are trading for their own account." Similarly, specialists were to be barred from trading for their own accounts or disclosing the contents of their future-order books to anyone, unless the data were available to all members of the exchange. Indeed, Section 10 invited the exchanges to go further and replace the specialists altogether with exchange officers or employees who could perform "the functions of specialists" but would have no rights to trade for their own accounts. Finally, to prevent brokers from touting new securities issued by their own firms when consulted for disinterested investment advice, Section 10 would have prohibited brokerage houses from acting as dealers or underwriters. To the floor traders and specialists who dominated New York Stock Exchange governance, Section 10 was tantamount to a declaration of war. If enacted, it would have ended all private transactions on the Exchange floor, permanently transforming the Exchange into a clerical agency for the execution of off-floor orders. But the section had equally radical implications for the stock brokerage firms that were the floor members' rivals in Exchange politics. Brokerage firms permanently would have lost the opportunity to share in the new securities issuance business. Rarely was a statutory proposal so well calculated to unite its opposition. The furor engendered by Section 10 briefly jeopardized the possibility of enacting any stock exchange proposal.

There was much more to the omnibus bill. The FTC also was to be given a general authority to regulate the interstate transactions of the over-the-counter markets. Since most over-the-counter transactions were intrastate, this provision was unlikely to be of much consequence, but Landis and Cohen were doubtful that purely intrastate securities sales could be regulated constitutionally.

Three related provisions of the bill empowered the FTC to require corporations selling securities traded on an exchange to file a registration statement with the exchange similar to that required by the 1933 act for new securities, update the statement with annual and periodic reports, and conduct corporate elections that employed mailed proxies subject to FTC regulations. The latter provision represented the Roosevelt administration's first efforts directly to regulate corporate governance. The electoral rules were recommended, Corcoran explained, because "proxies, as solicitations are made now, are a joke. The persons who control the machinery for sending out the proxies, with practically no interest in the corporation, can simply keep other people from organizing [and] get enough proxies to run the Company." It soon became known that the Roosevelt administration also was considering the possibility of developing a comprehensive federal corporation bill to fully replace the ineffective corporate governance provisions of state law.[61] The Senate Banking Committee, the Twentieth Century Fund, the Dickinson Report, and the New York Stock Exchange would each separately recommend a federal corporation act — although it was widely assumed that the NYSE's enthusiasm for corporate law reform was a tactic to deflect the momentum for a securities exchange law.

Finally, the "anti-Wiggin" provisions of the Fletcher-Rayburn bill required corporate directors, officers, or owners of 5 percent or more of a class of stock to file public reports of their trading in their own firm's stock and precluded their realizing "insiders' profits" by buying or selling securities and earning a profit within any six-month period.

Pecora, by then a master at scheduling hearings for maximum political advantage, attempted to galvanize support for the Fletcher-Rayburn bill by holding hearings highly embarrassing to the New York Stock Exchange just after the bill's introduction. From February 14 to the 22nd, the Senate Banking Committee heard evidence that the Exchange had been unable or unwilling to investigate effectively pool operations in alcohol stocks after Congress had voted to repeal Prohibition. Between July 18 and July 21, 1933, the price of American Commercial Alcohol abruptly fell from a high of 89⅞ to a low of 29⅛. Pecora immediately had taken a train to New York City and personally requested Richard Whitney to initiate a New York Stock Exchange investigation. Whitney reluctantly agreed, but then three months later reported to Pecora that "there were no material deliberate improprieties" in stock transactions in American Commercial Alcohol or five other alcohol firms investigated: "The repeal situation appears to have created a public interest in these stocks great enough to account for their activity." Incredulous, Pecora had assigned his own investigators to study American Commercial Alcohol's price fluctuations. They soon uncovered evidence that between May 3 and July 24, 1933, American Commercial's chairman of the board, Russell Brown, its specialist on the New York Stock Exchange, Charles Wright, and such notorious market operators as Thomas Bragg and Ben "Sell 'em" Smith had organized a pool operation that had helped push American Commercial's stock price up from a quotation near $20 to almost $90 by participating in as much as 75 percent of the stock's trades during that period. As the market rose, Brown had arranged to issue approximately 45,000 new shares of American Commercial stock to himself and other pool members. After the pool had sold off these and other shares, the pool ceased trading in American Commercial stock and its share price collapsed. During the February 1934 hearings, Pecora emphasized that the New York Stock Exchange neither at the time nor after the stock's suspicious market quotations had been called to its attention had been able to identify even the existence of a pool. How, Pecora suggested, could it be trusted to police its own members?[62]

For once Pecora's political theater failed him. He had come to view Richard Whitney and other officials of the New York Stock Exchange as obstructionists.[63] Roosevelt, too, believed that "the fundamental trouble with this whole Stock Exchange crowd is their complete lack of elementary education. I do not mean lack of college diplomas, etc., but just inability to understand the country or the public or their obligation to their fellow men."[64] For months, relations between Richard Whitney and the New Deal had deteriorated. The past October Whitney had been incensed when Pecora hired John Flynn, an acerbic critic of the Exchange, and asked Flynn to deliver personally to Whitney a draft of a questionnaire Pecora wanted the New York Stock Exchange to distribute to its members. On seeing Flynn, Whitney had abruptly left his office, returning several minutes later to deliver a furious lecture on why the New York Stock Exchange did not require government regulation, during the course of which Whitney delivered his memorable observation that "the Exchange is a perfect institution." Some days later, Whitney formally refused to distribute the questionnaire.[65] This had required the much-irritated Pecora to subpoena eleven stock exchange firms before successfully distributing his questionnaire to the balance of the Exchange's members. Whitney had his own causes for irritation. Late in October, the Exchange had tightened its auditing standards.[66] By February, Whitney was ready to announce three new Exchange rules barring members from participating in pools and prohibiting specialists from accepting stock options from anyone or disclosing information in their future-order books.[67] These rules were considerably more stringent than those recommended in the Dickinson Report. Yet in the days before his stock exchange message, Roosevelt had refused to speak to Whitney about the new Exchange rules or to discuss the administration's impending legislation.[68]

Whitney struck back. In February and March, he directed a highly effective business lobby. In spite of initial popular and press opinion in favor of stock exchange legislation, Whitney was able to force Pecora and Landis to withdraw their bill.

The campaign began four days after the Fletcher-Rayburn bill was introduced, when Whitney met with representatives of thirty brokerage firms. The following day Whitney wrote each member of the Exchange that the bill would "have very disastrous consequences to the stock market." A similar letter was forwarded to the presidents of all corporations listed on the New York Stock Exchange, emphasizing the "serious" effects the bill would have on their firm and its directors, officers, and principal shareholders. Soon Whitney had organized the 46,000 New York City brokerage house employees to protest the bill; Livingston & Company, a brokerage firm, began wiring its offices throughout the country with such messages as "Are your employees alive to the fact that with the passage of the bill a great many of them will be out of employment?" A second brokerage house compelled each employee to contribute to a lawyer's fund; a third, Jelke & Company, took to reprinting the Declaration of Independence in full in Washington papers to protest "the apparent 'New Deal' philosophy that engaging in a business for profit is unlawful."

The stock exchange lobby swiftly made itself felt in Washington. Congressmen reported receiving vast numbers of letters, telephone calls, and telegrams, variously warning that the bill "provides for the wholesale 'goose-step' regimentation of industry and commerce under the control of the Federal Trade Commission," "aids foreign competitors of American corporations to the detriment of American stockholders by making available confidential information not presently obtainable," "attempts an impossible degree of regulation of the credit agencies and business enterprises of the country, even to the point of requiring small and large companies to sign away constitutional rights as a condition to the continuance of their securities upon the public markets." "The issue involved," summed up the Standard Commercial Tobacco Company, "is whether political bureaucracy shall be permitted to stifle the initiative and creative genius of American enterprise."

Many of these statements were crude and hysterically overblown, but the lobbying efforts personally conducted by Whitney at first were not. Newspapers quietly were approached. Although nearly all daily papers in cities with populations of 50,000 or more initially supported the measure, by April Raymond Moley complained in a *Today* magazine article, "Day by day, almost, the ranks of the newspaper supporters of the bill have thinned." Repeatedly the NRA imprimatur was exploited; initially, in mid-February, when the investment brokers circulated rules of fair practice, which they argued made sections of the Fletcher-Rayburn bill unnecessary; later, when the New York Stock Exchange helped industrialists on the NRA "durable goods committee" disseminate a formal memorandum of proposed changes to satisfy business. Even Roosevelt's successor as governor of New York, Herbert Lehman, was persuaded to write the President that the state was counting on $40 million in stock transfer taxes in 1934–1935, and Lehman hoped that the interests of the Exchange "will be given careful and sympathetic consideration."[69]

Nowhere was the effectiveness of Whitney's lobbying campaign more evident than in the parallel House and Senate hearings on the initial Fletcher-Rayburn bill, held between February 14 and March 16. From the moment Landis and Corcoran completed their detailed explanation of the bill to Rayburn's House Commerce Committee, both sets of hearings were dominated by Whitney.

The stock exchange president broadly outlined his position in similar opening statements to both committees. The FTC's powers under the bill, he argued, were so great that the commission might not regulate but might "actually . . . supervise and manage all stock exchanges [and] establish indirectly a form of nationalization of business and industry which has hitherto been alien to the American theory of Federal Government." Even if the FTC exercised its powers with restraint, the bill would "destroy the free and open market for securities."

This was especially likely because of the rigidity of the proposed margin requirements and the arbitrariness of the rule barring specialists from trading in securities for their own accounts, which might lead to erratic oscillations in share prices heretofore prevented by specialists' purchasing and selling shares to ensure orderly price quotations. Whitney volunteered that the New York

Stock Exchange would support legislation establishing a stock exchange authority if it was composed of two members appointed by
the President, two Cabinet officers, one member appointed by the
Federal Reserve Board, and two stock exchange representatives.

> We suggest [concluded Whitney] that this coordinating authority be
> given plenary power to control the amount of margins which mem-
> bers of exchanges must require and maintain on customers' accounts;
> and further, that it would have plenary power to require stock ex-
> changes to adopt rules and regulations preventing not only dishonest
> practices but also all practices which unfairly influence the price of
> securities or unduly stimulate speculation.[70]

Whitney was succeeded at the witness table by Thomas Gay, outside counsel to the NYSE, who predictably opined that the Fletcher-
Rayburn bill was "not constitutional," then momentarily stunned
the House Commerce Committee by producing an opinion letter
James Landis had written for the New York Stock Exchange in 1932
while a law professor at Harvard; in it, he stated that a bill to regulate short-selling introduced by Congressman La Guardia was not
constitutionally acceptable. Gay argued that "the reasons which
Mr. Landis gave for entertaining the view that the La Guardia bill
was not constitutional are equally applicable . . . [to] this bill." *[71]

Then Whitney presented his most convincing argument: opposition to the bill was national; it was not limited to Wall Street bankers.

The New York Stock Exchange was hardly a popular institution
in 1934. Indeed, next to J. P. Morgan, it was the most obvious sym-
bol of New York City's often-resented financial community. But the
same hostility was rarely felt toward the smaller regional stock
exchanges, whose continued existence few employment-conscious
congressmen could afford to dismiss entirely. On five successive
House hearing days well-rehearsed representatives of twenty-four
separate local exchanges echoed Whitney's testimony. The tone of
the local representatives' testimony was set by Eugene Thompson,
president of the Association of Stock Exchanges, who, either paraphrasing or misstating a frequently expressed criticism of the
Fletcher-Rayburn bill, told the House Commerce Committee that it
was hardly necessary "to cure a case of hiccups by severing the head
of the patient." Less morbid, but probably more persuasive, was the
prediction of the Cincinnati Stock Exchange's W. D. Gradison that

---

* Landis later refuted Gay's argument, noting that his letter concerning the La Guardia bill had included the reservation "I am as yet unconvinced that a bill could not be
drafted to regulate security transactions on stock exchanges which would be constitutional." Landis insisted that the Fletcher-Rayburn proposal was that bill.[72]

the bill might "eliminate from existence" most regional exchanges, which the San Francisco Stock Exchange's president, Frank Shaughnessy, emphasized would make "the cost of capital to small firms . . . almost prohibitive." Several of the regional exchange representatives specifically criticized the draftsmen for so focusing on the model of the New York Stock Exchange that they failed to appreciate that a small exchange could not afford a segregation of brokers and dealers. Virtually every local exchange "heartily" endorsed Whitney's proposal of a stock exchange coordinating authority.[73] Similar sentiments were expressed by Dean Witter, appearing on behalf of 204 Pacific Coast dealers, the United States Chamber of Commerce, the National Association of Manufacturers, the Investment Bankers Association, the New York Curb Exchange, the usually politically liberal investment banking firm of Lehman Brothers, as well as a group of eighteen other investment houses. Even the President's cousin Archibald Roosevelt stated on behalf of the New York City Municipal Bond Dealers Committee that "if the bill goes through as it is, we will be put out of business."[74]

Undoubtedly, the opposition testimony that Pecora and Landis welcomed least was that of Edward A. Pierce, head of one of the nation's largest brokerage houses, E. A. Pierce & Company. The previous October, Pierce had cooperated with Pecora on the Senate Banking Committee's stock exchange questionnaire after Whitney refused to distribute it to Exchange members. Pierce, a leader of the Exchange's brokerage firm reform faction, often disagreed with Whitney's management of the Exchange.[75] But after studying the Fletcher-Rayburn bill, Pierce closed ranks with the Exchange's lobbyists. Terming the bill "destruction," Pierce testified that the margin provisions alone would result in a forced liquidation of several hundred million dollars' worth of stock.[76] Whitney received further unsolicited support from Assistant Commerce Secretary Dickinson, who sharply criticized the Fletcher-Rayburn measure, noting that he was particularly opposed to removing control over credit for stock market margin loans from the Federal Reserve Board.[77] Additional support for the New York Stock Exchange came from Alfred Bernheim, who had directed a recently published study of securities markets for the Twentieth Century Fund. Although the fund's study had urged Congress to enact a stock exchange bill, Bernheim testified that the Fletcher-Rayburn bill as introduced was so heavy-handed that it might "result . . . [in] the strangulation of some useful and beneficial activities."[78]

Before either the House or Senate hearings on the initial Fletcher-Rayburn bill were completed, James Landis conceded in a letter to

Felix Frankfurter that "the Stock Exchange bill is taking a terrific beating."[79] By then, congressional support was beginning to slip away. The flight from the bill was not slowed by statements of Corcoran and Pecora in late February indicating a willingness to modify the bill,[80] or by Rayburn's subsequent remark that the measure merely had been "introduced as a basis for consideration," and the House Commerce Committee soon would rewrite it.[81] On March 5, Senate majority leader Joseph Robinson took the Senate floor to announce "As to whether the Stock Exchange Regulation Bill may be ready for disposition during this session of Congress, no assurance at this time can be given."[82] With these words, the initial Fletcher-Rayburn bill was effectively dead.

The conspicuousness of the bill's defeat elevated the lobbying battle for a stock exchange act into a crucial test of Roosevelt's leadership. If no stock exchange bill could be adopted during the Seventy-third Congress, Roosevelt would have been perceived to have suffered his first major legislative defeat. He was by then too well identified with the corporate reform efforts of Pecora, Frankfurter, and Landis to avoid responsibility for the bill's fate by attaching to it the names of Fletcher and Rayburn.

With the prestige of his administration directly challenged, Roosevelt assumed personal direction of the effort to rewrite the bill. On March 7, the White House sharply responded to Senator Robinson, by announcing that President Roosevelt expected Congress to pass at the present session legislation for Federal regulation of stock exchanges.[83] Following a conference with Roosevelt the following day, Robinson concurred, with the face-saving proviso that "the bill would be simplified as much as practicable."[84] Relying primarily on Landis, rather than on the more uncompromising Pecora, Roosevelt initiated two separate revision efforts.

The first was largely intra-administration. Landis, Cohen, and Corcoran began meeting with officials of the Federal Reserve Board and Treasury Department.[85] Both agencies previously had opposed the bill, the board insisting in a memorandum to Senator Glass that control over margin accounts should not be vested "in a completely separate administrative authority like the Federal Trade Commission." With Roosevelt participating in some of the conferences, a compromise was struck returning to the Federal Reserve Board jurisdiction over margin requirements, but sharply limiting its discretion by providing in the revised bill that brokers could not lend more than 75 percent of the price of a security on a national securities exchange, nor more than 40 percent of the price of an unlisted secu-

rity. To meet the criticism that the bill would require the immediate sale of securities then held in margin accounts, the revised
draft provided that existing margin accounts would not be affected
until January 1939. Throughout the course of ten revisions of the
bill, drafted by Cohen and Corcoran between March 4 and March 19,
other compromises were made in an attempt to reduce business
opposition to the bill. Chief among them was a complex revision of
Section 10 meant to permit members of regional exchanges to act as
both brokers and dealers if granted permission by the FTC, but directing the Commission "to make a study of the feasibility . . . of the
complete divorcement of the functions of dealer and broker . . . [by]
January 1, 1936." State banks, denied in the initial draft power to
lend money to brokers for margin, were now given that power "in
localities where there are no [Federal Reserve] member banks, or to
meet emergency needs."[86]

In addition, after discussions with Fletcher, Rayburn, Landis, and
the Treasury Department's Herman Oliphant, Roosevelt approved
amendments to the 1933 Securities Act prepared by Landis to limit
recoverable damages to those resulting from misrepresentations or
omissions in a registration statement, limit underwriters' liability
to the extent of participation in a securities issue, and permit courts
to assess full costs against investors presenting unmeritorious
claims. Later he also agreed to shorten the act's statute of limitations. In effect, Roosevelt was willing to make every significant
change sought by the critics of the 1933 act except the demand that
purchasers prove reliance on a registration statement. Soon
Roosevelt and Landis began meeting with leading investment bankers, including Robert Christie of the Investment Bankers Association, Winthrop Aldrich of the Chase National Bank, Averell Harriman and Robert Lovett of Brown Brothers Harriman, and J. H.
Perkins of the National City Bank, to discuss these revisions.[87]

The revised Fletcher-Rayburn bill was introduced into the House
on March 19. Roosevelt's personal intervention had resulted in
unified administration support for the bill. Tom K. Smith, a St.
Louis banker then serving as assistant to the new Secretary of the
Treasury, Henry Morgenthau, Jr., informed the House committee
that now, since most of the Treasury Department's "suggestions
and changes . . . have been incorporated in the bill," the department
"approved" the bill.[88] Federal Reserve Board governor Eugene Black
unequivocally informed both committees that "the Board is . . .
prepared to approve the bill as revised."[89] Robert E. Healy, the FTC
chief counsel, emphatically testified in favor of the bill's grant of

authority to the Commission to prescribe corporate accounting standards.[90] Jesse Jones, Reconstruction Finance Corporation chairman, held a press conference at which he predicted that banks would soon lose their fear of both the 1933 Securities Act and the proposed stock exchange bill.[91] But the bill's most effective advocate was Roosevelt himself. Four days after the revised bill was introduced, he informed reporters that he favored a stock exchange bill "with teeth in it."[92] Roosevelt demonstrably considered this an apt metaphor. On March 26, just before departing for a vacation, he publicly released letters to Rayburn and Fletcher repeating his certitude "that the country as a whole will not be satisfied with legislation unless such legislation has teeth in it."* Noting that "a more definite and more highly organized drive is being made against effective [stock exchange] legislation . . . than against any similar recommendation made by me during the past year," Roosevelt made his first specific declaration of support for the revised Fletcher-Rayburn bill. "I do not see," he wrote, "how any of us could afford to have [the bill] weakened in any shape, manner, or form."[94] Prospects for the bill's passage further brightened when the Twentieth Century Fund's top officials also urged "speedy enactment" of the revised bill "without serious amendment."[95]

The stock exchanges remained adamantly opposed. As long as the Fletcher-Rayburn bill threatened to eliminate floor traders and the specialist system, it represented a personal threat to a substantial portion of the members of every stock exchange. Whitney signaled the intensity of the bill's opposition on March 22 when he began testimony to the House Commerce Committee by stating, "Our basic objections to the old bill apply with equal force to the new one."[96] Twenty-five regional exchanges concurred with Whitney that they could support the Fletcher-Rayburn bill only if it was sweepingly altered to create a new federal stock exchange commission in place of the FTC to enforce the act, grant the Federal Reserve Board unfettered discretion in setting margins, leave largely unchanged the existing system of specialists and floor traders, and not regulate corporate proxy elections.[97]

The perceived "punitive" nature of the bill continued to unify widely disparate elements of the business community in opposition. The commission brokers were especially antagonistic. Acting through Raoul Desvernine, a New York City attorney, they had

---

* Pecora, proponent of even more stringent legislation than Roosevelt, refused to be outdone. Reporters were informed he not only wanted a "bill with teeth in it," but also a bill "with strong jaws to work the teeth."[93]

attempted to negotiate with Landis and Cohen a compromise revision bill containing provisions similar to those Richard Whitney had proposed. Desvernine had offered the support of the moderate leaders of the brokerage houses if the New Dealers would agree to substitute a three-person national securities exchange commission, including "at least one commissioner . . . thoroughly experienced in stock exchange practices" for FTC enforcement, give the Federal Reserve Board a flexible power over margin limits, only modestly alter exchange membership, and eliminate sections in the bill dealing with corporate reports, corporate insider trading, and over-the-counter markets, since these were not "pertinent to exchange regulation." Each of Desvernine's proposals was rejected.[98] Paul Shields, a leading commission broker and Exchange moderate, angrily wrote Rayburn that the revised bill intended "to punish all people dealing in securities."[99] His sentiment was widely shared. By early April the Chambers of Commerce or Boards of Trade of forty-three cities had organized to arouse public opinion against the bill.[100] Twenty-eight prominent industrialists, claiming to speak for the nation's 486,000 corporations, soon also wrote to protest "provisions . . . unnecessarily severe."[101]

Lobbying against the bill turned increasingly vicious. Rumors characterized the bill's proponents variously as radicals or Bolsheviks or "a bunch of Jews out to get J. P. Morgan." James H. Rand, chairman of Remington Rand, told the House Commerce Committee that Dr. William Wirt, superintendent of schools in Gary, Indiana, had written to him of attending a dinner where unnamed individuals informed him that "Mr. Roosevelt is only the Kerensky of this revolution . . . the brain trusters would soon be able to use the police power of the Government and 'crack down' on the opposition with a big stick." Subsequent House hearings revealed Dr. Wirt's charges as malicious fantasies.

But the whisper campaign continued unabated. Corcoran privately wrote that the New York Stock Exchange publicists Edward L. Bernays and Ivy Lee engaged in a "very evident but unsuccessful attempt to make the press believe that the famous dinner [mentioned by Wirt] had been held" in the home he shared with Cohen. The press ignored the story until Congressman Fred Britten took the floor of the House to charge that the Fletcher-Rayburn bill itself had been "conceived in the little red house in Georgetown" by the "scarlet fever boys," Landis, Frankfurter, Cohen, and Corcoran, whose "real object . . . is to Russianize everything." The public and private campaigns of "the biggest and most highly paid lobby Washington has ever seen," concluded Corcoran, "*did* scare hell out of Congress," resulting in a "lack of sympathy of the southern political leadership."[102]

By the time the revised Fletcher-Rayburn bill was reported out, the respective House and Senate committees had revised it to incorporate several of the amendments publicly recommended by Richard Whitney. The most fundamental changes occurred in the Senate Banking Committee. By a vote of 10–8, the committee adopted a proposal by Carter Glass to replace the Federal Trade Commission and Federal Reserve Board as enforcement agencies with a new three-person Securities Exchange Commission.[103] Glass insisted that the amendment was offered to ensure that the Federal Reserve Board would not be "allied or aligned in any way with stock exchange transactions." That Glass had long been concerned with maintaining the board "as far from stock exchange transactions as possible" was well known, but this explanation of why he championed Whitney and Desvernine's proposal for a new commission was nevertheless ingenuous. A more probable explanation was that he, like the Exchange leaders, feared the FTC. With the 1933 appointments of Landis and George Mathews as commissioners, and the continued service of Robert Healy as chief counsel, the FTC, as Landis candidly put it, was controlled by "our group." Glass, deeply distrustful of Pecora and the New Deal reformers, initially recommended that the new Securities Exchange Commission include members experienced with Exchange practices, a proposal intended to ensure that Landis could not control the new commission.

Ultimately, as a consequence of New York Stock Exchange lobbying to weaken the Securities Exchange Act and Senator Glass's antipathy to the New Deal, the SEC would be born. Later Landis would acknowledge that he had been wrong to oppose the creation of a separate commission, since an agency with a narrow jurisdiction, like the SEC, had advantages in providing administrative expertise that an agency with a broader jurisdiction, like the FTC, lacked. But at the time, the SEC had not been sought by the New Deal. Its birth, in a sense, was an accident.

The Senate Banking Committee also adopted a second Glass amendment replacing fixed margin limits with a substitute provision empowering the Federal Reserve Board to specify margin requirements for loans from member banks to brokers. The proposed Securities Exchange Commission was to specify margin requirements for loans from brokers to investors.[104] In the House, less significant changes were made. The FTC was retained as the enforcement agency, and the Federal Reserve Board's discretion to regulate margins was still subject to a fixed formula, although the board could set loan limits as high as 55 percent of the current price of a security, or 100 percent of its lowest market price during the preceding thirty-six months. But the House bill dropped the anti-Wiggin provision barring insiders' purchases and sales of their own corporation's securities at a profit within any six-month period, and modestly altered the corporate reporting requirements.[105]

With these amendments, the stock exchange bill was assured of passage. Rayburn angrily defended the revised bill during the ensuing floor debate. Decrying "the most vicious and persistent lobby that any of us have ever known in Washington," he charged that some of the letters received in opposition to the bill were coerced, others forgeries. Without further amendment, the House adopted the stock exchange bill on May 4 by a vote of 281–84, with sixty-six abstentions.[106]

Fletcher soon demonstrated a comparable control over the Senate. After successfully appending to the revised bill James Landis's amendments to the 1933 Securities Act,[107] and a Pecora proposal to require disclosure documents from bankruptcy, reorganization, and other protective committees,[108] Fletcher frustrated attempts to add over twenty other amendments to the bill. By a vote of 62–13, the Senate approved the Fletcher-Rayburn Act on May 12. "Not in years," reported *The New York Times*, "has a bill of such a controversial nature been passed by so overwhelming a majority."[109]

Roosevelt and Fletcher, buoyed by the huge Senate majority, made a final attempt to restore the FTC as the administrative agency and to set fixed margin limits. Ignoring long-standing custom, Fletcher chose not to name senior Banking Committee members Glass and Robert Wagner to the Conference Committee, since both favored the new Securities Exchange Commisssion, and selected instead Senators Alben Barkley and James Byrnes, whom Fletcher described as "sympathetic to the legislation." Nearly simultaneously, Roosevelt informed a press conference that he "personally" preferred the House margin rules and FTC enforcement. A Landis memo was circulated to Congress, specifying as "reasons for making the Federal Trade Commission the Administrative Agency" a cost saving of $500,000 and avoidance of "the attendant delay and organizational difficulties . . . [of] setting up an entirely new governmental agency."

The move to reinstate the FTC misfired badly. After learning that he had not been named to the Conference Committee, Carter Glass fumed to the press, "It was a direct affront and a gratuitous indignity, and deliberately intended to be," and resigned from the Senate Banking Committee. Senator Barkley, a personal friend of Glass's, promptly also resigned from the Conference Committee. Majority Leader Robinson refused to accept either resignation, but agreed with Barkley that he and Byrnes could vote as "free agents" on the Conference Committee, not bound by the usual unit rule. Both men pledged to support Glass's new commission. Roosevelt, embarrassed by accusations that he had attempted to influence the Conference Committee and had not originally objected to Glass's proposal for a new commission, awkwardly retreated, informing the press that it was "not a frightfully important thing, one way or the other" which agency enforced the stock exchange bill.[110] In conference, the slightly more dignified Securities *and* Exchange Commission was brought into existence by compromise, the House conferees giving up the struggle for FTC enforcement, their Senate counterparts surrendering most of the Glass margin-limit amendment.

By late May, the long legislative battle was over. As reported out by the Conference Committee and swiftly enacted, the Securities Exchange Act of 1934 was a marvel of irresolution.[111] On most controversial substantive issues, Congress had been stalemated. Rather than providing the new Commission with a clear mandate, the legislators had granted the agency authority to study the controversy or issue its own rules. In effect, Congress had broadly defined the Commission's areas of expertise and invited it to forge its own mandate. The political processes that produced the jerry-built statute were allowed to continue.

The heart of the act was the Glass-inspired Section 4, which created the Securities and Exchange Commission. Related sections empowered the Commission to enforce the new law and to assume jurisdiction over the 1933 Securities Act. The new agency was to be composed of five commissioners appointed by the President, with the advice and consent of the Senate. No more than three commissioners could be members of the same political party. Each would serve a five-year term. This was a significant legislative victory for the Roosevelt administration, which succeeded, as Will Rogers phrased it, in putting "a cop on Wall Street" without agreeing that any member of the Commission would be a stock exchange member, as Whitney, John Dickinson, and Carter Glass had urged.

The administration also succeeded in retaining important portions of Benjamin Cohen's original draft. The act required the registration of the stock exchanges, vesting the SEC with authority to approve stock exchange rules. Firms issuing securities traded on an exchange were directed to file registration documents with that exchange. These firms also had to file annual and quarterly reports with the SEC. The Commission additionally was empowered to issue rules regarding corporate proxy elections and the over-the-counter markets. But with the exception of the noncontroversial anti-market-manipulation rules and the anti-Wiggin short-term profit sections, virtually all of the provisions retained from Cohen's original draft conferred on the SEC vague powers to use its discretion in issuing rules where appropriate "in the public interest or for the protection of investors."

Several other substantive provisions drafted by Cohen at Pecora's behest had been weakened. Where the bill originally had set fixed margin loan limits, the act almost entirely reversed this formula by providing that the initial extension of margin to investors could be no greater than the higher of 55 percent of the current market price of a security or 100 percent of the lowest price during the preceding thirty-six months, but then adding that the Federal Reserve Board was empowered to raise or lower these limits whenever it deemed appropriate. The New York Stock Exchange achieved an almost total victory regarding Exchange membership. Floor traders were allowed to continue, subject to SEC rules. The specialist system was very nearly unchanged. Broker-dealer segregation was not achieved. Congress deferred resolution of each of these issues until the SEC completed studies of Exchange membership and broker-dealer segregation, in 1935 and 1936 respectively. The Commission was directed to make a similar study of unlisted securities by 1936. Pecora's restrictions on protective committees were replaced by a directive for yet another study. The Senate Banking Committee counsel failed in his ambition to outlaw or severely limit short-selling.

Nonetheless, Pecora, like most in the New Deal, regarded the Securities Exchange Act of 1934 as a "happy compromise." With the creation of the SEC, the proponents of securities law reform had secured an ongoing agency to enforce the new statute and to continue studying the need for further corporate law reforms. With such considerations in mind, Pecora emphasized to Roosevelt the day the President signed the act, "It will be a good or bad law depending upon the men who administer it."[112]

4

Moley's Man

MR. MAPES. *The law ought to be made to apply to all alike and I hate the idea that some man can go to an administrative official and get something done that another fellow on the street cannot.*

MR. CORCORAN. *You have to have the power to make rules and regulations in every administrative body. The answer is to pick good men on your commissions.*

MR. MAPES. *Well, that sometimes is no answer at all.*

MR. CORCORAN. *It is the ultimate answer to any governmental problem.*

> — THOMAS CORCORAN
> Testimony on the Securities Exchange Act of 1934[1]

WITH THE PASSAGE of the 1934 Securities Exchange Act, it was widely assumed that James Landis would be the first chairman of the Securities and Exchange Commission. As early as May 27, *The New York Times* had headlined a front-page article J. M. LANDIS SLATED FOR STOCK MARKET CHIEF;[2] *Newsweek* reported that Washington "confidently expected" the appointment;[3] *Time* echoed the prediction, adding that Landis would "dominate" the Commission's proceedings;[4] *Business Week* took to referring to the SEC as "Landis' New Commission."[5] Endorsing the prevailing opinion, *Fortune* titled a feature article "The Legend of Landis."[6]

Behind the scenes, Thomas Corcoran, Ernest Gruening, and Ray

Stevens lobbied for the Landis chairmanship.[7] Felix Frankfurter implied his support in a bellicose letter to Roosevelt:

> What is involved is not merely the Stock Exchange Control Act.
> Nothing less is involved than to keep Wall Street in its place, to
> furnish a counterpoise against its aggrandisement of power, by which
> the Street all along the line resists efforts by the government for the
> common interest. And so, plainly, you need administrators who are
> equipped to meet the best legal brains whom Wall Street always has at
> its disposal, who have stamina and do not weary of the fight, who are
> moved neither by blandishments nor fears, who, in a word, unite
> public zeal with unusual capacity.[8]

That precisely was the public and the private perception of James
McCauley Landis. For close to a year he had advised, then led, the
Federal Trade Commission's Securities Division.[9] He had been a
hard-nosed administrator, developing rules and registration forms
that strictly complied with the 1933 Securities Act,[10] and, when he
felt it necessary, persuading the FTC to stop the issuance of, or
suspend the effectiveness of, thirty-three separate securities between July 1, 1933, and July 1, 1934.[11] In Congress, many had
bristled at his brilliance and self-assurance, and he had been deroga-
tively nicknamed "Cocksure" Landis. But his obvious intelligence
and zeal made him a well-publicized prototype of the New Deal
civil servant. Essentially humorless, usually photographed looking
tight-lipped, Landis was pictured by the press as an administrator so
dedicated that he sometimes slept on a cot in his office; an idealist
who once criticized the dean of Yale Medical School for suggesting
professors should be paid $25,000 a year because "a man should
follow a career for love of his work." *Fortune* reported that he always drove too fast, smoked two packs of Lucky Strikes a day, and
lunched on cups of black coffee. When his wife, who, it was recounted, "saw little of her husband," was asked to bring him to a
party, she replied wearily, "What husband?"[12] The press accounts of
Landis's overwork were thoroughly accurate. But in the crusade
atmosphere of Washington in 1934, such reports served to corroborate the point that Landis's supporters insistently made: James
Landis had earned the SEC's chairmanship.

Roosevelt's desire to conciliate the growing business opposition
to his administration ruled out Landis's appointment. As the
Securities Exchange Act battle neared its conclusion, Roosevelt
and Moley agreed there would "be a rather complete examination
and realignment of policy before September 1st [1934]."[13] Corcoran
reported to Frankfurter, "The plan of battle is to avoid any further

attempt at reforms that might bring down more criticism during the present Congress, arrange a 'truce of God,' reorganize the machinery down here to help along a business recovery this summer, and in every other way postpone all other considerations to the necessarily primary objective of winning the congressional elections."[14] Self-consciously, New Deal historians Arthur Schlesinger, Jr., and James MacGregor Burns would write that Roosevelt sought to reclaim his role "of National Father, of bipartisan leader, of President of all the people";[15] "to present himself as above the party battle."[16]

The "truce of God" with the business community lasted nearly a year, and was particularly apparent in the months preceding the 1934 election. Addressing a bankers' convention on October 24, Roosevelt, for example, stated, "The time is ripe for an alliance of all forces intent upon the business of recovery," generously conceding to his earlier scapegoats, "The Government is bending every effort through the Treasury, the Federal Reserve system, the Reconstruction Finance Corporation, the Securities and Exchange Commission, and the Federal Housing Administration to facilitate and encourage the revival of private investment . . . all of these new agencies are seeking consultation and cooperation with you bankers."[17]

The architect of Roosevelt's conciliatory strategy was Raymond Moley, who, though no longer a full-time government employee, remained one of Roosevelt's most influential policy advisers. Long an apostle of the need to revive business confidence, Moley had publicly reassured the New Deal's conservative opponents in May 1934, "With the passage of the Stock Exchange bill, the New Deal is practically complete."[18] When, shortly after, Roosevelt turned to Moley to suggest a list of people suitable for appointment to the Commission, the President implicitly took another step to fashion his truce of God with business. Arguing that James Landis was "better as member than as chairman because he is essentially a representative of strict control and operates best when defending that position against opposition from contrary view," Moley joined such Democratic Party conservatives as Bernard Baruch in successfully recommending Joseph P. Kennedy for chairman of the SEC "because of executive ability, knowledge of habits and customs of business to be regulated, and ability to moderate different points of view on Commission."[19]

From the point of view of many New Deal reformers, the choice of Kennedy to be the SEC's first chairman was absolutely, totally incredible. Throughout his varied business career, Kennedy had been a pool operator and a bear raider, periodically collaborating with

Charles Wright and other market manipulators whom the SEC soon would indict. Never accepted by J. P. Morgan and the financial establishment, Kennedy had amassed his fortune largely by running the stock department for the Hayden, Stone investment firm, reorganizing film companies, then exploiting his friendship with Franklin D. Roosevelt to secure the appointment as U.S. importer for British distillers Haig and Haig, John Dewar and Sons, and Gordon's once Prohibition was lifted. When Roosevelt failed to appoint him to a position in 1933 as a reward for his contributions and campaign efforts, Kennedy churlishly had demanded that the Democratic Party repay a $50,000 "loan" and bitterly denounced Roosevelt in private conversations with William Randolph Hearst. Hearing that Moley still favored his appointment, Kennedy offered him a slush fund. This presumably was not illegal in 1933, but it was extraordinary behavior for a man lobbying to become Secretary of the Treasury. It was not, however, unusual behavior for Joseph P. Kennedy. The exuberant son of a Boston saloon-keeper and local Democratic Party leader, he was typically direct, earthy in his language, and somewhat sloppy with both facts and ethics. In his day, it would be attributed to the "Irish" in Kennedy that he would inform *The New York Times* columnist Arthur Krock that he had been "a famous ballplayer" at Harvard who turned down a professional contract and achieved all of his success in administrative work, "not in market operations" — each of which statements was just as false as Joseph P. Kennedy's 1936 declaration that "I have no political ambitions for myself or for my children."

Most of this was known by Roosevelt in 1934, who took seriously Louis Howe's adamant opposition to Kennedy's appointment. But Roosevelt also was able to recognize much else. However questionable some of Kennedy's business career had been, Roosevelt believed Kennedy when he claimed that his greatest ambition was to be "a credit to his family." Crude though Kennedy sometimes might be in his speech and morals, his loyalty to Roosevelt in the 1930–1932 campaign for the presidency had been unflagging. Forsaking his fellow Roman Catholic Al Smith, Kennedy had raised money for Roosevelt and served as his conduit to the politically powerful publisher William Randolph Hearst for close to two years. At the nominating convention, the influential Arthur Krock credited Kennedy with helping persuade Hearst to release the decisive California delegates to Roosevelt. By the early New Deal period, Kennedy was Roosevelt's best-known advocate among businessmen. An articulate spokesman, Kennedy defended Roosevelt in numerous speeches and articles as a President who never "failed to assert or imply his belief in the essential capitalistic economy under which America and the American system have developed." As conservative opposition to the New Deal's "regimentation" of business grew, Kennedy stood almost alone in the business community when he wrote:

> An organized functioning society requires a planned economy. The more complex the society the greater the demand for planning. Otherwise there results a haphazard and inefficient method of social control, and in the absence of planning the law of the jungle prevails.

In time, Kennedy would write articles espousing aspects of the National Recovery Administration, the Social Security Act, the federal securities laws, the need for a federal corporation law, the need to reform investment trusts, and the need to eliminate "private" investment banking. It was this ideological affinity that led to Kennedy's appointment as SEC chairman.[20] Roosevelt needed an appointee who would conciliate and reassure the financial community, but he also wanted an SEC chairman he could trust. Joseph P. Kennedy, an improbable amalgam of political liberal and business opportunist, market operator and loyal party servant, of earthy directness and Harvard education, shrewd intelligence and amorality, seemed to Roosevelt the best available man to symbolize his politics of business conciliation.

Roosevelt casually tipped off the press that the rumors of the Kennedy appointment might be accurate when he began a June 29 press conference with the otherwise irrelevant observation "I sat up and drank beer with Barney Baruch and Joe Kennedy. I did not do any work at all, it was awful — two o'clock and I have no excuse for it."[21] The following day Roosevelt informed his Cabinet of his intention to appoint Kennedy SEC chairman. Interior Secretary Harold Ickes recorded in his diary:

> At Cabinet meeting yesterday afternoon the President talked over the appointments he had in mind on the new commissions that have been created by act of Congress. I am afraid I do not agree with him as to the chairman he is going to name for the Securities Commission. He has named Joseph P. Kennedy for that place, a former stockmarket plunger. The President has great confidence in him because he has made his pile, has invested all his money in Government securities, and knows all the tricks of the trade. Apparently he is going on the assumption that Kennedy would now like to make a name for himself for the sake of his family, but I have never known many of these cases to work out as expected.[22]

As word of the impending Kennedy chairmanship began to circulate, liberal and radical criticism of the choice mounted. Ferdinand
Pecora, financially strapped on his $3000-a-year salary as Senate
Banking Committee counsel, had looked forward to leaving Washington when the stock exchange practices hearings concluded and
returning to New York City, where his wife, who refused to live
anywhere else, was waiting. But in late June, after Pecora learned
that Roosevelt intended to nominate Kennedy, the press was informed that Senator Fletcher had delivered the message to Roosevelt
that Pecora would serve on the SEC for one year *if* he was named
chairman.[23] The press also was reminded that the Senate Banking
Committee recently had heard testimony that Kennedy had received profits from pool operations that manipulated Libbey-
Owens-Ford Glass Company stock during the summer of 1933.[24] To
Roy Howard of the Scripps-Howard newspapers, naming a stock ma-
nipulator to be SEC chairman was a breach of faith. In a personal
meeting with Roosevelt, and then in a *Washington News* editorial,
Howard insisted that the President "cannot with impunity administer such a slap in the face to his most loyal and effective supporters
as that reported to be contemplated in the appointment of Joseph P.
Kennedy."[25] Roosevelt stuck by his choice, announcing that Kennedy, Landis, Pecora, FTC commissioner George Mathews, and FTC
chief counsel Robert Healy were his nominees. As stipulated by the
1934 Securities Exchange Act, the initial Commission appointments were for staggered terms of five, four, three, two, and one
years. Roosevelt publicly signified his preference for a Kennedy
chairmanship by naming Kennedy to the five-year term. Since the
statute also provided that the SEC commissioners themselves chose
their chairman, Roosevelt had no power directly to install Kennedy
as chairman. But privately Roosevelt summoned Landis, Mathews, and
Healy to his office and urged them to "take a good look at Kennedy."
Landis was disappointed, but led the three FTC officials in agreeing
to do so. After a long meeting with Kennedy on the morning of July
2, Landis also persuaded Pecora to accept the one-year appointment
on the Commission and to support the Kennedy chairmanship.[26]

With the Kennedy chairmanship officially confirmed, liberal fury
reached firestorm proportions. "Had Franklin D. Roosevelt's dearest
enemy accused him of making so grotesque an appointment as
Joseph P. Kennedy to the chairmanship of his Stock Exchange Commission," *The New Republic* editorialized, "the charge might have
been laid to malice. Yet the President has exceeded the expectations
of his most ardent ill wishers."[27] "The appointment is appalling,"
scolded an incredulous John T. Flynn. "I say it isn't true. It is im-

possible. It could not happen."[28] Even naming Kennedy to the Commission, exclaimed Jerome Frank, general counsel of the Agricultural Adjustment Administration and himself a future SEC chairman, was "like setting a wolf to guard a flock of sheep."[29] Satirizing the reformers' disappointment, *The Magazine of Wall Street* described "the rulers of the stock market" as "four grave men and true, reformers and purgers of business by natural slant and experience, are led by a jovial master of the quick money-making art, a consummate product of the era they would bury. Four ascetics and a Sybarite out to trim the modern Sybaris! Four men in deadly earnest, chiefed by a good fellow, wise-cracker, successful speculator, high-liver — homes in Bronxville, Cape Cod, and Miami — generous spender."[30]

Among the indignant, Thomas Corcoran was one of the first to grasp the larger significance of Roosevelt's SEC appointments. "Oh well," he noted to Moley, "we've got four out of five anyhow."[31]

Corcoran's calculation was telling. Kennedy began his chairmanship on the defensive, distrusted by his colleagues and contemptuously regarded by an important faction of the nation's press. That in the next 431 days as SEC chairman he was able to convert such critics as Pecora, Fletcher, John T. Flynn, and Roy Howard into begrudging admirers was a considerable testament to his shrewdness and personal diplomacy. Kennedy's own version of the truce of God began even before he was sworn in. In separate *ententes cordiales*, he made his peace with Landis and Frankfurter and with Pecora.

The alliance of greatest consequence was with Landis and Frankfurter. Kennedy reassured Landis that the FTC Securities Division would be fully welcomed at the SEC on September 1, 1934, when the new Commission assumed responsibility for the 1933 Securities Act. Praising Landis as "one of the outstanding authorities in the country on the interpretation and application of statutes," Kennedy delegated to Landis primary responsibility for supervising all of the studies, reports, and regulations of the Commission.[32] Landis also wrote most of the SEC's first opinions. In the areas that mattered most to Landis, he would have had little more authority had he been chairman. At the same time, Kennedy courted Frankfurter. In a 1944 interview with the *Boston Globe*, Kennedy would defend himself against charges of anti-Semitism by stating, "It is no secret that I have not a high opinion of Felix Frankfurter — or of Henry Morgenthau, Jr., or of a number of Jews in high places, but that doesn't mean that I condemn all Jews because of my personal feelings for some."[33] Whatever his opinion of Frankfurter in 1944, in 1934 Kennedy consistently accepted his advice concerning SEC staff appointments[34] and successfully implored Frankfurter to write the first draft of at least one of the five major speeches given by Kennedy as SEC chairman.[35]

Somewhat more surprising was the speed with which Kennedy achieved an effective working relationship with Pecora. In the July 2 showdown between the two, Kennedy agreed to give Pecora primary responsibility for supervising the Stock Market Trading Division, the SEC division that would investigate market manipulations and regulate stock exchange floor members. Kennedy soon also impressed Pecora with his zeal in seeking out stock market fraud. So much so that Pecora wrote in his valedictory article about the Commission, "The chairman, Joseph P. Kennedy, is a business man with a wide experience in the practical affairs of Wall Street. I did not see any Wall Street brokers or experts come down to Washington who knew any more about the mechanisms of the Exchange and the methods of the Street than he does." When Pecora resigned his commissionership after six months to accept a New York judicial appointment, journalists at first assumed that there had been a clash between Kennedy and Pecora. Nearly the opposite was true. Pecora left the SEC to rejoin his wife and because he had been offered a New York judgeship with a $25,000-a-year salary. At about the time he left the SEC, in January 1935, Senator Fletcher's Banking Committee had the opportunity to hold confirmation hearings on Roosevelt's initial SEC appointments. Had there been major differences between Kennedy and Pecora, Fletcher, intensely loyal to Pecora, could have been expected to question Kennedy sharply. Instead, Fletcher whisked through all five appointments without hearings or floor debate.[36]

The first year's *Minutes* of the SEC reveal that only Commissioner Robert Healy often dissented. Healy had risen to the Vermont Supreme Court by 1928, when Calvin Coolidge selected his fellow New England Republican to direct the FTC's congressionally mandated investigation of the public utility holding companies. The experience radicalized the conservative Healy. Shocked to find that "you can capitalize in some States practically everything except the furnace ashes in the basement," he became an uncompromising advocate of accounting and public utility reform. Although he frequently dissented from early SEC accounting policies, Healy, too, generally supported Kennedy.[37]

The Commission's second required Republican appointee, George Mathews, had headed Wisconsin's Public Utilities Commission before receiving a Roosevelt appointment to the FTC. Although strongly supported by progressive Senator Robert M. La Follette, Jr., for the FTC nomination, Mathews was by instinct and political belief far more conservative than Healy.[38]

Simultaneous with Kennedy's efforts to harmonize relations within the Commission was his calculated use of public relations to increase his own and the Commission's clout. Assiduously, Kennedy cultivated the image of a Roosevelt intimate, entertaining the President at his lavish Maryland estate, so often calling on Roosevelt during the work day that Roosevelt once complained to Ickes "that he had to send for Joe Kennedy every few days and hold his hand." Roosevelt's sentiments toward Kennedy were generally warm, and the President afforded him a broad role in administration discussions of public works and business recovery.[39] Kennedy displayed a particular flair for transforming journalists into allies. His relationship with Arthur Krock bordered on the fraternal, with Krock's frequent commendatory columns in the *Times* early countervailing the barbs of *The New Republic*.[40] Kennedy not only lobbied the sympathetic Krock, but also visited and corresponded with Walter Lippmann, the *New York Herald Tribune*'s Robert Kintner, the *Wall Street Journal*'s William Raymond, his early foe Roy Howard, and countless publishers, including the *New York Times*'s Arthur Sulzberger, the *Washington Post*'s Eugene Meyer, the *Herald Tribune*'s Ogden Reid, and the *Washington Herald*'s Eleanor Patterson. It was characteristic of Kennedy's attention to press relations that when the SEC discovered a Tennessee firm attempting to sell fraudulent securities to schoolteachers, Kennedy mailed a copy of the ensuing Commission opinion with a personally signed cover letter to close to a hundred state and local school journals.[41]

The appearance of harmonious working relationships with the other SEC commissioners and a close personal relationship with Roosevelt enabled Kennedy rapidly and effectively to organize the Commission. This was Kennedy's most significant achievement as chairman. He was appointed shortly after Roosevelt's Budget Bureau had communicated to Congress a $300,000 estimate for the Commission's first fiscal year budget. Disagreeing, Landis had written Roosevelt of the need "to start off this new commission with an appropriation in the neighborhood of $1,500,000." Seizing the initiative, Kennedy demanded that the Budget Bureau recommend an appropriation of greater than $4 million for the Commission's second year. The bureau gagged at this staggering increase, but eventually approved a $2.3 million budget, which represented a considerable Kennedy victory. When the House Appropriations Committee reduced the recommended appropriation to $1.7 million, a week of Kennedy's lobbying resulted in Congress restoring virtually all of the Budget Bureau's recommended $2.3 million appropriation.[42]

A sufficient budget is merely the minimum requirement of an effective government agency. What distinguished the SEC was its ability to attract talented staff attorneys. In early understandings with Landis and Pecora, Kennedy had bargained away three of the five top staff positions of the Commission. Landis's two top assistants in the FTC Securities Division, Baldwin Bane and Donald Montgomery, were named, respectively, SEC executive assistant and chief of the Examination Division (soon renamed the Registration Division), which enforced the 1933 Securities Act. David Saperstein, Pecora's chief associate counsel on the Senate Banking Committee, assumed the leadership of the Stock Market Trading Division.[43] Kennedy insisted on naming his own general counsel, and chose Judge John J. Burns. Burns, a full professor at Harvard Law School by the age of twenty-nine, had been the youngest man ever appointed a Massachusetts Superior Court judge when he was so named at thirty.[44] The Burns appointment was important for two reasons: Kennedy sought a highly competent person for the key job of general counsel, and Burns, a friend of Frankfurter, was soon wiring his former Harvard Law School colleague to arrange interviews "with best [Harvard] Law Review men who might like work with our commission." The Burns appointment had a further consequence. So concerned was Kennedy about antagonizing Landis that when he learned that Ben Cohen had wanted the position of general counsel and that Landis believed Cohen "was entitled to it," Kennedy agreed that the Commission might begin with two general counsel. This generous though awkward arrangement was avoided only when Frankfurter insisted to Landis that the "suggested division of legal work [would be] practically impossible and fatal to the effective work of [the] Commission."[45]

Kennedy also deferred to Landis in the fifth top staff appointment. Section 211 of the 1934 Securities Exchange Act authorized the SEC to make a detailed study of bankruptcy, reorganization, and protective committes, a project intended to be a continuation of Pecora's Senate Banking Committee investigation. Landis urged Kennedy to appoint Yale Law School professor William O. Douglas.[46]

With the possible exception of Adolf Berle, Douglas was the nation's leading law professor of corporate finance. Between 1931 and 1934, he had written or co-authored five casebooks and nine law review articles on bankruptcy and corporate and securities law, an extraordinary achievement. Especially important to Landis was a

February 1934 *Harvard Law Review* article of Douglas's entitled "Protective Committees in Railroad Reorganization," which had run intellectual circles around a simplistic article written earlier by Pecora staffer Max Lowenthal, who was the only other serious candidate for the appointment. As with the appointment of John J. Burns, the designation of Douglas had further importance, since it gave the SEC a crucial connection to Yale Law School. Douglas named as his assistant a favorite student, Abe Fortas, who, like Douglas, was to become a Supreme Court Justice. During the Commission's first year, Douglas also was able to persuade Professor Thurman Arnold and Dean Charles E. Clark, both of Yale Law School, to agree to perform part-time work for the Commission.[47]

Each of the Commission's top five staff appointments was made by July 17, 1934, approximately two weeks after the commissioners themselves had been sworn in. During Kennedy's fourteen-month tenure, the staff expanded to 692 employees.[48] Regional offices were established in New York City, Boston, Atlanta, Chicago, Fort Worth, Denver, San Francisco, and Seattle.[49] As the staff grew, Kennedy was able to persuade the Commission to hire a small number of Wall Street investment firm partners or stock exchange officers — among them Leon Cohen, J. H. Case, Jr., and James A. Fayne — to work in the Commission as assistant division chiefs or technical advisers.[50]

Kennedy's primary substantive goal as SEC chairman was to revive the foundering securities markets. By late July, he had convinced his fellow commissioners that the SEC could aid Roosevelt's business recovery policies only if it won stock exchange and corporate acceptance. The policy of the SEC, Kennedy insisted, should be "balanced." Prosecution of security fraud should go hand in hand with encouragement of honest enterprise.[51]

On July 25, Kennedy heralded the Commission's "balanced" approach in his maiden address as SEC chairman, a speech nationally broadcast by radio. "Seldom," reported *Newsweek*, "have so many of Wall Street's busy inhabitants taken time off to hang over loudspeakers. Thousands gathered to listen in offices that afternoon. The future of their businesses depended on the policies set forth by the speaker."[52] After elaborately praising his fellow commissioners, especially "Mr. Pecora, whose striking contributions to public service are well known and deeply appreciated by the people of this country," Kennedy reassured Wall Street:

> We of the SEC do not regard ourselves as coroners sitting on the corpse of financial enterprise . . .

We are not working on the theory that all the men and all the women connected with finance, either as workers or investors, are to be regarded as guilty of some undefined crime . . .

We regard ourselves, as the President has said, as partners in a cooperative enterprise. We do not start off with the belief that every enterprise is crooked and that those behind it are crooks.

We want to see the wheels turn over and gather speed. We want to see the security business, by far the greatest in volume and most important in its effects of any in the country go forward on a broad scale.[53]

The Commission quickly put Kennedy's "cooperative" approach into action. Before each of the SEC's initial regulations was issued, conferences were held with representatives of the affected industry.[54] In retrospect, Kennedy would explain, the Commission

realized that the most effective enforcement of the Act would follow from the cooperation of people in the business. In the preparation of its forms and regulations, in drafting rules governing trading on exchanges, in considering the problems of the industry generally, no important step was taken without fully discussing it with those persons who would be affected. The interplay of ideas brought out in such conferences ironed out all essential differences between the industry and the Commission, so that I can honestly say that every constructive step which the Commission has taken accords with the letter and spirit of the legislation and is supported by a respectable majority of the industry as a whole.[55]

By the time the five SEC commissioners made a conciliatory visit to the floor of the New York Stock Exchange in mid-September,[56] the leaders of the Exchange had become outspoken votaries of the SEC. Richard Whitney especially appreciated the advantages of an alliance with the Commission. In public addresses, Whitney built on the obvious implication of the SEC's "balanced" policy to urge investors to "realize . . . the necessity of dealing with financial houses of reputation" like those associated with the New York Stock Exchange and "shun the wandering security salesman."[57]

Whitney's attempted use of the Commission to sanitize the NYSE seemed all the more plausible in light of the SEC's highly publicized campaign against stock manipulations and what Kennedy termed "fraudulent get-rich schemes."[58] During the SEC's first year, ten minor securities exchanges closed, including the New York Mining Exchange, known as "the penny stock exchange," and the Boston Curb Exchange, which Kennedy described as "a famous old playground for skip-shop promoters." An eleventh exchange, the New York Produce, discontinued its securities division. A twelfth, the

Baltimore Stock Exchange, was denied all unlisted trading privileges when evidence showed that firms not granted unlisted trading privileges were being traded on an unlisted basis.[59]

Twenty-three hundred individual cases of possible securities fraud were investigated.[60] Kennedy was particularly proud of his enforcement attorneys' methods. Personal cronies, brokers friendly to regulation, other brokers eager to make friends with the new Commission, were encouraged to pass on rumors. Learning of any suspected fraudulent securities salesman promoting a new venture or operating in a new location, an SEC investigator would engage in "whitemail" by interviewing the salesman to impress on him that he was under surveillance.[61] Yet for all of the Commission's much-publicized enforcement efforts, and Kennedy's recurrent threats to prosecute "sham securities" and "financial racketeers," not one major member of the New York Stock Exchange was civilly or criminally prosecuted the first year. This was not a policy decision, and several Exchange members soon would be. But the coincidence of the Commission's enforcement activities being directed primarily against minor exchanges and local traders enabled Kennedy to seek a détente with the leaders of the most influential exchange while maintaining a reputation for rigorous enforcement of the securities laws.

The first dividend from the SEC's policy of détente came in September. By promulgating initial regulations for the registration of securities exchanges that did little more than require the description of the exchanges' rules and procedures, the Commission avoided an early constitutional challenge to the 1934 Securities Exchange Act. Twenty-four exchanges, led by the New York Stock Exchange, duly applied for registration and on September 27 were certified as national securities exchanges.[62] Sensitivity to industry concerns also guided the Commission in its promulgation of requirements for listing business corporations on securities exchanges and the Commission's early unlisted trading regulations.[63] Before issuing the permanent listing requirements, for example, the Commission met repeatedly with the New York Stock Exchange's accounting and corporate officials. The requirements ultimately issued preserved for corporations and their accountants "a wide latitude in the manner of presenting the required data." A Commission press release emphasized "that corporations which are adhering to high standards of financial reporting will find it unnecessary to make anything but minor changes in their accounting practices as a result of the new requirements." The release also "call[ed] attention to that portion of the Securities Exchange Act which permits [the

SEC] to honor the requests of corporations to keep certain information confidential."[64] By the end of the first year, 2776 securities had been approved for unlisted trading, and 3345 securities were permanently registered, with another 1048 applications for registration still being processed.[65]

Securing a working relationship with the leading investment banks proved far more difficult for the Commission. The passage of the 1934 Securities Exchange Act did not end the capital strike. As late as November 1934, J. P. Morgan partner Russell Leffingwell was still trying to prove to President Roosevelt that the "Securities Act and the Banking Act have pretty much closed [the capital markets]."[66] Roosevelt refused to consider repeal or amendment of the Securities Act, and the bankers' strike continued. New securities effectively registered under the 1933 Securities Act dwindled from $113 million in July 1934, the month when the Commission began operations, to a minuscule $11 million in January 1935.[67]

Initially, Kennedy pursued a low-keyed approach in attempting to revive the securities market, emphasizing that the total expense of issuance of new securities under the 1933 act was averaging only 0.38 of 1 percent of the gross proceeds of securities flotations.[68] That argument had no discernible impact, and on December 5, the Commission instructed John J. Burns, the general counsel, to study the revision of the basic A-1 registration form and make "recommendations to the Commission . . . as soon as possible."[69] Kennedy himself leaked word of the Commission's impending "Christmas gift" to financiers a few days later to Arthur Krock. The New York Times columnist explained: "Mr. Kennedy has impressed his co-laborers and those who wrote the act itself that the test of the act is the amount of legitimate financing which flows from it."[70] Sensitive to the criticism that only new, speculative firms were issuing securities under the 1933 act, the Commission focused its revision efforts on the development of a new Form A-2, to be available only to seasoned firms that had already issued securities. Throughout December and early January, on a near-daily basis, the Commission discussed the revised form with Ben Cohen, Thomas Corcoran, and such leading critics of the act as Arthur Dean.[71]

"This is our answer," Kennedy stated in announcing the new Form A-2 on January 13, "to our pledge to make less onerous, less expensive, and more practical the registration of securities. We have tried this out with the most vociferous opponents of the Securities Act and with accountants . . . They feel that there is nothing in it which is unreasonable and will advise their clients to go ahead." Although the new form required all of the information specified in

Schedule A of the Securities Act, it permitted summary responses and eliminated several questions concerning the history of the issuing firm. To dramatize the point, Kennedy requested aides to produce the several large volumes of exhibits concerning patents that Republic Steel Corporation recently had filed with the Commission. Kennedy intimated that under the new form a mere recital of relevant patent office numbers and termination dates, along with a brief nontechnical discussion of the patents, would be sufficient in the future.[72]

Aware that $3 billion worth of seasoned corporations' outstanding securities were redeemable and could be reissued at the prevailing lower interest or dividend rates, Kennedy and Burns "packed their suitcases like traveling salesmen," wrote one SEC official, and traveled to meet with investment firms and corporate counsel to tout the new form.[73] In a February 8 address Kennedy criticized business leaders for attempting to avoid registration by the "private" issuance of new securities to only a few purchasers.[74] Then on March 19, in perhaps the most extraordinary speech that has ever been given by an SEC commissioner, Kennedy journeyed to New York City to tongue-lash the financial community as "cowardly and unmanly and un-American [in blaming] the government for its own lack of courage and enterprise." In lines equally unexpected from a "ruler of Wall Street," Kennedy darkly lamented, "Cassandra has dethroned Pollyanna. We have enshrined the poet Milton's gloomy 'loathed melancholy, of Cerberus and blackest midnight born in Stygian cave forlorn . . .' "[75]

Lower Manhattan's Stygian caves forlorn, however, soon were brightened by amendments that permitted corporate issuers to set forth certain information in the prospectuses for securities registered on Form A-2 "in condensed or summarized form";[76] permitted consolidated reporting of the income of subsidiaries in Form A-2 filings;[77] and eliminated the need for a registrant even to list subsidiaries, "unless such subsidiary is of material significance in relation to the total enterprise represented by the registrant and its subsidiaries."[78]

The "capital logjam" ended on March 7, 1935, when Swift and Company registered a $43 million bond issue[79] after the Commission directed new rules be drafted to assure the firm's directors that they would not be subject to an SEC enforcement action for earlier private offering negotiations.[80] Kennedy employed the Swift and Company registration both as a carrot and a stick. To potential corporate issuers, he stressed that the firm's fifty-nine-page registration statement was considerably simpler to assemble than the "about 20,000 pages" filed under the requirements of the earlier registration form by Republic Steel Corporation. To the established investment banks, Kennedy tauntingly noted that the relatively minor firm of Salomon Brothers and Hutzler had agreed to sell the bonds on a best-efforts basis for a commission of 0.4 of 1 percent, which was approximately one-tenth the average 4.3 percent gross underwriting spread for bond issues of $3 million or more sold during 1928.*[81]

Two days after Swift's filing, Pacific Gas and Electric registered a $45 million issue; on April 1,[83] Southern California Edison filed for $73 million.[84] The "trickling little stream of private corporation finance" soon reached "flood tide," as Kennedy put it.[85] In April 1935, $142 million of securities were effectively registered; in July, $530 million. The aggregate 1935 total of $2.7 billion of securities effectively registered was better than four times greater the 1934 total of $641 million.[86]

The success of Kennedy's campaign to register new securities won him considerable praise. In March 1935, it could hardly have been considered surprising to read the worshipful Krock hailing Kennedy's contributions to economic recovery. But Krock's opinion was widely shared, not only by businessmen, but also by John T. Flynn, who later termed Kennedy "the most useful member of the Commission,"[88] and *Time* magazine, which generalized that the SEC "has won the distinction of being the most ably administered New Deal agency in Washington."[89]

Only with respect to the development of accounting standards did Kennedy's conciliatory policy seriously divide the Commission. From the start, a majority of the commissioners took pains to reassure the accounting profession that the SEC would not soon exercise its statutory authority to develop uniform accounting principles..In a July 1934 meeting with accounting industry leaders, the Commission emphasized that it intended "moderation in exercising its power over accountants."[90] Commissioner Mathews was openly skeptical of the practicality of "forcing" uniform accounting standards.[91] Kennedy tended to view most technical accounting questions as relatively unimportant. As he put it in a spring 1935 remark

---

* Indeed, the most unassailable defense of the 1933 Securities Act was that it saved investors money. Paul Gourrich, the SEC's technical adviser, later calculated that gross underwriting spreads on high-grade corporate, railroad, and foreign bonds ranged from an average of 3 to 5.3 percent between 1920 and 1931. By 1936, with the Securities Act requiring clear disclosure of underwriters' fees, the gross spread on bond issues of $5 million or more ranged between 2.13 and 2.33 percent.[82]

to a reporter, "I'd hate to go out of here thinking I had just made some changes in accounting practices."

Even important accounting issues were of little interest to Kennedy compared with the task of persuading corporations to begin registering new securities issues.[92] Landis concurred with this priority, but Commissioner Healy disagreed. Many of the public utility frauds he had investigated for the FTC had been perpetrated by the "writing-up" of fixed assets from their original cost to an appraised value. When, in October 1934, the Northern States Power Company, a Minnesota public utility, filed a registration statement with a $16 million write-up of its fixed capital and investment accounts, Healy, seconded by Pecora, voted against permitting the firm to sell its securities to the public until it rewrote its balance sheet on a cost basis. These were the first dissenting votes at the Commission. Kennedy, Landis, and Mathews, eager to avoid discouraging other securities issuers from registering, merely required Northern States to indicate in footnotes that the results shown in the balance sheet would not have been the same if another accounting procedure had been followed and to summarize the results that would have been obtained had the other accounting procedure been employed. Within the Commission, the Northern States Power decision was an unpopular one. A "detailed expression of the circumstances and of the views of the majority and minority" promised by the SEC to be "made public at an early date" was never published.[93] Nor did the controversy end with the Northern States Power case. Healy and Pecora soon moved that Form A-2 require a ten-year review of surplus accounts, but they were outvoted by Kennedy, Mathews, and Landis.[94] Healy then sought to require subsidiary firms to disclose the funded debt of parent corporations, and lost by a 4–1 vote.[95] Healy was again defeated by a 4–1 vote on the issue of whether firms should disclose a ten-year analysis of their surplus when registering for listing on an exchange.[96]

The only major institution that the Commission did challenge during Kennedy's term was the New York Stock Exchange. And against the Exchange, the challenge was modest, and achieved, at best, indecisive results. Section 19(c) of the Securities Exchange Act of 1934 directed the SEC to "make a study and investigation of the rules of national securities exchanges with respect to the classification of members, the methods of election of officers and committees to insure a fair representation of the membership, and the suspension, expulsion, and disciplining of the members of such exchanges." The Commission's report was published in late January 1935. Although the statutory section referred to the "rules of national securities exchanges," the SEC report specifically treated only the New York Stock Exchange. Generally moderate in tone, the report was nevertheless an undisguised attempt to lessen floor member domination of Exchange governance by removing the obstacles to the commission brokers' exercising their numerical strength.

This in itself was the more conservative of the alternative strategies considered by the Commission. Under the New York Stock Exchange's constitution, only Exchange members who had purchased a seat could be members of the Governing Committee. No outside interest was directly represented in the government of the Exchange. But because "a successful administration of the [Securities Exchange] Act will be hampered if the governing boards are not inclined to give the commission effective cooperation," the SEC chose not to demand that outsiders be allowed to serve on the Exchange's Governing Committee. The SEC's 1935 governance report stated, "The admittedly important interests of the investor and of business . . . are presumably safeguarded [by the Commission's] powers to act rapidly and effectively against any abuse [through its field force and prosecutions]." For the same reasons, the SEC was not yet prepared to recommend that there be a nonmember president of the Exchange, or even a paid president.

But the report did make clear recommendations concerning the members of the Exchange's Governing Committee. As of 1934, the brokerage firms that dealt directly with the public owned 52 percent of the 1375 seats on the New York Stock Exchange. But only fourteen governors, about one-third of the Governing Committee, were representatives of the commission houses. The commission brokers' influence was also reduced by the requirement that only floor members of the Exchange could serve on the Governing Committee. Explained the report: "An anomalous condition thus exists. The less influential partners of large firms, who execute orders on the Exchange as the floor-member partners, are eligible for participation in the administration of exchanges, while the more consequential and significant partners, charged with the vital duties of managing these firms as office partners, may not participate in the government of the exchanges." A twofold "correction" was urged. First, commission brokers should hold a larger proportion of the Governing Committee's seats. Second, office partners of registered firms should be eligible for membership on the Governing Committee.

Closely related to the problem of fair representation on the Governing Committee was the method of electing members. A five-member committee of the New York Stock Exchange annually nominated the following year's members. Members of the Exchange theoretically could name an independent nominee if a petition was signed by forty members, but this was considered "open revolt" and infrequently done. This nomination system, insisted the SEC's report in its sharpest words, was "subject to just criticism. The results of its operation have been the self-perpetuation of the 'in' group . . . In its place should be substituted . . . nomination to the governing board by some method of petition and . . . a vote on the candidates so nominated by ballot of the membership."

Other recommendations were made to increase from one-fourth to one-third the proportion of the Governing Committee annually elected, nominate the Exchange president by petition, end restriction of membership of standing committees to members of the Governing Committee, and reform complaint proceedings. But consistent with Kennedy's "cooperative" approach, none of the SEC's eleven proposals was to be imposed. The report concluded: "The Commission does not now suggest that legislation be enacted to bring about these recommendations. Its recommendations can be put into effect by the voluntary action of the exchanges themselves without resort to legislation. It hopes that, in the main, these recommendations will be found acceptable and put into effect by the exchanges themselves."[97]

Initially, the report's divide-and-conquer strategy seemed to succeed. Whitney, infuriated by the report's criticisms, responded by hiring John W. Davis to prepare an "opinion letter" on the eleven-point reform program, a move assumed to be a prelude to a constitutional challenge to the 1934 Securities Exchange Act.[98] But the commission house trade association, the Association of Stock Exchange Firms, led by E. A. Pierce, Paul Shields, John Hanes, and others long discontented with Whitney, publicly endorsed the SEC recommendations,[99] and Whitney backed down. In a revealing aside during a February 7 address to five hundred brokers, Whitney conceded that he had been accused "of being arbitrary, antagonistic, noncooperative." Somewhat defensively he insisted, "Yet the only thing the Stock Exchange and its executives are trying to do is cooperate in order to make our business . . . workable under the Stock Exchange Commission."[100] Over the next few weeks, the Exchange agreed to increase the number of members on the Governing Committee from forty to forty-eight by adding eight brokerage house office partners, and voluntarily adopted several of the SEC's other recommendations.[101]

Emboldened, the commission house leaders decided to challenge Whitney directly in the 1935 Exchange elections. Pierce, at a February 25 meeting with the Nominating Committee, proposed that the Exchange hire a paid president and a press agent to replace its unpaid member president. A fair measure of the difference between the New Deal and even the most reform-minded Exchange members was Pierce's suggestion for president — "a man of the type of the late Calvin Coolidge."[102] Acknowledging that it had heard a "considerable divergence of opinion," the Nominating Committee soon took the unusual step of proposing three nominees for Exchange president: Whitney, a critic of Whitney, John Hanes, and a compromise nominee, Charles Gay, a brokerage house senior partner, personally friendly to Whitney.[103] Hanes promptly withdrew.[104] Gay, however, like Pierce, believed that the Exchange needed better "public relations" if its slack share volume was to revive. Although cordial to Whitney and his emissaries, Gay insisted that he would stay in the race. Two days before the April 8 meeting at which Exchange officer nominees were officially announced, Whitney reluctantly withdrew from the campaign for the presidency and accepted a nomination to a seat on the Governing Committee.[105]

Whitney's withdrawal had little practical effect on Exchange governance. Gay, a self-made man educated in Brooklyn's public schools, outwardly could not have appeared less like the aristocratic Whitney. Yet a decade's experience on the Exchange's Governing Committee had inculcated Gay with views similar to Whitney's.[106] As Gay's statement accepting nomination emphasized, in lines Whitney himself could have delivered, "There is a widespread misunderstanding of the Exchange; what it really is . . . It is not a private club. It is a national institution filling a national need of first importance."[107] The May election results were a further vindication of Whitney and his floor member allies, by then popularily known as the Old Guard. The former Exchange president received more votes than any other candidate, including Gay, who ran unopposed. Hanes and two other candidates for the Governing Committee named by the Nominating Committee were defeated by an Old Guard slate of independent candidates nominated by petition. Gay immediately named E. H. H. Simmons, Old Guard member par excellence — indeed, Whitney's close friend and predecessor as Exchange president — to be his vice president. Except for the symbolic loss of the top office, the Old Guard's domination of Exchange politics was undiminished.[108]

There was, in April 1935, an indication of how little the Exchange's policies were affected by the elections. The 1934 Securities

Exchange Act empowered the SEC to regulate exchange floor members. In the fall of 1934, Kennedy had persuaded the Commission to defer consideration of segregation of brokers and dealers and reform of the role of specialists until 1936, when a statutorily directed study was required to be delivered to Congress. Trading rules, however, were negotiated with the exchanges. But given the Commission's strong desire not to jeopardize its "cooperative" relationship with the New York Stock Exchange, and the continuing domination of the Exchange by the specialists and floor traders of the Old Guard, the sixteen trading rules promulgated succeeded only in outlawing the best-known devices for manipulating share prices through pool operations. Many of these devices had earlier been outlawed by the New York Stock Exchange. Whitney's firm stance prevented the issuance of a rule that measurably limited short-selling.* A last-minute telegram from Whitney prompted the SEC to rewrite the Tenth Rule, "Trading by Specialists," to avoid the possibility of interference in specialists' market-making functions. After Whitney's faction triumphed in the May 8 elections, the Commission agreed that the NYSE could adopt its rules after making additional minor modifications. Somewhat defensively, the Commission in its *First Annual Report* characterized the trading rules as "experimental" and noted that they might "be changed if further study indicates a necessity therefor."[109]

Kennedy's period as chairman ended less happily than it began. As a market operator, political operative, and Hollywood mogul, Kennedy had exhibited an extraordinary sense of timing. By May 1935, he sensed that it was time to resign. His reputation by then was secure. It then must have seemed doubtful that any SEC chairman soon could surpass Kennedy's achievements in his organization of the Commission or in breaking the capital logjam. He anticipated that the work of the Commission would be increasingly technical. "Consequently," Kennedy would write, it would be "necessary that lawyers should predominate in the Commission."[110] A nonlawyer, easily wearied by detail work, Kennedy on May 27 literally was walking to the White House to resign when he learned from a *Washington Star* newsboy that the Supreme Court had declared the National Industrial Recovery Act unconstitutional. Because of per-

---

* The Sixteenth Trading Rule prohibited Exchange members from effecting "a short sale of any security . . . at a price below the last sale price of such security on the Exchange." The rule proved ineffective in preventing short sales from accentuating a market decline, since it permitted short sales to be made at the market price. Early in 1938, the SEC issued a more effective regulation after the 1937 stock market crash made obvious the weakness of this trading rule.

sonal loyalty to Roosevelt, Kennedy returned to his office and tore up his resignation letter.[111]

The Supreme Court's unanimous *Schecter* decision did more than end the NRA, the most heralded of Roosevelt's early recovery programs; it placed in question the constitutionality of a host of New Deal statutes, including the Securities Act of 1933 and the Securities Exchange Act of 1934.[112] Although the New York Stock Exchange's Governing Committee announced that it did "not comtemplate any action looking toward a test of the Securities Exchange Act,"[113] the SEC soon conceded that its plan to register the over-the-counter brokers and dealers by July 1 had been thwarted as a result of *Schecter*.[114] By late June, J. Edward Jones, a securities promoter, had mounted a constitutional challenge to the 1933 Securities Act. Until April 1936, when the Supreme Court upheld the constitutionality of the 1933 act in the *Jones* case, no one at the Commission could be entirely confident that the agency would survive.[115]

Kennedy was routinely re-elected chairman on July 1, 1935. But changes in the tenor of Roosevelt's policy direction continued to make him uncomfortable. Roosevelt's truce of God with business had ended. The combination of the Supreme Court's constitutional challenge to the New Deal and the business community's unremitting hostility signified to Felix Frankfurter and others close to Roosevelt that "the Administration plainly has reached a new stage." On June 10, 1935, Frankfurter reflected the President's own mood when he wrote to Jerome Frank, "From now on it must be to a large extent trench warfare."[116]

Roosevelt, personally, had been in part responsible for exacerbating the hostility between the New Deal and business. Soon after the Democrats' unexpected gains in the 1934 congressional elections, he had directed administration drafting teams to prepare anti–public utility holding company legislation. Even as moderated before enactment by Congress, the Public Utility Holding Company Act of 1935 was the most radical reform measure of the Roosevelt administration. To deal with the sprawl and inefficiency of public utility empires, such as that of Samuel Insull, Section 11, the controversial "death sentence" provision of the act, empowered the SEC to limit each holding company "to a single integrated public-utility system" by compelling divestiture of most geographically dispersed subsidiaries.

Kennedy was opposed to the breadth of the proposed death sentence provision. Taking the unusual step of offering his "personal view" to the Senate Commerce Committee, he stated, "I cannot be too vehement in urging upon you my feeling that [the death sentence] section . . . is most unfortunate." "By far" Kennedy's "most important objection" was "that it is not a wise policy to vest in any one group of men the tremendous responsibility involved in this grant of power. Certainly, this is true unless such a grant is hedged with precise and defined standards set up by Congress itself."[117]

Soon after the enactment of the Public Utility Holding Company Act, Kennedy resigned. Under his leadership, the SEC had played a conciliatory role, achieving prominence for its stimulation of private investment. With the enactment of the Holding Company Act, the agency's emphasis would shift to business reform; its character inevitably would become more confrontational. Kennedy's sense that his usefulness had passed was heightened in August, when Roosevelt named J. D. Ross, former manager of Seattle's municipally owned public utility, to Pecora's long-vacant seat. As was true of Commissioner Healy, Ross's primary expertise was in public utility regulation.[118] Unlike any of the SEC's original five commissioners, Ross was totally ignorant of securities regulation. Kennedy was well aware that Ross had been enthusiastically recommended by Frankfurter. It was obvious that Frankfurter's anti–Wall Street counsel had fully replaced Moley's policy of business–New Deal harmony. On nearly the same day that Roosevelt signed the Public Utility Holding Company Act into law on August 26, 1935, Kennedy circulated to the White House the first draft of his resignation letter.[119]

Kennedy's resignation officially was accepted on September 20.[120] His last act as chairman was to participate in the unanimous election of James Landis as his successor.

5

James Landis and the Administrative Process

Standards, if adequately drafted, afford great protection to administration. By limiting the area of the exercise of discretion they tend to routinize administration and to that degree relieve it from the play of political and economic pressures which otherwise might be harmful. The pressing problem today, however, is to get the administrative to assume the responsibilities that it properly should assume. Political and official life to too great an extent tends to favor routinization. The assumption of responsibility by an agency is always a gamble that may well make more enemies than friends. The easiest course is frequently that of inaction. A legalistic approach that reads a governing statute with the hope of finding limitations upon authority rather than grants of power with which to act decisively is thus common.

— JAMES LANDIS
The Administrative Process

A YEAR AND THREE MONTHS before, *Time* had characterized James Landis as a "true economic radical";[1] Henry Stimson had labeled him "the most dangerous man in the country."[2] Yet after Landis had served for fifteen months as an SEC commissioner, Wall Street had come to view him with something close to approbation. By then his support of Kennedy's policy of business-government cooperation was well known. It was assumed that Landis as chairman would be cautious, undogmatic, a mediator between the conflicting claims of such parties as investors and securities issuers, the New York Stock Exchange and the smaller, regional exchanges, Exchange floor members and commission house members. Charles Gay, the Exchange president, led a chorus of establishment voices in expressing pleasure at Landis's election.[3] Aptly, *Business Week* titled an article about Wall Street's reaction "Not Afraid of Landis,"[4] tilting its editorial posture to "Landis Satisfies"[5] after the new chairman stated at his first press conference, "Everybody knows that we will continue to work in harmony. Mr. Kennedy's policies are the commission's policies and there is no reason for changing them."[6] By contrast, so concerned was *The New Republic*'s John T. Flynn by the financial community's enthusiasm for Landis that he warned, "It is certain as sunrise that any regulation that pleases Wall Street will be a total failure . . . I hope, therefore, that [Landis] may be spared the humiliation of having regulated Wall Street to its entire satisfaction."[7]

Still, there was something to be said for *Time*'s initial perception of Landis. As a theorist, James Landis was no radical. But he was an articulate advocate of an expanded role for the federal regulatory agencies. Doubtful that unregulated firms in industries like banking, insurance, utilities, shipping, or communications could function adequately to meet public needs, or even function efficiently in the narrower economic sense, Landis viewed the primary purpose of an administrative agency to be "the guidance and supervision of the industry as a whole," rather than to play the simpler role of policeman.

So that the administrative agencies effectively could perform this supervisory role, Landis urged the agencies' right to a near-exclusive jurisdiction over technical regulatory problems and the agencies' right to combine in a single regulatory body the functions historically embodied by the Constitution's three conceptually separate branches of government.

> It is obvious [Landis would insist] that the resort to the administrative process is not, as some suppose, simply an extension of executive power. The administrative differs not only with regard to the scope of its powers; it differs most radically in regard to the responsibility it possesses for their exercise. In the grant to it of that full ambit of authority necessary for it in order to plan, to promote, and to police, it presents an assemblage of rights normally exercisable by government as a whole. Administrative power, though it may begin as an effort to adapt and make efficient police protection within a particular field, moves soon to think in terms of the economic well-being of an indus-

try. The creation of that power is, in essence, the response made in the light of a tripartite political theory to the demand that government assume responsibility not merely to maintain ethical levels in the economic relations of the members of society, but to provide for the efficient functioning of the economic processes of the state.[8]

However bold Landis could be in his theoretical writings, he had far less confidence in himself as SEC chairman. An adjective former Commission associates often used in describing Landis was "complicated." This ambiguous word was meant to pay homage to Landis's brilliance and indefatigable work habits, and also to acknowledge the most obvious manifestations of Landis's insecurity: his coldness in personal relationships, his difficulty in accepting criticism from journalists or different points of view from staff members, his incipient alcoholism, and his occasional indecisiveness.

The combination of Landis's theoretical beliefs about government-by-administrative-agency and his personal self-doubts precluded his being either punitive or evangelical as chairman. Landis sought instead to reform the securities industry on the basis of "findings arrived at as scientifically as seemed possible."[9] The hallmark of his chairmanship would be an insistence on the technical competence of the Commission. His were the virtues commended by the *Harvard Law Review:* insistence that technical issues be empirically studied on a case-by-case basis rather than be resolved by reference to general moral or ethical principles; insistence that no administrative proposal be made until the agency thoroughly understood its practical consequences; insistence that no action be taken by the agency that could not survive review by the then-hostile Supreme Court. The bitterest internal controversies at the SEC during his chairmanship would be Landis's struggles with the Commission's economic and technical advisers, whose reform proposals Landis considered inadequately analyzed.

Landis's insistence on the professional excellence of the SEC soon gave the Commission staff its esprit de corps, its enduring standards of high quality, its attractiveness to talented attorneys. But Landis's effectiveness was limited by a tactical conservatism that increasingly was to isolate him from the forefront of the Roosevelt administration's reform efforts, efforts that Landis earlier had helped lead. In particular, Landis was reluctant to confront industry leaders the SEC was required to regulate, and he had difficulty articulating the substantive goals needed to galvanize political support. It was with such considerations in mind that William O. Douglas, the SEC's third chairman, disparagingly assessed his predecessor: "James M.

Landis . . . was born to be dean of a law school."[10] By dint of his intellect, preparation, and commitment, Landis also had been born to be SEC chairman. But he lacked the toughness and political flair that were to make his successor a more accomplished SEC chairman.

* * *

The greatest showdown between Washington and Wall Street did not concern the Securities Act of 1933 or the Securities Exchange Act of 1934, but, rather, the Public Utility Holding Company Act of 1935. The restructuring of the public utility industry historically has been the SEC's single most useful accomplishment. It was also by far the most difficult to attain.

The structure of few industries was so influenced by investment banking practices as that of the public utility industry before the 1929 stock market crash. By 1932, three super-holding companies, J. P. Morgan's United Corporation, Insull's utility empire, and the Electric Bond and Share Company, were responsible for 45 percent of the electric energy generated in the United States. Sixteen holding companies had ownership interests in properties producing about 92 percent of the electrical output of the nation's privately owned companies. Four holding company groups controlled more than 56 percent of the total mileage of the country's natural gas transportation system. Natural and manufactured gas production was concentrated in a similar handful of dominant firms.[11] Persuasive arguments were made that utility firms larger than local operating plants were necessary to finance efficiently local construction and least expensively maintain central engineering, construction, and managerial staffs.[12] But the far-flung geographic dispersion of the utility holding companies and their immense size far exceeded economies of scale. And the stock market crash and ensuing depression rebutted the utilities' claims of efficiency. Although, between 1929 and 1936, utility operating companies' revenues dropped only about 15 percent from their highest historical levels, fifty-three utility holding companies with $1.7 billion worth of securities outstanding went into receivership or bankruptcy. Twenty-three other utility holding companies with about $535 million of outstanding securities defaulted on interest payments and voluntarily offered readjustment plans. During the same seven-year period, fifty-three operating companies with $600 million of outstanding securities either were forced into bankruptcy or receivership or voluntarily sought a readjustment plan.[13]

The concentration of the utility industry precipitated what may have been the most extensive study of an American industry ever conducted. Between 1928 and 1935, the Federal Trade Commission published eighty-four volumes of hearings and documentary evidence on utility corporations. Beginning with the populist assumptions that "no large holding-company structure has grown to its present size without the aid of investment bankers" and that "managements apparently often give greater attention to the counsel of bankers than to the interests of widely scattered stockholders,"[14] the FTC's concluding summary report depicted in detail how individuals like Insull or banks like J. P. Morgan and Company were able to control holding company empires with minority common stock ownership through such means as stock "pyramiding," nonvoting stock, voting trusts, classified boards of directors, interlocking directorates, and contractual relationships. Most often minority control was achieved by the purchase of voting control only in a top holding company, most of whose capital was raised by the selling of bonds or nonvoting preferred stock. To control an entire holding company system, the top holding company then would buy a majority voting interest in a series of sub-holding companies, each of which also largely would be capitalized through the sale of bonds or nonvoting stock. The sub-holding companies, in turn, would own voting control in the utility operating companies. Through such pyramiding of control, five public utility holding company systems were controlled in 1931 by the holders of common stock worth less than 1 percent of the entire system's assets. In the most extreme case, Standard Gas and Electric Company, with a total investment of $1.2 billion, was controlled by $23,100 of common stock.[15] A principal consequence of financing public utility systems with large proportions of debt securities was a significant increase in the risk of business failure, since the fixed interest charges on debt securities had to be paid, regardless of the earnings of the utility. By contrast, dividends to stockholders usually are paid at the discretion of a board of directors and may not be paid at all when a firm lacks an available "surplus." Excessive debt-to-equity ratios were the primary cause of the utility holding company bankruptcies during the 1929–1936 period.[16]

The FTC *Utility Corporations Report* also emphasized the unsound accounting techniques employed by those who controlled the top holding companies. It was found that the combined capital assets of the 151 firms studied were written up by $1.4 billion (16 percent of claimed aggregate capital assets of $8.6 billion) to inflate earnings and justify dividends.[17] Top holding companies further swelled their profits by providing engineering, construction, accounting, and managerial services to operating firms, exacting in some instances profits ranging from 50 percent to over 300 percent of the actual cost of such services.[18] The appearance of even greater profits was created by such unsound accounting methods as failing to recognize adequately depreciation expenses for physical assets,[19] recognizing income from the undistributed earnings of subsidiaries, and recognizing income from the sale of properties to controlled subsidiaries at figures higher than market value.[20] The FTC's exhaustive study concluded with recommendations that Congress seek to abolish all top holding companies and many sub-holding companies through tax measures or statutory prohibitions.

At virtually the same time the FTC was carrying out its utility corporation study, Congressman Rayburn's House Interstate Commerce Committee was conducting an independent investigation, directed by Special Counsel Walter M. W. Splawn. Far less ambitious than that of the FTC, the Splawn study was most notable for its finding that fifteen different individuals each sat on the board of directors of at least a hundred separate utility corporations. Two individuals, in fact, sat on over two hundred boards of directors.

Roosevelt, himself an uncompromising advocate of holding company abolition, created the National Power Policy Committee in the summer of 1934 to formulate his administration's legislative proposals. Secretary of the Interior Harold Ickes was named chairman. Benjamin Cohen soon was hired as general counsel; Robert Healy, among others, served on the committee. In March 1935, shortly before the conclusions of the FTC *Utility Corporations Report* were published, the Power Policy Committee recommended to Congress the practical abolition of most holding companies. It asked for legislation directing a federal administrative commission to see to "the elimination of unnecessary corporate complexities and of properties which do not fit into an economically and geographically integrated whole."[21] The recommended concept of geographic integration was similar to Senator Burton Wheeler's oft-quoted sentiment "A utility is essentially a local institution. It should be locally controlled and locally owned."[22] The committee also recommended that a federal administrative agency supervise the issuance of securities by utility companies, the acquisition of new securities and properties, prevent utility holding companies from owning nonutility ventures, prevent electric utility and interstate gas transmission or production firms from being commonly owned, and police holding company service, sales, and construction arrangements to ensure that controlled operating companies received "the performance of their work at cost."

The Public Utility Holding Company Act of 1935[23] as enacted achieved most of the policy aims of the National Power Policy Committee. Drafted chiefly by Benjamin Cohen, the act followed the by then familiar general structure of the 1933 and 1934 Securities Acts. After a section declaring that public utility holding companies were engaged in interstate commerce and had committed a long catalogue of abuses, the act went on to forbid the utilities from engaging in interstate commerce unless they registered with the Securities and Exchange Commission. There was only one significant exemption for intrastate holding company systems.

The most far-reaching provision of the act was Section 11, the controversial death sentence provision. The final compromise version of the section required the SEC as soon as practicable after January 1, 1938, to limit the operations of each holding company system to a single integrated system "and to such other businesses as are reasonably incidental or economically necessary or appropriate to the operations of such integrated public-utility system," provided, however, that a holding company system could continue to control one or more additional public utility systems if it could show that the additional systems were in the same state or an adjoining state and that joint control would result in substantial economies. At the same time, the corporate simplification subsection of Section 11 vested the SEC with the power to restructure any holding company whose structure was unduly or unnecessarily complicated.

In thirty-four terse pages the act additionally empowered the SEC to regulate the sale of all utility securities issuances, in the manner of a blue sky law commission, both by requiring truth in prospectuses and by barring altogether new securities issuances when the SEC considered the securities not reasonably adapted to the financial structure of the firm, or when it considered the underwriting costs too great or found any other terms of the issues "detrimental to the public interest." Similar grants of power authorized the SEC to regulate the purchase by a utility system of any securities, utility assets, or interest in any other business. The Commission was directed to bar altogether loans by one utility firm in a holding system to a second utility in the same system and to prohibit utility company dividends unless the Commission was satisfied that they could be made without jeopardizing a utility firm's "financial integrity." Section 13 authorized the SEC to supervise all utility service, sales, and construction contracts performed by subsidiaries of holding companies or independent mutual service companies to ensure that they were performed "economically" and "at cost" for the benefit of operating companies. All remaining holding companies and each new mutual service company was required to report periodically to the SEC, employing a uniform system of accounts if the Commission deemed it in the public interest to develop uniform accounting methods.

In the broadest sense, the Holding Company Act gave the SEC power to refashion the structure and the business practices of an entire industry. Except in wartime, the federal government never before had assumed such total control over any industry, not even in banking, railroad transportation, or communications, over which federal regulatory powers long had existed. Also noteworthy was the act's underlying assumption about the politics of regulatory agencies. As with the two federal antitrust laws, the emphasis of the Holding Company Act was on a significant one-shot intervention into a dysfunctioning industry, rather than the continuing regulation of an industry's structure. By directing the SEC to simplify the public utility systems "as soon as practicable after January 1, 1938," Roosevelt and his draftsmen acted on the belief that changing an industry significantly had to be done swiftly after the passage of an enabling act, while its political supporters remained in power.

There never was any real likelihood that the utility industry would initially cooperate with the SEC in the enforcement of the Holding Company Act. Throughout the bitter legislative battle leading to the enactment of the act, the Edison Electric Institute, the public utilities' principal lobbying organization, steadfastly had maintained that "the true purpose of the bill is to socialize the business of providing the homes of the nation with electric light and power."[24] Passage of the bill in largely intact form only exacerbated such fears. The utilities, declared Philip H. Gadsen, chairman of the Committee of Public Utility Executives, in a nationwide radio broadcast, were "frankly engaged in a desperate struggle to survive."[25] John W. Davis, lead attorney for the Edison Electric Institute, repeatedly thundered his concurrence: the act was "vicious . . . the last word in federal tyranny . . . the gravest threat to the liberties of the American citizen that has emanated from the halls of Congress in my lifetime."[26] A law of such fundamental importance, insisted Edward F. Hutton, chairman of the General Foods Corporation, required all industry to "gang up" to oppose the national government — and its "radical socialists."[27]

On September 12, 1935, just seventeen days after the passage of the Holding Company Act, the Edison Electric Institute announced that it had retained, in addition to Davis, former Secretary of War Newton Baker and former Solicitor General James Beck to test the constitutionality of the act "as soon as possible."[28] The test came with unexpected suddenness. Although no utility was required to register with the SEC, even on an initial temporary basis, until December 1, 1935, on September 16 the trustees of the American States Public Service Company, a minor utility system then being reorganized under the provisions of the Bankruptcy Act, and one Fred Lautenbach, a dentist who owned $2500 of the firm's bonds, petitioned federal district court judge William Coleman for a declaration that the Public Utility Holding Company Act was unconstitutional.

Landis's chairmanship began a few days later in an atmosphere of crisis. In several letters written late in 1935, Landis remarked that the act's enforcement kept him "busy day and night . . . busier than I have been at any time since the organization of the Securities and Exchange Commission," leaving him "barely time to even turn around."[29] None of the conciliatory tactics that had worked so effectively for Kennedy in enforcing the securities laws aided Landis in enforcing the Holding Company Act. After summoning the leading utility executives to Washington in an attempt to develop a cooperative approach to the act, Landis was informed on September 25 that the utility firms intended to fight the act "to the last legal ditch."[30] A nationwide radio broadcast by Landis three days later, offering his assurances that the utility law would be enforced "without vindictiveness, with an open mind," proved equally unpersuasive.[31]

The destiny of the Public Utility Holding Company Act was to be decided by the federal courts. And in the courts, the SEC at first found itself outmaneuvered. By September 27, when SEC General Counsel Burns, flanked by Cohen and Corcoran, arrived in Judge Coleman's Baltimore Federal District Court to appear in the *American States Public Service Company* proceeding, it was already obvious that the judge intended to declare the act unconstitutional. On September 16, James Piper, counsel for the trustees of American States, had requested Coleman to instruct him as to whether the act was constitutional and therefore required the company to register with the SEC, or was so likely to be declared unconstitutional by the Supreme Court that the holding company could risk not registering. Since that action by Piper, there had been no one in court to defend the act. Judge Coleman, a rabid anti–New Dealer appointed by President Coolidge, announced that he regarded the act as unconstitutional and scheduled a formal hearing on its constitutionality for September 27. To ensure that the hearing would be sufficiently adversarial in form to justify a decision declaring the act unconstitutional, the judge accepted attorney Ralph Buell's petition to declare the act *constitutional*. Buell, representing a number of American States' bondholders, argued with superficial plausibility that his clients would profit most by immediate liquidation of the utility and that this would be facilitated if the Holding Company Act was upheld. The sincerity of his argument, however, was open to question since he had been an outspoken opponent of the act before its passage, and his firm also represented the International Utilities Corporation, which intended to seek a declaration that the act was unconstitutional. Coleman also permitted Davis, then among the best-known appellate attorneys in the country, to appear in court and attack the act on behalf of Fred Lautenbach, and invited the SEC to intervene.

The Commission declined to appear formally as a party in the proceeding, but it did agree to advise the court as an informal *amicus curiae.* In a blistering forty-five-minute opening statement, Burns attacked the adversary proceeding for having been "prearranged" by attorneys Piper, Davis, and Buell. Terming this "professional impropriety" and "collusion," since Buell did not represent an interest truly adversary to those represented by Piper and Davis, Burns demanded that the court make a "thorough investigation in order to ascertain whether or not these proceedings are collusive." Since the SEC had no likelihood of prevailing on the merits in Judge Coleman's court, Burns's collateral attack presented the only possible way the Commission could prevent an early declaration of the act's unconstitutionality.

Furious, Davis responded that Burns's accusation of collusion "would have been offensive to the dignity of a police court in his state of Massachusetts." Referring to Burns, Cohen, and Corcoran, Davis then passionately continued:

> They stoop to seize a handful of mud in each hand and think by throwing it at the litigants and their counsel that in some way they can influence the action, even the power of this court. I say it is an unworthy, an undignified and a contemptible presentation. And when I realize it comes from the official representatives of the government of the United States, I say if that represents their conception of official duty and their temper toward citizens, then on bended knee I pray, "God save the Securities and Exchange Commission and the people of these United States!"

Though he agreed to hold a hearing on Burns's extraordinary charges, Judge Coleman denied Burns a delay so that the SEC could further investigate his allegations. During the balance of that day's proceedings, Burns nonetheless adduced testimony from witnesses that seemed to corroborate much of his opening statement. Pinning down the supposed official defender of the act, Ralph Buell, Burns showed that Buell was unable or unwilling to offer any explanation for his abrupt conversion from a fervent opponent of the act to an advocate of its constitutionality. A bewildered Fred Lautenbach acknowledged that he had never met John W. Davis, had never intended personally to hire an attorney, and certainly had no intention of paying Mr. Davis a fee. To the best of his knowledge, he merely had signed some papers that had something to do with the reorganization of American States Public Service Company. Davis waspishly interrupted, "I submit that I do not have to have social relations with my client to defend his interests." Lautenbach then granted Davis authority to argue on his behalf, after Davis emphasized to Lautenbach that his representation would be "of course without expense to you." Judge Coleman soon dismissed Burns's charges as uncorroborated, thus setting the stage for an early test of the act's constitutionality — and its foreordained result.[32]

"Funny Business in Baltimore," *The New Republic* called it.[33] Landis publicly labeled the proceeding a "sham."[34] In the office of the SEC's general counsel, even Ben Cohen's sardonic attempt to lessen the gloom by expressing tongue-in-cheek praise for Davis's "magnificent charitable concern for that dentist" produced little mirth.[35]

On November 7, the inevitable Coleman decision was handed down. Condemning the act as "grossly in excess of any lawful congressional power [and] the extreme of dictatorial control," the judge declared the Public Utility Holding Company Act "void in its entirety." "So devoid," Coleman opined, "are its provisions of any attempt properly to distinguish between intrastate and interstate commerce that, were dissection attempted, scarcely a clause would survive, save perhaps the preamble."

The next day public utility stocks rose between one and three points.[36] But for the SEC the decision was the beginning of a nightmare. From the date of the passage of the Holding Company Act, John Foster Dulles, managing partner of the leading Wall Street firm of Sullivan and Cromwell, had urged the major utility firms not to register with the Commission, but to "resist the law with all your might."[37] The Coleman decision precipitated a stampede among the utility firms to follow Dulles's advice. Fifty-eight separate lawsuits were brought on behalf of over a hundred companies in thirteen different federal district courts to enjoin the enforcement of the act. Three hundred and seventy-five firms sought a declaration of exemption.[38] As the act's December 1, 1935, deadline for temporary registration expired, a mere fifty-seven utilities, mostly minor firms, had formally registered with the SEC. Nearly all of these firms availed themselves of the Commission's offer to file while reserving their constitutional rights, including the right simultaneously to bring an action to have the act declared unconstitutional.[39]

At the Commission, the leading litigators of the Roosevelt administration rapidly assembled. By late November, joining Landis, Burns, and recently appointed Justice Department special assistants Benjamin Cohen and Thomas Corcoran were Robert Jackson, the assistant general counsel of the Treasury Department, who recently had gained widespread notice for his prosecution of former Secretary of the Treasury Andrew Mellon for tax evasion, and James Lawrence Fly, general solicitor of the Tennessee Valley Authority, who had successfully prosecuted a celebrated antitrust case against the Sugar Institute.[40] It was a striking and fully accurate reflection of how important Roosevelt considered the act's defense that when Supreme Court Justice Van de Vanter retired in May 1937, seven of the ten people whom *The New York Times* reported that official Washington "speculated" might be named to Van de Vanter's seat had played prominent roles in either the enactment or courtroom defense of the utility legislation.*[41]

With unexpected suddenness, on November 26 the Commission began its own test case to establish the constitutionality of the Holding Company Act, catching its chosen defendant as surprised as the Commission itself had been by the commencement of the *American States Public Service Company* proceeding.

The chosen target was the Electric Bond and Share Company, the nation's second-largest utility system, responsible in 1932 for production of 14 percent of national electrical generation and, significantly for a constitutional test of the interstate commerce clause, an undeniably "interstate" system, operating in thirty-one separate states stretching from Florida to Washington. For weeks Landis had been meeting with C. F. Groesbeck, Electric Bond and Share's chairman, trying to persuade him to register the utility system with the Commission. At the climactic meeting on November 26, Groesbeck

---

* Leading the list was Landis. Also listed were Attorney General Cummings and Solicitor General Stanley Reed, both of whom delivered key oral arguments in the utility litigation, Jackson, Cohen, Corcoran, and Frankfurter, who had drafted the final version of Section 11 and was a key lobbyist for the act. Roosevelt soon named Senator Hugo Black to Van de Vanter's place. Black was considered the senator most responsible for the Public Utility Holding Company Act's 1935 passage. He was later joined on the Supreme Court by Reed, Jackson, and Frankfurter, as well as by William O. Douglas, who would play a significant role in the early enforcement of the act.

insisted that Electric Bond and Share would join virtually every other major public utility system in seeking an injunction to bar the SEC from enforcing the holding company law against it. Groesbeck's statement had been anticipated. Within minutes after he departed from the chairman's office, Landis telephoned an SEC employee waiting in New York City's federal courthouse and arranged for a complaint to be filed in the court of Judge Julian Mack.[42] Filing first was crucial. By beating Electric Bond and Share's lawyers to court, the SEC was able to ensure that the case would be tried by one of the nation's most liberal federal district court judges, a judge as predisposed to favor the constitutionality of a reform law as Judge Coleman had been predisposed to oppose it; a judge, moreover, who was a personal friend of Felix Frankfurter and who once had employed Ben Cohen as a law clerk; the very judge who had presided over James Lawrence Fly's successful prosecution of the Sugar Institute. Since all federal district court decisions may be appealed, even more significant to the Commission than the likelihood that Judge Mack would rule in its favor were the advantages that filing first gave the SEC in framing the appealable issues. Had Electric Bond and Share brought suit first, it would have challenged the entire first title of the Public Utility Holding Company Act, including its controversial death sentence provision. By beginning the suit, the SEC was able to limit the case to a test of the constitutionality of two far less controversial provisions, Sections 4 and 5, which prohibited a utility from engaging in interstate commerce until it had filed a registration statement with the SEC.

In this posture, there was little likelihood that Electric Bond and Share could prevail even before "the horse and buggy" Supreme Court of the day. Electric Bond and Share was a super-holding company with controlling interests in five multistate holding companies, which, in turn, controlled 187 domestic subsidiaries that provided electricity and gas to a population of nearly fourteen million people in the United States and served approximately thirteen million additional people abroad. Electric Bond and Share also held 100 percent interests in eight service and construction company subsidiaries. Through these service companies, the firm systematically had milked its operating company subsidiaries. During the seven years 1922–1928, 64 percent of Electric Bond and Share's income had been derived not from the yield on securities it held in its subholding companies, but from fees for providing construction, engineering, management, and underwriting services to its controlled operating firms. As best as the FTC could calculate, the profit on such service relationships averaged over 100 percent. Some fees, such as commissions Electric Bond and Share charged for selling operating company securities to investment bankers, seemed to have no economic value whatsoever to the operating subsidiaries. Other fees charged by Electric Bond and Share's Texas Construction Company or Phoenix Engineering Corporation were for necessary services, but not at market rates. Instead, standard Electric Bond and Share contracts laid down fee schedules based on percentages of a construction project's total expense, the amount of a security issuance, or the monthly income of a subsidiary, regardless of the actual cost of providing the service. Further to inflate Electric Bond and Share's apparent worth, the assets of operating subsidiaries frequently were written up when the firms were initially organized, merged, or reorganized. The same assets regularly were underdepreciated. In 1929, the capital surplus account of Electric Bond and Share may have been overstated by as much as $383 million.[43]

However, the skill with which the SEC's lawyers framed the Electric Bond and Share complaint did little to end the utility firms' registration boycott. Indeed, the very magnitude of the utility system's size slowed the litigation to a snail's pace. Even with Electric Bond and Share's lawyers agreeing to waive a trial of the facts, and joining the SEC in stipulating the facts in a 376-page record, it was not until November 12, 1936, nearly a year after the complaint was filed, that Judge Mack could schedule the oral argument. Then, Benjamin Cohen made a rare courtroom appearance to urge Judge Mack, his former employer, to dismiss Electric Bond and Share's cross-bill and limit the case to a consideration of Sections 4 and 5.[44] In the meantime, Attorney General Cummings and SEC general counsel Burns were able to persuade the Supreme Court of the District of Columbia to hold in abeyance all suits filed against the Commission in its home jurisdiction until the *Electric Bond and Share* or another test case could be brought before the U.S. Supreme Court.[45] By the Holding Company Act's terms, the courts in jurisdictions other than the District of Columbia could not compel the SEC to be a party, so the Commission was able to ignore most of the fifty or so suits brought against it outside Washington, D.C., or to seek their dismissal.[46] But to avoid conferring jurisdiction in courts other than that of Judge Mack, the SEC had to refrain from attempting to enforce the civil or criminal penalties for noncompliance with the act.[47] With the SEC effectively prevented from enforcing the act, and most utility systems refusing to register voluntarily, the Commission's role under the Holding Company Act was almost entirely frustrated.

Late in January 1937, Judge Mack's predictable decision affirming the constitutionality of Sections 4 and 5 of the act was published.[48]

Since Judge Mack's sympathies were as well known as Judge Coleman's, even Mack's thorough vindication of the Commission's legal
arguments did little to reduce the utilities' registration boycott. In
the immediate aftermath of Mack's ruling, two major utility systems, the North American Company and the American Water
Works and Electric Company, withdrew suits against the SEC and
announced that they would register.[49] In mid-March, a third major
system, American Light and Traction Company, registered.[50] But
when, in June 1937, the United States Supreme Court refused to
expedite review of the *Electric Bond and Share* case and instead
directed that Mack's decision first be considered by the Second Circuit Court of Appeals,[51] the resolve of the remaining unregistered
utility systems stiffened. Even the Fourth Circuit Court of Appeals'
earlier partial reversal of Coleman's ruling in the *American States
Public Service* proceeding[52] encouraged few firms to register. When
Landis resigned his chairmanship in September 1937, only ninety or
so utility firms, holding about one third of the assets of all companies subject to the Holding Company Act, had registered.[53] Although the Commission during Landis's chairmanship was able to
promulgate detailed Holding Company Act regulations, including a
Uniform System of Accounts,[54] that achievement was far eclipsed
by the major utility systems' boycott. For James Landis and the
Commission, the first two years' experience in enforcing the act was
a period of near-total frustration. It would not be until 1938, when
the United States Supreme Court affirmed Judge Mack's decision in
Electric Bond and Share,[55] that enforcement of the Public Utility
Holding Company Act effectively could begin.

*   *   *

"I only hope," Landis had written E. A. Pierce early in the public
utility court struggle, "that our energies will not be so diverted by
[the holding company problem] that my first and real love, the securities markets, will suffer."[56] Throughout his chairmanship, the securities markets remained Landis's "real love." In interpreting and
expanding the mandate of the 1934 Securities Exchange Act, Landis
made his most enduring contributions to the Commission.

The New York Stock Exchange had been the logical first concern
of stock market regulation. It was the largest and most influential
securities exchange. But merely to regulate listed securities on the
organized stock markets would not have effectively reduced securities fraud so much as rechanneled it to the unlisted departments of
the smaller exchanges and to the over-the-counter markets.

By definition, unlisted securities were securities admitted to trading privileges on an exchange at the initiative of an exchange member instead of the issuing corporation. Since unlisted securities typically had not provided investors with financial reports comparable with those of listed securities on the New York Stock Exchange, the initial 1934 securities and exchange bill had called for the abolition of all unlisted trading. Unified opposition by twenty-four regional exchanges had resulted in the compromise Section 12(f). The SEC was directed to study unlisted trading and report to Congress by January 3, 1936. But unless Congress adopted new legislation, all unlisted trading was to end on June 1, 1936, the "death sentence" date for unlisted securities.[57]

By January 1936, Landis had come to regard the problem of unlisted trading as more complex than a matter of unequal investor information. Discarding a draft of the unlisted trading report prepared by A. Wilfred May under the supervision of Kemper Simpson, the Commission's economic adviser, Landis had directed an assistant, attorney Milton Katz, to prepare a new report, focusing on the structure of the securities markets.[58]

The Katz draft, published as the SEC's "Report on Trading in Unlisted Securities Upon Exchanges," and related Commission statements depicted the organized stock market system on the verge of becoming noncompetitive. In the period from July 1, 1935, to June 30, 1936, 85 percent of the market value of securities transactions on all organized exchanges occurred on the New York Stock Exchange, which traded only listed securities. Eleven percent of the market value of securities transactions on an organized exchange took place on the New York Curb Exchange, 80 percent of whose trading was in unlisted securities. About half the securities traded on the other twenty-two exchanges were unlisted.[59] If unlisted trading were to be abolished, Landis testified, the New York Curb Exchange "would suffer seriously [and] many small exchanges would be forced to close."[60] Ultimately, the previously unlisted shares would be largely redistributed to the New York Stock Exchange, which would then account for an even higher proportion of transactions on the organized stock exchanges, or to the over-the-counter markets,[61] some of which Landis had recently described as persisting in "practices which could not have been indulged in even on the least reputable of our stock exchanges."[62] Characteristic of such a stock market system would be a near-total absence of competition. The New York Stock Exchange, the New York Curb Exchange, and the over-the-counter markets, which generally did not compete, would continue to control all trading in securities, and there would be few or no regional exchanges to offer competitive price quotations or competitive commission rates. Such a stock market system would also be more difficult to police. As the SEC's report emphasized:

> Exchanges constitute an organized mechanism of control which can be utilized to good advantage. Manipulative or deceptive practices in the comparatively unorganized over-the-counter markets are more difficult to detect and prevent. In consequence, if our purpose is the effective regulation of trading practices, it would be profitless to drive securities from the exchanges into the over-the-counter markets.[63]

Both to increase inter-exchange competition and to ensure more effective regulation, the Commission's January 1936 report recommended retention of unlisted trading.[64] But the SEC deferred making a specific legislative proposal until it could prepare a bill that also addressed the more complicated question of regulating the over-the-counter markets.

Section 15 of the 1934 Securities Exchange Act had granted the SEC carte blanche authority to regulate the over-the-counter markets as long as its rules and regulations gave investors protection "comparable" with that provided by the act "in the case of national securities exchanges." Chairman Kennedy had concluded early in 1935 that "the problem of the over-the-counter markets . . . is probably the most difficult and most complex single problem before the Commission."[65] Kennedy interpreted Section 15 to require that the over-the-counter markets be subject to the same degree of regulation as the organized stock exchanges.[66] But achieving such "nondiscriminatory" regulation seemed both impractical and constitutionally impermissible.

Through 1936, the amount of over-the-counter trading dwarfed securities transactions on the organized exchanges. Although the Commission found "authentic data were lacking," it was estimated that two to four times the amount of trading on the exchanges was transacted over the counter. Where 6260 issues were traded on all exchanges registered with the SEC, 90,000 issues were quoted for over-the-counter trading in the National Quotation Bureau's semi-annual stock and bond summaries. The SEC termed the over-the-counter markets "one of the enigmas of our financial system," not so much because of the size of the over-the-counter markets as because of their variety. The 1934 Securities Exchange Act described over-the-counter trading with the phrase "otherwise than on a national securities exchange." Within this capacious definition coexisted several distinct types of securities trading. At one extreme the over-the-counter markets were "preeminent in those securities having the least amount of risk." Virtually all United States Treasury bonds and notes, federal Farm Loan bonds, Home Owners Loan bonds, and state and municipal bonds were traded over the counter. Similarly, in 1958 it would be estimated that about 80 percent of all transactions in corporate bonds were traded over the counter. As much as 95 percent of the trading in bank and insurance common shares also were traded over the counter. At the other extreme were over-the-counter markets trading local issues or new issues where trading volume was too sparse to justify the issues being listed on an exchange. His experience in enforcing the 1933 Securities Act for the Federal Trade Commission had convinced Landis that the most speculative oil and gas, gold mine and liquor securities usually were traded by local, sometimes fly-by-night, over-the-counter dealers. Finally, the over-the-counter markets provided some competition with the exchanges by trading bonds, preferred stocks, and other fixed income securities. "Even with respect to some common stocks admitted to exchange trading," reported a 1936 SEC study, "the volume of trading over the counter frequently exceeds that on the exchange."

But over-the-counter trading did not occur on a discrete number of exchange floors. Each of the nation's five thousand to six thousand over-the-counters brokers and dealers could become a "market-maker" in a designated security merely by signifying to other over-the-counter traders an intent to deal in particular securities. No seat on an exchange need be purchased. No exchange disciplinary rules need be obeyed. The principal over-the-counter firms were unified only by "a nationwide web of telephone and telegraph wires."

The very informality of the over-the-counter markets invited sharp dealing, particularly in small, local common stock trading. Even the most wide open of the precrash securities exchanges functioned as an "auction market," requiring specialists to match the highest bid and lowest offer in each transaction. When trading was sufficiently active in a security, the funneling of most transactions to a specialist resulted in price quotations being relatively stable, rarely including erratic price jumps. By contrast, over-the-counter dealers were not bound to deal with any particular market-maker. Purchase transactions typically occurred when an over-the-counter dealer bought a security from a market-maker at one price and resold it to a customer at a higher price. The customer was not informed of the price at which the over-the-counter dealer had purchased the security, and the SEC later learned of a great many instances in which over-the-counter firms pocketed profits as high as

25 percent or more per transaction. In one notorious instance, the Commission found that an over-the-counter dealer had taken a profit of 380 percent by purchasing a security at $5.00 and reselling it to a customer at $24. The newspaper quotations for securities traded over the counter contributed to the possibility of unfairness. Dealers did not disclose the "inside" market prices at which they were interested in buying or selling over-the-counter securities from other dealers; rather, separate "outside" market prices were printed, reflecting the levels at which local dealers estimated they would be interested in buying or selling from the public.[67]

During Landis's chairmanship, the SEC considered several regulatory approaches to the "enigma" of the over-the-counter markets. In late 1934, the Commission began studying means by which securities traded in over-the-counter markets could be made subject to the same periodic disclosure, proxy, and insider trading rules as securities registered on a national exchange. But the Commission's options were believed to be severely limited by the Supreme Court's discussion of the Constitution's interstate commerce clause in cases such as *Schecter*. So the January 1936 *Unlisted Trading Report* could go little further than discuss the comparative merits of indirectly trying to pressure issuers to register securities through such means as barring over-the-counter brokers and dealers from using the mails until the securities had been registered, allowing over-the-counter securities to be purchased on margin to the same extent that securities on an exchange could be but only if they were registered with the SEC, or publicly disclosing the income tax returns of issuers of over-the-counter unregistered securities. Ultimately, the constitutional law and the practical difficulties with each of these and other approaches seemed insurmountable, and Landis's SEC did not propose a comprehensive scheme to provide ongoing disclosure and proxy regulation of over-the-counter securities. This created an anomalous gap in the SEC's otherwise comprehensive scheme of securities regulation that fully justified Harvard Law School professor Louis Loss's later criticism: "It seems self-evident that the disparity of regulation is without justification. If the public interest requires the application of [the ongoing disclosure, proxy, and insider trading rules of the 1934 Securities Exchange Act] to companies with listed securities, the need is certainly no less in the case of large companies with widely distributed securities whose managements do not choose to register and assume the statutory obligations."[68] With memories of Charles Mitchell's delisting of the National City Bank's stock still vivid, Landis undoubtedly agreed. But it was a guiding principle of his SEC that the Commission would not recommend a rule that could not withstand Supreme Court scrutiny, so the SEC's 1936 proposal to regulate over-the-counter securities was extremely limited.

Landis focused the Commission's efforts on regulating the over-the-counter brokers and dealers whose activities often clearly were in interstate commerce. In a November 1935 speech,[69] Landis proposed a two-pronged approach to regulation of the over-the-counter dealers. It called first for the Commission to seek the registration of all brokers and dealers active in the over-the-counter markets, "together," Landis explained, "with the imposition of a few regulations mainly confirming their fiduciary duties." The registration program, in fact, had already begun, and by December 31, 1935, would result in the registration of 5083 over-the-counter brokers and dealers.[70] But Landis emphasized that such "large-scale" registration could accomplish little more than "winnowing out . . . the black sheep" by denying registration to brokers or dealers who had criminal records or were guilty of violating the securities laws. Thus, Landis stressed "the second method of control," an SEC attempt "to help in the organization of a self-disciplinary agency of dealers. Just as the disciplinary committees of the exchanges have been invaluable to us in our efforts to supervise the activities on the exchanges," Landis explained, "similar machinery would seem to be of value for the over-the-counter markets." Protracted negotiations first conducted by Landis would result in 1938 in congressional approval of a self-disciplinary agency for over-the-counter dealers.

The SEC's February 1936 legislative proposals were directed primarily toward rationalizing the relationships among listed securities, unlisted securities, and the over-the-counter markets. The Commission proposed amending Section 12(f) of the 1934 Securities Exchange Act to permit continued trading of unlisted securities if trading had occurred before March 1, 1934, if the security was listed on a second exchange, or if the SEC found that the issuer voluntarily provided information to investors "substantially equivalent" to that required by the 1933 and 1934 acts. The new section strengthened the New York Curb and the regional exchanges. Not only was each of the smaller exchanges allowed to continue trading in unlisted securities that had been traded before the 1934 act, but each was allowed to trade the most active listed securities on other exchanges if it could convince the SEC that there would be "sufficient public trading activity" on its floor to provide an orderly market.

A proposed amendment to Section 15 of the 1934 act codified the SEC's earlier-effected system of registering over-the-counter brokers and dealers. It also required each over-the-counter security with a share value of $2 million or more, registering under the 1933 Securities Act, to provide periodic financial statements, as if it were listed on an exchange. This provision applied only to over-the-counter securities making new offerings after the effective date of the 1936 amendments. "A program of this character," recognized the *Unlisted Trading Report*, "should not be expected to bring about registration of these over-the-counter securities except over a period of years." At most, it would result in periodic reporting by a small proportion of securities traded over the counter.[71]

Only a few officials of statewide over-the-counter dealer associations opposed the SEC legislative proposals.[72] But since the dealers' opposition was largely a reflection of their disappointment that the SEC had not recommended the abolition of unlisted trading, it had no discernible political impact. With little modification, the 1936 amendments to the 1934 act were passed unanimously by both Houses of Congress and signed into law by President Roosevelt on May 26.[73] Consistent with the disclosure philosophy of the 1933 and 1934 Securities Acts, the amendments went as far as Landis believed constitutional law and practicality would permit "to obtain," as Commissioner Douglas put it in a Landisian statement, "from the issuers of securities traded over-the-counter and traded unlisted on exchanges, corporate information equivalent . . . to the information required by law from issuers of listed securities."[74] At the same time, the amendments sought to protect investors both by favoring the organized exchanges over the unorganized over-the-counter markets and by strengthening the smaller regional exchanges so that they could compete directly with the New York Stock Exchange in the trading of the most active issues.

*   *   *

The very qualities that led to Landis's success in extending the 1934 act to unlisted trading and the over-the-counter markets — his aversion to dogmatic positions, his insistence on thorough study, his preference for moderate, incremental action — soon led him to issue the most controversial study of his chairmanship, the SEC's June 1936 *Report on the Feasibility and Advisability of the Complete Segregation of the Functions of Dealer and Broker.*

It had been an article of faith with Ferdinand Pecora and such influential Senate Banking Committee staff members as John T. Flynn and Max Lowenthal that stock exchange members should be limited in their activity to the brokers' function of executing orders for the public and should not be allowed simultaneously to trade for their own accounts. To them, "the heart" of the 1934 securities exchange bill had been Section 10 of Ben Cohen's original draft, which categorically barred "any person who as a broker transacts a business in securities . . . to act as a dealer in or underwriter of securities." Flynn, who inspired Section 10, considered it "the most important business of the Commission" for an "obvious" reason:

> An exchange that consisted of brokers who were limited to executing the buying and selling orders of the public would be a socially useful instrument in the capitalist money economy. But this is not what we have. We have an exchange in which a few of the members are brokers and nothing more, while almost all of them are heavy speculators for their own account; where perhaps a third represent public buyers as agents and at the same time carry on extensive speculations for their own profit, and where the balance are primarily speculators, some openly as floor traders, others covertly as floor brokers and specialists, all using the instrumentalities of the market place to buy and sell and gradually unload their holdings upon the public they are supposed to represent and serve. This is not a public utility, but a public abomination.

To Flynn, on this issue there could be no appropriate compromise. The issue was ethical, not technical.

> So far as I am concerned [he would later write], there is really nothing to be argued about the question of separation of the functions of broker and trader. It is a very simple question. It gets down to a question of fundamental honesty and integrity in dealing. I lay it down as a truism that no man whose primary function is a fiduciary one — that of an agent — should be permitted to enter the market in which he appears as an agent for others and to trade in that market for himself . . . If that proposition is not sound, then any attempt to introduce simple decency into business relations is utterly impossible. We are face to face with a fundamental concept of commercial civilization.[75]

The bitterest defeat for Ben Cohen and Pecora, as well as for Flynn, in the lobbying for the 1934 securities exchange bill had been the deletion of the original uncompromising Section 10 and the enactment of Section 11(e), which directed the SEC to study the feasibility and advisability of the complete segregation of the functions of dealer and broker and to report the results of the study to Congress. The segregation study represented the second, and presumably last, chance for Flynn and a fair number of like-minded stock exchange reformers to remake the New York Stock Exchange in the image of a public utility.

Kemper Simpson, the Commission's chief economic adviser, and Willis Ballinger, chief of special studies, were assigned to prepare the report on the segregation study. Although the Simpson-Ballinger draft of the *Segregation Report* did not call for complete segregation, as Flynn urged, it did recommend an almost total elimination of members floor trading for their own accounts, the barring of brokerage houses from also underwriting new securities, and the strengthening of the smaller regional exchanges at the expense of the less well-organized over-the-counter markets. Landis, appalled by the report's cursory consideration of the practical consequences of segregation in the organized exchanges, persuaded the Commission to reject the Simpson-Ballinger draft and assign David Saperstein, director of the Trading and Exchange Division, and Thomas Gammack, his executive assistant, to work with Landis in rewriting the report. The withdrawal of the report embittered all concerned. A copy of the Simpson-Ballinger draft found its way to the *Herald Tribune.* Landis soon fired Andrew Ten Eyck, Simpson's legal adviser. In late 1936, the full Commission eliminated the positions of economic adviser and chief of special studies, effectively dismissing Simpson and Ballinger. A bitter Simpson departed, publicly railing against a "Commission dominated by those interested primarily in technical detail and legal phraseology."[76]

The final *Segregation Report* released in June 1936 was not so much technical in detail as cautious in its conclusions. In language that even Flynn and Simpson approved, the report began with an extensive criticism of stock exchange floor traders and specialists. Approximately 24 percent of trading on the New York Stock Exchange between June 24, 1935, and December 14, 1935, the report found, had been trading by members for their own accounts. When trading on the stock exchange floor, a member enjoyed extraordinary advantages over nonmember investors, primarily because his physical presence on the floor gave him the advantage of having crucial information. The report stated:

> He sees instantly the outbreak of activity in a stock, the nature of the trading, and the direction of prices. He is in a position to discount or revise his market appraisals almost instantaneously. Upon the basis of information which he derives while on the floor he can increase, decrease, or cancel his orders more rapidly than a non-member to whom the same information is only made available at a later time. This is particularly true when the "tape is late," i.e., when reports of transactions which are conveyed to the outside world by means of a ticker system are delayed because of unusual activity on the floor. During such periods the member on the floor has immediate knowledge of the latest prices while the non-member must rely upon prices which may no longer be current.

The specialists, who served as exchange market-makers, enjoyed each of these advantages, and could on some occasions, the *Segregation Report* found, anticipate price trends in the securities they traded by reference to their future-order books or through personal contact with the corporate officers or principal shareholders of the securities in which they specialized. "Recognizing . . . the existence of abuses arising from the combination of broker and dealer functions," the report nonetheless stopped short of calling for the complete segregation of the functions of brokers and dealers. Concerned by a study they had conducted in preparing the report that suggested that specialists trading for their own accounts tended to stabilize market prices, the writers of the report took the position, characteristic of Landis, that there was insufficient evidence yet available to predict the likely effects of segregation and that therefore it was preferable to pursue "an evolutionary approach . . . to test the waters by gradual approaches rather than to dive headlong into them."

Accordingly, the SEC report recommended that no legislation be enacted requiring the complete segregation of the functions of dealer and broker. Instead, the Commission would use its existing rule-making authority to effect "partial segregation" primarily through the functional segregation of all members on the exchange floor with the exception of specialists. "Under such a requirement floor traders could not act as brokers, and commission brokers could not . . . initiate orders for their own account." This was a significant "evolutionary step," which would have reduced the number of New York Stock Exchange floor brokers dealing for their own accounts. But its significance was considerably reduced by the fact that the recommended "functional segregation" did not extend to dealing that took place off the floor. Thus, a commission broker barred from trading for his own account on the exchange floor could do so in the over-the-counter market. Nor did the report specify any new limitations on specialist trading beyond indicating that the SEC would study "appropriate restrictions governing the conditions under which the specialist may trade with his book." Finally, and by far most significantly, the *Segregation Report* shied away from the most important implication of its empirical findings. Given the report's findings concerning the abuses of member trading and its insistence that liquidity should not be regarded as a "fetish," the report well might have renewed the call for the abolition of floor traders, the stock exchange members who traded only for their own accounts. Even a cautious report might have considered means to abolish floor traders gradually, say, by prohibiting future New York

Stock Exchange members from floor dealing unless they were specialists.[77]

Few influential political reformers understood the complexities of stock market trading well enough to comment on the *Segregation Report*. Those who did were harshly denunciatory. Flynn wasted no time in condemning the report for deciding on "a futile gesture of regulation": "It proposes to force brokers to abstain from trading in shares while on the floor. They may, however, trade for themselves while not on the floor, and their firms and their partners may trade for themselves and may even give the orders to the exchange member of the firm. Naïveté can go no farther."[78] Max Lowenthal, Flynn's former colleague on the Senate Banking Committee staff, went even further than Flynn in personalizing his criticism. The Landis chairmanship, he wrote to Frankfurter, "however vernal may have been the hope with which it started, faded out in a dismal autumn fashion."[79] Landis, stung by Flynn's repeated attacks, wrote Bruce Bliven, *The New Republic*'s editor, to complain of the magazine's "failure to understand" the Commission's work.[80]

To the stock exchanges, the *Segregation Report*, even with its limited, preliminary recommendations, was, as both Landis and *The Literary Digest* independently judged it, "a bombshell."[81] When Landis made plain to a New York Stock Exchange committee on November 18, 1936, that the SEC intended to see its plan for functional segregation of exchange members put into effect regardless of the wishes of the Exchange,[82] the value of a seat on the Exchange began a precipitous drop, declining $38,000, to a value of $89,000 by December 1, 1936.[83] W. W. Spald, president of the Associated Stock Exchanges, lambasted the SEC for subjecting the organized stock markets to a greater degree of regulation than the over-the-counter markets. "Stock exchanges," claimed Spald, "have entered the dying industries classification by reason of the discriminatory operation of the Securities and Exchange laws."[84] For the exchanges, partial segregation of brokers and dealers was almost as intense a pocketbook issue as the proposed abolition of floor traders had been in 1934. To cushion the economic impact, Landis did not attempt to regulate all floor transactions, nor did he seek to apply the partial segregation recommendation to exchanges less financially strong than the New York Stock Exchange and New York Curb Exchange. This did little, however, to reduce the intensity of the exchanges' opposition. After accepting SEC proposals that member trading not be effected on margin and minor changes in specialists' trading, the New York Stock Exchange adamantly opposed all of the other *Segregation Report* reforms.[85]

Even before securities prices sharply slumped in the fall of 1937, NYSE president Charles Gay publicly blamed SEC and other federal regulatory bodies for creating "abnormal market conditions" that threatened to destroy a "broad, liquid market."[86]

At his final press conference, Landis scornfully dismissed Gay's remark that excessive regulation had lessened the liquidity of the market and sharply questioned the objectivity of stock exchange officials like Gay, whose living depended on creating the greatest possible share volume.[87] Against the strong opposition of the Exchange, however, he was unable to negotiate a partial segregation rule during his chairmanship. And when the market began a severe slump in mid-August 1937, the SEC, in spite of Landis's earlier insistence, did not impose such a rule.[88]

* * *

The defeat of partial segregation was a rare setback in the SEC's efforts during the Landis chairmanship to reduce fraud on the securities exchanges. Although Landis personally disliked the policeman's role, the SEC he led was imaginative and effective in its enforcement activities. By the end of his chairmanship, the SEC had evolved a strategy of informal enforcement procedures and occasional highly publicized exemplary prosecutions that allowed the Commission to maximize the impact of its enforcement resources.

At the Federal Trade Commission, Landis had frequently resorted to use of the 1933 Securities Act stop order powers. At the SEC, his review of larger securities issues managed by the leading underwriters convinced him that the mere threat of a formal proceeding was sufficient to persuade most underwriters to withdraw an issue and rewrite the securities registration statement in compliance with the SEC's perception of what was an accurate and complete disclosure. As Landis later explained: "The ability to sell a substantial block of securities depends upon creation of a belief that that issue is, like Calpurnia, above suspicion . . . the threat of initiating a proceeding, because of its tendency to assail the reputation of an issue and because it will mean delay, is sufficient in the normal case." By May 1936, SEC informal "deficiency letters" and conferences had led to the withdrawal of registration statements covering approximately $300 million in securities, compared with new securities worth approximately $100 million blocked through formal stop and refusal orders. The use of informal procedures to enforce the Securities Act was nonpunitive. By avoiding the formalities of evidence discovery, Commission hearing, and possible court review, the SEC was able to increase the number of allegedly false or misleading securities prospectuses that it prevented from reaching investment markets.[89]

At the same time, Landis's SEC focused its formal enforcement activities on a few widely publicized prosecutions of egregious fraud or manipulation, often against well-known defendants. The first SEC action to suspend a New York Stock Exchange member began late in 1935, against Michael Meehan. Meehan had been among the best-known market operators during the 1920s' bull market, a specialist in RCA common stock who amassed a fortune estimated to be worth between $25 and $50 million allegedly by manipulating "Radio," whose shares rose from $85 in 1924 to $570 in 1929. A flamboyant, gregarious man, Meehan reportedly had given every one of four hundred employees a full year's salary as a Christmas bonus in 1927. The enactment of the 1934 Securities Exchange Act apparently had caused him little concern. In the summer of 1935, the Commission detected an extraordinary increase in the volume of trading of Bellanca Aircraft Corporation. While as few as six hundred Bellanca shares had been traded during the entire month of January 1935, ninety-two hundred shares were traded on June 10 alone. On that day, Meehan had been responsible for the sale of nine thousand of these shares. More important, he had also bought five thousand of the nine thousand shares that were sold. Indeed, between June 8 and 18, Meehan had been responsible for the sale of 29,000 of the 40,900 Bellanca shares sold, purchasing back 15,400 to boost the share price from 4 to 5½. An exhaustive SEC investigation was able to piece together a network of fifteen or so traders who had worked with Meehan to match orders and boost Bellanca's price. Meehan was expelled from the three stock exchanges of which he was a member.[90] Similar well-publicized fraud actions against onetime Kennedy cohort Charles Wright, White, Weld and Company, and Thomas Gagen gave the Landis SEC a reputation for being a vigilant watchdog of Wall Street.[91]

The effectiveness of the Commission's enforcement activity, combined with the primitiveness of its initial hearing procedures, engendered intense animosity. The anti-SEC hostility first became evident in the aftermath of the Supreme Court decision in *Jones* v. *SEC.*[92] J. Edward Jones, in 1935 the nation's largest dealer in oil royalty securities, in May 1935 had filed a registration statement that the SEC considered so misleading that it telegraphed Jones one day before the statement was to become effective and demanded that he show cause why a stop order should not be issued. Instead, Jones moved to withdraw the registration statement. When the SEC refused to permit him to do so, citing a Commission rule that withdrawal could occur only with SEC consent, Jones began a federal court challenge to the constitutionality of the 1933 Securities Act and the SEC's rule preventing withdrawal of his registration statement. In March 1936 his case reached the Supreme Court. Justice Sutherland's subsequent decision ignored questions of the act's constitutionality, allowing court of appeals holdings affirming the act's constitutionality to stand as controlling law. But a six-to-three Court majority ruled that, the act being silent on the appropriate procedure, the SEC should have followed controlling equity court rules and permitted withdrawal. This was a defeat for the SEC, but on a technical point, remediable in the future by waiting until the registration statement became effective before instituting a stop order proceeding.

Although Sutherland's decision implicitly acknowledged that the SEC's actions were at most "petty encroachments" or "minor invasions of personal rights," he closed his decision by comparing the Commission's procedures with the "unlawful inquisitorial investigations" and "intolerable abuses of the Star Chamber." Landis attributed Sutherland's tirade to the anti–New Deal sentiments of the Court's majority, taking some pleasure in telegraphing Roosevelt the bristling rejoinder to Sutherland in Justice Cardozo's dissent: "A commission which is without coercive powers, which cannot arrest or amerce or imprison though a crime has been uncovered or even punish for contempt, but can only inquire and report, the propriety of every question in the course of the inquiry being subject to the supervision of the ordinary courts of justice, is likened with denunciatory fervor to the Star Chamber of the Stuarts. Historians may find hyperbole in the sanguinary simile."

The *Jones* decision, nonetheless, was widely hailed, not only by securities promoters, with their obvious self-interest, but by such usually sympathetic observers as *The New York Times* and journalist Robert Kinter. Kinter appreciated the basic issue underlying Sutherland's outburst. The arrival of government-by-administrative-agency meant a revolution in constitutional norms of government structure and procedural fairness. As Landis argued, the interests of expertise and agency authority, flexible enough to supervise the protean variety of industry, required that the agency itself not only issue regulations but also prosecute and judge noncriminal violations of its enabling act. This gave an agency the ability to evolve rules on a case-by-case basis, rather than limiting the agency to occasional industrywide rules. By combining in a single commission the prosecutor's discretion to choose appropriate cases for prosecution and the judge's power to author a decision, agency case decision could be a crucial mechanism for an agency's interpretation of its enabling act. Landis, championing the need to expand the province of government-by-agency, firmly maintained that agency professionalism and judicial review were adequate to protect individual defendants from wrongful prosecution.

But the combination in a single agency of prosecutional and judicial functions *appeared* unfair; it seemed totally contrary to the detachment and independence expected of a judge. This was particularly so for an agency like Landis's SEC, with vague enabling statutes, an aggressive staff, and evolving hearing procedural rules. In an otherwise inexcusably exaggerated article from so astute a journalist, Robert Kinter well stated this fundamental criticism: "It is difficult . . . to reconcile any nobility of purpose with the present discretionary authority of the SEC, which permits its officials to act as plaintiff, witness, prosecutor, judge and jury."

Precisely because their discretion overlapped the traditional responsibilities of each of the three branches of government, Roosevelt's agencies even in what Landis called their "lusty youth" were already jealously regarded. Sutherland's tirade against the SEC was as much a defense of judicial supremacy as a polemic against the New Deal. The fevered excesses of the Liberty League and Alf Landon's 1936 "Down with the Alphabet [Agencies]" presidential campaign would draw their justification from the traditional tripartite scheme of the Constitution that Landis's theoretical writings and the SEC in practice disputed as inevitable. Even Roosevelt's own Committee on Administrative Management early in 1937 would inveigh against the independent regulatory commissions that threatened in time to become "a headless fourth branch of the government, not contemplated by the Constitution, and not responsible administratively either to the President, to the Congress, or to the Courts." Lacking the legitimacy accorded by the Constitution through periodic election or judicial appointment, agencies like the SEC were inherently vulnerable.[93]

Beginning in 1934 the American Bar Association began a twelve-year campaign to reduce the judicial powers of the administrative agencies. The association's annual report that year warned, "The judicial branch of the federal government is being rapidly and seriously undermined . . . So far as possible, the decision of controversies of a judicial character must be brought back into the judicial system." To correct "the fundamental evil" of combining "judicial with executive or legislative functions," an American Bar Association committee suggested in 1936 the creation of a new administrative court. This suggestion was soon dropped, but a 1938 American Bar Association committee's legislative proposals were the inspiration for the Walter-Logan administrative law bill, introduced in 1939. The Walter-Logan bill proposed to increase dramatically judicial review of administrative agency actions. Significantly, Sections 4 and 5 of the proposal not only would have permitted judicial review of the final orders of the SEC — as was already the law — but also, apparently, virtually all decisions of a procedural or administrative nature, such as a Commission decision to file an injunction or a trial examiner's ruling on the admissibility of evidence. "If this is a correct interpretation of the bill," one official SEC comment insisted, "administrative proceedings may thereby be interminably hampered and delayed in a manner not permitted with respect to judicial proceedings in the lower [federal] courts." James Landis, by then dean of Harvard Law School, asserted, in a slashing attack on the Walter-Logan bill, that it would "cut off here a foot and there a head, leaving broken and bleeding the process of administrative law." But despite the combined opposition of the Roosevelt administration, Sam Rayburn, and such Wall Street stalwarts as John Foster Dulles and the Administrative Law Committee of the Association of the Bar of the City of New York, the Walter-Logan bill was passed by both Houses of Congress late in 1940.

Roosevelt vetoed the bill. In a December 17, 1940, message he urged that it was advisable to await the report of a Committee on Administrative Procedure, earlier appointed by the Attorney General, before adopting new legislation. The 1941 report of the committee — known as the Acheson Committee after its chairman, Dean Acheson — effectively ended the movement to enact procedural legislation to hamstring such controversial agencies as the SEC and the NLRB. The 474-page final report began with an elaborate case against interference with the administrative agencies. Pointedly noting that thirty-four of the existing fifty-one administrative agencies had been created before the New Deal, the Acheson Report argued that the agencies were a pragmatic necessity to handle routine governmental matters, enforce preventive rather than punitive legislation (such as the SEC's securities registration statute), and carry out a vast range of discretionary rule-making functions. The less restrictive legislative recommendations of the Acheson Committee became the basis of the Administrative Procedure Act enacted in 1946. Since the SEC by then had voluntarily adopted sophisticated hearing rules and independent trial examiners, the act itself resulted in virtually no change in the Commission's procedures.[94]

* * *

Within the Roosevelt administration, there was relatively little criticism of Landis, but those who did criticize inevitably echoed the remarks made by Kemper Simpson. Landis, it was said, was too much the technician, the legalist, too deliberate and too cautious, to effectively reflect the overthrow of the old financial order Roosevelt attempted to achieve between 1934 and 1937. These impressions intensified during the 1936 presidential election campaign. The contrast between Landis's passionless "scientific" approach to securities exchange reform and the rhetoric of Roosevelt's political crusade against "economic royalists" could not have been more striking.

Yet Roosevelt's support for his restrained SEC chairman was unstinting. Roosevelt accepted Landis's December 20, 1935, recommendation that William O. Douglas be named to Kennedy's slot on the Commission (after Landis's first choice, John J. Burns, declined to be considered for the nomination).[95] He also accepted Landis's May 1936 recommendation that Judge Healy be reappointed.[96] When Harvard University offered Landis the opportunity to become dean of the law school, Roosevelt wrote Harvard president James Conant asking him to extend Landis's leave of absence so that Landis could remain longer in Washington before returning to Cambridge. At one point, Roosevelt offered Landis the opportunity to become Under Secretary of the Treasury. Conant refused to extend Landis's leave of absence, placing Landis in a difficult position. He could become dean of the law school or lose his tenure at Harvard. On January 11, 1937, it was publicly announced that Landis would become Harvard Law School's next dean. So reluctant was Roosevelt to see Landis depart that the President employed the heavy-handed tactic of stating at a May 20, 1937, press conference that he hoped Landis would continue as SEC chairman "as long as possible." Four days later Landis agreed not to resign in June, as he had intended, but to remain at the SEC until September, when the law school's next academic year began.[97]

During his eight months as a lame duck chairman, Landis's experience at the Commission became progressively less pleasant. After Landis announced his intention to resign, Commissioner Douglas began a campaign to succeed Landis as chairman. With the completion of the first five parts of his massive Protective Committee Study by May 1937 and introduction of three proposed bills incorporating the study's legislative recommendations,[98] Douglas believed that he had earned the chairmanship. He was miffed that Landis refused to support him. So bitter was Douglas that he would recall in his autobiography, written thirty-seven years later, his belief that

Landis prolonged his stay in Washington for the deliberate purpose of preventing Douglas from becoming chairman, since Douglas had been named Yale Law School's dean and intended to return to New Haven at the start of that school's academic year — which, Douglas recalled, began "one or two days before Landis had to be at Harvard" — unless he was first named chairman.[99]

As the rivalry between Landis and Douglas heated up, Douglas began making speeches far more critical of Wall Street than Landis as SEC chairman was prepared to make,[100] winning praise from the same John T. Flynn, *New Republic*, and *Nation* that regularly assailed Landis.[101] Increasingly, Douglas, like Healy, dissented from SEC opinions.[102] He cultivated relationships with Joseph P. Kennedy and Thomas Corcoran, who, in 1937, were particularly influential in advising Roosevelt on financial issues.[103] It was characteristic of Douglas that when Roosevelt stunned his own administration in February 1937 by proposing the "packing" of the Supreme Court, Douglas quickly joined Corcoran and Cohen in helping Roosevelt mobilize his administration to lobby for the proposal. Landis, by contrast, had to be persuaded to deliver a speech endorsing the plan.[104] Douglas later attributed his selection as the SEC's third chairman to Joseph Kennedy's supportive "intervention."[105]

When Landis officially tendered his resignation as chairman on September 11, 1937, he wrote Roosevelt a gracious letter, concluding, "Our Commission and our work sprang from your mind, your utterances, your ideals."[106] An equally appropriate encomium could have been stated of Landis for his role in helping to draft the 1933 and 1934 Securities Acts and the regulations, opinions, and reports issued during the SEC's first three years. Yet both sympathetic and critical commentators concurred with the assessment in a *New York Times* editorial that, as an administrator, he had been "diligent, unsensational and, on the whole, conservative."[107] Douglas lost no time in emphasizing at his first press conference that his chairmanship would "be a period of action"; on issues such as segregation and regulation of the over-the-counter markets, Douglas considered the Commission's steps to that date to have been a "prologue." His own SEC would "move more swiftly."[108]

6

The Man Who
Got Things Done

*Under Joe [Kennedy] the gains made toward protecting the rights
of investors through President Roosevelt's legislative program
were consolidated. Under Jim [Landis] we were taught how to get
things done. And we're now going to go ahead and get them done.*

— WILLIAM DOUGLAS
October 1937

WILLIAM ORVILLE DOUGLAS'S career as a Supreme Court Justice
was so long and so controversial that it all but obliterated memory
of the achievements during the Roosevelt administration that led to
his elevation to the Court. This is unfortunate. As distinguished as
Douglas's contributions as a Justice were, they would never have
occurred but for his nineteen months as chairman of the Securities
and Exchange Commission. Between March 1938, when the Richard
Whitney embezzlement scandal broke, and April 1939, when he was
elevated to the Supreme Court, Douglas led the SEC on a crusade
that attempted to complete the Commission's logical mandate by
consolidating SEC enforcement of the over-the-counter markets,
commencing enforcement of the geographic integration and corporate simplification provisions of the Public Utility Holding Company Act, and replacing state standards of corporate finance, accounting, and corporate governance with SEC-enforced federal rules.
No other SEC chairman ever addressed so many fundamental prob-

lems simultaneously. Not all of Douglas's initiatives succeeded. But
his chairmanship was the most accomplished in the SEC's history,
in part because it articulated a coherent policy framework for federal
corporations law that was to guide the next two generations of corporate reform efforts.

It was, nevertheless, a profoundly conservative chairmanship,
chiefly concerned with strengthening business competition and industrial productivity by removing opportunities for self-interested
transactions and abuses of economic power. In Douglas's own
words, the work of the SEC was "concerned with the preservation of
capitalism." His chairmanship was distinguished from that of his
predecessors by its tactics, not by its ideals. Like Frankfurter and
Landis, Douglas was a progressive deeply affected by the views of
Louis Brandeis. As SEC chairman, Douglas would decry the gravita-
tion of finance to New York City and the giant corporations' curse
of bigness, and encourage regional finance and "the small companies"
that have been "the backbone of this country's progress." He also
fully shared the Frankfurter-Landis commitment to the need for
technical expertise in the management of administrative agencies.

But Douglas had a more adversarial conception of the role of the
SEC than had Landis. In his first press conference as chairman,
Douglas would emphasize that the SEC should be "what I might call
'the investor's advocate.' We have got brokers' advocates; we have
got Exchange advocates; we have got investment banker advocates;
and we are the investor's advocate." Douglas's hostility to "the
goddam bankers" was scathing and passionate. His first public bid
to succeed Landis as SEC chairman was made in a luncheon address
to New York City's Bond Club on March 24, 1937. The audience,
primarily New York City investment bankers, was reported to have
been "shocked" by Douglas's unrelenting attack on the noncompetitive conditions prevailing in the investment banking business.
Douglas pointedly insisted that competitive bidding for corporate
securities sales was necessary to stop "bankers . . . dispensing to
themselves the patronage of a monopoly," that investment banking
had severely disrupted "economic balance and stability" through
"overissuance and oversalesmanship" of securities, and that "the
key to the solution of current industrial problems is to be found in
large measure in a process of democratization of industry" by making corporate managements more responsive to labor, the investor,
and the consumer. Elsewhere Douglas would assail "financial ter-
mites," brand "the Morgan influence . . . the most pernicious one in
industry and finance today," and devote his professorial career to
exposing the abuses of "insider control."

Yet no matter how passionate were Douglas's public statements, he always exhibited a shrewd operational sense. Alone among New Deal reformers he had opposed the *"in terrorem"* liability provisions of the 1933 Securities Act as being self-defeating.

His *bel idéal* was industry self-regulation under the close supervision of a government agency. The concept seemed at odds with his Brandeis-like enthusiasm for economic and governmental deconcentration. But it was typical of Douglas to prefer a pragmatic solution, one that would be effective and enduring, to a philosophically pure solution. To Douglas, industry self-regulation under government supervision was profoundly different from the "cooperative" approach espoused by Kennedy and Landis. Industry, in Douglas's view, had to retain the initial responsibility for preventing fraud or unfairness, both because it could act swiftly and more subtly than a government bound by due process standards and could avoid "the bureaucratic blight" of a too intrusive government police force. But an agency like the SEC had to move aggressively when industry self-discipline failed to maintain high ethical standards.

In mechanical terms, Douglas outlined the approach he later applied to stock exchange and over-the-counter regulation in a 1935 letter to Willis Ballinger, describing how he would have regulated investment bankers:

> I proposed that the investment bankers and issuers be forced to police their own industries. I suggested a code authority for that purpose. I believed that the bankers were among the least socially minded groups in society. I had seen them either wink at or close their eyes to the practices of their brethren for years. My idea was to force them to approve or disapprove in public fashion the practices in the field. I felt this would accomplish two things: (1) it would help to clean up some of the worst practices which could not stand the light of public endorsement; and (2) it would make the bankers more vulnerable at the hands of the commission and other agencies of the government. They would so to speak be on the spot.[1]

The nineteen months of Douglas's chairmanship coincided with the political epigee of the Roosevelt administration. It began eight months after Roosevelt unveiled his court-packing plan, the worst miscalculation of his administration and a political fiasco from which the New Deal never fully recovered. Just before Douglas's SEC chairmanship commenced, the economy began the most serious recession since 1929–1933. Between May 1937 and June 1938, the Federal Reserve Board's index of total industrial production fell 33 percent. During the same general period, durable goods' production declined over 50 percent, profits 78 percent, payrolls 35 percent.

The rate of unemployment doubled. Almost six million people lost their jobs. "Roosevelt's recession" shattered the President's claim that the 1933–1937 recovery occurred "because we . . . planned it that way." The 1938 congressional elections were another New Deal debacle. The number of Republicans in the House of Representatives swelled from 88 to 170 and increased in the Senate by eight.[2]

Douglas's chairmanship of the SEC was to prove one of the few bright spots in the New Deal's waning years. Like the rest of the Roosevelt administration, Douglas began his chairmanship on the defensive. The 1937–1938 recession was accompanied by a stock market crash almost as severe as that of 1929. Stock prices plummeted 38 percent between August 14 and October 18, 1937, as compared with a price collapse of 45 percent between September 7 and November 13, 1929.[3] Leading financial spokesmen sought to blame the stock market collapse on the SEC. Most influential of the Commission's critics was Winthrop Aldrich, chairman of the Chase National Bank. On October 14, 1937, Aldrich strongly endorsed Charles Gay's thesis that SEC regulation had impaired the efficiency of the stock market, rendering it able to absorb "a greatly reduced volume of sales only with very serious breaks in prices."[4] Other critics of the SEC demanded a more conciliatory attitude toward the public utilities. They asked that the SEC not seek enactment of three bills drafted by Douglas's Protective Committee Study — the Lea Committee bill, the Chandler bankruptcy revision bill, and the Barkley trust indenture bill — and that the Commission generally adopt a less hostile and less "crusading" spirit toward business.[5] Within the Commission it was then widely believed that if a Republican were elected President in 1940, a serious attempt would be made to repeal the securities laws, or cripple their effectiveness with inhibitory amendments or unsympathetic Commission appointments. Abe Fortas, Douglas's closest aide, would insist that Douglas's greatest achievement as chairman was in changing business's attitude toward the SEC. "Douglas was primarily responsible for completing the acceptance of public responsibility by financial institutions, for persuading a reluctant Wall Street that it was an appropriate subject for legal mandates."[6] But Douglas's "revolution" or "domestication of Wall Street," as Fortas alternatively termed it, was by no means foreordained.

Roosevelt's initial response to the rising criticism of the SEC was an attempt to appease the business community. On October 25, 1937, he received Commerce Secretary Roper's Business Advisory Council.[7] The following day, after Douglas met with Roosevelt, Douglas informed reporters that matters were in a state of flux,[8] an elliptical way of conceding that Roosevelt had prevailed on Douglas to accept a Federal Reserve Board recommendation, which Douglas had vehemently opposed, lowering margin rates from 55 to 40 percent.[9] Six weeks later, simultaneous with the nomination of Douglas's long-time friend Jerome Frank, Roosevelt nominated John W. Hanes to be an SEC commissioner. Hanes was the first member of the New York Stock Exchange selected for the position. Although he was a reformer among Exchange members, his appointment was recognized as a conciliatory gesture; as Douglas put it in his autobiography, Hanes was chosen because of great pressure on Roosevelt "to 'protect' the interests of Wall Street."

Once on the Commission, Hanes spearheaded an in-house campaign to repeal those sections of the 1933 Securities Act that required a twenty-day waiting period, barred solicitation of orders before registration was effective, and required dealers to deliver a prospectus to investors before each new security's initial sale. Hanes's moves prompted Flynn to complain, in the title of a *New Republic* article, "Hoover Days Are Here Again."[10]

That Douglas under these circumstances was able to initiate a program of stock exchange reform primarily was a consequence of the deepening division among the New York Stock Exchange's members. That Douglas's reform program succeeded as completely as it did was the result of the Richard Whitney embezzlement scandal. Richard Whitney's self-destruction by now is.a better than thrice-told tale.[11] Its psychology and the class significance have been analyzed by commentators whose views ranged from those of John Brooks and John Kenneth Galbraith to those of Ferdinand Lundberg. But what has not been examined is the way in which Douglas used the Whitney scandal to restructure the governance of the New York Stock Exchange and to complete, to a large degree, the SEC's reform of corporate finance.

The events leading to stock exchange reform began in August 1937, when Charles Gay published the New York Stock Exchange annual report accusing the SEC and other federal regulatory bodies of endangering the securities market. Gay's report ended the appearance of SEC–New York Stock Exchange "harmony" that had prevailed since the creation of the Commission by abruptly spurning James Landis's effort to negotiate a rule at least partially segregating exchange floor members.

The looming confrontation led Paul Shields, E. A. Pierce, John Hanes, and other leading commission brokers who had maneuvered Gay's election in 1935 to break with Gay. By August 1937, the securities brokerage business was badly sagging. Bond-trading in

1937 was to reach its lowest level, with two exceptions, since 1918. In August 1937 new securities issuances were running at a rate barely 50 percent of a year before. In the vernacular, "grass was growing on Wall Street" and "the market was dead." Brokers were asking, "How can we keep from starving to death?" The Shields-Pierce faction insisted that only the appearance of cooperation between the SEC and Wall Street could rebuild investor confidence. Shields had been furious when Gay rationalized his uncompromising rejection of Landis's partial segregation initiative as unavoidable, since the floor traders and specialists associated with Richard Whitney's Old Guard commanded a majority of the Exchange's Governing Committee. Having labored to deprive Whitney of the Exchange presidency in 1935, the Shields-Pierce faction made no attempt to hide its bitterness that Whitney continued to dominate the Exchange through a factotum.[12]

At his first press conference, Douglas emphasized his intent to confront the NYSE by repeatedly asserting that the SEC would "proceed immediately on a course of swift and direct action where the facts justify it," coupling to this implied threat a none-too-subtle signal: "I should think that the best elements in finance . . . would find here the fullest cooperation." On October 16, Shields and Pierce journeyed to Washington to respond to Douglas's implicit invitation with an explicit invitation of their own: Would the SEC back them in a fight to reorganize the Exchange? Douglas, flanked by fellow commissioners Robert Healy and George Mathews, promised full support. Joseph Kennedy, on whom Douglas then heavily relied for advice and communications with the White House, also agreed and soon informed Shields of Roosevelt's support. To symbolize Roosevelt's commitment, Douglas, Kennedy, and Shields made a well-publicized trip to Hyde Park and met with the President the following week.

At Shields's initiative, the SEC began negotiations with the Exchange in an effort to restore a cooperative relationship.[13] Three matters dominated the next month's discussions. First, Douglas's insistence that the management of the Exchange had to be removed from the Old Guard's control and placed in the hands of a paid president with his own professional staff. Second, Douglas's threat that unless the Exchange agreed to reorganization, the Commission would impose new trading rules. And third, the SEC's insistence that the Exchange draft a letter to the Commission formally requesting reorganization discussions and including a paragraph acknowledging that the Commission had not been responsible for the 1937 market break. To the Commission, retraction of Gay's accusation was critical. With the market in a near-collapse, Douglas feared that Congress would investigate Gay's charges to see whether they could be corroborated. This could lead to the repeal of some of the Commission's powers. At the very least, it would complicate lobbying for new enabling legislation. Throughout the discussions, Douglas emphasized his belief that the Exchange had failed to make and enforce effective antimanipulation rules. To substantiate this belief, early in October Douglas had instructed the SEC's New York regional office to examine the records of over a hundred Exchange members to determine the extent to which floor member trading had accelerated the market's steep decline between September 7 and 25, 1937, through short sales or concerted activity.[14] Whether Douglas directly discussed the regional office's study in his negotiations or not, the extent of the SEC investigation alone implied that unless the Exchange retracted the criticism made by Gay, the SEC was prepared to publish a report blaming the market's abrupt decline on floor member trading.

On November 22, 1937, the negotiations collapsed. Although as many as twenty draft letters for the Exchange to forward publicly to the Commission were prepared by SEC and Exchange lawyers, the Exchange's Old Guard, which dominated the Law and Governing committees, refused to commit themselves to a paid president or to language exonerating the SEC from responsibilty for the 1937 market crash.

The following day, Douglas, with the unanimous approval of the Commission, issued a press release strongly implying the nature of new trading rules that the SEC would issue unless the New York Stock Exchange committed itself to reorganization.

The first paragraph succinctly made public Douglas's private threat. The Commission had reached a point where it had to decide whether to continue "the past policy of leaving to the Exchanges much of the regulation of their own business" or to seek "an immediate and more pervasive administration directly by the Commission of all phases of Exchange business coming within the purview of the Securities Exchange Act of 1934":

> Operating as private-membership associations, exchanges have always administered their affairs in much the same manner as private clubs. For a business so vested with the public interest, this traditional method has become archaic. The task of conducting the affairs of large exchanges, especially the New York Stock Exchange, has become too engrossing for those who must also run their own businesses. And it may also be that there would be greater public confidence in exchanges (and the prices made thereon) which recog-

nized that their management should not be in the hands of professional traders but in fact, as well as nominally, in charge of those who have a clearer public responsibility.

In Douglas's view, the conflicts of interest of the professional floor traders created problems more "fundamental" than archaic governance. Describing at length the results of the regional office's study of Exchange member trading in September and October 1937, Douglas implied "that members of the Exchange trading for their own account — particularly the specialists — either create the daily price fluctuations or else contribute materially to their severity" specifically by accentuating a "declining market by short-selling for speculative profit." The regional office's study of trading in selected leading securities on the New York Stock Exchange then was summarized to document "that short-selling represented as much as 31 percent of the total trading in one of these market leaders and constituted almost a quarter of the trading in . . . five leading stocks. Of this amount 46 percent, or almost half of the entire volume of short sales, was that done by members for their own accounts." Strongly suggesting a willingness to limit or abolish most members' floor trading for their own accounts and severely to restrict short-selling, Douglas argued:

> These figures as a group are a challenge to the validity of the common assertion that the existence of the specialist and the floor trader is justified on the basis of their stabilizing influence on the market, and their resultant benefits to the members of the public who enter the market. In a market in which there is such an enormous public interest — in which not only 300,000 small traders but 10,000,000 investors have a stake, it is essential that no element of the casino be allowed to intrude and that all such elements be obliterated.[15]

Douglas's November 23 press release soon achieved its desired effect of shocking the New York Stock Exchange into reorganization. This was not the consequence of Douglas's tough words alone. Tough words can always be answered in kind. Rather, President Gay and much of the Old Guard realized how much more financially expensive SEC-imposed trading rules and a public feud with the Commission would be than reorganization. No one after the issuing of the release could seriously believe that Douglas, like his predecessor Landis, was bluffing when he threatened to impose new rules. This reality rendered all but irrelevant the Old Guard's confidence that the 1940 presidential election would eliminate "the SEC problem." For over three years they might first have to live with Douglas. And Douglas had made obvious that the rules the SEC might impose could abolish or substantially reduce much of the Exchange's floor members' business. Nor was a public confrontation with the SEC likely to eliminate this risk. The Shields-Pierce faction was determined to undercut any further attacks by Gay on the Commission. Moreover, it was inconceivable that Douglas would have made so threatening a statement without assurances of Roosevelt's support.

Six days after Douglas's press release was issued, Gay capitulated, not so much to the SEC as to the Shields-Pierce reform faction of Exchange members. Responding "in the friendliest spirit, and in the firm belief that cooperation between the Exchange and the Commission is essential," Gay promised to begin reorganization by appointing "a special committee to study this whole matter and to report as promptly as possible."[16] *The New York Times* published its belief that Gay's committee was a public relations gimmick, commenting cynically, "November 9, 1940, is the logical date for the report."[17] But Gay was sincere. On December 10, 1937, he appointed a nine-man committee "to consider all aspects of a further development of the organization and administration of the Exchange, including, among others, the advisability of making the presidency a salaried office, of transferring greater administrative responsibility to executives, and of making the function of standing committees supervisory rather than administrative." The committee's membership was most notable for its failure to include a single Exchange member associated with Whitney's Old Guard. Instead, the Exchange's future organization was placed in the hands of three corporate executives: Carle Conway, chairman of the board of Continental Can, known to favor Exchange reorganization, Kenneth Hogate, president of the *Wall Street Journal*, and Thomas McInnerney, president of National Dairy; three current Exchange members, one of whom, thirty-year-old William McChesney Martin, Jr., had made no secret of his reform sentiments; and three "outside" members, Adolf Berle, who had been a charter member in Roosevelt's brains trust and was an enthusiastic supporter of Douglas, Trowbridge Callaway, an investment banker who was then president of the Better Business Bureau of New York, and John Prentiss, a partner in Hornblower and Weeks, who had once been president of the Investment Bankers Association. Four days later Conway was named chairman of the committee and immediately traveled to Washington to solicit Douglas's advice and to promise a report by the end of January.[18] Ganson Purcell, director of the SEC's Trading and Exchange Division, soon delivered to the Conway Committee an outline of the Commission's recommendations, most of which subsequently were adopted. The SEC recommended proportional representation on the Board of Governors of the various classes of members "(such as specialists, commission brokers, etc.), each such class to be entitled to representation on the Committee in the ratio which it bears to the entire body of members." This was meant to increase considerably the power of the underrepresented commission brokers. To provide the Exchange "with a degree of executive efficiency of as nearly a disinterested nature as possible," the Purcell outline next provided "for a full-time salaried president with a background of executive and business experience, who should not be, or have been, a member of the Exchange . . . or in any way engaged in the securities or banking business." Additionally, "all standing committees of the Exchange should be provided with expert staffs competent to discharge the functions and duties assigned to the committee," the size of the Governing Committee should be reduced to make it more effective, and consideration given to naming one, two, or more industrial representatives to the Governing Committee.[19] The SEC recommendations, in aggregate, were formulated to create a checks and balance system within the Exchange, with a disinterested professional staff and a brokerage house governing board majority intended to prevent the floor members from engaging in manipulation or sharp trading, which might jeopardize public confidence in the integrity of the Exchange.

The very composition of the Conway Committee ensured that its report would recommend a substantial reorganization of Exchange governance. But precisely because Gay had excluded Old Guard representatives from the Conway Committee, the reception a reform report would be accorded by the Exchange's Old Guard–dominated Governing Committee was less predictable. Cognizant of the Exchange floor members' general hostility to reorganization, on January 24, 1938, the SEC forcefully indicated what type of trading rules it was likely to adopt if the Conway Committee report was rejected. Invoking its own rule-making authority, the Commission significantly limited short sales in a declining market by requiring each short sale to be made at a price above the last transaction in the security. This precluded floor members from accentuating general market declines by the systematic short sale of leading securities. The short-sale rule was the first that the SEC imposed, rather than persuading the Exchange to issue as its own trading rule. It also was the first trading rule promulgated without any prior consultation with the New York Stock Exchange, a distinct departure from the "cooperative" policy of predecessor chairmen Kennedy and Landis.[20]

Three days later the Conway Committee issued its report. Although painstakingly inoffensive in its phrasing, the report's recommendations represented a nearly complete adoption of the reorganization proposals earlier urged by the SEC. Ultimate governing power was to be removed from the existing Old Guard–dominated fifty-member Board of Governors and vested in a reconstituted thirty-two-member board. The new board's electoral rules were meant to ensure that it would be controlled by the commission house brokers. Besides the Exchange president and the Board of Governors' chairman, three of the new board members would be public representatives and twelve would be nonmember partners of firms doing a brokerage business for the public. Thus, the Old Guard faction of floor traders and specialists would be eligible to seek election only to the minority of fifteen slots on the board reserved for New York Stock Exchange members. But they could not secure even all of these slots, for the Conway Report insisted that "these governors should be selected with due regard to the various interests represented in membership." The most important function of the reconstituted Board of Governors was to select a full-time paid president, who would serve as the Exchange's chief executive officer and "be the point of contact with governmental agencies and the general public." The president was to have his own staff and general responsibility for public relations. To further ensure commission house broker control of the future governance of the Exchange, additional recommendations guaranteed that the brokers would be a majority of the Nominating Committee, which selected members of the Board of Governors. If adopted, the Conway Report was intended to end the Old Guard's historic control of the New York Stock Exchange. Exchange governance no longer would be dominated by floor traders and specialists who traded largely for their own accounts. Control of the Exchange was to be transferred to the commission house brokers who regularly transacted business for the public, not to the SEC.[21]

This was the crucial point in the Conway Committee scheme. It was soon explicitly endorsed by Douglas as "showing wisdom and courage in an effort to solve a perplexing problem."[22] By choosing to reconstitute Exchange self-governance, not to supplant it, Douglas made a decisive compromise. In return for a more cooperative Exchange management, the SEC, as a practical matter, restricted its ability to impose rules. As the Conway Report explained, "a close working relationship" between the SEC and the Exchange was conditioned on the understanding that "standards of conduct must be largely self-executed, rather than imposed." Subsequently this would prove a highly expensive compromise. The SEC's deference to Exchange rule-making in the two decades after World War II would result in the Commission long ignoring the costs to investors of the Exchange's fixed brokerage commission rate structure. But in early 1938, with the Conway Committee plan for Exchange governance in effect, the SEC had the security of knowing that regardless of how the 1940 elections turned out, the Exchange's governors would be sympathetic to the Commission's existence. Had the SEC instead sought more direct control of the Exchange, it would have united all factions of the Exchange in a general opposition that could have proved effective after the 1940 elections. As it was, by choosing to support the leading commission brokers in their effort to take over the governance of the Exchange, the Commission received an immediate political dividend. The Conway Report concluded by publicly repudiating the accusations in Gay's 1937 annual report: "Neither the Stock Exchange nor the SEC," explained the report, "can be held responsible for major fluctuations in the price of securities. These depend on fundamental business and economic conditions."

* * *

The Exchange's Board of Governors adopted the Conway Committee's report on January 31, 1938, a mere four days after its publication. By late February, a three-man committee, named by Charles Gay and comprising Conway Committee secretary William McChesney Martin, Jr., former Exchange president E. H. H. Simmons, and commission broker Charles Harding, had drafted proposed constitutional amendments based on the report.[23] With ratification of the amendments inevitable, Douglas undoubtedly considered his immediate effort to reform the New York Stock Exchange substantially complete. By a shrewd combination of public and private pressure, he had enabled the Pierce-Shields faction of commission brokers to take over management of the Exchange. He did intend to bargain with the Exchange's new governors on such "fundamental" problems as those associated with floor traders, but his immediate priority was to re-establish a harmonious relationship.

It was then that the Whitney scandal broke. During the afternoon of March 7, 1938, Exchange president Gay telephoned Douglas that he would arrive in Washington that evening. With him would be Howland Davis, chairman of the Exchange's Disciplinary Committee. They had a matter of importance to discuss with Douglas that could not be explained over the telephone. At approximately eight o'clock that evening Douglas met Gay and Davis at the Carleton

Hotel. Douglas was informed that shortly before Gay and Davis had left New York City, the Exchange's Board of Governors had held a special meeting and voted charges of misconduct against Richard Whitney. Although they were not yet sure of the full extent of Whitney's illegal activities, they had heard evidence that Whitney had embezzled or unlawfully pledged securities belonging to the New York Stock Exchange Gratuity Fund (which paid $20,000 to the heirs of each Exchange member on his death) and at least two customers. A public hearing before the Exchange's Board of Governors was scheduled for March 17.

At 10:05 the next morning, Robert L. Fisher, the secretary of the Exchange, unexpectedly rang the gong that suspends trading. As puzzled Exchange members crowded around the rostrum, Charles Gay read a letter from Richard Whitney and Company that stated, in its entirety, "We regret to advise you of our inability to meet our engagements." Gay tersely announced that the Whitney firm had been suspended for insolvency, but he could not bring himself to state publicly that Whitney had been involved in criminal misconduct. Immediately after Gay hurried from the rostrum, an Exchange press release was distributed. It began, "In the course of an examination of the affairs of Richard Whitney & Company, the Committee on Business Conduct discovered on March 1, 1938, evidence of conduct apparently contrary to just and equitable principles of trade and on Monday, March 7, 1938, at 1:30 P.M., presented to a special meeting of the Governing Committee charges and specifications." That sentence meant that Whitney was not only bankrupt, but allegedly dishonest. Two journalists reported, "There was a dead silence, then a wild babble of voices." Market prices jolted sharply lower; then trading in the afternoon all but ceased.

The immediate effect of the Whitney scandal was momentous. It was as if the floor had dropped out from under Wall Street. Chester Lane, SEC assistant general counsel, was in San Francisco to give a speech the day the scandal broke.

> You could see the change overnight in the attitude of the San Francisco financial community [he recalled]. They saw the handwriting on the wall. This was not a fraud in securities practice; it was not financial immorality of the kind which the SEC was set up to eliminate; it was nothing but out-and-out stealing by the most respected and prominent of all the figures of the financial world in the country . . . You could see a deepening sense of gloom over just those few days in the faces of the people I was meeting. They knew Douglas was preparing to buck, and they knew now that he was going to be successful.[24]

After the scandal broke, events began to move with dizzying rapidity. On March 9, 1938, Richard Whitney issued a statement assuming personal responsibility for all "actions [that] have been wrong."[25] The next day New York County district attorney Thomas E. Dewey personally arrested Richard Whitney and indicted him for grand larceny and misappropriating $105,000 of securities from a trust fund established by his late father-in-law. Within twenty-four hours, New York State's attorney general secured a second grand larceny indictment, charging Whitney with the theft of $153,200 of securities from the New York Yacht Club, of which Whitney was treasurer. By March 17, Whitney had pleaded guilty to both indictments and had been expelled from the New York Stock Exchange by unanimous vote.[26]

In his memoirs, Douglas would describe Roosevelt as close to tears when informed that his fellow Groton graduate had pleaded guilty to larceny. "Not Dick Whitney!" Douglas recalled he exclaimed. "Dick Whitney — Dick Whitney," Roosevelt repeated. "I can't believe it."[27]

Douglas's own reaction was totally without sentiment. The scandal offered him and the SEC a once-in-a-lifetime opportunity. As long as Douglas could protract and publicize the revelations of the Whitney scandal, he would neutralize the ability of the financial community to oppose SEC efforts further to reform the Exchange or seek additional enabling legislation. Douglas immediately seized this opportunity. Within minutes of being informed by Charles Gay on March 7 of Whitney's defalcations, Douglas had directed Commissioner John W. Hanes and General Counsel Allen Throop to initiate an investigation of Whitney. A formal investigative order was voted by the full Commission the next morning, forty-five minutes before Gay made the first public disclosure of the scandal.

Although Richard Whitney, the New York Stock Exchange, and Thomas Dewey were eager to end the scandal as quickly as possible on the basis of Whitney's repeated assertion that "none of my partners, none of my business associates or connections, in fact no one but myself has or had any responsibility," Douglas was determined to show that Whitney's conduct was not just that of a single self-destructive individual; it also implicated other financiers, in particular J. P. Morgan, Jr., in whose firm Richard Whitney's brother, George, was a partner.

On March 22, 1938, Douglas wired Dewey and the state attorney general's office to request a delay in Whitney's sentencing so that the SEC could complete "an investigation of all phases of the circumstances which resulted in the insolvency of Richard Whitney & Company and the indictments of Richard Whitney."[28]

Since the Justice Department was seeking to develop a third indictment against Whitney based on criminal violations of the federal securities laws, none of the other four SEC commissioners initially agreed with Douglas that public hearings should be held. At six consecutive Commission meetings in early April, Douglas argued that the need to build public interest in new financial safeguards restricting Exchange members outweighed any possible prejudice to Whitney's rights if he did face a third criminal indictment. Douglas's argument was strengthened by the celerity of District Attorney Dewey and the state attorney general. In their race to the courthouse, both had omitted to indict Whitney for the theft of funds from the New York Stock Exchange Gratuity Fund, yet the SEC attorneys conducting a private investigation already were convinced that this was the most serious Whitney misconduct.[29] On April 6, 1938, the SEC unanimously ordered a public hearing "to examine the circumstances surrounding the failure of the firm of Richard Whitney and Company," stating that the primary purpose of the hearing would be to enable the Commission to recommend additional rules, regulations, or legislation. To preserve the ability of the Justice Department subsequently to bring criminal indictments, the Commission took the unusual step for a legislative hearing of permitting counsel for each witness to conduct cross-examination and present exculpatory evidence.[30]

For fourteen hearing days between April 8, 1938, and June 28, 1938, SEC attorneys publicly examined fifty-two witnesses, focusing on the knowledge or complicity of other Exchange members in Whitney's misconduct.[31] It was shown that over a twelve-year period, Whitney had borrowed, without collateral, $6,172,800 from sixteen Exchange members, mostly to cover financial losses he experienced in disastrous investments in firms distilling applejack, marketing peat humus, and mining colloids. At least eighteen other individuals had refused to make loans. To one non–Old Guard Exchange member, this pattern of loans was evidence that Whitney was "broke and borrowing money all over the street." But almost no other Exchange member considered the loans a cause for official concern. Not until January 1938 did a single creditor demand repayment from Whitney. What made such forbearance suspect was the Gratuity Fund incident, which Dewey and the state attorney general failed adequately to investigate. Since 1935, Whitney had served as one of five elected trustees who managed the $2.5 million fund to provide death benefits to Exchange members. Whitney also served as the fund's broker. Beginning in February 1937, Whitney had retained some $900,000 of the fund's bonds entrusted to his care and misappropriated $221,508 in cash. On November 22, 1937, the failure of Whitney to return the fund's assets was brought to the attention of the other trustees by the fund's accountant. Promptly after the meeting, one of the trustees, Whitney's friend and predecessor as Exchange president, E. H. H. Simmons, requested that Whitney return the fund's cash and bonds. Since Whitney had pledged most of the misappropriated securities, he could not immediately comply. Desperate, on November 23 Whitney had called on his brother George to secure an emergency loan of $1,082,000. Whitney informed his brother that he had misappropriated the trust fund's assets. To save his brother, George Whitney had sought help from Thomas Lamont, the Morgan firm's managing partner, informing him of Richard Whitney's defalcations from the trust fund. George Whitney and Thomas Lamont delivered the $1,082,000 to Richard Whitney on November 24, enabling him to return the wrongfully pledged securities to the Gratuity Fund. Neither reported his knowledge of Richard Whitney's embezzlement to any responsible figure. Lamont later testified that he considered a report unnecessary, since Whitney's misappropriation was a "perfectly isolated thing," public testimony all but guaranteed to convey the impression that the House of Morgan considered itself above the law. Nearly as destructive of the Old Guard's reputation was the testimony of J. P. Morgan, Jr. Although he apparently knew nothing of Richard Whitney's misappropriations, he gratuitously testified that he would not have informed Exchange authorities even if he had, which likely was the most self-destructive testimony volunteered in a federal hearing since Morgan earlier warned a Senate Committee, "If you destroy the leisure class, you destroy civilization."[32] The same week that the SEC's public hearings in the Whitney case ended, Joseph Alsop and Robert Kintner reported the obvious: "The end of Richard Whitney was the end of the Old Guard also."[33]

Douglas's campaign against the Old Guard continued for the balance of his term as chairman. Shortly after the SEC's report "In the Matter of Richard Whitney" was published in November 1938, Chester Lane, then the Commission's general counsel, forwarded a copy to the Department of Justice, directing its attention to the conduct of George Whitney and Thomas Lamont in late November 1937 "in [assisting] Richard Whitney in concealing his activities."[34] Although George Whitney and Thomas Lamont may have been guilty of the rarely prosecuted common law crime of misprision of a felony, the Justice Department declined to prosecute. In his autobiography, Douglas bitterly assailed Brien McMahon, the Justice Department attorney who refused to indict Whitney and Lamont, for the frequency with which McMahon "cast our reports into the dustbin." "I did not always know the reason," Douglas wrote, suggesting darkly, "Somewhere in the background was a powerful figure with money and political connections."[35]

The Commission employed more aggressive tactics in urging the New York Stock Exchange to discipline George Whitney, Thomas Lamont, and E. H. H. Simmons. The day the report on Whitney was published, Douglas forwarded a copy to the Board of Governors, directing its attention "specifically to the possibility of violation by persons who appeared and testified (of the section in the Exchange's constitution granting the board power) to suspend any member adjudged guilty of any act determined . . . to be 'detrimental to the interest or welfare of the Exchange.'"[36] By then, Douglas's close friend, University of Chicago president Robert Hutchins, had been selected as one of the three public representatives on the board. At the December 14, 1938, meeting of the governors, Hutchins urged that the Exchange conduct a public hearing to determine whether George Whitney, Lamont, or Simmons had violated the Exchange's constitution. Hutchins subsequently wrote:

> I said that I found the testimony of Mr. Simmons [that he had not suspected Richard Whitney's embezzlements in November 1937] incredible. I said that George Whitney and Mr. Lamont should not have permitted Richard Whitney to continue to perpetuate his frauds for almost four months after they knew of them. I raised the question whether the ties of blood or friendship were a sufficient excuse or one that could avail to prevent some disciplinary action by the Exchange.

Not one member of the board agreed with Hutchins. By a vote of 27–1 the board decided not to proceed, in part because of a statement from J. P. Morgan and Company asserting that in late November 1937 Exchange officials were aware of Richard Whitney's embezzlement.[37] The Morgan statement, quite simply, was false and contradicted earlier testimony given by George Whitney and Thomas Lamont.[38] Hutchins promptly resigned.

Douglas's reaction to what he termed the "Whitney white-wash" was Vesuvian. On December 18, he prepared a draft of a statement to be released by the Commission, including the accusation:

> When persons of outstanding wealth are involved, the Exchange cannot be trusted to do its own house-cleaning. Unhappily we are forced to conclude that discipline by the Exchange authorities of its own

members will be exerted only if the offending person is of relatively little importance, that there is, so far as the Exchange is concerned, one law for the very powerful or wealthy and another for those of little wealth and influence.

Douglas recommended that the SEC consider

> [reopening] the Whitney hearing to consider the following evidence: (a) The assertion in the Morgan press release that the Exchange authorities knew, in November 1937, of Richard Whitney's embezzlement. (b) The reasons for the Board's recent determination to take no action. (c) The bases of Hutchins's resignation. (d) What new rules by the Exchange or by us are required, or what new legislation is needed, to prevent a repetition of such a white-wash.[39]

Since the publication of such a statement would have discredited the NYSE reform government that Douglas had helped elect eight months before,[40] the SEC instead issued a brief reassurance that "the action on the Whitney case has not caused a change in the cooperative program which we launched," ambiguously adding that "the problem of better coordination and allocation of the policing and disciplinary functions between the Exchange and the Commission" later could be "constructively explored."[41]

Douglas's fury did not subside. His last major action as chairman was to persuade Roosevelt to name Robert Hutchins as his successor. This would have been a symbolic act almost as humiliating to the Exchange's reform government as the unpublished December 18 draft statement. Hutchins declined. To many, including some senior officers of the SEC, Douglas's relentless pursuit of the Old Guard was unnecessarily vindictive.[42]

Yet it was exactly Douglas's reputation for uncompromising toughness that made possible the 1938 reform of the New York Stock Exchange. Kennedy's "cooperative approach" had moved the Exchange but little. Landis's patient negotiation had resulted in stalemate. It was Douglas's exploitation of the political differences among the Exchange members and the Whitney scandal that got things done. Douglas himself would justify his approach in purely operational terms. "Political and economic power only rarely diverge," he once explained to Milton Katz, a Landis executive assistant, "and when they do, you must move rapidly."[43]

The second phase of Douglas's efforts to reform the Exchange began within hours of Richard Whitney's expulsion on March 17, 1938. That afternoon the constitutional revisions inspired by the Conway Committee were adopted by a vote of 1013–22.[44] Five weeks before, the SEC had issued a press release denying that it had

approved or sponsored any person to be the Exchange's new president.[45] The Whitney scandal eliminated the need for further public
discretion. On March 19, Douglas made abundantly clear his electoral preferences. In a press release "categorically" denying the improbable rumor that the SEC "favored the retention in the government of the Exchange of representatives of the group which
formerly was in control," Douglas emphasized that their retention
"may seriously endanger the plans of the forward-looking majority
of the Exchange membership to extricate the Exchange from the difficulties from which it is striving to emerge . . . the reorganization of
the Exchange should not be a mere sham but thoroughgoing
and complete in actual fact. The former philosophy of Exchange
government should be abandoned not merely on paper but in
practice."[46]

On April 11, 1938, the Exchange's Nominating Committee
named a genuine reform slate for election to the reconstituted Board
of Governors. Old Guard representatives were almost totally excluded. Of the thirty-two chairmen and vice chairmen of the seventeen Exchange standing committees in existence before the Whitney scandal, only three were nominated for re-election to the Board
of Governors. Even former Exchange presidents Simmons and Gay
were denied customary "elder spokesmen" nominations. Within a
month all twenty-eight of the reform slate's nominees had won
unopposed election to the Board of Governors. Paul Shields, the
leader of the reform slate, soon claimed a slot on the three-man
committee to name a new full-time Exchange president as well as
the chairmanship of the new Committee on Public Relations. Like
his Exchange ally Pierce, Shields was convinced that the revival of
investor confidence required the selection of a president who symbolized the same kind of probity that Judge Kenesaw Mountain
Landis had brought to baseball after the 1919 Chicago "Black Sox"
corruption scandal. As many as two hundred candidates were considered by Shields's presidential selection committee before it determined to retain its interim figure of self-rectitude, temporary president William McChesney Martin, Jr., as president.[47]

Martin unquestionably was a publicist's dream. Profoundly reli-
gious, he did not smoke, drink, or gamble, and was wont to refer to
the Exchange as a "savings bank for securities." At thirty-one, he
was a symbolic antidote to the Whitney scandal. A plethora of magazine feature articles soon explained to readers that Martin had been
a tennis champion at Yale, lived a spartan existence in New York
City's Yale Club, often eating at automats, had been shocked by the
machinations of floor traders when he first joined the Exchange,

voted for Roosevelt in 1932, and never missed a Broadway play, although, true to form, he always sat in the balcony to save money and would repair to Sardi's afterward to drink a hot chocolate. A *Time* cover story accordingly dubbed him Mr. Chocolate. *Collier's* hailed "the Lamb of Wall Street." Even so cynical a reporter as John T. Flynn wrote: "It can happen here . . . He does not belong to any of the swanky New York clubs, does not fraternize with powerful bankers and promoters, has never been on a participation list, does not play the stock market himself, does not move about in altitudinous New York society, and aside from his time in the theatre, the tennis court and church, he spends most of his spare moments in his room as a student."

William McChesney Martin, Jr., indeed was a serious student of economics, and for this reason won Douglas's support. He was the son of the president of the St. Louis Federal Reserve Bank. After graduating from Yale, he had briefly worked for his father as a Federal Reserve Bank examiner before joining A. G. Edward & Sons, a commission brokerage house, as head statistician. In May 1931 he had moved to New York City to work as A. G. Edward's floor broker while taking graduate courses in economics at Columbia and the New School of Social Research. In 1935, he was a successful reform candidate for the Exchange Board of Governors. Charles Gay, among others, admired his abilities and named him both to the Conway Committee and to the three-man committee that translated the Conway Committee's recommendations into amendments to the Exchange's constitution. Martin was widely credited with having written much of the Conway Report. Impressed, Paul Shields had asked Martin to head the reform slate in April 1938 as the nominee for chairman.

Like Douglas, Martin viewed the Exchange "as a vital and indispensable part of the national economy," with no other legitimate purpose. "The days of the Exchange as a private business are past," he would explain in July 1938. The Exchange is a "public service institution [that] will be operated as a public business." From another man, these words might have been hollow platitudes. Martin understood their operative meaning in the same sense that Douglas did. To Flynn — whom Whitney and the Old Guard loathed — Martin would explain, "I suggest that, for any who fear too much government intervention, the correction lies in themselves and their own deeds." To avoid SEC imposition of rules, the Exchange had to "demonstrate by action . . . [that] it would be unnecessary for government to interfere." Douglas did not demand Martin's selection as Exchange president, as he pointedly had demanded the exclu-

sion of the Old Guard from the Exchange's reconstituted Board of
Governors. But he did openly campaign for Martin. On May 13,
1938, Douglas had brought Martin, the new chairman of the Board
of Governors, to meet President Roosevelt, and had stood silently
while Martin informed reporters, "I am convinced as a result of
my meeting with the President and Mr. Douglas, that if we can
get together on these problems we can make the New York Stock
Exchange the national public institution it ought to be." Then,
shortly before Shields's presidential selection committee reached
its climactic deliberations, Douglas concluded a meeting with
Exchange representatives by throwing an arm around Martin's
shoulders and exclaiming, "Here's a fellow I can really work
with!"[48]

With a reform Board of Governors elected, Douglas used the occasion of a May 20, 1938, dinner honoring the Conway Committee to
outline the balance of the SEC's program for Exchange reform. It
was an address simultaneously calculated to build public support for
the Exchange's first reform government and to pressure it to complete the elimination of the "casino element" from "what should be
an old-fashioned, open auction." "Our enemy," Douglas stated, "is
not ourselves but deep economic problems. This government needs
you and you need this government in attacking those problems. Let
us not be deluded into mistaking personalities for issues." Both
"healthy capitalism" and "healthy democracy" required "that honest business [have] opportunity to make honest and substantial
profits." But the Exchange best aided the financing of honest business when it was "above suspicion. To satisfy the demands of investors there must be in this great market place not only efficient
service but also fair play and simple honesty. For none of us can
afford to forget that this great market can survive and flourish only
by grace of investors." To Douglas, the course of immediate action
was clear. The Exchange would have to assume the primary burden
of policing manipulative trading, withdraw the trading advantages
of insiders, and prevent broker misuse of customer funds. If the
Exchange would eliminate these last sources of irritation, Douglas
promised that the SEC would not only be the investors' advocate,
but also "your advocate."[49]

In private "round-table" conferences with Martin, the ubiquitous
Paul Shields, and other Exchange representatives, beginning on May
18, 1938, Douglas bargained hardest for two principal concerns. To
protect customers from the kind of losses resulting from broker
misconduct or insolvency illustrated by the Whitney scandal, Douglas proposed the establishment of a brokers' trust company to han-

dle "those aspects of the brokerage business having to do with receipts and deliveries of securities, receipts and payments of cash, the
obtaining of credit for security purchases, [and] clearing of securities." Both in his May 20 speech honoring the Conway Committee
and in the private negotiations, Douglas emphasized that a brokers'
trust institution was his first priority. In late August, he deferred
publication of Part II of the report on Whitney for what turned out to
be a two-month period to give Martin and Shields time to use their
"best efforts" to persuade the Exchange "to bring about the adoption, first, of a central depository for customers' funds and securities
and, secondly, of a trust institution which would assume, subject to
customers' order, full control of customers' funds and securities."
The central depository had "great appeal" to Douglas because "it
would simplify the [SEC's] task of making inspections of the margin
accounts of our far-flung brokerage community and also the handling of the other details which are the necessary incidents of enforcement or self-regulation," as well as reduce or eliminate the
risks associated with brokers "holding and commingling of the
funds and securities of their customers." To underline how necessary Douglas considered the brokers' trust institution, he bluntly
informed Martin and Shields that he would "promptly release the
Whitney report" if their efforts to bring about a trust institution
proved unsuccessful and "might find it necessary to recommend to
the Congress a program of legislative action, segregating the brokerage and banking functions or subjecting brokerage firms to the
same type of suspension as banks."

With considerably less vehemence Douglas also proposed complete segregation of all floor members of the Exchange. Douglas
urged both that floor members be limited to performing the function
either of broker or dealer and that specialists be permitted to perform only dealers' functions. Since this proposal went well beyond
Landis's earlier efforts to secure partial segregation of floor members, and also exceeded the recommendations of the Douglas Commission's Trading and Exchange Division, it apparently was meant
to be a bargaining chip with which to induce the Exchange's floor
members to support the brokers' trust institution. As such, it
proved only modestly effective.[50] After five months of negotiation,
the SEC and the Exchange agreed to an elaborate compromise.[51] In
return for the Commission's not then imposing any segregation
rule, the Exchange's Board of Governors on October 26, 1938,
adopted a thirteen-point reform program. The key features of the
program committed the Exchange to more frequent and detailed
audits of member firms; prohibited brokers doing business with the

public from maintaining margin accounts; established a fifteen-to-one ratio between a broker's indebtedness and his working capital; required members to report all uncollateralized loans to other members; reported that the Exchange had hired Haskins & Sells, an accounting firm, to study the feasibility of a central depository; and encouraged each member firm to form a corporate affiliate to handle dealer and underwriter activities, as a compromise means of insulating brokerage customers from the risks inherent in underwriter and dealer operations.[52]

Nearly simultaneously, the SEC published "In the Matter of Richard Whitney." While praising the Exchange for "a constructive approach," the SEC publicly repeated its "opinion that full realization of effective regulation of the industry in the public interest is to be found in the establishment of trust institutions to assume the banking and custodial functions of the brokerage business." Although the SEC annual reports of the next two years were highly critical, the Exchange and leading commission house brokers, including Pierce and Shields, continued to oppose the brokers' trust institution because of its initial cost and tendency to disrupt the broker-customer relationship. In August 1939, an Exchange committee recommended an alternative program to protect brokerage customers; it required that customers' accounts be fully segregated and that the Exchange's examining force be increased and conduct audits on a surprise basis.[53]

When Douglas had first contemplated reform of the Exchange in September 1937, his paramount concern had been reducing insider manipulation. He had indicated his approach to the problem with the colorful phrase "You need a snoop to catch a jiggle."[54] Within thirteen months, the Douglas SEC put into effect reforms different from those Douglas had originally contemplated. Instead of floor segregation or a brokers' trust institution, he had forced the Exchange floor members to accept an in-house "snoop" in the form of a broker-dominated Board of Governors, a full-time president, and an increased Exchange disciplinary force. Over time the significance of these reforms dissipated. Within a few years after Douglas left the SEC, Exchange floor members again dominated Exchange governance. Repeatedly during the next three decades the SEC would attempt to abolish floor traders; in the late 1960s the need for a central stock depository would again be evident. Yet Douglas's "revolution in financial morality" should not be underestimated. Until Douglas and the Whitney scandal, the politics of the Exchange had been dominated by its concern to preserve the trading privileges of floor members. This concern has never abated. But after Douglas, the

Exchange exhibited a greater commitment to the philosophy of the
major brokerage houses, which emphasized the need to assure customers that they could invest safely on the New York Stock Exchange. In part, the enormous post–World War II expansion in securities trading occurred because Douglas-type reforms did reduce the
likelihood of manipulation on the New York Stock Exchange. When
a major stock market scandal next occurred, in the late 1950s, it
involved the American Stock Exchange, which Douglas's reform
efforts largely had ignored. The New York Stock Exchange's built-in
disciplinary system, backed by the SEC's enforcement attorneys,
has now operated for over four decades without a comparable floor
member scandal. This has been both a profoundly conservative and
a highly ironic achievement. As Douglas said during his May 20,
1938, address, he viewed "the aims of this government and the
objectives of business as wholly compatible." Both were committed
to an expanded private sector that would reduce the need for direct
government finance. Yet, ironically, the very toughness of SEC enforcement activities that reassured investors they could safely purchase securities has perennially caused the financial community to
fear and resent its government protector.

* * *

The Supreme Court's affirmance of Judge Mack's decision in the
Electric Bond and Share[55] case on March 28, 1938, gave Douglas an
early opportunity to employ the political benefits of the Whitney
scandal to toughen the Commission's enforcement of the Public
Utility Holding Company Act. Although Landis had unstintingly
endorsed the constitutional law defense of the act that resulted in
the *Electric Bond and Share* decision, he made plain within the
Commission his intention to pursue a conciliatory policy in enforcing the geographic integration provision, at one point expressing
concern for the preservation of the SEC itself if the Commission
attempted to enforce the Holding Company Act too rigorously.[56]

While disagreeing with Landis's enforcement approach, Douglas
initially found the act as frustrating as Landis had. On the defensive
during the 1937 stock market crash, Douglas greeted the Second
Circuit Court of Appeals' November 8, 1937, affirmance of *Electric
Bond and Share* with the Landisian observation that the SEC would
"go more than half way to make it possible for the companies to
meet the standards prescribed by the Act."[57] Three months later, in
an address entitled "A Call for Leadership," Douglas appealed to
utility operating managers to free themselves from "the whiphand

of New York finance" and cooperate with the SEC.[58] The very nature of Douglas's appeal required him to stress voluntary action rather than strict SEC enforcement of the Holding Company Act.

The combination of the Supreme Court's decision in *Electric Bond and Share* and the Whitney scandal offered Douglas the opportunity to redirect the Commission's public utility enforcement program. At first, Douglas proceeded cautiously, trying to secure enforcement of Section 11 through a combination of aggressive speeches and voluntary industry compliance. It was only after Douglas's voluntary compliance approach had failed that he reorganized the leadership of the Public Utilities Division, making possible the SEC's 1940–1942 litigation, which ultimately led to the restructuring of the nation's public utility industry.

Within a week of the Supreme Court's *Electric Bond and Share* decision, every major utility system had registered with the SEC or had announced its intention to register.[59] This set the stage for a second showdown between the utility industry and the SEC over enforcement of the Holding Company Act. On April 20, Electric Bond and Share's chairman, C. E. Groesbeck, and the North American Company's J. F. Fogarty communicated to Douglas their intention to form a utility industry committee to negotiate enforcement of the act with the Commission.[60] Douglas assumed that the Section 11 death sentence provision, "is apt to be the major bone of contention." To prepare "for the onslaught," on April 26 Douglas requested that Commissioner Healy supervise a statistical survey of geographically integrated and disintegrated holding company systems to illustrate "the validity of the theory of Section 11."[61] The anticipated onslaught began within ten days. On May 5, executives from several of the largest utility systems joined Groesbeck and Fogarty in a written request to the SEC for a meeting to discuss enforcement of Section 11. In the crucial paragraph of their May 5, 1938, letter, Groesbeck and Fogarty implicitly promised utility industry cooperation with the SEC if the Commission would forgo rigorous enforcement of the death sentence provision. Describing their fellow utility officers' views, they explained: "These executives . . . expressed their belief that the fundamental principle of diversity of investment, which is represented here by both geographic location of operating properties and character of business served by them, is a very important factor in the raising of additional capital, and that such principle should be preserved in the public interest."[62] In a subsequent meeting with SEC commissioner Jerome Frank, Groesbeck went further and expressed the hope that "as the Commission worked with the industry and became familiar with its problems, the Commission would come to believe that the statute should be amended so as to preserve the principle of diversity of investment and that the Commission would then join with the industry in recommending to Congress an appropriate amendment to the statute to eliminate that part of Section 11 which is inconsistent with that principle."[63]

The day after Groesbeck's meeting with Frank, Douglas forwarded an icy letter to Groesbeck and Fogarty to correct any misapprehension the utility executives might have that Section 11 would be abandoned or not enforced. The statute, insisted Douglas, was capable of only one interpretation. It would be strictly enforced in accordance with its terms.[64]

A few weeks later, in an address to the American Bar Association, Douglas presented an uncompromising defense of the geographic integration concept. Comparing the financial reports of ten integrated utility systems and eight geographically "scattered" firms, he reported that the geographically integrated firms "were *less* vulnerable to business depression than the scattered or diversified systems," since they had experienced less severe declines in earnings between 1929 and 1934.

> If an investor wants diversification in his utility investments [explained Douglas], he can best get it by direct investment in a number of companies . . .
> To argue that the pattern of present-day holding-company systems should be maintained because of a "principle of diversity of investment" is to beg a basic question. Holding-company systems have not been organized upon any such scientific-sounding "principle" . . . In the roaring twenties and before, they were slapped together merely on the theory of putting together every utility property that the dominant interests could acquire. Diversity of risk was merely a slogan for the security salesman and not a standard for the promoter. Where it did exist, diversity of investment was frequently the more or less accidental result of a policy of acquiring properties, wherever located, mainly for the purpose of promoting the sale of equipment, of profiting from the sale of securities, or of realizing fees for financial, construction, or management services.[65]

On August 3, Douglas requested that sixty-six major public utility systems submit plans no later than December 1, 1938, describing what steps they intended to take to comply with Section 11 of the Public Utility Holding Company Act. Douglas's letter and a related press release offered to accept "tentative suggestions, plans, and programs," conceded that full geographic integration and corporate simplification would "take years," but emphasized, "to get on with our task we must insist on progress."[66]

Douglas's effort to secure voluntary compliance with Section 11 almost totally failed. Although nearly every utility system submitted a "plan" for geographic integration,[67] only a few of the utilities' integration proposals were to prove adequate.[68] The failure of the SEC's holding company voluntary compliance program brought to a head a long-simmering dispute within the SEC over the enforcement of the act. In return for Mathews's support in the New York Stock Exchange reorganization struggle, Douglas had elevated Mathews's associate, C. Roy Smith, to the directorship of the Public Utilities Division, while trying to administer the division through the assistant director, Douglas's protégé, Abe Fortas. With Commissioner Healy, the official "sponsor" of the division, personally loyal to Smith, clashes between Smith and Fortas soon became, in Commissioner Jerome Frank's word, "nasty." But Douglas long declined to resolve the dispute. As Frank would later write to Thomas Corcoran, "Bill had the problem of a general who doesn't want battles on all fronts — with dissension in the army." Although calling Douglas "a great general," Frank had come to believe that Smith was barely competent to lead the division and was frustrating enforcement of the act by communicating to the utilities his belief that there need not be strict compliance with Section 11. In November 1938, Frank forwarded a detailed memorandum to Healy, urging him to dismiss Smith. Although Healy shared the view of Douglas and Frank that there had to be strict enforcement of the act, he was greatly offended by Frank's memorandum, and protested that Smith's inadequacies as an administrator were mainly the consequence of "the failure of the Commission to support [Smith] fully," specifically assailing Fortas for directly communicating with the full Commission on occasion "without the knowledge of Smith."

When it became clear early in 1939 that Douglas's program of voluntary compliance with the geographic integration provision of the Holding Company Act had failed, Corcoran communicated to Douglas the President's "urgent request" that the SEC's Public Utilities Division be reorganized. By then, recalled Robert O'Brien, a "crisis atmosphere . . . had formed":

> Old faithful backers of the legislation were disappointed and disgruntled and talked about a congressional investigation to examine the reasons for the Commission's mismanagement and nonenforcement of the statute. Senator Norris, a mainstay of the statute, was

threatening repeal. Burton Wheeler and Sam Rayburn, whose names identified the act, were disappointed and complaining about what was being done and not being done with the act. The *Wall Street Journal*, *The New York Times*, the *New York Herald Tribune*, *Washington Post*, and *Washington Star* carried articles describing the desultory conditions in the division. Literally nothing had been accomplished. The staff was in a shambles, the morale was low, and a bitter split between the top officers hamstrung operations. By any measure it was a disastrous state of affairs.

On April 1, 1939, Douglas persuaded a reluctant Smith to agree to resign by the summer. Healy and Mathews voted against acceptance of the resignation, later making plain the intensity of their displeasure at the abruptness with which the resignation was arranged by voting against Jerome Frank's nomination to be Douglas's successor as SEC chairman.[69]

Smith's dismissal made possible effective enforcement of Section 11. To replace Smith, Douglas arranged for the appointment of Joseph Weiner and Robert O'Brien to lead the division. Joseph Weiner, who had been Mayor La Guardia's counsel for public utility litigation in New York City before serving at the SEC as special counsel to the Reorganization Division, was named director. Joining Weiner as associate director was Robert O'Brien, previously SEC assistant general counsel. Roger Foster, Fortas's "ablest lieutenant," remained. Weiner, O'Brien, and Foster, unlike Smith, were committed to the vigorous enforcement of the Holding Company Act. Their decision, supported by the Commission and Roosevelt, "to institute proceedings practically simultaneously against all the major [holding company] systems" beginning in early 1940, rather than to continue attempting to negotiate compliance with the act or proceed through test cases, proved to be the key to the effective enforcement of Section 11 of the Public Utility Holding Company Act.[70]

* * *

The Whitney scandal also eased passage of the 1938 Maloney Act amendments to the Securities Exchange Act, which led to the creation of the private National Association of Securities Dealers to police over-the-counter brokers and dealers. In this project, as in several others, Douglas built on studies initiated during Landis's chairmanship. As early as November 1935, Landis publicly had promoted "the organization of a self-disciplinary agency of dealers."[71] Douglas's contributions to the Maloney Act were tactical. Adopting Landis's approach to enforcement of O-T-C regulations, Douglas lobbied the bill through the Roosevelt administration and Congress within a few months after its introduction by rapidly recognizing what compromises were necessary to its passage and by exploiting the legislative opportunity created by the Whitney scandal.

The stock market crash and the Pecora hearings had severely embarrassed securities dealers. To restore their reputation, Adolf Berle in July 1933 urged the leading investment bankers to form a "Committee of Public Safety" and "be their brothers' keepers": "When it is realized that the reputation of their brothers is in the last analysis their own reputation, that their own life and death interests are bound up in the transactions of every member of their guild, it is plain that they have a quite definite personal interest, as well as a legitimate public interest, which must be served."[72] This view was shared by the Investment Bankers Association. Under the National Industrial Recovery Act, the association secured NRA-approved codes of fair competition and fair trade practice, allowing an Investment Bankers Code Committee to serve as the industry's semi-official policeman.[73]

With the NRA limping toward collapse in April 1935, the Investment Bankers Code Committee and the NRA requested that the SEC assume the duty of administering the provisions of the Investment Bankers Code.[74] Commissioner Robert Healy and SEC technical adviser Paul Gourrich opposed the SEC's "entangling itself with the cooperative efforts of the industry." Gourrich warned that the Commission's doing so would undermine its ability to pursue policies unacceptable to the securities industry:

> It is one thing to steer and inspire a cooperative body and another thing to be identified with it as an administrator. The Commission, if it were to become associated with the administration of the Code, would be in the position of serving the interests of the industry and, at the same time, trying to formulate rules to direct investment banking in accordance with its longer views, which at a given time might not be acceptable to the industry.[75]

After the *Schecter* decision sped the abolition of the NRA, the SEC encouraged the Investment Bankers Code Committee to form a permanent organization to "cooperate" with the SEC in "bringing about fair practices among investment bankers and eliminating fraud in the selling of securities."[76] The first attempt at securities industry cooperation with the Commission proved frustrating. In September 1936, leading investment bankers from such firms as J. P. Morgan, Kuhn, Loeb, and Goldman, Sachs formed the Investment Bankers Conference, Incorporated, to serve as a nationwide volun-

tary organization to police the over-the-counter markets, "standard-
ize fair business practices, and maintain high principles in the
investment banking business, aiming at ultimate development of
self-regulation in the securities business." The conference earlier
had received the blessing of the SEC and been approved by a national
meeting of over-the-counter brokers and dealers.[77] It proved to be an
ineffectual policeman. Only seventeen hundred of the country's six
thousand securities dealers ever joined. In 1937, the SEC sent a few
attorneys and accountants on a "flying survey" of three over-the-
counter areas outside the largest financial centers: Cleveland, Detroit, and the Pacific Northwest. Within a few months, thirteen
individuals were criminally convicted. Sixteen more were indicted,
seventeen other corporations and forty-one other individuals were
enjoined, and two firms expelled or obliged to withdraw from national securities exchanges, all for elementary violations of the securities laws. "It would be folly to imagine," Commissioner
Mathews later testified, "that the problem is less serious in other
parts of the country."[78]

Douglas remained committed to over-the-counter self-regulation.
Like Landis, Douglas believed it was "impractical, unwise, and unworkable" for the SEC directly to regulate the six thousand or so
o-t-c brokers and dealers trading in 1938.[79] Since they were not
centralized on a few stock exchange floors, but could "make a market" in an over-the-counter security anywhere in the country, "the
problem of direct government regulations of the over-the-counter
market," Mathews would explain, "is a little bit like trying to build
a structure out of dry sand. There is no cohesive force to hold it
together, no organization with which we can build, as authorita-
tively representing a substantial element in the over-the-counter
business."[80]

In December 1937, Douglas invited leaders of the investment
banking community to discuss means of better coordinating enforcement activities. At the meeting several bankers agreed with an
SEC proposal to amend the Securities Exchange Act to give voluntary associations like the Investment Bankers Conference an official
status similar to that of the organized exchanges "in order to enable
the associations to undertake effective programs of enforcement."[81]
Douglas soon emphasized to a congressional committee that if effective self-regulation of the securities exchanges was to succeed,
the SEC could not compromise its enforcement role, but should play
a residual role: "Government would keep the shotgun, so to speak,
behind the door, loaded, well oiled, cleaned, ready for use but with
the hope it would never have to be used."[82] Amplifying this theme

in a January 7, 1938, address to the Hartford Bond Club, Douglas urged allowing voluntarily organized over-the-counter associations "ample contractual powers over members to take a hand in enforcing the law." Self-regulation would have "unquestioned advantages" over direct SEC enforcement: "By and large, government can operate satisfactorily only by proscription. That leaves untouched large areas of conduct and activity; some of it susceptible of government regulation but in fact too minute for satisfactory control; some of it lying beyond the periphery of the law in the realm of ethics and morality. Into these large areas self-government, and self-government alone, can effectively reach."[83]

Virtually simultaneously, Connecticut senator Francis Maloney introduced SEC-drafted legislation to implement Douglas's approach to over-the-counter regulation. The Maloney bill permitted the formation of national associations of brokers or dealers if it appeared to the Commission that each association permitted all over-the-counter brokers and dealers (or all within specific geographic areas) the right to membership, assured democratic voting procedures, and enforced disciplinary rules to prevent fraud, promote just and equitable principles of trade, and "to perfect the mechanism of a free and open market" by forbidding price discrimination "between customers, or issuers, or brokers or dealers" and barring rules designed to permit the fixing of minimum profits or commission rates. The SEC's "shotgun in the closet" was emphasized. The Commission was given the power to review all disciplinary decisions, abrogate any association rule or request, then itself alter or supplement most rules.[84] In late January 1938, Douglas quickly secured Roosevelt's support with the prudent arguments that the Maloney bill would "afford . . . investors in the over-the-counter markets protection comparable to that afforded under the Exchange Act in the case of exchanges [at] a small fraction of the sum which would be necessary, should the alternative system of direct commission action be adopted."[85]

Negotiations with the securities industry proved considerably more difficult. Soon after Douglas's December 1937 meeting with the industry's leading investment bankers, both the Investment Bankers Association and the Investment Bankers Conference approved the Maloney bill "in principle."[86] In part, industry support was the consequence of a subsection that provided that if the Maloney Act conflicted with "any provision of any law of the United States," the Maloney Act "shall prevail." This subsection was intended to shield the governance of the over-the-counter markets from the reach of the antitrust laws, a protection that only an Act of Congress could provide a "self-regulatory" group.[87] Yet even this "sweetener" was insufficient to retain the Investment Bankers Association support. At Senate Banking Committee hearings on February 8, 1938, the association's president, Francis Frothingham, criticized the "inherently dangerous" powers delegated to the Commission. But with the considerably larger Investment Bankers Conference already having endorsed the bill, the Investment Bankers Association's legislative specialist, John Starkweather, conceded the futility of opposition to the entire Maloney bill by noting that the association's membership "almost unanimously" could accept the bill if the SEC would content itself with the power to abrogate securities association rules, rather than also seeking the power directly to promulgate rules regulating over-the-counter brokers' fraud, rates of commission, financial responsibility, and business solicitation. Since the power directly to promulgate over-the-counter rules was crucial to persuading brokers and dealers to join "voluntarily" a securities association, the SEC did not accept the association's offer. Ultimately, the association was able to persuade Congress to withhold from the SEC several minor powers, including the authority "to regulate the manner, method, and place of soliciting business."[88]

The SEC fared less well against a more potent political opponent. During the Roosevelt administration, no business lobby proved nearly as effective against the SEC as the nation's municipal securities issuers and municipal securities dealers. Strengthened by the appearance of defending local government, not big business, with political allies in both parties and almost every state, the municipal securities lobby was able to wrest exemption from the 1933 Securities Act and the 1934 Securities Exchange Act, and, as will be shown later in this chapter, virtually alone defeat the Lea Committee bill, the most significant defeat William Douglas experienced as an SEC commissioner.

When the municipal securities lobby began its campaign for exemption from the Maloney bill, Senator Maloney made a nationwide radio address to argue that the general pattern of exemptions for municipal securities dealers could be justified on no principled basis:

> What claim have municipal dealers to a holier-than-thou attitude? If they engage in fraudulent practices, should they escape regulation? If their acts are deceptive or manipulative, should not investors be protected against them also? Should not they be held to the same conservative standards of financial responsibility as other dealers? . . . The answers are obvious. If they are exempted from this type of regulation,

it would be the grossest form of discrimination against other dealers, fully as reputable, fully as honest, fully as competent as they.[89]

As was always the case during the New Deal, such logic proved unpersuasive. On March 1, 1938, the Senate Banking Committee voted 7–3 to exempt dealers in municipal securities from the Maloney bill.[90] This placed Douglas in a quandary. Commissioner Healy undoubtedly reflected the full Commission's belief when he publicly stated that the exemption for municipal securities dealers "smack[ed] of unfair competition."[91] But Douglas as SEC chairman always balanced ethical considerations with operational ones. By the spring of 1938 he had fully assimilated the advice Felix Frankfurter wrote in January 1934 to the considerably more idealistic Professor William Douglas: "The French proverb 'Let not the better be the enemy of the good' has marked application in the history of legislation."[92]

Douglas refused to allow the unfairness of the municipal securities dealer exemption to jeopardize passage of the Maloney bill. Soon after the Whitney scandal broke in early March, Douglas committed the SEC to seeking the bill's earliest possible enactment. No attempt was made to reverse the municipal securities dealer exemption on the Senate floor, and it passed the Senate on the unanimous consent calendar on March 31, 1938.[93] When the House Commerce Subcommittee considering the Maloney bill communicated to Douglas its preference for the Senate-passed municipal securities dealer exemption on April 29, 1938, "in order that the chances of the Bill's passing the House would not be prejudiced," the SEC drafted the necessary amendment. With only the few previously noted minor concessions to the Investment Bankers Association necessary for steering the Maloney bill through the House Rules Committee, the SEC draft was enacted and signed in June 1938.[94] Fourteen months later, the SEC approved the registration of the National Association of Securities Dealers (NASD) as the one and, to this date, only over-the-counter regulatory organization. Within two decades, NASD's membership exceeded 80 percent of the over-the-counter brokers registered with the Commission, in large measure because of an important economic advantage of NASD membership. Broker-dealers who were members of NASD were charged a "wholesale" price when they purchased or sold securities from other NASD members; non-NASD members had to pay the same price as the public.

The Landis-Douglas approach to over-the-counter regulation was a practical necessity if the SEC was to enforce what Investment Banking Code Committee chairman B. Howell Griswold aptly termed "the traffic regulations" of the securities industry.[95] Not only would direct SEC enforcement have been unwieldy because of the number of broker-dealer firms, it would have been politically difficult. During the New Deal period, the over-the-counter firms had considerable capacity to galvanize congressional support, because they were a nationwide constituency, and, Abe Fortas would write, "as contrasted with the New York Stock Exchange, there was no single organization [of over-the-counter members] which was the target of political wrath and the focus of public indignation."[96]

Nonetheless, self-regulation of the over-the-counter industry did not come without cost. By creating NASD to serve as the over-the-counter dealers' disciplinarian, the SEC also granted quasi-official status to a trade association that thereafter often opposed — frequently successfully — further SEC legislative initiatives. Nor could the SEC escape the dilemma Paul Gourrich described in his 1937 memorandum opposing Commission administration of the Investment Bankers NRA codes. To ensure that o-t-c broker-dealers joined NASD, the SEC was required to negotiate its formation both with the remnants of the Code Committee and the less conciliatory Investment Bankers Association. Inevitably, this process demanded some compromise of the policies the SEC would have pursued had it directly regulated the industry through licenses and rule-making. Yet the greatest weakness in SEC "self-regulation" of the over-the-counter market was the risk that during periods when the Commission was led by less activist chairmen than Douglas or hamstrung by budget stringency, the SEC would cease to prod NASD to discipline its members vigilantly. As Douglas recognized, without an SEC "shotgun in the closet," there was little incentive for an industry self-regulatory organization to perform the unpleasant task of disciplinarian. During the Truman and Eisenhower administrations, the SEC did not effectively oversee NASD self-regulation. The lack of disciplinary vigor both of the SEC and of NASD undoubtedly was responsible in part for the discernible increase in securities fraud during the 1950s.

* * *

Until he assumed the chairmanship in September 1937, Douglas's principal work at the SEC was supervising the Commission's Protective Committee Study, a study notable, like the Pecora investigation, for its protracted public hearings. Eventually the study produced an eight-part, four-thousand-page report, which, in the manner of Brandeis's *Other People's Money* and the Senate Banking Committee's 1934 "Stock Exchange Practices Report," was an adversarial brief, largely devoted to making the case for displacement of insider control of corporate bankruptcies, reorganizations, and debt security sales. The report also urged stringent reform of foreign and municipal debt adjustments, and of real estate bond sales. The cumbersome length of the report and its adversarial excesses — ridiculed by Robert T. Swaine, a leading corporate bankruptcy attorney, as giving the study the "colorful verbiage of a dime novel of the nineties" and the "dramatic excitement" of "a modern Hollywood gangster thriller"[97] — may have reduced the legislative impact that the Protective Committee Study otherwise might have enjoyed. The study did lead to the enactment of two minor corporate reform measures, Chapter X of the Chandler Bankruptcy Revision Act and the Trust Indenture Act. But when introduced in May 1937, both were meant to complement a more far-reaching measure proposed by Congressman Clarence Lea called the "committee bill."[98]

Although never enacted, the committee bill represented a milestone in Douglas's evolution from academic theorist to political tactician. As drafted by Douglas and his Protective Committee Study staff, the Lea Committee bill would have subjected all municipal and foreign debt arrangements, corporation reorganizations, and voluntary corporate readjustments to similar patterns of regulation. In each type of reorganization, there would have been required disclosure of material background information, including the fees to be paid Protective Committee members. Incumbent corporate management, underwriters, and other interested persons would have been barred from serving on the reorganization committees. On request of a court, the SEC would have been empowered to file a report concerning the fairness of a reorganization plan. Where a reorganization involved more than $5 million, the SEC would have had the power to intervene in a court proceeding and, under some circumstances, to arbitrate differences between protective committees and security holders. As drafted, the committee bill well realized the law professor's favored virtues of constitutionality, unambiguous language, internal consistency, remedial provisions rationally related to the "necessity for regulation" described in the bill's findings of fact, and economy, in the sense that the proposal addressed technically similar problems under a generic regulatory framework. The bill, however, was politically artless. Having made no serious effort, even within the Roosevelt administration or Congress, to build a coalition to support the bill, the drafters hopelessly overreached themselves. Provisions like that forbidding incumbent management to direct a reorganization when it was voluntary and effected through means such as a merger that could instantly infuse a hard-pressed firm with adequate capital were opposed as inflexible and counterproductive, even by such usually reform-minded commentators as Harvard Law School professor E. Merrick Dodd. Moreover, by seeking to regulate in one bill such diverse debtors as foreign governments, municipalities, and business corporations, the committee bill achieved the improbable result of uniting in opposition liberal congressman Adolph Sabath,[99] the Foreign Bond Associates, Incorporated, and myriad spokesmen for municipal corporations with such predictable opponents as the Investment Bankers Association.

In part, this was the consequence of Douglas's inability to bargain with Congressman Sabath, who had chaired extensive hearings on corporate, real estate, and municipal protective committees and introduced his own bankruptcy bill, which Douglas disparaged as loosely drawn, ignoring "a substantial and important portion of the reorganization field," imposing "intolerable" administrative burdens on the SEC (the Commission was to act as a trustee in every corporate bankruptcy involving indebtedness of more than $50,000), and creating the possibility of "endless conflict" by vesting the Commission and the federal courts with overlapping jurisdiction. Douglas's inability to work with Sabath, whose committee then was the only other group in Washington seriously studying protective committees, bruised a particularly sensitive congressional ego. As Abe Fortas predicted in an October 1935 memorandum to Douglas, introduction of a rival bill would cause "the Sabath Committee [to] be angry with us and [to] stop our legislation in the House," with the result "that the fruits of our study [will] be lost." When the Lea bill later was introduced, Sabath and other congressmen testified against it. One, Congressman Milton West, opposing the bill on behalf of municipal corporations, expressed doubt that Congressman Lea had even read the bill before introducing it at SEC request: "I am convinced this bill was conceived in the mind of a theorist and brain-truster and given birth by one who has never had any practical experience." After initial hearings were held in June and July of 1937, the Lea Committee bill quietly disappeared.

By contrast, the SEC's 1937–1938 campaign for enactment of Chapter X of the Chandler bankruptcy revision bill was an illustration of Douglas's rapid political maturity. As early as 1926, there had been considerable bipartisan support for amendment of the Bankruptcy Act of 1898. In 1929, federal district court judge Thomas Thatcher of the Southern District of New York appointed Colonel William J. Donovan to conduct a comprehensive investigation into the administration of bankruptcy proceedings. Donovan's report roundly criticized both the courts and bankruptcy trustees for a system that "has been ineffective, burdensome, and generally inefficient." Subsequent studies by the Department of Commerce,

Judge Thatcher when he became President Hoover's Solicitor General, the House Judiciary Committee, and Yale University's Institute of Human Relations reached similar conclusions. By 1932, a private bar-dominated National Bankruptcy Conference was established to develop a revised bankruptcy bill. But the conference's efforts soon were overtaken by events. Hastily drafted emergency bankruptcy acts were passed in 1933 and 1934. Bills drafted by the National Bankruptcy Conference were the subject of extensive House Judiciary Committee hearings in 1935 and 1936.

William Douglas, however, soon emerged as the dominant figure in the bankruptcy reform efforts. In no corporate-related field were Douglas's intellectual abilities more widely recognized than bankruptcy. Between 1928 and 1934, he had been a special adviser to Colonel Donovan, had collaborated with the Department of Commerce in its bankruptcy studies, had directed bankruptcy studies for Yale's Institute of Human Relations, and had written on the subject the leading law school casebook, articles for the *Encyclopaedia Britannica* and the *Encyclopedia of the Social Sciences*, as well as several law review articles. Congressman Walter Chandler agreed to hold up an effort to pass a new bankruptcy act until Douglas's Protective Committee Study completed its relevant reports and to allow Douglas to participate in drafting the revision bill.

In fact, Douglas's Protective Committee Study group wrote virtually all of the bill. On May 10, 1937, the Protective Committee Study published Part I of its report, a nine-hundred-page document entitled "Strategy and Technique of Protective and Reorganization Committees." The Protective Committee Study made fourteen specific legislative recommendations, two of which were of fundamental importance. First, the study recommended that in every corporate bankruptcy a qualified and disinterested trustee should be appointed to "supplant the system of leaving [the corporate bankrupt's insiders] in possession or of appointing 'friendly' trustees." Equally independent counsel also should be required. The independent trustee should be responsible not only for preparing a reorganization plan, but for investigating

> the condition of the company and of the events antedating the failure, with the threefold objective (1) of ascertaining the facts necessary for formulation of a plan; (2) of evaluating the worth of the existing management and the desirability of its retention by the reorganized company; and (3) of disclosing and diligently pursuing corporate assets in the form of claims against directors, officers, their affiliated interests and others who may have misused corporate control for their personal benefit.

Second, the Securities and Exchange Commission was to be available to the federal court "as an aid in the administration of the [bankruptcy reorganization] and in the analysis of the fairness, equity, and soundness of plans."

At Chandler's direction, Douglas compromised differences with the National Bankruptcy Conference. In return for Douglas's agreement to support repeal of a provision in an emergency Bankruptcy Act allowing creditors with claims as small as $1000 to institute a federal court bankruptcy proceeding and other technical concessions, the conference agreed to support virtually all of the Protective Committee Study draft of what came to be known as Chapter X of the Chandler Bankruptcy Revision Act. The Whitney scandal enabled the SEC to push through a draft of Chapter X in June 1938 that reflected the Commission's preferences on most subsidiary points that had been opposed by the National Bankruptcy Conference.

As enacted, Chapter X of the Chandler Act required a court to appoint an independent trustee to investigate the background of each bankruptcy involving $250,000 or more of indebtedness. The trustee could not be a director, officer, employee, or underwriter of the bankrupt firm, but the trustee was required to report any evidence that corporate insiders had been involved in fraud, misconduct, mismanagement, or other irregularities. Where the bankruptcy involved more than $3 million of indebtedness, the federal district court judge conducting the bankruptcy proceeding was required to submit to the SEC for examination and advisory review any reorganization plan the judge deemed worthy of consideration. On request or approval of the bankruptcy judge, the Commission was allowed to intervene and participate in other phases of the bankruptcy proceeding. SEC insistence secured passage of a novel provision giving labor unions or employees' associations the right to be heard on the economic soundness of the reorganization plan where it affected the interests of employees. A comparable "democratization" gave corporate insiders, any creditor, and any stockholder the right to be heard in a bankruptcy proceeding. Other SEC-inspired provisions barred the issuance of nonvoting stock by the reorganized firm and required full disclosure of all fees and expenses incurred in a bankruptcy reorganization.[*][100]

The second legislative consequence of the Protective Committee Study was the Trust Indenture Act of 1939. Although a study of debt securities was not explicitly authorized by Section 211 of the Securi-

---

[*] In 1978, Chapter X of the Chandler Act was repealed and a new bankruptcy act adopted. The 1978 act substantially alters the role of the SEC in bankruptcy proceedings.

ties and Exchange Act (which mandated the Protective Committee Study's work), by November 1934 Douglas was convinced of the need for a legislative reform of the trustee system that then was responsible for approximately $40 billion in corporate debt securities issued under indenture agreements.[101]

In June 1936, the Protective Committee Study published the most influential of its eight reports, entitled "Trustees Under Indentures." The report benefited from several fortuities. Even in the most generous view, an analysis of corporate debt securities was tangential to the Protective Committee Study's mandate. Mindful of this, the main body of "Trustees Under Indentures" was a mere 112 pages in length — a pamphlet by Protective Committee Study standards — and limited to discussion of a "few exemplary major points," editorial decisions that had the result of making the report the easiest to read Protective Committee Study document. Unlike the rest of the Protective Committee Study's work, which ranged in somewhat desultory fashion over several different legislative topics, such as municipal debt adjustment, foreign bonds, and real estate bond protective committees, "Trustees Under Indentures" was focused on a single legislative problem: long-term corporate debt. This meant not only that the report could be easily translated into a legislative proposal, but also that the legislative proposal would be opposed only by a single group of industry lobbyists. Finally, and most fortuitously, much of the report was inspired by Edward Levi, then a Yale Law School graduate student (later president of the University of Chicago and Attorney General of the United States) whom Douglas allowed to review the Protective Committee Study's debt security research for a school paper he was then preparing. The paper was never published, but Douglas, with Levi's permission, incorporated many of Levi's arguments into the trust indenture report.[102]

The thesis and tone of "Trustees Under Indentures" was similar to that of the bankruptcy report: disorganized and scattered investors often were treated unfairly by self-interested inside management and allied bankers. As the trust indenture report explained, when corporate bonds and other long-term debt securities were sold, the investors' basic protector was a trustee, usually a commercial bank, which was required by a formal indenture agreement to enforce remedial provisions if the corporate issuer defaulted on its obligations to investors. But "Trustees Under Indentures" found that "typically the trustees do not exercise the elaborate powers which are the bondholders' only protection." Instead, the "so-called trustee" typically acts as "merely a clerical agency." This trustee passivity jeopardized the investors' position throughout the life of a debt security. Usually the trustee did not participate in drafting the indenture, allowing the corporate issuer and its underwriter to decide what safety features would protect investors. Not surprisingly, these protective features often proved illusory. For example, when corporate debt securities were sold, it was common for the issuer to advertise negative pledge clauses by which it promised not to incur other debts during the life of the loan. Because an investors' representative did not participate in the drafting of negative pledge clauses, these clauses often contained ingenious loopholes. Trustee inaction could be equally dangerous to investors after the initial indenture agreement was written, as investors in Krueger and Toll discovered shortly after the 1929 stock market crash, when they learned that their trustee had permitted Ivar Kreuger to substitute as collateral for $25 million worth of sound European bonds, Yugoslavian and other poorly rated bonds with an identical face value but an actual value of $9.75 million.

The report was most critical of passive trustees when a corporation defaulted on its indenture obligations. In 63 percent of the indentures studied, trustees were not required to complain of a default, even if they had actual knowledge of it, unless formally requested by holders of a specified percentage of the outstanding debt securities. As "a general practice," trustees often exercised their discretion and ignored known defaults. Since the trustee often as a practical matter had the exclusive power to bring a lawsuit to enforce investigators' rights, this usually meant investors had no effective legal protection unless holders of specified percentages of outstanding debt securities (usually 50 percent or more) compelled the trustee to institute a lawsuit.

> Even this [stated the Protective Committee Study report] does not tell the whole story. It is not enough that the required percentages of security holders, having in some manner been assembled, shall give notice of default and make the demand upon the trustee. Almost uniformly there is this further barrier; the indenture expressly provides that the trustee has no obligation to take any action which in its opinion is likely to involve it in expense or liability unless the security holders furnish it with indemnity.

Dismal as the performance of passive trustees was, the Protective Committee Study argued, it was inevitable. The trustee of a corporate debt security usually was selected by the corporate issuer or the underwriter or both. Invariably the trustee was inadequately remunerated for the assumption of more than minimal duties. In a typical example, the Chase National Bank received $1100 a year for acting as trustee under an indenture covering $10 million of the debentures of the National Electric Power Company. Yet even this minimal fee was characterized as "grotesquely exorbitant for the negligible services performed" by Judge Samuel I. Rosenman in the *Hazzard* v. *Chase National Bank* case, because exculpatory clauses with which most debt-securing indentures "fairly bristle" exonerated a trustee from all misconduct except that caused "by its own gross negligence or bad faith," a level of misconduct almost never proven in a court of law. Finally, the report noted that it was unlikely trustees would become more active until "compelled to purge themselves of conflicting interests," such as associations with an underwriter more interested in marketing future securities for a corporation than in protecting existing debt security holders.

Enactment of the Trust Indenture Act of 1939 was facilitated by policy differences between the two principal bank lobby organizations, which Douglas skillfully exploited. Soon after "Trustees Under Indentures" was published, R. G. Page, chairman of an ad hoc committee of the American Bankers Association, the commercial bankers' lobbying organization, wrote his fellow commercial bankers that the report was "most drastic" and "astonishingly unfair to corporate trustees as a class," but since "any fair-minded person must admit that there have been abuses," he had accepted an SEC invitation to confer. Between October 1936 and March 1938, Douglas and the American Bankers Association negotiated the provisions of what ultimately became the Trust Indenture Act. Because commercial bankers' concern with the bill was for the most part limited to preserving the power of trustee banks to lend money to a corporate debt issuer and to limiting trustees' exposure to negligence liability, the SEC won pledges that the commercial banks would not oppose the trust indenture bill, with relatively few concessions. This isolated the Investment Bankers Association in opposition and undermined many of their arguments against the bill, because they no longer could claim that most bankers found the bill impractical. Douglas, mindful that securing the nonopposition of the investment bankers would ensure passage of the bill, attempted to negotiate with the Investment Bankers Association until December 1938. The Investment Bankers Association, however, never deviated from its public position opposing any trust indenture bill except one limited to disclosure provisions. Equally emphatically, the SEC rejected so limited a bill. As SEC commissioner Edward Eicher later would testify:

> It is clear from three years of experience under the Securities Act . . .
> that even the fullest disclosure of the terms of an indenture is not
> sufficient to bring about the necessary improvements, and that the
> desired objectives will not be attained so long as the form of the
> indenture is determined exclusively by the conventions of the obligor
> and its underwriters.

Passage of the bill became inevitable in early May 1939, when the
Senate voted 40–19 in favor of a final SEC–American Bankers Association draft. The opposition, led by Senator Robert Taft, had little
with which to counter repetition of the findings of the SEC's "Trustees Under Indentures" but citation of the Investment Bankers Association's unanimous rejection of the bill.

The Trust Indenture Act of 1939 itself, to invoke a favorite phrase
of James Landis, was closely articulated. Most corporate debt securities thenceforth were required to comply with the Trust Indenture
Act as well as with the disclosure provisions of the Securities Act of
1933. The Trust Indenture Act, when applicable, required each corporate debt security to be protected by at least one trustee with a net
worth of $150,000, free of nine specified conflicting associations
with other debt issues, the corporate issuer, the underwriter, or
voting stockholders. Although a commercial bank also could be a
creditor of the corporation, a detailed section of the act, laboriously
negotiated by the SEC and the American Bankers Association, prohibited the bank trustee from improving its creditor position at the
expense of debt security holders within four months of a default
unless a genuine "reserve" or "distress" loan was made. To facilitate debt security holders' enforcement of their rights, the act required lists of debt security holders to be readily available, required
periodic reports both from the trustee and the issuer (including
certificates of fair value when collateral was substituted), barred
exculpatory provision after known defaults, and allowed debt security holders direct rights of action whenever principal and interest
payments were past due.[103]

*   *   *

While an SEC commissioner, William Douglas had disagreed with
the Kennedy-Landis policy of leaving the promulgation of accounting principles almost entirely to the accounting profession. In 1936
and 1937, Douglas and fellow commissioner Robert Healy pressed
the Commission to "take the lead in formulating accounting principles as it was empowered to do under the 1933 Act."[104] Douglas was
the first chairman to challenge the laxness of the Commission's

accounting policies, raising appropriate questions for SEC internal study and modestly reforming the Commission's accounting policies. But his efforts were not sufficiently far-reaching to be effective. By default, Douglas would contribute to the SEC's historic reluctance to assume direct responsibility for accounting principles, a reticence that long endured as the weakest link in the Commission's corporate disclosure program.

Kennedy and Landis had viewed accounting reform as subordinate in importance to capital flotation. Following the Commission's November 1934 *Northern States Power* decision, the SEC permitted, in the words of a 1937 staff study, "financial statements reflecting improper accounting practices to remain unchanged provided such statements were footnoted to set forth the proper procedure which should have been followed together with a statement of the manner in which the accounts would have been altered had they been set up properly." Minimalist as this policy may have seemed, coming from a Commission that had been expected by many to promulgate uniform accounting principles, Landis's Commission further shackled the SEC's reform of accounting standards by permitting the broadly worded requirements of Form A-2. Superficially, the Form A-2 stipulation that an accountant was required to certify his opinion of "the accounting principles and procedures" employed in a registration statement seemed like a practical limitation on a corporate management's ability to select self-serving accounting principles. However, as the SEC's November 1937 staff study found, "The Commission has not been disposed to make an issue of accounting practices which are deemed improper by the registration division but which are approved by the independent accountant in his certificate with the registration statement." Only when "the accountant's exceptions and the explanatory footnotes were so numerous that the statements were particularly confusing" would the Commission compel a corporation to redo its financial records along lines directed by the Commission.[105]

In December 1936, Landis publicly complained, "The impact of almost daily tilts with accountants, some of them called leaders in their profession, often leaves little doubt that their loyalties to management are stronger than their sense of responsibility to the investor." After resigning as chairman, Landis would express a considerably more heated view in a March 1939 letter: "What is really needed is a good spanking for the accountants as a whole rather than refinement of the accounting form."[106] But as SEC chairman, Landis was unwilling to be the accounting profession's disciplinarian. Instead, he appointed Carman G. Blough to be the Commission's chief accountant. Blough was not directed to develop uniform or industry-wide accounting principles; he pursued a policy of cooperation with the accounting profession. In a 1937 article, Blough explained that the Commission

> depended a great deal upon the ability of the independent public accountants, and has not attempted to lay down hard and fast rules regarding the type of audit or the specific form of the financial statements required. Certain minimum requirements are specified in each form, but much is left to the judgment of the accountant.[107]

Douglas, though critical of Landis's quiescent approach to accounting practices, did not have a clearly defined approach toward accounting problems when he became chairman. As he explained at his first press conference:

> I think that the Commission must be the pacesetter in the accounting field, crystallizing the most conservative practices of the best elements in the accounting profession and seeking by education, by precept, perhaps by rule and regulation, to bring the accounting profession up to the highest levels of its best elements."[108]

Soon after becoming chairman, he directed the Registration Division and the Office of Chief Accountant to prepare studies of existing practices. But Douglas was never able to use these studies effectively.

Douglas's accounting policy was announced in April 1938. In the seven preceding months, his attention had been focused almost entirely on the political implications of the 1937 recession, his struggle with the New York Stock Exchange, the Whitney scandal, lobbying for the Maloney, trust indenture, and bankruptcy bills, and debates within the Roosevelt administration on the problems of small business, government-sponsored regional banks, deficit spending, and the Temporary National Economic Committee. By necessity, Douglas could do little more in pursuing accounting reform than associate himself with the approach to accounting principle-setting espoused by Judge Healy.

Douglas recalled in his autobiography that in late December 1937, Healy, an enthusiast of the common law's method of incremental case-by-case development, spoke also for Douglas when he described "the next step in accounting":

> The staff as the result of instructions has for some time been studying the proposal to issue some rules dealing with accounting principles. We are not thinking of a mass of rules or innovations in accounting. We are trying to express a few standards as to principles which we

believe are accepted by a majority of good accountants, especially of those who do not assume the role of special pleaders for their more lucrative clients.[109]

This approach proved inadequate. The ideal of comparable corporate financial statements, as distinguished from the common law's ideal of individualized justice, can be effectively pursued only within a comprehensive accounting framework. But Chief Accountant Blough had convinced a majority of the Commission earlier in December that his office lacked sufficient time and staff to do "the extensive research necessary to formulate the correct accounting principles" even in *individual* accounting controversies.[110] Nor was the limited Healy-Douglas policy ever fully effected. A majority of the SEC commissioners (Mathews, Frank, Hanes) opposed Commission formulation of accounting principles. Mathews, long the conservative stalwart of the Commission, later explained, "One need only recognize that the principles of the science of accounting are in a state of flux and rapid development to be hesitant in wresting guardianship from the hands of the profession."[111]

A compromise was engineered among the five SEC commissioners in late March by which the chief accountant was authorized periodically to issue accounting releases expressing his interpretation of accounting standards on major accounting questions "for the purpose of *contributing* to the development of uniform standards" (italics added).[112] One month later the Commission, with Mathews dissenting, modestly tightened the looseness of the Kennedy-Landis footnote policy with the adoption of Accounting Series Release No. 4, which stated in its entirety:

> In cases where financial statements filed with this Commission pursuant to its rules and regulations under the Securities Act of 1933 or the Securities Exchange Act of 1934 are prepared in accordance with accounting principles for which there is not substantial authoritative support, such financial statements will be presumed to be misleading or inaccurate despite disclosures contained in the certificate of the accountant or in footnotes to the statements provided the matters involved are material. In cases where there is a difference of opinion between the Commission and the registrant as to the proper principles of accounting to be followed, disclosure will be accepted in lieu of correction of the financial statements themselves only if the points involved are such that there is substantial authoritative support for the practices followed by the registrant and the position of the Commission has not previously been expressed in rules, regulations, or other official releases of the Commission, including the published opinions of its chief accountant.

The advance in accounting rigor portended by this release proved to be very slight. Two SEC staff attorneys pointedly noted in 1939 that the Commission had left unresolved virtually all accounting controversies by failing to define "substantial authoritative support." Accordingly, standards for such basic accounting concepts as cost of sales, depreciation, inventories, and surplus continued to "seem very inadequate."[113]

* * *

A perennial conundrum of the securities laws is how to treat small business fairly. Historically, considerable evidence has corroborated Landis's belief that a substantial proportion of securities fraud is committed by the promoters of new, small speculative firms.[114] Fully to exempt small business from the reach of the securities laws would deprive investors of protection in some of the instances where investors need protection most. On the other hand, there is no question that when small firms issue new securities, they pay a proportionately higher price for commissions, accounting, legal, and filing costs than larger businesses. For some small firms, the costs of a public securities distribution are prohibitive. Thus, unless it is national policy to give large business firms advantages over the small in capital formation, it is essential to create compensatory programs to stimulate the financing of small firms.

For Douglas, a proponent of economic deconcentration, this was a particular priority. During his chairmanship, a debate over whether the 1933 Securities Act should in whole or in part be repealed was transformed into the economically more significant debate about the most effective way to equalize the capital-raising opportunities of large and small business. Although Douglas's proposal for a regional investment banking system never was adopted, his economic analysis contributed to a broadening of the Reconstruction Finance Corporation's mandate in 1938 and, indirectly, to the similar mandate of the Small Business Administration in 1958.

SEC analysis of 217 representative securities issued in 1937[115] went far to sustain the conclusion of a subsequent Temporary National Economic Committee (TNEC) report "that the capital markets are simply not organized for small issues, and consequently closed to small business."[116] By securities type, the 1937 SEC study found, the expense of issuing common stock in blocks of $250,000 or less under the 1933 Securities Act equaled 22.4 percent of the gross amount of money received from investors; for common stock issues of $1,000,000 to $4,999,000, 15.7 percent. With preferred stock and debt securities these disparities were considerably greater.

The expense of floating $250,000 or less in preferred stock equaled 17.3 percent; preferred stock issues between $5 and $10 million cost a mere 3.7 percent. Similarly, for debt security issues under $250,000, the expense was 9.2 percent, which was approximately four times the 2.3 percent cost of debt issues of $25 million or more.

To Douglas, such data, far from establishing a case for the partial or total repeal of the Securities Act, illustrated "that the problem of small issuers is a result of fundamental defects in our capital market machinery." Eighty to 90 percent of security distribution costs were found to be investment banker gross commissions, not the costs directly associated with filing a registration statement with the SEC. These costs would have been paid by corporate securities issuers in the absence of a securities law, and, indeed, SEC studies throughout the 1930s consistently found, "Insofar as comparable issues can be selected, it appears that, at least for bonds, the gross spread to underwriters has, if anything, been lower since the Securities Act than prior to it." Douglas believed the principal obstacle to small business finance was not the costs associated with an SEC filing; it was the unwillingness of investment banks to make a firm commitment to underwrite the smaller firms' securities. After agreeing on business terms with an underwriter, most large firms usually were guaranteed a sale of 100 percent of a security issue, because a syndicate of investment banks would assume the full risk of the issue. For most small corporate issuers, however, investment banks would make no such firm commitment, but promised only to extend their best efforts. As a result, Douglas wrote Federal Reserve Board chairman Marriner Eccles:

> Despite the completion of registration with the Commission, issuers of such securities, by and large, fail to raise the funds which they desire. Of 152 operative companies which had effective registrations some time between July 27, 1933, when the Securities Act became effective, and the close of 1936, 17 or 11% of the total number failed to sell any of the registered securities within a period of at least six months and generally much longer following registration. Another 63 or 41% failed to sell as much as 50% of the amount which they had registered.[117]

When the 1937 recession continued into 1938, pressures mounted to roll back the 1933 Securities Act. Chairman Eccles, for example, wrote Douglas of his impression "that the Securities Act of 1933 has been a factor impeding the flow of investment funds into the capital market, particularly so far as smaller issues are concerned."[118] A small business conference organized by Commerce Secretary Daniel

Roper communicated a similar message to the White House in early February. Initially, in response to the renewed criticism of the 1933 act, Douglas wrote Roosevelt on January 29, 1938, about "the desirability of setting up a system of industrial banks to service the capital requirements of legitimate business."[119] A subsequent memorandum, dated March 1, set forth in a manner, Douglas calculated, most likely to convince Roosevelt, the economic and political advantages of creating a nationwide system of regional industrial banks. Such banks, Douglas wrote, would provide "an adequate amount of capital necessary for the task which lies ahead" and would also "displace the Morgan influence in the various regions [with] a new and enlightened leadership in the business . . . decentralize financial and industrial control . . . do more than anything else to develop the United States regionally, [and] have enormous public support, outside of New York City." In mid-March, Douglas began circulating within the Roosevelt administration a draft of the industrial finance bill. It called for the creation of a five-member Industrial Finance Board to supervise up to fifteen regional banks, mostly funded by public bond sales, to finance local industry through loans, securities purchases, or the underwriting of small firms' securities issues. The banks after a few years were to be privately owned.[120]

With the recession deepening throughout March 1938, Douglas's regional bank initiative became bound up with a broader economic debate within the Roosevelt administration. During a telephone conversation on March 25, Roosevelt requested Douglas to outline a more comprehensive recovery program. Affiliating himself with Harry Hopkins, Leon Henderson, Marriner Eccles, Thomas Corcoran, and others within a divided administration, Douglas the next day urged Roosevelt immediately to increase federal spending through the Works Progress Administration to boost consumer purchasing power, adopt an emergency program for the ailing railroad industry, and provide Reconstruction Finance Corporation guarantees for bank loans to small businesses. But Douglas continued to emphasize "the device of regional industrial banks." He wrote, "Without some method of opening up the capital market, I am fearful that the normal investment banking machinery will not function adequately."[121]

With Roosevelt's apparent encouragement, Douglas attempted to win support for the regional bank proposal within the administration. Treasury Secretary Morgenthau soon communicated his opposition to creation of a new parallel banking system.[122] In early April Douglas joined Morgenthau, RFC chairman Jesse Jones, and others on a Special Committee to study credit requirements of large and small businesses.[123] After the Special Committee on April 4 endorsed Senator Carter Glass's bill to broaden the authority of the RFC to extend credit to business firms, Douglas wrote Agriculture Secretary Henry Wallace that the Glass bill alone would not be adequate. Douglas doubted that emergency government loans alone could fill the capital gap. In an earlier letter to Congressman James Mead, Douglas had noted that RFC and Federal Reserve Board industrial loans had not been of major significance: "In three and one-half years, the two agencies disbursed total funds of less than $250,000,000, and by 1937 such loans had tapered off to very insignificant amounts."[124] Moreover, Douglas wrote Wallace, straddling small businesses with interest-bearing obligations, rather than helping them market common stock, would lead to unsound capital structures. Thus, Douglas reasoned, the Glass bill amending the Reconstruction Finance Corporation statute alone would do little to aid recovery:

> (1) In the first place, it does not authorize the Reconstruction Finance Corporation to invest in any securities whatsoever except interest-bearing obligations. (2) In the second place, it omits the important and desirable element of regionalization. (3) In the third place, it does not adequately provide for the participation of private capital in new investing machinery. (4) Furthermore, that Bill is deficient in the following respect: The agencies which we need must be equipped to do a complete *investment banking job* with respect to analysis of and revamping of capital structures, strengthening and ascertaining of financial conditions, and the adequacy and balance of assets.[125]

On April 13, the Glass amendment to the RFC statute was enacted, empowering the corporation to make loans to business enterprises and to purchase business securities and obligations.[126] The following day Roosevelt ended the immediate administration recovery program debate with the Keynesian recommendation that Congress appropriate $3 billion for recovery agency grants and loans. To appease the small-business community, Roosevelt also requested "that the Securities and Exchange Commission consider such simplification of regulations as will assist and expedite the financing, particularly of small business enterprises."[127] This, the SEC promptly did. Within twenty-four hours it announced plans to broaden the exemption for issues under $100,000 and to require a new simplified form for issues involving less than $5 million.[128]

But it was soon apparent that the Roosevelt administration's approach in 1938 to the recovery of small-business activity was inadequate. The SEC's minor rule changes achieved little. The RFC's

stock-purchasing powers were unused. SEC research published in
1941, however, found that small business firms were almost universally hostile to proposals for government purchase or underwriting
of their stock. As SEC chairman Jerome Frank wrote Roosevelt in
April 1941, "The managements of most small businesses do not
want a partner, i.e., to sell stock, because they do not want to
weaken their control. They would rather run the risk of failure."[129]
But Douglas was correct in believing that a new federal loan agency
specifically oriented to the concerns of small business was needed if
small-business funding was to be measurably increased.[130] SEC
officials testified in 1941 that the RFC had not met small-business
needs because the corporation had been unwilling to make greater
use of its powers unless it could act consistently with conservative
banking practices.[131] Largely for this reason, the problem of small-
business funding in 1958 was delegated to a specially tailored loan
agency, the Small Business Administration.

* * *

The chief unfinished business in the Roosevelt administration's
program of federal corporations law was the enactment of a statute
regulating corporate governance. There was irony in this omission.
Many of the unethical or illegal actions reported by the Pecora Committee, the SEC's Protective Committee Study, and SEC enforcement programs involved the misconduct of senior corporate managers and directors, not investment bankers. Section 14 of the 1934
Securities Exchange Act, which gave the SEC power to regulate
corporate proxy elections, had been widely recognized as a minor
first step, to be succeeded by a more comprehensive federal corporate governance statute. President Roosevelt favored such an act. So
did many in his Cabinet, as well as a majority of the people questioned in public opinion polls,[132] the AFL,[133] several members of
Congress, the SEC, and even the New York Stock Exchange. Nevertheless, until the very end of the New Deal, a federal corporate
governance statute was not a Roosevelt administration priority.
And when the Roosevelt administration did commit itself to the
enactment of such a law, it all but defeated its own efforts by linking
enactment of provisions regulating corporate governance to an omnibus corporate-licensing bill intended also to revitalize the antitrust laws and broaden employees' rights.

Professor William Douglas was a leader in the movement to secure enactment of a federal corporate governance statute. Indeed, as
early as 1934, he was the most prominent academic proponent of a
federal incorporation act. After the 1933 Securities Act was adopted,

Douglas published a celebrated criticism of that law in the *Yale Law Review*. He defended his criticism in a December 1933 letter to Felix Frankfurter: "The act is of secondary importance in a comprehensive program of social control over finance. Publicity of affairs, control over capital structures, control over directors, regulation of speculation, regulation of holding companies, protection of minorities are primary."[134]

In an expansive subsequent letter to Frankfurter, Douglas added:

> Federal incorporation does not mean to me merely drafting a statute and determining what rule of *ultra vires*, stock dividends, directors' liability, etc. to adopt. Those are next to clerical in significance. The real problem is to determine what social and economic values are at stake; what is wanted; what should be destroyed? What types of holding companies do you want? What room shall be left for the little fellow, the Henry Fords of the future or the corner grocery store of the next decade?[135]

Douglas never proposed a legislative formula to answer these questions. But in June 1934 he published what has endured as his best-known law review article, "Directors Who Do Not Direct." In a philosophical sense, the article is best appreciated as a companion piece to Landis's *The Administrative Process*. It represented Douglas's attempt to provide for corporate governance the same type of expert, disinterested leadership that Frankfurter and Landis sought for the federal agencies. The article began by implying agreement with the assertion of the House report accompanying the 1933 Securities Act: "Directors should assume the responsibility of directing and if their manifold activities make real directing impossible, they should be held responsible to the unsuspecting public for their neglect." But in Douglas's view recent court records and Senate hearings showing such abuses as "secret loans to officers and directors, undisclosed profit-sharing plans . . . dividend policies based on false estimates . . . and trading in securities of the corporation by virtue of inside information" meant that "considerable refashioning of codes of conduct — in business as well as in law — must be effected if the next cyclical trend is not to produce as many malpractices and abuses as has the current one."

The primary concern in regulating large corporations, Douglas insisted, was "[to avoid] or [make] impossible the vicious practice of having the board controlled or dominated by the managers." While disparaging as well "inside" directors who were corporate executives subservient to senior management and "outside" or nonemployee directors chosen solely for their prestige, Douglas saw a solution in taking away control and dominance of the board from executive management and vesting it instead in an independent board with sufficient power and responsibility to "supervise those who [manage the enterprise] and [formulate] the general commercial and financial policies under which the business is to be conducted." Douglas meant such directors to be "experts . . . sufficiently detached from the business to be able to see it in relation to its competitors, trade trends, etc.," not mere public representatives to serve as "corrective influences." "Hence, they should have a position of dominance and power on the board rather than the subordinate position to which some reformers would relegate them." As a "partial agenda" of means to create such a supervisory board, Douglas urged preventing management domination over corporate elections by withdrawing their control of the proxy machinery (by which shareholders who could not personally attend meetings were required to sign over their votes to incumbent management's representatives), barring nonvoting stock, and magnifying the opportunities for scattered minorities to express themselves through cumulative voting.[136] While he was SEC chairman, Douglas delivered a related address, urging smaller boards made up of adequately paid directors, whose primary business would be to serve on the boards of a few corporations so that each director could "acquire a thorough knowledge of the corporations."

> With no conflicting interests whatsoever, the paid director could give his full attention to his company's affairs. He could visit the factories and the warehouses. He could know if the plant was being carried at too high a value; he could look not merely at statements of inventory but at the inventory itself. He would be able to penetrate the mysteries of the balance sheet and see the realities that lie behind it. He would not be merely a director at board meetings; he would be a director between board meetings as well. He could give the directing job more time in a week than many a director gives it in a year.[137]

As SEC chairman, however, Douglas initially did not seek a federal corporate governance statute. With so many initiatives already begun, Douglas was reluctant to begin an additional campaign for a corporate governance statute. Instead, early in 1938, Douglas directed Chester Lane, then assistant general counsel, to draft a federal corporation registration act to extend the periodic disclosure requirements of the 1934 Securities Exchange Act to firms with outstanding securities worth $1 million or more.

Douglas wrote Roosevelt on February 18 that such a bill would close the gap left in the Commission's corporate disclosure program created by excluding from the 1934 act firms traded over the counter. Douglas requested permission for the SEC to sponsor this "limited" measure, urging that a federal incorporation bill be considered later.[138]

Roosevelt was unwilling to commit his administration to Douglas's timetable, nor did he exhibit enthusiasm for so technical a bill. In August 1935, shortly after the Supreme Court's *Schecter* decision held unconstitutional the National Industrial Recovery Act, Wyoming's populist senator Joseph O'Mahoney had proposed in its stead a federal incorporation act, meant simultaneously to achieve the disparate goals of more effective antitrust enforcement, advancement of employees' right, and protection of shareholders by requiring every firm engaged in interstate commerce to secure a license from the Federal Trade Commission. Each license, in addition to requiring equal treatment for female employees, barring child labor, and guaranteeing employees the right to bargain collectively, would have barred dishonest or fraudulent trade practices. A second title would have guaranteed stockholders equal voting rights, disallowed bonuses or commissions to corporate officers unless voted by stockholders, required the distribution to stockholders of corporate surplus above a specified percentage of capital stock, and authorized the Civil Service Commission to accredit corporate representatives to serve as proxy-holders. A final title would have excluded the interstate shipment of goods produced in whole or in part by child labor.[139] The concept of a federal licensing act, though not O'Mahoney's admixture of provisions, appealed to Roosevelt.[140]

In January 1937, Idaho's William Borah, a senator more respected by the Roosevelt administration than O'Mahoney, introduced a second corporate licensing bill. Having as its basic purpose the prevention of monopolies, the bill authorized the FTC to refuse to license or to revoke the license of any interstate firm violating the antitrust laws.[141]

The Borah approach, basically a death sentence for antitrust-law violators, was consonant with Roosevelt's own view. With Roosevelt's tacit support,[142] Assistant Attorney General Robert Jackson and Interior Secretary Harold Ickes delivered a series of virulent antimonopoly addresses in December 1937 and January 1938. At approximately the same time, O'Mahoney and Borah decided to combine the substantive features of their respective bills into a new jointly sponsored corporate-licensing bill.[143] However, as the 1937–1938 recession deepened, the policy differences among Roosevelt's principal economic advisers sharpened. The administration's leading conservatives, including Treasury Secretary Morgenthau, Commerce Secretary Roper, the RFC's Jesse Jones, and Joseph Kennedy, urged the President to conciliate business by, among other actions, declaring a moratorium on reform initiatives.[144]

Roosevelt resolved this conflict within his administration with his ill-fated Temporary National Economic Committee proposal. On April 22, 1938, Roosevelt first publicly announced substantial agreement with Senator Borah on the monopoly issue.[145] But he did not endorse either of Borah's proposals to enforce the antitrust laws through federal licensing of corporations. Instead, one week later, Roosevelt asked Congress to appropriate $500,000 so that the FTC, the SEC, and the Department of Justice could make a comprehensive study of the concentration of economic power in American industry.[146] By linking the passage of any new federal corporations statute to Borah's death sentence for antitrust-law violators, and implicitly to O'Mahoney's labor reform legislation — and deferring passage of each until a major interdepartmental economic study was completed — Roosevelt doomed the chance of any federal corporate governance law being enacted during the New Deal. New Deal historian Ellis Hawley has suggested that, given the divisions within the Roosevelt administration, this may have been Roosevelt's intention.[147] More likely, it was inadvertent. Roosevelt initially requested funding for an Executive Branch study, whose direction would have been controlled by men such as Robert Jackson, Thurman Arnold, and Douglas. In their hands, the appropriation probably would have been used to conduct public hearings dramatizing the need for new legislation in much the same fashion as Pecora earlier had used the stock exchange practices hearings to build support for the securities laws. Instead, Congress authorized $500,000 for the unwieldy Temporary National Economic Committee (TNEC), composed of six members of Congress and representatives from six federal agencies.[148]

Practical control of the TNEC rested with Senator O'Mahoney, who had introduced the authorizing resolution and was selected its chairman. O'Mahoney stifled the potential of the TNEC to function as an adversarial body by insisting that its hearings "impute no blame." Indeed, so concerned was O'Mahoney with reassuring the business community that the TNEC was "not a punitive expedition" that at one point he explained to a panel of industry witnesses, "We of the committee might just as well be sitting on the other side of the table. Our interests are really the same." As a consequence, the TNEC hearings were, in O'Mahoney's own word, "dull."[149] Yet, while refusing to use the TNEC hearings for adversarial purposes, O'Mahoney remained wedded to the omnibus concept of "national

charters for national business." Through the conclusion of the
TNEC investigation, in March 1941, O'Mahoney remained an advocate of a single generic law embracing antitrust, shareholder, labor,
and ultimately consumer reforms as the basic legislative aim of
TNEC.[150] However much sense O'Mahoney's all-embracing corporate-licensing proposal might have made as a liberal political party's
platform, it divided the TNEC. Eventually even the final SEC representative, Sumner Pike, voted against it, in part because
O'Mahoney, in order to secure a TNEC majority in favor of the
corporate-licensing concept, made his description of the proposal
increasingly vague.

After Roosevelt's antimonopoly study message, the SEC briefly
campaigned for a comprehensive corporate governance statute. On
May 10, 1938, Part VII of the *Protective Committee Study* was published. It concluded with the recommendation that it was "impera-
tive . . . to eliminate the abuses in our corporate system made possible by lax state corporation laws." The report recommended the
adoption of a federal incorporation law or use of the federal tax
power to prevent state "chartermongering."[151] An SEC Monopoly
Study unit soon was established to investigate corporate practices
(as well as investment banking and the insurance industry) as the
Commission's research contributions to the TNEC. But Douglas
subsequently became convinced that it was unlikely that the TNEC
would lead to the adoption of any new federal corporate governance
statute. Beginning in December 1938, Douglas attempted to persuade O'Mahoney to allow the SEC to seek adoption of the narrow
corporate registration bill he earlier had presented to Roosevelt.
These efforts did not succeed either in Douglas's remaining months
as chairman or during Jerome Frank's subsequent chairmanship.[152]

*   *   *

William Douglas's chairmanship ended somewhat sooner than he
had expected it would. Early in 1939, Douglas sent word to
Roosevelt that he intended to accept the Yale Law School deanship
for the academic year beginning September 1939. By that time,
Douglas believed "the work of the Commission in the field of
finance [would have been] rounded out." The Securities, Securities
Exchange, and Holding Company Acts would have been proven "to
be workable and sound." Indeed, Douglas already was envisioning
"some future time [when] it should be possible to merge or consoli-
date the various registration or reporting requirements of the three
Acts to the end that information filed by a corporation under one
statute would serve the purposes of all three statutes." Douglas

accurately anticipated that trust indenture and investment company legislation would be enacted, and early in 1939 he still hoped that his corporate registration bill could be. The preservation or enactment of these measures, Douglas believed, would complete the Commission's mandate "in the field of finance and would still keep [the Commission] within permissible size limits."

Soon after Justice Louis Brandeis retired, on February 13, 1939, however, Douglas abruptly changed his career plans. Aided by *The New York Times*'s Arthur Krock, Thomas Corcoran, Benjamin Cohen, Senator Borah, and others, Douglas campaigned hard for Roosevelt's nomination to succeed Brandeis on the Court.

Roosevelt had publicly indicated that his next Court appointee would come from the West. Although Douglas had been raised in Yakima, Washington, his adult years had been spent at such Eastern institutions as the Columbia and Yale Law schools. In 1939, he was a resident of the State of Connecticut. Not until Senator Borah, then the ranking Republican member of the Judiciary Committee, held a press conference to announce that he regarded Douglas as a Westerner did Douglas feel he had any chance for the appointment. But he faced substantial opposition. The other leading Western candidate was Washington's senator Lewis Schwellenbach, then one of the most radical members of Congress. By contrast, Douglas appeared to be a conservative, leading *The New Republic* and journalists like I. F. Stone and Max Lowenthal to campaign against Douglas as a "pawn of Wall Street." Such accusations were fatuous, but of sufficient concern that when representatives of seventeen stock exchanges, on March 14, 1939, proposed amendments to the 1933 and 1934 Securities Acts, Douglas not only led the SEC in rejecting the proposals but persuaded the Commission to issue a press release within twenty-four hours blasting the proposals as an attempt to "bring the pool operator back into the market," which could work only to the benefit of "the insider and the market rigger [and] destroy . . . investor confidence." Orally, Douglas labeled the proposals "phony." Since the proposals had been made before and were advanced in good faith, the intensity of Douglas's response bewildered New York Stock Exchange president William McChesney Martin, who soon requested a meeting to clarify "misunderstandings." But Douglas's "red-hot criticism" of Wall Street achieved its intended result, muting the charges that Douglas was "too conservative." Four days later, Roosevelt sent the Senate Douglas's nomination.

On April 16, Douglas would recall, "there was a farewell party at the SEC, the whole staff attending. It was a sad occasion, for an old regime had ended and a new one was about to be launched. We would go different ways, and old friends would now disappear."[153] With Douglas's departure, the SEC passed its historic zenith. Never again would the Commission receive such strong support from the White House, Congress, and the public. As the memory of the stock market crash, Pecora's investigation, and the Whitney scandal faded, the Commission's ability to initiate new reforms would dissipate. Increasingly, it would be known for its technical proficiency, not for its legislative reform role. Moreover, Washington itself would change. During the New Deal, the SEC had loomed large because it was the lead agency in addressing one of the half-dozen or so major problems that the Roosevelt administration was committed to solve. But the federal government would expand enormously in the post–World War II period, reducing the Commission to one of the smallest of the alphabet of agencies. And even before the postwar expansion of Washington, World War II itself began the diminution of the Commission that had been built up by Kennedy, Landis, and Douglas.

7

The End of the New Deal

*The Securities and Exchange Commission was a wartime casu-
alty. Moved from Washington to Philadelphia as a nonessential
agency, lessened in importance due to the doldrums into which
the private capital markets fell because of the war and the supremacy of governmental financing, the Commission turned from
a "glamor" agency of the New Deal into something of a "forgotten
man."*

— J. SINCLAIR ARMSTRONG
SEC chairman, 1955–1957[1]

ON MARCH 31, 1939, after Germany's annexation of Czechoslo-
vakia, Great Britain and France declared that they would defend
Poland. From that date until V-J Day, six and a half years later,
World War II overshadowed all other events in official Washington.
As early as April 11, 1939, SEC chairman Douglas met with Treasury Secretary Morgenthau, Agriculture Secretary Wallace, and the
Federal Reserve Board's Marriner Eccles to develop a contingency
plan to close all securities and commodities exchanges in the event
of a wartime market panic.[2] It was never used, but Jerome Frank,
Douglas's successor as SEC chairman, in an April 1940 address to
the Army Industrial College soon initiated a three-year Commission campaign to administer a program modeled after the World
War I Capital Issues Committee "to police and supervise all private
capital issues to determine whether the financing is consistent with
the defense program." In spite of the support of Roosevelt, Morgen-

thau, and the National Association of Securities Dealers, the opposition of the military prevented the SEC from assuming responsibility for capital issue control or any other significant wartime role.[3] In March 1942, the Commission, considered a "nonessential" agency, was physically transferred to Philadelphia. There, one third of its staff would be furloughed for military service, its budget would be reduced, and throughout 1942 and 1943 its stop order enforcement activities would cease.[4]

Yet World War II was to have little lasting effect on the SEC. The Commission's most important work, the geographic integration program under the Public Utility Holding Company Act, advanced in spite of the war. The anti–New Deal Seventy-sixth Congress (1939–1940), not the looming European conflagration, lessened the Commission's power to secure its final New Deal enabling acts, but did not prevent the SEC from winning passage of the compromise 1940 Investment Company and Investment Advisers Acts. As long as Roosevelt lived, the Commission was able to defeat all efforts to amend significantly the Securities Acts. The SEC was a "wartime casualty" only in the sense that during World War II the Commission lost its ability to initiate new reform programs.

＊   ＊   ＊

Jerome Frank, the SEC's fourth chairman, was one of the most memorable personalities of the New Deal.[5] Gifted with a photographic memory, able to read as many as two hundred pages of technical literature an hour, and work as many as twenty hours a day, he would in his lifetime write learnedly of psychoanalysis, economics, semantics, historiography, religion, drama, physics, political theory, moral philosophy, and urban transportation while devoting most of his published writings to strictly legal topics. Richard Rovere, who had collected material for a biography of Frank, once speculated, "It seems entirely possible that he has read more than anyone else alive today" and declared Frank "a species of universal genius." To his close friend William O. Douglas, Frank was a man who "traveled the world in his library"; to Second Circuit Court Judge Learned Hand, Frank's life was "a perpetual cerebration."

Jerome Frank, however, would leave his mark on the New Deal largely because of his technical virtuosity as a corporate lawyer and statutory draftsman, his unremitting compassion for the powerless and the poor, and his adversarial spirit. He was, in Abe Fortas's view, a "spark plug" of the early New Deal, but also a prickly and pugilistic polemicist, a humorous, ebullient, warm-hearted spirit to his friends, an overly sensitive and contentious opponent to innumerable journalistic, scholarly, and governmental foes.

For all his erudition, the politcal education of Jerome Frank was an intensely practical one. Born into a cultured upper-middle-class German-Jewish family in 1889, Frank was the only son of a successful New York City lawyer. When Frank was young, his family moved to Chicago, where, at the age of sixteen, he entered the University of Chicago and soon became a disciple of Professor Charles E. Merriam, a La Follette Progressive and a leading political scientist of his day. At his father's "overpowering" insistence, Frank entered the University of Chicago Law School in 1909, later graduating with the highest academic average any student had yet achieved.

Following graduation Frank began a fifteen-year association with the Chicago corporate law firm of Levinson, Becker, Cleveland and Schwartz. There he would become an expert in the law of railroad reorganizations. Frank's greater enthusiasm was for municipal politics. He had interrupted his legal education for a year to serve as Charles Merriam's secretary when Merriam was elected a reform alderman to the Chicago City Council. Against the likes of aldermen popularly known as Hinky Dink and Bath House John, Frank honed a political style that was never to be known for its subtlety nor its reticence. Fifteen years later, as SEC chairman, he would write slashing letters to Walter Lippmann, Max Lerner, Arthur Krock, Raymond Moley, John T. Flynn, and countless other journalists he believed in error with the same bristling intransigence with which he had earlier learned to answer politicians whom he considered "notorious" exponents of "bare-faced graft." The same bruising style would pervade his more polemical articles and books.

In Frank's spirited view, Albert Einstein and Christopher Columbus Langdell, the father of American legal education, were "neurotics," the legal philosopher Roscoe Pound, an intellectual sneak thief in the night. At the same time, Justice Oliver Wendell Holmes, Jr., was the "completely adult jurist"; life was "not worth living" without William Douglas. Frank was capable of quoting Aristotle, St. Thomas Aquinas, Dante, Calvin, Cotton Mather, Chesterton, and Will Rogers to explain why he believed public utilities should be refinanced with equity, rather than debt, securities; and also of losing his first important job in the Roosevelt administration by rushing the resolution of a crucial policy issue while an adversary was out of town.

In the mid-1920s, Frank began a serious study of the psychoanalytic theories of Sigmund Freud. In his own words this period "was a turning point" in his life. In 1927–1928, he completed a psychoanalysis in six months by attending twice-daily sessions. At about the same time, he permanently left Chicago to join a New York corporate law firm and published his first book, *Law and the Modern Mind*.

Shortly after publication of *Law and the Modern Mind*, Frank was appointed a lecturer at the New School for Social Research and became a research associate at the Yale Law School. At Yale, he began his friendship with Douglas by co-authoring a technical article, "Landlord Claims in Reorganization," and *amicus* briefs. After Roosevelt's election, Frank wrote to Felix Frankfurter, "I know you know Roosevelt very well. I want to get out of this Wall Street racket anyhow. This crisis seems to me to be the moral equivalent of war and I'd like to join up for the duration." With Frankfurter's aid, Frank landed the position of general counsel of the Agriculture Adjustment Administration. In his fiery two-year career at the AAA, Frank fought the meatpackers and processors to protect consumers, finally losing his job by pressing too hard to secure legal rights for sharecroppers. Simultaneously, he helped draft the Agricultural Adjustment Act, the National Industrial Recovery Act, and other early New Deal legislation.

After Frank's dismissal from the AAA, he spent two and a half years as a journeyman New Dealer, briefly serving as a special counsel to the Reconstruction Finance Corporation, specializing in railroad reorganizations, before returning to a New York City law practice. During 1936 and 1937 he worked on a per diem basis as a special legal counsel for the Interior Department. He also wrote *Save America First*, a book-length tract urging the United States to remain economically and politically isolated from Europe and to reform its own economy, largely through public works, minimum wage, and kindred programs to increase laborers' and farm-workers' income. Frank also urged the restoration of an NRA-type agency with a new inter-industry council to prevent capital-intensive industries like steel from engaging in "industrial sabotage" by reducing output to maintain artificially high prices.

Roosevelt chided Frank for the isolationist title and argument of *Save America First*, and did not consider seriously the book's proposals to seek a reconstituted NRA. But he regarded Frank as one of his "loyal shock troops" who had "fought the good fight" in the AAA, the RFC, and the Department of Interior; in December 1937 he acceded to Douglas's request that Frank be named to the Commission to countervail the appointment of investment banker John Hanes. Although Frank occasionally disagreed with Douglas,[6] the irony of his three and a half years at the SEC was the extent to which he set aside advocacy of his own Tugwell-type economic views to support and continue Douglas's initiatives. Like Douglas, Commissioner Frank viewed the SEC in Brandeisian terms as an "investor's advocate" to offset the power of inside management and bankers' control, as an advocate of regionalism, and as a "physician" to "cure past ailments" in the public utility, securities exchange, and investment company fields. Frank believed that the SEC, unlike the AAA and NRA, was "not primarily creative," but rather "a conservative institution striving in its own legitimate field patiently, sensibly, but persistently to assist in the work of conserving by improving our profit system."

After Robert Hutchins declined the job, Frank was Douglas's choice to succeed him as SEC chairman. Roosevelt reluctantly concurred, insisting on April 19, 1939, that the SEC "at once" designate Frank chairman, but with the understanding that Frank would be succeeded as chairman within a few months by Leon Henderson, Harry Hopkins's economic adviser, then spearheading the TNEC investigation, whom Roosevelt named to fill Douglas's vacancy on the Commission. When Henderson declined the chairmanship in favor of war-related responsibilities, and Ben Cohen also declined the job, Frank became a full chairman. Roosevelt's reluctance to vest Frank with the chairmanship was, in part, a consequence of Frank's repeatedly communicated preference for a judicial appointment. Roosevelt also was concerned that Frank's strained personal relationships with Commissioners Healy and Mathews after Douglas dismissed Public Utilities Division director C. Roy Smith at Frank's behest,* might jeopardize the SEC's restructuring of the public utility industry. It was only after Frank completed Douglas's reorganization of the Public Utilities Division and supported the thirty or so major lawsuits that led to the restructuring of the power industry that the White House reposed complete confidence in Frank.[7]

* * *

---

* Fallout from the Smith dismissal was to continue throughout Frank's chairmanship, most publicly in October 1940, when the still bitter Smith would write a statement for the Republican National Committee saying that while he was in charge of the Public Utilities Division he "personally, though reluctantly, directed a politically inspired investigation" of a public utility once led by Wendell Willkie, the Republican presidential nominee. The charge did not hold up, but Frank, alarmed, unsuccessfully attempted to have the Commission fire the SEC staff attorney who conducted the investigation, which, in turn, provoked a bitter dispute with Chester Lane, then the SEC's general counsel.[8]

Throughout his two years as chairman, Frank was preoccupied with the enforcement of the Public Utility Holding Company Act. He viewed the act as "vital not only to the success of the Securities and Exchange Commission, but also to the success of the New Deal,"[9] and took particular pride in writing Roosevelt in March 1941, when he left the SEC for a Second Circuit Court of Appeals judgeship, "We have broken the back of the utility integration problem . . . From now on, what is needed in that field is quiet firmness and technical competence."[10] Lack of a Supreme Court quorum delayed a definitive construction of the Holding Company Act's integration and simplification section until 1946, deferring full realization of the results of the SEC's restructuring of the utility industry until the Truman administration.[11] Much of the work necessary for the industry's restructuring, however, was accomplished before the definitive Supreme Court decisions.

The earliest consequences of the Frank Commission's aggressive enforcement of the Holding Company Act came instead in the field of public utility finance, most notably in the SEC's issuance of Rule U-50, which demanded compulsory competitive bidding for the underwriting of utility securities. "The competitive bidding controversy," Vincent Carosso, an investment banking historian, later would conclude, was "the most bitterly fought issue facing investment bankers since the passage of the Securities Act, if not in the entire history of the industry."[12]

The April 1941 promulgation of Rule U-50 was to be the Commission's most direct challenge to the House of Morgan's historic dominance of utility new security origination. The enactment of the 1933 and 1934 securities laws had not altered the dominance of the securities origination business by a half-dozen Wall Street investment banks. As a 1940 SEC Public Utilities Division study found, "During the five and one-half year period [January 1934 to June 1939], six leading New York bankers managed 62 percent of all registered, managed bond issues and 57 percent of all registered, managed bond, preferred stock, and common stock issues." Morgan, Stanley and Company, the J. P. Morgan investment bank formed after the 1933 Banking Act required its divorce from the J. P. Morgan commercial banking operations, in particular had benefited from what the SEC study alleged to be "an unwritten code whereby once a banker brings out an issue, the banker is deemed to have a recognized right to all future public issues of that company."* Since its

---

* The Investment Bankers Association disputed the SEC's allegation concerning the extent of concentration in the underwriting business, arguing that the crucial index

formation in September 1935, Morgan, Stanley alone had managed 81 percent of all first-grade registered bond issues. Major regional investment banks, such as Chicago's Halsey, Stuart and Company and Cleveland's Otis and Company, effectively were denied the opportunity to compete with Morgan, Stanley and other leading Wall Street firms like Kuhn, Loeb, Lehman Brothers, and Goldman, Sachs when the New York firms had a pre-existing relationship with a securities issuer.[15] In the public utility industry, the concentration of the securities origination business was particularly great, with Morgan, Stanley alone managing 70 percent of first-grade public utility bond issues. By 1940, the primary limitation on the size of utility security–underwriting spreads was the growing practice of directly selling high-grade utility debt issues to insurance companies.[16]

Although it was not within the SEC's mandate to require competitive bidding in any other industry, the Public Utility Holding Company Act required the SEC to establish "arm's-length bargaining" and "maintain competitive conditions" in utility firm securities offerings. But the Commission proceeded slowly in enforcing these requirements. In a 1936 case it exhorted utilities to introduce competition in securities underwriting, but, by a 3–2 vote, permitted the Kansas Electric Power Company to place noncompetitively a securities issue with an affiliated investment bank.[17] The following year, Commissioner Douglas made his celebrated New York Bond Club address, urging compulsory bidding in all new securities sales. Although the Interstate Commerce Commission since 1926 had required compulsory competitive bidding for railroad equipment trust issues, and three states and the District of Columbia then enforced competitive-bidding requirements for public utilities,[18] the SEC in late 1938 adopted Rule U-12F-2, which did not require compulsory bidding. Instead, it barred affiliated investment banks from underwriting securities unless their participation was less than 5 percent

---

was not the percentage of all issuances managed by a lead underwriter, but rather "the actual underwriting *participation* of each underwriter."[13] Since the lead underwriter determined the underwriter and dealer spreads,this argument did not directly respond to the SEC's basic point, which was that lack of competition among lead underwriters resulted in higher underwriting costs. The Investment Bankers Association also challenged the SEC's implied allegation that the lack of competition in the industry was a result of agreements in violation of the Sherman antitrust law. A 1953 district court opinion, *United States* v. *Morgan*,[14] would concur that the leading investment bankers had not violated the antitrust laws. But, again, that finding did not contravene the SEC's basic argument that the customs and structure of the investment banking industry resulted in higher underwriting costs than there would have been in a more competitive industry.

of the offering and their fee was computed at the same rate as that of other underwriters, or unless the affiliate had been awarded the security issuance as the most favorable bidder in an open competition.[19] The rule soon proved ineffective. No use was made of the competitive-bidding procedure that Rule U-12F-2 was meant to encourage, nor did the rule loosen the historic bonds between the major utility systems and affiliated investment banks. The result, Jerome Frank complained in the *Consumers Power* case, was that "the issuer may not receive as good a bargain as if it dealt with independent underwriters."[20] Moreover, since the rule often required the Commission to hold hearings to judge the presence or absence of an "affiliation" between the utility and the lead underwriter, it was disliked almost as intensely by the SEC's Public Utilities Division as it was by the utility industry and investment banks.

Soon after the Federal Power Commission adopted a compulsory-bidding requirement in 1939, Joseph Weiner and Robert O'Brien of the Public Utilities Division began lobbying the full Commission to adopt a similar rule. The five commissioners were at first somewhat tentative in their enthusiasm. In February 1940, the division was instructed to make a full study of the issue, and nearly simultaneously the leading investment banks and registered utility systems were invited to comment on the wisdom of adopting a competitive-bidding rule.

The "Public Utilities Division Report," issued on December 18, 1940, was an adversarial document presenting the case for competitive bidding with four primary arguments:

> 1. Competitive bidding may be expected to remove the threat (and actuality) of banker domination of utility finance policies . . . 2. [It] should result in genuine arm's length bargaining for securities thus sold . . . 3. [It] may be expected to reduce the concentration now found in the underwriting management of new utility issues . . . 4. It should produce reasonable prices and fees . . .

Although acknowledging that almost all investment banks opposed the rule — only the major regional firms, Halsey Stuart, and Otis and Company, favored it — the division proposed that the right to distribute nearly all public issuances of utility securities above $1 million in aggregate amount be auctioned off to the highest investment bank or other bidder.[21]

The Investment Bankers Association and Morgan, Stanley's Harold Stanley carried the main burden of the opposition, most persuasively arguing that the reduction of underwriting income might jeopardize the existence of the nationwide networks of generally small broker-dealer houses through which underwriting syndicates distributed new issues.[22] In part to assay the actual risk to local broker-dealers, the Commission held a four-and-a-half-day "town meeting," beginning in late January 1941, which was attended by as many as two hundred "interested parties," most of whom were in the securities business.

Senator Harry Truman, then completing supervision of a twenty-three-volume study of the causes of railroad bankruptcies, was widely credited for delivering the decisive argument in favor of the Public Utilities Division's rule. Asserting that the noncompetitive banking associations of J. P. Morgan and Company with the Missouri Pacific Railroad, and Kuhn, Loeb with the Pennsylvania Railroad, had cost the railroads "exorbitant sums," had not resulted in short-term emergency loans to stave off bankruptcy, and had led banks to offer self-serving advice, Truman concluded that, where it was applicable, the ICC's competitive-bidding rule for railroad equipment trust certificates had "wiped out with one stroke the many types of abuse which, as our record abundantly illustrates, cluster about the traditional types of underwriting arrangements."[23] Also of significance to the Commission were assurances from Jesse Jones that if the leading underwriters refused to bid for utility bonds, the RFC would frustrate such a "bankers' strike" by itself bidding for them.[24]

In April 1941, the SEC promulgated Rule U-50, which was the Public Utilities Division's compulsory competitive-bidding rule with minor modifications.[25] Although the rule led to only a modest increase in the number of investment banks serving as lead underwriters in the utility field, it did significantly increase competition among the leading investment banks, making it possible for such firms as Halsey Stuart, and later Merrill Lynch, Pierce, Fenner and Smith, to compete rigorously with Morgan, Stanley and the handful of other banks that earlier had dominated utility finance. Cost savings consistently were reported. An SEC study of the underwriting spreads during the five-year period 1935–1940 had found that the average spread for 159 utility bond issues had been 2.49 percent. In the first three years of Rule U-50's existence, the spread on thirty-seven bond issues sold to underwriters by competitive bidding averaged 1.21 percent. In the 1944–1949 period, the spread on 179 utility bond issues averaged less than 1 percent.

Such "tremendous economies" led even the *Public Utilities Fortnightly* as early as 1951 to publish an article titled "Competitive Bidding Proves Out." More recent evidence suggests that competitive-bidding procedures also may reduce issuer costs by leading to lower yield rates.[26] For this reason, two articles published in 1979 by the *Journal of Finance* recommended that corporations and state and local governments begin generally employing competitive bidding to avoid the "significantly higher new issue borrowing costs" produced by negotiated sales.[27]

*　*　*

The SEC's greatest legislative defeat during the Roosevelt administration involved the compromises necessary to win enactment of the Investment Company Act of 1940.*

The SEC officially would observe that the law represented "the minimum workable regulation of investment companies," in part justified because it provided the Commission with a basis from which to seek "major amendments . . . if and when amendment seems advisable."[29] Unofficially, the act represented the most the SEC could achieve in the anti–New Deal Seventy-sixth Congress, a half-a-loaf compromise made with the investment company industry because of uncertainty that any law could be enacted after the November 1940 presidential elections or the start of American participation in World War II.

Before the 1929 stock market crash, the history of American investment companies had been comparatively brief. Although one Massachusetts investment trust may have been formed as early as 1823, investment companies played a relatively minor role in the United States economy until 1926. It was only in the frenzied years just before the stock market crash that investment companies became, in John Kenneth Galbraith's words, "the most notable piece of speculative architecture of the late twenties, and the one by which, more than any other device, the public demand for common stocks was satisfied." Where approximately 160 investment trusts with combined assets of less than $1 billion were actively in business in 1926, close to 600 new investment companies were formed in the next three years, increasing total assets to over $8 billion just before the 1929 market break.

Three considerations were emphasized in the high-pressure sales campaigns that stimulated the investment companies' abrupt growth. First, American promoters stressed the successful record of the earlier-formed English and Scottish investment trusts. Second,

---

* The accompanying Investment Advisers Act was of considerably less consequence, originally providing little more than a pro forma registration requirement for personal investment advisers with fifteen or more clients, and antifraud provisions.[28]

small investers were informed that only through an investment company could they economically diversify their shareholdings and reduce their risk. Finally, tremendous emphasis was placed on the quality of the investment company's management. As one saying went, the investment companies formed by the Dillon, Read investment bank provided "an opportunity to let the public in on [Clarence] Dillon's investment brains."

Given the nature of the pre–stock market crash sales promotion, it was hardly surprising that 97 percent of the industry's assets in 1929 were held by management companies that provided little or no restriction on the type or frequency of investments a company could make, almost all of the largest investment companies were organized and managed by leading investment banks, and a majority of common shareholders held investments of $500 or less.

Because the virtually unregulated investment companies provided obvious opportunities for their managers to exploit ill-informed small investors, the firms were suspiciously regarded even before the 1929 stock market crash. A prescient March 1929 *Atlantic Monthly* article by investment company manager Paul Cabot, for example, complained of the "dishonesty; inattention and inability; and greed" in the investment trust movement, warning that without the remedies of publicity and education, a period of "disaster and disgrace" would be "inevitable."[30] Similar considerations, less melodramatically expressed, dissuaded the New York Stock Exchange from permitting even the tentative listing of investment trust securities until June 1929.[31]

After the 1929 stock market crash, the reputation of the investment companies declined even more rapidly than it had grown in the previous three years. With aggregate investment company assets shrinking to $2.8 billion and at least twenty-two companies declaring bankruptcy, the investment companies were criticized by the *New York Journal of Commerce,* the *American Bankers Association Journal,* and *Barron's* between October 1929 and February 1930. *The New Republic's* John T. Flynn effectively commenced his career as the generation's best-known critic of Wall Street with an April 1930 article, "Investment Trusts Gone Wrong." Soon Flynn was joined by the *Harvard Law Review,* which in November 1930 published a discussion of the need for statutory regulation of investment trusts.[32]

Legislation was to be almost a decade in coming. Although the Pecora hearings would investigate several investment companies and the final report denounce the "veritable epidemic of investment trusts [that] afflicted the nation,"[33] the abuses of the investment companies were overshadowed by the far more publicized misdeeds of J. P. Morgan and Company, Charles E. Mitchell, pool market operators, and purveyors of then near-worthless foreign bonds. The SEC was responsible for sustaining concern. In July 1935, Paul Gourrich, the Commission's technical adviser, prepared at Commissioner James Landis's request a memorandum summarizing "prima facie evidence of the need of a thorough investigation of the investment companies." The memorandum said, "So many misdeeds and malpractices are revealed in this study, so shocking are some of the findings, that the following summary is virtually a bill of indictment."[34] At approximately the same time, Commissioner Robert Healy, who had directed the FTC's seven-year investigation of public utility holding companies, communicated his belief that investment companies subsequently might be employed by those seeking to evade the public utility holding company bill, then nearing enactment.*[35] At the recommendation of the SEC, Section 30 was added to the legislation. It directed the Commission to deliver a study of investment companies to Congress no later than January 4, 1937.

The SEC's six-year study of investment trusts and investment companies, supervised by Healy, closed a decade of government investigation of financial scandals with a 5100-page report. By delaying publication of most of the report until 1939 and 1940, the SEC was able to describe two generations of investment company misconduct and to show that the unsupervised reorganization of the industry after the crash had created problems almost as serious as the promoters' abuses that stimulated the investment companies' 1927–1929 growth.

The basic sin of the investment bankers who formed investment companies before the 1929 crash had been self-interest. Excessive fees were a commonplace of the period, with promoters often profiting from the distribution of securities in the investment companies themselves and from the purchase and sale of a portfolio of securities, as well as from management contracts, stock options, and the unloading of slow-moving securities. Illustrative were Dillon, Read's two giant investment companies, the United States and Foreign Securities Corporation and the United States and International Securities Corporation.

When it was begun in 1924, the United States and Foreign Securi-

---

* At the time over 40 percent of the so-called investment companies were, in fact, holding companies, most in the public utility field, including such well-known firms as Insull Utility Investments and J. P. Morgan's United Corporation.

ties Corporation was considered by Hugh Bullock, an investment company executive, to be "by far the most eminent of the trusts of the early 1920s." The public was sold 250,000 shares of first preferred stock at $100 a share for $25 million; Dillon, Read purchased 50,000 shares of second preferred stock for $5 million. Anyone purchasing the preferred stock received as a bonus a common stock share with each share of preferred. Dillon, Read also awarded itself 250,000 common shares for its considerably smaller preferred stock investment and sold itself an additional 500,000 shares of common stock for $100,000. Thus, at the formation of the firm, Dillon, Read not only received a standard $1 million underwriting fee, but also locked up 75 percent of the possible profits of the company on an investment one-fifth as large as that made by public investors. In a rising market, Dillon, Read's common stock was worth over $17 million by September 1928. But the company also would profit from the United States and Foreign Securities Corporation by acting as its broker in purchasing and selling securities for its investment portfolio, directing the investment company in at least sixteen instances to purchase blocks of new securities originated by Dillon, Read, and causing the firm to buy large blocks of railroad securities from Dillon, Read in a slumping market.

In October 1928, Dillon, Read amplified its opportunities to profit from captive brokerage and underwriting sales by using $10 million of the surplus profits of the United States and Foreign Securities Corporation to purchase all of the second preferred stock and two million shares of common stock in a new subsidiary investment firm, the United States and International Securities Corporation. With public investors advancing $50 million for first preferred stock and a minority of the common shares, Dillon, Read, by that date, had succeeded in creating a controlled pool of $80 million on its own initial investment of $5.1 million. As long as the market rose, all of the public investors did receive a 6 percent annual return on their preferred stock investment. But after the crash, the excessively leveraged United States and International Securities Corporation went bankrupt, and the original United States and Foreign Securities Corporation sustained losses amounting at one time to $26 million.[36] Such results were common for the more highly leveraged investment companies. "By the end of 1937," the SEC would report, "the average dollar which had been invested in July 1929 in the index of leverage investment company common stocks was worth 5¢, while the nonleverage dollar was worth 48¢."[37]

Following the stock market crash, approximately half of the investment companies organized between 1927 and 1936 went out of business. With the market values of shares in investment companies at times averaging 35 percent less than asset values, a considerable number of investment companies were acquired by scavenger firms like Floyd Odlum's Atlas Corporation. The scavengers preyed on yet another vulnerability of the nonvoting public preferred stockholders. Although the preferred shareholders technically were entitled to a prior claim on all investment company assets in the event of bankruptcy or dissolution, only the common stockholders could vote a voluntary dissolution. Since it would have tarnished the reputation of an investment bank controlling an investment company to be publicized as responsible for a business failure, many investment banks preferred to sell their control block of common stock to a scavenger firm. In a few documented instances, the scavengers bribed investment company directors or officers to vote in favor of a transfer of control or to recommend a transfer. For example, after receiving a payment of $75,000, C. Shelby Carter, a director and vice president of the All American General Corporation, agreed to use his "best efforts" to persuade the corporation's shareholders to accept Atlas Corporation stock worth $17.70 in return for All America shares with an asset value of $26.

Once a scavenger firm acquired control of an investment company, it often engaged in a second "mop-up" step to force the sale or redemption of the remaining publicly held shares. These early progenitors of exchanges, later known as "going-private" transactions, typically involved the merger of the acquired firm into the scavenger firm, with the shareholders of the investment firm offered a cash sum equal to less than the actual asset value of their shares. Although the public shareholders usually had the right under state corporations statutes to demand an appraisal and receive fair value, few did so. The costs of an appraisal procedure were often prohibitively high, and few public shareholders recognized the extent to which they were being exploited. The disclosure provisions of the 1933 Securities Act were not then interpreted as applying to such transactions. Only three states required automatic review of going-private mergers by an independent appraiser. The scavenger controlling the common stock of the investment company wrote the merger plan, wrote the accompanying solicitation, and often omitted mention of state appraisal rights or other material information.[38]

Even before the introduction of the SEC-drafted bill, its provisions for regulating investment companies were compromised in order to increase the possibility of the bill's enactment by the anti–New Deal Seventy-sixth Congress. After conferences of SEC staff with investment company industry leaders, beginning in late January

1940, SEC proposals to divorce completely investment companies from the investment banking firms, impose a death sentence on previously issued debt securities and preferred stock, and redistribute securities voting rights were dropped.[39] As introduced, the SEC bill was judged "moderate and well considered" by *The New York Times*.[40] Unlike the Public Utility Holding Company Act, it directed no reorganization of an industry. Instead, a variety of techniques employed in earlier securities laws were to be used to ensure that investors would receive fair value in future investment company transactions. Following the examples of the 1933 Securities Act and the Maloney Act amendments to the 1934 Securities Exchange Act, for instance, investment companies and their directors, managers, and advisers were to be registered with the SEC. Conflicts of interest were to be minimized by the flat prohibition of such practices as investment company underwriters' selling the investment company other securities. The companies would be internally policed through a requirement that a majority of each investment company's board of directors be composed of outside, unaffiliated people. Excessive promotion of investment companies was to be discouraged by barring persons from serving as officers of an investment company if they had promoted a second investment company within the preceding five years. To prevent investment companies from serving as disguised holding companies, maximum-size limits were to be imposed. Shareholders were to have the opportunity to approve any fundamental change in an investment company's policy and its manager's remuneration contract. In the future, with very few exceptions, all new issues of investment company securities were to be common stock with equal voting and dividend rights. The most far-reaching provisions to the bill focused on investment banking arrangements. Stock options and warrants for investment company underwriters were to be proscribed. Investment banker exploitation also was to be prevented by prohibiting underwriters from buying investment company securities except at the same price they were sold to the public (minus conventional underwriting fees) and by empowering the SEC to stop "unconscionable or grossly excessive sales loads." Fairness in the reorganization or dissolution of investment firms was to be realized by a comparable Commission power to block such transactions if found "not fair and equitable to all persons . . . affected."[41]

Although even the SEC's most conservative commissioner, George Mathews, considered the Commission's bill barely sufficient,[42] it was clear, after eighteen hearing days before a Senate Banking Subcommittee in April 1940, that the initial SEC bill would not be adopted by the Seventy-sixth Congress.[43] Many conservatives in Congress shared with Senator Robert Taft a dislike of giving the SEC or any regulatory agency "infinite . . . discretionary power . . . to tell a man how he shall conduct his business."[44]

Other congressional opponents of the bill were impressed by the arguments of the Lehman Corporation's Arthur H. Bunker, who during the hearings was the investment company industry's leading spokesman. Addressing himself primarily to the dozen most far-reaching provisions of the bill, Bunker argued that the SEC draft went "further than is necessary to safeguard the interests of investors," with the result that "it is quite possible [the] legislation [may] hamstring and shackle the operations of investment companies to such an extent that their usefulness may cease to exist."[45] Paradoxically, however, Bunker and most other investment company industry leaders were as eager as the SEC to secure passage of an investment company bill before the Seventy-sixth Congress adjourned. Only by enactment of a law, Bunker believed, could "the cloud" under which the industry long had operated be removed and investment companies regain the ability to market new securities. SEC support also was believed necessary to secure Internal Revenue rules that would subject all investment companies to equal tax treatment.[46] With Bunker's pledge that the investment company industry was "not only willing, but anxious to cooperate" with the SEC,[47] backed by a joint statement of investment company leaders accepting nearly all of the less consequential provisions of the SEC draft,[48] David Schenker, the SEC Investment Company Study director, and investment company attorneys Alfred Jaretzki and Warren Motley began in early April to negotiate a mutually satisfactory bill.[49]

The Investment Company Act was the product of five weeks of subsequent SEC-industry negotiations. Meeting daily in the same Carleton Hotel where James Landis and Benjamin Cohen seven years before had secretly written the Securities Act, Schenker, Jaretzki, and Motley labored throughout May 1940 to fashion a compromise bill. A breakthrough came on May 13, when the negotiators drafted a revised bill that proved acceptable both to the Commission and almost all investment companies. The final bill, though not purely a disclosure measure, contained several major SEC concessions. Principally, the SEC agreed to the following: it would not require registration of investment company officers; it would require that only a 40 percent minority of each investment firm's directors be disinterested outsiders; it would eliminate investment company maximum-size limits; eliminate limitations on the number of investment companies a person could sponsor; withdraw the flat prohibition against issuance of new debt securities or preferred stock in favor of a limitation on the amount each firm could issue; and would all but totally eliminate the Commission's fairness jurisdiction by limiting its power to enjoin reorganizations to instances where investment company security holders requested SEC intervention and a federal district court found a reorganization plan "grossly unfair." Since most of these concessions had been publicly requested by Arthur Bunker, and the investment companies' own concessions were comparatively less significant, one law review commentator condemned the compromise "for removing the most important features of the original bill."[50] The investment company bill *was* the only New Deal securities law unequivocally endorsed by the Investment Bankers Association.[51] The SEC, nonetheless, supported the watered-down bill, employing the election-year logic that if it failed to secure the Investment Company Act in the Seventy-sixth Congress, it ran the risk of getting no investment legislation in the foreseeable future.

Two months after the compromise bill publicly was endorsed by the SEC and the investment company industry, it was unanimously passed by both Houses of Congress.[52] Senator Wagner noted with approval that the bill "has the distinction of having the virtually unanimous support of the persons for whose regulation it provides, as well as of the regulatory agency by which it is to be administered."[53] President Roosevelt, less sanguine, used the occasion of the August 23, 1940, signing of the Investment Company Act to "look back" at the five earlier securities laws enacted during his administration, implying that "we have come a long way since the bleak days of 1929" primarily because of more stringent legislation, such as the Public Utility Holding Company Act of 1935.[54]

Besides providing less effective regulation of the investment company industry, the legislative defeat had a second and broader significance. Throughout the New Deal period, the Commission's draftsmen had evolved a more sophisticated concept of the SEC's appropriate enduring role. The Securities Act of 1933, the Commission's initial enabling act, popularly had been termed an antifraud measure because it explicitly required the SEC to ensure accurate dissemination of material facts to investors, rather than approve or disapprove securities issues. Yet it soon had been recognized that the principal usefulness of the act was not in preventing fraud, but in discouraging such activities as investment banker or corporate executive overreaching, which were not, as a matter of law, fraudulent, but often were deterred when held up to public scrutiny. Subsequent SEC statutes had more directly addressed the question of insider unfairness. Notably, the 1935 Holding Company Act empowered the Commission to impose fairness standards in reorganizing the capital structures of holding companies; the 1938 Chandler Act directed the SEC to advise federal courts concerning the fairness of bankruptcy reorganizations. Underlying the drafting of these acts and of the unenacted Lea Committee bill was the New Deal SEC's recognition that disclosure alone often did not effectively protect investors.

In the original investment company bill, the SEC endorsed the position that ensuring fairness to investors required not only full disclosure, but also that the Commission itself be empowered to enforce a fairness standard, that all stocks have the self-protection of a vote, and that a majority of investment company directors not be insiders.

When the Seventy-sixth Congress refused to grant the SEC power to enforce fairness requirements for investment companies, it sealed the impression that the SEC's primary role was to monitor a corporate disclosure system. As the character of the investment company industry before 1940 well illustrated, this was a second-best solution, permitting the Commission to be an effective "investor's advocate" when it could prove fraudulent misrepresentations or omissions, but making it a toothless watchdog when investors were exploited because they had less ability to appraise the worth of a securities transaction than did corporate insiders. Thirty-four years later, William Cary would urge that a Federal Corporate Uniformity Act be enacted to provide minimum federal fiduciary standards and "prescribe fairness as a prerequisite to any transaction." Echoing the SEC's arguments for the original investment company bill, Cary would write:

> Disclosure alone is not enough. It is absurd that a corporate transaction, clearly unfair though perhaps not fraudulent, should be subject to attack in the federal courts only upon the ground that it has not been disclosed to the shareholders rather than because of its inherent inequity . . . Even if it said that the securities laws focus exclusively upon protection of the securities market, confidence in the market generally and in any particular stock may depend as much upon the probity of management as upon the mechanism of the market. If we accept the soundness of the securities laws, then there should be a federal interest in providing a standard of conduct for management and the corporation on which much of the economy depends.[55]

For most post–World War II advocates of corporate reform, like Cary, the "first step" was a federal fairness standard.

* * *

After Chairman Douglas in March 1939 attacked as "phony" the recommendations of the New York Stock Exchange's Hancock Committee to amend the 1933 and 1934 Securities Acts,[56] relations between the Commission and the Exchange deteriorated. For two years Jerome Frank's SEC and William McChesney Martin's New York Stock Exchange engaged in a bruising confrontation concerning Martin's efforts to increase Exchange trading volume. Yet it was a struggle markedly different from the earlier New Deal wars between the Commission and the Exchange. The SEC sought to impose no new rules on the Exchange; merely to maintain a status quo among all national securities exchanges during a thin trading period. The Exchange did not seek to diminish fundamentally the Commission's power to regulate the securities markets. Indeed, the Exchange's most striking proposal was a recommendation that Congress *increase* the SEC's regulation of the over-the-counter markets so that all securities exchanges would be subject to an equal regulatory burden. By the end of the New Deal, relations between the SEC and the NYSE had evolved into the uneasy coexistence that was to characterize the SEC–New York Stock Exchange relationship after World War II. An adversarial relationship, usually somewhat distrustful, often tense, was to continue. But in Douglas's 1937–1939 reorganization, the SEC surrendered its opportunity to regulate the Exchange more directly. And during the presidency of William McChesney Martin, the Exchange just as plainly conceded that it lacked the power to lobby through any substantial withdrawal of statutory power from the SEC.

The precipitant of the last major New Deal SEC–New York Stock Exchange confrontation was a condition of near-panic on Wall Street during the prolonged 1938–1941 trading slump. After the 1937–1938 recession, the annual share volume on the NYSE had fallen from 721 million shares in 1936 to 196 million shares in 1941. Even with one out of three securities salesmen leaving the profession during approximately the same period, almost half of the New York Stock Exchange's member firms lost money in the first six months of 1941.[57]

As the trading slump continued, the position of the New York Stock Exchange's reform president Martin grew more vulnerable. A speech by Jerome Frank in June 1939, publicly calling for the same "brokerage bank" institution that Douglas had pressed the Exchange to adopt in private round-table discussions, provoked so angry a reaction among Exchange members (concerned about the bank's cost and impact on their already diminished brokerage business) that Martin had to threaten to resign to push through a minor trading rule he had earlier promised the SEC would be adopted.[58] Thereafter, Martin focused his Exchange presidency on persuading the SEC to allow the securities business "to catch its breath," periodically echoing the sentiments of his predecessors with public remarks like that of September 1, 1939: "The impact of regulation has already severely impaired the vitality of the market."[59] Martin's policy reversal strained his personal relationship with Chairman Frank, who indignantly accused Martin of duplicity on at least one occasion during the summer of 1939.[60]

Relations deteriorated further on September 28, 1939, when Martin appointed the Special Committee on Multiple Exchange Trading in Securities Listed on the New York Stock Exchange to study whether the Exchange should begin enforcing a generally ignored section of its constitution, initially adopted in 1863, which provided that any Exchange member who "deals publicly outside the Exchange in securities dealt in on the Exchange . . . may be suspended or expelled." If enforced, the section would have prevented NYSE members from trading securities listed on the Exchange on the floor of any other exchange, thereby preventing the "diversion" of trading equal to 4.4 percent of the Exchange's 1938 volume to the regional exchanges. To Martin, the loss caused by multiple trading of New York Stock Exchange securities was a matter of "deep concern." A rapid growth in multiple trading had taken place after the 1936 amendments to the Securities Exchange Act authorized the SEC to approve unlisted trading of Exchange securities on the regional exchanges, as one means, in the words of a Senate Banking Committee report, of "creating a fair field of competition among exchanges." Between 1937 and 1939, regional exchange trading in securities listed on the New York Stock Exchange increased over 60 percent, with further increases likely after the Boston Stock Exchange began advertising for additional business in 1939.[61]

Chairman Frank, during reconciliation efforts in September 1939, had expressed sympathy for Martin's efforts to increase Exchange members' income by volunteering SEC support if the Exchange raised commission rates, authorized brokers to collect new service charges, or sought enactment of an amendment to the Securities Exchange Act equalizing SEC regulation of the over-the-counter and exchange markets.[62] But a ban on multiple trading that would jeopardize the existence of the financially fragile regional exchanges was quite another matter. Exchange enforcement of its rule against member multiple trading would conflict with the purpose of the 1936 Securities Exchange Act amendments and the policy of the antitrust laws. The ban also flatly contradicted the decision of the Exchange in 1936 not to oppose that year's Securities Exchange Act amendments. As Exchange attorneys W. H. Jackson and Roland Redmond stated to Chairman Landis, there was a recognized "public interest" in "permitting New York Stocks to be dealt in other exchanges [since] it was important for local exchanges to exist in order to make an exchange market for local securities" and because "it was doubtful whether many of these exchanges could exist purely upon the revenues that they derived from trading in local securities."[63]

A subsequent SEC study would find that "during 1939 . . . the New York Stock Exchange succeeded in obtaining over 95 percent of the total round-lot and odd-lot trading on all national securities exchanges in stocks on its list. Competitive trading by regional exchanges in stocks listed on the New York Stock Exchange does not, therefore, constitute a serious immediate problem to the New York Stock Exchange, compared to their total volume." On the other hand, withdrawal of the comparatively small amount of multiple-trading business from the regional exchanges might have caused the failure of some of these exchanges. If all the regional exchanges had failed, as many as seven hundred securities that were traded exclusively on the local exchanges would have been relegated to the over-the-counter markets, where investors would pay higher costs for trading them, generally receive lower collateral values, and receive less complete information in corporate disclosure documents.[64]

Soon after the New York Stock Exchange's Board of Governors announced, on February 28, 1940, its intention to begin formal enforcement of its rule against multiple trading, the SEC tacitly communicated its disapproval by directing its Trading and Exchange Division to study the likely consequences of the governors' decision. Simultaneously, the regional exchanges began to lobby against the rule. Five of the six regional exchanges directly affected filed formal protests with the SEC, two claiming that they might have to dissolve if the rule was enforced, a third publicly threatening an antitrust suit. Republican Senate leaders Henry Cabot Lodge, Jr., and Robert Taft and Democratic congressman John McCormack also communicated their concern for the local exchanges.[65] Nevertheless, on July 12, 1940, the NYSE announced that, beginning September 1, 1940, it would discipline any member trading on another exchange securities listed on the New York Stock Exchange.[66] A late August SEC request that the Exchange delay enforcement of its policy for at least sixty days, until the Commission had completed its study of multiple trading,[67] was refused, although Martin offered sixty-day "stays of execution" to any Exchange member firm that made an individual request.[68]

Until the 1940 presidential elections, the SEC's response to the Exchange's campaign to ban multiple trading was restrained. Sumner Pike, a Republican businessman who succeeded Commissioner George Mathews, attempted to negotiate Exchange withdrawal of its rule against multiple trading. In October 1940, the Trading and Exchange Division published a preliminary report labeling "the action of the New York Stock Exchange . . . inimical to the interests of the investor and to the public at large" and recommending that the Commission take "appropriate steps to bring about the rescission [of the Exchange resolution to enforce the rule against multiple trading]."[69] But it was only after the Trading and Exchanges Division's final report, "The Problem of Multiple Trading on Securities Exchanges," issued in late November 1940, that the Commission formally requested the Exchange to change its rules "to make it clear the rules of the Exchange or their enforcement shall not prevent any member from . . . dealing upon any other exchange outside the City of New York of which he is a member."[70]

When the SEC, in the phrase of a *New York Times* headline, was "flouted again by [the] Exchange,"[71] the confrontation reached a vituperative dénouement. The Commission scheduled a January 1941 hearing to decide whether it should invoke its power, never previously employed, to cause an exchange to alter one of its own rules. Martin, whose effectiveness as Exchange president had been sharply diminished by continued low trading volume and the SEC's opposition to his most conspicuous proposal to increase Exchange volume, vented his frustration in March with a speech characterizing the SEC's commissioners as "ignorant," having "no fundamental concept of the broad picture of a market," and subverting volume on the Exchange through "unintelligent administration" of the securities laws.[72] These were remarkably foolish statements, easily answered in kind by SEC commissioner Pike, a former Wall Street investment adviser, who blasted Martin for "an unwillingness to face realities and to take steps indicated by plain common sense and good business judgment," and by SEC publication of a letter from General R. E. Wood, president of Sears, Roebuck, who had refused in June 1940 to stand for re-election as a "public" representative on the Exchange's Board of Governors because "the Stock Exchange even yet has no realization of its full duty to its customers."[73] When

Martin, the following month, answered a Selective Service Board's draft call and resigned from the NYSE, one Wall Street wag, seeing a newspaper photograph of the former Exchange president with the caption "Private William McChesney Martin," sarcastically dubbed him "the Happy Warrior."[74]

The Exchange quickly took steps to repair its tattered relationship with the SEC by appointing as its new president Jesse Jones's protégé and hand-picked successor as RFC chairman, Emil Schram. Schram, an Indiana-bred bookkeeper and eight-year veteran of New Deal politics, knew little about securities markets, but well understood that he had been hired to harmonize the relationship between the Exchange and Washington. "It is illogical," he urged in his June 1941 maiden address as Exchange president, "to suppose that the Securities and Exchange Commission is intent upon either the destruction of the Exchange or the strangulation of security markets . . . cooperation must be the keynote of the hour."[75] A final repudiation of Martin's confrontational approach came in October 1941. Three weeks after the SEC ordered the Exchange to rescind all prohibitions against its members' trading in Exchange-listed securities on other exchanges,[76] Schram wrote the Commission that the NYSE would not seek a court review of the SEC's order, but instead would give up its two-year battle to end multiple trading.[77]

Paralleling the Exchange's campaign to end multiple trading was its collaboration with the Investment Bankers Association, the New York Curb Exchange, and the National Association of Securities Dealers (NASD) in a less-heated three-year effort to secure amendments to the 1933 and 1934 Securities Acts. The effort was effectively begun when Martin appointed the Hancock Committee in January 1939 to work with fifteen other exchanges in recommending revisions of the 1934 Securities Exchange Act "to facilitate the flow of capital and improve the functioning of the securities markets."[78] It received expressions of support from the National Chamber of Commerce, the Investment Bankers Association, the National Association of Manufacturers, the New York Curb Exchange, the American Bar Association, and Senator Taft.[79] However, Wall Street's efforts to seek amendments to the securities laws were not considered a serious threat by the Commission until June 14, 1940, when House Interstate Commerce chairman Clarence Lea unexpectedly announced that during the following week John M. Hancock, who had led the New York Stock Exchange's amendment efforts, and Howard Coonley, chairman of the National Association of Manufacturers, would testify about the extent to which the securities laws had caused a "partial stagnation of capital investment."[80]

Privately, one congressman informed Commissioner Healy that the
hearing and two bills earlier introduced by Lea to amend the securities laws had been developed by Lea after consultation with the
Investment Bankers Association lobbyist John Starkweather and
that Chairman Lea, a Democrat unsympathetic to the New Deal,
planned future hearings "generally to investigate the activities of
the SEC."[81]

SEC chairman Frank, alarmed, requested top Roosevelt aide Colonel Edwin M. (Pa) Watson, then Roosevelt himself, to call on
House Speaker Sam Rayburn to prevent the initial anti-SEC hearing.
This, Rayburn was able to do, but only after the SEC agreed to meet
with the Investment Bankers Association, the NASD, and the stock
exchanges to discuss mutually acceptable amendments to the 1933
and 1934 Securities Acts, an opportunity that "delighted" the Investment Bankers Association president E. F. Connely.[82] In a related
effort to dampen efforts to amend the securities laws, the SEC acceded, on June 25, to a long-pressed Investment Bankers Association
demand to seek congressional authority to shorten the 1933 act's
statutory twenty-day waiting period before a new security registered
with the Commission could be sold to the public. This largely symbolic amendment was adopted as a rider to the Investment Company Act in August 1940, but thereafter was rarely employed by the
Commission.[83]

SEC conferences with the Investment Bankers Association, the
NASD, and the two New York stock exchanges officially began at
the staff level in October 1940 and continued through June 1941,
with the SEC ultimately agreeing with the financiers on fifty-five
technical amendments to the 1933 and 1934 Securities Acts.[84] But
the financiers' efforts to seek substantive amendments to the securities laws were frustrated, in part, by a fundamental policy dispute
between the Investment Bankers Association and the New York
Stock Exchange. Both organizations favored significant revisions to
the 1933 act, such as permitting offers on a new security to be made
on the basis of a "limited prospectus" before the Commission had
completed its review of the full statutory registration statement.
And both organizations agreed on several revisions of the 1934 act,
including withdrawal of the SEC's power to segregate exchange floor
members and repeal of the anti–insider trading Section 16(b).

The Investment Bankers Association, however, viewed the
amendment negotiations as an opportunity to seek a fundamental
reduction in the Commission's power and effectiveness. This intent
was most clearly reflected in proposals pressed by the association to
remove enforcement of the Public Utility Holding Company Act

from the Commission and to increase the number of SEC commissioners and departmentalize their authority.[85] By contrast, even during his most bitter assault on the SEC's commissioners, William McChesney Martin reaffirmed his general support for the 1934 Securities Exchange Act.[86] The Exchange's priority was to equalize SEC regulation of the over-the-counter and exchange markets, rather than seek a fundamental reduction in the statutory authority of the Commission.[87] But the Investment Bankers Association did not support the Exchange's "equalization" proposal, and the National Association of Manufacturers was so opposed to the Exchange's recommendation that it reversed an earlier position and recommended in December 1941 that Congress not adopt *any* amendments to the 1933 and 1934 acts, because of the risk that they would "add new burdens to American business."[88] Although the House Commerce Committee held hearings between October 1941 and January 1942 on proposals to amend the securities laws, SEC opposition to substantive revisions and the business community's internecine differences defeated the New Deal period's only significant effort to reduce the Commission's mandate.* Subsequently, the post–World War II revival of the securities business undercut the financial community's argument that the securities laws or the Commission measurably limited new securities flotations or stock exchange trading volume.

* * *

After Jerome Frank left the SEC for his Second Circuit Court of Appeals appointment in the spring of 1941, the Commission was chaired for nine months by former congressman Edward Eicher. Eicher was a figurehead, selected solely because war preparedness had deprived the Commission of more logical candidates for the job, like Commissioner Leon Henderson or Public Utilities Division director Joseph Weiner.[90] In December 1941, Eicher was nominated to be chief justice of the United States District Court for the District of Columbia, and was succeeded as SEC chairman by Ganson Purcell.

---

* The only legislative consequence of Wall Street's prewar drive to amend the Securities Acts was a 1945 amendment to the Securities Act to permit exemption of securities issues of up to $300,000 rather than the earlier small-issue exemption of $100,000.[89]

A more significant consequence of the 1940–1942 SEC-industry negotiations was that they effectively began the scholarly career of Louis Loss, who served as the junior SEC staff attorney at the negotiations. In the ensuing decades, Loss emerged as the leading legal scholar of securities regulation, not only writing the definitive treatise in the field, but also heading highly influential efforts to codify both state and federal securities law.

Purcell, an SEC careerist, had directed the Trading and Exchange Division from 1937 to 1941 before taking Frank's seat on the Commission and effectively running the SEC during Eicher's chairmanship. As with the contemporaneous appointments of Reorganization Division director Edmund Burke and Public Utilities Division director Robert O'Brien to be SEC commissioners, the selection of Purcell as chairman was part of a conscious Roosevelt effort to ensure the continuity of the SEC during and after World War II.[91]

Purcell's wartime leadership of the SEC was a personally frustrating one for the thirty-six-year-old Douglas protégé, who had been the SEC's field marshal for the Richard Whitney investigation and the subsequent New York Stock Exchange reorganization. In spite of what the five SEC commissioners termed a "legislative crisis,"[92] the SEC's headquarters was moved to Philadelphia three months after the United States entered World War II. After the formal declaration of war, in December 1941, new legislative initiatives were a political impossibility. Even Commission adoption of new proxy rules late in 1942 provoked a fierce outcry. The new rules did not include a proposal earlier considered by the staff to empower non-controlling shareholders to use the corporate proxy machinery to nominate directors. But the proxy revisions did require certain senior executives to disclose their compensation before seeking re-election or reappointment, allowed shareholders to circulate 100-word statements at the corporation's expense, proposing changes in corporate charters or by-laws, and directed that an annual report to shareholders accompany or precede the proxy.[93]

The regulations prompted what *Business Week* called "a storm of protest." Newspaper and magazine editorials complained that the SEC was "Bureau-crazy" and was "fettering business by proxy" while "American industry is doing such a magnificent job in helping win the war." A subsequent House Commerce Committee hearing investigating the new rules culminated with a congressional attack on the rule's draftsman, SEC attorney Milton V. Freeman, for his alleged communist sympathies,[94] prompting Roosevelt publicly to denounce businessmen for undercover efforts to get rid of the SEC and remind House Commerce Committee chairman Lea of an earlier understanding that no amendment to the SEC's statutes would be considered during the war.[95]

In April 1945, President Roosevelt died. The impact of his death on the Commission was almost immediate. Purcell had hoped to commence the postwar period with a Douglas-like effort to abolish floor trading on the two New York stock exchanges. A detailed staff study published in January 1945 made the case for prohibiting any stock exchange member from trading purely for his own account, because of the substantial advantages floor traders enjoyed over public customers and their tendency to "give rise to excessive speculation, resulting in sudden and unreasonable fluctuations in the price of securities." The New York Stock Exchange, predictably, was adamantly opposed to an abolition of floor trading. At a June 22, 1945, meeting, Exchange president Schram threatened "a cat and dog fight" if the SEC voted to abolish floor trading, stating that he would "go to Congress for changes in the statutes" if an SEC rule outlawing floor traders was issued. This proved unnecessary. On August 8, 1945, the SEC tentatively voted to abolish floor trading. On August 22, recalled Raymond Vernon, then a member of the Commission's Trading and Exchange Division, Chairman Purcell informed a Commission meeting that the White House had ordered the SEC to rescind the rule abolishing floor trading. Vernon, who was the only Commission official present at the August 22 meeting still living when this history was researched, could recall Purcell offering no explanation for this highly unusual intervention by the White House, but he speculated that the Truman administration, preoccupied with the conclusion of World War II, considered an SEC–New York Stock Exchange controversy a "trivial" and "diversionary" concern. As ordered, the SEC on August 22 withdrew its prohibition of floor trading, with the understanding that the NYSE would issue its own modestly restrictive floor trading rules. In the *SEC Minutes*, the Commission officially "expressed itself as doubting that the rules proposed by the Exchange would meet the more serious problems arising out of floor trading, especially the tendency of such trading to exaggerate market movements and aggravate fluctuations." The *Minutes* also included the SEC's conclusions "that floor trading as now conducted gives an undue advantage to floor traders over the public; that frequently it accelerates market movements and accentuates fluctuations in particular securities or groups of securities; that more often than not it detracts from the stability or liquidity of the market."

Since the SEC doubted that the New York Stock Exchange's rules could adequately deal with the problems created by floor trading, the Commission indicated that it would consider prohibiting floor trading if subsequent evidence showed that the Exchange's rules "are not sufficiently effective in minimizing the harmful effect of floor trading to justify their continuance."*[96]

---

* Ten months later, a report to the Commission by the Trading and Exchange Division indicated that studies it conducted "leave no doubt that the rules are grossly

By the spring of 1946, Purcell was openly skeptical that Truman wanted him to continue as SEC chairman. Truman had made it known that he considered Douglas, Purcell's mentor, a political rival. In June 1946, Purcell's resignation as SEC chairman became effective.[98]

---

inadequate for their purposes . . . To be sure, the volume of floor trading seems to have been somewhat reduced; but that reduction is in some aspects illusory. The volume of trading by leading floor traders is as great as it was before the adoption of the rules; the chief difference is that whereas such traders formerly initiated few transactions off the floor, they now initiate about one-third of their trades in that manner. By a judicious resort to frequent off-the-floor trades, floor traders appear to have found the means for minimizing the restraints of the rule while retaining the advantages of a floor location."[97] Nineteen years later, a Trading and Markets Division study would reach a similar conclusion about the SEC's 1964 rule to regulate floor traders. See Chapter 10.

8

The Public Utility
Holding Company
Commission

*A combination of corporations is not a mess of scrambled eggs but
a network of legal contracts. It is not a Gordian Knot which cannot be untied. What the ingenuity of corporation lawyers has put
together the ingenuity of other lawyers and the courts can take
apart.*

— DR. FRANK FETTER
TNEC, *Final Report* (1941)

THE SEC began a fifteen-year postwar decline during the presidency
of Harry Truman. As President, Truman had little interest in the
day-to-day administration of the Commission. Truman well characterized his attitude in December 1945, when he remarked at a
press conference, "I have had so many things to think about that I
haven't looked at the stock market, because I have never been interested in the stock market personally." A 1948 staff report of the
Hoover Commission on Organization of the Executive Branch of the
Government similarly observed, "Since the war, President Truman
has asked little more than to be kept informed of the activities of the
[Securities and Exchange] Commission."[1] Emblematic of Truman's
lack of personal interest in the SEC was the delay, until 1948, in
return of the Commission's headquarters from Philadelphia. Nor

was the SEC permitted to resume occupancy of its prewar office at 1758 Pennsylvania Avenue, a block and a half from the White House; it was housed in a "temporary" building constructed during the war. The SEC was to remain in the "tempo" for the next eighteen years.[2]

Although corporate law reform was never a priority of his administration, Truman was committed to the continuance of the SEC. Following Roosevelt's example, Truman named three former staff members among his first six Commission appointments. He personally questioned at least one other appointee about his sympathy toward the SEC's statutory mission before forwarding his name to the Senate for confirmation.[3] When World War II ended, the SEC had a staff of approximately 1150 employees. Until the Korean War began, in June 1950, Truman's Bureau of the Budget regularly approved SEC budgets sufficient to increase modestly the Commission's personnel.[4]

Yet Truman, to some degree, subverted the effective continuance of the SEC by the mediocrity of his Commission appointments. The appointments process, generally, was the Achilles' heel of the Truman administration. Throughout Truman's presidency, he was regularly criticized for appointing "party hacks," "cronies," or "fixers" to leading federal positions while dismissing, demoting, or pressing for the resignations of such leading New Dealers as Henry Wallace, Harold Ickes, James Landis, and Marriner Eccles. One sympathetic student of Truman's independent regulatory appointments estimated that "over half of Truman's selections involved political considerations."[5] No modern President, including Roosevelt, has avoided using some of his judicial and executive appointments as bargaining chips with which to gain congressional support or campaign contributions. Truman's presidency was not unique in this regard. It, however, was unique among post–World War II presidencies in the extent to which political considerations and cronyism dominated the appointments process and the number of scandals that subsequently wracked Truman's Justice Department, Internal Revenue Service, and Reconstruction Finance Corporation.[6]

Truman's SEC appointments were made with the same erratic regard for merit as the appointments made throughout much of the rest of his administration. Illustrative were Truman's three choices for SEC chairman. After Ganson Purcell resigned, the SEC was led for eighteen months by James Caffrey, a Roosevelt appointee who had served for nine years as administrator of the SEC's Boston and New York regional offices.[7] Truman took no part in the Commission vote that elected Caffrey chairman.[8] When Caffrey resigned, Truman persuaded the Commission to elect Edmond Hanrahan chairman. In 1946, Hanrahan had been appointed by Truman to the Commission as a reward for his prowess as a New York City Democratic Party fund-raiser.* Hanrahan was, SEC general counsel Roger Foster recalled, an "honest Tammany politician" with a "back-slapper's temperament." Although an attorney, Hanrahan had no background in securities law. When first named to the SEC, in July 1946, he had voted in favor of himself to succeed Purcell as chairman. So lacking in qualifications for the job had he been that SEC commissioner Robert McConnaughey not only voted against Hanrahan, but took the unusual step of recording in the *SEC Minutes* his belief that the SEC's "Chairman should be a person with experience in the Commission's affairs."[10]

Little better qualified was Harry McDonald, whom Truman recommended as SEC chairman after Hanrahan retired in 1949. Although McDonald for fourteen years had been a member of a Detroit investment bank, his primary business experience was in the dairy industry. Appointed to the Commission in 1946 at the recommendation of Truman's foreign policy ally Senator Arthur Vandenberg, McDonald was the first Republican to serve as SEC chairman, and he was named to that position because of his close personal friendship with Harry Truman. As fellow commissioner Robert Millonzi recalled, "Both men were Shriners, both men were Masons." In the evenings, when Truman would relax with friends and play his piano, McDonald often was called on to sing "Wagon Wheels," a song Truman particularly enjoyed. McDonald must have had a remarkably affecting voice. Three former SEC senior officials separately suggested during interviews that McDonald literally sang his way to the SEC chairmanship. *Forbes* magazine apparently credited the story. A 1950 profile said:

> Iowa-born Harry McDonald, whose ascendance came as a pleasant surprise to the business and financial community, is not cast in the smooth Ivy League Wall Streeter mold normally associated with the term "investment banker" . . . Before 1932 he was the McDonald of Detroit's McDonald Creameries and became known as the "singing milkman," a nickname which has stuck with him ever since. Singing, he insists, was just an avocation, but it helped pay his way through

---

* Two other Truman SEC appointees were successfully recommended by Paul Fitzpatrick, chairman of New York State's Democratic Party. They were Robert Millonzi, a Buffalo attorney specializing in banking matters, who had been suggested to Fitzpatrick by Hanrahan, and J. Howard Rossbach, attorney-in-chief of the New York City Legal Aid Society, a grandnephew of New York's Senator Herbert Lehman.[9]

school and made him a local celebrity when he sang oratorios with the Detroit Symphony. Now he just sings to be sociable — at the drop of a hat.

McDonald himself was candid about his lack of qualifications; he began his maiden address as SEC chairman with "My election as chairman . . . was a complete surprise to many, including myself." As chairman, McDonald largely followed the advice of such senior Commission staff members as Associate General Counsel Louis Loss or fellow commissioner and former staff member Donald Cook, who in 1950 was named to be the Commission's first, and thus far only, vice chairman, because, as Cook explained, "McDonald did not understand the securities statutes."[11]

Cook, Truman's final SEC Chairman,* was an able attorney and business school graduate with seven years' experience in the Commission's Public Utilities Division, where he had risen to become assistant director, before leaving in 1945 to become Attorney General Tom Clark's executive assistant. Like Hanrahan and McDonald, however, Cook was appointed a commissioner primarily because of political considerations. As Cook explained in an interview, during World War II he had served as counsel to Senator Lyndon Johnson's Naval Subcommittee and had befriended both Johnson and House Speaker Sam Rayburn. When, in 1949, President Truman had informed Rayburn that he could name the next SEC commissioner, Rayburn selected Cook. Out of loyalty to his political sponsors, Cook served from 1950 to 1952 as chief counsel to Senator Johnson's Committee on Korean War Preparedness while simultaneously directing the SEC, first as vice chairman, then, beginning in February 1952, as chairman.[13]

Truman's politicization of the appointments process harmed the SEC, in part because his SEC appointees tolerated practices that would have been sharply questioned by earlier chairmen like Douglas and Landis, who had a higher regard for the Commission's value. In February 1952, Senator Paul Douglas opposed Truman's nomination of SEC chairman Harry McDonald to be chairman of the Reconstruction Finance Corporation, arguing that the SEC during McDonald's chairmanship had "permitted . . . a very bad practice of allowing former members of the Commission, former chief counsel, and former heads of divisions to resign and then almost immediately to represent private [legal] clients before the SEC itself." Senator Douglas described several examples of this practice, which

---

* Pursuant to the provisions of the Reorganization Act of 1949, the President was given the power to choose directly the SEC's chairman beginning in 1950.[12]

began in 1937 with John J. Burns, the SEC's first general counsel, and continued through former chairmen Purcell, Caffrey, and Hanrahan. "When these men are retained," explained Senator Douglas, "they may be retained for their ability. They may be retained for their special knowledge; but they may also be retained for their influence." In two cases, involving Caffrey and Hanrahan, Paul Douglas alleged that the chairmen's clients had benefited from "extraordinary procedural rulings."[14] Since Senator Douglas referred to these two clients as "X Company" and "Y Company," it was not possible to establish the truth or falsity of his allegations.

Indeed, it is important to emphasize that no charge of improper influence-peddling was formally proven against any SEC official during the Truman administration. But the appearance of possible impropriety did tarnish the SEC's reputation. By the last years of the Truman administration, it had become common for firms with legal matters before the Commission to hire a former SEC commissioner or senior official immediately after his retirement. For example, Edward McCormick resigned as an SEC commissioner in 1951 to become president of the New York Curb Exchange (which in 1953 was renamed the American Stock Exchange). Ten months after leaving the SEC in 1952, former commissioner Robert Millonzi agreed to represent two Canadian uranium-mining firms whose securities were restricted from sale in the United States under an SEC enforcement procedure.[15]

The most publicized instance of a firm with business before the SEC hiring former Commission officials involved the United Corporation, the one-time J. P. Morgan and Company–controlled holding company, which, before the enactment of the Public Utility Holding Company Act of 1935, had controlled directly or indirectly the largest utility holding company system in the United States. From 1943 to 1951, the United Corporation fought an ultimately successful litigation battle to be allowed to become an investment company and retain a small minority interest in certain of the utility firms it had previously controlled, rather than be dissolved. During that period, United's president was William Hickey, who briefly had served as assistant director of the SEC's Public Utilities Division in 1936. United's vice president was E. Carey Kennedy, a nine-year veteran of the Public Utilities Division; United's counsel was former SEC general counsel John J. Burns. At the behest of a minority shareholder of United and investment banker Cyrus Eaton, Congressman Louis Heller supervised a year-long House of Representatives subcommittee investigation in 1951–1952 to determine whether there had been improper influence exerted on behalf of United.[16] The

Heller Subcommittee generally exonerated the SEC, concluding, "in many phases of its work, the Commission has done a commendable job in protecting the public." But the subcommittee's report sharply criticized the SEC for permitting "opportunities [to] have existed for former Commission personnel to exercise improper influence and to receive preferential treatment from the Commission."* [17]

The Commission paid a price for its inattention to appearances. For over a year, the Heller Subcommittee's initial allegations against the Commission regularly were recounted in newspaper and magazine articles describing other federal agencies in which actual misconduct had been proven. During this same period, the SEC was notably unsuccessful in combating the severe budget cuts occasioned by the Korean War.

The attempt by the Heller Subcommittee to prove that former SEC officials had been guilty of misconduct obscured a far more serious consequence of Truman's politicization of the SEC appointments process. During the Truman administration, the SEC was recognized by the 1949 Hoover Report on Regulatory Commissions as "an outstanding example of the independent commission at its best" because of the quality of the Commission's staff. At the same time, the Hoover Task Force concurred in the popular complaint that the SEC had become a captive of its staff. As the Hoover Committee's report on the SEC stated, "The complaint has often been made that the staff really determines Commission policy."[19] The complaint was largely true, and it represented the most serious result of Truman's SEC appointments practices.

By failing to appoint to the SEC a single leading academic or thinker in the corporate law field, Truman ensured an intellectually stagnant Commission. In spite of considerable growth in the securities business during Truman's presidency and a backlog of unfinished projects bequeathed by the New Deal, the SEC after Purcell's 1946 departure did not initiate a single major study for the balance of the Truman administration. The only significant legislation recommended by Truman's SEC was the 1950 Frear bill, which would have enacted William Douglas's 1938 proposal to subject securities traded over the counter to the same level of regulation as securities traded on a national securities exchange. In part, the Commission's inactivity was the result of chairmen who lacked the background or the ability to study effectively the SEC's regulatory performance. It was men like Hanrahan and McDonald whom James

---

* In February 1953 the SEC adopted a regulation requiring former SEC members or employees to file a statement with the SEC if, during the first two years after leaving the SEC, they represented a client before the Commission.[18]

Landis probably had in mind in 1960 when he reported to President-elect Kennedy that resolution of important SEC regulatory problems had been delayed for years in the post–World War II period because of the "incapacity of the commissioners themselves to grasp the essence of these problems and the significance of their resolution to the financial community."[20]

The intellectual limitations of Truman's SEC appointees deprived the Commission of leaders who could lobby effectively in the Executive Branch and Congress for new legislation or adequate funding for SEC staff or studies. But the intellectual limitations of Truman's SEC appointees had less effect on the quality of the SEC's ongoing enforcement programs. From the earliest weeks of Joseph Kennedy's chairmanship, the character of the Commission's registration and enforcement programs had been determined chiefly by the agency's senior staff. Fortified by long-established precedents and generally superior understanding of the SEC's regulatory process, the Commission's senior staff, to some degree, countervailed the inexperience and occasional hostility of the Truman and the Eisenhower administrations' SEC commissioners.

★ ★ ★

The pivotal role of the SEC's senior staff was particularly evident in the completion of the restructuring of the public utility industry, the predominant concern of the Commission during the Truman years.[21] Notwithstanding the Commission's move to Philadelphia during World War II and the generally mediocre SEC appointments made in the years immediately following the war, the SEC's geographic integration and simplification of the utility holding companies historically has been the agency's single most significant achievement. It was accomplished largely under the staff leadership of three successive Public Utilities Division directors: Joseph Weiner, Robert O'Brien, and Milton Cohen.

Several authors have observed that the Public Utility Holding Company Act of 1935 represented "the most stringent corrective measure ever applied to American business," "the most ambitious legislation of the depression-inspired federal attack on concentrated economic power," an "unequaled" and "severe" law.[22] But much less consideration has been given to the way in which the SEC, in the period from 1940 to 1952, was able substantially to restructure the utility industry. Since the enforcement of Section 11 of the Holding Company Act was the most effective antitrust enforcement program in United States history, as well as an important illustration of the administrative process, it is a topic worth considering in some detail.

Throughout its entire history, the enforcement of Section 11 was deeply influenced by considerations of litigation strategy. Benjamin Cohen's original draft of the provision had been a true "death sentence," requiring the dissolution of every public utility holding company immediately after January 1, 1940, except for the very few local utility holding companies that could obtain

> from the Federal Power Commission a certificate that the continuance of the holding-company relation is necessary for the operation of a geographically and economically integrated public-utility system serving an economic district extending into two or more contiguous States or into a contiguous foreign country and the merger or consolidation of such registered holding company with its subsidiary company or companies is impossible under the applicable State or foreign law.[23]

Focusing on this provision, public utility lobbyists had forced an elaborate compromise. Section 11(b) of the final act had been divided into two parts. Subsection 11(b)(1) empowered the SEC "to limit the operations of the holding-company system of which such company is a part to a single integrated public-utility system and to such other businesses as are reasonably incidental, or economically necessary or appropriate to the operation of such integrated public-utility system." There was a crucial exception, popularly known as the (A)(B)(C) clause:

> The Commission shall permit a registered holding company to continue to control one or more additional integrated public utility systems, if . . .
> (A) Each of such additional systems cannot be operated as an independent system without the loss of substantial economies which can be secured by the retention of control by such holding company of such system;
> (B) All of such additional systems are located in one State, or in adjoining States, or in a contiguous foreign country; and
> (C) The continued combination of such systems under the control of such holding company is not so large (considering the state of the art and the area or region affected) as to impair the advantages of localized management, efficient operation, or the effectiveness of regulation.

Section 11(b)(1) if read alone could have been construed to permit many of the holding company systems existing in 1935 to continue.

The SEC eventually succeeded in enforcing the intent of Cohen's original draft because the Roosevelt administration's lobbyists secured passage of three other crucial provisions and controlled the

drafting of the act's congressional reports. In the final compromise
of the Holding Company Act, considerable attention had focused on
the "great-grandfather clause" in Section 11(b)(2), which required
the dissolution of any holding company that had a subsidiary that
itself had a subsidiary company that was a holding company. Section 11(b)(2) also empowered the SEC to restructure a holding company whenever necessary "to ensure that the corporate structure or
continued existence of any company in the holding-company system does not unduly or unnecessarily complicate the structure, or
unfairly or inequitably distribute voting power among security holders, of such holding-company system."

Of nearly equal significance to the enforcement of the act was the
less-debated language of definitional Subsection 2(a)(29) and Subsections 1(b) and 1(c). Subsection 2(a)(29) influenced the interpretation
of a permissible holding company system under Subsection 11(b) (1)
by defining an "integrated public utility [electrical] system" as one
whose "utility assets . . . are physically interconnected or capable of
physical interconnection." While the (A)(B)(C) clauses of Subsection 11(b)(1) could be read to permit holding companies to retain
several separate holding companies if they were located in adjoining
states, collectively achieved operating economies, or were merely
efficiently managed, Subsection 2(a)(29) provided the SEC with a
basis for arguing that a permissible holding company almost always
had to be limited to a single physically interconnected system.

Complementing the interpretative thrust of Subsection 2(a)(29)
were Subsections 1(b) and 1(c). Subsection 1(b) commenced by asserting that Congress had concluded, on the basis of facts disclosed
by Judge Robert Healy's massive FTC study of the utility industry
and other named congressional studies critical of the holding companies, that there was a necessity to control holding companies.
This finding suggested that the courts should take into account the
disclosures in these studies when construing the act. Subsection 1(b)
then listed several practices that Congress found adversely affected
utility investors and consumers, such as lack of financial disclosure,
frustration of state utility commission regulation, "fictitious"
write-ups of utility assets, holding company excessive charges for
services, and lack of efficiency. Section 1(c) "declared to be the policy of this title, in accordance with which policy all the provisions
of this title shall be interpreted to . . . eliminate the evils . . .
enumerated in this section . . . and for the purpose of effectuating
such policy to compel the simplification of public-utility holding-
company systems and the elimination of properties detrimental to
the proper functioning of such systems . . ."

The language of the Holding Company Act alone, however, could not ensure that the utility industry would be restructured. A hostile Judiciary could have ruled the act unconstitutional or construed Subsection 11(b) on the basis of a judicially identified "plain meaning," ignoring the interpretive guidance of Subsections 2(a)(29), 1(b), and 1(c). During the first five years of the act's enforcement, the SEC pursued what then Public Utilities Division attorney Roger Foster termed "the Fabian tactic" of avoiding giving the largely Republican-appointed Judiciary opportunities to construe Section 11. Besides persuading the Supreme Court to limit its initial review of the act to consideration of the constitutionality of the act's registration provisions in the 1938 *Electric Bond and Share* case, the SEC compromised enforcement of Section 11 in its early Section 11 cases to discourage appeals to the Judiciary.

The most significant Section 11 decision during the 1935–1939 period involved the American Water Works and Electric Company.[24] In *American Water Works*, the Commission's first Section 11 decision, the SEC unanimously ruled that a holding company could retain both gas and electric subsidiaries, allowed a top holding company to retain ownership of three subsidiaries with utilities stretching across five states despite a lack of physical interconnection among the three subsidiaries, and permitted the holding company to retain interests in a variety of other businesses, including electric railways, bus companies, and bridge businesses, largely because they "contributed a stable source of revenue" or "were an inheritance from an earlier age" and difficult to sell for a satisfactory price. Each of the principal holdings in the *American Water Works* decision later was contradicted by SEC decisions in other Section 11 cases. But at the time the decision was reached, it evoked little controversy within the SEC, since the tactic of avoiding an early court test of Section 11 was well understood, and it was hoped that by generally concurring in American Water Works' voluntary plan to comply with the act, the SEC would encourage other utilities to comply voluntarily with Section 11.*

By 1940 the SEC had less reason to fear the Judiciary. Five of the nine Supreme Court Justices (Hugo Black, Stanley Reed, Felix Frankfurter, William Douglas, and Frank Murphy) were Roosevelt appointees, and they reasonably could be assumed to favor the act's enforcement. Throughout the duration of Roosevelt's administration, the process of replacing pre–New Deal Justices with Roosevelt

---

* When, in 1941, the Commission began contradicting the key holdings in *American Water Works*, the SEC took pains to characterize the *Water Works* decision as an "advisory opinion," not a "controlling" precedent.[25]

appointees continued. By the time of Roosevelt's death, in 1945, only two of the nine Justices then sitting had not been appointed by him. Parallel changes occurred in the lower federal courts. This contributed to the success of the SEC's aggressive litigation strategy after 1940. In the 280 judicial proceedings completed under the Public Utility Holding Company Act by June 30, 1952, only two were terminated adversely,[26] a record so one-sided that Second Circuit judge Learned Hand once introduced an SEC attorney with the caustic observation, "Now we will hear from that sacred cow, the Securities and Exchange Commission."[27] Although the SEC's Public Utilities Division included extraordinarily talented attorneys, the Commission's Holding Company Act litigation record would have been inconceivable before a less sympathetic Judiciary.

As it became clear both to the Commission and to the utility industry that all reasonable Commission interpretations of the Holding Company Act were likely to be upheld by the federal courts, the SEC began the second phase of its program to enforce Section 11. In February and March 1940 the SEC initiated integration proceedings against nine of the thirteen largest registered holding company systems. By June 1943, the SEC had instituted 127 Section 11 proceedings, involving almost all of the fifty-five utility systems registered with the Commission in 1940.[28] Given the number of holding company systems registered under the act and the time required for contesting antitrust litigation, it never was considered desirable by the SEC to impose divestiture plans on each utility. Moreover, had the SEC sought to impose reorganization plans, it would have run a considerable political risk. Congressional sentiment in favor of effective antitrust structural legislation in this century has been fleeting and infrequent. Even under the most favorable political circumstances, the compromise Section 11 of the Holding Company Act had been passed in the Senate by a single vote. If the SEC had imposed a single divestiture order that appeared to harm either utility investors or consumers, it risked a congressional re-examination of the act under less favorable political circumstances. During the twelve crucial years of the act's enforcement, 1940 to 1952, the SEC's Public Utilities Division senior attorneys thus recognized, in Roger Foster's words, that: "the Commission could not afford to give a valid basis for even the most minor amendment for fear that really crippling amendments would emerge, since it would be difficult to mobilize again the public understanding of the holding company evils which had made it possible to push through the Holding Company Act over resourceful and determined opposition."[29]

The essence of the Commission's enforcement strategy after 1940 involved creating incentives (and removing disincentives) so that the utilities themselves would offer acceptable divestiture and simplification plans. This was known as the 11(e) strategy, since the Holding Company Act authorized enforcement of Subsection 11(b) under either Subsection 11(d), which empowered the SEC to seek a federal district court order requiring compliance with a Commission reorganization plan, or Subsection 11(e), which authorized the SEC to approve and, if necessary, seek court approval of a reorganization plan offered by a utility. Although the threat of imposing the more draconian Subsection 11(d) was "deemed indispensable" to the enforcement of the act by the Commission,* it was employed only once in the 1940–1952 period.[30]

The SEC's 11(e) strategy quietly commenced in 1939, when Chairman Douglas persuaded Congress to postpone the recognition of capital gains or losses under the Internal Revenue Code when the securities or property of registered holding companies were exchanged "in obedience to an order of the Securities and Exchange Commission." In 1942, Congress exempted public utilities that complied with Subsection 11(b) of the Holding Company Act from the tax code's stamp tax on issuances and exchanges of securities.[32]

The key to the SEC's 11(e) strategy was doctrinal. Largely between 1941 and 1943, the Commission construed Subsections 11(b)(1) and 11(b)(2) in an uncompromising manner, making plain to any utility that required the SEC to enforce those provisions through an 11(d) proceeding that it would be subjected to as comprehensive a divestiture order as was permissible under a reasonable interpretation of the act. Three lines of cases were of paramount significance in interpreting the geographic integration Subsection 11(b)(1). First, flatly contradicting its earlier *American Water Works* opinion, the SEC held in its 1941 *Columbia Gas and Electric* and *United Gas Improvement* opinions that a "single integrated public utility system" could not retain both electric and gas properties.[33] Second, in its *United Gas Improvement* and 1942 *North American Company* opinions, the SEC construed the language permitting an integrated

---

* In the vernacular, Section 11(b) had "teeth in it" not only because it allowed the Commission directly to impose a divestiture order when it received court approval, but because it authorized the court to appoint the SEC a sole trustee to hold, administer, and dispose of the assets of any company subject to an SEC Section 11 order. The act's Subsection 11(e) voluntary compliance scheme was modeled on the Supreme Court's divestiture orders in a series of early Sherman Act monopolization cases, including the celebrated 1911 *Standard Oil* and *American Tobacco* "Rule of Reason" decisions.[31]

public utility system to retain "such other businesses as are reasonably incidental, or economically necessary or appropriate" as allowing retention of other businesses only when they resulted in "economies in the operation of an integrated utility system." "Other businesses" without a functional relationship to an integrated electric or gas system could not be retained. Dicta in the *American Water Works* opinion permitting retention of nonfunctionally related "other businesses" because of a history of joint ownership, stability of income, or difficulty of sale were disregarded.[34] Third, Commission opinions in the *United Gas Improvement, Engineers Public Service,* and *North American Company* cases stringently limited the opportunities for a holding company to retain an additional public utility system beyond the single physically interconnected utility system permitted by definitional Subsection 2(a)(29). To achieve this result, the SEC held that an additional public utility system could be retained only if all three of the requirements in the 11(b)(1) (A)(B)(C) clause were satisfied.*[35]

In practice, this proved difficult. In what the Commission termed "the most important interpretative issue arising under Section 11(b)(1)," the SEC construed clause (B), soon known as Big B, as permitting the retention of an additional system only if it was located in the state in which the principal system operated or in an adjoining state or country. This "one-area" interpretation of clause (B) allowed the SEC to order the divestiture of utility properties on the basis of proof no more complicated than a map diagramming the location of a holding company's subsidiaries. One legal commentator, alert to the strategic use the Commission made of Big B, later wrote, "This brief requirement of the Act has probably been more disastrous to the sprawling utility empires than any other provision of the law . . . At the outset the Commission seized upon the requirements of this provision to pair large segments of existing utility combinations before the more difficult and abstruse standards of the Act were applied."[36] Moreover, the SEC could still urge divestiture of any holding company's additional system, satisfying clause (B)'s one-area rule, if the utility could not show that severance of the additional system would result in the loss of substantial economies, as required by clause (A), or that the utility's size was not so large as

---

* While this construction of the (A)(B)(C) clauses found literal support in a text that linked the clauses with the word "and" rather than the word "or" and subsequently was affirmed by the Judiciary, it nonetheless was a somewhat surprising construction, which might have been questioned more skeptically by a less sympathetic Judiciary.

to impair the advantages of localized management or effective state regulation, required by clause (C).[37]

Simultaneously, the Commission interpreted the proscription against "unduly or unnecessarily complicated corporate structures" in Subsection 11(b)(2) as requiring the elimination of holding or sub-holding companies "which serve no useful purpose." Under the SEC's interpretation, heavily leveraged holding company systems such as *Electric Bond and Share* could be dismantled if it was shown that specific constituent firms had no productive function or had been used primarily to increase the leverage of the controlling share-holders in the top holding company.[38]

The cumulative effect of these interpretations gave the SEC the bargaining power to persuade many holding company systems to offer a sufficiently far-reaching voluntary divestiture plan under Subsection 11(e) to satisfy the Commission. This was often done in one of two ways. By agreeing to divest additional integrated utility systems, several major holding companies, including the Middle West Corporation, the Columbia Gas and Electric Corporation, American Gas and Electric Company, and the Commonwealth and Southern Corporation, were allowed to retain geographically larger principal integrated systems than they otherwise might have.[39] In other instances, divested operating companies were allowed to re-tain both gas and electric properties, although the Commission usu-ally forbade a registered holding company to do so.[40]

At the same time, other SEC decisions created financial rewards for the security-holders of holding companies that completed 11(e) voluntary proceedings. Holding company preferred shares usually sold at a substantial discount below their liquidation value. As long as utility executives opposed SEC efforts to simplify holding com-pany capital structures by retiring "unduly or unnecessarily com-plicated structures," there was uncertainty as to whether preferred shares would ever be exchanged for their liquidation values. Holding company common share prices generally also were depressed be-cause preferred stock dividend arrearages (past-due dividends) made it legally impossible for the company to pay common stock divi-dends and because there was uncertainty as to whether the common shares would be entitled to any payment, in the event that the SEC did compel liquidation, if preferred shares were paid their full con-tractual liquidation value.[41]

SEC decisions generally increased the market value of both pre-ferred and common stock. Had the SEC followed traditional bank-ruptcy law's absolute priority rule and required all preferred share-holders to receive their full contractual liquidation payment before common shareholders were entitled to receive any portion of the corporation's assets, several issues of common stock would have been rendered valueless. Thus, it was probable that, in any holding company lacking the assets to pay off fully the liquidation value of the preferred shares, the common stockholders, who usually alone elected the decision-making board of directors, would encourage every effort to prevent or delay the dissolution of the firm.

The SEC, however, declined to enforce the absolute priority rule. Instead, drawing on statements in the Senate report accompanying the Holding Company Act that described one SEC function as the prevention of undue "losses to security-holders from investment dislocations," the Commission employed what it termed "the investment value theory."[42] This involved using an estimate of the relative value of the preferred and common stock that would have continued had the SEC not compelled a recapitalization as the basis for preferred and common share distribution when its proceedings resulted in the retirement of classes of stock. Such a calculation of going-concern values involved a comparison of the preferred stock's contractual liquidation value and the common stock's likelihood of future earnings. When a holding company lacked sufficient assets to pay off the full liquidation value of preferred shares, SEC application of the investment value theory typically resulted in preferred shareholders receiving 90 to 95 percent of the corporation's assets; common shareholders, 5 to 10 percent. In other instances, the common shareholders enjoyed even more important financial benefits from SEC decisions that called for the retirement of "unduly or unnecessarily complicated" preferred stock. When the preferred shares had dividend arrearages, their retirement enabled common stockholders to begin receiving dividends immediately.

The tendency of an SEC-approved 11(e) plan to increase both preferred and common share values was first widely recognized in the aftermath of the Commission's March 1943 approval of United Gas Improvement's 11(e) plan. UGI was a sub-holding company of the United Corporation, which itself controlled eighty subsidiaries. To facilitate the retirement of UGI's preferred stock, the SEC approved an 11(e) plan under which UGI's preferred shareholders exchanged their shares for cash and common stock with a dividend preference in the Philadelphia Electric Company, UGI's largest subsidiary. UGI's common shareholders received common shares in Philadelphia Electric and other UGI subsidiaries, with the result, according to the Commission, that "UGI's common stockholders, upon consummation of the proposed plan, will have had removed the prior claims of the preferred stock to UGI's assets and earnings and will be in a position to receive the benefits not now enjoyed which are incident to the direct ownership of UGI's portfolio securities."[43] In dollar terms, UGI common stock rose from $4.00 per share before UGI filed its 11(e) plan to nearly $10 just before UGI completed its recapitalization.[44] By mid-1943, financial analysts like Standard and Poor's, Moody's Stock Survey, and Barron's predicted that comparable financial benefits would be enjoyed by security-holders of other holding companies after they filed 11(e) plans. On June 7, 1943, Standard and Poor's, for example, stated:

> Holding company stocks have benefited from integration or liquidation plans filed with the S.E.C. in recent months . . . Since utility holding company stocks normally sell at a discount from their liquidating value . . . the filing of liquidation plans has caused the price of securities involved to advance sharply to approximately those values.
>
> This was the experience of the common stocks of Federal Water & Gas, National Power & Light, Niagara Hudson Power, and United Gas Improvement, all of which have lately filed integration plans, as well as the preferred stocks of Standard Gas & Electric and United Light & Power. Many of these issues more than doubled in price with the announcement that liquidation or integration of the holding company was planned . . . Additional utility holding companies will probably file integration or liquidation plans, which should prove beneficial generally to the market price of their securities.[45]

The securities markets created further incentives for holding companies to seek a voluntary reorganization under 11(e). Throughout the war, it was possible for many utilities to redeem bonds and preferred stock and refinance at lower interest rates. But unless a holding company was willing to accompany a redemption and new security sale with an 11(e) plan, it was virtually impossible for it to take advantage of the wartime interest rates. "Quite apart from the legal restrictions imposed by section 7 of the Act," recalled Roger Foster, "it had become impossible to sell bonds and preferred stock of holding companies which would, for the most part, be backed by nothing but junior stocks of operating companies. The impracticality of selling holding company common stocks for new capital was manifest from the fact that the outstanding stocks sold on the market substantially below their estimated underlying asset value."[46] Joseph Weiner, the Public Utilities Division director who initially supervised the 11(e) strategy, relied on such market pressures. From Weiner's point of view, recalled associates, the doctrinal basis of challenging a specific holding company system "was relatively unimportant . . . the Commission [strove] to find some way of compelling *some* major step in simplification for each major holding company system . . . since removing a single log might well loosen the jam to the point where the current of economic forces would itself compel major breakups of most of the holding company systems."[47] Weiner's belief substantially was corroborated by events. As early as January 1944, the SEC was sufficiently "encouraged [by] the apparent recognition by holding company executives of the practical business advantages of compliance with the Act and the increasing cooperation that has developed in the formation and filing of plans" to assert that "the completion of the task of conforming various public utility holding company systems to the standards of Section 11 is in sight."[48] By June 30, 1945, holding company systems had divested properties worth over $5 billion.[49]

After Supreme Court decisions in 1945 and 1946 held that Subsections 11(b)(1) and 11(b)(2) were constitutional and approved SEC interpretations of these subsections,[50] the pace of voluntary compliance under Subsection 11(e) accelerated. Between 1945 and 1948, holding companies divested themselves of assets worth approximately $7 billion.[51] Consistent with Weiner's assumption, the end of opposition to Section 11 after World War II was as much a result of stock market pressures as of Supreme Court decisions. Aggregate electrical utility industry capital expenditures had proceeded at a minimal rate during the late depression and war years, 1935 to 1945, averaging approximately $420 million per year. Antiquated facilities and growing consumer demand required the electrical utility industry to increase construction expenditures nearly fivefold in the 1946–1950 period to an average of $1.8 billion per year.[52] Nearly all of the industry's expansion program had to be financed by security sales.[53] Although many holding company systems could have deferred final enforcement of Section 11 by requiring the SEC to prosecute an 11(d) action, the need to finance plant and equipment construction provided a final, decisive incentive for voluntary compliance under 11(e). By the end of the Truman administration, the SEC's mission under Section 11 was over 90 percent completed.[54] At one time or another, holding companies registered with the SEC had controlled 1983 subsidiaries. By June 30, 1952, 1603 had been divested. On July 1, 1940, fifteen separate holding companies supplied electric or gas service in ten or more states, and seventeen other systems supplied power in five to nine states. By June 30, 1951, no utility holding company operated in ten or more states; only seven operated in five to nine states. In 1959, when

Section 11 enforcement was almost complete, only three registered holding companies would operate in more than four states.[55]

The magnitude of the SEC's geographic integration of the electric utility industry can be seen in the fate of the Electric Bond and Share Corporation, the largest holding company system to register with the SEC.

As of December 31, 1940, Electric Bond and Share controlled five sub-holding companies, which, in turn, controlled 234 direct and indirect subsidiaries with aggregate consolidated assets of $3.44 billion. Within the United States, Bond and Share's four domestic sub-holding corporations controlled 131 domestic subsidiaries, which provided electricity or gas services in thirty-two separate states, supplying over 13 percent of the electricity generated by all utility companies in the United States during 1940. Over a twenty-year period concluding in 1960, Electric Bond and Share was reorganized into an investment company. It was allowed to retain a controlling 55 percent interest in its foreign sub-holding corporation, American and Foreign Power Company, Incorporated, but was required to sell or distribute all of its domestic holdings except for a 4 percent interest in United Gas and a 1.15 percent interest in Ebasco Services.[56] Each of Bond and Share's sub-holding companies simultaneously was reorganized.

Before the enactment of the Public Utility Holding Company Act, three of Electric Bond and Share's sub-holding companies — American Power and Light, Electric Power and Light, and National Power and Light — had been purely "paper companies," with no independent staff or productive function. In an effort to avoid a Subsection 11(b)(2) lawsuit, Bond and Share in November 1935 had vested each of the three with its own officers and employees and a separate suite of offices in the Electric Bond and Share building. The effort was unsuccessful. In 1941 and 1942, first National Power and Light, then American Power and Light, and Electric Power and Light were ordered to dissolve because they created undue and unnecessary complexities in the Electric Bond and Share system. At the time of the dissolution orders, the National, American, and Electric sub-holding companies collectively controlled thirty-five utility and fifty-one nonutility subsidiaries. Over a twelve-year period, the utilities were geographically integrated, then divested to form sixteen local or regional electric operating or holding companies, two gas companies, and one electric and gas operating company.[57]

The fate of American Gas and Electric Company, Electric Bond and Share's fourth domestic sub-holding company, was considerably different. Before the 1935 reorganization of Bond and Share, American Gas and Electric had functioned as an independent corporate entity, essentially administering three integrated electrical utility systems. Eighty-six percent of American's assets were held by its central system, whose geographical extremities, as of January 1945, stretched from Benton Harbor, Michigan, at the northwest end, to Steubenville, Ohio, in the northeast, Newport, Tennessee, in the southwest, and Danville, Virginia, in the southeast. This was an area of approximately ninety thousand square miles, with a population of over three million. Public Utilities Division director Milton Cohen recalled that dealing with the central system was "the toughest case the division faced." If American Gas were allowed to retain the entire central system, it would have administered the largest integrated utility system in the country. Yet the system, large as it was, had long been considered a model for the industry. Because it was completely interconnected, an extensive Commission proceeding concluded, the system's "fuel costs and losses between point of generation and point of delivery are well below the national average, and plant thermal performance is substantially better than the national average." The SEC accordingly permitted the retention of the central system, noting in its decision that "we are of the opinion, however, that the central system approaches the maximum size which we believe is consistent with the standards of localized management, efficient operation, and effectiveness of regulation contained in Section 2(a)(29) and 11(b)(1)."* American's two other utility systems, located in northwestern Pennsylvania and southern New Jersey, were divested.[59]

In 1938, at the time of the Supreme Court's decision in the *Electric Bond and Share* case, three holding company systems — Electric Bond and Share, the United Corporation, and the nonbankrupt holding companies once controlled by Samuel Insull — directly or indirectly controlled 50 percent of the $15 billion of assets owned by registered holding companies.[60] The cumulative effect of the SEC's 11(b) proceedings against Electric Bond and Share, the United Corporation, and the Insull interests was to transform three super-holding companies that directly or indirectly had controlled about half of the nation's electrical generation into approximately forty-five regional, state, or local utility companies.[61]

---

* In 1946, the SEC refused to permit American Gas and Electric to purchase the Columbus and Southern Ohio Electric Company despite estimated savings equal to approximately 10 percent of Columbus and Southern's gross electric operating revenues. The Commission's decision, largely based on the size of American Gas and Electric, was one of the few it made that appeared to be economically inefficient. Thirty-four years later, however, the SEC did permit this acquisition.[58]

Though this represented one of the most far-reaching accomplishments of the Roosevelt administration, it has been, curiously, almost unrecognized in the New Deal histories published to date. From the turn of the century to the Truman administration, a priority of progressive politics had been the redistribution of the power of an alleged Wall Street "money trust" and an alleged nationwide "power trust." That today such terms are rarely employed is another measure of the SEC's achievement under Section 11.

The Commission's enforcement of Section 11 benefited the utilities and their investors. The guiding principle of the geographic integration program had been to increase the economic efficiency of the utility industry. With electric utility firms, the SEC concentrated on two different types of efficiency — plant and firm efficiency.

As a general matter, in the electrical industry, the lowest unit costs will occur when production is increased to the maximum point before the cost of transporting electricity offsets the cost savings resulting from the lower unit investment cost and operating expenses of the largest possible plant. Further cost savings may be achieved by interconnecting adjacent electrical plants, because the reserve capacity each plant must maintain may be reduced by the pooling of reserve capacity. Through 1952 one comprehensive economic study of Section 11 proceedings was able to identify only two instances in which an SEC Section 11 proceeding resulted in the separation of previously interconnected operating facilities. In neither instance did it appear that losses of plant economies occurred. On the contrary, the study found that "while losses of plant economies due to forced geographic integration have been negligible, gains in plant economies have been large." They resulted when SEC proceedings eliminated duplicative urban facilities in cities like St. Louis and Erie, Pennsylvania, allowing a single firm to operate with lower unit costs. Plant economies also occurred when SEC proceedings connected adjacent plants.[62]

SEC Section 11 proceedings also achieved some firm efficiencies. Firm costs are those associated with management and capital costs. Theoretically, costs should decline as size increases to the point where the firm can sell securities at the lowest yields and its percentage of administrative expenses cannot be reduced by further efficiencies. In the public utility industry before 1935, however, cost savings resulting from increases in operating company size coexisted with unnecessary expenses associated with the structure of the holding company. The 1935 act anticipated cost savings by prohibiting holding company subsidiaries from providing services to operating companies except "at cost" and implicitly requiring competitive bidding for registered utilities' securities. After the SEC began enforcing Section 11(b)(2), it became clear that the elimination of "unduly or unnecessarily complicated" firms from a holding company system also could decrease a utility's costs by reducing the expense of required government reports and intercompany contracts. Firm capital costs also were reduced because of the greater flexibility that a larger consolidated operating company enjoyed in the use of its funds as compared with a series of smaller operating companies managed by a holding company where fund transfers often were not legally possible.[63]

The SEC's enforcement of the Holding Company Act further aided utility firms by strengthening the financial structure both of registered holding companies and of operating companies (before they left the SEC's jurisdiction). "A major objective" of the SEC's regulation of public utility securities, explained the Commission's *Tenth Annual Report,* "has been to achieve a balanced capital structure with a substantial amount of common stock equity. A balanced capital structure provides a considerable measure of insurance against bankruptcy, enables the utility to raise new money most economically, and avoids the possibility of deterioration in service to consumers if there is a decline in earnings." SEC policies encouraged electric utilities to increase the percentage of common stock in their composite capital structure from 23.6 to 36.3 percent between 1937 and 1957 while decreasing debt from 58 to 51.7 percent. With utility earnings rising, this resulted in a reduction of the percentage of operating revenues necessary to pay interest from 13.1 to 6.3 percent between 1937 and 1958.[64]

On January 1, 1937, a Federal Power Commission study of the more than three hundred companies subject to its jurisdiction found that the utilities' $6.8 billion of plant assets had been written up by $1.6 billion in excess of their original cost. Joint efforts of the FPC, state utility commissions, and the SEC resulted in the elimination of virtually all of the $1.6 billion in write-ups over a fifteen-year period.[65]

Simultaneously, utility depreciation and dividend practices were placed on a conservative footing. A 1940 SEC study entitled "Financial Statistics for Electric and Gas Subsidiaries of Registered Public Utility Holding Companies, 1930–39" had found marked discrepancies between the depreciation charges that utilities claimed as deductions in their federal income taxes and the expenses they recorded in financial reports to shareholders. For the ten-year period 1930–1939, 168 operating companies were allowed depreciation tax deductions of $1.77 billion, although the depreciation expenses charged against income in their reports to shareholders were only $1.15 billion. This discrepancy was significant both because it had facilitated the payment of $349 million more in dividends than these firms actually had earned and because utilities generally were maintaining inadequate reserves for the maintenance or replacement of depreciating assets. As early as 1937 the SEC first adopted rules to prohibit the payment of dividends except from earned surplus unless a utility obtained Commission approval. Between 1935 and 1947, a subsequent SEC study of seventy utilities found, Commission efforts increased average depreciation reserves from 8.75 to 22.5 percent of total utility assets.*[66]

The cumulative results of the SEC's related efforts to achieve plant and firm efficiencies through geographic integration or corporation simplification proceedings and to strengthen utility firms' financial practices corroborated the 1935 prediction of the Senate report accompanying the public utility bill that "the individual investor in present-day holding companies should come out of any reorganization process under the title with far better securities than those with which he went into it." An SEC study of the common stock performance of the largest public utility holding companies between the date of their registration under the act and September 24, 1951, found in nine of twelve cases that common stock had increased by a greater percentage than either the Dow Jones Utilities Average or the Dow Jones Composite Average during the same period. Notably, Electric Bond and Share common stock had increased by 449 percent while the Dow Jones Utilities Average had increased by 166 percent and the Dow Jones Composite Average had increased by 192 percent. Engineers Public Service common had increased seven and a half times more than either average; the Middle West Corporation, five times faster than either. On average, the twelve common stocks had increased in value 327 percent, which was over twice the average 160 percent increase in the Dow Jones Composite Index or the 147 percent increase in the Dow Jones Utilities Index. A study of the preferred stock performance for the same twelve public utility systems found a comparable increase in value of 267 percent.[68]

The operating efficiencies that resulted from the SEC's integra-

---

* SEC recapitalization plans and required protective provisions also eliminated approximately $370 million in preferred stock arrearages between 1938 and 1951.[67]

tion program also helped reduce consumers' utility costs. Between January 1, 1938, and January 1, 1951, the average monthly electric bill for users of 25 kilowatts of service fell by 14 percent, and the average monthly electric bill for users of 100 kilowatts per month fell by 10 percent.*[69]

The SEC's enforcement of Section 11 of the Public Utility Holding Company Act illustrated the potential benefits of antitrust structural relief. The Commission's Section 11 program also showed the extent to which antitrust enforcement under even the most politically favorable circumstances may have to compromise to succeed substantially. The SEC's enforcement of Section 11 most notably fell short of the efficiency and social objectives specified by the act in its litigation strategy of encouraging voluntary compliance with Section 11(b) by allowing some operating companies to retain both electric and gas properties. As the SEC itself explained, "To expect vital competition between the two types of service when controlled by the same interests is, in our opinion, highly unrealistic."[71]

Yet even taking into account the compromises the SEC made to enforce Section 11, the Commission's geographic integration and corporate simplification of the utility industry remains the most comprehensive structural relief ever achieved by an agency of the federal government. The SEC's enforcement of the Holding Company Act also was an illustration of the advantages of the administrative process. Crucial to the SEC's effort was a large and sophisticated staff in its Public Utilities Division able to study not just a single case, but an industry. Equally crucial was the ability of the Commission to coordinate doctrine, timing of litigation, and negotiations with holding companies in such a manner as to persuade an entire industry ultimately to comply voluntarily with the geographic integration provision of the act. It is highly unlikely that the initial prosecution of several separate holding company actions before separate federal district court judges would have led to an equally effective dissolution program, for the act's effective enforcement required, above all else, continuity of effort. Beginning with the FTC's comprehensive study of the utility industry and continu-

---

* Consumer benefits would have been larger had the SEC not followed as conservative an approach to debt-to-equity ratios. Under the Internal Revenue Code, interest on debt securities is a business expense, but stock dividends are not. Hence, when the corporate income tax rate is about 50 percent, as it was during the 1950s, a firm must earn twice as much to pay a $1.00 stock dividend as it must to pay $1.00 in interest on a debt.[70]

ing through the legislative battle to enact Benjamin Cohen's draft of the holding company bill, the 1935–1938 litigation battle to establish the constitutionality of the act and then stretching for another fourteen years during which the SEC substantially completed its Section 11 program, the effort to restructure the holding company industry was pursued by highly competent people with generally similar political ends. Such a continuity of objective and competence is the hallmark of an effective administrative agency.

9

The Budget Bureau's SEC

My own feelings about the changes in the financial world were summed up when the SEC celebrated its twenty-fifth anniversary. It was 1959 and Dwight Eisenhower was President . . . An early speaker had mentioned the big drive on "boiler rooms," the covert switchboards where a bevy of high-powered salesmen worked over sucker lists for sales of securities that had no more realizable value than the blue sky above us.

Many other speeches were made, and when it came my turn the hour was late and I made it short.

I said, "The main difference I see between the old SEC and the new one is that we put in prison a much higher type of person."

— WILLIAM O. DOUGLAS

DURING THE EISENHOWER ADMINISTRATION, the Securities and Exchange Commission reached its nadir. Although the SEC retained a reputation as the best of the independent regulatory agencies, its enforcement and policy-making capabilities were less effective than at any other period in its history. This was not because the Eisenhower administration per se was hostile to the effective administration of the securities laws. By 1953, the disclosure and anti-fraud rules of the securities statutes commanded general bipartisan support. When Arthur Dean, John Foster Dulles's law partner, opined in 1952 that "the Securities and Exchange Commission stands out as a very model of what an administrative agency should be," he reflected the consensus of Wall Street and moderate Republican opinion.[1] With market volume still ascending from its late New Deal depths, the organized exchanges and corporate issuers generally regarded the SEC's disclosure program and antifraud enforcement as desirable to maintain market confidence.

The effective enforcement of the securities laws and the necessary expansion of the SEC's jurisdiction nevertheless were frustrated by the Eisenhower administration's greater commitment to a balanced budget, elimination or prevention of what it termed "excessive" federal regulation, and its general preference for amicable federal government–private business relations.

The conflict between effective enforcement of the securities laws and the general political goals of the Eisenhower administration was most sharply drawn in the budget process. No domestic political goal was more cherished by Dwight Eisenhower than the reduction of the federal budget. In his 1952 campaign, Eisenhower set as "a goal of the new administration to cut federal spending, to eliminate the budget deficit, and to reduce taxes." This was a goal Eisenhower unrelentingly pursued. "When my administration took over the reins of government in 1953," Eisenhower recalled, "there was no one among my immediate associates not dedicated, in principle, to the proposition that both federal expenditures and the public debt must be reduced." On February 2, 1953, Eisenhower stressed "the elimination of the annual deficit" as his first order of business. In 1958, Eisenhower derived satisfaction from his belief that "over the past five years it seems to me that I have put in two thirds of my time fighting increased expenditures in government." Sherman Adams, long Eisenhower's closest associate, memorialized the administration with a similar observation: "Eisenhower was more deeply concerned with economics than most people realized. He once told the Cabinet that if he was able to do nothing as President except balance the budget he would feel that his time in the White House had been well spent."

Eisenhower made his most uncompromising efforts to balance the 1954 and 1955 budgets. The 1954 budget (for the period from July 1, 1953, to June 30, 1954) had been drafted by the Truman administration and called for $78.6 billion in expenditures, $71 billion of which went for the national security program or such "uncontrollable" major items as interest on the national debt. In spite of this lack of "elbow room," Eisenhower's Budget Bureau scaled down the 1954 budget to $72 billion in the early months of 1953. Efforts to reduce the 1955 budget began almost immediately. In November 1953, Eisenhower approved a memorandum prepared by his Budget Director, Joseph Dodge, meant, in Eisenhower's words, "to serve as a weapon in his economizing efforts with federal agencies." The memorandum's three principal points read:

(1) ... Both appropriations and the level of expenditures for fiscal year 1955 must be reduced substantially below those for the 1954 fiscal year.

(2) To achieve this objective every possible reduction will have to be made and every item included in the Budget must meet the test of necessity rather than of desirability. This policy of reduction must be applied with relative uniformity, though equitably, to all agencies.

(3) Pressures to protect favored expenditures or programs must give way, except in the most unusual cases, to the greater pressure to reduce overall Government expenditures.[2]

Eisenhower's parsimony, compounding reductions in the SEC staff made during World War II and the Korean War, severely curtailed the Commission's enforcement programs. At its height, the SEC had employed 1723 persons in 1941. During the Truman administration, the Commission reached its highest level of employment in 1947, when it employed on average a staff of 1200. At that level, the bipartisan Hoover Commission found, the SEC had a backlog in its examination of annual reports filed by corporations under the 1934 Securities Exchange Act and was unable to inspect brokers and dealers annually. Since the SEC believed that the "examination of the records of securities firms by the Commission . . . is no less significant to millions of investors than is the work of a superintendent of banks to depositors," in 1948 the SEC urged that "its enforcement activities need to be strengthened."

The Korean War instead resulted in further personnel cuts. By the conclusion of the 1953 fiscal year on June 30, 1953, the SEC staff had been reduced to 773. Approximately 150 jobs had been eliminated without harm to the Commission's capabilities as the public utilities integration program concluded. The elimination of three hundred other employees between 1947 and 1953 "drained much of [the Commission's] vitality," wrote Truman SEC commissioner J. Howard Rossbach. On March 3, 1953, Commissioner Richard McEntire stated, "Because of the necessity of curtailing our operations to the extent that we have, the Commission is not able to do an adequate job in administering the seven statutes entrusted to it." Privately, holdover chairman Donald Cook circulated a memorandum to the Eisenhower Budget Bureau describing "serious delays" in the work under the Holding Company Act, a "29 percent increase in the backlog of examining work in the Division of Corporation Finance," "drastic reductions" in fraud investigations, broker-dealer

inspections, and market surveillance, and "uneconomical performance of service activities because of lack of personnel." Cook's
confidential warning was echoed by the 1952 report of the Heller
House Subcommittee, which urged "careful and thorough study" of
the SEC's "help shortages" after finding "most disturbing shortcomings in the Commission's broker-dealer inspection program."[3]

Even before Eisenhower's first SEC chairman was confirmed, the
Budget Bureau recommended cuts in the SEC's 1954 budget that
resulted in a 10 percent reduction of the Commission's staff, leaving
the SEC 699 employees on June 30, 1954. Donald Cook criticized
the impending staff cut in an April 1953 public statement, expressing his "firm belief that people will be defrauded by the hundreds in
ways that we could check and would be able to stop if we had the
staff we need."[4] Ralph Demmler, confirmed as Eisenhower's first
SEC chairman in June 1953, soon implicitly agreed. On July 13,
1953, Demmler wrote Senator Leverett Saltonstall, chairman of the
Senate Subcommittee on Independent Offices Appropriations, that
any further budget reduction "might have the effect of crippling [the
Division of Corporation Finance's] ability to clear registration statements within the time schedules imposed by the issuers and underwriters [and] would automatically curtail the enforcement activities
of the Commission." On November 17, 1953, Demmler wrote
Budget Director Dodge that a proposed 8 percent cut in the SEC's
1955 budget "would be reflected primarily in curtailed enforcement
activities and in delayed regulatory proceedings. The Commission
considers that to the extent such curtailments and delays occur it
will be failing to discharge its statutory responsibilities." Despite
Demmler's warnings, the Budget Bureau insisted on a 6 percent cut.
By June 30, 1955, the SEC's staff had been reduced to 666 persons,
the lowest level in the post–World War II period.[5]

Exactly as Demmler predicted, the SEC's enforcement program in
1954 and 1955 was curtailed. Memoranda were circulated to SEC
regional administrators, encouraging them to rely on state authorities whenever possible to investigate and prosecute securities
violations as one means "to save manpower." SEC enforcement
officials also were encouraged to rely on the National Association of
Securities Dealers, securities exchanges, or the states to inspect broker-dealers to "eliminate unnecessary duplication of effort and ex-
penditure," despite known weaknesses in each alternative broker-
dealer inspection program. The SEC had no choice. As Demmler
testified on February 10, 1955, the SEC annually could inspect the
books of only about a thousand of the nation's 4100 broker-dealers
because "it does not have the staff to carry out regular periodic

examinations." SEC investigations in 1955 led to the conviction of only seven persons for securities fraud, the lowest figure in the Commission's history. The preceding year, the Commission instituted no stop order proceedings and sought suspension of only one security for fraudulent claim of a small-issue exemption.[6]

Underlying the SEC's "budget starvation" during the Eisenhower administration were beliefs about the appropriate role of the federal government held by Treasury Secretary George Humphrey, who supervised the initial SEC appointments, the Eisenhower Budget Bureau, and a majority of Eisenhower's early SEC appointments. In marked contrast to Roosevelt's SEC, Eisenhower's SEC began with the assumptions that business was overregulated, that large business institutions like the New York Stock Exchange usually could discipline themselves, and that fraud or unfairness almost always would be found in small, local businesses, especially those associated with organized crime.

These beliefs were most visibly reflected during the term of Chairman Ralph Demmler. Demmler, a securities law practitioner from a leading Pittsburgh corporate law firm, arrived at the SEC affirming that "the principles behind the Acts which the Commission administers are basically sound." He repeatedly underscored his loyalty to the SEC with such statements as, "It goes without saying that the Commission as presently constituted does not intend to sabotage the statutes it administers. The Federal Securities laws are not in the hands of their enemies." But Demmler also considered himself one of the "many representative, responsible, and informed people who think that the Commission in certain areas has from time to time gone beyond its statutory powers in an excess of regulatory zeal; that it has been dominated by its staff; that both staff and Commission have sometimes been high-handed; and that the Commission has been careless of other peoples' time and money in imposing on issuers and underwriters useless and duplicative paper work." During his chairmanship Demmler requested General Counsel Roger Foster and Associate General Counsel Myron Isaacs to resign because of philosophical differences. Demmler found his conviction that "there was some dead wood that could be dispensed with without any damage to work" corroborated by the presence of one senior SEC official, with the title of "Foreign Economic Adviser," whose job had long outlived its usefulness, a regional administrator who had suffered a mental breakdown, and a former director of the Corporation Finance Division who had been retained as an executive assistant after developing a drinking problem. Demmler pressured all three to leave, as well as Anthony

Lund, the director of the Trading and Exchanges Division. Demmler, however, ultimately won high marks from the SEC staff because of his obvious intelligence, his willingness to modify preconceptions when presented with persuasive counterarguments, the high caliber of the senior staff members he recruited, notably General Counsel William Timbers and future commissioners Philip Loomis and Ray Garrett, Jr., and his support of the most talented holdover senior staff officials, such as Byron Woodside and Manuel Cohen.

Yet Demmler also was loyal to the values of the Eisenhower administration. He began his chairmanship by stating his intention to comply with a Bureau of the Budget request for "suggestions for methods of reducing expenditures for Fiscal 1955." This, Demmler philosophically was prepared to do. Although he repeatedly noted that he sought to retain "those things in our procedures which are good and valid," with equal frequency he indicated his intention to eliminate SEC regulations and forms "which are unnecessary or unduly cumbersome." The complementary goals of reducing expenditures and eliminating unnecessary regulation largely determined the policies of Demmler's SEC.[7] Early in his tenure as chairman, Demmler announced that "budgetary considerations" had persuaded him to "substantially curtail discretionary intervention by the Commission" in bankruptcy proceedings.[8]

To reduce the "paperwork" burden on business registrants, Demmler's SEC unsuccessfully lobbied to have Congress raise the 1933 Securities Act small-issue exemption from $300,000 to $500,000[9] and revised a number of SEC regulations, forms, and procedures.[10]

The most controversial changes were the SEC's 1954 amendments to the proxy rules. In 1942, the SEC had adopted proxy rules permitting shareholders to circulate proposals for corporate action at the expense of the firm as one limited means of achieving what a District of Columbia Court of Appeals in 1970 aptly termed "the philosophy of corporate democracy which Congress embodied in Section 14(a) of the Securities Exchange Act of 1934." The SEC's 1942 proxy regulations never were particularly far-reaching. In 1945 the Corporate Finance Division had officially expressed the view that matters "of a general political, social, or economic nature" were not proper subjects for inclusion in a shareholder's proxy proposal. This test was used in 1951 to prevent a shareholder of the Greyhound Corporation from circulating a proposal called "A Recommendation that Management Consider the Advisability of Abolishing the Segregated Seating System in the South." Even though it agreed that the proposal "appeared germane to the business of the company," the "Commission determined that the primary motive of the shareholder was the advancement of a cause with which the stockholder had a close association rather than the solution of a problem pertinent solely to the corporation itself."

In 1954, the Demmler SEC, apparently concerned about such "corporate gadflies" as Lewis Gilbert and Wilma Soss, markedly narrowed the scope of the proxy rules. Shareholders were barred from circulating a proposal if it was not a proper subject for action by stockholders under the laws in the state in which the corporation was chartered, if it was submitted primarily to redress a personal grievance, or if it was related to the conduct of the ordinary business operations of the corporation. The corporation was not required to circulate any proposal unless it was received at least sixty days before a shareholders' meeting. The firm could exclude any proposal submitted once within the previous three years if it had not received a 3 percent vote; if twice submitted, a 6 percent vote; or if submitted three times, a 10 percent vote. Although the revised rules did not, as some critics feared, totally "strangle corporate democracy," the rules did maintain shareholder activity at a low ebb. In the months succeeding their circulation, to cite three examples, the SEC interpreted its rules to permit Liggett and Myers to exclude Lewis Gilbert's proposal that stockholders request "information as to the amount [the firm] spent on advertising," since this was considered both impermissible under the relevant state's law and a matter related to the conduct of the company's ordinary business operations; allowed Butler Brothers to exclude a shareholder proposal that the firm's Board of Directors appoint a committee to fill board vacancies and retain stated percentages of net earnings for expansion; and the Atlantic Refining Company to omit a proposal that no relative of a corporate executive be eligible for a corporate executive position, because the SEC concurred with the company that the proposal was circulated primarily to redress a personal grievance.

While the Third Circuit Court of Appeals in a leading 1947 decision denominated the proxy rules a mechanism to remind a firm's executives that a "corporation is run for the benefit of its stockholders and not for that of its managers," the SEC's 1954 amendments began with the near opposite premise, recorded in the *SEC Minutes*, that a corporation should be permitted "to omit any proposal which impinges upon the duties and functions of the management."[11]

At the same time that the SEC used what Demmler termed "sickle and pruning shears"[12] (as distinguished from the less sensitive "ax and scythe") to cut back what Demmler considered unnecessary regulations and forms, Demmler could not recall "any serious discussion" of substantive legislative initiatives at the

SEC during his chairmanship.*[13] As he explained during his confirmation hearing, he did not think it was "part of my job as one of five commissioners to carry the flag on new legislation."[15] Instead, he took the position that the SEC should endorse legislation only when there was mutual agreement among Congress, the SEC, and such industry organizations as the Investment Bankers Association, the National Association of Securities Dealers, and the New York Stock Exchange. Demmler maintained a similar hands-off approach with respect to stock exchange rule-making. In 1962, New York Stock Exchange president Keith Funston explained to SEC chairman William Cary that until 1952–1953 it had been customary for the Exchange to seek SEC approval of each "important action" that it took. "At the time when Ralph Demmler came in he talked with [Exchange officials] and said from here on they are on their own and for that historical reason . . . policy has been consistently independent since that time."[16] In 1953, the NYSE raised commission rates an average of 18 percent[17] and rescinded certain of its rules restricting floor trading.[18] The Demmler SEC's approach to the Exchange's actions was illustrated by the *SEC Minutes* for August 6, 1953. On being informed that the Midwest Stock Exchange objected to certain features of the New York Stock Exchange's rate increase, Demmler, speaking for the SEC, indicated to the two exchanges that the Commission would take no official position on the issue unless the Midwest Exchange formally petitioned the SEC to invoke a Section 19(b) proceeding under the 1934 Securities Exchange Act. At Demmler's suggestion, the two exchanges privately settled their differences, the *SEC Minutes* recording, "Mr. Demmler disclaimed any intention on the part of the Commission to try to influence the representatives of the two Exchanges in their decision as to what, if anything, should be done under the circumstances." On September 10, New York Stock Exchange officials returned to the Commission to discuss other Exchange rule changes. The *SEC Minutes* state that "the Commission . . . indicated a 'hands-off' attitude. That is to say, the representatives of the Exchange were advised that the Commission was expressing neither approval nor disapproval of the proposed rules. It was stated that the Commission should have a completely free hand under Section 19(b) of the Secu-

---

* In 1954, Congress passed what Demmler termed "modest housekeeping amendments" to the 1933 Securities Act, which gave statutory approval to practices that the SEC had long permitted by rule or custom, such as allowing an issuer to distribute a preliminary prospectus to potential investors during the statutory waiting period while the SEC formally reviewed a registration statement for accuracy and completeness.[14]

rities Exchange Act of 1934." During Demmler's chairmanship, the SEC never initiated a Section 19(b) proceeding.

*   *   *

After the Democrats regained control of Congress in November 1954, the Eisenhower administration's management of the SEC came under sharp attack. Between September 1953 and January 1955, Standard and Poor's index of 480 common stocks rose by 50 percent. Accompanying the market rise was evidence of the most widespread pattern of speculative activity and securities fraud to occur since the late 1920s.[19] Beginning in the spring of 1954, an unparalleled number of "penny" uranium company securities were sold, employing a 1933 Securities Act small-issue exemption.

Over a five-year period Walter Tellier raised money for more than sixty uranium-mining companies. Some of Tellier's securities issuances were fraudulent, including those of the Consolidated Uranium Mines, Incorporated, which falsely claimed it owned or operated 85,000 acres of uranium leases. As a result of investigations initiated during Demmler's chairmanship, Tellier was convicted of criminal securities fraud. Other uranium securities promoters did not engage in securities fraud, though their activities raised obvious public policy questions. One analysis of the uranium securities found underwriters charging fees as high as 33⅓ percent. Similarly, an SEC study of 224 uranium issues distributed in 1953 and 1954 found that "in a great many cases promoters and management owned shares very much out of line with the capital they have contributed." In one instance, that of the Pioneer Uranium Corporation, promoters received 62.5 percent of the firm's securities although they invested no capital.[20]

The early 1950s also saw a vast increase in "boiler rooms," where, typically, twenty to thirty telephones would be manned by former carnival workers, pitchmen, confidence game operators, or bookmakers who would promote fraudulent or highly speculative securities to lists of unsophisticated investors.[21]

Simultaneously, Walter Winchell in his weekly radio and television broadcasts fed the speculative climate by offering such "tips" as his April 1953 statement that the "biggest oil strike in North American history . . . may be confirmed tomorrow by Amurex Oil Development Company." Winchell's tips were not illegal, since he was not paid to make them and usually culled his information from published sources, but they frequently sent corporation stock prices jolting upward by several points. "In January 1955," Wall Street historian Robert Sobel wrote, "Winchell claimed that had a person purchased round lots in all the forty or so stocks he had mentioned in the previous year, he would have a paper profit of around a quarter of a million dollars." Winchell's claim was not true, but the confabulations of a man who had once been the nation's most popular radio commentator, reported Sobel, "drew many thousands of speculators into the markets."[22]

The SEC's response to the 1950s' revival of securities speculation and the "Winchell Market" convinced *Time* magazine, among others, that, as an article title put it, in providing "Protection for Investors: The SEC is Unequal to the Job."[23] Testifying before the Senate Banking Committee in March 1955, Demmler indicated that the SEC had sought an increase of twenty-six staff members, but he believed that the securities markets and brokerage houses "are being operated in a manner consistent with the public interest" for numerous reasons, including "the continued maintenance of consultation and liaison between the exchanges and the Commission [and] the fact that unlawful activity on the floor of an exchange cannot easily escape the notice of others on the floor." "Above and beyond these things," Demmler emphasized, the SEC "must place considerable reliance on the disposition of most people to obey the law."[24] The Senate Banking Committee disagreed, reporting in May 1955, "The evidence . . . indicates unmistakably that there has been an increase in unhealthy speculative developments in the stock market since the fall of 1954."[25] At approximately the same time, Congressman John Bennett criticized Demmler for proposing to increase the Securities Act small-issue exemption from $300,000 to $500,000 during a penny stock securities fraud wave. In July 1955, a House Commerce Subcommittee began hearings to consider Bennett's recommendation that the small-issue exemption be abolished.[26]

For purely personal reasons, Demmler resigned as SEC chairman in May 1955. Criticism of the Eisenhower administration's SEC continued for the balance of the year. By statute, no more than three of the SEC's five commissioners may be members of the same political party. In June 1955, the Eisenhower administration nominated Harold Patterson as a commissioner. Patterson was the fifth commissioner nominated by the Eisenhower administration and the second registered Democrat with a background primarily in investment banking. When Senators Wayne Morse and Herbert Lehman adduced testimony at Patterson's confirmation hearing that the appointment had been cleared by the Republican National Committee, which Morse characterized as "the Republican patronage organization," substantial opposition to Patterson's confirmation developed. Six of the fourteen members of the Senate Banking Committee voted against Patterson's confirmation after Lehman charged that the statutory requirement that the SEC "should be bipartisan has been flagrantly disrespected." Since the three Republican SEC commissioners whom the Eisenhower administration previously had nominated had been corporate attorneys, the Banking Committee minority also complained that Patterson's presence on the SEC would "make industry representation on the SEC unanimous." On August 29, 1955, former President Truman echoed the charge, asserting that the SEC was packed as never before with people who came from the ranks of the industries it was supposed to regulate.[27]

The Commission's involvement in the Dixon-Yates controversy resulted in further accusations that the SEC was subject to a private industry orientation. Early in his administration, Eisenhower described the expansion of the Tennessee Valley Authority (TVA) as a form of "creeping socialism," exclaiming at a July 31, 1953, Cabinet meeting, according to associate Emmet Hughes, "By God, if ever we could do it, before we leave here, I'd like to see us *sell* the whole thing, but I suppose we can't go that far."[28] Similar sentiments prevailed throughout the Eisenhower administration. In his January 9, 1953, budget message, outgoing President Truman had recommended a $30 million appropriation for the TVA to begin work on what was known as the Fulton steam plant to enable the authority to meet its contractual commitment to supply power to Memphis, Tennessee. On May 13, 1953, the Eisenhower administration revised the TVA's 1954 budget, eliminating funds for the Fulton plant. To prevent the further growth of the TVA, successive Eisenhower Budget Bureau directors Joseph Dodge and Rowland Hughes supervised a complex arrangement, announced in the 1955 budget, whereby the Atomic Energy Commission (AEC) would cease purchasing from the TVA some 500,000 to 600,000 kilowatts a year for its Paducah, Kentucky, installation, and the TVA would use that capacity to supply Memphis.

In order to power the AEC's Paducah installation, the Eisenhower Budget Bureau encouraged the AEC and the TVA to contract with Middle South Utilities, whose president was Edgar H. Dixon, and the Southern Corporation, whose president was Eugene Yates, to build a new private plant. After considerable negotiation, Dixon, Yates, and the AEC agreed, on November 11, 1954, that a new firm, known as the Mississippi Valley Generating Company, would build a plant in West Memphis, Arkansas, to supply power to the AEC using TVA interconnections. The Dixon-Yates contract with the AEC and the TVA fell apart in late June 1955, after it was revealed that Adolphe Wenzell had served as an unpaid adviser to the Eisenhower Bureau of the Budget in drawing up the Dixon-Yates plan while simultaneously receiving a salary as vice president of the First Boston Corporation, the investment bank that had been granted the contract to sell securities for the Mississippi Valley Generating Company.

For the balance of the year, a subcommittee led by Senator Estes Kefauver questioned the propriety of the SEC's approving, under the Holding Company Act, the formation of the Mississippi Valley Generating Company and its securities sales. After twice claiming executive privilege, J. Sinclair Armstrong, Ralph Demmler's successor as SEC chairman, acknowledged in July 1955 that Sherman Adams had requested him to delay a hearing the preceding month concerning the Mississippi Valley Generating Company's debt-financing. Adolphe Wenzell was expected to testify publicly at the hearing, but it coincided with a vote by the House Committee on Appropriations on transmission lines for the TVA to interconnect with the Dixon-Yates plant.[29] One historian later would conclude of the Dixon-Yates controversy, "The greatest damage to the Administration resulted from the reluctant testimony of SEC chairman J. Sinclair Armstrong, who finally acknowledged that he had postponed hearings of the SEC on the day Wenzell was to testify because of the intervention of Presidential Assistant Sherman Adams."[30]

In December 1955, the role of former chairman Demmler also was questioned after it was disclosed that in September 1954 he had prepared a memorandum for AEC chairman Lewis Strauss, advising Strauss how the Dixon-Yates contract would satisfy the requirements of the Public Utility Holding Company Act in spite of its 95 percent debt ratio and the lack of physical interconnection between the proposed West Memphis plant and the Southern Corporation's nearest plant. Demmler, citing two earlier instances in which SEC chairman Donald Cook similarly had advised the AEC, defended the memorandum as appropriate, since "we all work for the same Government." Congressional critics of the Dixon-Yates contract viewed Demmler's conduct in a more sinister light. The most extreme view was held by Senator Joseph O'Mahoney, acting chairman of the Senate Antitrust and Monopoly Subcommittee, who in July 1956 released a staff report that concluded, "The administration of law by the SEC was brought into disrepute because of the SEC's flagrant departures from accepted interpretations of the Public Utility Holding

Company Act and its succumbing to pressures from higher authority emanating from the White House."*[31]

After Demmler's departure, the SEC was led for two years by Chairman J. Sinclair Armstrong, then for the balance of the Eisenhower administration by Chairman Edward Gadsby. With even the New York Stock Exchange lobbying to expand the Commission's staff,[33] the SEC was able to increase its personnel to 1087 during the last six years of the Eisenhower administration. But, as was recognized by Armstrong and Gadsby and by a Booz Allen and Hamilton study contracted by the Eisenhower Budget Bureau,[34] the SEC's staff increases never kept pace with the booming securities markets. Between 1955 and 1961, the SEC staff grew by 63 percent. During the same period, the number of investors, representatives of New York Stock Exchange firms, and the value of shares traded on the NYSE approximately doubled; the number of registered NASD representatives increased by 130 percent. Stimulating this growth was a soaring Dow Jones Average, which rocketed from a low of 388.2 in 1955 to a high of 734.9 in 1961. In the longer view, between 1945 and 1961 the SEC's staff decreased by 6 percent.[35] Over this sixteen-year period, the value of mutual funds increased from $1.3 to $22.8 billion; the dollar value of trading of over-the-counter shares increased eightfold; the dollar value of new securities increased fivefold.[36]

The late 1950s' bull market was accompanied by the type of speculative climate in which securities fraud thrives. During the late 1950s, not only boiler rooms and marginal brokerage houses,

---

* During the 1956 presidential campaign, the Dixon-Yates contract was a Democratic Party campaign issue. Although the Democrats lost the White House, on February 5, 1957, House Speaker Sam Rayburn recommended the creation of a committee to investigate whether the laws administered by the independent regulatory commissions were "being carried out or whether a great many of these laws are being repealed or revamped by those who administer them." The subsequently created Special Subcommittee on Legislative Oversight was best remembered for revelations that Sherman Adams had intervened in FTC and SEC proceedings against Bernard Goldfine after receiving a vicuña coat and other gifts from Goldfine. Adams soon resigned. Although Adams's intervention at the SEC had no practical effect on the Commission's litigation against Goldfine to compel him to file statutorily required annual reports, the subcommittee did discover that the SEC had not compelled Goldfine's East Boston Company to file an annual report for six years from 1948 to 1954, in spite of the Commission's knowledge of Goldfine's delinquency as early as 1948. The subcommittee appropriately criticized the SEC for "failure . . . to adopt adequate administrative procedures to prevent flagrant violations of their requirements." This failure was consistent with the general weakness of SEC enforcement efforts between 1945 and 1961 while the Commission was seriously understaffed.[32]

but some New York Stock Exchange firms employed get-rich-quick advertisements. In one, a New York Stock Exchange firm recommended "six securities which we believe should be able to double over the next few months."[37] "Hot" issues dominated the new securities markets. The SEC's *Special Study of the Securities Markets* later was to report:

> From 1959 until the market decline of early 1962, the distribution of securities by companies that had not made a previous public offering reached the highest level in history. This activity in new issues took place in a climate of general optimism and speculative interest. The public eagerly sought stocks of companies in certain "glamour" industries, especially the electronics industry, in the expectation that they would quickly rise to a substantial premium — an expectation that was often fulfilled. Within a few days or even hours after the initial distribution, these so-called hot issues would be traded at premiums of as much as 300 percent above the original offering price. In many cases the price of a "hot" issue later fell to a fraction of its original offering price.[38]

In a market in which one financial writer claimed, "Almost any issue with a Buck Rogerish tinge to its name was bound to go into orbit,"[39] former ballroom dancer Nicolas Darvas's *How I Made $2,000,000 in the Stock Market* sold more than 100,000 copies within five weeks of its publication date.[40] The increasingly speculative securities market further strained SEC resources. Understaffing, for example, led to a near-tripling of the time required by the SEC to review securities registration statements, from a median of twenty-two days in 1955 to fifty-five days in 1961.[41] "The problems of the Securities and Exchange Commission are relatively simple," James Landis would write President-elect Kennedy in 1960; "much of the delays that characterize its operation stem from the fact that it, more than any other agency, has been starved for appropriations. Even the recent increases have not restored the amounts formerly available."[42]

The SEC's regulatory efforts deteriorated throughout the Eisenhower administration also because of a crucial shift in the agency's operative assumptions. During the New Deal period, the SEC had focused its enforcement efforts on the New York Stock Exchange and the leading securities broker-dealers on the assumption that sustained scrutiny of the industry's leaders would stimulate the most vigorous industry self-regulation. By contrast, the SEC during the Eisenhower years tended to share with the NYSE the assumption that securities fraud was unlikely to be perpetrated on the leading exchanges or by the leading broker-dealers.

In a 1959 article, for example, SEC chairman Gadsby implied his belief that the Commission's enforcement efforts should not be focused on the leaders of the securities industry, since "responsible professional and business leaders . . . have evolved existing patterns of conduct based upon the principles of honesty, fair dealings, and full disclosure underlying the securities acts."[43] Instead, successive Eisenhower chairmen Demmler, Armstrong, and Gadsby emphasized the strengthening of regional offices to combat boiler rooms, fraudulent penny stocks, and exploitative local broker-dealers. Between 1950 and 1960, the proportion of SEC employees in regional offices grew from 31 to 41 percent,[44] with aggressive SEC enforcement attorneys like New York regional office director Paul Windels garnering headlines for dramatic increases in the number of SEC enforcement actions directed at boiler rooms.[45] It was a highly selective enforcement policy. Although Windels stated that "criminal prosecution is the only language the boiler rooms understand," he was considerably less eager to initiate investigations of the stock exchanges, as he illustrated in May 1959, when Chairman Gadsby asserted that a small group of floor traders bore some responsibility for recent erratic swings in certain stock prices. At approximately the same time, Windels publicly stated, "Thank Heaven for the floor traders. I love 'em! They back up the specialists in giving us price continuity and reasonably responsive markets."[46] Inevitably, such attitudes translated into enforcement practices. Three years later, Philip A. Loomis, then director of the SEC's Trading and Exchanges Division, would conclude that the SEC's enforcement attorneys were not sufficiently "alert" to the possibility of securities fraud being committed by Exchange floor members: "The primary enforcement problems over a period of a good many years had been registration violations and fraud and misrepresentation in the sale of securities. The result of this was that the investigation and enforcement staffs, both in regional and in the home office, were just not oriented to Exchange operations."[47]

The combination of SEC understaffing and emphasis on regional office antifraud actions left wide gaps in the Commission's enforcement program. The Commission's 1963 Special Study of Securities Markets was particularly critical of the SEC's passive role in supervising securities exchange and NASD self-regulation, finding that "responsibilities at the heart of the Commission's role of protecting public investors . . . such as continuous examination of changing market circumstances and regulatory needs, appraisal, and reappraisal of the adequacy of the existing regulatory measures, and in particular, evaluation and oversight of the operation of the self-regulatory agencies" had been largely ignored. To dramatize the significance of this criticism, the Special Study's report pointedly noted:

> The Commission's relative inattention to these latter areas is mirrored in the contents of its annual reports and other public pronouncements. For example, with respect to matters of continuous and routine administration — registrations, suspensions, delistings, etc. — its annual reports are storehouses of information as to its activities. But with respect to such vital matters as the performance of specialists, the stock exchange commission rate structure, the over-the-counter quotations systems, automation of market or ancillary mechanisms, competitive markets, or the achievements and deficiencies of self-regulation, the reports are virtually silent.[48]

Criticism of SEC regulation of the leading broker-dealers was nearly as severe. During the late 1950s, the securities brokerage industry collectively experienced a rapid expansion, with the result that, as SEC Chairman William Cary testified in 1961, "many securities salesmen work on a part-time basis; many have no particular qualifications to sell securities; and most important, many are not subject to the kind of supervision which ensure high ethical standards."[49] With the SEC able to inspect broker-dealers on average only once every three years, and to inspect brokerage houses located in New York City on average only once every five or six years,[50] the SEC's 1963 Special Study of Securities Markets identified several instances in which leading brokerage houses had engaged in what Cary delicately termed "questionable merchandising techniques." In one striking instance, the Special Study found that brokers employed by Merrill Lynch, the nation's largest brokerage firm, sold 99,400 shares of Aquafilter Corporation, a firm that manufactured a water-impregnated filter for cigarettes, on the basis of such representations as "Aquafilter production could not keep up with demand" and "a favorable Dun and Bradstreet report had been obtained on [Aquafilter's] president." Not only were these and similar claims false, but the overzealous salesmen had broken several internal rules supposedly enforced by Merrill Lynch, including one requiring brokers to consider the suitability of a high-risk security for each customer to whom it was recommended, a second requiring Merrill Lynch brokers to consult with the brokerage house's research department before recommending a previously unknown security, and a third rule barring Merrill Lynch brokers from recommending any security that claimed a small-issue exemption under the 1933 Securities Act.[51]

Comparable weaknesses existed in the SEC's supervision of investment companies. In two addresses in 1962 and 1963 William Cary explained, "From the enactment of the 1940 [Investment Company] Act until 1961, there had been inspection of only thirty investment companies." Given the number of investment companies, this meant each firm would be inspected once every twelve years, a frequency Cary termed "inadequate, indeed absurd."[52]

Ultimately, the gaping weaknesses in the Eisenhower administration's SEC enforcement program resulted in the near-complete collapse of self-regulation on the American Stock Exchange, the most serious stock market scandal since Richard Whitney's defalcations were revealed in the spring of 1938. Unlike the situation in the New York Stock Exchange after the Whitney scandal, the governance of the New York Curb Exchange had not been effectively reorganized. From January 1953, when the Curb Exchange was renamed the American Stock Exchange, through May 1961, when the SEC initiated a comprehensive staff investigation of the exchange, governance of the American Stock Exchange was dominated by four men, Joseph Reilly, Charles Bocklet, James R. Dyer, and John J. Mann. All four were exchange specialists or former specialists. This meant that governance of the American Stock Exchange was in the hands of floor members, not brokers who dealt with the public. It was exactly the pattern of governance that the SEC had attempted to end on the NYSE after the Whitney scandal.[53]

In 1951, the Curb Exchange had hired Edward McCormick to be its president. McCormick, who for seventeen years had worked for the SEC, had become a commissioner, in part, as a result of writing in 1948 one of the earliest scholarly books on the Commission, *Understanding the Securities Act and the SEC*. McCormick's principal job as exchange president, however, was not regulating floor transactions; it was obtaining new listings of securities for the exchange. Throughout his ten years as exchange president, McCormick made so many trips throughout the country to meet with officials of corporations that potentially could list their securities on the American Stock Exchange, "that McCormick was considered by the membership principally as a salesman rather than as an administrator," reported an SEC staff study in 1962.[54] American Stock Exchange specialists also were encouraged to seek new listings because of a rule, in effect until 1961, entitling any specialist whose efforts led to the listing of a company's stock to register as the specialist in that stock. This created a financial incentive for specialists to join McCormick in recruiting new securities,[55] and helped boost American Stock Exchange total annual trading volume by over 400 percent between 1953 and 1961.[56]

The salesmanship of the American Stock Exchange (Amex) early resulted in a number of securities of dubious quality being listed on the exchange. In the early 1950s the SEC was highly concerned about the sale of Canadian mining and oil securities in the United States. Twelve such Canadian issues were listed on the exchange in 1952 alone. By December 31, 1960, 104 Canadian securities were traded on the Amex, over half of which had lost money in two of the three preceding fiscal years. Relaxation of listing requirements led to the listing of several other securities of marginal companies. In 1955, for example, the exchange had acceded to the request of one of its leading specialists and agreed to list New Pacific Coal and Oils Ltd., despite the fact that the firm had reported no income during any of the previous three years.[57] At the same time, McCormick indicated in his 1953–1954 *Report of the President of the American Stock Exchange* that the exchange was "bending every effort to cultivate a greater interest in securities by persons in the lower and middle income groups." Throughout the 1950s, the Amex was the highly conspicuous hub of a securities speculation revival.

Regulation of the American Stock Exchange by the SEC was largely passive. In May 1953, the Commission requested that the exchange, as one means of deterring market manipulation, adopt a rule requiring specialists to report to the exchange purchases of securities they made off the floor. It was characteristic of the Commission's exchange regulation during this period that it was not until 1959 that the SEC discovered that the rule adopted by the American Stock Exchange applied only to purchases made during hours when the exchange was open, entirely frustrating for six years the intent of the Commission's 1953 recommendations.[58] A second expression of concern was communicated in a 1956 speech by SEC chairman Armstrong at the annual outing of the American Stock Exchange, when he described "an observable tendency for people to be more lax in adhering to the federal securities laws" and urged, "Guard the reputation of your American Stock Exchange. If your exchange is used only for purely speculative activity and the public gets hurt, you will reap the adverse public reaction."[59] Yet during the first seven years of the Eisenhower administration, the Commission made no effective efforts to review or alter the exchange's governance, listing, or floor-trading practices.

In 1955, or at the latest in 1956, the Commission became aware of serious securities violations committed by two leading American

Stock Exchange members in connection with a distribution of Crowell-Collier convertible debentures. Crowell-Collier, then best known as the publisher of the struggling *Collier's* magazine, had sustained such substantial operating losses in 1953 and 1954 that it was advised by investment bankers that a distribution of common stock would be impossible. By May 1955, bank creditors were pressing the company. It was anticipated that large loans due in August 1955 would not be extended unless additional long-term financing was obtained from other sources. The firm's financial circumstances then were so precarious that a House of Representatives subcommittee later found that had Crowell-Collier made the public disclosures required by the 1933 Securities Act, "the disclosures probably would have vitiated efforts to raise additional capital." Instead, Crowell-Collier turned to American Stock Exchange broker-dealer Edward Elliot, who proposed a "private placement" of $4 million of debentures convertible immediately into common stock.

It always had been the law under the Securities Act that if a security was sold to a sufficiently small number of investors "able to fend for themselves" in a nonpublic offering, no registration was required. At the time, it was widely believed that a private placement had to be limited to no more than twenty-five people, none of whom could act as an underwriter and resell the security to others. In 1955, Elliot sold $3 million of debentures to twenty-seven purchasers, securing from each an investment letter representing that "said debentures are being purchased for investment and the undersigned has no present intention of distributing the same." The investment letters were generally ignored, with the result that the debentures were, in fact, distributed to seventy-nine purchasers representing eighty-eight people. Since none of the purchasers was fully informed of the precarious financial condition of Crowell-Collier, the distribution involved patent violations of the 1933 Securities Act. In 1956, the same investment letter procedure was employed to sell another $1 million of debentures.

Among those to whom Elliot sold the debentures was James Gilligan, a general partner of Gilligan, Will, then the leading specialist on the American Stock Exchange. In October 1955, Gilligan succeeded in having Crowell-Collier common stock listed on the Amex with himself as its specialist. Gilligan also helped to distribute $500,000 of the debentures, violating the 1933 Securities Act by reselling the unregistered securities to friends and associates.

On August 8, 1955, a Crowell-Collier shareholder wrote Chairman Armstrong to complain about the low conversion price on the Crowell-Collier debentures, inquiring, "Can the Securities and Exchange Commission . . . be of any help in having this action rescinded?" Within ten days, a pro forma response was mailed to the shareholder, indicating that the Commission lacked jurisdiction. Approximately one year later the SEC commenced an investigation of the Crowell-Collier private placement, tentatively concluding in November 1956 that the firm had illegally claimed a private placement exemption. But the Commission's prosecution of this offense was restrained. No disciplinary action was taken against Crowell-Collier after it agreed to file a registration statement in June 1957. In August 1957, the Commission commenced an administrative proceeding, which in 1958 resulted in a twenty-day suspension from the NASD of Elliot and Company, Edward Elliot's brokerage firm, and a five-day NASD suspension of Gilligan, Will.

Apparently no effort was made by the SEC to learn whether Elliot and Company or Gilligan, Will had participated in other similar distributions. Nor was an effort made to learn why the American Stock Exchange had not questioned the claimed "private placement" of the Crowell-Collier securities when the securities were listed, despite the revelation in 1957 that Edward McCormick had purchased $15,000 of the illegally distributed Crowell-Collier debentures. Nor was any effective effort made to discover whether Elliot and Company or Gilligan, Will was in violation of other securities laws. So passive was the Commission's investigation and prosecution of the *Crowell-Collier* case that in January 1959 the House Special Subcommittee on Legislative Oversight published a detailed report concerning the Commission's performance in the case. It concluded:

> The record indicates that from July 1955 to December 21, 1956, a period of 18 months, the Commission failed to take any affirmative action even though it had notice of numerous specific instances where the violations had officially come to its attention. Because of the Commission's failure to take immediate effective action, many subsequent violations by all the participants occurred.
>
> Despite illegal actions by participants, the Commission imposed only nominal penalties on but 3 of the broker-dealers involved — suspension for 5 to 20 days from membership in the National Association of Securities Dealers, Inc. Thus, they and numerous other participants in the financing effected through evasion of the requirements of the 1933 act were able to keep the fruits of their lawbreaking with immunity from any effective administrative sanctions.

Had the SEC pressed its investigation, it might have learned that in 1955 Gilligan, Will had orchestrated a distribution of 200,000 shares of Guild Films to 172 people, employing an equally questionable claim of private placement exemption. James Gilligan later testified that the Commission's five-day suspension of him from NASD "had no effect whatsoever on him financially," since he was primarily a specialist, not dependent on NASD membership for his livelihood. A 1962 SEC staff report would find that in the five years after the Commission began its 1956 investigation of the Crowell-Collier distribution, Gilligan, Will participated in the distribution of unregistered securities for at least six other corporations: Acme-Hamilton, Chromalloy, Occidental Petroleum, El-tronics, Hazel Bishop, and New Idria. The report concluded that most of these distributions were accompanied by violation of a Securities Exchange Act rule that forbade price manipulation by an underwriter.

In other instances, the report found, Gilligan, Will had benefited from inside information as a result of a close relationship with a corporate issuer's management or had made off-board purchases of securities in which it was a specialist, in violation of an American Stock Exchange rule. The report also found that questionable floor-trading activity systematically had occurred at the Gilligan, Will post on the American Stock Exchange. It was apparent that Amex officials were sufficiently aware of "the entire pattern of activities conducted by Gilligan, Will . . . that the exchange might have been expected to act promptly in putting a halt to them." Yet the SEC in 1962 woud find "that Gilligan was immune from disciplinary action by the exchange. He testified that he has not been the subject of a disciplinary action of the exchange for at least twenty years." The Commission in 1962 suggested that a primary reason for Gilligan's immunity from prosecution may have been the control of exchange governance by other specialists. Gilligan also had consistently given securities or presented desirable opportunities to buy securities to American Stock Exchange leaders, including President McCormick, Joseph Reilly while he was chairman of the exchange's Committee on Floor Trading, and Michael Mooney, the exchange's general counsel.[60] Only in February 1962, after publication of the SEC's staff report on the American Stock Exchange, was James Gilligan effectively sanctioned; he was barred from serving as an Amex specialist for five years.[61]

The same SEC passivity that emboldened James Gilligan and Edward Elliot permitted the more serious securities law violations committed by their fellow Amex specialists, the father-and-son team of Gerard A. (Jerry) and Gerard F. Re. Between 1954 and 1960, the Res illegally distributed over $10 million of securities on the American Stock Exchange. They manipulated the prices of several securities. They illegally touted shares. They bribed brokers to tout shares. They took advantage of inside information. They caused to be published false and misleading prospectuses by at least four firms. They systematically failed to keep required records, and routinely ignored Section 11(b) of the 1934 Securities Act, which provides that if the Commission permits specialists to act as dealers, the SEC shall "restrict his dealings so far as practicable to those reasonably necessary to maintain a fair and orderly market." All told, the Res may have violated ten separate provisions of the 1933 and 1934 Securities Acts and an equal number of rules of the American Stock Exchange, well justifying the SEC's subsequent conclusion that the Commission's two leading market manipulation cases to that date, 1930s' actions against Michael Meehan and Charles Wright, "became almost trivial" by comparison.

In 1961, a bristling SEC brief would lead to the expulsion of the Res from the American Stock Exchange for their "prostitution of the specialists' important role [which] resulted in many millions of dollars of harm to thousands of unsuspecting investors." But the Re scandal was most shocking because it occurred nearly thirty years after the creation of the SEC. "Almost unnoticed," financial journalist Frank Cormier would write, "Jerry and Gerard Re had turned back the clock to an earlier era, reviving some of the very practices that had led to federal regulation of Wall Street. The two specialists were living proof of the fact that history repeats itself — if men lack the wisdom and fortitude to learn from the mistakes of the past."

Between 1954 and 1959, the SEC underinvestigated the Res in spite of clear signals of serious wrongdoing at least as early as 1957. The scandal effectively began in May 1954, when financier Lowell Birrell and Jerry Re purchased a controlling interest in the Swan-Finch Oil Corporation. During the period from about July 1954 to about April 1957, the Res distributed at least 578,000 shares of Swan-Finch common stock with a market value over $3 million without filing a registration statement, as required by the 1933 Securities Act. Over half of the illegally distributed shares were funneled through the dummy securities account of Charles Grande, who was an old friend of Jerry Re's and an itinerant horse trainer with no experience in the securities business. Rather than register Swan-Finch securities with the SEC when they were to be issued, Re would deliver the shares to the Grande account. Over time, Grande illegally would sell the shares to the public.

All of this was understood by the SEC by April 15, 1957, when the Commission obtained a temporary restraining order to halt trading in Swan-Finch common stock. The following day the Amex also suspended trading in the security on discovering that Swan-Finch

Oil Corporation had not filed required reports for several years. On June 27, 1957, Lowell Birrell, the Res, and Charles Grande consented to permanent injunctions from selling Swan-Finch common stock or any other security in violation of the Securities Act. But even with Birrell fleeing to Havana after receiving a subpoena to testify about his activities in Swan-Finch,* neither the SEC nor the American Stock Exchange further investigated the Res or Swan-Finch.

Some months later, the Amex Committee on Floor Transactions found that the Res had failed to perform their specialist functions in connection with the stock of American Manufacturing Company. No penalty was imposed. This was typical of Amex discipline at that time. Between March 1957 and December 1959, ten specialists were called before the Committee on Floor Transactions to answer serious charges. None was disciplined.

In November 1959, the Amex Committee on Business Conduct charged that the Res had illegally short-sold shares of Trans Continental Industries. The case was referred to the Amex Board of Governors. By a vote of 18–5, on December 19, 1959, the specialist-dominated board exonerated the Res. But under pressure from the SEC, which had uncovered evidence that the Res also might have been involved in illegal sales of Skiatron Electronics and Television and I. Rokeach & Sons shares, the Amex did suspend Jerry Re for thirty days for failure to keep adequate records. One exchange governor acknowledged that the penalty was exacted chiefly because "it was in the interests of the exchange from the standpoint of public relations and relations with the SEC."

It was only then that the SEC initiated an effective investigation of the Res. Deeming the Amex board's thirty-day suspension of Jerry Re entirely inadequate, Ralph Saul, associate director of the SEC's Trading and Exchanges Division, assigned the SEC's leading investigator, Edward Jaegerman, to begin an investigation of the Res. By May 12, 1960, the division had assembled sufficient evidence to request that the SEC hold a public hearing to determine whether it was necessary or appropriate to expel the Res from the American Stock Exchange. The SEC's May 12 order described an unprecedented pattern of securities law violations. The order alleged that the Res, employing first the dummy account of Charles Grande, then the accounts of Benjamin Wheeler and the Swiss bank account

---

* Birrell, long suspected by SEC attorneys of being involved in criminal wrongdoing, in 1958 was indicted for grand larceny in connection with the looting of another corporation. Three more criminal indictments against Birrell were returned in 1961.

of an apparently imaginary José Miranda, had illegally distributed securities for nine separate firms. Illegal securities distributions of seven of these firms continued after June 27, 1957, when the SEC secured its injunction against the Res as a result of the Swan-Finch distribution. In five cases, the order charged that the Res had manipulated share prices during an illegal distribution through carefully timed purchases or short sales. While in control of I. Rokeach & Sons, the Res allegedly had used their inside knowledge of an impending merger to increase their shareholdings before a public announcement of the merger predictably boosted the stock's price. In the prospectuses of Rokeach and three other corporations, the Res allegedly had fraudulently omitted disclosures concerning their shareholdings. On August 24, 1960, the SEC amended its order to allege further that the Res had illegally manipulated an October 1954 issue of 118,000 convertible preferred and 118,000 common shares of Thompson-Starrett Company through wash sales and payments "to certain persons . . . for soliciting others to purchase Thompson-Starrett common stock."

The Res never contested any of the facts described in the SEC's order. On May 4, 1961, within six days after the Trading and Exchanges Division completed its formal investigation, the SEC expelled both Res from the American Stock Exchange. In 1963, they were convicted and sentenced to six months in prison for criminal share manipulation of Swan-Finch Oil Corporation's shares between 1954 and 1957.[62]

Revelation of the apparently criminal securities violations committed by the Res persuaded the SEC in May 1961 to authorize a comprehensive staff investigation of the American Stock Exchange. The SEC staff study of the American Stock Exchange concluded in January 1962 that the exchange's "manifold and prolonged abuses by specialists and floor traders . . . make it clear that the problem goes beyond isolated violations and amounts to a general deficiency of standards and a fundamental failure of controls." No one disputed this conclusion. But a candid discussion of how so prolonged "a fundamental failure of controls" could exist after the creation of the SEC did not appear in the study's report. There was one frank commentary, however, in a 1962 memorandum by Philip Loomis, director of the Division of Trading and Exchanges, written for the benefit of Chairman William Cary. Loomis acknowledged, "In the light of hindsight, it is reasonably apparent that the staff of the Commission should have realized that something was seriously wrong on the American Stock Exchange considerably earlier than it did, probably in 1957 or early 1958, if not earlier." Loomis emphasized that during the period in question the SEC was understaffed and its small staff "was confronted with unprecedented enforcement problems which did not appear to stem from the exchanges," especially the high-pressure sales campaigns of the boiler room and illegal distributions of unregistered securities. But Loomis felt there was a second primary cause nearly as important. To the SEC of the 1950s, "Exchange regulation was not approached as an enforcement problem, it being assumed, until the contrary became evident, that the American Stock Exchange was basically aware of its responsibilities and honestly conducted." This was an avoidable contributing cause of what Loomis termed the "breakdown" of "self-regulation on the American Stock Exchange."[63]

10

Revitalization Under Cary

The failure of the self-regulatory agencies to operate at maximum capacity and with full regard for the public interest in certain areas is in part attributable to the Commission's own failure to provide the necessary continuing guidance and oversight.

—WILLIAM CARY
Special Study Transmittal Letter
(August 8, 1963)

TWO DAYS after his election as President, John Kennedy signified his determination to revitalize the federal regulatory agencies by announcing that former SEC chairman James Landis had agreed "to undertake a study in an area of long concern to us both, a study of the federal regulatory agencies." Landis's "Report on Regulatory Agencies to the President-Elect," published in late December 1960, together with other documents Landis prepared in the early months of the Kennedy administration, outlined the practical steps that the new administration was prepared to take to revive the SEC and the other independent regulatory agencies. The Landis Report also effectively implied the limits of the Kennedy administration's support for the Commission. Not only did Landis all but omit discussion of new SEC enabling legislation,* but the rationale for his controver-

---

* Landis did recommend "the extension of the Commission's power of forcing appropriate disclosures with securities in the over-the-counter market," noting this was "an extension long urged by the Commission," but concluded that the only other SEC-related legislation required would be procedural.

sial White House "agency czar" proposal presaged the considerable difficulties the SEC would have initiating new legislation on its own during the Kennedy administration.

"The prime key to the improvement of the administrative process is the selection of qualified personnel," Landis repeatedly emphasized. "No other single step can accomplish as much." Both the Landis Report and private memoranda circulated by Landis within the White House recommended a return to what might be termed the Roosevelt formula for the selection of SEC commissioners. This involved appointing a combination of leading academics or others with broad policy-planning ability and elevating senior SEC staff members. Landis was particularly concerned that qualified staff members regularly be advanced to commissionerships, viewing this as important to the SEC's ability to retain a high-caliber staff. The Kennedy administration first offered the SEC's chairmanship to Harvard Law School professor Louis Loss, then best known as the author of the multivolume treatise *Securities Regulation*. When Loss declined, the chairmanship was offered to Columbia Law professor William Cary, the author of the most widely used law school casebook on corporations.

Cary accepted. Shortly after, Cary and Landis exhorted Kennedy to name Manuel Cohen and Philip Loomis, the SEC's two most highly regarded staff members, to the Commission. In October 1961, Cohen was appointed. At Cary's recommendation, Byron Woodside, who earlier had been elevated from the staff, was reappointed by Kennedy.*

Landis's description of the SEC's "budget starvation" helped persuade the Bureau of the Budget and Congress to add 250 new employees to the SEC's staff during the Kennedy administration's first fiscal year. Landis also pointed out that many commissions, including the SEC, had neglected their policy-making functions. Primarily to enable the SEC's commissioners to supervise investigations of the magnitude of its New Deal Protective Committee and Investment Company studies and to perform other planning functions, Landis drafted for President Kennedy an SEC reorganization plan, which would have permitted the delegation of several types of routine work to the Commission's senior staff. Although the plan was rejected by Congress in 1961, a similar SEC reorganization bill was enacted the following year.

* Instead of Loomis, Kennedy appointed Jack Whitney, a former Cary law student who had the support of Senator Everett Dirksen. Only in the appointment of former Delaware senator J. Allen Frear did Kennedy make a primarily political SEC appointment.

Landis, however, recognized that for the SEC and the other independent regulatory agencies to realize a full revitalization would require a White House office committed to serve as a "protagonist of the agencies" before Congress and the Bureau of the Budget. By 1961, it was obvious that no President regularly could devote as much attention to any of the regulatory agencies as Roosevelt had devoted to the SEC. Without a White House protector, Landis anticipated that the agencies neither would receive adequate support for legislative initiatives from the White House's lobbyists nor be sympathetically treated by the typically business-oriented Bureau of the Budget.[1] Nonetheless, the Kennedy administration soon concluded it could not afford Landis's proposed White House agency czar. Kennedy's 1960 election had been accompanied by the loss of twenty liberal Democrats from the House of Representatives, making the House far more conservative than the White House. For Kennedy to secure passage of even his less controversial legislative initiatives required husbanding "bargaining power for its most effective use," as Arthur Schlesinger, Jr., later wrote. Although Landis's idea for the Office of Oversight was abandoned after expressions of congressional concern that it might lead to White House "dictatorial power over the commissions," the office, in fact, would have required a political commitment to the regulatory agencies that the Kennedy administration proved unwilling to make.[2] The SEC, for example, received no effective White House support in seeking passage of new enabling legislation between 1961 and 1963. Chairman William Cary did not once see President Kennedy on official business, and found that Ralph Dungan, the White House aide expected to oversee the Commission, also "literally had no free time to talk with us." Even when Cary was concerned that the Kennedy administration's Comptroller of the Currency was attempting to sabotage the Commission's 1963 Securities Acts Amendments bill, the White House did not effectively intervene.[3]

The absence of White House support for new SEC legislation, coupled with the conservative leadership of the House of Representatives, fundamentally affected the SEC during the chairmanship of William Cary. In retrospect he described himself as "convinced that no major step forward can be achieved by an old-line regulatory agency in the absence of support from some of the leaders in the industry it regulates . . . Even as to rule-making, if none of the industry's spokesmen feel there is a need and complaints mount, congressmen are likely to intervene and commence inquiry, and a committee may either stall the proposal or kill it."[4] During Cary's chairmanship, only one legislative initiative was advanced, the "noncontroversial" Securities Acts Amendments bill. More far-reaching legislation, such as a bill to reform the mutual fund industry, was deferred.

Yet the Kennedy administration's noninterference with the SEC, its tangible support for the Commission through the budgetary and appointments process, as well as the administration's air of idealism and reform, did contribute to the SEC's revival. Not the least of the Kennedy administration's contributions was the appointment of William Cary as chairman. Cary provided a link to the spirit and goals of the New Deal's SEC. At Yale Law School in 1934, he had been a student in one of the last corporate finance courses taught by William Douglas. He had served on the SEC's staff between 1938 and 1940, initially under Chairman Douglas. Although Cary did not regard himself as one of Douglas's "fair-haired boys" either at Yale or at the Commission, as chairman he reflected an intellectual style and outlined policy goals reminiscent of Douglas's SEC chairmanship. Like Chairman Douglas, Chairman Cary insisted on balancing reform aims with technical rigor. He often quoted Karl Llewellyn's aphorism "Technique without ideals is a menace; ideals without technique are a mess."

It was characteristic of Cary that he would recall Douglas's SEC as "one of the two best law offices in Washington"; and that he would warn law students that "a St. George in Washington might perhaps resemble Don Quixote." But Cary was a determined reformer. In the field of tax law, Professor Cary long had been a respected gadfly. His 1955 *Harvard Law Review* article "Pressure Groups and the Revenue Code" echoed the tone and liberal convictions of Douglas's earlier piece, "Directors Who Do Not Direct." A subsequent law review article, written by Cary after his chairmanship, "Federalism and Corporate Law," would prove to be the most influential study of state corporations law in the postwar period.

In the field of securities law, during his chairmanship Cary revived efforts to complete several unfinished projects first attempted during the New Deal, including the enactment of a statute extending the Securities Exchange Act's requirements to all unlisted firms above a minimum size and a highly publicized attempt to abolish floor trading. This sense of revival of the New Deal's SEC was cultivated by Cary. Troubled by the intransigence of the New York Stock Exchange, Cary renewed Douglas's accusation that "the Exchange, though a public institution, still seems to have certain characteristics of a private club." Like the Douglas SEC, Cary's Commission kept as a mission the reduction of opportunities for Exchange floor members or corporate insiders to take advantage of their positions, as well as a general commitment to raising fiduciary standards.

At the same time, the differences between Cary's SEC and that of the late New Deal were equally striking. William Cary was a far more taciturn man than the New Deal's SEC chairmen. He gave few speeches and usually preferred to allow an SEC report to speak for itself, instead of issuing a press release. While William Douglas or Jerome Frank considered himself involved in a political reform movement, Cary "felt it important to behave like a lawyer." To Cary this meant not being a "public relations man" or one who would use a public hearing to depict a "chamber of horrors" rather than "demonstrate a problem." In his memoirs, Cary underlined his belief that "every program of re-examination and policy-planning need not take the form of a crusade."

Cary brought to the Commission the political instincts of a Stevenson reform Democrat. Instinctively he preferred to maintain as great an independence as possible from the White House or Congress to shield the SEC from Sherman Adams–type of political interference. In Cary's Landisian view, the leadership of a commission required overcoming obstacles to independence from partisan politics or regulated industries so that an agency would be able to attract the most able policy-makers. Although Cary's meritocratic approach was to serve him well in recruitment for the SEC, it proved less effective in discussions with Oren Harris, the Arkansas Democrat who chaired the pivotal House Commerce Committee. Later, Cary would recall "constantly" having to convince the states-rights and local-business-oriented Harris that "he was not an ogre or excessive bureaucrat." Often Cary would find Harris's political machinations frustrating; at times, incomprehensible.[5]

A further difference between the New Deal's SEC and that of the New Frontier was a purely intellectual one. The work of the New Deal's SEC had been preceded by a generation of study of the securities markets and corporations law. The Pecora hearings, the Federal Trade Commission's study of public utilities, the SEC's own reports on stock exchange governance, segregation of brokers and dealers, protective committees, and investment companies, had provided an informed basis for major SEC policy initiatives. Each of these studies also had afforded the SEC the opportunity to employ commissioners or staff members with broad expertise in an industry or industries subject to the SEC's jurisdiction. No comparable studies had been made of the securities markets for over twenty years when Cary arrived. As the securities industry expanded and qualitatively changed, the pathbreaking studies of the New Deal period had grown increasingly dated.

Cary began at the SEC with "no overall policy view,"[6] but with a determination to restore the Commission's policy-making capability and to increase its attraction to highly competent staff members. The principal vehicle for achieving both aims proved to be the 1961–1963 Special Study of the Securities Markets. Early in his chairmanship, Cary began the practice of hiring consultants to make "critical studies . . . of the Commission in the light of present-day problems." Among others, Cary hired Joseph Weiner, one-time director of the Public Utilities Division, to review the Commission's performance under its principal enabling statutes; Professor Frank Coker of Yale Law School to evaluate the earlier-commissioned Wharton School Investment Company Size Study; Yale economist Raymond Goldsmith to analyze the SEC's research and statistical activities; and, later, securities attorney Carl Schneider to study the extent to which the requirements of the 1933 and the 1934 Securities Acts could be integrated by SEC rules.[7]

As early as May 15, 1961, Goldsmith recommended that the Commission seek a separate appropriation and separate staff to make special studies of the over-the-counter market, small securities issues, and investment advisory services. When Congressman Peter Mack, chairman of the House Commerce Subcommittee with responsibility for oversight of the SEC, expressed concern about the implications of the SEC's investigation of the American Stock Exchange, about indications of increased securities speculation, and about a statement by the NASD that $1.4 billion of securities had not been delivered to investors on time, Cary urged Mack to introduce a resolution authorizing the SEC "to make a study and investigation of the adequacy, for the protection of investors, of the rules of national securities exchanges and national securities associations." In early September, Congress appropriated $750,000 to the Commission to complete by January 1963 what came to be known as the Special Study of Securities Markets.[8]

The appropriation enabled the SEC to hire Milton Cohen, also a former director of the Public Utilities Division, and a professional staff of forty attorneys, economists, statisticians, financial analysts, and investigators to work full time for close to two years. It was a stellar staff, several of whose members, among them Eugene Rotberg, Stanley Sporkin, and Sheldon Rappaport, were to continue to make contributions to the Commission long after the study was completed.

Still, substantial questions could be raised about the character of the Commission's Special Study. Ideally, the investigation should have been conducted by Congress. Chairman Cary was totally candid when he acknowledged in his memoirs that the SEC had "welcomed" the Mack resolution because "a Congressional investigation might have had the tendency of focusing on the SEC rather than upon major developments in the market." But any investigation of the securities markets in 1961 had to focus to a considerable degree on the Commission. Such matters as the breakdown of self-regulation of the American Stock Exchange, the revival of securities speculation, and the late-delivered securities noted by Congressman Mack raised clear questions about the quality of the SEC's performance. As Congressman Robert W. Hemphill asked at the hearings that preceded adoption of the Mack resolution about the need for an SEC investigation of the American Stock Exchange, "Why is that necessary at this late date after having had a Securities and Exchange Commission for going on twenty-seven years now?"[9]

House Speaker Sam Rayburn, the "father of the securities acts," however, was unwilling to permit the House Commerce Committee to conduct a comprehensive investigation of the SEC and the securities markets.[10] To ensure the independence of the Special Study group, Director Milton Cohen insisted on an unusual procedure. Cohen took the position that he would not head up the study if its work had to be formally approved by the five SEC commissioners. Instead, the SEC agreed with Cohen that the findings of the Special Study would be a report to the SEC from a quasi-independent group within the Commission. Cohen regarded this arrangement as "absolutely essential to the quality of the study," since it obviated the inevitable compromises that would have occurred if the entire report had to secure the official support of the SEC.[11] The ability of the Special Study to assess critically the Commission was further aided by the stature of the men who led the study and the sense that they largely were reviewing the actions of an earlier SEC, which had labored under more stringent budget restraints in a different political climate.

There were, however, limits to the Special Study group's independence. Although the report of the Special Study was not published as an SEC report, the entire manuscript was reviewed before publication by the full Commission and was discussed with the Special Study group. Chairman Cary in public statements suggested that he, at least, was eager to avoid a "flamboyant anti–Wall Street publicity venture." *The Report of Special Study of Securities Markets* was, in Cary's characterization, "not a sensational document — quite consciously."[12]

Several members of the study group were and remained highly regarded SEC staff members. They brought to the study their practical knowledge of the securities markets. But in at least some instances they also helped internalize within the study group the operative assumptions of the Commission at that time, including a preference for SEC regulation rather than unregulated competition, and a recognition that there were practical limits as to how far the Special Study could urge reform of the New York Stock Exchange. In a few sections of the study's report, such as those covering fixed commission rates and New York Stock Exchange specialists, the Special Study reached conclusions that stopped short of the implications of its findings in a manner that later House and Senate reports on the securities industry usually did not. The study's failure to analyze Rule 394 of the New York Stock Exchange, which hindered securities dealer competition by generally prohibiting exchange members from transacting business with nonmembers, also was a striking anomaly, reflecting the belief of many SEC senior members that it was wiser to centralize securities trading on a single exchange than increase the difficulties of market regulation by encouraging competitive market-makers.[13] These limitations of the study, although significant, should not be exaggerated.

There seems little question that the quasi-independent Special Study group was able to make recommendations with less regard for their impact on stock market prices or SEC-industry relations than an official SEC study could have. The greater practical constraints on the SEC were well illustrated by Chairman Cary's letter of transmittal accompanying the first segment of the *Special Study*. Cary, writing officially on behalf of the Commission, took pains to reassure Wall Street that

> the report demonstrates that neither the fundamental structure of the securities markets nor of the regulatory pattern of the securities acts requires dramatic reconstruction. The report should not impair public confidence in the securities markets . . . Serious shortcomings are apparent and the report, of course, has concentrated on their examination and analysis. Yet it is not a picture of pervasive fraudulent activity and in this respect contrasts markedly with the hearings and findings of the early thirties preceding the enactment of the Federal securities laws.

In fact, the text of the study report, insofar as it focused on the growing role of institutional investors, the need to automate the securities industry, and the anticompetitive practices associated with the New York Stock Exchange's fixed-commission-rate structure, suggested that the fundamental structure of the securities markets did, or soon would, require dramatic reconstruction. Although it arguably was true that the *Special Study* did not present "a picture of pervasive fraudulent activity," it was also true that it did depict an industry beset with the same type of conflicts of interest, excessive transaction costs, and high-pressure sales techniques that three decades earlier had motivated the Pecora investigation and the New Deal's SEC to reach far more sweeping conclusions than Cary's transmittal letter was prepared to state. Most of the fundamental reforms achieved in the securities industry during the dozen years after the publication of the *Special Study* were anticipated, at least in part, by the study group. It is doubtful that a study directly supervised by the SEC could have made so innovative a contribution.

The decision of the Special Study group to conduct only twelve days of public hearings was debatable. Originally the group had planned to hold hearings on a number of topics. Milton Cohen recalled that it was a "great disappointment to us" that more hearings were not held; it became "purely a question of time and money, public hearings effectively took, say, ten times the resources as proceeding through private hearings or questionnaires."[14] The group concentrated its efforts on publishing the most comprehensive securities market study possible within its time and money constraints rather than employing a public hearing process to galvanize congressional support for SEC reforms in a more limited number of areas. This provided a more informed basis for subsequent SEC reform efforts than otherwise would have been possible and had the subsidiary advantage of avoiding SEC–Wall Street confrontations during a period when the SEC was attempting to work with securities industry leaders to reorganize the American Stock Exchange and secure passage of the 1964 Securities Acts Amendments bill.

But the study group's decision to largely forgo public hearings may not have been the wisest political course. There were tremendous time lags before the SEC effectively was able to act on certain of the study's most important findings in such areas as fixed commission rates and the securities market structure. These time lags, in part, occurred because the fact findings were not effectively communicated at the time of the study and at first evoked little or no congressional interest. In the 1930s, a different strategy had been employed. The Pecora hearings and the SEC's Whitney and Protective Committee hearings were used to build public and congressional sentiment for statutory reforms opposed by the financial industry. It is at least arguable that the Special Study's minimal use of public hearings may have unnecessarily delayed SEC efforts to secure reforms of far greater practical consequence than those wrought by the 1964 Securities Acts Amendments.

Given even these substantial questions about the Special Study, its report undoubtedly was the single most influential document published in the history of the SEC; it provided a foundation for most of the reforms that occurred in the securities industry during the ensuing fifteen years. In large measure, the *Special Study* was a factual documentation of the limits of self-regulation in the securities industry. Although Cary's transmittal letters and the report itself repeatedly stated a "continued belief in self-regulation as an ingredient in the protection of the investor," the report's findings illustrated that without the "pointed stimuli" of the SEC, securities industry self-regulation consistently had been self-interested and self-protective, often failing to produce standards of conduct superior to those that existed before the enactment of the securities laws. Significantly, in most of the principal areas covered by the report — for example, entry requirements, selling practices, back-office problems, exchange floor members, fixed commission rates, mutual fund selling practices, and exchange disciplinary procedures — similar disadvantages of securities industry self-regulation were found. In several instances, like floor-trading regulation, the SEC's postwar passivity had, in fact, permitted a deterioration of standards.[15]

Illustrative of the study's findings were chapters in the report on the qualifications of people in the securities industry and on commission rates. In the securities industry, in which the income of all broker-dealer firms and of virtually all sales personnel is directly related to new and secondary issue sales volume, there exists a constant danger that brokers irresponsibly will attempt to boost sales through such means as excessive trading of discretionary accounts, misrepresentations to investors, or recommendation of unsuitable securities. Unethical or fraudulent sales practices can be policed either after the fact through disciplinary proceedings or before the fact through entrance requirements and training. Neither approach is foolproof. During the 1950s neither the SEC nor industry self-regulatory organizations performed either function well. At the time of the Special Study, there were approximately six thousand broker-dealer firms in the United States. Three fourths of these firms were members of the National Association of Securities

Dealers, making the NASD the industry organization with the widest self-regulatory functions. Yet even during a period when budget stringency precluded the SEC from performing a major role in broker-dealer inspections, the NASD inspected main offices of broker-dealer firms only once every three years and branch offices once every ten years, employing inspection procedures that all but ignored the possibility of investor abuse through fraudulent misrepresentations.[16]

Simultaneously, securities industry entrance requirements remained negligible. The NASD prescribed no training period; it merely required new members to pass an entrance examination. That examination was little more stringent than the written portion of a state driver's license test. The examination consisted of 100 questions drawn from a pool of 344 questions (later increased to 441), which were published, along with the correct answers, in an easily memorized booklet distributed to applicants. Typically, less than 2 percent of applicants failed the examination.[17] The ease of the examination facilitated a dramatic increase in the number of part-time securities sales personnel in the late 1950s;[18] permitted over 50 percent of the broker-dealer firms that did not specialize in mutual funds or belong to a securities exchange to give no on-the-job training;[19] and resulted in over 95 percent of the sales personnel specializing in mutual funds having no prior securities industry experience.[20]

A lack of uniform minimum capital requirements aggravated problems created by an absence of meaningful competency requirements. Although thirty-three states required broker-dealers to maintain either minimum capital or a surety bond, the SEC, the NASD, and such important states as New York and Illinois did not have the requirement. Thin capitalization was common for new broker-dealer firms. In one typical six-month period in 1956, among 215 new broker-dealers registered with the SEC 27 percent reported an initial net capital of less than $1000, and 60 percent reported initial net capital of less than $5000. In one extreme case, a securities firm was begun in 1958 with an adjusted net capital of $42.

To a considerable degree, the securities industry's low level of required capitalization was the consequence of a 1942 SEC decision prohibiting the NASD from adopting a minimum capital requirement. The decision reflected the SEC's concern that the securities industry would arbitrarily exclude new entrants. By the time of the Special Study it was plain that this policy had not worked well. The study's findings strongly suggested that new, usually undercapitalized, broker-dealer firms had been responsible for the underwriting of a large portion of the unsuccessful new securities issues in the 1950s and early 1960s. In part, the prevalence of fraudulently or unsuitably marketed new issues had been the result of many newer broker-dealers considering themselves "judgment-proof" since they lacked the assets to pay damages claims. Thin capitalization also made it unlikely that new firms could employ experienced securities sales personnel or afford the costs of training new sales personnel, and it increased the likelihood that new broker-dealer firms would lack adequate record-keeping or securities clearance capabilities.[21]

The Special Study's criticism of low entrance requirements in the securities industry necessarily focused on the shortcomings of new securities firms, most of which were not members of a securities exchange. The *Special Study* report recommended that the industry's entrance requirements approach the standards required by the most rigorous exchanges and broker-dealer firms. Such an elevation of standards reasonably could have been anticipated to receive the support of the NASD and the exchanges.* Although the exchanges and the NASD had been notably deficient in enforcing disciplinary and entrance standards in the 1946–1961 period, more rigorous standards clearly were in their economic self-interest, principally because such standards would lessen the likelihood that the misconduct of some broker-dealer firms would reduce investor confidence in securities investment generally.

A principal benefit of the Special Study, however, was that it marked a return in the Commission's focus from the fiduciary issues, which had been the SEC's predominant concern in the 1946–1961 period, to consideration of market structure issues, which had last been emphasized during the New Deal's SEC. The significance of this aspect of the study's findings was not fully appreciated during Chairman Cary's tenure, although, in retrospect, it appears to have been the most important contribution made by the study.

During the 1946–1961 period, SEC oversight of the securities market structure had been minimal. Characteristic of the SEC's approach during this time was its review of New York Stock Exchange commission-rate increases. Under Section 19(b) of the 1934 Securities Exchanges Act, the SEC was directed to regulate "the

* Indeed, in December 1962, Investment Bankers Association president Amyas Ames already had signified his willingness to support stricter standards when he noted, of the securities industry's postwar growth, "Mistakes have been made. To name a few: We have grown too fast; we have taken on too many men without training them thoroughly enough; we haven't trained enough managers; some people have come into the business who aren't qualified."[22]

fixing of reasonable rates of commission." Twice during the New Deal period, in 1938 and 1942, the SEC interposed no objection to NYSE's commission-rate increases. The SEC's response in both instances primarily was stimulated by declining brokerage income, occasioned by lower trading volume. Before the 1938 increase, average daily volume had declined to 1,492,000 shares, approximately one third the 1929 level. Before the 1942 increase, volume had undergone a further severe decline, to an average daily total of 619,000 shares. During the postwar period, however, with trading volume rising, in 1961, to a level of 4,085,058 shares traded on average daily, there existed no comparable justification for SEC passivity in reviewing New York Stock Exchange commission rates. Nonetheless, in 1947, 1953, and 1958, the SEC had permitted the Exchange to raise its commission rates. In none of these instances did the SEC set forth a standard for determining "reasonable rates of commission," nor, found the Special Study, did it ask for sufficient data from broker-dealers about firm and transaction costs to evaluate fully the reasons for the rate increases.[23]

By the time of the Special Study, lack of rate competition among New York Stock Exchange members encouraged four major types of anticompetitive practice in the securities industry. First, it had become common for the large brokerage houses to engage in non-rate competition, usually through such ancillary services as investment research, safekeeping of customers' securities, or collection and delivery of investor dividends, rights, and warrants. Since the New York Stock Exchange had used brokerage house cost data to justify its 1947, 1953, and 1958 rate increases, the "bundling" of brokerage services provided a mechanism for raising brokerage rates (and brokerage house income) even if the costs of executing transactions had not increased. For many investors who did not utilize the ancillary services, the bundling of brokerage house functions resulted in an increase in transaction costs without any corresponding increase in value. Within the broker-dealer market, the prohibition of rate competition, coupled with non-price competition, made it more difficult for competent and adequately capitalized small brokerage firms to compete. As one such firm wrote the New York Stock Exchange, "Smaller member firms such as ours are clearly at a severe disadvantage in competing for business against [the] huge promotional expenditures of large firms, ladled out freely as 'statistical and advisory publications and services.'"[24]

Institutional and other investors who purchased large blocks of securities formally were prohibited from negotiating volume discounts in spite of the lower per-share cost of large-volume purchases. In some instances when securities listed on the New York Stock Exchange also were traded on a regional exchange or over the counter, it was possible to negotiate lower commission rates off the NYSE. But when a competitive market-maker was not available, the New York Stock Exchange's antirebate rule required large-volume investors to pay the standard commission rate and receive the equivalent to a price discount in such forms as investment research or installation at the broker's expense of a direct wire.[25]

In the mutual fund field, the absence of volume discounts regularly resulted in a practice known as "give-ups." Although Exchange members were prohibited from rebating commissions to nonmembers, they were permitted to give up portions of their commissions to other Exchange members. Thus, a mutual fund could arrange for a broker to give up part of the commission to a second Exchange member, who, typically, benefited the fund by selling the mutual fund's shares. Give-ups were, in effect, an additional commission paid by mutual funds managers to retail sales organizations. Give-ups also sometimes raised the costs of administering mutual funds by requiring the funds' directors to use research or other services that they might otherwise consider unnecessary, rather than receive volume discounts. In practice, give-ups were running as high as 60 percent of commission rates by the time of the Special Study. This was some indication of the cost of the New York Stock Exchange's noncompetitive rate structure in large-volume transactions.[26]

Finally, the Exchange's rate structure encouraged Exchange members to raise investors' costs through reciprocal trading and service arrangements. The New York Stock Exchange required that nonmember broker-dealers pay full commissions for executing orders on the Exchange. For nonmember broker-dealers, the combined expense of paying an NYSE member a full commission plus bearing their own overhead costs when executing an order for a customer created a powerful financial incentive to develop alternative markets for the trading of securities listed on the Exchange. To reduce this incentive, the Exchange permitted its members to reduce the nonmember broker-dealers' costs by providing reciprocal commission business.* The *Special Study* found, "This reciprocal commission business is generally placed under arrangement involving 'reciprocal ratios' of 2 to 1, 3 to 1, or similar ratios, that is, the NYSE member will direct $1 in commissions to the nonmember

---

* Alternatively, the Exchange member might provide reciprocal services such as installation and maintenance of wire services, office space, or research.

for each $1.50, $2, or $3 of commissions received." Like non-price competition, the provision of services to large-volume investors, and give-ups, reciprocal commission business was a mechanism by which Exchange members shared some of the profits created by a noncompetitive commission-rate structure with nonmembers to preserve the noncompetitive rate structure. Inevitably, reciprocal commission arrangements delayed or decreased the likelihood of competitive market-makers evolving and thus raised investor costs.[27]

At the time of the Special Study, the SEC did not initiate a course of action concerning the New York Stock Exchange's commission-rate structure. The study report itself finessed its recommendations and conclusions. It recommended that the SEC further study volume discounts and "consider the feasibility and desirability of (1) a separate schedule of rates for the basic brokerage function and for ancillary services, or alternatively (2) a schedule of maximum rates, or minimum-maximum rates, covering all services." But the report emphasized that "so drastic a step" as establishing maximum rates or minimum-maximum rates "is not intended as a suggestion for action but only as a course of further study." Among the Special Study group's leadership, it was believed that the market was not ready for negotiated rates; this was so fundamental a reform that it could occur only when at least some industry leaders favored it. Milton Cohen defined the primary function of the report's chapter on commission rates largely in terms of producing the first effective description of the New York Stock Exchange's fixed rate structure rather than resolving the policy questions involved. David Silver, a senior staff official, recalled that most of the study group's discussions focused on demonstrating the need for a volume discount for institutional transactions; there was little substantive discussion about the wisdom of abolishing fixed rates.[28] Similarly, during William Cary's chairmanship study of abolition of fixed New York Stock Exchange commission rates was not treated as a priority. Challenging the NYSE's commission-rate structure would have resulted in a direct conflict between the SEC and the Exchange on the issue of greatest dollar-and-cents significance to the Exchange. This, Cary's SEC was not prepared to do. Cary's strategy consistently was to achieve as much as he could in cooperation with the Exchange before confronting the Exchange on issues that would produce conflict. Cary made this point publicly, explaining to the Investment Bankers Association in 1962, "At this time our internal job is consolidation and improvement. We are not interested in growth as such."[29] To the extent that "growth as such" meant the SEC would

assume its responsibilities under Section 19(b) of the 1934 Securities
Exchange Act and regulate the reasonableness of commission rates,
this objective was not realized at any time during Cary's chairmanship.

* * *

An early benefit of the Cary SEC's nonconfrontational approach
was the rapid reorganization of the American Stock Exchange. By
the time Cary was sworn in as SEC chairman on March 27, 1961,
Trading and Exchanges Division director Philip Loomis and associate director Ralph Saul had nearly completed the Re investigation. Cary, who had a high regard for both men, almost immediately
committed himself to an expansion of the Trading and Exchanges
Division's investigation. On May 4, 1961, the Commission considered the division's brief recommending the revocation of Gerald A.
Re's and Gerald F. Re's registrations as brokers and their expulsion
from the American Stock Exchange. Cary startled the Trading and
Exchanges Division's enforcement attorneys by insisting on the
novel procedure of expelling both men that day instead of waiting
until the publication of a formal opinion. The rapidity of the expulsion, like the scathing language of the opinion that he wrote, was
meant, in Cary's words, "to be a dramatic way of announcing
shock." Eight days after the expulsion, the SEC approved a Trading
and Exchanges Division recommendation to investigate the rules,
policies, practices, and procedures of the American Stock Exchange.
In early September, when the Special Study was voted by Congress,
Ralph Saul became its associate director. The American Stock Exchange investigation continued under joint auspices of the Trading
and Exchanges Division and the Special Study.[30]

By then, evidence already accumulated indicated how fundamentally deficient was the self-regulatory system of the American Stock
Exchange. Yet neither its president, Edward McCormick, nor the
four specialists who long had dominated its management, Joseph
Reilly, Charles Bocklet, James Dyer, and John Mann, had taken
steps to commence a housecleaning. Cary wrote:

> Under these circumstances, if anyone in government wanted head-
> lines, this was a unique opportunity. Like Galahad, we could have
> publicly denounced the American Stock Exchange. If the SEC had
> worried about its "image," we should have sought immediate pro-
> ceedings and publicly forced through a reorganization plan. Then we
> might have been hailed as "vigorous and tough" — politically attrac-
> tive labels.[31]

Both Cary and Loomis were convinced that such a confrontational approach would backfire. Although it would have led to a reorganization of the Amex, Cary believed it would have caused such resentment in the securities industry that leading financiers would not have aided the SEC in revamping the American Stock Exchange. Cary also feared it later would have been more difficult to secure industry support for the legislation he already assumed the SEC would offer at the conclusion of the Special Study.

Instead, Cary employed the technique by which William Douglas had forced through the 1937–1938 reorganization of the New York Stock Exchange and, if anything, utilized it more deftly. Douglas had worked with the brokerage house–dominated Conway Committee to wrest control from the floor members who then controlled the New York Stock Exchange's governance. Analogously, Cary recruited the considerably greater relative influence of the New York Stock Exchange's leading brokerage firms to reorganize the Amex.

Although the leading New York Stock Exchange brokerage firms also were members of the American Stock Exchange, they had had almost no involvement in its governance. A fall 1961 meeting with Cary, Loomis, and others of the SEC led to an abrupt change in attitude. Cary emphasized that the problems on the Amex eventually could threaten investor confidence in the NYSE as well. Specifically, the SEC made plain that if the financial community's leaders would not take responsibility for cleaning up the Amex, the SEC would be compelled to hold public hearings, a course of action that might well lessen investor confidence in securities investment. The SEC's willingness to forgo hearings was deeply appreciated by the New York Stock Exchange's leadership. Former Exchange vice president Edwin Etherington, who a few months later would assume the Amex's presidency, recalled:

> An important decision was made when the Commission called for the investigation. A crucial decision was made when it received the report and presented the findings and comments to the Exchange and the public. At a moment when the Commission might have ordered a public hearing, it chose to rest on the impact of public disclosure. Instead of reaching for power, it looked to those closest to the scene to respond constructively. It assumed what ought to be done, would be done.

Similarly, Goldman, Sachs's influential partner Gustave Levy, who, in October 1961, agreed to head a committee of New York Stock Exchange leaders to recommend steps necessary to reform the Amex, soon stated, "I think that every house on Wall Street wants to help the Curb at this time."[32]

Although the Levy Committee publicly assumed responsibility for the Amex reorganization, the SEC supervised virtually every step of the reorganization. On December 11, 1961, after it was learned that in 1955 Edward McCormick had permitted Alexander Guterma, who subsequently was convicted of securities manipulation, to pay off a $5000 gambling debt incurred by McCormick, the Amex Board of Governors accepted McCormick's resignation and that of his close associate, the Amex's general counsel, Michael Mooney. Eight days later Joseph Reilly, chairman of the Amex Board of Governors, and Charles Bocklet, the vice chairman, appeared before the SEC to explain the events that had led to McCormick's resignation. They also indicated that the existing Board of Governors had commenced looking for a new president and that the Nominating Committee "probably" had completed the selection of nominees for the Board of Governors' election, to take place in February 1962. After extensive Commission discussion, Cary telephoned Gustave Levy and Joseph Reilly on December 20 and 21 to suggest that board nominations and selection of a new president be deferred until after the SEC published its American Stock Exchange report in early January. Cary indicated that the Commission would take no position concerning nominees, "only with respect to policy." But after being informed by Levy that Reilly claimed that the SEC desired Reilly to remain as Amex chairman, Cary advised Levy that this statement "was not true." Cary also explained to both Reilly and Levy, "The [SEC] staff report would be very critical of the administration of the American Stock Exchange." On December 28, Reilly announced that he would not be a candidate for re-election as chairman.

On January 5, 1962, a copy of the SEC's *American Stock Exchange Report* was delivered to the Amex Board of Governors. The next day it was published. The SEC report pointedly faulted "a small self-perpetuating group dominated by specialists" for the Amex's "fundamental failure of control." On January 7, according to *Newsweek*, Gustave Levy met with the Amex Board of Governors and secured understandings that the four specialists the SEC blamed for mismanagement of the Amex would not stand for re-election.* By January 8, the Amex Nominating Committee had named Edwin Posner to succeed Joseph Reilly as the exchange's chairman. Two days later Posner and Levy met with the Commission. Shortly after the conference ended, the *SEC Minutes* state, "the Commission directed the

---

* On January 22, 1962, Joseph Reilly resigned as Amex chairman. Also on that day, Charles Bocklet, James Dyer, and John Mann resigned as board members.

staff to prepare, for the Commission's consideration, a list of steps to be taken by the exchange to cure the problems now existing."[33]

Meanwhile, the Levy Committee, in interim reports dated December 21, 1961, and January 30, 1962, and its final report of February 15, 1962, detailed the constitutional changes necessary to end the specialist hegemony of the Amex. As the Conway Committee twenty-four years earlier had recommended to reform the New York Stock Exchange after a similar debacle, the Levy Committee urged that the Board of Governors be the sole policy-making body of the Amex, with specialists limited to a small minority of its membership. Administrative responsibility for the management of the exchange would repose in a president and a professional staff, rather than in specialist-dominated standing committees. Indeed, the Levy Committee went beyond the Conway Committee in this aspect of its reform proposal and recommended that the Amex's standing committees be abolished. Other portions of the Levy Committee reports detailed measures to reform listing requirements, membership structure, and enforcement. Nearly all of these recommendations subsequently were adopted.[34]

The SEC continued to monitor closely the Amex reform program after the publication of the final Levy Committee reports. In March, at the suggestion of members of the committee, the Amex's board elected Edwin Etherington president, to take office in September. Etherington had served as a special consultant to the Levy Committee and was a proponent of the view that "the SEC's duty to administer the securities laws makes it the natural ally and not the natural enemy of the securities industry." Under Etherington, the Amex staff was increased by 104 persons, notably including William Moran, a former senior SEC enforcement attorney, who was named to direct the exchange's enforcement activities, and Rolf Kaltenborn, a former member of the Commission's Special Study, who became a special assistant to Etherington responsible for ensuring that new listings were "of high quality."[35]

Months before Etherington formally assumed the Amex presidency, the SEC began working with him. The Commission's report on the American Stock Exchange had been particularly critical of the exchange's floor surveillance and disciplinary procedures, describing how "ineffective" the exchange's audit and report procedures were and how the Committee on Floor Transactions "found members guilty of charges brought against them but has failed to punish them in any effective way." On May 10, 1962, the SEC concluded that "it was dissatisfied with the lack of progress on the

part of the exchange in this area." Staff attorney Arthur Rothkopf
was directed to meet with Etherington. After Etherington assumed
the exchange presidency, Amex enforcement officials undertook
131 disciplinary investigations, resulting in disciplinary action being taken against twenty members.[36] In a parallel development,
twenty-five securities that did not meet listing standards recommended by the Levy Committee were removed from trading on the
American Stock Exchange in 1962.[37]

"Probably never," concluded John Brooks, "has any stock exchange reformed itself so thoroughly so fast."[38] The SEC at all times
controlled the course of the reorganization, though not its precise
details nor the choice of the Amex's new leadership. By allowing the
Levy Committee to design the exchange's new constitution and
select the Amex's new leadership, the SEC was able to act for the
most part through unpublicized conferences and to effect improvements in the caliber of the Amex's enforcement activities
without political or financial costs to the Commission.

* * *

After leaving the SEC's Public Utilities Division in 1947, Special
Study director Milton Cohen had become a partner in the Chicago
law firm of Dallstream, Schiff, Hardin, Waite and Dorschel. His
private law career primarily involved counseling or representing
major business corporations. William Cary recognized that in
selecting Cohen to lead the Special Study he had chosen an extraordinarily competent man, but one who was also a moderate or conservative in corporate and securities law policy issues. Similarly,
Ralph Saul, the study's associate director, had long experience as a
corporate lawyer, serving for several years as an in-house attorney at
RCA Victor. In 1965 Saul would leave the SEC to assume a series of
executive positions successively at the Investors Diversified Services, the American Stock Exchange, and INA Corporation. Like-
wise, Dr. Sidney Robbins, the study's chief economist, hardly was
an inveterate opponent of the private sector. After completion of the
Special Study, Robbins would emerge as the leading academic critic
of the SEC's mutual fund legislative proposals.[39]

Although the study's staff, to use William Cary's term, included
its "evangelists," its leaders were not men instinctively doubtful of
the stock exchanges' capacity for good faith or self-regulation.
Among the 175 recommendations in the *Special Study* were suggestions that voluntarily "the self-regulatory agencies . . . [speak] out on
particular questions in the form of cautionary messages, policy

statements, codes of ethics, or rules of fair practice." When the study recommended that the SEC act, it most frequently urged further study of a problem, Commission efforts to negotiate new stock exchange– or NASD-promulgated rules, or consultation with industry before the SEC issued its own rules. Nevertheless, the Special Study group concluded its work by recommending that new laws concerning twelve separate problem areas be enacted, including statutes to regulate mutual fund contractual plans, the segregation of customers' securities held by broker-dealers, the operation of over-the-counter quotations systems, reckless dissemination of investment advice and corporate publicity, and securities credit.[40]

Lacking both a congressional sponsor to introduce new securities legislation or an understanding that President Kennedy would endorse a securities bill,*[41] Cary's SEC early determined that its initial 1963 legislative proposals would be far narrower than the full list recommended by the Special Study. For five months, beginning in January 1963, the SEC internally debated its list of legislative priorities. The most controversial of the Special Study's legislative recommendations, the regulation of mutual fund contractual plans and segregation of customers' securities held by broker-dealers, never were seriously considered for the initial securities bill. Internal memoranda, and Chairman Cary's April 3, 1963, transmittal letter accompanying the first part of the *Special Study*, both indicated that the SEC intended to recommend either five or six legislative proposals: a new law extending the 1934 Securities Exchange Act's regulations to unlisted securities with three hundred or more shareholders, a proposal authorizing standards of character, competence, and financial responsibility as requirements for entry into the securities business, an amendment of the 1933 Securities Act increasing from forty to ninety days the period during which a prospectus had to accompany a new security issue, a statute regulating private firms that published over-the-counter quotations, an act barring fraudulent corporate publicity, and, possibly, legislation concerning securities credit.[43] After discussions with representatives of

---

* President Kennedy never did personally endorse the SEC's 1963 securities bill, although his administration's Bureau of the Budget did state that the bill was "in accord with the program of the President." As a practical matter, the Kennedy Budget Bureau's endorsement was of little value compared to President Johnson's February 1964 personal endorsement of the bill in his special message on consumer interests. Moreover, Johnson's White House did some lobbying on behalf of the SEC's bill and, perhaps most significantly, Johnson, in 1965, fulfilled a long-held desire of House Commerce Committee chairman Oren Harris by nominating Harris to be a federal district court judge.[42]

the securities industry and the Federal Reserve Board, the SEC announced on June 3, 1963, that it had further pared its initial legislative package by deferring submission of proposals to regulate over-the-counter quotations, securities credit, and false and misleading corporate publicity.[44]

The essence of Chairman Cary's strategy to secure enactment of the 1963 legislative proposals was to win general securities industry support for a "noncontroversial" bill. Later, one liberal member of Congress was to criticize the SEC's bill precisely because "there isn't a single provision opposed by the industry."[45] Yet given the lack of White House and congressional support for the bill, Cary may have been correct in his assessment that passage of any bill in the Eighty-eighth Congress would have been "impossible" without substantial securities industry support.[46]

The process of building industry consensus for the 1963 securities bill began long before the SEC drafted legislation. As the first part of the *Special Study* neared publication, the SEC held informal conversations with securities industry leaders concerning its legislative recommendations. On December 12, 1962, for example, Milton Cohen discussed a key part of the Commission's likely legislative program with the NASD's executive director, Wallace Fulton.[47] One month later Investment Bankers Association president Amyas Ames circulated a memorandum to his Board of Governors, stating, "If concrete proposals for legislation or rules go beyond what we think are reasonable or practical for the industry, we will fight, but we have everything to gain by accepting Bill Cary's offer of a cooperative approach to the problems of self-regulation."[48]

After the first part of the *Special Study* was published, on April 3, 1963, the Commission's discussion of its legislative proposals with the financial community was formalized. At the SEC's request, representatives of the New York Stock Exchange, the American Stock Exchange, the Investment Bankers Association, the Association of Stock Exchange Firms, and the Investment Company Institute, among others, formed the Industry Liaison Group to negotiate a mutually acceptable bill. Meetings were held with the Industry Liaison Group and separately with the Investment Bankers Association throughout the latter half of April and May 1963.[49] SEC compromises resulted in virtually the entire leadership of the securities industry testifying in favor of the Commission's 1963 bill. During June 1963 Senate hearings, the New York Stock Exchange, the American Stock Exchange, the Midwest Stock Exchange, the NASD, and the Association of Stock Exchange firms unconditionally endorsed the bill. The Investment Bankers Association expressed "strong support" for the proposal but urged changes in the bill's coverage.

On June 18, New York Republican senator Jacob Javits welcomed Chairman Cary to the legislative hearings by noting that "coming from the city in which the primary securities market of the country is located, I am perhaps better able than most to testify to the fine receptivity of the financial community to the work which has been done. It is rare that such comprehensive work has been carried on with such an apparent feeling that, whether there are disagreements or not, certainly every effort has been made to minimize them." There was, agreed Amex president Etherington, "an unprecedented merger of opinion within our industry."[50]

The SEC's Securities Acts Amendments bill was introduced in the House and the Senate on June 4, 1963.[51] The most significant provisions of the bill proposed to apply the periodic disclosure, proxy, and insider-trading sections of the 1934 Securities Exchange Act to all securities issuers with a class of stock held by five hundred or more investors and total assets exceeding $1 million. Popularly known as the Frear-Fulbright bill, since Senators J. Allen Frear and J. William Fulbright earlier had introduced similar bills,[52] legislation to apply the 1934 act to unlisted firms above a minimum size first had been seriously considered in 1938, when SEC chairman Douglas privately recommended to President Roosevelt that all corporations with $1 million or more in assets be subject to the periodic disclosure provisions of the 1934 act, and a New York Stock Exchange report publicly proposed a comparable initiative. As described in Chapter 6, Roosevelt ignored Douglas's recommendation and instead endorsed a more far-reaching federal licensing bill. Both the SEC and the NYSE had continued for the next twenty-five years to recommend the enactment of a bill that would, from the SEC's point of view, better protect investors primarily by increasing disclosure and proscribing quick-turnover insider trading and, from the New York Stock Exchange's point of view, increase the attraction of an exchange listing by equalizing the regulatory burden of all listed and unlisted securities issuers above a minimum size.

There never was any real question that Cary's SEC would recommend the Frear-Fulbright bill. The only question was when. In early March 1962, the SEC had debated recommending the Frear-Fulbright bill before the completion of the Special Study. After Cary held conversations with members of Congress, the SEC decided to defer recommendation of the proposal until the Special Study's report was written. Cary was impressed with the argument made by the House Commerce Committee chairman Oren Harris of Arkansas that it might be advisable to tie the Frear-Fulbright bill, then generally favored by the securities industry, to other legislative proposals for which the industry might have less enthusiasm. Special Study director Milton Cohen also was concerned that the introduction of a bill in 1962 would divert the time and attention of the Commission from the task of completing the study.[53]

Part III of the *Special Study* assembled more persuasive empirical data to show the need for a Frear-Fulbright bill than the SEC earlier had offered in 1946, 1950, and 1956 reports endorsing similar legislation. The most important findings were summarized in a few sentences:

> The study has surveyed every case of fraud under either the Securities Act or the Exchange Act which was reported in either a litigation release or other Commission release during a period of 18 months beginning January 1961 . . . Of 107 proceedings in which the name of the security was mentioned, all told 99 (93 percent) involved issuers that were not subject to the continuous reporting requirements of the Exchange Act. Sixty-five involved companies of which the Commission had no record whatsoever and 34 involved issuers that had offered a fully registered or regulation A offering at some time but were not required to file periodic financial reports. It is of course true that fraud is possible and does exist even when there is complete disclosure by the issuer; the records demonstrate, however, that during the period surveyed the preponderance of fraud cases related to securities about which the public had not accurate data. To the extent that companies which have publicly traded over-the-counter issues outstanding are allowed to operate in the dark, the very conditions that encourage a resort to fraud and manipulation are fostered.

The *Special Study* emphasized that "relatively unknown, insubstantial, and unseasoned issues should be subjected to more, not less, light than their fellows." As the senior partner of a major brokerage house testified:

> It is almost incredible that . . . small companies, often undercapitalized, with new or untried and unseasoned managements, engaged in new and hazardous fields of endeavor, often with new products in a growing competitive field, many with nothing more than a new idea or a newly developed but untried product, are not required to make any disclosure or reports to stockholders beyond that of the original registration statement if they sold new securities, and not even such information if no new securities were issued, despite the fact that they may have many new stockholders.*[54]

---

* At the time of the SEC Special Study there was little economic controversy or even literature concerning the costs or benefits of the SEC's corporate disclosure program.

At Chairman Cary's direction, Part III of the *Special Study* focused on the major unresolved substantive questions raised by the earlier efforts to enact the Frear-Fulbright bill. First, what should be the scope of the bill? The study recommended that all 5500 over-the-counter firms with 300 or more shareholders, irrespective of firm assets, should be subject to Sections 13, 14, and 16 of the 1934 Securities Exchange Act. To lessen the SEC's administrative burden, the study recommended that the act be phased in over four years: for the first two years to add unlisted issues with 750 or more shareholders; for the next two years, issuers with at least 500 shareholders; and then permanently to require compliance by issuers with at least 300 shareholders.

Second, should banks, already subject to federal or state banking regulations, be required to comply with the Frear-Fulbright standards? The *Special Study* noted that approximately a thousand banks had 300 or more shareholders. Although the banks were subject to periodic inspection by the Comptroller of the Currency, the Federal Reserve Board, the Federal Deposit Corporation, or state authorities, the regulation primarily was intended to protect depositors. A sample of 358 banks with 300 or more shareholders showed the same deficiencies in shareholder reporting and proxy statements found in unlisted firms generally. For example, 67 percent of the banks did not send their shareholders a profit-and-loss statement; in over 90 percent of proxy solicitations, neither the names of directorial nominees nor the remuneration of officers was disclosed. In five of nine then-recent bank mergers that required a shareholder vote, shareholders were not provided with financial statements of the merging banks; in two instances they were asked to approve a merger plan without any description of the plan. Accordingly, the study recommended that banks with 300 or more shareholders should be subject to the 1934 act's disclosure, proxy, and insider-trading provisions, with the soon-to-be-controversial caveat that the

---

Testimony in favor of the extension of the 1934 act's disclosure requirements to unlisted firms, besides showing that a vast majority of securities fraud occurred among firms not subject to the SEC's periodic reporting requirements, also showed that the prices of unlisted insurance securities tended to exhibit wide price fluctuations — a finding consistent with a conclusion of George Stigler's pioneering 1961 article, "The Economics of Information": "Price dispersion is a manifestation — and, indeed, it is the measure — of ignorance in the market." Testimony further showed that the cost to unlisted firms of complying with the 1934 act was minimal. American Stock Exchange president Edwin Etherington, for example, testified that "the total cost of annual compliance with all of the requirements now applicable to listed companies apparently would be in the area of $1500 to $3000 for the smaller industrial companies covered by this bill except in most unusual circumstances."[55]

SEC could exempt banks subject to federal or state regulatory authorities that enforced equivalent requirements. For the same reasons, the study also recommended that insurance companies with 300 or more shareholders, although subject to state insurance commission regulation, also should be subject to the Frear-Fulbright bill.

Finally, the study recommended that Section 16(b) of the 1934 act, which proscribed profitable insider trading within a period of six months or less, should be applied to any investment bank that made a market in a corporation's securities over the counter, even if this discouraged the investment bank's partners from serving on that firm's board of directors. The study termed "greatly exaggerated" the predictions that this would deprive over-the-counter securities of market-makers.

Chairman Cary wrote in his April 3 transmittal letter that the SEC would recommend legislation adopting the Special Study's Frear-Fulbright standards. But as a result of SEC negotiations with the securities industry's representatives in late April and May, the Commission made three notable compromises of its initial draft bill before transmitting it to Congress in early June. Approximately sixteen hundred firms were excluded from the coverage of the bill because the ultimate jurisdictional test was raised from at least three hundred shareholders to at least five hundred shareholders and at least $1 million in assets. This compromise, in effect, split the difference with the securities industry. The Investment Bankers Association in late June would indicate that it preferred that the new bill be applied only to unlisted corporations with at least a thousand shareholders. Next, the SEC fully acquiesced to industry insistence that investment banks that made a market in over-the-counter securities be exempt from the Section 16(b) prohibition of profitable short-term insider trading. The SEC agreed with the *Special Study* that investment banks whose members served both as market-makers and as corporate directors in a given security had the opportunity to exploit inside information, but the Commission decided to rely on its general power to prosecute insider-trading abuses and new rule-making authority to deal with the problem. Congressman John Dingell later would term this compromise a "license to steal" and accuse the SEC of having made a "contract" with the securities industry on this issue. Of course the SEC had. But without its acquiescence on this issue, the Commission might not have been able to retain the support of the Investment Bankers Association and the NASD for the rest of the Frear-Fulbright bill, which, after enactment, was expected to extend the 1934 Securities Exchange Act's periodic disclosure, proxy, and insider-trading provisions to 3900 new firms in what would be the most significant extension of the securities laws since 1940.

Finally, the securities industry convinced the SEC that the bill should at first exempt foreign securities, with the understanding that the SEC could require such securities to be subject to the act when it found that substantial trading existed in the United States or that it was necessary to protect investors.*[56]

The second cluster of provisions in the SEC bill submitted to Congress on June 5 sought to remedy the deficiencies in securities industry entrance requirements and disciplinary procedures identified by the *Special Study*. Chairman Cary's April 3 transmittal letter stated that the SEC would attempt to strengthen broker-dealer self-regulation by recommending legislation that required all broker-dealers, including those who transacted business solely intrastate, belong to a self-regulatory association such as the NASD; required the NASD and any other broker-dealer associations that evolved to set and enforce minimum standards of character, competence, and financial responsibility; and granted the SEC new direct disciplinary controls over individuals (as contrasted with firms), including intermediate sanctions short of expulsion or suspension.

The practical significance of the SEC's self-regulatory association-related provisions was that they would bring the thousand or so broker-dealer firms registered with the SEC and an unknown number of solely intrastate broker-dealers that were not members of the NASD under the auspices of a self-regulatory association and raise entrance and disciplinary standards for all broker-dealer firms. As was the case in the legislative process preceding the 1938 Maloney Act amendments that led to the creation of the NASD, the SEC emphasized that self-regulation would reduce government cost, shifting part of the financial burden of securities markets regulation from taxpayers to the broker-dealer firms themselves. Moreover, since 4750 firms were members of the NASD, a 1964 SEC staff memorandum observed, "It would seem anomalous and inefficient for the Commission to establish and administer standards for a small group [of broker-dealer firms] while the self-regulatory agencies do so for the vast majority." The NASD persuaded the SEC to remove language from its initial draft bill empowering the Commission to change the NASD rules, as it could stock exchange rules, largely with the argument that the NASD, unlike the NYSE, never had fought an SEC rule recommendation once the Commission's position was settled. The securi-

---

* The House Commerce Committee later insisted that the bill be changed back to the SEC's original language. Industry and the Senate reluctantly agreed.[57]

ties industry also negotiated removal of SEC power to close broker-dealer firm branch offices and language empowering the NASD to set standards of "integrity" in addition to "character." With these and other technical changes, the SEC in late April and May 1963 secured united securities industry support for a bill minimally changed from the SEC's initial draft.[58]

The final part of the SEC's June 1963 legislative package proposed to reduce investor ignorance concerning hot issues by extending from forty to ninety days the period during which a securities dealer must deliver a copy of a prospectus to each purchaser of a security registered under the 1933 act. This alone was unlikely to lessen the number of fraudulent issues marketed during the securities industry's episodic speculative periods and, in fact, after enactment, had no known effect in reducing the dangers of the next generation of hot issues in the late 1960s. The alternative to a disclosure approach to new securities issues was empowering the SEC to disapprove new securities issues as if it were a state blue sky commission. This approach had not been adopted in 1933 and was politically inconceivable in 1963 in spite of the general perception that a relatively small number of fraudulently marketed new issues could markedly injure investor confidence. Implicitly, the SEC in 1963 determined to rely on increased enforcement activity after new securities were issued rather than prior approval power to minimize the danger of fraudulent new securities sales.

The Senate, by voice vote, passed the SEC's 1963 securities bill on July 30, 1963, less than two months after its introduction. Senate Banking Committee chairman A. Willis Robertson of Virginia was principally responsible for the rapidity of passage. Subcommittee hearings began two weeks after the bill's June 4, 1963, introduction, with Robertson's assurance to Cary that "I am sure that, in due course of time, we will have legislation on this subject," preceded by a colorful description of the itinerant "stock flim-flammers" who had victimized the farmers of Robertson's home county in the aftermath of World War I. Subcommittee chairman Harrison Williams and ranking Republican Jacob Javits, impressed by the unanimity of securities industry support for the bill, also soon signified their support. The only substantial opposition to the bill came from Comptroller of the Currency, James J. Saxon, who was in the process of issuing his own disclosure provisions for banks subject to his office's regulation and resented the Commission's argument that the Comptroller's requirements would not be "at least equal in effectiveness to those imposed by the SEC." Since the Comptroller regulated only a portion of the banks that would have been subject to the SEC's bill, the total exemption for banks from the bill that Saxon wanted might have resulted in some banks with more than five hundred shareholders and $1 million in assets having no shareholder disclosure requirements and all banks above that size following no effective proxy and insider-trading rules. Instead, Senators Williams and Javits successfully offered an amendment, endorsed both by the American Bankers Association and the SEC, requiring the three federal banking agencies to enforce the applicable standards of the 1934 Securities Exchange Act for all banks subject to their jurisdiction. Although the SEC's June 4 draft bill probably would have led to the same result, the Williams-Javits amendment facilitated swift Senate enactment of the securities bill by ending opposition from the American Bankers Association.

Comptroller Saxon, however, remained displeased. The following February Saxon circulated a letter to the chief executive officers of all national banks, renewing his total opposition to inclusion of banks in the SEC's bill. Although Saxon was requested by the White House to cease his opposition and was criticized by the American Bankers Association for misrepresenting the bank-related provisions of the bill, he persisted and, as will be shown, later almost single-handedly defeated the Commission's bill in the House Rules Committee.[59]

The Securities Acts Amendments bill received a far less enthusiastic reception in the House, where it was to linger fourteen months before final passage. For the first ten of these months, Cary recalled feeling at the "mercy" of Congressman Oren Harris, the Commerce Committee chairman who "so dominated the situation by reason of his knowledge and experience that no action was taken until he saw fit."[60] Harris was a Southern Democrat comfortable with the moderately progressive leadership that House Speaker Sam Rayburn and Senate Majority Leader Lyndon Johnson had exercised in Congress during the late 1950s. Although he confessed unfamiliarity with securities markets, Harris supported the SEC Special Study and the philosophy of the 1933 and 1934 Securities Acts because he did not "believe you will find anybody today that has anything to do whatsoever with the securities business that would recommend the repeal of those acts of 1933 and 1934" and because the late Sam Rayburn had told Harris about the passage of the 1933 and 1934 acts "time after time."

At the same time, Harris somewhat more enthusiastically supported Southern business interests, once interrupting Chairman Cary's analysis of why there were so many stock insurance companies in the South issuing promotional securities to insist "What I am trying to find out is why is it that this area is subjected to greater promotional activity than any other? I am trying to find out. If I can help build up the insurance business or any other business in the South or Southwest I want to do it." Throughout the Commerce Committee's extended consideration of the Securities Acts Amendments bill, Harris pressured the SEC to negotiate compromises with the insurance industry and state securities and insurance officials in the same manner as it earlier had done with the leaders of the national securities industry and the American Bankers Association. In so doing, Harris reflected the values of state government and local business, particularly questioning the "unlimited power" over broker-dealers that he believed the securities bill granted the SEC and the propriety of compelling any business firm to belong to an organization like the NASD, a compulsion Harris found disturbingly reminiscent of the union shop. However, Harris, a shrewd veteran of the legislative process, "recognized in these regulatory matters that our economy has reached such a stage at this point . . . that it is pretty difficult in matters of this kind to hew to the state line." Eventually, the congressman sought to mediate the differences between state government and the SEC, not to use the dogma of localism to defeat the securities bill.[61]

Harris's approach to the Securities Acts Amendments bill was easier to discern in retrospect than it was at the time. Cary recalled, "For a long time I was not sure whether Harris would support the bill." SEC general counsel Philip Loomis never believed Harris "was cordial to securities regulation."[62] For several months after Cary testified before the House Commerce Committee on April 3, 1963, about the first part of the *Special Study*, Harris refused to schedule hearings on the SEC's securities bill "until the entire report is filed."[63] As the SEC neared publication of the final part of the *Special Study* early in August 1963, it became evident that Harris's concern about the securities bill was not merely a matter of avoiding "piecemeal" legislation. On July 26, 1963, Dr. Andrew Stevenson, a member of the House Commerce Committee's professional staff, telephoned Cary to question the desirability of empowering the SEC to file civil suits against broker-dealers without proof that the challenged transactions were in interstate commerce.[64]

Soon after, Harris began a protracted effort to negotiate a compromise between the SEC and the insurance industry. Before the Senate Commerce Committee, several insurance lobbying organizations had made a last-minute effort to secure a full exemption for insurance firms from the Frear-Fulbright bill. By a 9–6 vote, the Senate Commerce Committee rejected an amendment that insurance companies be required to file with the SEC only the financial statements they already filed with state insurance commissioners.[65] The insurance industry lobbyists, joined by the state insurance commissioners, continued their efforts in the House.

At Harris's request, Cary met privately on at least three occasions with Harris and representatives of the insurance industry or the state insurance commissioners, notably including the insurance commissioner of Arkansas. At these meetings and in subsequent public colloquy, Harris expressed concern that the SEC's bill would weaken the authority of the state insurance commissioners, who historically had regulated the insurance industry. Cary initially opposed any special treatment for insurance companies, arguing that the annual shareholder reports of unlisted life insurance firms had been termed "among the poorest of any major industry in the United States" in 1960 by a group within the National Federation of Financial Analysts Societies. An SEC analysis of 1961–1963 price fluctuations of unlisted stock insurance corporations provided a factual basis for Cary to argue further that prices of insurance securities were "volatile and exhibited wide price fluctuations," presumably because there were few "data available for a sound evaluation of each company." Congressman Harris publicly acknowledged to Cary that "very frankly, I think you have made a very good case." But he disputed the SEC's position that the fifty states' insurance commissioners were incapable of improvement and held up Commerce Committee consideration of the SEC's bill for six months until "it became apparent," wrote Cary "that a compromise was a political necessity."

Under pressure from Harris, the National Association of Insurance Commissioners (NAIC), the organization of state insurance commissioners, conceded that the state insurance commissioners "had not given a great deal of thought or concern or consideration to investors." In December 1963, NAIC published a "Stockholder Information Supplement" to the insurance industry's uniform annual reporting form. The insurance commissioners of all fifty states and the District of Columbia wrote the House Commerce Committee that they would require insurance companies to provide stockholders with the information required by the supplement. Harris, in turn, required the SEC to accept an exemption in its Frear-Fulbright bill for all insurance companies subject to state regulation of annual statements and proxies equal to the standard prescribed by NAIC and a state statute substantially the same as the short-swing insider-trading provision of the 1934 Securities Exchange Act. This compromise subjected unlisted stock insurance companies to roughly the same pattern of regulation as the American Bankers Association earlier had secured for unlisted banks.[66]

The SEC chafed under the seemingly interminable delays imposed by Congressman Harris, particularly his refusal for four months to schedule public hearings on the securities bill. The Commission found an ally in *The New York Times*, which published an article critical of the House Commerce Committee inaction and, on October 9, 1963, an editorial entitled "Why the Stalling, Mr. Harris?" The *Times* lobbying apparently was effective. On October 14, Cary had lunch with House Commerce Committee's Dr. Andrew Stevenson. Cary reported to his fellow commissioners that Stevenson "was not upset by *The New York Times* article or the editorial, but in general seemed to feel that with all of this speculation in the press . . . there will most certainly be hearings in November, probably around the middle of the month." One week later, hearings were scheduled to begin on November 19, 1963.[67]

The hearings as originally structured, however, were not designed to lead to a swift enactment of the SEC's bill. The SEC was requested to prepare testimony concerning voluntary reforms made by the securities industry in response to the recommendations of the Special Study and the SEC's own efforts to implement the study's recommendations by rules. Similarly, the House Commerce Subcommittee examined the securities exchanges, the NASD, and the Investment Bankers Association on the broad effects of the Special Study, with the result that the inquiry stretched over thirteen hearing days scheduled intermittently until February 19, 1964. To the extent that the hearings focused on the SEC's bill, they emphasized enduring controversies. Not only was the insurance industry given ample opportunity to be heard, but the protracted hearings allowed Harris to adduce testimony from state securities commissioners who shared the congressman's opposition to compelling membership in a broker-dealer association such as the NASD and to abolishing the intrastate exemption for broker-dealers.[68] The *Times* again sharply criticized Harris's inaction. A November 17, 1963, article, published just before the Commerce Subcommittee's hearings began, bluntly accused Harris of artificially trying to cause conflict over the securities bill as a means of personally garnering national news attention. Subsequent *Times* editorials dated November 29, 1963, and January 19, 1964, insisted that "it is absurd to let misgivings about the SEC's powers vis-à-vis the states hold up passage of the present securities bill" and "in its concern for state authorities, which will still have supervisory responsibility, the Committee is ignoring the public."[69] In late January, the SEC secured the aid of a more influential lobbyist. President Johnson endorsed the Securities Acts Amendments bill in his budget message. Two weeks later, in his February 5, 1964, "Special Message on Consumer Interests," Johnson devoted considerable attention to the bill, concluding, "Legislation . . . has already passed the Senate and is pending before the Interstate and Foreign Commerce Committee of the House . . . I recommend prompt enactment of this disclosure legislation for over-the-counter securities."[70]

Since early December, Congressman Harris had indicated that the House Commerce Subcommittee's hearings were scheduled for an early conclusion.[71] But both the *Wall Street Journal* and *The New York Times* reported that the congressman's enthusiasm for the Securities Acts Amendments bill was perceptibly greater after President Johnson's endorsement.[72] Nonetheless, Harris held the securities bill before the House Commerce Subcommittee and full Commerce Committee another three months, until the SEC accepted a series of additional revisions: the earlier-described exemption for insurance companies, which Harris had termed "the one big issue" before the subcommittee; language sought by Harris clarifying the pre-existing implied exemption for farmers' cooperatives; language retaining the intrastate exemption for broker-dealers; and a compromise provision determinedly sought by Insurance Securities, Incorporated, a direct seller of mutual funds, and by Harris, allowing broker-dealers who preferred not to belong to an industry self-regulatory organization to subject themselves instead to comparable direct SEC regulation.[73]

There was a final hold-up. Before a bill could be considered by the full House, it usually required a "rule" from the House Rules Committee. By the time the House Commerce Committee voted out the Securities Acts Amendments bill, the Eighty-eighth Congress was nearing adjournment. This meant, as a practical matter, that securing a rule would require the personal approval of the House Rules Committee's chairman, "Judge" Howard W. Smith of Virginia, who also served as chairman of the board of the Alexandria National Bank. On June 3, 1964, the SEC was informed by Congressman Harris that "Judge Smith was proving reluctant to let our Bill out of the Rules Committee," because Comptroller of the Currency Saxon had persuaded Smith to insist on an amendment to the Frear-Fulbright portion of the bill to the effect "that the Comptroller of the Currency shall not be under a duty to exercise the powers given him under our Bill." This would have meant that the Comptroller had the power to exempt banks subject to his jurisdiction, a power that would have been intolerable to the SEC and Harris, as well as to the insurance industry, which reluctantly had accepted a legislative regimen equal to — but not greater than — that imposed on banks. With the intercession of Senate Commerce chairman Robertson, Smith's colleague from Virginia, a compromise was engineered that at last satisfied both Saxon and the SEC: the Comptroller and other banking agencies in carrying out their responsibilities under the SEC's bill were required to issue regulations "substantially similar" to those issued by the Commission unless they found that "implementation of substantially similar regulations . . . are not necessary or appropriate in the public interest or for the protection of investors, and publish such findings, and the detailed reasons therefor, in the Federal Register."[74] The Securities Acts Amendments were signed into law on August 20, 1964, a little over fourteen and a half months after the "noncontroversial" bill was introduced. To Cary, the legislative process demonstrated how limited was the capacity of an independent regulatory agency like the SEC to initiate legislation in the post–New Deal period. "Without the cooperation of both Congress and the Executive," Cary wrote in his memoirs, "little constructive can be achieved. To reemphasize the point, an agency is literally helpless if either branch is uninterested or unwilling to lend support." The tortuous process that led to the 1964 Securities Acts Amendments specifically demonstrated, Cary wrote, that "no matter how small, a lobby can induce Congress to shy away from a bill which no member is strongly pushing." This was a fundamental reason, Cary concluded, that the SEC usually would be "a conservative or gradualist institution."[75]

*   *   *

In its report accompanying the 1964 Securities Acts Amendments bill, the House Commerce Committee accurately had observed that the bill was "but a part, and not too large a part at that, of the full program needed to strengthen the protection afforded to the investing public by the various securities laws."[76] Most of the Special Study's recommendations for new standards required implementation by SEC, stock exchange, or NASD rules.[77] Beginning in the fall of 1963, the Commission conducted protracted negotiations with the securities exchanges, the NASD, the Investment Bankers Association, and the Association of Stock Exchange Firms. As a result of these negotiations, there were changes in a number of rules of the SEC and self-regulatory organizations concerning competency examinations, net capital, selling practices, supervision, advertising, and investment advice. Exchange and NASD brokerage house inspection efforts were increased. A new SEC rule required publication of over-the-counter wholesale quotations. Earlier, only adjusted retail quotations were published, a practice the *Special Study* had termed "indefensible."[78]

The Cary SEC's most significant rule-making negotiations were conducted in accordance with a felt need to minimize confrontation similar to that which typified the Commission's legislative negotiations with industry. The political limitations of the Cary SEC's rule-making were most clearly illustrated in the 1963–1964 period by the Commission's negotiations with the New York Stock Exchange concerning floor members. Soon after Douglas's departure from the SEC, the reforms in the New York Stock Exchange's governance structure negotiated in 1938 began to erode. The Exchange's floor leaders, led by Robert Stott and John Coleman, first secured a formal expansion of their power in 1941 with the creation of an Advisory Committee, to which the Board of Governors delegated certain disciplinary questions and the power to recommend the allocation of securities to specialists. The Advisory Committee generally followed the recommendations of the floor leaders. In the 1949–1950 period, a so-called Committee of 17 negotiated a series of amendments to the New York Stock Exchange's constitution that changed the power of the NYSE floor members, including a new provision requiring that ten of the Board of Governors' thirty-three members spend "a substantial part of their time on the floor of the Exchange." Since nine members of the board were commission brokers who worked elsewhere than in New York City and attended policy meetings only periodically, this constitutional amendment, as a practical matter, ensured the re-emergence of floor-member domination of the Board of Governors. By the time the Special Study was undertaken, the floor governors also held a majority of seats on the Exchange's Nominating Committee and had restructured the Exchange's governance so that discipline of floor members was dominated by the floor governors. The *Special Study* pointedly criticized the floor governors' informal procedures for the disposition of specialist and floor-trader violations, specifically noting that the Exchange's system of specialist surveillance was "not generally geared to the detection of cases of major improprieties." The *Special Study* further found "an apparent reluctance . . . to impose disciplinary sanction on floor traders, despite repeated violations of the floor-trading rules."

The study had documented that the root of the continued floor-member dominance of Exchange governance was the "seat concept" of voting. As of May 1962, there were 1366 seats outstanding on the

Exchange, of which floor members held 668, commission house partners held 648, and 50 were inactive. The floor-member majority was attributable to an undemocratic anomaly in the Exchange's rules. A floor member could not operate without owning a seat. In order to expand floor operations, additional seats were needed. As a consequence, the associate brokers and partners affiliated with the two major odd-lot firms owned approximately 125 seats; four specialist firms owned eight or more seats. On the other hand, a brokerage house could build a national network of branch offices and have several thousand brokers but needed to own only a single seat. This created an anomalous situation in which brokerage houses accounting for 50 percent of the Exchange's commission income and 48 percent of its registered representatives held only 7 percent of the total number of seats, but firms consisting primarily of floor members accounting for 10 percent of commission income and employing 10 percent of total registered representatives held 60 percent of the seats. The *Special Study* had recommended that the situation be corrected by extending full or partial voting rights to allied members of any firm holding a seat on the Exchange. Because of the substantially larger number of allied members in the commission houses, such a voting scheme would have ended the floor members' voting majority. In addition, the study had recommended increasing the number of slots reserved for commission house office partners on the Exchange's Board of Governors, Advisory Committee, and Nominating Committee.[79]

The SEC discussed each of the study's recommendations with Exchange president Funston, beginning in December 1963. Funston, according to a January 8, 1964, file memorandum written by Cary, "expressed his continued feeling of being 'burned up' with the Special Study on the proposition that the floor dominates the Exchange." However, he soon informed the SEC "that the Exchange's Steering Committee would submit to the Board of Governors certain organizational changes designed to diminish the influence of floor members on the Government of the Exchange, including one that would give non-floor members a majority on the Nominating Committee." In March the Exchange's Board of Governors, after receiving the recommendations of the Exchange's Steering Committee, agreed to increase the commission brokers to a four–three majority on the Advisory Committee and add three commission brokers to the twelve floor members on the Floor Affairs Committee. In a March 17, 1964, letter, Chairman Cary noted the absence of any recommendation concerning the Nominating Committee, then stated:

Although the Exchange has provided for greater non-floor participation in its government and affairs, these recommendations do not begin to deal adequately with the basic problem of Exchange organization described in the *Special Study* — the continued preponderant influence of floor professionals. The Commission believes that the Exchange must address itself to this problem and that it should propose a satisfactory program to its members which will give greater representation in the government of the Exchange to office partners from firms primarily doing a public business.

Approximately one month later, the Exchange's Nominating Committee announced its nominations for the 1964–1965 Nominating Committee and Board of Governors. Only trivial changes were made. The floor members' six–three majority on the Nominating Committee was reduced to a five–four majority. The floor members' thirteen-man faction on the Board of Governors was reduced to twelve. Since nine of the seventeen office partners on the board were from out of town and thus, concluded Ralph Saul, "can be expected to exert only a minor influence on Exchange government . . . 12 floor governors, plus Funston, are able to effectively dominate the Exchange." The *SEC Minutes* for April 29, 1964, similarly recorded that since the Nominating Committee's action on April 13 "indicated an apparent determination to keep control of the Exchange government in the hands of floor members, notwithstanding Mr. Funston's previous indication that certain organization changes were to be submitted to the Board of Governors by the Steering Committee designed to diminish the influence of floor members on the government of the Exchange, including one that would give non-floor members a majority on the Nominating Committee," the Commission decided to schedule a conference with Funston on Exchange organization at an early date. For the balance of Chairman Cary's term, however, none of the additional Exchange governance reforms considered by the SEC in April 1964 was pursued vigorously. The *SEC Minutes* for July 15, 1965, for example, record that the Exchange had made no new proposals concerning governance during the previous fifteen months. Instead, the SEC chose to maintain sufficiently good relations with the Exchange to ensure enactment of the 1964 Securities Acts Amendments bill by limiting its conflicts with the Exchange to an earlier-initiated effort to reform floor trading. Ralph Saul, then director of the SEC's Division of Trading and Markets (formerly the Division of Trading and Exchanges), subsequently explained that the SEC's focusing its reform efforts on NYSE governance changes would have been like "tilting at windmills"; it was considered wiser "to get done what you could get done."[*][80]

In the view of both the SEC's Special Study group and Cary's Commission, floor trading was morally and, arguably, legally wrong. Both the study and the Commission agreed that floor trading on occasion quite literally did provide "a license to steal" by allowing floor traders to be physically present on the floor of the Exchange, where they had the opportunity to take advantage of information that would affect stock prices more rapidly than all other investors, who relied on tape reports and quotation systems. This competitive advantage was vividly illustrated in the *Special Study*'s description of floor trading in the Sperry Rand Corporation on January 25, 1961. Just before noon, Sperry's Board of Directors decided to declare a 2 percent stock dividend in lieu of its usual cash dividend. Since a stock dividend has no intrinsic value, the board's decision reasonably could be assumed to lead to a reduction in Sperry's stock price. The Sperry board's decision was known on the Exchange floor at 1:48 P.M.; it was effectively communicated to the public at 2:32 P.M. by the Dow Jones broad tape. Before 2:32 P.M. floor traders were able to sell close to 20,000 Sperry shares, most of which presumably were purchased for investors ignorant of the dividend reduction.[82]

Section 10(b) of the 1934 Securities Exchange Act had been held, in the SEC's 1961 *Cady, Roberts* opinion,[83] to be violated when a partner in a broker-dealer firm with advance knowledge of an impending dividend reduction sold securities on an exchange before the reduction was publicly announced. In March 1964, Commissioner Byron Woodside posed the central ethical and legal question about floor trading. If it was fraud for an office partner to take advantage of the public through the use of inside information, was it not "equally reprehensible" for a floor trader to take advantage of comparable knowledge that would affect stock prices before it was effectively disseminated to the public?[84] For both the Special Study and the Commission, the question answered itself. The study concluded, "Floor trading in its present form is a vestige of the former 'private club' character of stock exchanges and should not be per-

* Following the publication of the 1971 Martin Report, the Exchange did change its Board of Directors. The total number of directors was reduced from thirty-three to twenty-one; the number of non-Exchange or "public" representatives on the board increased from three to ten. The immediate inspirations for these changes were the 1967–1970 back-office crisis and subsequent congressional criticisms of the New York Stock Exchange.[81]

mitted to continue." Published statistics indicated that there were approximately thirty full-time floor traders on the New York Stock Exchange and three hundred intermittent floor traders responsible for 2.1 percent of total Exchange volume in 1961.* Earlier studies and the Special Study's own research consistently showed that floor traders were a "significant destabilizing factor in the market," since they tended to accentuate price movements in the market as a whole and in individual securities by buying when specific securities were rising and selling when they declined.

In defense of floor traders, the exchanges argued that floor traders contributed to the liquidity or "marketability" of given securities by increasing the number of people available to buy or sell stock and that they also provided both greater price continuity and price stability in the market. The Special Study wholly rejected these rationalizations, because floor traders usually traded in active securities rather than inactive securities; the evidence already noted consistently showed that floor traders artificially accentuated price trends and that floor trading tended to cease altogether when volume measurably declined. Each of these points had been clear to the SEC as long ago as 1936, when its *Segregation Report* stated, "Floor trading, as disclosed by the evidence, reveals a tendency, on the average, both to concentrate in stocks where activity is already present and to accentuate price trends. The liquidity it creates is too often superfluous. It misleads, for under stress it vanishes."[86]

The study's factual conclusions were further corroborated by the testimony of several floor traders who testified that they had no interest in trading inactive stocks, because, as one put it, "I can't beat them."[87] In the view of the study, there was only one possible justification for floor trading. A "unique species" of floor trader occasionally volunteered to help stabilize a specific security's prices by temporarily acting as a specialist. The study therefore recommended that all full-time or part-time floor trading be abolished

---

* These data may have understated both the number of intermittent floor traders and the volume of floor trading. In February 1964, James Dowd, an employee of the consulting firm of Cresap, McCormick and Paget hired by the New York Stock Exchange to prepare an "independent" study of floor trading, resigned from the firm after the draft of a study of floor trading he prepared was modified to satisfy the New York Stock Exchange. As explained later in the text, Dowd met with SEC officials and described the Exchange's actions. A February 28, 1964, memorandum prepared by Ralph Saul reports, "Mr. Dowd was perhaps most vehement on the inadequacies of present surveillance of floor traders. He indicated that the floor-trading reports understate floor trading by between 25 to 50 percent through deliberate evasion and thorough misinterpretation of the rules . . . He called the Floor Department of the NYSE 'incompetent' and under the domination of floor members."[85]

unless SEC or stock exchange studies demonstrated that some floor traders could perform a formal role as "auxiliary specialists."

Six days after the publication of the Special Study's analysis of floor trading, the SEC, on July 23, 1963, distributed a press release that seemed to agree with the study's conclusion. The release stated in part:

> In light of the very serious and basic problems presented by the continuation of floor trading, as brought out by the *Report of the Special Study* and as evidenced by prior studies, and of the lengthy and apparently unsuccessful efforts to resolve them, the Commission agrees that a rule proposal abolishing floor trading on the New York and American Stock Exchanges should be developed unless those exchanges demonstrate that its continuance would be consistent with the public interest.[88]

This release, in fact, camouflaged a basic policy disagreement within the Commission. Chairman Cary, as a matter of principle, sought the unconditional abolition of floor trading. The balance of the Commission essentially agreed with the study's analysis but sought to preserve the opportunity to rechannel floor trading into a constructive role.[89]

The Exchange soon took advantage of the SEC's offer to prepare a study of a possibly constructive role for floor trading. On October 24, 1963, a New York Stock Exchange vice president wrote the SEC that the Exchange had hired the firm of Cresap, McCormick and Paget, a consulting firm with experience in the securities industry, to prepare an independent analysis of floor trading.[90] According to the Cresap report, the firm had been hired by the Exchange to prepare "an independent comprehensive study of floor trading as currently conducted on the floor of the New York Stock Exchange" with the understanding that the firm had the authority "to reach whatever conclusions and to formulate whatever recommendations the study's findings appeared to warrant," including "complete agreements with the Special Study."*[91]

On January 15, 1964, the Cresap firm submitted its report to the Exchange. After review of pertinent Exchange internal reports, fifty hours of visual observation of floor traders, analysis of its own questionnaire, and interviews with Exchange members and officials as

---

* Since this understanding appeared in the version of the Cresap report rewritten by order of the New York Stock Exchange, there apparently was no dispute about the original understanding. At any rate, it is difficult to conceive how a consulting firm could be "independent" unless it operated under an understanding that its conclusions would be its own.

well as members of the SEC's Special Study, the firm submitted a report that substantially agreed with the factual conclusions of the Special Study. Its initial report, according to Ralph Saul, who had the opportunity to read it, "envisaged a fairly far-reaching program of reform, including a recommendation that floor trading as presently conducted be discontinued, and that a new function be provided to create additional capital and experience needed to effect large transactions and dampen price swings." On February 3, 1964, James Dowd, the Cresap investigator who prepared the report, and William Boken, the Cresap partner in charge of the project, met with New York Stock Exchange officials, including President Funston. The Exchange officials informed Dowd "that his recommendations were unacceptable and they would have to be changed." The next day Dowd informed the Cresap firm that he would resign if the firm's final report did not conform to his views. Dowd indicated that the two other Cresap employees who worked with him on the report agreed with his conclusions. The Cresap firm nevertheless decided to modify its report to satisfy the Exchange. As modified, the report was submitted to the Exchange on February 14, 1964.[92]

Dowd and one other Cresap employee subsequently resigned. Before leaving Cresap, Dowd telephoned Ralph Saul and arranged to meet with him on February 14, 1964, to prevent the Exchange "from dealing [the SEC] one from the bottom of the deck." The SEC, apparently, fully believed Dowd's version of events. The day after his telephone call, the Commission authorized the Division of Trading and Markets to conduct an earlier-proposed investigation of possible fraud in floor trading. The investigation soon was expanded to take testimony from Dowd and two other Cresap employees.[93] On February 20, 1964, the SEC tentatively agreed to schedule a public hearing on floor trading before the end of March. Exchange representatives were informed on March 13, 1964, according to the *SEC Minutes*, "of the facts in the Commission's possession which indicated that the so-called 'Cresap report' on floor trading was not, in fact, an independent report."[94] In an interview William Cary subsequently stated that "there was a cover-up on the part of the Exchange."[95] Contemporaneous newspaper articles in *The New York Times* implied the same.[96]

Even as modified, the Cresap report was hardly a ringing endorsement of floor trading. The modified report stated that 231 of 679 Exchange members who responded to the Cresap questionnaire had observed "questionable floor-trading practices," typically the congregating by floor traders around the post of an active security or their dominating the market in a security. Both practices could permit floor traders to take advantage of public investors by completing transactions before knowledge that might affect securities prices was disseminated to the public. The Cresap report also found that the Exchange's surveillance of floor trading had been "inadequate"; corroborated the *Special Study* by disclosing that 49 percent of all floor trading during a two-week test period had been concentrated on five securities; and further agreed that "very often" floor trading was "primarily destabilizing." Nonetheless, the modified Cresap report insisted that "some, though not all, floor traders exert a beneficial effect on the market" and opposed the indiscriminate abolition of floor trading. The modified Cresap report recommended transforming floor traders into "registered dealers," subject to a minimum capital requirement, who would be permitted to trade for their own accounts only if 60 percent or more of their transactions were executed at prices opposed to price trends and hence, presumably, "stabilizing." In the official view of the SEC, the recommendation of the modified Cresap report did not represent "meaningful changes in existing practice" but, rather, "constituted only a series of rules little different from those which had been tried at one time or another during the long history of ineffectual regulation."[97]

Under the circumstances, the SEC proceeded with considerable restraint. If ever there was an opportunity for the Commission to seek the complete abolition of floor trading, it was present immediately after the publication of the modified Cresap report. The SEC, however, did not fully press its bargaining advantage. Instead, the Division of Trading and Markets was directed to meet with the New York Stock Exchange and negotiate an SEC rule that would severely restrict the opportunities of floor traders to exploit their competitive advantage or make destabilizing trades but not call for the outright abolition of floor traders. On March 4, 1964, New York Stock Exchange representatives met with Ralph Saul and other SEC staff members and outlined a program for the future regulation of floor traders similar to the modified Cresap report. Strikingly, the SEC's negotiators framed their response as a series of "modifications" to the Exchange's program. On March 9, the SEC recommended that all "casual" or "amateur" floor trading be ended and floor trading be restricted "to professionals having substantive capital and capable of supplementing the activities of specialists." Floor traders in the future would not be entitled to priority over public orders, and at least 80 percent of all floor traders' transactions would have to be against the price trend.[98]

The key differences between the Exchange and the SEC were quantitative. The Exchange sought a $100,000 floor trader minimum capital requirement; the SEC wanted a much higher figure to ensure the abolition of intermittent floor traders. The Exchange would have required 60 percent of all floor trader transactions to be against the price trend; the SEC, 80 percent. But the Exchange representatives refused further compromise of their program. In Keith Funston's view, had the Exchange accepted "the SEC staff's proposed changes, we would, in effect, be abolishing floor trading." On March 14, 1964, the Exchange's representatives indicated that they would not agree to the SEC's proposal, and the SEC broke off negotiations. The Commission informed the Exchange that it would proceed to issue a proposed rule and hold a public hearing on the rule in mid-April.[99]

Exchange president Funston, like his predecessor Emil Schram nineteen years earlier when faced with a similar SEC effort concerning floor trading, appealed to the White House. On March 14, Funston published a letter, addressed to all Exchange members, justifying the Exchange's bargaining position. Specifically accusing the SEC of possessing a "dangerous concept of our free enterprise system" and of proceeding on the "theoretical and academic" analysis of the Special Study, Funston argued that "the absence of the floor trader . . . would substantially reduce the liquidity of the market [and] work to the disadvantage of public investors," in part, because "floor traders' transactions tend to improve the market by entering at points and prices, and on the side of the market, where there is a momentary lack of public interest." Each of these assertions was contravened by the empirical findings of both the *Special Study* and the modified Cresap report. Nonetheless, after the Exchange's Board of Governors voted on March 19, 1964, to institute the Exchange's program of regulating floor traders, Funston wrote Ralph Saul, "We do not believe that now, when the Government is doing all that it can to encourage the nation's economic growth, is the time to run the risk of adversely affecting public confidence in the economy by unnecessarily tinkering with the delicate mechanism of the country's principal securities markets."[100]

Funston had arranged to meet with President Johnson on March 25. William Cary relates in his memoirs that Funston's intention to discuss the SEC's floor-trading proposal with the President "came to the attention of the press." On March 23, *The New York Times* published an article entitled "Stock Exchange to Ask Johnson for Support Against the SEC; Funston to Meet President This Week in Attempt to Head Off Agency's Plan to Curb Floor Traders." The article outlined the SEC's approach to the floor-trading negotiations. Johnson refused to intervene, and, indeed, somewhat mischievously used the meeting as an occasion to ask the New York Stock Exchange's support for legislation to increase the salaries of high-ranking government officials, including, Funston disclosed, the "heads of independent agencies."[101]

On approximately the same day as Funston met with Johnson, Chairman Cary met with James Kellogg, the president of the commission brokerage houses' lobbying organization, the Association of Stock Exchange Firms. Kellogg informed Cary that the brokerage houses did not fully support Funston and offered to aid the SEC staff in negotiating a final compromise. The leading brokerage houses, many of which did no floor trading, were eager to resolve the controversy rapidly and with as little additional newspaper publicity as possible.[102]

With such leading brokerage houses as Merrill Lynch and F. I. duPont unwilling to support Funston's bargaining position, the New York Stock Exchange's resistance to the SEC's floor-trading rule quickly dissipated. By March 31, the Exchange's negotiators tentatively had accepted the SEC staff position that future floor trading be limited to "a small professional group" of approximately twenty to thirty traders, each with a minimum of $250,000 in capital, who would be capable of supplementing the activities of specialists. In a slight revision of the SEC staff's earlier plan, the floor traders, who thereafter were to be called "registered traders," would be required to make 75 percent, rather than 80 percent, of their trades against the price trend. Crucially, registered traders would be prohibited from executing brokerage orders and floor trading in the same security during a single trading session. Soon after Ralph Saul had been authorized to advise the Exchange that "the Commission saw no need for a public hearing" if the Exchange approved the SEC's proposal, the Exchange's Board of Governors signified its agreement. On April 9, 1964, the SEC formally issued its proposed rule restricting floor trading. The rule was adopted six weeks later and went into effect on August 3, 1964.[103]

By prohibiting floor brokers from executing brokerage orders and floor trading in the same security during a trading session and adopting substantial capital requirements, the SEC did succeed in the virtual elimination of "casual" or "part-time" floor traders. Subsequent statistical analysis showed that these reforms ended approximately three fourths of all floor trading. Floor trading was reduced from 2.48 percent of total transactions on the New York Stock Exchange for the year ending July 31, 1964, to 0.66 percent for the following year.[104] In retrospect, Ralph Saul, who was substantially responsible for negotiating the SEC's floor-trading rule, was satisfied with the rule, since he believed the part-time or casual floor traders were the main source of floor-trading abuses and the full-time floor traders with a great deal of money at stake tended to act more responsibly and were useful on the floor to help transact large-block trades.[105]

The SEC's scheme for ensuring that the remaining full-time floor traders did not exploit their competitive advantages, however, was open to serious objection. The requirement that 75 percent of all floor traders' transactions be "stabilizing" or against the price trend was to be enforced by the so-called tick test, which both the *Special Study* and the Cresap report concluded was ineffectual. The test assumed that any change in the price of a security by as little as an eighth of a point was a "trend" and that any purchase on a one-eighth decline or sale on a one-eighth rise was "trading against the trend." The *Special Study* found the test to be largely worthless, because even when a security price generally declines, there will be numerous instances when the price temporarily will advance by an eighth of a point. A floor trader could receive a 100 percent score on the tick test even though he was, in fact, always trading with the price trend. The *Special Study* noted that a high score in most events was likely, since the requirement that a floor trader purchase on minus ticks and sell on plus ticks did no more than direct him "to buy low and sell high, a course he is led to more simply by his profit incentive." Moreover, even if the tick test had been thoroughly effective, it usually required a floor trader to sacrifice only an eighth of a point each time he sought to take advantage of his position on the floor to execute a transaction before the public could respond to an event likely to affect a security price.[106]

The ineffectuality of the tick test was illustrated by an SEC study of floor-trading activities during the first six months of the 1964 rule. It found that floor traders averaged 90 percent stabilization percentages under the tick test. But an analysis of floor traders' performances in two securities that had experienced sharp price breaks found floor traders to have "dominated" or "contributed" to price trends "by means of key destabilizing purchases and sales" that "washed out in the monthly stabilization computations." The tick test was too crude a device for detecting the destabilizing transactions of a floor trader who rapidly moved in and out of a volatile stock.

The SEC study of the first six months of the floor trader rule also criticized the New York Stock Exchange for its lack of effective enforcement of the rule, specifically noting inaccuracies in floor traders' reports of their trading activity and a significant increase in off-floor transactions by members of firms with floor-trading accounts. In one instance a floor trader apparently violated the 1964 rule by employing a "card system" to signal members of his firm to execute off-floor transactions.[107] For such reasons, William Cary subsequently deprecated the SEC's 1964 floor-trading rule, stating, "We waffled and wound up with a series of rules that did not achieve much."[108]

To the SEC's senior leadership, including Cary, Special Study chief economist Sidney Robbins, and Office of Policy Planning director Walter Werner, floor trading, though important in principle, was not significant in practical terms relative to other contemplated securities exchange reforms. Floor trading, Cary believed, was "a peanut issue." At the time, SEC officials expressed surprise at the intensity of the Exchange's opposition to the abolition of floor trading.[109]

There could have been no comparable surprise concerning an SEC initiative to revamp the New York Stock Exchange's specialist system. This was, as a *Fortune* magazine article title stated, "Wall Street's Main Event."[110] The Exchange's 360 specialists were the market-makers who administered the Exchange's continuous auction market. By acting as brokers' brokers who executed purchase or sell orders when the market price reached stipulated prices, the specialist and his order book centralized at a single post on the Exchange floor the execution of customers' orders not slated for immediate execution. By serving also as dealers in lists of "specialty" securities, the NYSE argued, specialists increased the liquidity (that is, the immediate marketability) of securities, provided securities price continuity (that is, the closeness in price of successive transactions), and depth (that is, closeness in price even when there were temporary imbalances in supply and demand). "In his unique capacity," the SEC staff's *American Stock Exchange Report* explained, "the specialist stands at the heart of the Exchange market mechanism. He has intimate knowledge of the past market action of the stocks in which he specializes. He also has sole access to the specialist book showing outstanding orders both below and above the market, which affords him a great competitive advantage over the public. In addition, he exercises a significant influence on the public appraisal of a security, since he is the one who quotes the market."[111]

During the New Deal, the propriety of specialists serving both as brokers, with their unique ability to anticipate price trends because of their physical presence on the exchange floor and possession of the specialists' order books, and dealers, with opportunity to profit personally from trades with those less well-informed or less able to influence securities prices, had been the single most controversial issue in exchange regulation.[112]

Events during Cary's chairmanship rekindled the historical controversy concerning specialists. The Commission's brief in the *Res* expulsion proceeding emphasized that

> the core of this case is the willful and planned violation by the Res of their fiduciary duties as Exchange specialists. As we will point out, statute, common law, and custom place immense trust and responsibility and a correlative potential for harm in the hands of specialists. It is the prostitution of the specialists' important role ... which provided the *modus operandi* for the operations [that] resulted in many millions of dollars of harm to thousands of unsuspecting investors who had every reason to expect that the exchange market in which they dealt was honest and fair.[113]

The SEC's *American Stock Exchange Report* found similarly that the "entire pattern of activities of the specialist firm, Gilligan, Will and Company were . . . so clearly contrary . . . to the statute and rules of the exchange [that] any program of reform must concentrate heavily on the dominant role of the specialist."[114]

Specialists on the New York Stock Exchange also were severely criticized during Chairman Cary's tenure. On May 28, 1962, the Dow Jones Industrial Average suffered a severe 34.95 decline. In twenty-three of a sample of fifty securities the SEC studied, specialists reduced their holdings on May 28 to the minimum permitted. According to the *Special Study*, specialists trading in leading securities, such as American Telephone and Telegraph, IBM, and Korvette, "tended to be passive at best and possibly destabilizing in nature." Generalizing, the study concluded, "a few specialists seemed to contribute to the 'pounding down' of prices by their selling."[115]

After the study's analysis of specialists was published, but before the SEC began specialist-rule negotiations with the New York Stock Exchange, President Kennedy was assassinated. In the twenty-seven minutes between the time his assassination became known on the Exchange floor and the closing of the Exchange, volume was extraordinarily heavy, with the Dow Jones Industrial Average falling approximately twenty-five points. SEC analysis of twenty-five securities again found that specialist performance varied widely. In four securities — Korvette, International Telephone, American Motors, and American Photocopy — the SEC reported, "The specialists sold substantial quantities of stock almost immediately after the news of the assassination . . . Not only did their selling contribute to the disorderliness of the market, but the specialists were able to use their central market position to liquidate their positions ahead of the public."[116]

The *Special Study*'s chapter on specialists was noteworthy for its pioneering computer study of specialist trading. On the basis of the most sophisticated and detailed evidence ever accumulated on the subject, the study concluded that the specialist system "in its present form . . . appears to be an essential mechanism for maintaining continuous auction markets and in broad terms appears to be serving its purposes satisfactorily."[117] Considerable evidence was published demonstrating that specialist dealing usually was against the price trend.[118] This evidence tended to justify permitting specialists to combine broker and dealer functions. Such evidence, in the words of David Silver, author of the chapter, led the study to believe "that segregation of functions was a lost battle in an old war."[119] Nonetheless, the study's chapter raised fundamental questions about the performance of specialists. And the *Special Study*'s recommendations to increase SEC and exchange regulation of specialists were among the most debatable recommendations in the study, largely because there was no analysis of the extent to which competition among market-makers might also have been employed to ensure that specialists performed consistently with the public interest.

Among the most significant data the *Special Study* published concerning specialists described changes in the nature of competition among securities market-makers. When the 1933 Securities Act was passed, there were 466 stocks traded on the New York Stock Exchange with competing specialists. Active stocks frequently were handled by more than one specialist, with some securities having as many as six competing specialists. The SEC's 1936 *Segregation Report* had emphasized that competition among specialists had served a highly constructive function by offering commission brokers the opportunity to choose among competing specialists and "entrust their brokerage orders to the specialist who stands ready at all times to narrow the quoted market and prevent price fluctuations." The desire of competing specialists to attract commission business, reported the *Segregation Report*, was "an important incentive to maintain a fair and orderly market."[120] By the time the *Special Study* was published, there had occurred "a drastic decline in com-

peting specialists," with only thirty-seven securities traded by competitive specialists.* The *Special Study* wrote of the decline in specialist competition:

> At present, competition is unsatisfactory for several reasons. Com-
> mission firms are often confused as to who is quoting the market in
> active stocks. The commission firms do not shop for the best service
> but often give each competitor half their brokerage business. In addi-
> tion, neither competitor accepts full market-making responsibilities,
> thus adding to the Exchange's regulatory problems."[121]

This was an accurate description of the experience of brokerage
firms directing orders to the few remaining competitive specialists
on the New York Stock Exchange during the early 1960s. But it
raised a fundamental question. If specialist competition had become
"unsatisfactory," was it desirable to reform the rules of the New
York Stock Exchange to permit other forms of market-maker competition?

Later chapters of the study described the increasing percentage of
securities volume initiated by such institutional investors as pension funds, investment companies, or insurance firms, which by
September 1961, according to the New York Stock Exchange, were
responsible for approximately 26 percent of share volume on the
Exchange.[122] Increasingly, the study found, the fixed commission-
rate structure of the New York Stock Exchange and the difficulties
specialists had in handling large-volume transactions had led institutional investors to purchase or sell New York Stock Exchange–listed securities in the over-the-counter market. Price considerations, the *Special Study* reported, were significant. When the
institutions were asked to describe the circumstances that affected
their determination to buy New York Stock Exchange–listed securities over the counter, "three quarters of the respondents indicated
price and cost considerations as determining factors." When institutions were asked what suggestions they might have for changes in
the practices or structure of the exchanges, "the most frequent suggestion was for a volume discount or lower commission rates for
larger blocks on the New York Stock Exchange."[123]

These findings suggested that, at least with large-block orders,
better prices sometimes were available because over-the-counter
dealers competed with New York Stock Exchange specialists. Anec-
dotal evidence assembled by the *Special Study* also was consistent
with the findings of the *Segregation Report* that competition among

---

* By 1967, there were no longer any NYSE-listed securities traded by competing
specialists.

market-makers tended to result in exchange specialists and competitive market-makers narrowing price spreads.[124]

At the very least, a *Special Study* that explicitly recognized the SEC's responsibility "to create a fair field of competition" and "directly intervene," when necessary, "in furtherance of the public interest"[125] might well have recommended or studied the mechanisms by which market-maker competition further could be increased. For example, the study might well have tried to determine whether it was possible to increase opportunities for individual investors to enjoy the net cost savings that sometimes resulted from competitive over-the-counter trading of securities listed on the Exchange by removing restrictions on Exchange member trading off the Exchange floor. "The evidence," concluded the *Special Study* in a passage outside its chapter on specialists, "points to the conclusion that the benefits of (dual or multiple markets for securities) competition outweigh any possible effects on the depth of the existing markets."[126] This was not a conclusion the study synthesized into its recommendations concerning specialists.

The failure to analyze how specialists might have been subjected to greater competition seemed particularly significant in light of data the *Special Study* published suggesting that some NYSE specialists were engaging in greater dealing than was necessary to perform effectively their market-making functions and that the Exchange long had experienced difficulty in enforcing its rules against excessive trading.

The study reported that aggregate specialists' dealing for their own accounts increased by approximately 50 percent during the period from 1952 to 1959. Strikingly, the study found that specialists' dealing for their own accounts averaged 15.5 to 21.2 percent of total trading during the period from 1937 to 1952. This was a period of extreme fluctuations in Exchange volume, but also a period when SEC exchange regulation had been emphasized. Starting in 1953, specialists' dealing for their own accounts "increased sharply until it exceeded 29 percent in 1959, 1960, and 1961." This was a period of aggregate volume increases, when SEC exchange regulation had been least effective. It was also a period, reported the *Special Study*, when the New York Stock Exchange "generally pursued a policy of favoring high dealer participation" and tended to ignore the "problems of excessive specialist participation *per se.*"*[127]

---

* Nor could it be persuasively argued that specialists needed high dealer profits in actively traded securities to subsidize dealer losses in less actively traded securities. In 1976, the NYSE supplied data to the SEC covering specialists' income on all common stock activity for 1974. The data showed that when both specialist agency

In the study's own interpretation of specialist profit data, it acknowledged that the data suggested, at least for the largest specialist units, that trading may become an end in itself. The inference that, for at least some specialists, trading profits, not market
stabilization, were a primary motivation for specialists' dealing
seemed inescapable in the light of the *Special Study*'s findings that
there was "extremely wide diversity" among specialist units, with
certain "aggressive" specialists earning as much as 80 percent of
their income from trading profits. The specialist units ranked in the
top 10 percent of all units by total income earned 38 percent of total
specialist income both in 1959 and 1960. Among this top 10 percent
of all specialist units, 69 percent of their income was derived from
dealing for their own accounts in 1959 and 62 percent in 1960.[129] As
early as 1941, SEC staff economist Raymond Vernon explained the
significance of such data: "If [specialist] dealer transactions in a
given issue were responsible for the major part of his income, it
might be inferred (although the inference might well be subject to
some challenge) that his interest in his brokerage business in that
issue was secondary to an aim to profit from operations as a dealer."
By contrast, if a "specialist actually suffered losses from his
dealer trades" it could be inferred that the specialist's dealer
activities contribute to a more satisfactory execution of his brokerage duties.[130]

The *Special Study* also concluded that "the Exchange's regulatory
and surveillance programs [had] been inadequate ... in the area of
the conflicts of interests which arise from the specialist's unique role
as both broker and market-maker." Specialist discipline, in large
measure, was meted out by fellow floor members.[131] There were
good reasons by the time of the *Special Study* to doubt that this was
an effective system of regulation. The study expressed particular
concern about its discovery that the SEC's 1952 rulings prohibiting
not-held (or discretionary) specialists' orders were ignored by the
Exchange floor governors for close to a decade.[132] The study also
observed that as orders were executed on a specialist's book, the
book as a record of the specialist's transactions was, in part, de-
stroyed. "This means," explained the study, "that it is extremely
difficult actually to reconstruct the book as it was at any particular
point in time. To do so requires working with a mass of orders,
executions and cancellations, and even then such efforts may not be

---

and dealing income were taken into account, specialists earned money on their trading
activities on all common stocks, including the one hundred least active common
stocks, even during the year of the lowest NYSE volume in the 1971–1980 period.[128]

wholly successful. Thus, what should be a primary source of data in the surveillance of specialists' activities cannot be effectively utilized."[133] Nor was the Special Study satisfied that the tick test or other surveillance tests then employed by the Exchange adequately policed specialists' excessive dealing or conflicts of interests.[134] The study recommended that automated surveillance of specialists be employed in the future.[135] The last point apparently was particularly significant to the Special Study group. After the study was published, Sidney Robbins, who had been its chief economist, expressed doubt that any surveillance method that did not involve a computer's retention of the transaction-by-transaction records of specialists' trades in a given security was "likely to be fully effective."*[136]

Given the Special Study's conclusion that as of 1963, New York Stock Exchange regulation of specialists was "inadequate," the wisdom of not analyzing whether the existing specialist system was preferable to a system with greater market-maker competition was debatable.

The *Special Study*'s own data suggested that greater competition among market-makers could lead to better prices, provide more capital to handle institutional orders, and reduce reliance on Exchange floor governors to prevent excessive dealing.

The *Special Study* section on specialists concluded by recommending the adoption of a new SEC specialist rule incorporating a number of modest reforms, including reiteration that dealing should be limited to the 1934 statute's "reasonably necessary" standard, a new affirmative obligation requiring specialists to deal when dealing was necessary to maintain a fair and orderly market — such as during the rapidly falling markets of May 28, 1962, or November 22, 1963 — and a higher minimum capital requirement.[138]

Seventeen years after the publication of the *Special Study*, William Cary recalled that he informally proposed to his fellow SEC commissioners a more far-reaching approach. To eliminate the inherent conflict of interest in the specialists' dual broker and dealer roles, Cary discussed having Exchange employees assume the specialist role. "The New York Stock Exchange had the capital," Cary argued. "It could cover any dealer losses."[139] This essentially had been the recommendation of Benjamin Cohen, the original draftsman of the 1934 Securities Exchange Act. Cary remembered that

* During its 1964 specialist-rule negotiations, the SEC did not insist that the NYSE implement an effective system of automated surveillance. Although the SEC was criticized by a Senate staff study in 1972 for its failure to develop (or require the exchanges to develop) an automated surveillance system,[137] through 1981 no such system had been implemented.

there was "no serious consideration given" to the proposal that the New York Stock Exchange itself perform the specialist's functions. Fellow commissioners Manuel Cohen and Byron Woodside, in particular, were opposed, considering Cary's proposal "an extreme step."

On February 11, 1964, the SEC sent to the New York Stock Exchange a proposed rule to regulate specialists that essentially followed the *Special Study*'s recommendations. As contrasted with the floor-trading rule negotiations, it was universally agreed that the SEC–New York Stock Exchange specialist rule negotiations were amicable. Controversy was limited to a single significant issue. The SEC wanted a Commission rule to define the specialist's "negative" obligation not to deal excessively and "affirmative" obligation to deal when essential to stabilize the market. The SEC argued that, without a Commission rule, it could not directly sanction a specialist, since "the Commission is not . . . empowered to enforce rules of the Exchange." The New York Stock Exchange agreed to the substance of both obligations but insisted that they be enforced by an Exchange, not an SEC, rule. During negotiations, the Exchange, according to a subsequent United States Senate staff study, expressed two primary objections to an SEC rule:

> First, the Commission for the first time would be able to establish and enforce standards of specialist performance without the intermediation of the exchanges' floor committees and boards of governors. As one NYSE representative stated the point at a meeting, the rule would give the SEC the power to reach a specialist without the "shield of the governors." Second, and far more important, the proposed rule would expose the exchanges and their specialists to the possibility of civil liability for the failure of a specialist to fulfill his dealer obligations.

Over the course of negotiations conducted between May and August 1964, the SEC reversed itself and agreed that the New York Stock Exchange could issue the rule requiring specialists to obey both negative and affirmative trading obligations. The SEC limited its enforcement powers to an awkward indirect procedure: if, after notice and a hearing, the SEC found a specialist had excessively traded for his own account, the SEC could order the Exchange to cancel or suspend the specialist's registration in one or more securities, unless the Exchange earlier had done so. In that case, the SEC agreed it could not impose any further sanction except where it found substantial or continued misconduct by a specialist. In the ensuing seven years the SEC did not once invoke this procedure, prompting the 1972 Senate staff study to state, "Under the rule the SEC cannot enforce the specialist's 'affirmative' obligation at all, and it can enforce the 'negative' obligation only indirectly and then only in a limited and time-consuming manner."[140]

As with the SEC's ineffectual 1964 attempt to reorganize Exchange governance and its unsuccessful attempt to abolish floor trading, a principal consequence of its limited specialist regulatory rule was that the issue had to be faced again within a relatively few years. In 1970, the SEC's staff again studied whether specialists were engaged in excessive trading. The SEC's 1970 staff investigation concluded, "The data in this report clearly raise significant questions as to the adequacy of NYSE specialists' performance under the NYSE rules and the rules of the Commission."

The first step taken by the SEC staff in 1970 was to compare aggregate specialists' purchase and sale balances in all stocks with the movement of the Dow Jones Industrial Average for the period of March 1 to June 30, 1970. According to a 1972 Senate staff summary, the SEC found some of the data "extremely disturbing." On 30 percent of the days on which the market advanced or declined more than ten points, specialists on balance acted in a destabilizing fashion — that is, they were net buyers when the market rose and net sellers when it declined. With the market experiencing a sharp decline during the four-month test period, the SEC's inspection team found that specialists as a group were "heavy" short-sellers. The SEC inspection team next studied individual specialist performance on eighty-eight stock days (each stock day represented the performance of one specialist in one specialty stock on one trading day), selected on the basis of large price changes or extreme volatility employing three tests: the tick test, a ratio of the specialists' trades for their own accounts to total volume, and a comparison of a specialist's daily net purchases or sales with the daily price change for that stock. The SEC's analysis of specialist performance during these eighty-eight stock days revealed thirty-one instances in which specialists failed one or more of the three tests. According to the Senate staff summary: "In the SEC's view, a specialist's failure of one or more of the tests was an indication that further inquiry into his performance was appropriate, not as conclusive evidence that his performance was poor." For fourteen of the thirty-one stock days in which there had been such failure, the SEC assembled transaction-by-transaction records. The SEC concluded that in nine of the fourteen cases, "the specialist's performance was poor and may well have deserved some enforcement action by the Exchange." As for the remaining five cases, "the performance of the specialist involved was unsatisfactory and while deserving at the minimum some informal action by the Exchange was not as egregious" as in the other nine cases. In none of the fourteen cases analyzed by the SEC had the New York Stock Exchange taken formal or informal action against the specialist involved. After the SEC brought these fourteen cases to the attention of the Exchange, the Exchange's Committee on Floor Affairs (seven of whose eleven members were specialists) "unanimously disagreed" with the SEC that any of the cases required disciplinary action. The committee cited such extenuating circumstances as "unusual market conditions" or "thinness of the book" to justify the performance of each specialist.[141]

In 1971 and 1972, the SEC reversed itself and emphasized, both in the transmittal letter accompanying its *Institutional Investor Study* and in its "Policy Statement on the Future Structure of the Securities Markets," that the creation of competition among securities market-makers should be a key tool for the regulation of specialists. That this decision in part was made because of perceived inadequacies of the SEC's previous specialist regulation was implied by the 1972 "Future Structure Statement," which said:

> The Commission believes that the liquidity needs of individual and institutional investors can best be provided by policies fostering the development of competition among dealers who are specialists, market-makers, and block positioners. Such competition will mitigate the very difficult problem which now exists of developing and enforcing rules designed not only to prevent specialists from abusing their privileged position, but also to motivate them to perform satisfactorily under widely differing circumstances and in the light of varying risks and pressures.[142]

*   *   *

Only with respect to securities litigation did Cary's Commission consider itself unrestricted by the political limitations that bound its legislative and rule-making program. In broadening the bases for private litigants to bring damages actions against corporate officers and directors who exploited inside information or distributed false and misleading proxy statements, Cary's SEC fundamentally altered securities law enforcement.

As indicated, Cary had arrived at the SEC in March 1961 with "no agenda." But there was one priority he did have from the start of his chairmanship. That was, to use Section 10(b) of the federal 1934 Securities Exchange Act to reverse, in effect, state corporations law decisions concerning insider trading, such as the Massachusetts Supreme Judicial Court's 1933 opinion *Goodwin* v. *Agassiz*.[143] The question in *Goodwin* had been a classical one in securities law:

Could a corporate director with nonpublic (or "inside") knowledge of facts that would increase the share price of a security purchase stock from an uninformed shareholder without informing him of these facts? Some state courts had held that this was impermissible if done under the "special circumstances" of a face-to-face transaction. But *Goodwin* had held that the purchase of stock by a director with inside knowledge was permissible if done "impersonally" through a stock market. The Massachusetts Supreme Judicial Court reasoned: "An honest director would be in a difficult situation if he could neither buy nor sell on the stock exchange shares of stock in his corporation without first seeking out the actual ultimate party to the transaction and disclosing to him everything which a court or jury might later find that he then knew affecting the real or speculative value of such shares." The court also had stated: "Business of that nature is a matter to be governed by practical rules. Fiduciary obligations of directors ought not to be made so onerous that men of experience and ability will be deterred from accepting such office. Law in its sanctions is not coextensive with morality."

Cary also did not believe the law could be "coextensive with morality," but he insisted that it was shocking for either courts or business executives to believe that it was permissible conduct for executives to use inside information for their personal benefit.[144] Putting morality or fairness entirely aside, few actions were more likely to reduce confidence (and, ultimately, aggregate investment) in the securities markets than the failure to enforce rules guaranteeing, as far as the law could, that all investors trading on stock exchanges have relatively equal access to material information.

Within months of assuming the chairmanship, Cary wrote an SEC administrative opinion, *In the Matter of Cady, Roberts & Co.*,[145] that not only contravened *Goodwin* v. *Agassiz*, but also expanded the utility of Rule 10b-5 as a basis for private causes of actions. This rule was soon to be of such significance in securities law that Harvard Law School's Louis Loss would remark in 1969, "The great Rule 10b-5 seems . . . to be taking over the universe gradually."[146]

Section 10(b) of the 1934 Securities Exchange Act was a catch-all or residual antifraud provision meant to outlaw types of manipulation not specifically proscribed by the act's more precise denunciation, in Section 9, of touting, wash sales, and other forms of stock market fraud identified by the Pecora hearings. By its terms, the Section provided that "it shall be unlawful . . . to use or employ, in connection with the purchase or sale of any security . . . any manipulative or deceptive device or contrivance in contravention of such rules and regulations as the Commission may prescribe." Since nearly identical language in Section 17(a) of the 1933 Securities Act prohibited fraud in the offer or sale of securities, Section 10(b) was not employed by the SEC until March 21, 1942, when the Commission adopted Rule 10b-5. The rule provided that it shall be unlawful for any person in connection with the purchase or sale of any security "(1) to employ any device, scheme, or artifice to defraud, (2) to make any untrue statement of a material fact or to omit to state a material fact necessary in order to make the statements made, in the light of the circumstances under which they were made, not misleading, or (3) to engage in any act, practice, or course of business which operated or would operate as a fraud or deceit upon any person."

In 1943, the SEC issued a report concerning the Ward LaFrance Trucking Corporation's purchases of its own stock. In the report, it "called attention" to the existence of Rule 10b-5. The rule, however, was relatively little used during the next eighteen years because of uncertainty as to whether it applied to purchases or sales effected through securities exchanges.[147] This was the decisive issue in *Goodwin* v. *Agassiz* and the decisive issue that *Cady, Roberts* resolved with its holding that a person possessing inside information must either disclose it to others from whom he seeks to purchase or sell stock or abstain from trading until the inside information becomes publicly known, regardless of whether the person engages in securities transactions face to face or over a securities exchange. Because the person possessing inside information in *Cady, Roberts* happened to be a securities broker, the decision was of concern to the New York Stock Exchange. Cary recalled that shortly after his opinion was published, Keith Funston telephoned and read a strongly critical letter that he was about to send to the SEC characterizing the *Cady, Roberts* decision "as an unwarranted step toward raising standards to an unrealistic level."[148] Cary defended the decision and did not hesitate to inform Funston that the letter would not influence the Commission. It was, in fact, never sent.

Cary's SEC also supported private enforcement of the securities law through the SEC's successful appearance as *amicus curiae* in the Supreme Court's 1964 case *J. I. Case* v. *Borak*.[149] In *Borak*, the Court held that stockholders had an implied statutory right to bring damages actions when they were defrauded by corporate proxy solicitations, agreeing with the SEC's argument that "private enforcement of the proxy rules provides a necessary supplement to Commission action. As in antitrust treble damage litigation, the possibility of civil damages or injunctive relief serves as a most effective weapon in the enforcement of the proxy requirements."

The cumulative effect of the SEC's actions in *Cady, Roberts* and *Borak* was rapidly apparent. The *Annual Report of the Director of the Administrative Office of the United States Courts* noted that a total of 171 private civil cases filed in United States district courts were based on the federal securities, commodities, and exchanges statutes in 1961, the year *Cady, Roberts* was decided. By 1963, the number of private cases had more than doubled, to 388; by 1970, it had reached 1091. Although it is generally treacherous to cite such aggregate data for such a factual demonstration, there is little doubt that private litigation based on Rule 10b-5 was a primary cause of this rapid increase in private litigation. In Professor Loss's 1961 treatise, *Securities Regulation*, Loss enumerated the number of private Rule 10b-5 actions as "somewhat larger [in] number" than fifteen. By 1967 law professor Alan Bromberg would require an entire treatise to analyze private and SEC cases brought under the 1934 act's Rule 10b-5.[150]

* * *

No President, not even Roosevelt, professed that such elaborate benefits flowed from the securities laws as did Lyndon Johnson during the first year of his presidency. The securities laws "authored [by] my very dear, beloved friend, the late Sam Rayburn ... has helped make all of us a nation of capitalists," Johnson insisted. The SEC itself was a "dramatic demonstration" of the federal government's leadership and wisdom, responsible, in part, for boosting "the market value of stocks listed on the New York Stock Exchange [to] a new high of $465 billion [on July 31, 1964] as contrasted to a value of $23 billion prior to the enactment of the first federal·securities law in 1933."[151]

Johnson's White House consumer lobbyists effectively aided the enactment of the 1964 Securities Acts Amendments, as they would in 1967–1968 determinedly work to try to enact the SEC's mutual fund legislation.

Yet it was obvious soon after Kennedy's assassination that Johnson did not want the Commission to play so crusading a role that it prevented the business community from supporting his administration.[152] Johnson's legislative priorities initially were civil rights and poverty legislation, both causes that he believed business could support, especially during the painful aftermath of Kennedy's assassination.[153] Greeting the heads of the independent regulatory agencies on December 3, 1963, Johnson bluntly told the commission chairmen not to rock the boat: "We are challenged . . . to concern ourselves with new areas of cooperation [with industry] before we concern ourselves with new areas of control." Although Johnson did not subvert the SEC's 1964 effort to limit floor trading, around the time when it was being negotiated he made two highly conservative SEC appointments. In March 1964, former Oklahoma securities commissioner Hugh Owens was designated to succeed the already retired Commissioner Frear; then in June, Johnson nominated Hamer Budge, a former Republican congressman from Idaho, to replace Commissioner Whitney. The selection of Budge, obviously a political appointee, who, unlike Owens, had no background in securities law, was criticized. "An Unprofessional Appointment," chastised *The New York Times*; "Mr. Johnson Flunks," echoed *The Nation*. Johnson, not unaware of how such editorials often were inspired, angrily telephoned Chairman Cary after the *Times* piece appeared and accused him of planting the editorial — which Cary denied. Johnson then menacingly informed him, "You know, I'm something of a populist myself."[154]

As soon as Cary was convinced that the Securities Acts Amendments bill was likely to pass, he publicly announced his intention to resign. He officially resigned as chairman the day the legislation was signed. Just before Johnson signed the Securities Acts Amendments and the order designating Cary's fellow commissioner Manuel Cohen to be the new SEC chairman, Johnson publicly announced to "my friend, Manuel Cohen" that Cohen, too, would be expected not to rock the boat: "A new era of regulatory relationship is coming, a relationship sincerely devoted to confidence, to understanding, to a responsible role on the part of government in helping and not harassing our American capitalistic system."[155] Throughout the Johnson presidency, the SEC staff size essentially remained static at the 1390–1400 employee level.[156] Johnson's final two SEC appointees, Francis Wheat and Richard Smith, were capable, though conservative, corporate attorneys. Johnson may indeed have been "something of a populist," but as far as the Commission was concerned during the 1963–1968 period, his SEC budget and appointments measurably limited the Commission's capacity to respond effectively to the dramatic changes occurring in the securities industry.

11

The Midlife Crisis of the SEC

Things have been quiet around the Commission this week. Of course, this is only Wednesday. Since the commission rate hearings resumed yesterday, I am sure things will pick up again. There are days, however, when I hanker for the time when the SEC was criticized for being a listless middle-aged agency and a captive of the industry.

— MANUEL COHEN
Address (September 18, 1968)

BY THE SUMMER of 1964, when Manuel Cohen began his chairmanship, the SEC was thirty years old. Throughout most of its post–World War II years, the Commission had interpreted its statutory responsibilities narrowly, focusing primarily on the noncontroversial tasks of administering a corporate disclosure system and preventing fraud. It had devoted considerably less attention to its statutory responsibilities concerning "reasonable" brokerage commission rates, supervising or promulgating accounting standards, and regulating corporate proxy elections as well as to its implicit statutory mission, to be the federal agency expert in the economics of the securities industry.

In part, the SEC's post–World War II performance was the consequence of the low priority that successive Presidents and successive Congresses had assigned to securities regulation. Reforming Wall Street ceased to be a matter of urgency in Washington after

Roosevelt's death. Conservative or mediocre Commission appointments, coupled with inadequate or maintenance budgets, allowed the SEC to endure, but not to expand. There was a sense, as William Cary once wrote, that the White House expected to be involved with an agency like the SEC only when something went wrong.[1] It is a fair generalization that Congress in the first twenty post–World War II years had no greater interest in the work of the Commission.

Underlying much of the difficulty the SEC was to experience during Manuel Cohen's chairmanship also was the lack of an economic theory about the regulation of stock exchanges and mutual funds. The Commission's less-than-enthusiastic devotion to the antitrust laws' economic theory of competition often placed the SEC in conflict with the Justice Department's Antitrust Division and the Federal Trade Commission, weakening the SEC's ability to garner congressional support for its regulatory policies.

The lack of a clear economic theory also affected the presidential appointment of commissioners and Commission staffing. Virtually all of the post–World War II SEC commissioners appointed during the Truman, Eisenhower, Kennedy, and Johnson administrations were corporate attorneys or SEC staff members with little or no background either in economics or the antitrust laws. During most of the period covered by these administrations, the SEC functioned without an economic staff. When the Office of Policy Planning was created after publication of the 1963 *Special Study*, it was understaffed and had relatively little influence within the Commission.

Nor did SEC commissioners or the agency's senior staff during the first two decades after the war generally believe the Commission should play a more prominent role in determining the economic structure of the securities industry. It was widely believed within the SEC that its favorable reputation was, in part, a consequence of its not prescribing rate levels or industry structure, as did other then less well-regarded federal agencies, such as the Interstate Commerce Commission. If the SEC directly regulated the economics of the securities industry and thereby increased its ability to affect the industry's profitability, it was assumed it would risk the loss of considerable industry support and be subjected to far more frequent and intense political pressures. Rather than being an "umpire" of securities industry disputes well regarded for its technical competence, the SEC would become a different agency. It would be vulnerable to charges of being an "industry captive" if its leadership was quiescent, at loggerheads with the securities industry if its leadership was activist, and in either case, less likely to maintain its highly regarded reputation or such insulation from partisan politics as it did possess, regardless of its technical competence.

Moreover, SEC commissioners and senior staff generally doubted that the economic structure of the securities industry required regulatory attention. During this period, as Leonard Leiman, Manuel Cohen's first executive assistant, recalled, the New York Stock Exchange was thought to be "the envy of the world,"[2] far preferable to the more fragmented securities markets then common in Europe.

Throughout the chairmanship of Manuel Cohen, these conservative influences persisted. But a combination of economic, technological, and political influences also affected the SEC, partially reversing the SEC's long pattern of narrow interpretation of its statutory responsibilities.

The securities industry fundamentally changed during the 1960s. Trading and new-issue volume reached unprecedented levels. Between 1960 and 1968 the total annual dollar volume of stocks traded on the New York Stock Exchange increased nearly fourfold, from $38 billion to $145 billion, a rate considerably exceeded by the eightfold increase in the dollar volume of trading on the American Stock Exchange from $4.2 to $34.8 billion and the 534 percent increase in trading on the regional exchanges from $3.1 to $16.6 billion. Between 1960 and 1969, the number of new securities annually registered with the SEC increased from 1426 to 3645, with the dollar value of new issues increasing from $14.4 to $86.8 billion. This staggeringly rapid increase in volume led to a tenfold increase in pretax profits of New York Stock Exchange members between 1962 and 1968, but the SEC, in the words of the Commission's *Thirty-fourth Annual Report*, was "almost overwhelmed by the sheer volume of activity." Even with the agency adopting expedited procedures to review new-issue registrations, by 1969 a median of sixty-five days was necessary to review a registration statement, over three times the twenty-day waiting period prescribed by the 1933 act.[3]

Simultaneous with the enormous 1960s' growth in trading volume was a rapid institutionalization of the stock markets. In the postwar period up until the SEC's 1963 *Special Study*, aggregate stock trading by mutual funds, commercial bank trust departments, insurance companies, pension funds, and other institutional investors ranged, according to various studies and samples, between 17 and 28 percent of total New York Stock Exchange volume. In the next six years, the dramatic rise in aggregate institutional trading "transformed those institutions," reported the SEC in 1971, "into a major, if not the dominant factor in the equity market." By 1969, institutional investors accounted for 52 percent of NYSE volume, with individual and nonmember broker-dealer trading for the first time reduced to a minority of transactions on the Exchange.[4]

The simultaneous surge in aggregate stock exchange volume and in the proportion of institutional trading by the late 1960s threatened to alter fundamentally the structure of the stock exchanges. Between the last quarter of 1964 and the first quarter of 1969, the percentage of total New York Stock Exchange volume transacted through block trades of ten thousand or more shares grew from 2 to 12 percent. The difficulties Exchange specialists experienced in handling large-block trades, together with the rigidity of the Exchange's fixed commission-rate schedule and related membership rules that afforded institutional traders neither volume discounts nor the right to become Exchange members, created tremendous incentives for institutional investors to trade New York Stock Exchange–listed securities off the Exchange floor on the over-the-counter "third market." Institutional traders often were prevented from securing the price and liquidity advantages of third-market trading by New York Stock Exchange interpretations of its Rule 394, which usually forbade an Exchange member from trading Exchange-listed securities over the counter. Nonetheless, institutional trading with over-the-counter dealers who chose not to become Exchange members and could deal in New York Stock Exchange–listed securities off the Exchange floor reached approximately 5 percent of total New York Stock Exchange volume by late 1968.[5] With the NYSE's fixed commission-rate schedule, absence of a volume discount, prohibition of institutional membership, and Rule 394, each the potential target of an antitrust suit, far more significant challenges to the Exchange's dominant role in securities trading seemed probable by the last years of Manuel Cohen's chairmanship.

By the end of Cohen's tenure as chairman, plans to automate securities trading operations were sufficiently advanced to portend another fundamental pressure to alter the historic structure of the stock markets. Two communications systems, AutEx Corporation and Institutional Networks Corporation (Instinet), were scheduled to begin operations in 1969, both being designed to permit institutional subscribers and third-market dealers to communicate directly with each other their interest in the purchase or sale of large securities blocks. The Instinet system also was designed to execute orders. The AutEx and Instinet systems suggested the technological feasibility of a "fourth market," predicted by the *Special Study*, in which institutional investors would directly purchase and sell securities from each other, eliminating the need to pay either Exchange or over-the-counter commissions.

The SEC's 1968 annual report also predicted, "Automation is on the threshold of revolutionizing the system of quotations for unlisted securities." In 1968, the National Association of Securities Dealers (NASD), after four years of consultation with the SEC, hired the Bunko-Ramo Corporation to build and operate NASDAQ, a national electronic data-processing and communications system to provide instantaneous over-the-counter price quotations from over-the-counter market-makers for each security listed within the NASDAQ system. Though an effective fourth market threatened to reduce the volume of securities trading transacted on the hardwood floor of the New York Stock Exchange, NASDAQ suggested that the stock exchanges themselves might be on the verge of obsolescence, soon to be replaced by a national system of brokerage-house desk consoles administered by a centralized computer service. Reluctantly, the New York Stock Exchange began to automate its own facilities. In 1969, the Exchange initiated the Central Certificate Service, achieving, in part, SEC chairman Douglas's proposal of thirty years before, for a central broker's bank to handle the clearing of stock certificates. The following year the Exchange was scheduled to begin direct competition with the AutEx and Instinet communications systems through its own Block Automation System (BAS) service. A measure of the urgency the New York Stock Exchange attached to its dilatory efforts to automate was provided in 1967, when NASD president Robert Haack succeeded Keith Funston as the Exchange's president. Haack had had a major role in the development of the NASD's NASDAQ system. At the New York Stock Exchange as well, Haack commented soon after assuming the Exchange presidency, "My job is to move these people into the twenty-first century."[6]

The forty-three-month-long Dow Jones price rise, beginning in June 1962, was instrumental in stimulating the decade's record trading volume. It also stimulated a protracted period of securities speculation immortalized by *The New Yorker*'s financial correspondent, John Brooks, as the "go-go years." By Brooks's definition, "the term 'go-go' came to designate a method of operating in the stock market . . . characterized by rapid in-and-out trading of huge blocks of stock, with an eye to large profits taken very quickly, and the term was used specifically to apply to the operation of certain mutual funds, none of which had previously operated in anything like such a free, fast, or lively manner."

The speculation of the go-go years also created a pressure to reverse the SEC's post–World War II period of narrow interpretation of its statutory responsibilities. Trading volume over the American Stock Exchange and the over-the-counter markets in speculative issues resulted in rapid price run-ups in securities ranging from Kentucky Fried Chicken, selling at close to a hundred times its last reported earnings in April 1967, to Boothe Computer, a minor computer-leasing firm, which rose from 18 to 46 on the first day it was offered to the public. The Amex, foundering after the Res scandal with a mere 6.8 percent of total stock exchange volume in 1962, nearly tripled that percentage in the next six years, primarily as a result of the go-go period's fascination with the newer and smaller firms listed there, as contrasted with the New York Stock Exchange's list of older, larger, and less speculative firms. As Brooks emphasized, the most publicized actors during the go-go years were mutual fund managers who adopted the strategy of seeking the most profitable short-term "performance," typically by emphasizing a greater proportion of investment in speculative or "growth" common stocks than mutual fund managers historically had. In a few instances mutual fund managers engaged in the far more speculative practices of buying on margin, short-selling, and purchasing stock options or unissued letter stock.[7]

Initially less evident than the rapid 1960s' volume surge, the growing institutionalization of the stock markets, or the revival of securities speculation were political changes in the federal government that also placed enormous pressure on the SEC to assume a more activist role. By the late 1960s, the market self-correcting premises of the mainstream of economic theory were so widely accepted by both the Democratic and Republican parties that the Justice Department Antitrust Division and the Federal Trade Commission under both President Johnson and President Nixon would adopt nearly identical positions in urging the SEC to use its statutory authority to abolish price-fixing in the stock markets and the mutual fund industry.

It was during the chairmanship of Manuel Cohen, 1964 to 1969, that the SEC effectively began the process of redefining its primary functions in light of the fundamental changes then occurring in the structure of the securities markets, the go-go years' revival of securities speculation, and the greater political influence of the economic theory of competition.

By dint of his twenty-two years' previous experience as an SEC staff attorney and SEC commissioner, Cohen was better prepared to assume the Commission's chairmanship than any chairman in the SEC's history. As Leonard Leiman wrote, with only slight exaggeration:

Manny knew more securities law than nearly anyone else; he knew all the statutes, their legislative history, and their interpretations, and what he called the lore as well as the law of securities regulation. Second, he knew more about the SEC than anyone else. He had spent more than twenty years there, and he knew the staff, organization, budgets, problems, and where the bodies were buried. His expertise made it difficult for the staff to argue with him; while he was Chairman, we never heard the complaint that the staff ran the Commission. Finally, Manny Cohen knew Washington. He knew the congressional staffs and the key people everywhere who could help the SEC.

Cohen began his chairmanship as a demanding and determined taskmaster and was only briefly slowed by a heart attack early in 1965. The son of a milk deliveryman, who had earned his law degree in Brooklyn Law School's night program while driving a taxi by day, Cohen believed in hard work, in promotion solely on merit, and in the federal government and the SEC. These beliefs were reflected in his intense loyalty to the Commission. Meyer Eisenberg, Cohen's third executive assistant, recalled, "Manny was impatient with everyone who worked for him, as he was impatient with himself. He wanted the Commission to perform better; he wanted the staff to perform at the highest level of any government agency. He held everyone to his standards. No piece of paper ever left his office unmarked or unedited."

As Cohen had progressed within the SEC, he developed what those closest to him characterized as a "limitless faith in his ability to talk anybody into anything." To David Ratner, Cohen's second executive assistant, this faith was the product both of Cohen's considerable self-confidence and of his understanding that in Washington "the person who argues longest rather than the person with the best arguments often wins legal or political battles. A joke from one of Manny's speeches contains more truth than humor. Someone reportedly asked Manny's wife what her husband actually *did* as SEC chairman. Her reply was, 'I can't describe it exactly, but if *I* did it, it would be called nagging.'" Leiman would credit Cohen's perseverance with persuading the Budget Bureau to approve an appropriation for a new SEC building "because the Budget Director found it easier to yield to Manny's incessant personal badgering than to hold the line on budget increases." He also believed that Cohen persuaded the Justice Department's Antitrust Division to allow the SEC as many as three additional years to attempt to negotiate a resolution of the antitrust issues implicit in the New York Stock Exchange's commission-rate structure before the division itself directly intervened. Ratner would cite Cohen's same "entrepreneurial talents" as responsible for convincing reluctant House and Senate chairmen to schedule hearings on the Commission's 1967 mutual fund legislative proposals. Eisenberg would recall that "after a meeting between Manny and President Johnson, an aide to the President reported in wonder that this meeting was the first one he had attended in which *the agency head did all the talking*" (italics added).

The policy views of Cohen, particularly during his first years as chairman, were deeply influenced by his nineteen years as an SEC staff member. Cohen joined the Commission in 1942, roughly at the beginning of the Commission's long post–New Deal decline. By 1952, his legal ability was well recognized and he was named chief counsel of the SEC's Division of Corporate Finance, then considered the elite division of the agency. Working closely with the division's director, Byron Woodside, Cohen played a leading role in fashioning the SEC's and federal courts' approach to interpreting the 1933 Securities Act.

His technical proficiency was as highly regarded by Eisenhower's SEC chairmen Demmler, Armstrong, and Gadsby as it would be later by Chairman William Cary and Kennedy administration adviser James Landis. Former SEC chairman and close friend of President Johnson Donald Cook also admired Cohen and in 1964 would persuade Johnson to name him SEC chairman. When Byron Woodside became an SEC commissioner in 1960, Cohen succeeded his longtime chief as director of the Division of Corporate Finance. James Landis's recommendation led to Cohen's appointment as a commissioner in 1961. William Cary, in a letter to President Kennedy urging Cohen's 1961 Commission appointment, underlined Cohen's long experience as the counsel and intellectual leader of the Corporate Finance Division: "He is the lawyer's lawyer par excellence, and is so recognized by the corporate bar of this country." In terms of sheer technical ability to employ the antifraud concepts of the securities laws, Manny Cohen, among the Commission's staff in the 1950s, unquestionably was, as Irving Pollack wrote, "Mr. SEC."

Cohen also assimilated the political assumptions of the 1950s' SEC. He began his commissionership with the narrow view of the SEC's role characteristic of the Commission's leadership during the Truman and Eisenhower administrations, emphasizing consultation with the securities industry and antifraud litigation as the SEC's primary regulatory tools. This regulatory philosophy was publicly articulated by Cohen in a series of law review articles he published between 1960 and 1964. The most important article took issue with the criticism of federal Court of Appeals judge Henry Friendly that the regulatory agencies of the 1940s and 1950s had been too reluctant to use their rule-making authority and too prone to regulate piecemeal through adjudication. Cohen countered that not only was case-by-case adjudication often essential to avoid excessively broad rules that might unnecessarily disrupt an industry, but also that adjudication often was politically desirable:

> Adjudication . . . seems to provide an advantage for the enunciation of policies because of the different reactions by interested persons and the Bar to a policy stated in a case and to one enunciated in a formal rule. When an agency publishes a proposed rule for comment there is a tendency to evaluate it in terms of the maximum possible scope of its language . . . By contrast, a statement in an adjudicatory opinion is evaluated against the specific factual context. There is a general understanding that the precedential value of an opinion is limited by the underlying facts. Though an opinion foreshadows future developments, there is an awareness that its dictum will not be applied literally in every conceivable circumstance.

Characteristically, during his chairmanship Cohen would extend the campaign against insider trading begun by Cary's 1961 *Cady, Roberts* decision, not with a new SEC rule but by instructions to "his enforcement division to develop a series of enforcement actions in which the Commission and the courts gradually espoused clear principles of law," recalled Arthur Mathews, an SEC enforcement attorney during that period.

In March 1964, after Cary's plans to leave the SEC were known within the Commission, Cohen publicly articulated a theory of SEC–securities industry relations in an address to the Investment Bankers Association entitled "Cooperative Regulation." In terms calculated to appeal to President Johnson, Cohen said, "Perhaps the most striking yet most ignored feature of [the *Special Study*'s] recommendations is that they evidence a considerable amount of faith in the self-regulatory agencies, since more of them call for action by the self-regulators than for action by the Commission." With this, Cohen expressed accord, arguing that "the self-regulators must be permitted to enjoy such autonomy as will enable them to act as responsible partners in a cooperative enterprise and that the Commission's direct and oversight powers are to be used with restraint."

Subsequent events would transform Cohen into one of the most activist SEC chairmen of the postwar period, one not reluctant to employ Douglas's metaphoric shotgun. But he began his chairmanship, as he explained in the March 1964 address, with this belief:

> A new rule must not have a shotgun effect. Rather, the approach must be affirmative and selective. It will involve, even at this stage, the

cooperation of the industry . . . Neither the Commission nor the industry can allow a disagreement to lead to a breakdown in the lines of communication or to a failure of cooperation in other tasks.

Cohen's appointment as chairman beginning in August 1964 was greeted, several newspapers reported, with "jubilation" by the SEC staff. He was the first staff member to rise through the ranks to the chairmanship in close to thirty years. Cohen reciprocated the staff's loyalty. He never forgot Chairman Demmler's politically motivated dismissal of SEC general counsel Roger Foster in 1953, and rehired the semiretired Foster to be an SEC special counsel. Determined not to mistreat the SEC's career staff, Cohen retained a few individuals in authority who he himself doubted were fully equal to their responsibilities. Arthur Mathews recalled, "Cohen was the last guy to bring in an 'outsider.'" As with the New Deal's SEC and Cary's Commission, Cohen encouraged "staff freedom." In discussions, rank was rarely claimed. Members of the staff could knock on a commissioner's door, walk in, and present a new idea.

At the same time as in-house "intellectual insubordination" was favored as essential to agency creativity, Cohen strove to be a "consensus-maker" among the SEC's commissioners so that he could present a united front to the public. Consensus leadership inevitably depoliticized the Commission, reduced personality conflicts, and emphasized areas of SEC technical competence, but it also tended to slow and compromise SEC initiatives and too often led to the belief that it was important to "do something" in a problem area rather than achieve a specific type of reform. The most notable failures of Cohen's chairmanship, such as the hodgepodge proposals in the 1966 mutual fund report or the long delay before the commission-rate cluster of issues was effectively addressed, to some degree were the consequence of Cohen's determination to achieve Commission unanimity.

As with most in the Commission's senior staff, Cohen had a Landisian faith in the SEC's regulatory expertise and jealously guarded the Commission's jurisdiction. As chairman, he frequently voiced his concern that a purely antitrust approach to the structure of the securities industry might remove an SEC responsibility to federal courts less familiar with securities regulation.

Cohen's greatest strength as chairman was his capacity to lead the SEC through a period of substantial policy change. As with his onetime fellow staff member Louis Loss, who wrote the first comprehensive securities regulation treatise while serving as the SEC's associate general counsel during the Commission's somnolent Truman administration period, Cohen made an extensive study of corporation and securities laws during his years as a senior SEC staff member. After winning a Rockefeller Public Service Award in 1956, which allowed him to spend a year studying the securities markets of Europe, Cohen also became an avid student of comparative corporate and securities laws.

In his first address as chairman to the Investment Bankers Association, in December 1964, Cohen obliquely signified his determination to change the SEC's "future direction," implying his conviction that "the abuses of years gone by — the pools, the manipulators — were of the grossest and most obvious sort" and now should be replaced as SEC priorities by the challenges of a fundamentally changed securities industry: automation, inter-securities market competition, commission-rate levels, and institutional investors, particularly the enormous growth of the mutual fund industry. Although Cohen continued to emphasize his concern that securities regulation "can be accomplished within the present framework of the industry and established controls, without drastic upheavals," his chairmanship, in essence, became a monument to the practical limitations of his preferred "evolutionary approach."[8] In each of the principal policy issues that Cohen's SEC addressed — mutual fund reform, the restructuring of the securities markets, the 1960s' conglomerate merger wave — he came to believe, as he stated during the last months of his chairmanship, that "Wall Street must change with the times and it rarely moves toward reform unless it is pushed." Constrained by a conservative majority throughout all four and a half years he led the SEC, Cohen added, "I sometimes wonder whether we have pushed hard enough."[9] He made the same point more forcefully after he left the SEC, during a 1971 debate with economist George Stigler. "The most prominent current weaknesses of the securities industry," Cohen said, "can be attributed not to excessive regulation but to a failure of regulation." Instead of disclosure, occasional fraud actions, and consultation with industry, Cohen now emphasized "the infusion of competition [as] one of the principal reasons for the success of regulation of the securities industry," a regulatory tool necessary to remove "arbitrary impediments to fair and free markets."[10] Cohen's disposition late in his career to use government power to create "fair and free markets" was conveyed most memorably in his October 1968 response to presidential candidate Richard Nixon's criticism that the SEC had been engaged in "heavy-handed bureaucratic regulatory schemes." "Regulation," insisted Cohen, "is not a dirty word. We should not be ashamed to regulate."[11]

Cohen's progress from a "lawyer's lawyer" and advocate of "cooperative regulation" to a votary of securities industry competition and regulatory activism crudely paralleled the SEC's institutional redirection during the 1960s. But the SEC as an institution changed less than did its chairman. The commissioners who led the SEC in the 1964–1969 period were unwilling fully to support Cohen's priorities or his attempts to increase competition in the mutual fund industry and securities markets. As a consequence, Cohen's SEC, in general, progressed slowly, occasionally was unable to explain clearly its regulatory proposals, and left Cohen personally at the conclusion of his chairmanship with the conviction that "in so many ways, we have just begun."[12] This was also an appropriate historical judgment. The revitalization of securities regulation initiated by Cary and the Special Study and furthered by Cohen was not completed during Cohen's chairmanship, and in such important areas as restructuring the securities markets, commission-rate reform, improvement of accounting standards, and SEC regulation of corporate misconduct had "just begun."

*   *   *

Cohen's long experience at the SEC enabled him to rapidly take steps to strengthen the SEC's enforcement program. During the Truman and Eisenhower administrations, the enforcement program of the home office of the SEC's Trading and Exchanges Division had been minimal, generating a total of fifty cases during the 1950s. In large measure, the program was "a paper-pushing outfit," recalled future Enforcement Division director Stanley Sporkin, whose function was to process requests from the regional offices for formal investigations and answer investors' complaint letters. With the regional offices understaffed and their enforcement efforts focused on local broker-dealer practices and the illegal sale of new securities, the SEC during much of the Eisenhower administration essentially had no enforcement program to prevent corporate executives, mutual fund advisers and officers, or stock exchange floor members from engaging in securities fraud.

There was one exception to the SEC's generally deficient home office enforcement program staff. His name was Edward Jaegerman. During the New Deal, apparently at William Douglas's behest,*

---

* Jaegerman studied under Douglas at Yale Law School. Enforcement attorney Arthur Mathews recalled when he interviewed Justice Douglas in connection with the SEC's 1969 civil injunctive action against the Parvin Dohrmann Company, Douglas began the interview with his own question: "How are my boys, Jaegerman and Callahan?"

Jaegerman and his fellow Yale graduate Tim Callahan had been assigned what *Fortune* aptly termed "a roving commission" to investigate securities fraud anywhere in the country. Callahan later worked out of the SEC's New York City regional office, while the peripatetic Jaegerman, at least nominally, remained attached to the Commission's home office, where he was considered the SEC's finest investigator.

The resuscitation of the Trading and Exchanges Division's home office enforcement program began during the Gadsby and Cary chairmanships. The 1950s' revival of the boiler rooms had increased SEC concern about its enforcement efforts, but there was still, Ralph Saul noted when he began at the SEC in 1958 as associate director of the Trading and Exchanges Division, a sense that the "exchanges were off limits. There was a feeling you just didn't touch the heartland of Wall Street." Saul and Trading and Exchanges Division director Philip Loomis were responsible for ending this self-imposed restraint. Soon after Saul began at the Commission, Jaegerman requested permission to investigate American Stock Exchange specialists Gerard A. and Gerard F. Re. Saul encouraged the investigation and assigned Ira Pearce to help Jaegerman do the legwork. As described in Chapter 10, Chairman Cary broadened the SEC's investigation of the Res into a wider study of the American Stock Exchange, which focused on the Amex's leading specialist firm, Gilligan, Will, and the exchange's specialist-dominated leadership.

The 1961 SEC action expelling the Res also convinced Chairman Cary, Stanley Sporkin recalled, that "the Commission needed a home office pre-emptive strike capability." Later in 1961, Cary transferred Assistant General Counsel Irving Pollack, then the SEC's expert in developing securities fraud cases for referral to the Justice Department for criminal prosecution, to the Trading and Exchanges Division to be its associate director and rebuild the home office's enforcement program. Pollack brought in Thomas Rae from the SEC's Los Angeles regional office to be a top assistant and hired approximately twenty other attorneys by the time the Special Study ended. He then further augmented the Trading and Exchanges Division enforcement staff by persuading Ira Pearce to return and by recruiting Stanley Sporkin. During the three years of Cary's chairmanship, the home office of the Trading and Exchanges Division initiated approximately as many cases as it had in the previous twenty-six years of the SEC's existence, averaging forty new cases per year as compared with the 1950s' annual average of five.

Manuel Cohen promoted the expansion of the home office enforcement program of what was by then named the Trading and Markets Division. From the beginning of his chairmanship, Cohen encouraged enforcement actions to expand the potential targets of SEC civil litigation and the interpretive contours of the securities laws. The most significant action, *SEC* v. *Texas Gulf Sulphur*, was filed in 1965. *Texas Gulf Sulphur* was the first major postwar case brought against officers and directors of a large business corporation for fraudulent insider trading on a securities market. The SEC's action against Texas Gulf Sulphur resulted in a landmark 1968 Second Circuit Court of Appeals decision that sustained the SEC's factual allegations that several Texas Gulf Sulphur Company directors, officers, and employees had violated Rule 10b-5 by purchasing stock and stock options without disclosing their knowledge of an extraordinary mineral discovery in Timmins, Ontario. The Second Circuit's decision was doctrinally significant for its definition of when information was "material," its application of the *Cady, Roberts* rule that a corporate insider possessing nonpublic material information about his corporation could not buy or sell corporate securities until the information becomes public, and its comment that "tippees" or outsiders receiving nonpublic material inside information also could be held liable if they purchased a security before the nonpublic information was disseminated. Enforcement attorney Arthur Mathews recalled, "The Commission seized this comment as an opportunity to extend insider-trading sanctions to these outside beneficiaries of the information by filing a broker-dealer disciplinary action on this theory just thirteen days after publication of the *Texas Gulf* decision." The SEC soon established a precedent for the rule that "tippees" could be held liable by securing a consent judgment against Merrill Lynch, Pierce, Fenner and Smith, then the nation's largest commission brokerage firm.

Similar doctrinal ingenuity was employed by the Cohen Commission in its 1966 action, *SEC* v. *VTR, Inc.*, with which the Commission began a long series of civil cases obtaining ancillary relief, rather than merely an injunction against further misconduct, by persuading a federal district court to approve the appointment of independent directors, and the restitution of approximately $1.2 million. Five years later, the SEC's action against Texas Gulf Sulphur would culminate in a similar restitution proceeding requiring the company's officers and directors who profited from their insider advance knowledge of the Ontario mineral strike to "disgorge" their profits for the benefit of the defrauded securities sellers.

By the end of the Cohen chairmanship, the enforcement program of the home office of the SEC's Trading and Markets Division had grown to a staff of over a hundred people. The program continued to initiate an average of forty new cases a year during the 1965–1969 period, and also played a role in developing an increased number of criminal prosecutions under the securities laws. Largely because of Cohen's role in providing the staff and doctrinal support for the SEC's enforcement efforts, Stanley Sporkin would describe the Cohen chairmanship as "truly the Golden Age of the Commission." From the point of view of the SEC's Enforcement Division this was an appropriate judgment.[13]

* * *

Inevitably, reform of the mutual fund industry was the SEC's legislative priority during Cohen's chairmanship. Between 1940, when the Investment Company Act was adopted, and 1966, mutual fund net assets had increased from $450 million to $38.2 billion, growing from a minority 21 percent share of the total investment company industry to a predominant 83 percent share. At the same time, the number of mutual fund investors had increased twelvefold, from approximately 300,000 investors in 1940 to more than 3.5 million in 1965. By the mid-1960s, the funds had become a matter of widespread controversy. Discarding historically cautious investment approaches, fund managers, led by the much-publicized Gerald Tsai, throughout the 1960s emphasized "performance" by concentrating their investment portfolios in growth stocks rather than in "balanced" portfolios. In the early 1960s, Tsai popularized a new style of institutional investment management, emphasizing quick turnover of large blocks of securities. The new performance-oriented approach was widely emulated; the Investment Company Institute calculated that an average mutual fund turned over 13 percent of its common stock holdings in 1953 and 17.6 percent in 1960, but turnover reached 46.6 percent in 1968 and 55.6 percent during the second quarter of 1969.[14] The "cult of performance" raised questions about the riskiness of mutual funds and about the impact of their large-block transactions on the securities exchanges. Off-shore fund holding companies, like Bernard Cornfeld's Fund of Funds, suggested a less profound inquiry: Were foreign-based mutual fund holding companies being employed as vehicles for tax evasion? It was difficult to understand why United States citizens would pay double the notoriously high sales loads of domestic mutual funds but for the italicized enticement of the Fund of Funds' prospectus: *"The names and addresses of all investors are held in strictest confidences at all times."*[15]

That the SEC did not develop legislative recommendations

concerning mutual funds until December 1966 was a matter of considerable embarrassment at the Commission.[16] In 1958, the SEC had commissioned the University of Pennsylvania's Wharton School of Finance and Commerce to prepare a study of the implications of the mutual funds' growth. This was the only research study of any consequence initiated by the SEC during the Eisenhower period. A 1960 address by Commission chairman Edward Gadsby underlined the agency's concern. Speaking at a time when approximately fifty lawsuits had been instituted against eighteen registered investment companies, alleging that their management fees were excessive, Gadsby described the typical management of mutual funds by outside investment advisers as an "anomaly" that resulted in "what might be termed monopoly prices," which raised questions about "whether mutual funds have become captives of particular advisers, and whether directors of or investment advisers to the funds are fully acquitting their duty to shareholders."

SEC concern about mutual fund costs intensified during Cary's chairmanship. Between 1961 and 1963, most of the mutual fund shareholder suits alleging excessive advisory fees were settled out of court. The three fully litigated cases held that shareholders failed to prove the fees excessive, since the controlling "waste" doctrine authorized courts to intervene only when remuneration was "unconscionable" or "shocking."[17]

In 1961, Chairman Cary requested Joseph Weiner, then acting as a consultant to the Commission, to prepare a study of "The Administration of the Investment Company Act." Weiner's study, one of a series he made on the securities laws, was not published but was widely circulated within the Commission. Weiner concurred with the "sagacious words" of Gadsby's 1960 address, setting forth an argument that would be repeated in several published SEC reports and statements during the next decade:

> Unlike any other form of business enterprise, [mutual funds] are not managed by their nominal managers but by investment advisers. The typical compensation is a percentage of the assets of the investment company, ordinarily at the rate of ½ of 1 percent per annum. This of course means that any purchase of [mutual fund shares] . . . automatically results in an increase in the advisory fee. With the long-continued bull market and the increasing success of mutual fund salesmen the advisory fees have grown to astronomical proportions.
>
> The result of this has been that in the large funds today the fees paid to investment advisers have no substantial relation to the cost of performance of the service or to its results, they do not reflect the

economies of scale, and are obviously not the product of arm's-length bargaining. They sometimes resemble a toll levied on the investment company as a result of the strategic position occupied by the investment adviser.[18]

Weiner further reported that the marketing of mutual funds presented problems "fully as acute" as the "exaction of monopoly prices" by mutual fund advisers. "Under the present typical method of compensating the investment adviser any increase in the number of outstanding shares automatically increases the advisory fee. This creates a great incentive to secure increased sales." Since mutual funds usually were "sold" by salesmen, not "bought" by unsolicited investors, the sales load paid on mutual fund shares had increased during the 1950s as rival funds had competed to *increase* commission rates "to have the salesmen push their product in preference to the products of others." As the SEC's 1966 *Report on Investment Company Growth* would put it, "Faced with the choice of appealing to price-conscious investors or to compensation-conscious fund retailers, most load fund underwriters have followed the latter course." This was in marked contrast to the usual workings of the competitive process, in which rival sellers sought to increase sales by *reducing* their price. Weiner was particularly critical of the front-end load on periodic payment plan mutual funds, the most extreme type of what Manuel Cohen later would call "this perverse" form of competition. Under the Investment Company Act of 1940, up to one half of the payments made in the first year of a periodic payment plan purchase of a mutual fund typically running ten years could be deducted for the salesman's commission. Weiner wrote that although this "creates a strong incentive for the salesman . . . it produces obvious hardship for persons who discontinue the plan in early years." Since "it is difficult for the type of purchaser who is the usual prospect for these sales to comprehend the consequences of the contractual arrangement," Weiner recommended that the "front-end sales load" be abolished by legislation requiring that sales commissions be spread uniformly over the life of periodic payment plans.[19]

In 1962, the SEC published the Wharton School's *Study of Mutual Funds*. Although the Wharton School study made no legislative recommendations, its factual findings suggested the need for fundamental reforms. The most publicized finding of the Wharton study was that for the 1952–1958 period the average performance of mutual funds did not differ appreciably from what would have been achieved by a randomly assembled portfolio of securities with the same division among asset types.*[20] The Wharton study found no significant relation between the rates of management fees and performance results nor between the initial sales charges and performance results.

Like Weiner's earlier memorandum, the Wharton study concluded that "the most important current problems" of the funds largely appeared to "involve potential conflicts of interest between fund management and shareholders" and "the possible absence of arm's-length bargaining between fund management and investment advisers." The study found that almost all funds were controlled by their investment advisers, who typically organized the fund and entered a contract with it before shares were sold to the public. Under the Investment Company Act, no more than 60 percent of a mutual fund's board of directors could be affiliated with the investment adviser. But the requirement of the act that 40 percent of the directors be unaffiliated had proven ineffectual, since "the term 'affiliated' was narrowly defined in the act of 1940 and does not necessarily bar from this category close personal friends, relatives, or business associates."

Testimony concerning the extent to which investment advisers dominated mutual fund directors would be offered five years later, when Manuel Cohen noted that in the entire history of the mutual fund industry, "with one possible minor exception," the directors of a mutual fund had never "dislodged an adviser who was willing and able to continue." The wide dispersion of mutual fund shareholdings, redemption privileges, the lack of sophistication of many fund investors, and the interest of investors in acquiring the services of a specific investment adviser, found the Wharton study, made the voting powers of the mutual fund shareholders an equally weak restraint on investment adviser control.[22]

---

* In 1967, this result would be unscientifically corroborated by Senator Thomas McIntyre, who assembled a portfolio of common stocks by casting darts at a list of NYSE securities. In spite of selecting Industria Electria de Mexico, American Shares, a security the senator found had "an unfailing genius for declining in price," the growth of his randomly assembled portfolio from $10,000 to $25,300 during the ten-year period January 1, 1957, to December 31, 1966, compared favorably with the growth from $10,000 to $22,500 of the average common stock mutual fund and approximately equaled the slightly less than $25,000 result of the average capital growth mutual fund. While mutual funds typically charged an initial 8.5 percent sales load and 0.5 percent annual advisory fee, McIntyre observed, "The costs of managing this portfolio, amortized over a 10-year period, amount to about 29½ cents per year, to cover the initial cost of the dart, the dart board, the newspaper from which the market list was obtained and the four thumbtacks."[21]

Lack of arm's-length bargaining between mutual funds and their investment advisers led to considerably higher advisory fees than were charged other clients. Before the enactment of the 1940 Investment Company Act, Merrill Griswold, chairman of a leading internally managed investment company, had testified about the predictable results of economies of scale:

> It is now almost axiomatic in the trust business that operating costs decline proportionately as the size of a trust increases . . . Whether a company is a $1 million company, a $10 million company, or a $100 million company, it has to maintain an office, pay rent, pay for long-distance telephone calls, retain experts, clerks, stenographers, all the numerous expenses that go with it; and those expenses do not go up proportionately [as an investment company increases in size].

Griswold predicted that as investment company assets grew, proportionate costs would be reduced, "with resulting benefit to all shareholders."[23] The Wharton study, however, found there usually was no resulting benefit to shareholders. While three fourths of a sample of investment advisers for individual clients scaled their fees according to the amount of money to be managed or by negotiation, 85 percent of a second sample of investment advisers charged mutual funds a flat rate, usually 0.5 percent per annum, regardless of the size of the fund to be managed. "This was true," according to the study, "despite the fact that operating expenses of the adviser were generally lower per dollar of assets managed with increases in the size of assets under the adviser's control." In 45 percent of the examined cases of mutual fund advisers with other clients, the effective rate charged mutual funds was two or more times that charged their other clients. The Wharton School study characterized this as a consequence of the lack of competition among investment advisers to manage particular mutual funds, concluding that the "principal reason" for the difference in rates charged mutual funds and other investment adviser clients was that other clients negotiated fees and could hire a different adviser if they were dissatisfied with the level of a fee, but fees charged mutual funds "are typically fixed by essentially the same persons who receive the fees."

The advisory fee rates of mutual funds also tended substantially to exceed the management costs in the small number of internally managed mutual funds. In 1966, the SEC *Report on Investment Company Growth* would calculate that the median advisory fee of fifty-seven externally managed funds in 1965 was 0.48 percent, roughly twice the 0.25 percent estimated median management cost of eleven leading internally managed funds. Similarly, the Wharton study would find that the median pretax rate of returns for mutual fund advisers in 1958–1959 was 29.5 percent, nearly twice the median for business service corporations generally in that fiscal year. In 1965, the median pretax rate of return of the fourteen largest investment advisory organizations making public reports would equal 42.6 percent.[24]

The Wharton School and subsequent SEC staff studies further substantiated Weiner's belief that competition among mutual fund underwriters in general had raised rather than lowered mutual fund commission rates in the post–World War II period. By 1962, the typical commission or sales load on a mutual fund ran between 8 and 8.5 percent, with retail sales organizations receiving between two thirds and three fourths of the load. Of the thirty largest mutual funds in 1950 for which data were available in 1966, thirteen increased and none decreased their sales load during that sixteen-year period; eighteen of the funds increased the proportion of the sales load distributed to retail sales organizations.[25] That mutual funds usually were sold, not bought, seemed amply corroborated by the insignificance of no-load funds, which made no direct sales efforts and charged no initial commission. Although the no-load funds generally gave investors 8 to 8.5 percent greater value than load funds and on average performed as well as load funds, as of 1963, the thirty existing no-load funds accounted for a mere 3 percent of the total assets of the investment company industry.[26]

The Cary Commission's response to the Wharton study was deliberately low-keyed. Both among the staff and the commissioners, there was agreement with Chairman Cary's decision "not to push mutual fund reform until the 1964 Securities Acts Amendments were passed."[27] But the staff and the Commission were bitterly divided over the character of the SEC chairman's letter of transmittal to accompany the publication of the Wharton study. Yale law professor Frank Coker, then serving as a special consultant, urged the SEC to use its "large educational and hortatory powers" to emphasize the significance of the Wharton study's findings. Coker drafted a lengthy release calling attention to specific Wharton study findings about the size of mutual funds, sales loads, advisory fees, the lawsuits concerning fees, and other matters, arguing in a June 19, 1962, memorandum, "The appearance of the Wharton Study without active response by the Commission to the report . . . will inevitably have some effect of acquiescence in existing attitudes and patterns."* Coker was supported by Allan Conwill, director of the

---

* Tragically, Professor Coker suffered a heart attack and died while making an oral presentation of his views to the SEC on June 28, 1962.

SEC's Division of Corporate Regulation, which then regulated mutual funds.[28] Other staff leaders of the Division of Corporate Regulation, backed by Commissioner Jack Whitney, urged the Commission to accord the study minimal attention; in Whitney's words, to denominate the study "one part of an assortment of materials which will contribute to a degree not now measurable to the Commission's ultimate conclusions."[29]

Cary muted the intramural disagreement with a bland letter of transmittal that praised the Wharton study, briefly noted that it raised important questions, especially about sales practices, then diplomatically concluded:

> Although it would be premature at this time for the Commission to attempt an evaluation of the conclusions and comments in the Study, it is apparent that the Commission's rules under the 1940 Act and indeed some of the provisions of the statute itself may require reassessment. The Commission accordingly has directed its staff to undertake a detailed analysis of the Study with the view to making such recommendations as may seem appropriate.[30]

The referral of the Wharton study to staff evaluation achieved Cary's key objective, which was delaying Commission action on mutual funds until the initial legislative package evolving from the 1963 Special Securities Market Study was enacted. Yet Cary also was intent on seeing that SEC interest in mutual fund reform did not dissipate. As promised in his letter of transmittal, on September 26, 1962, the Commission ordered a staff investigation of mutual fund sales loads, advisory fees, boards of directors, and conflicts of interest to supplement the Wharton study.[31] Earlier, Cary's SEC had directed the Special Securities Market Study to investigate a few questions concerning mutual funds not addressed by the Wharton study, including the training and supervision of mutual fund sales personnel and investor experience with the front-end load on mutual fund periodic payment plans.

The *Special Study Chapter* on mutual funds, published in August 1963, concluded that "serious consideration should be given to the elimination of future front-end load plans." Contracts to buy investment company shares on a periodic payment basis were first offered to the public in 1930. By the time the SEC published its New Deal–period report *Investment Trusts and Investment Companies*, these funds' potential for exploiting unsophisticated investors was recognized. Total commission charges on completed contract plans in some cases amounted to 20 percent of the sum invested. Usually, all of the first year's payments were deducted for sales load and other charges, leaving the investor with little or no investment if shares were redeemed early. These findings prompted Congress to enact Section 27 of the Investment Company Act of 1940, limiting sales loads to 9 percent of the total proposed payments on contractual plans and prohibiting the deduction of more than 50 percent of the first year's payments for sales commissions.

In the late 1950s there recurred the widespread employment of contract plans with first-year front-end loads equal to the 50 percent statutory limit. The Special Study "conservatively estimated" that, though front-end loading had been an infrequent practice as late as 1956, by 1962 "more than one-fourth of the 2.6 million persons investing in mutual funds are doing so through contractual plans." This was treated as an alarming development. For those investors desirous of purchasing mutual funds over time, so-called voluntary plans with a uniform 8.5 percent sales load and no penalty for failure to complete a five- to twenty-five-year contract were available. By contrast, contract plans with a front-end load normally charged a 10.5 percent fee (exceeding the statutory 9 percent limit by dividing the fee into an 8.5 percent sales charge and a 2 percent custodial fee). A Special Study sample of 1437 investors' experience with contract plans over a three-and-a-half-year period, beginning in February 1959, found that one sixth of all contractual plan purchasers, as a result of redemptions and payment lapses, paid an effective commission of 50 percent of the amount they invested. An additional one-sixth paid an effective sales load in excess of 18 percent. The *Special Study* characterized as "unpersuasive" the chief industry justifications for contract plans: the "penalty" was necessary to stimulate people to regular savings habits, and the advance payment was necessary to compensate adequately sales personnel for bringing the benefits of equity investments to people of modest means. The study concluded:

> The combined factors of the incentive to high-pressure selling which the front-end load provides to salesmen, the essentially unsupervised nature of home selling of plans, the complexity of the security sold, and the lack of financial sophistication of so many of the purchasers of plans creates a problem of a fundamental nature which cannot be solved through the mere application of the doctrine of disclosure.[32]

Thus, by the time Manuel Cohen began his chairmanship in August 1964, the SEC had been studying the mutual fund industry for six years. Cohen concurred in the Wharton study's conclusion that the "conflict of interest between mutual fund managers and shareholders" inherent in the structure of the funds resulted in mutual fund shareholders "incurring excessive costs in the acquisition and management of their investments."[33] Cohen reoriented the SEC staff study of mutual funds then in progress toward the preparation of specific legislative proposals. As ultimately published in December 1966, the *Report of the Securities and Exchange Commission on the Public Policy Implications of Investment Company Growth* represented the Cohen Commission's official view on how the mutual fund industry should be reformed. More than any other study of the period, it also illustrated the fundamental intellectual conflict between the Commission's ad hoc legalistic approach to economic regulation and the competition-oriented theory of the antitrust laws. As Dr. Sidney Robbins aptly was to write of the Commission's 1966 mutual fund report, the SEC "forgot its economics."[34] Less charitably, Walter Werner, director of the Commission's Office of Policy Research during the Cary chairmanship, wrote in a 1968 *Columbia Law Review* article, "In a key area of economic regulation, which *is* the subject of its report, the SEC lacks competence: more specifically, it is incapable of evaluating developments in the investment company industry and of recommending sound change in its regulation."[35] Harsh as was Werner's judgment, it was widely shared. On the crucial resale price maintenance issue, the report's analysis was to be rejected virtually unanimously by economists, including MIT's Paul Samuelson, later a Nobel laureate, Yale's Henry Wallich, the University of Chicago's George Stigler, Irwin Friend, principal author of the 1962 *Wharton Study of Mutual Funds*, and Donald Farrar, who was to serve as director of the SEC's 1968–1971 Institutional Investor Study. In addition, the report's analysis would be rejected by President Johnson's Council of Economic Advisers, the Justice Department's Antitrust Division, and, in 1972, when, as a practical matter, it was too late, a subsequent SEC staff report.[36]

The fundamental issue in mutual fund regulation during the postwar period was the persistence of higher sales loads and advisory fees than would have occurred if there had been effective competition. Payment of an 8 to 8.5 percent sales load was irrational given the existence of no-load funds with comparable performance records. Similarly, the standard 0.5 percent annual advisory fee then was about twice the median fee that investment advisers charged individual clients or that internally managed mutual funds charged their shareholders. Yet externally managed mutual funds dominated the industry.

In large measure, the persistence of mutual fund extracompetitive costs was the result of federal laws and regulations prohibiting or

inhibiting competition. The 1933 Glass-Steagall Banking Act prohibited banks from selling shares in commingled investment accounts, which are the functional equivalent of mutual funds. Since
banks could manage commingled investment accounts without
charging an initial sales commission, these accounts represented
the major potential competitive restraint on mutual fund extracompetitive sales loads. Through 1971, the SEC did not squarely consider the wisdom of recommending an amendment to the Glass-
Steagall Act to permit banks to enter the mutual fund industry.
Instead, in 1966 the SEC authorized the First National City Bank to
register as an investment company and sell units of participation in
a commingled investment account on a no-load basis, charging the
typical mutual fund annual management fee of 0.5 percent. With
the Federal Reserve Board, the Comptroller of the Currency, and the
Federal Deposit Insurance Corporation each having ruled that the
commingled investment account did not violate the Glass-Steagall
Act, the SEC approved the bank's registration "on the assumption
that the proposal does not violate the banking laws." Five years later
the Supreme Court disagreed, holding that two sections "of the
Glass-Steagall Act appear clearly to prohibit this activity by national banks." In the ensuing decade these sections of the act have
remained unamended, preserving intact a significant shield against
mutual fund competition.[37]

The SEC itself prevented the no-load funds from paying securities
brokers a commission when they recommended no-load securities
(this, of course, would have changed no-loads into low-loads) and
strictly limited the newspaper advertisements of all mutual funds.
The combination of infrequent recommendations by stock brokers
and ineffectual advertising prevented the no-loads from effectively
competing with the sales efforts of the load funds that then dominated the mutual fund industry. Recognition of the role the SEC
itself played in inhibiting no-load sales would be reflected in a 1972
SEC staff study, which stated, of the no-loads, "Their problem is
essentially one of bringing their message to the public. If they had
the requisite information, most people would prefer to save money
by buying no-load funds rather than load funds."[38] In a 1967 statement to the United States Senate, Irwin Friend recommended that
the SEC employ its historically preferred technique of "full disclosure" to improve the competitive opportunity of the no-load funds.
This would have required the publication on the front page of the
prospectus of each mutual fund (including any sold with the typical
8 to 8.5 percent commission rate) of information "in a manner prescribed by the SEC," comparing the performance and costs of the

fund being offered with the corresponding group averages for load and no-load funds.[39]

Given the Special Study's findings about the lack of sophistication of many mutual fund investors, it is difficult to understand how any technique short of that proposed by Friend could ensure that the relatively large proportion of inexperienced investors who purchased mutual funds did so on an informed basis. But the SEC's 1966 *Report on Investment Company Growth* did not make legislative recommendations that would have enabled the no-load funds to be more competitive.

The most controversial statutory restraint on mutual fund industry competition was Section 22(d) of the 1940 Investment Company Act.[40] Section 22(d) long has been recognized as a "notable exception to the general congressional policy against price-fixing." It prohibits retail securities dealers from selling mutual funds "except at a current offering price described in the prospectus." This prevented price competition among mutual fund retailers and, in the often-echoed view of the SEC's 1966 *Report on Investment Company Growth*, was responsible "in part" [for] the failure of competition among principal underwriters to bring price benefits to mutual fund investors." The SEC's 1966 report explained:

> In a freely competitive market the load-raising effects of the vigorous competition among principal underwriters for the favor of dealers and salesmen could be restrained by countervailing downward pressures stemming from price competition among retailers for investor patronage. By precluding competition at the retail level, section 22(d) suppresses the downward pressures that normal market forces might otherwise exert.

Against this economic and regulatory background, the SEC's 1966 *Report on Investment Company Growth* must be accounted among the most poorly reasoned studies ever prepared by the Commission, striking both for its failure adequately to analyze central policy questions and for the extent to which the report's legislative recommendations were influenced by political expediency rather than the needs of investors or the theory of competition that elsewhere regulated the economy through the antitrust laws.

These deficiencies were most serious in the report's analysis of the Section 22(d) resale price maintenance issue. As SEC chairman Cohen was to testify in 1967, "It is difficult to exaggerate the significance of Section 22(d)."[41] Both SEC general counsel Philip Loomis and special counsel Richard Phillips, the two men who supervised the preparation of the Commission's 1966 *Report on Investment Company Growth*, recommended to the Commission that Section 22(d) be repealed, as did an early unpublished draft of the report.[42] Chairman Cohen obviously sympathized with the staff's recommendation. In 1967, he testified before a House Commerce Subcommittee, in words reminiscent of the earlier Senate testimony of Paul Samuelson:

> The essential question . . . becomes whether federal law should continue to insulate mutual fund sales organizations, which have probably grown oversized and inefficient . . . from . . . price competition . . . High sales loads may be of some help to the weak in the securities industry. But the general public pays a tremendous price for that help. And most of that price goes into the pockets of the largest and the most affluent securities firms who are well able to fend for themselves.[43]

Nonetheless, the SEC in 1966 did not propose the repeal of Section 22(d). Formally, the SEC 1966 *Report on Investment Company Growth* offered two explanations of the Commission's decision. First, the abolition of Section 22(d) might lead more mutual funds to distribute their securities through directly employed sales personnel rather than independent retail organizations. But unless the SEC intended to subsidize inefficient sales personnel, this was a result it presumably should have favored. Second, retail price competition would permit knowledgeable investors to achieve greater cost savings than those investors most in need of protection.[44] This argument, too, was not persuasive. "Knowledgeable" investors presumably already purchased no-load funds. If abolition of Section 22(d) alone was insufficient to lead to greater retail price competition, nothing prevented the SEC from also recommending changes in mutual fund advertising and prospectus requirements to increase the information available to potential mutual fund investors.

In public testimony, SEC officials did not emphasize these formal explanations for retaining Section 22(d). Chairman Cohen stressed:

> When the industry was informed that such a proposal had been suggested to the Commission, it went into action with a frenzy. We were deluged with protests . . .
> We were told that, for reasons never made quite clear to us, the mutual fund business was one that just couldn't stand competition; that, though investors are willing to pay today's high sales loads, they would not pay the lower sales loads that retail price competition would make available to them; that dealers would no longer bother to sell fund shares; and that the funds would be depleted by redemptions, shrivel up, and die.[45]

Although Cohen consistently stated that he considered such industry arguments "exaggerated," a majority of the Commission apparently was less confident that the industry's dire predictions were
exaggerated.

A major reason for the SEC not recommending the repeal of Section 22(d) in 1966 and 1967 thus appears to have been the failure of
the SEC's 1966 *Report on Investment Company Growth* to study
the economic implications of repeal for investors and the industry.
In 1969 testimony, Commissioner Hugh Owens offered this as a
justification for the Commission's action:

> We were apprehensive [Owens explained in response to a question
> from Senator McIntyre] that as a regulatory agency we could not tell
> you gentlemen where a repeal of 22(d) would take us. There was
> apprehension and there still is, I might add, that we don't know what
> conditions will result in the marketplace if 22(d) is repealed. We are
> told that wild-catting and price cutting will be ruinous to the indus-
> try. It well might be. We don't know the answers to those questions
> and to those possible results. It is because of that area of darkness that
> we didn't feel we had enough economic background and strength to
> come up here and recommend a repeal of this section.[46]

The conservatism and lack of economic training of some of Johnson's appointees to the Commission obviously also had some bearing on the SEC's refusal to recommend that Section 22(d) be repealed, as did the concern of some commissioners that repeal would
put a large number of small broker-dealers out of business.[47] But
Owens's apprehension was a valid one. The SEC's 1966 study discussed a fundamental reform of mutual fund sales practice without assembling any evidence on how this would affect the industry.
Lack of study of the economic consequences of repeal of Section
22(d) later also would discourage the Senate Banking Committee
from recommending abolition of the section, although the committee indicated that it otherwise had been inclined to do so.[48] When
the SEC at the Senate Banking Committee's request did make a
study of "the potential economic impact of a repeal of Section 22(d)"
in 1972, it found that repeal would lead to lower sales costs, "most
of the savings would go to small investors," the impact on the securities industry and on most retail sellers of mutual fund shares
would be "extremely modest" except on part-time sales personnel,
who represented the least efficient segment of the industry, and that
"the repeal of Section 22(d) is unlikely to lead to protracted net
redemptions on an industrywide basis." William Casey, then the
SEC chairman, wrote of the 1972 staff report, "Its findings certainly

suggest there is not compelling public interest in continued retail price maintenance in this field and that the repeal of Section 22(d) would on balance be desirable." *

This failure of the 1966 SEC *Report on Investment Company Growth* to prepare an economic analysis comparable to that prepared by the agency in 1972 well illustrated the agency's "midlife crisis." Faced with a regulatory problem that involved market structure rather than fraud, the Commission lacked the staff and the theoretical basis to develop a methodology effectively to study the problem. Instead, the 1966 SEC report group proceeded as many trial lawyers would. It assembled data comparing the 8 to 8.5 percent typical mutual fund sales load with the usually lower commission rates paid on securities purchased on an exchange, over the counter, and from a new issue. Apparently because the National Association of Securities Dealers then limited dealer spreads to 5 percent, the SEC's 1966 report recommended that the Investment Company Act be amended to provide that sales charges for mutual funds be limited to 5 percent.[50]

There were similar analytic shortcomings in the second principal recommendation of the SEC's 1966 *Report on Investment Company Growth*, that investment advisers be limited to a "reasonable" fee when managing mutual funds, taking into account the nature and extent of services, the quality of services, economies of scale, and other factors "as are appropriate and material." In the federal district courts where it was to be enforced, the SEC's "reasonableness" standard undoubtedly would have been more effective in limiting advisers to fees equal to an arm's-length bargain than the "waste" doctrine then applied by the state courts. This was a traditional lawyer's solution to the problem of compensating a monopolist. As federal Second Circuit Court of Appeals judge Henry Friendly testified to the Senate Banking Committee in 1967, "Determining whether charges or other business practices are reasonable is nothing new for courts."[51]

But neither the SEC's 1966 *Report on Investment Company Growth* nor Commission testimony adequately explained why a reasonableness standard should be preferred to the compulsory internalization of mutual fund management. In economic theory, it

---

* There was, however, no repeal. After public hearings on the issue, the SEC in 1974 chose instead to "move toward price competition on a limited basis" by amending its rules concerning advertising, allowing no-load funds to pay brokers a fee, and broadening the regulatory exceptions to Section 22. The Commission apparently was influenced by the depressed securities market at the time, which had caused net redemptions of mutual funds and the growth of the no-loads by then to a significant proportion of the industry.[49]

usually is assumed that the costs of a single firm efficiently performing a function will be less than the costs for performing a function
that includes a transaction between two firms. Savings from the
elimination of transaction costs and duplicative overhead, in fact,
had been a clear efficiency achieved by the SEC in its simplification
of public utility holding companies. That savings also could be
achieved by eliminating external advisers in the mutual fund industry was suggested by both the 1962 Wharton School and the 1966
SEC investment company studies, which found that the expenses of
the small number of existing internally managed mutual funds
tended to run about half those of the much larger number of externally managed funds. Such savings later led plaintiff's attorney Abe
Pomerantz to testify in favor of compulsory internalization of
mutual fund management:

> Why can't the Mutual Fund do what every other American corpora-
> tion does: internalize its management, i.e., hire and pay for its execu-
> tive talent? I wonder what the stockholders of General Motors would
> say if their company, for a whopping fee, farmed out its manufactur-
> ing business, its distribution business — all its business — to a cor-
> poration privately owned by its directors, leaving General Motors a
> shadow corporation. I believe a hue and cry would go up which would
> resound throughout the land. What is so different about the Mutual
> Funds to justify such a corporate abdication? After all, Massachusetts
> Investment Trust, the country's oldest mutual fund, has a built-in
> or internal advisory department, as do many other investment com-
> panies. And the record does not prove that the vastly more expensive
> external adviser has a better performance record than the internal
> one.[52]

The SEC never satisfactorily answered this question, instead arguing that its reasonableness standard was less "drastic" than compulsory internalization, more "cautious," and "genuinely conservative." Such arguments hardly constituted a substitution for an
empirical study of the practicality of compelling internalization.

Building on the earlier research of the 1963 Special Securities
Market Study, the Commission's third principal mutual fund proposal was to abolish front-end loads on contract plans through
statutory language prohibiting "the amount of sales load deducted
from any one payment [exceeding] proportionately the amount deducted from any other payment." The SEC's 1966 *Report on Investment Company Growth* also included a number of other legislative
proposals of less consequence, such as provisions to regulate off-
shore fund holding companies and to increase the "disinterestedness" and responsibilities of mutual fund directors. A bill based on

the Commission's 1966 *Report on Investment Company Growth* was introduced in Congress on May 1, 1967.[53]

Long before the SEC's bill was introduced, the mutual fund industry began assembling a lobby to defend existing practices. The lobby was unparalleled in its employment of former SEC commissioners and senior staff officials. James Landis, having left the White House staff in 1961, was employed as the chairman of the Association of Mutual Funds Plan Sponsors in 1962 to draft statements defending the front-end-load feature of contract plans. Eisenhower SEC chairman Ralph Demmler served as an attorney to the Investment Company Institute during 1967 legislative hearings. Demmler's criticism of the SEC's motives in seeking mutual fund legislation would be prominently featured in a front-page *Barron's* article entitled "Power to Destroy: That's What the SEC Is Seeking Over Mutual Funds." A second Eisenhower SEC chairman, Edward Gadsby, in 1960 a critic of investment adviser "monopoly prices," by 1968 would be a registered lobbyist for several funds. By then, also, Sidney Robbins, chief economist of the SEC's Special Study, would be an unaffiliated director of the Oppenheimer Fund and would write, with Oppenheimer Fund president Leon Levy, an adversarial article opposing the Commission's mutual fund legislative proposals.[54]

After the SEC's *Report on Investment Company Growth* was published in December 1966, the Investment Company Institute, the mutual fund industry's primary trade association, supported by the National Association of Securities Dealers, the Investment Bankers Association, and the New York Stock Exchange, employed a number of arguments to oppose the Commission's legislative proposals. It was argued that the dramatic postwar growth of the industry rebutted the need for new legislation; that other financial institutions, including banks through savings accounts, life insurance companies, and pension funds, provided ample competition to the mutual fund industry; and that the SEC's limitations on mutual fund sales loads and advisory fees, according to an NASD study, in 1966 would have caused "three out of five of our members [to operate] at a loss," most seriously hurting "small firms deriving a very large percentage of their gross income from mutual fund sales." It also was argued that the SEC's proposed limits on sales loads would harm investors, because "retail salesmen simply could not afford to seek out, inform, and educate the small investor as to the unique advantages of mutual funds." The SEC's proposal to limit sales loads to 5 percent was criticized both because it was arbitrary and because the SEC data depicting the lower comparative costs of other types of securities purchases were termed irrelevant and also unfair, since the expense of odd-lot stock purchases and sales could exceed the typical 8.5 percent mutual fund sales load. The SEC's reasonableness standard was attacked because advisory fees had declined during the 1960–1967 period and because the standard put "the Commission squarely in the rate-making business," vesting it with "inordinate power to control management fees."[55]

The most effective mutual fund industry criticisms of the SEC's legislative proposals focused on the analytical deficiencies of the Commission's 1966 *Report on Investment Company Growth.* Five days after the report was published, *The New York Times,* long the SEC's most influential journalistic ally, joined the mutual fund industry in arguing that the report had a "major defect": "The report fails to . . . provide economic justification for its demand that the initial sales load be limited to 5 percent." This inadequacy, the *Times* reported, was "the result of the SEC's orientation, which is legal, not economic." Although the *Times* subsequently would publish an editorial criticizing the mutual fund industry's lobby and state that "by and large, the SEC's package of reforms is fair and reasonable," the same editorial would repeat the *Times*'s earlier argument that the Commission "failed to provide sufficient economic justification for its proposal to reduce sales charges to 5 percent."[56] The *Times,* with its qualified support, was typical of those who later testified in favor of the SEC bill, among them the Justice Department, the Council of Economic Advisers, Paul Samuelson, Irwin Friend, Abe Pomerantz, and securities law professor Richard Jennings, each of whom directly or by implication faulted the Commission for its failure to address effectively the economics of the mutual fund industry.[57]

Even before Senate Banking Committee hearings began on the SEC's 1967 mutual fund bill, Committee chairman John Sparkman circulated a compromise proposal to the Investment Company Institute, the NASD, and the New York and American stock exchanges. In place of the SEC bill's 5 percent limit on sales charges, Sparkman asked, would the industry support a provision requiring the NASD to set reasonable mutual fund sales loads subject to SEC oversight? The provision was endorsed within a week by the NASD and both securities exchanges, with the Investment Company Institute alone insisting that no new legislation was necessary.[58] Sparkman's compromise was the first of a series of substantial alterations made by the Senate before it enacted the SEC's mutual fund bill on July 26, 1968.[59] Although the SEC's original bill had recommended the abolition of the front-end load on mutual funds purchased through a periodic payment plan, under which as much as 50 percent of the payments made by the investor during the first year could be deducted for commissions, the Senate bill limited the load to no more than 20 percent in any one year or more than 64 percent over the first four years. The Senate bill retained the SEC's reasonableness standard for assessing investment adviser fees, but added a rebuttable presumption that fees were reasonable if ratified by a majority of shareholders and disinterested directors. These Senate modifications substantially weakened the SEC's bill. Nonetheless, the Commission reluctantly supported the Senate bill, with the agency taking no official position on a fourth Senate alteration, an amendment introduced by Senator McIntyre to authorize banks to enter the mutual fund industry through their management of commingled investment accounts.[60]

However, in a highly unusual event, a 4–3 majority of the House Commerce Subcommittee on Commerce and Finance refused to report out any version of the mutual fund bill for consideration by the full Commerce Committee, and the bill died in the House in September 1968. Newspaper accounts attributed the surprise vote to the waning influence of the lame duck Johnson administration and the lobbying activities of the mutual funds, noting particularly the prominent role played by J. Edward Day, former Postmaster General, on behalf of the Association of Mutual Fund Sponsors, the trade association of the front-end-loading contractual plans.[61] Georgia Congressman W. S. (Bill) Stuckey, who led the House Commerce Subcommittee's move to bottle up the mutual fund bill, argued that the Senate bill would breed nuisance suits against the funds, grant excessive power to banks, and drive mutual fund salesmen out of business, although Stuckey "never heard any reasons" for mutual fund sales loads being reduced.[62] Further questions were raised about the mutual fund industry's lobby early in October 1968, when it was disclosed that presidential candidate Richard Nixon, until 1968 a director of the Investors Diversified Services, the largest mutual fund complex, had sent a letter to leaders of the securities industry criticizing the SEC for proposing "heavy-handed bureaucratic regulatory schemes" to impose "rate-fixing" on the "highly competitive" mutual fund industry. According to the *Wall Street Journal* and Senator McIntyre, the letter Nixon signed, in fact, had been written by an "issues committee," whose counsel, Charles Colson, then was a lobbyist for several mutual funds.[63]

After President Nixon accepted Manuel Cohen's resignation as SEC chairman in February 1969, the mutual fund bill passed by the Senate in July 1968 was further compromised before its enactment into law in December 1970. From the mutual fund industry's perspective, three compromises were of paramount importance. The 1968 Senate-passed bill would have authorized banks to operate commingled investment accounts in direct competition with mutual funds. The 1970 act dropped this provision, leaving the Glass-Steagall Banking Act as controlling law. Early in 1971, the Supreme Court held that the Glass-Steagall Act bars bank-managed commingled investment accounts.

The 1970 act also altered the reasonableness standard for appraising investment adviser fees initially recommended by the SEC and passed, with qualification, by the Senate in 1968. The Senate-passed reasonableness standard went far toward limiting advisory fees to amounts equal to an arm's-length bargain by defining "reasonable" as taking into account fees paid by other clients of an adviser, the nature and extent of services provided, and other relevant and material factors, presumably including economies of scale, the fees charged by rival investment advisers, and the management costs of internally managed funds. By contrast, the 1970 act, without definition either in the statute or congressional reports, provided that "the investment adviser of a registered investment company shall be deemed to have a fiduciary duty with respect to the receipt of compensation for services." An SEC annual report later stated that the breach of fiduciary duty standard was "equivalent in substance" to the reasonableness test. This was unclear, given the failure of Congress to define the term. The 1970 act's requirement, however, that "the plaintiff shall have the burden of proving a breach of fiduciary duty" clearly meant that the evidentiary burden of a plaintiff proceeding under the 1970 act in some instances would be greater than it would have been under the reasonableness standard of the 1968 Senate bill.

In addition, the 1970 act loosened the 1968 Senate-passed bill's front-end-load limitation. The Senate-passed bill, itself a significant compromise of the SEC's effort to abolish front-end loads on mutual fund periodic payment plans, had provided that the sales load on a contract load could be no more than 20 percent of the first year's payments or 64 percent of the first four years. The 1970 act retained this standard, but provided that the sponsors of the mutual fund alternatively could elect to sell funds with a 50 percent front-end load as long as the funds retained no more than a 15 percent commission if the securities were redeemed within the first eighteen months. This alternative meant that SEC efforts to eliminate the 50 percent front-end load possible under the 1940 Investment Company Act had been totally defeated in instances when funds chose the alternative load restriction and their shareholders did not formally redeem their shares for a year and a half.

The 1970 act did retain Senator Sparkman's compromise sales-load provision. In place of the SEC's proposed 5 percent limit on mutual fund sales loads, the act directed the NASD to prohibit its members from charging an "excessive sales load but shall allow for reasonable compensation for sales personnel, broker-dealers, and underwriters, and for reasonable sales loads to investors." The rules subsequently adopted by the NASD permitted its members to continue to charge the traditional 8.5 percent fee, except on large-volume purchases of $10,000 or more, as long as a mutual fund reinvested dividends without further fee and offered rights of accumulation.[64]

The Commission's unsatisfactory justification of its 1966–1967 legislative recommendations undoubtedly was responsible, in part, for the agency's meager 1970 statutory harvest. By failing to make a rigorous analysis of the economics of the mutual fund industry or to recommend the abolition of a pattern of price-fixing that in virtually every other industry would be prohibited by the antitrust laws, the SEC was vulnerable to industry charges of performing inadequate research, and received only qualified support from other agencies of the Johnson administration. The full significance of the SEC's ad hoc approach to mutual fund legislation became clear beginning in 1969. Despite candidate Richard Nixon's attack on the SEC's "heavy-handed bureaucratic regulatory schemes," the Nixon administration's Justice Department consistently testified in favor of the repeal of the Investment Company Act's resale price maintenance provision, a reform potentially more far-reaching in its cost savings for investors than the SEC's initial proposed 5 percent sales-load limit.[65] The political lesson was plain. SEC reform initiatives that relied on marketplace competition to protect investors were far more likely to command bipartisan support from liberal consumer-minded members of Congress and conservative exponents of "free enterprise" than direct agency rate regulation. In the Johnson and Nixon administrations, this was a lesson the Commission's leadership reluctantly, but inevitably, assimilated.

* * *

No issue did more to bring into question the historic reputation of the SEC as "an outstanding example of the independent commission at its best" than the Commission's handling of a related cluster of stock exchange commission-rate and membership rules in the 1963–1973 period.

To Paul Samuelson, the SEC's historic indifference to efficient competition in the securities industry was "sad, if not scandalous."[66] The University of California's Lawrence Shepard in an often-cited book, *The Securities Brokerage Industry*, would make the more extreme point that in commission-rate regulation the SEC had performed like a captive agency, "championing [the interest of] the regulated," permitting "noncompetitive pricing and entry practices [to] flourish" under the Commission's regulatory umbrella.[67] So "timid a watchdog" did journalist Louis Kohlmeier believe the SEC in mutual fund and commission-rate regulation that he urged in his 1969 book, *The Regulators*, that the Commission be "abolished as it now exists."[68]

As with the mutual fund industry during the Cohen chairmanship, the principal regulatory problems concerning stock exchange commission rates involved economic, not antifraud, regulation. Also, as in the mutual fund field, the SEC's investigation of stock exchange commission rates was dilatory, its fact-finding initially partial and inadequate. But, as distinguished from the SEC's lengthy evasion of the fundamental economic issues in the mutual fund field, in the last year of Cohen's chairmanship the SEC did set in motion an investigatory process that eventually led to a fundamental restructuring of the securities exchanges, including the total abolition of fixed commission rates in 1975. This result was, in part, the consequence of pressure brought by Congress, the Department of Justice, and private parties on the SEC to assume the responsibility of creating competition in the securities markets. The political pressures were effective because of uncertainty after the Supreme Court's 1963 *Silver* v. *New York Stock Exchange* decision, about the extent to which stock exchange price-fixing and exclusionary membership rules were permissible under the antitrust laws.

The Cohen SEC's early passive approach to commission-rate issues was publicly announced late in 1964.* Earlier that year the New York Stock Exchange's Committee on Costs and Revenues informally had indicated to the SEC's staff "its present thinking" that a "modest increase" in the Exchange's commission rates "might be necessary."[70] The SEC treated the Exchange committee's discussion with the staff as an occasion to communicate its policy toward review of the group of questions about commission rates raised by the Special Study. On November 23, 1964, the *SEC Minutes* relate "it was the sense of the meeting" that the SEC would not consider changes in commission rates until the Exchange's Board of Governors presented "definitive proposals, and documented arguments in support thereof." In other words, rather than the Cohen

---

* Between 1964 and 1966, the Cohen SEC, however, did study and require the NYSE to change the differential paid by odd-lot investors.[69]

SEC making a comprehensive study of commission rates on its own initiative, it limited its role to reviewing New York Stock Exchange proposals to change the existing commission-rate schedule. Chairman Cohen explained this approach in a December 1, 1964, address to the Investment Bankers Association: "The Commission must satisfy its statutory responsibility to see that *any changes* in the structure or level of rates or charges have a rational basis and are consistent with the needs of the public. We will expect full documentation of *any proposals* so that we will be able to exercise that statutory responsibility" (italics added).[71] This was the minimum role the SEC could perform in the commission-rate area. Taking its cue from such communications, the Exchange indicated in April 1965 that it had "shelved" its proposed commission-rate increase.[72] In the immediate aftermath of that decision, the SEC largely limited its initiatives concerning commission rates to periodic discussions with the Exchange and attempts to revise the broker-dealers' income and expense report form.[73] When Exchange president Funston "was quite vehement in his opposition" at an October 29, 1965, SEC-Exchange conference, the SEC dropped consideration "of the possible necessity of a public hearing" on the Exchange's commission-rate structure.[74] Mounting political pressures on the Commission forced the SEC to discard this minimalist approach toward commission-rate issues two and a half years later.

The statutory basis for these political pressures was Section 19(b) of the 1934 Securities Exchange Act, which empowered the SEC "to alter or supplement" registered stock exchange rules when "necessary or appropriate for the protection of investors or to insure fair dealing" with respect to thirteen categories of exchange rules, including "the fixing of reasonable rates of commission." By its plain language, Section 19(b) did not expressly exempt exchange commission rates from the anti-price-fixing rules of the antitrust laws. Nor did congressional debate, congressional reports, or testimony in 1934 decisively indicate whether an antitrust exemption was to be implied or how the Securities Exchange Act was to be harmonized with the antitrust laws.[75]

The Supreme Court first faced the issue in 1963, when it decided the case of *Silver* v. *New York Stock Exchange*.[76] Harold J. Silver was not a member of the New York Stock Exchange. In June 1958, Silver had established Municipal Securities, Incorporated, in Dallas, Texas, to trade municipal and corporate securities. In that year, he was granted "temporary approval" by the NYSE to install direct private telephone wires to ten member firms of the Exchange, as well as a direct teletype connection to one member firm and a stock ticker service that came directly from the Exchange itself. In February 1959, without any explanation, the New York Stock Exchange ordered the member firms to discontinue all wire and teletype communications with Silver, and simultaneously withdrew its own stock ticker service. As a practical matter, these steps effectively put Silver's Municipal Securities, Incorporated, out of business. Since the actions of the Exchange and its member firms were what is called in antitrust law a group boycott or concerted refusal to deal, the Supreme Court held, "It is plain, to begin with, that removal of the wires by collective action of the Exchange and its members would, had it occurred in a context free from other federal regulation, constitute a *per se* violation of Section 1 of the Sherman [Antitrust] Act." Nor, in these circumstances, was the Court willing to grant the New York Stock Exchange immunity from liability by implying an antitrust exemption:

> The Securities Exchange Act contains no express exemption from the antitrust laws or, for that matter, from any other statute. This means that any repealer of the antitrust laws must be discerned as a matter of implication, and "it is a cardinal principle of construction that repeals by implication are not favored." Repeal is to be regarded as implied only if necessary to make the Securities Exchange Act work, and even then only to the minimum extent necessary.

Justice Arthur Goldberg added, "The antitrust laws are peculiarly appropriate as a check upon anticompetitive acts of exchanges which conflict with their duty to keep their operations and those of their members honest and viable . . . Denial of their applicability would defeat the Congressional policy [of ensuring competitive freedom] reflected in the antitrust laws without serving the policy of the Securities Exchange Act." The Supreme Court in *Silver* held that an anticompetitive act of a stock exchange could be implicitly exempt from the antitrust laws only when it both was "within the scope and purposes of the Securities Exchange Act" and either subject to direct SEC review or observed such procedural safeguards as the notice, explanation, and fair hearing the Court held that the Exchange should have afforded Harold Silver before effectively destroying his business.

Concerned that the *Silver* decision might inhibit "vigorous performance by the exchanges of their self-regulatory responsibilities," Chairman Cary indicated in a letter of transmittal accompanying the *Special Study* that "legislation may be required . . . to avoid any possible problems."[77] In a July 1965 letter to Senate Banking Committee chairman A. Willis Robertson, Chairman Cohen went further and suggested that the exchanges be accorded a full antitrust immunity in areas subject to SEC review.

Cohen explained that his concern, like Cary's, was that the threat of antitrust prosecution would discourage the securities exchanges from performing their self-regulatory functions in preventing securities fraud.[78] Nonetheless, his suggestion that the exchanges receive a statutory exemption from the antitrust laws in areas subject to SEC review was emphatically rejected by Congressman Emanuel Celler and Senator Philip Hart, the chairmen respectively of the House and Senate Antitrust subcommittees, with both underlining their preference for the "application of established antitrust policies" to the stock markets.[79]

After *Silver*, several other private litigants challenged the securities exchanges, employing the antitrust laws. The first case directly to attack the New York Stock Exchange fixed-commission-rate structure was *Kaplan* v. *Lehman*,[80] decided by a federal district court in February 1966. The plaintiff, apparently prompted by a desire to avoid the considerable expense of fact discovery, urged that all fixed commission rates established by the New York Stock Exchange be declared illegal per se. Since the Securities Exchange Act allowed securities exchanges to fix rates if the SEC in its supervisory role found the rates to be "reasonable," the suit was almost frivolous in its legal theory and was summarily dismissed by District Court judge Julius Hoffman. There might have been a far different result had the plaintiff challenged the particular commission-rate schedule then being enforced as unreasonable; for example, because it failed to provide a volume discount even though the cost of a large-volume transaction was less per share than a small-volume transaction. In January 1967, a court of appeals affirmed the dismissal of Kaplan's case and the Supreme Court declined to review the appeals court decision later that year. Chief Justice Warren dissented from the Court's decision not to review the appeals court decision in *Kaplan* v. *Lehman* because of his reluctance to see the important question of "the compatibility of the Exchange's rate-fixing practice with this nation's commitment, embodied in the antitrust laws, to competitive pricing . . . lie where it has aimlessly fallen by virtue of the scanty opinion below." Warren seemed to sympathize with the petitioner's contention "that for many reasons the possibility of SEC review is an insufficient substitute for application of the antitrust laws":

> For example, the SEC's review of rates is discretionary. Further, the regulatory scheme fails specifically to enjoin the SEC, in determining

what rates are reasonable, to "enforce the competitive standard" . . . [but also] neither the SEC nor the Exchange has ever articulated any standard of reasonableness. Petitioners also claim that the underlying data used by the SEC in reviewing each of the five rate increases since 1934 have been essentially those supplied by the Exchange, and have been very limited in scope and content. Finally, they claim that if and when the SEC exercises its discretion to review rates, it is not required to hold a hearing, and because the matter is committed to the SEC's discretion, there is no effective judicial remedy to require it to initiate a rate proceeding.

Warren's dissent was treated by the SEC like a warning from the Supreme Court. Two weeks after it was published Chairman Cohen informed the Investment Bankers Association, in November 1967, that the commission-rate issue had been "tossed squarely back to the exchanges and to us by the courts in the *Kaplan* case," requiring the SEC "to re-examine promptly the propriety of a commission structure which demands a level of charges so high that the brokers who receive them are continually straining their ingenuity to discover more and more complicated methods of giving them away to meet the requests of professional managers of certain institutional investors." Cohen added, "I hope that by the time you convene again next year, there will have been substantial changes in the basic commission-rate structure and in related rules of the securities exchanges. A substantial part of our time over the next year will necessarily be devoted to this endeavor."[81]

An even more significant antitrust challenge to the rules of the New York Stock Exchange had begun in December 1964, when non-Exchange member Morris Schapiro indicated to the SEC his intention to file a lawsuit contesting New York Stock Exchange Rule 394.[82] At that time, Rule 394 read in its entirety, "Except as otherwise specifically exempted by the Exchange, members and member organizations must obtain the permission of the Exchange before effecting a transaction in a listed stock off the Exchange, either as principal or agent." Government and corporate bonds generally were exempt from the rule, as was a list of "high-grade preferred stocks." But Rule 394, as then interpreted, prohibited a member of the Exchange from buying or selling nearly all Exchange-listed common stocks in the over-the-counter market even if an over-the-counter dealer could provide a better price or lower transaction costs. Under the *Silver* case's holding that the rules of the New York Stock Exchange were to be considered implicitly exempt from the antitrust laws "only if necessary to make the Securities Exchange Act work, and even then only to the minimum extent necessary," it was doubtful whether Rule 394 could have survived an antitrust challenge before the Warren Supreme Court. A 1965 SEC staff study of Rule 394 found that a principal effect of the rule was to minimize competition between New York Stock Exchange specialists trading listed stocks and over-the-counter (then popularly called third-market) dealers making competitive markets in the same securities. The SEC staff study found that the minimization of competition between market-makers tended to raise investor costs both because the rule eliminated competitive third-market dealers, to whom New York Stock Exchange members could turn when they quoted better prices than the Exchange specialist, and because it generally resulted in an Exchange member receiving two commissions rather than one when he acted as an intermediary in a transaction between a nonmember public customer and a nonmember dealer or financial institution.

Rule 394 also raised questions under the Securities Exchange Act. The rule minimized the extent to which Exchange members could benefit from the capital of nonmembers in executing large-volume transactions. This was a particularly serious question during a period of increased institutional large-block transactions. Merrill Lynch's senior executives would report to Eugene Rotberg, the report's principal author, "It was becoming increasingly difficult for the Exchange floor to absorb the orders." Further, the rule appeared to require an Exchange member to violate his fiduciary duty under the securities laws "to get the best price for his client," a duty the SEC had ruled as long ago as 1936 applied to members of an exchange, "even though that price is only obtainable off the floor of the exchange."[83]

The history of Rule 394 strongly suggested that the rule was not "necessary to make the Securities Exchange Act work." In 1939, the New York Stock Exchange's Board of Governors became concerned about trading by its members on regional exchanges and appointed a committee to determine whether these members were in violation of Article XVI of the Exchange's constitution, which forbade a member to "deal publicly outside the Exchange in securities dealt in on the Exchange." The following year, as related in the discussion of the *Multiple Trading* case in Chapter 7, the Exchange announced it would begin to enforce Article XVI against members who traded listed securities on a regional market. The SEC requested in December 1940 that the Exchange reverse itself and make clear that neither its rules nor their enforcement would "prevent any member from . . . dealing upon any other exchange." The Exchange refused. In October 1941, the SEC ordered the New York Stock Exchange to amend

Article XVI of its constitution to state "Nothing herein contained shall be construed to prohibit any member . . . from . . . dealing . . . *on another exchange.*" Presumably, the same SEC which issued that opinion prohibiting the New York Stock Exchange from enforcing rules to prevent its members from trading Exchange-listed securities on a regional exchange also would have prohibited the NYSE from enforcing Rule 394 to prevent its members from trading Exchange-listed securities over the counter. For the SEC's 1941 *Multiple Trading* opinion concluded,

> At best, the Rule is an attempt by the NYSE to implement its minimum commission rule. Whether or not that object might be justifiable, we are of the opinion that it cannot properly be achieved by measures such as this Rule which, as we have previously pointed out, would seriously impede the functioning of important instrumentalities of interstate commerce, would unreasonably restrain interstate commerce and would have other undesirable consequences.[84]

But the issue of Exchange members' trading Exchange-listed securities over the counter was not before the SEC in 1941, and the Commission's 1941 opinion was silent on the subject.

Exchange members' trading of Exchange-listed securities over the counter first became a concern to the New York Stock Exchange in May 1948, when Blyth & Company circulated a letter to Exchange members stating that it had begun to make an over-the-counter market in fifteen listed stocks, including such market leaders as American Telephone and General Motors. At that time, the New York Stock Exchange constitution required that an Exchange member obtain the approval of the Exchange "before effecting a transaction in a listed stock [over the counter]." The same requirement was expressed in the 1948 Member Firm Circular No. 52, part of which was denominated Rule 394 in 1957. Approval to trade over the counter initially was given liberally whenever the off-the-Exchange price was better or if a customer directed an off-board trade. The SEC 1965 staff study of Rule 394 found in the June 1948–May 1949 period that "705 requests for approval for off-board trades were granted of 857 applications received."

During the next fifteen years the Exchange, without changing the text of Rule 394, radically changed its interpretation. For example, in 1956, one New York Stock Exchange staff member involved in decisions to approve off-board member trades of Exchange-listed securities noted, "In view of the present attitude of the governors which looks to putting all possible trades on the floor, the staff does not approve *any* requests during trading hours, and only in exceptional cases at any other time." By the 1960–1965 period, Rule 394 generally was interpreted to prohibit Exchange members from soliciting the interests of nonmembers for an off-board trade. The 1965 SEC staff report on Rule 394 generalized, "At the present time the fact that a customer might obtain a better execution in an off-board trade is not considered to be an appropriate justification for an off-board trade . . . The early position in the 1940s that the 'customer's interest comes first' is now secondary to the interest of the Exchange in preserving the market as it is now constituted and preserving the minimum commission-rate schedule." Similarly, the report found, "Member firms almost uniformly reject the principle that they have a duty to seek out the best market for a customer if such activity involves trading off floor with a nonmember." The report stated that this "reluctance" to seek the best price for a customer on a competitive market was the result "of the member firm's experience that the Exchange would not grant permission to execute such orders off board." By the early 1960s, Rule 394 had become as effective an inhibition of securities market competition as the New Deal's SEC feared the New York Stock Exchange's 1940 policy of prohibiting members from trading Exchange-listed securities on the regional markets would have become had the SEC not intervened.

The 1963 SEC *Special Study* obliquely expressed concern. Without extended discussion of Rule 394, the study concluded its chapter on market interrelationships with the assertion that "restrictions on members doing business away from the primary market . . . may sometimes motivate other than best executions from the customers' viewpoint." More pointedly, the study declared in a footnote, "The pertinent NYSE rule does allow off-board transactions with specific permission, but where permission is sought and given under this rule it is apparently always in terms of capacity of the auction market to handle the particular business, not in terms of best executions as such," a circumstance the footnote went on to suggest violated the broker's fiduciary duty to ensure that he obtained the best price for his clients. The *Special Study* signified the import it attached to the rule by recommending, "Among the subjects that appear to need further and continuous attention . . . are . . . factors contributing to or detracting from the public's ready access to all markets and its assurance of obtaining the best execution of any particular transaction."[85]

Over-the-counter securities dealer Morris Schapiro's December 1964 threat to initiate an antitrust suit challenging Rule 394 stimulated the SEC to make its first detailed investigation of the rule. Schapiro was a politically well-connected New York City securities dealer who claimed annually to transact $78 millon of business in bank stocks with New York Stock Exchange members. After the 1964 Securities Acts Amendments required banks with stocks traded over the counter to make periodic disclosures comparable to those required for securities listed on an exchange, a number of banks, led by the Chase Manhattan, determined to list on the New York Stock Exchange. Once the bank stocks were listed, New York Stock Exchange members would be prohibited by Rule 394 from purchasing or selling these bank stocks from or to nonmember dealers like Schapiro. To avert this "potentially very costly" event, in the early fall of 1964 Schapiro attempted to persuade the New York Stock Exchange to place Chase Manhattan stock on the "exempt list" of bonds and preferred shares that were not subject to Rule 394 and could be traded off the Exchange floor by Exchange members. The Exchange officially declined Schapiro's suggestion on October 24, 1964. Six weeks later, Schapiro and his attorney, George Reycraft, paid a visit to SEC chairman Cohen to report, according to the *SEC Minutes* for December 14, 1964, that they "were considering the filing of a lawsuit against the New York Stock Exchange attacking Rule 394 of the Exchange."[86]

Also accompanying Schapiro during his December 1964 visit to Cohen was House Judiciary Committee chairman Emanuel Celler. The *SEC Minutes* made clear that Celler expressed his interest in Schapiro's case in no uncertain terms: "Chairman Celler also indicated that he had been asked, but had not decided as yet, to introduce at the next session of Congress a bill to exempt from the Securities Acts, as amended, any issuer whose deposits were guaranteed by the FDIC."* [87]

Soon after the Schapiro and Celler visit, the SEC ordered a comprehensive staff investigation of Rule 394.[89] Over the next six months, Eugene Rotberg, chief counsel of the SEC's Office of Policy Planning, directed an inquiry that took approximately two thousand pages of transcript from witnesses and, employing subpoena powers, gathered extensive documentary materials from the New York Stock Exchange and other exchanges. In September 1965, a 211-page

---

* In the next six months, Celler also urged the Justice Department's Antitrust Division to investigate Rule 394. By March 1965, New York Stock Exchange president Keith Funston would report to the SEC "that the Department of Justice had issued a civil investigative demand to the Exchange for information with respect to the Exchange's Rule 394 and its commission rates." As early as December 14, 1965, Ralph Saul, the director of the SEC's Division of Trading and Markets, informally urged Funston to reconsider Rule 394.[88]

staff report on Rule 394 was circulated within the Commission. It was endorsed by SEC general counsel Philip Loomis and SEC Division of Trading and Markets director Irving Pollack.

The fundamental issue, recognized by the report, was the future structure of the securities markets. The report began with a detailed elaboration of the New York Stock Exchange's rationale for the rule: "Exchange members state that Rule 394 is designed to preserve·and maintain the depth and liquidity of the auction market and that any fragmentation of that market by permitting orders to be executed other than on the floor of the Exchange damages the primary market." The Exchange argued that only on its floor could securities customers be assured "the fairest market . . . in which all orders are entitled to an execution based on the best price available as qualified by rules concerning precedence, parity, and priority of orders." The Exchange market also provided a specialist system to narrow the spread of bid and asked prices, which the Exchange "realistically evaluated" as required "for most, if not all securities" to maintain a central market. But, argued the Exchange, "if the specialist is required to maintain a fair and orderly market by taking positions and supplying securities where needed, he can reasonably be expected to do so if he is assured that he will see *all* the buy and sell orders entered by the public through member firms." Finally, the Exchange asserted "that its market is a regulated market." By contrast, over-the-counter trading of Exchange-listed securities occurred on "a market which does not have rules and regulations with respect to the obligations of market-makers to assure a fair and orderly market; there are no rules concerning short-selling; there is no tape print and no public reporting of transactions."

Rotberg's staff report evinced considerable respect for each of these arguments. However, on balance, the report predicted that Rule 394 would be held illegal under the *Silver* case's application of the antitrust laws to the New York Stock Exchange because:

> The existence of [other stock] markets without such restrictions as are enforced under Rule 394 and the ability of the exchanges to use alternative means to obtain the minimal self-regulatory benefits of the Rule seem to militate against its propriety. The mass of discriminatory exceptions, the relationship of the Rule to the preservation of the minimum commission rate schedule under circumstances where its rationale is questionable, the fact of its recency as a response to competition, its arbitrary method of enforcement and its conflict both with the concept of promoting competition and the fiduciary duty of the broker to the client also raise most serious questions concerning the propriety of the Rule under our anti-trust laws.

Acknowledging that Rule 394 "does contribute to the depth and liquidity of the market in the sense of bringing all orders to the floor," the Rotberg staff report offered two alternative proposals designed to maintain market depth without sacrificing competition in the securities markets. The "preferable" approach, recommended by Merrill Lynch's senior executives, involved revising the commission-rate structure to permit Exchange members to execute orders with nonmember dealers on the Exchange floor with only a single commission to be charged by the member firm. Such an approach would result in all transactions with over-the-counter dealers appearing on the Exchange tape and being subject to the Exchange's fair-dealing rules. It would also increase the dealer capital available on the Exchange floor for handling large-block trades and benefit securities customers by giving them the advantage of the over-the-counter dealers' competitive prices. Alternatively, the staff report recommended that Exchange members be allowed to buy or sell Exchange-listed securities off the floor whenever over-the-counter dealers offered a better price than the Exchange's specialist. This was considered a less preferable alternative because it did "not provide for the publicity of the tape nor is it within the formal Exchange regulatory framework." Merrill Lynch opposed this approach because its branch offices then communicated directly with the floor of the New York Stock Exchange: "As a result, it would be quite difficult for branch offices to check two or three markets in New York." Its executives also feared such a rule might increase the firm's liability to customers for failure to obtain best prices.[90]

The SEC's response to its staff's report represented the rock-bottom low point of the Cohen Commission. On November 24, 1965, a contingent of New York Stock Exchange officials, led by Exchange president Keith Funston, met with the SEC's commissioners and stated that "they cannot live with [the staff report's] proposals." Their position was generally unyielding. Although the Exchange had conducted no research or analysis of its own, the SEC conference memorandum reported that "the Exchange representatives urged that there should be no substantive revision in or exceptions to its Rule 394, lest the 'depth and strength' of the New York Stock Exchange two-way auction market be impaired, to the detriment of the investing public."[91] Subsequently, Funston would make the same point more colorfully in public, stating early in 1966, "Rule 394 is one of the pillars of the Exchange and we cannot, and will not, budge on this issue."[92]

Believing that further negotiation with the Exchange would not be fruitful, "unless we advise the Exchange of the intention to release the report," Trading and Markets Division director Pollack and his staff soon recommended that the SEC "publish the report in order to invite comments and alternative solutions."[93]

The full SEC refused to publish the report. Indeed, it was not to be made public for six years, until Morris Schapiro successfully sued the Commission to gain access to it under the Freedom of Information Act.[94] Instead, Chairman Cohen mailed President Funston a letter on December 22, 1965, inviting the Exchange to "offer alternative answers or solutions to meet and resolve the problems raised [by Rule 394]."[95] Although Cohen's letter also stated that "the Commission believes the recommendations of the staff have considerable merit," the SEC's unwillingness to impose the staff's recommendations on the Exchange was repeatedly signaled in Cohen's letter by statements that the Commission desired "to assist the Exchange" in its attempt to revise the commission-rate structure. The full significance of the December 22 letter deserves to be underscored. By neither publishing the report on Rule 394 nor placing pressure on the Exchange to accept a new pro-competitive rule, the Commission deprived Morris Schapiro, the Justice Department, or any other potential litigant of the basis for what might have been a successful antitrust lawsuit challenging Rule 394, and lessened the incentive for the Exchange to negotiate an effective new rule.

Over the next six months, the New York Stock Exchange essentially offered only one "alternative answer" to the problems identified by the SEC report on Rule 394, a new proposed Rule 397, permitting Exchange members to solicit nonmember market-makers to participate in transactions of ten thousand or more shares on the floor of the Exchange. While this rule change would have brought some additional capital to the Exchange floor for a small number of large-block transactions, it so completely ignored the competitive securities markets and best execution price issues raised by the staff report that even a conservative Commission ultimately felt it had to draw a line. On May 11, 1966, the SEC forwarded a letter to President Funston, informing him that the Exchange's proposed rule "did not adequately [meet] the problem."

After four more months of discussion, the SEC formally acceded to an Exchange proposal outlined in a letter from Keith Funston to Manuel Cohen, dated September 15, 1966.[96] The proposal, soon to be recorded as NYSE Rule 394(b), permitted an Exchange member to solicit an over-the-counter market-maker to participate in the execution of an order off the floor of the Exchange only if several conditions were satisfied, including "a diligent effort to explore the feasibility of obtaining a satisfactory execution of the order on the floor"; trading being limited to over-the-counter dealers who satisfied specified SEC capital and other requirements; and the filing of a written report concerning the transaction. The rule further required that just before the transaction was executed with the over-the-counter dealer, the Exchange member was to give the specialist and other floor brokers present a second chance to meet the over-the-counter dealer's price. At the Exchange's request, to increase the likelihood of clothing the rule with an antitrust immunity, the SEC formally directed the Exchange to adopt the new rule, officially finding it to be "necessary and in the public interest."[97]

Immediately after Rule 394(b) went into effect, the Exchange interpreted it to prohibit an Exchange member from requesting a quotation from an over-the-counter dealer before checking the Exchange specialist's price and contacting an Exchange floor governor. If an Exchange member did request a quotation from an over-the-counter dealer in advance, the Exchange disqualified the member from subsequently executing a transaction under Rule 394(b) because of failure to check the floor first. As a practical matter, this unpublicized interpretation of Rule 394(b) almost fully subverted whatever effect the rule might have had in increasing securities market competition. In the first year of the rule's operation, Morris Schapiro, for example, was to complete only one 500-share transaction under Rule 394(b). Weeden and Company, the largest third-market dealer, qualified to trade in two hundred Exchange-listed securities, similarly completed only fifty-one trades, with twenty other transactions canceled by the Exchange because of "technical violations" of the rule. In all, the SEC staff estimated in October 1967, less than 1 percent of all third-market trading occurred under Rule 394(b).[98] While the SEC's 1941 *Multiple Trading* decision had been decisive in preserving regional exchange competition with the New York Stock Exchange in Exchange-listed stocks, the SEC's 1966 Rule 394 negotiations had been almost totally ineffectual in increasing over-the-counter dealer competition in Exchange-listed securities.

* * *

Other pressures mounted on the SEC to initiate a comprehensive review of the New York Stock Exchange's commission-rate schedule. The NYSE long had restricted its membership to persons and firms who actively devoted the major portion of their time to the securities business. Until 1970, the New York Stock Exchange denied membership to any publicly held corporation. These rules were meant to prevent institutional investors and other "customers" from joining the Exchange and reducing their costs by eliminating the need to pay brokerage fees. As the percentage of securities transactions initiated by institutional investors soared during the 1960s, the Exchange's prohibition of institutional membership became another "pillar of the Exchange," nearly as important as Rule 394 in maintaining a commission-rate schedule at a higher-than-competitive level.

Beginning in 1965, the New York Stock Exchange ban on institutional membership was challenged. Early that year, a brokerage subsidiary of Waddell and Reed, the investment manager for United Funds, the nation's fourth-largest mutual fund organization, was formed for the express purpose of joining the Pacific Stock Exchange as a means of reducing brokerage costs when purchasing or selling New York Stock Exchange–listed securities dually listed on that exchange. At the time the Pacific Coast Exchange did not prohibit institutional members. Under threat of an antitrust suit, the exchange reluctantly permitted Waddell and Reed's brokerage subsidiary to join, but it hurriedly adopted an exclusionary rule denying membership to any firm or its affiliates whose shares were publicly held. The Pacific Coast Exchange's new ban on institutional members almost immediately was challenged by legal representatives of Investors Diversified Services, the nation's largest mutual fund organization, which succeeded in securing Pacific Coast Exchange membership for its own securities brokerage subsidiary, as did two other mutual fund organizations. They managed to do this before the Pacific Coast Exchange succeeded in barring additional institutional investors with a new rule barring members who were controlled by persons or firms outside the securities business. A grandfather clause permitted already admitted members controlled by mutual funds to retain their Pacific Coast Exchange membership. Although the SEC debated intervening and preventing the Pacific Coast Exchange from adopting its various rules barring future institutional members, the Commission proved too divided either to object to the exchange's rules, or, for that matter, formally to assent to them.

The institutional membership controversy was renewed late in 1967, when the faltering Philadelphia-Baltimore-Washington Stock Exchange determined actively to recruit institutional members to increase its trading volume. Within a relatively short period, fifty institutional members were generating approximately 40 percent of this minor exchange's business. The trading in New York Stock Exchange–listed securities diverted either to the Pacific Coast

Exchange or to the Philadelphia-Baltimore-Washington Stock Exchange did not measurably reduce New York Stock Exchange volume. But the existence of institutional members on these two regional exchanges was a visible reminder that the NYSE's own prohibition of institutional members might not survive an antitrust suit under the *Silver* case's rule permitting anticompetitive practices "only if necessary to make the Securities Exchange Act work, and even then only to the minimum extent necessary."[99]

Only with respect to one of the cluster of rules concerning commission rates was the Cohen Commission able to assemble a majority in favor of a significant reform. That issue was the "give-up." As explained in Chapter 10, the give-up was a device by which an institutional investor could receive an indirect form of volume discount. In its simplest form, a mutual fund would direct a New York Stock Exchange member to give up 50 to 80 percent of its commission on a large-block sale to a second Exchange member as a reward for the second member's sale of shares in the fund itself or provision to the mutual fund of other services, such as research. Since the Investment Company Act of 1940 placed a statutory maximum on the rate of commission a mutual fund could pay retail sales organizations, the give-up provided a method by which mutual funds could reward securities retailers for successfully selling their funds' securities by paying a give-up bonus on top of a regular commission. The New York Stock Exchange forbade its members to rebate commissions to nonmembers. Thus, the mutual funds' desire to use give-ups also created an incentive to trade NYSE-listed securities on a regional exchange, where give-ups could be directed to non-NYSE members who effectively sold mutual fund shares. Between 1964 and 1968, the amount of investment company–directed give-ups effected through New York Stock Exchange member firms increased more than 700 percent, from $11.4 million to $91.7 million, meaning that in 1968 Exchange members gave up 38 percent of the $243 million in commissions they received from investment companies. During those same four years, give-ups effected on regional exchanges increased 1900 percent, to approximately $19 million in 1968.[100] "Give-ups and reciprocal business practices in connection with institutional trading," the SEC would report early in 1968, "have become so widespread that it may plausibly be argued that, in the case of large institutional orders, there is in economic substance no fixed commission rate" but rather an anomaly: "Competition in the securities industry between institutional managers and brokers and between exchanges has operated to reduce very substantially the amount of commissions actually *retained* by executing brokers — but with relatively little impact or effect as yet on the commissions actually *paid* by the public investors who invest through institutional media."[101]

To economists, led by Paul Samuelson, the widespread use of give-ups was a "dramatic way of revealing the [New York Stock Exchange's] distorted rate structure." The failure of the Exchange either to allow rates to be competitively set or to provide a volume discount for large-block transactions whose proportional transaction costs were less than the cost of smaller trades necessitated give-ups as "a kind of loophole through which a little competition could asthmatically breathe." Far preferable, urged Samuelson, "from the standpoint of efficient and equitable operation of our capital market," would be to allow competition to operate directly in the securities industry by abolishing fixed commission rates and by eliminating restrictions on access to the facilities of the New York Stock Exchange.[102]

During the 1965–1968 period, the SEC's commissioners did not approach give-ups as a problem of economic regulation, nor act officially to revamp the commission-rate and access rules of the New York Stock Exchange that, as give-ups so clearly illustrated, were resulting in higher-than-competitive-level transaction costs. Instead, the SEC officially condemned give-ups for reasons more familiar to corporation and securities lawyers. In the Commission's analysis, give-ups were most objectionable because of the conflict of interest that occurred when mutual fund managers used them to build mutual fund sales and thus increase their advisory fees, rather than attempt to secure a volume discount on securities transactions and benefit the funds' shareholders.[103]

The Commission's ability to approach the give-up problem with the familiar corporate law rubrics of fraud and conflict of interest enabled it on this single commission-rate issue, and this issue alone, to concur with its more reform-minded Division of Trading and Markets staff in a two-year campaign to abolish give-ups. But this partial approach to the cluster of commission-rate issues ultimately was to be perceived by the Department of Justice's Antitrust Division as so inadequate that in April 1968 the division would publicly intervene, prompting the 1968–1971 hearings that subsequently led to the abolition of all fixed securities brokerage commission rates.

SEC consideration of a ban on give-ups effectively began after the New York Stock Exchange's presentation, on November 23, 1965, of a package of proposals to revise its commission-rate structure. Most significantly, the proposals included a 25 percent discount from the standard commission rates for nonmember broker-dealers, a proposal the New York Stock Exchange favored only if the SEC used its power to require that rules concerning commission-rate schedules and discounts apply uniformly to all registered securities exchanges. Division of Trading and Markets director Pollack excoriated the Exchange proposal two weeks later as a transparent device to prevent the regional exchanges from providing commission-rate competition; he wrote that the proposal "would probably seriously damage the regional exchanges without giving significant compensatory advantages to the market. Indeed, the fact that the New York Stock Exchange also suggests that the regional exchanges be limited to a 25 percent give-up makes it clear that the NYSE proposal is designed to recapture institutional business from the regionals." Pollack recommended as a preferable alternative that "the Exchange [adopt] a meaningful volume discount so that the savings of large orders can be passed on directly to the shareholders represented by the institutional investor."[104]

The SEC formally rejected the Exchange's proposal on December 22, 1965, with Manuel Cohen commenting in a letter to Funston "that a volume discount is necessary and appropriate" and that the SEC believed "it would be desirable to frame rules" defining the circumstances under which Exchange members would be permitted to split commissions with nonmembers.[105] On March 3, 1966, the Division of Trading and Markets recommended that give-ups in any form be abolished.[106] The SEC officially endorsed its staff's recommendation on May 19, 1966, approving a letter to be forwarded to the New York Stock Exchange that stated in part: "We believe that the prohibition of give-ups will simplify the mechanical problems in devising a workable volume discount . . . we do not believe, however, that the development of an appropriate and effective volume discount should delay putting into effect promptly other aspects of the commission structure proposals."[107] On this issue, as distinguished from its actions on Rule 394, institutional membership, and Exchange access rules, the SEC relatively rapidly enunciated a clear policy position and pursued its implementation with a degree of firmness.

In mid-July 1966, Irving Pollack wrote the presidents of all registered securities exchanges and the president of the NASD that "the 'give-up' practice in the exchange communities has developed to a point where it threatens the integrity of wide segments of the securities industry." Accordingly, the SEC recognized "that the solution of the problem may require coordinated action by each of the national securities exchanges, by the NASD and by the Commission."[108]

The pressure was kept up by the SEC throughout the balance of 1966. The *SEC Minutes* indicate that Chairman Cohen wrote the New York Stock Exchange concerning give-ups on September 20, 1966, and again on October 19, 1966, stating in the later letter that the give-up "is a practice . . . which the Commission believes should be eliminated without delay."[109] When it was objected that the give-up was necessary to ensure the continued viability of some broker-dealers whose principal business was retailing mutual funds and of certain regional exchanges, Cohen responded in a November 1966 address that giving smaller broker-dealers "economic access to the New York Stock Exchange, by permitting them to share commissions with Exchange members on a realistic basis when they originate transactions in listed securities, might be a more constructive approach to . . . helping smaller broker-dealers" than the give-up.[110]

Despite Cohen's response, the SEC deferred for another thirteen months officially promulgating a rule to abolish give-ups, precisely because of concern that such a rule would harm the regional exchanges and because of the hope that the securities exchanges would act on their own to abolish give-ups.

By mid-March 1967 the SEC had received private comments from the New York and American stock exchanges, the Investment Bankers Association, and Weeden and Company on a draft of Rule 10b-10, the rule to abolish give-ups.[111] Rather than promptly rewriting the rule and again circulating it for private or public comments, the SEC for the next eight months considered alternative "middle" positions, such as Eugene Rotberg's June 1967 suggestion that "give-ups might be prohibited only in the case where a fiduciary was directing its beneficiaries' assets to another firm to perform no function"[112] or attempting to limit give-ups through the holdings of an SEC administrative action rather than a rule. The SEC's hesitation appeared to be strongly influenced by such comments as that received from Pacific Coast Stock Exchange president Thomas Phelan, "that the Commission's urging of a volume discount or the elimination of certain give-up practices sounds the death knell for the Pacific Exchange."[113] The Commission also on at least one occasion in July 1967 forwarded a letter to the exchanges officially reminding them of the SEC's concern about the lack of progress in solving the give-up problem.[114] By late November 1967 the SEC agreed with Pollack that "it is becoming patently clear that the self-regulatory organizations are unwilling or unable to take the initiative in putting an end to these practices. It appears necessary, therefore, for the Commission to exercise its rule-making power under the Exchange Act to provide a solution in order to eliminate a system of trading which is recognized as being improper and inimical to the public interest."[115]

The New York Stock Exchange's new president, Robert Haack, met with the Commission on December 4, 1967. When Haack acknowledged to the SEC that, as the day's *Minutes* report, "concerning the commission-rate structure . . . the Exchange had 'accomplished absolutely nothing,'" the tempo of events accelerated.[116] Within a month, Haack returned to the SEC with an Exchange "package." Rather than abolish give-ups altogether, the New York Stock Exchange was prepared to limit the percentage amount that might be given up while simultaneously adopting a volume discount and permitting nonmember dealers to direct transactions to the NYSE floor at a discount if the SEC would use its powers to order a prohibition of institutional membership on any exchange and aid in prohibiting give-ups above a specified amount on other securities exchanges.[117]

On January 10, 1968, Eugene Rotberg, then associate director of the Division of Trading and Markets, met with President Haack to clarify the ambiguities of the Exchange proposal. Haack emphasized, *"The amount of give-up would have to be the same on all exchanges"* (italics on original). Rotberg's analysis of the Exchange's January 1968 "package" was almost identical with Irving Pollack's analysis of the similar Exchange proposals offered in November 1965. In a memorandum dated January 11, 1968, Rotberg predicted, "I do not think that any regional exchange could continue to exist if the NYSE proposals were put into effect," since the "regional exchanges would have no way to compete with the NYSE by offering 'more' to either sole members, nonmembers, or the public (i.e., institutional membership)." Rotberg added, "The third market might survive despite the volume discount, but [its] viability would be seriously threatened if the Exchange continued the substantial give-ups to members and nonmembers, thereby motivating institutional managers to continue to avoid the third market."[118]

The day after Rotberg's analysis was circulated, the Commission directed the staff to draft a release inviting public comments on its proposed anti-give-up Rule 10b-10, which prohibited "investment company managers from requiring brokers executing transactions for an investment company to divide their compensation, if any, with other brokers unless the benefits of such division accrued to the investment company or its shareholders." The Commission simultaneously invited comments on the proposals of the Exchange.[119]

By the time of the January 26, 1968, Rule 10b-10 release, the strategy of Chairman Cohen and Eugene Rotberg, his closest adviser on commission-rate issues, had undergone a profound transformation. Throughout most of his chairmanship, Cohen had attempted to persuade the New York Stock Exchange to reform its fixed-rate schedule in a manner that could survive an antitrust challenge. He suggested that the Exchange institute a significant volume discount and voluntarily abolish give-ups. Leonard Leiman, Cohen's executive assistant in the 1964–1966 period, recalled, "While trying to persuade the Exchange leadership to make the necessary changes, he was almost single-handedly restraining the Antitrust Division of the Department of Justice and some members of Congress, pleading for time to allow the industry to correct itself without judicial or legislative interference." There were several causes for the Cohen-Rotberg jawboning strategy, including doubts that the courts or Congress could reform the Exchange's commission-rate structure as quickly or as expertly as the SEC; a belief that no reform as momentous as the abolition of fixed rates could be effected until at least some securities industry leaders favored it; uncertainty about the impact of the abolition of fixed rates on small broker-dealers, regional exchanges, and the third market; a recognition that it would be strategically easier for the SEC to control the self-regulatory efforts of the exchanges if it had power to approve rate increases than if they were determined by negotiation; and anxiety that unfixed rates might lead to lower rates for institutional investors but higher rates for small individual investors. Cohen and Rotberg preferred that, if possible, the SEC function as a referee between competing industry and government forces, and that it not simply dictate a resolution. The jawboning strategy had the advantages, in theory, of avoiding the possibility that the SEC might impose a "wrong" or controversial solution that would place the securities industry at war with the Commission and lessen Legislative and Executive Branch support. It had the further virtue of allowing Cohen and Rotberg to insist to the Exchange's leaders that the commission-rate reforms they advocated were more in the Exchange's interest than the competitive rate structure an antitrust suit or Congress might impose if the SEC's negotiations with the Exchange failed to produce results.

Had the Exchange been less stubborn in its response to Chairman Cohen's arguments, much of the momentum for unfixing commission rates might have been slowed. But the Exchange confounded Cohen by not pursuing rationally its self-interest, and Cohen, increasingly alarmed by the size and prevalence of mutual fund give-ups, which mocked every argument the Exchange offered to justify its fixed rate schedule, began to pursue an alternative strategy, that of building securities industry and congressional support for the ultimate abolition of fixed commission rates. The publication of the SEC's Rule 10b-10 release was the first public notice of Cohen's new strategy. David Ratner, then Chairman Cohen's executive assistant, later explained that the simultaneous publication of the Exchange's package and the SEC's proposed Rule 10b-10 was "designed to spotlight the fact that the NYSE was trying to preserve its fixed minimum commissions and at the same time preserve the devices by which its members evaded that rate schedule for their own benefit." Rotberg, author of the 10b-10 release, believed it publicly dramatized the point that "if a substantial portion of commission income is directed to firms who perform no function which reduces the expense of executing firms, then the present rate level cannot be justified on reasonable grounds." Yet Cohen did not, in January 1968 or at any time in the remaining thirteen months of his chairmanship, directly demand the abolition of all fixed rates. He continued to believe it was wiser for the SEC to encourage securities industry initiatives for negotiated rates rather than have the SEC assume the political risks of so controversial a reform. Moreover, Cohen was far out in front of most or all of the other four SEC commissioners, who did not yet agree that all fixed rates should be abolished.[120]

Thus, paradoxically, while Cohen's Rule 10b-10 strategy eventually did help facilitate the abolition of fixed commission rates, the purpose of the proposal was little understood at the time. As Paul Samuelson subsequently was to say of the SEC's "very small progress" toward effective competition in the securities industry during this period, "Where was the SEC in all those years? . . . the Securities and Exchange Commission should long ago have acted to promote equitable and efficient competition and to control private monopoly."[121] Four and a half years had passed since the *Special Study* recommended that the SEC make a comprehensive study of the New York Stock Exchange's commission-rate structure. During those years, the SEC had discussed with the Exchange volume discounts, nonmember access to the Exchange floor, Rule 394, and banning give-ups. But the SEC had never articulated an economic analysis that justified why fixed commission rates should exist in the first place nor gathered sufficient empirical data to prepare such an analysis. On the single most significant dollars-and-cents issue subject to the SEC's authority, the Commission, quite simply, was ill prepared to act effectively. The SEC's Rule 10b-10 release itself conceded, "The Commission recognizes that the proposed rule is not a substitute for full re-examination of the structures and rates of

commission on the national securities exchanges."[122] What the release did not explain was why, through that date, a full re-examination had been neither conducted nor initiated.

It was at this point that the Justice Department intervened.
Aware of the divisions among the SEC's commissioners that had for
a long time limited the SEC's ability to address the commission-rate
issues,[123] the Justice Department's Antitrust Division on April 1,
1968, filed a sixty-seven-page comment on the SEC's proposed Rule
10b-10.[124] The comment was based on the premise, second nature to
any practicing antitrust attorney but rarely set forth in official SEC
documents during the postwar period, that "the most obvious interest of the investing public" in regulation of the stock exchanges was
"to be protected from excessive commission charges." The Antitrust Division also assumed that the New York Stock Exchange
fixed-commission-rate schedule was not furthering the second
public interest in stock exchange regulation, that of maintaining an
efficient auction market, but, in fact, was helping to fragment the
market in Exchange-listed securities by inducing institutional and
other investors, when they could, to trade on the regional exchanges
or use the over-the-counter third market, where competitive rates
sometimes were available. Accordingly, the division recommended
that the SEC "promptly" institute public hearings to determine the
extent to which fixed commission rates or restrictions on nonmember access to the Exchange floor was "required by the purposes of
the Securities Exchange Act."

Given the Justice Department's ability under the *Silver* case to
initiate an antitrust action and attempt to show that fixed commission rates and the New York Stock Exchange's restrictive membership rules were "not necessary to make the Securities Exchange Act
work," Ratner reported, "the intervention of the Antitrust Division
was in itself sufficient to trigger the calling of a public hearing on
stock exchange commission rates" by the SEC.[125] Chairman Cohen,
long frustrated by the SEC's conservative majority, made no secret
of his relief that the Justice Department had intervened, publicly
stating in a 1971 address, after he left the Commission, that the
initiation of the commission-rate hearings and related studies *"may
have been the only means* by which the problems could have been
brought to public attention and provision made for a vehicle
through which the objectives of all relevant national policies could
be fulfilled on a basis that would ensure the continuing public
confidence in the securities markets" (italics added).[126] Even before
the commission-rate hearings commenced on July 1, 1968, Cohen

was able to employ the Justice Department's antitrust threat to persuade a Commission majority to demand on May 28, 1968, that the New York Stock Exchange abolish fixed commission rates for transactions in excess of $50,000 or put into effect a schedule of volume discounts specified by the SEC, and, in either event, reduce or eliminate charges for nonmember transactions on the NYSE. Both in his May 28 letter and in an address delivered that day, the chairman emphasized that these were only interim measures. The SEC intended to consider the abolition of all fixed rates, the elimination of give-ups, institutional membership, Rule 394, and competition in the securities market generally during the commission-rate hearings, Cohen's letter stated, precisely because "of the Commission's responsibilities to consider the national policies embodied both in the securities laws and in the antitrust laws."[127]

Three days before the SEC's commission-rate hearings began, the New York Stock Exchange's Board of Governors agreed to a series of interim reforms as its response to Cohen's May 28 letter. In an action publicly acknowledged to have been taken to fortify its defense against an anticipated government attack on its minimum commission schedule, the Exchange agreed "in principle" to put into effect volume discounts of unspecified size, phase out give-ups over a one-year period if the SEC used its power to prohibit give-ups on all other registered exchanges, and adopt a one-third discount for nonmembers.[128] During subsequent technical discussions with the SEC, the Exchange considerably retrenched. Although it agreed to an immediate abolition of give-ups on December 5, 1968,* the Exchange limited its volume discount to trades of 1000 or more shares, a far higher figure than the 400-share "switching point" that Eugene Rotberg and his associate, Fred Siesel, had persuaded the SEC to request in Cohen's letter to the Exchange. The Exchange also deferred putting into effect a one-third discount for nonmembers until the SEC's commission-rate hearings were concluded. The Exchange's interim reforms of its commission-rate schedule were, in fact, quite modest. Nonetheless, the SEC was able to report, soon after the commission-rate hearings began, both that give-ups would be abolished by the end of the year and that the Exchange's interim volume discount, if in effect in 1967, would have reduced total

---

* The abolition of give-ups did not end a number of other reciprocal practices that could be employed to evade the NYSE's fixed-commission-rate schedule and antirebate rule. Certain reciprocal practices persisted through September 1973, when the SEC indicated that it would require the abolition of all fixed commission rates on May 1, 1975.[129]

commissions paid to New York Stock Exchange members by 7 percent, or approximately $150 million.[130]

The New York Stock Exchange's interim commission-rate reforms had the practical effect of focusing the SEC's hearings[131] on the most fundamental issue: whether the Exchange should be permitted to fix rates through a minimum commission schedule or whether all rates should be negotiated and rate levels determined by competition. In mid-August 1968, essentially for the first time in its history, the New York Stock Exchange attempted publicly to justify price-fixing in the securities brokerage industry with the publication of a 137-page analysis of "economic effects of negotiated commission rates on the brokerage industry, the market for corporate securities, and the investing public."

The Exchange's economic analysis, a highly adversarial document, presented a worst-case scenario of the possible consequences of abolishing fixed commission rates. The analysis emphasized the "possible chaos" that would occur if the abolition of minimum fixed rates led to a further fragmentation of the market in trading Exchange-listed securities.

> At the present time [explained the Exchange], the existence of minimum commissions represents a primary incentive for retaining NYSE membership. A member may trade on the floor of the Exchange by paying the prescribed charges to floor brokers, while the nonmember must pay the higher commission rate applicable to the public. Without some effective rate differential between members and nonmembers, the incentive to join the NYSE — thus bringing trades to the NYSE floor, and thereby contributing to the liquidity of the market — would quickly disappear.

Without fixed rates, the Exchange's economic analysis predicted, few large commission brokerage firms would remain members of the New York Stock Exchange:

> Any time they wanted to execute orders on the floor of the Exchange, they would only have to agree upon an appropriate rate with a floor broker . . . The result would be a shrinking of the NYSE to a mere association of floor brokers and specialists. Brokerage firms would take their orders to the floor only when they could not be executed as crosses in their offices or as principal trades in dealer-created third markets.

According to the Exchange's analysis, this could only harm investors, particularly small investors:

> The decline of the specialist system would thus be the first step in the weakening of the overall central securities market to the detriment of

all investors. Stock price swings would tend to become more pro-
nounced than at present. A weakening of specialist support could at
times lead to sudden collapses (or undue rises) of stock prices on
announcement of unexpected news.

Fragmented trading in Exchange-listed securities also would produce, the Exchange predicted, "wider spreads in quotations," since
trading on the New York Stock Exchange would be "thinner." This
prediction, in part, was based on a study published earlier in 1968 by
economist Harold Demsetz, which concluded, "The cost of ex-
changing a security (as reflected by its spread) declines as trading
activity in that security increases. It would seem that centralization
of trading activity on the NYSE can be explained by the lowering of
transaction costs thereby achieved." Other harms, argued the Exchange analysis, would follow when the abolition of fixed commission rates reduced the incentives for the large commission house
brokers to remain Exchange members: "Office crosses and transactions in other markets would not be published and the advantages to
investors of the full print on the tape — including both volume and
changing prices — would be largely lost. In fact, the print on the tape
might even become somewhat misleading."

The Exchange analysis concluded its initial argument against
negotiated sales by predicting that, with a plethora of market-
makers in Exchange-listed securities, each with thin volume, and no
reliable record of price and volume, whatever savings investors
might achieve from lower commission rates probably would be
more than offset by poorer executions:

> The splintering of the central auction market would disadvantage
> individual investors in particular. Their orders would no longer be
> brought to one place where most bids and offers are concentrated.
> Instead, orders would often be executed in the offices of securities
> firms to which they happened to be entrusted.
> In these circumstances, there would be very little likelihood that the
> best executions would or indeed could be obtained. The individual
> broker would find it impractical to check each fragmentary market for
> each customer's order. As a result, neither individuals nor securities
> firms would know for certain whether each order received the best
> available price at the time it was executed.

The second principal argument of the Exchange in its August
1968 economic analysis was that the elimination of fixed commission rates would result in periods of "destructive competition"
whenever trading volume declined, causing many efficient firms to
be eliminated "while many inefficient firms, because of their size

and diversification, would survive." The Exchange based this prediction on a series of complex interrelated arguments that most simply
may be restated as follows. Fixed costs, if they included clerical and
related personnel costs, were very high in the securities industry,
equal to an average of 51 percent of total costs. Demand was unpredictable, but securities firms needed to maintain excess capacity in
slack periods to meet periodically heavy volume. Without fixed
commission rates, during periods of low volume negotiated commission-rate levels could be driven down to levels insufficient for
many firms to cover fixed costs — a likely result, the Exchange
theorized, since reduced commission charges alone were unlikely to
increase volume. Thus, the firms most likely to survive would not
be the most efficient firms (that is, those that executed transactions
at the lowest cost), but the largest and most diversified firms, able to
survive financial losses from intermittent periods of low demand.
Smaller securities firms, "regardless of their efficiency," would be
eliminated, since "the prerequisite for survival would be not
efficiency but financial power."

Simultaneous with this increase in concentration in the securities
industry, the Exchange argued, would be price discrimination,
which would tend to harm smaller and less sophisticated investors.
Reasoned the Exchange: while institutional investors would be able
to negotiate lower commission rates if the minimum commission
schedule was abolished, their transactions might make little or no
contribution to fixed expenses, but would only cover or slightly
exceed the variable cost of brokerage fees. "The result would be to
shift these [fixed overhead] costs to smaller, less-powerful traders —
and even to smaller institutions with less bargaining power —
whose demand is less responsive to price." Here the Exchange
scored a debating point by noting that even the Justice Department,
in its April 1968 comment, had suggested

> that it might be necessary to set rate maxima in small trades, presum-
> ably to avoid just such a shifting of costs to small investors. This fear
> of inequitable pricing constitutes a recognition that, without
> minimum commission rates, discriminatory pricing might well
> plague the industry and its smaller customers. But, the determination
> of an appropriate schedule of maximum commissions would involve
> exactly the sort of problems which the Justice Department alleges
> make minimum rate-setting so difficult.

The Exchange's final principal argument was that small investors
would be further harmed through the "unbundling" of securities broker services. Without minimum commission rates, so this argu-

ment went, brokerage firms would sharply curtail investment research and information services. Discount brokers "would probably become dominant in the securities business," for "negotiated rates would force most firms to discontinue or reduce all services other than the execution of orders." The Exchange recognized that most economists would consider this desirable, because it would permit investors to pay for only the brokerage services they wanted — for example, investors could separately subscribe to a research advisory service if or when they wanted one while separately paying brokerage commissions only high enough to cover the cost of executing securities transactions and not high enough to include the cost of research services that these investors did not use. Nonetheless, the Exchange claimed, "the matter cannot be disposed of that easily." Since "the proliferation of brokerage discount houses would probably reduce informational services to the lowest common denominator," this might harm all investors, including those who usually did not avail themselves of the opportunity to study commission house information services. "This is because the presence of public information affects the prices which investors pay or receive in purchases and sales . . . Better information leads to more informed opinion and less haphazard price making." Moreover, "as serious as the elimination of data dissemination would be the reduction in research services. Registered representatives would still be asked by their clients to recommend stocks, but they would no longer have the backing of any serious research effort . . . Registered representatives would recommend stocks on the basis of their own limited resources and knowledge. This would be similar to a clothing store selling the same suits to all customers without attempting to fit."

The New York Stock Exchange's economic analysis concluded, "All of the benefits of a competitive system, without the serious drawbacks of negotiated rates, can be achieved by designing an appropriate schedule of minimum commission rates. A new schedule of regulated commission rates has been proposed with better potential benefits and without the drawbacks of the Justice Department's proposal." Presenting the New York Stock Exchange economic analysis at the SEC commission-rate hearings, President Haack added one further argument designed to appeal to the SEC's cautious majority:

One does not remove the keystone to an industry which is responsible for billions of dollars of public money, which operates the largest securities market in the world, and which facilitates the raising of the bulk of new capital for this country without presenting irrefutable evidence. We are dealing with a delicate mechanism. This is not an area where one experiments, tries a new system, and returns to the old if the results are unsatisfactory. Destruction of the minimum commission rate would produce irreversible consequences. An erroneous decision will have far-reaching effects. I am sure the Commission shares our view that, in this area, one must proceed with extreme caution.

The New York Stock Exchange's economic defense of fixed commission rates was subjected to a two-pronged attack. Consistent with the strategy of the SEC's January 1968 Rule 10b-10 release, the SEC's staff did not call directly for the abolition of fixed commission rates during the initial months of the commission-rate hearings, but instead presented several weeks of testimony, Eugene Rotberg explained, "designed to discredit fixed rates by showing that fixed rates neither, in fact, existed nor were essential to the exchanges' viability." The character of the SEC staff's indirect challenge to the New York Stock Exchange's fixed-commission-rate structure was well illustrated by Rotberg's interrogation of Exchange vice president Robert Bishop on July 1, 1968, the first day of the hearings. Throughout the course of a day-long examination, Rotberg made obvious that the New York Stock Exchange could not satisfactorily answer such questions as why the commission on a hundred shares of $10 stock was $17 while the commission on a hundred shares of $80 stock was $47, in spite of the fact that no greater work was involved for a broker to execute one order than the other; why there was no volume discount; or how the Exchange's antirebate rule could be harmonized with give-ups or such reciprocal business practices as an insurance firm placing orders with a brokerage house only if the brokerage house agreed to purchase insurance from it. Repeatedly, Bishop insisted, "We are not trying to rationalize and defend this; we intend to change it." In other instances, Bishop, the official responsible for enforcing the Exchange's commission-rate rules, acknowledged that he could not offer a "definitive" answer as to why an Exchange interpretation of its antirebate rule was so. At another point, Bishop conceded he was "confused" by Rotberg's description of a particularly Byzantine reciprocal practice. Bishop was succeeded by such witnesses as Michael Heaney, a floor member of the American Stock Exchange, who testified that he would give up as much as 90 percent of the commissions he received from a mutual fund for a large order after the fund sent a little note to the effect, "Mike, send X dollars to so and so. We think you've had that money long enough." As early as July 8, 1968, the *New York Daily*

News published an article praising the Cohen-Rotberg strategy, characterizing it as the most amusing "inside joke" in Washington.[132]

Four months later, the Justice Department's Antitrust Division began a second attack on the New York Stock Exchange's defense of fixed commission rates, directly calling for the abolition of fixed rates. For several days, beginning October 30, 1968, the department presented the testimony of four of the country's leading economists, MIT's Paul Samuelson, Princeton's William Baumol, the University of Chicago's Harold Demsetz, and Yale's Henry Wallich, as well as the testimony of Boston College economist Michael Mann, then serving on the Department of Justice staff. Although the five men differed somewhat in analytic approach, all agreed that fixed commission rates could not be justified and that a competitive commission-rate system was both preferable and workable.

To the economists, there were two principal defects of the New York Stock Exchange fixed-commission-rate system and related exclusionary practices, such as Rule 394 and the prohibition on institutional membership. First, the failure of the commission-rate schedule to reflect actual brokerage costs had resulted in excessive or monopolistic profits. Paul Samuelson testified:

> The true incremental or marginal costs of transacting five hundred shares of a listed stock is much less than five times that of transacting a hundred shares . . . The fact that commissions have long had to be the same for subsequent round lots as for the first one is itself, to a trained economist, the sign of monopoly . . . Without being told that this lopsided structure of rates has been the result of coercion by the stock market over the minimum commission any other member may charge, an economist could have inferred the existence of interference with free competition from the facts of inflated markups themselves.

In dollars-and-cents terms, fixed commission rates had resulted in a greater than sixfold increase in brokerage income in the 1961–1968 period, with aggregate securities commission income of New York Stock Exchange members increasing from $613 million to $3.245 billion, making Wall Street, *Forbes* magazine stated in June 1968, "perhaps the greatest growth industry in the U.S." In 1967, at most one of the 330 New York Stock Exchange firms engaged in the public commission business had sustained a net loss; the general profitability of Exchange membership had meant that the price of a seat on the Exchange cost as much as $550,000 in 1968, more than twice the highest price of $250,000 paid just three years earlier.[133] By shielding Exchange members from the rigors of competition, fixed rates had the further consequence of sheltering inefficiency. Most dramatically, this would result in Exchange members' dilatory efforts to automate their rapidly growing volume of paperwork, a type of inefficiency that would significantly contribute to the Exchange's 1968–1970 "back-room" crisis.[134]

The Justice Department's independent expert economic witnesses unanimously concluded that none of the New York Stock Exchange's defenses of fixed commission rates justified the securities brokerage industry's greater-than-competitive-level profits or its inefficiency.

The economists also agreed that the incentive of high commission rates was not necessary to maintain a centralized trading market. "On the contrary," argued Harold Demsetz, noting that the Exchange had misconstrued the results of his research, "there is good economic evidence that a central market will always draw the preponderance of trading activity in a given security because of its inherent efficiencies, unless external costs, such as high commissions, impede the natural growth of the market." Lower competitive commission rates were likely to increase the volume of trading on the New York Stock Exchange and improve its liquidity. Principally, this was because, contrary to an assertion of the Exchange, a decrease in rates would be likely to increase trading volume. It was Samuelson's belief that "it follows from the most fundamental of economic principles that a larger volume of total transactions will take place at lower charges" and several studies cited by Henry Wallich had found that relatively small changes in transaction costs would increase the demand for securities. The conclusion of these theoretical studies long had been assumed. The London Stock Exchange, for example, in 1968 decided to lower commission rates to stimulate trading volumes. Similarly, several New York Stock Exchange commission brokerage houses had opposed contemplated or actual exchange rate increases through the 1940s and 1950s because of concern that higher rates would decrease volume.

Moreover, both the economists and leading third-market dealers, including Morris Schapiro and Donald Weeden, recognized that far from fragmenting trading in New York Stock Exchange–listed securities, lower commission rates likely would recapture volume lost to the regional exchanges and the third market. Thus, the practical consequence of eliminating fixed rates would be to centralize more fully the market in NYSE-listed securities while reducing the profits of the securities brokerage industry to competitive levels. If this occurred, investors would benefit from lower commission charges and conceivably also closer bid-ask spreads; only Exchange members who purchased seats based on the expectation of monopolistic levels of profit would suffer.

The Exchange's second principal justification, that fixed commission rates were necessary to avoid "destructive competition" among Exchange members with resulting injury to the public, was rejected with equal unanimity by the economists on both practical and theoretical grounds. The simplest basis for rejecting this argument was that negotiated rates already were charged in the over-the-counter markets, and to institutional investors who could avail themselves of give-ups, without any manifestation of destructive competition. Justice Department staff economist Michael Mann additionally demonstrated that the fixed costs of the securities brokerage industry were far lower than those claimed by the Exchange. Clerical and administrative personnel salaries representing 59 percent of what the Exchange denominated "fixed costs" could be reduced during periods of low demand through the obvious expedient of personnel lay-offs, as, in fact, was utilized during the 1962 period of reduced demand and would be again in 1970. Nor were scale economies so great in the securities industry that only a few firms could be expected to survive rate competition; low economics of scale suggested that entry to the industry would remain easy and concentration levels low.

The New York Stock Exchange's price discrimination justification was rebutted, in substantial degree, by the arguments of the Exchange's own economic analysis. The elimination of fixed rates would make it possible for discount brokers to charge lower rates to all investors, including small investors. This would reduce the likelihood that other brokers could subsidize below-cost rates to institutional investors by charging excessive prices to small investors.

As predicted by the Exchange's analysis, the independent economists had little sympathy for the Exchange's "unbundling" argument. Mann testified, "The SEC has recently raised the possibility that the small investor does not obtain the same quality or timeliness of information as the large investor," an allusion to *Texas Gulf Sulphur* and other insider-trading cases. "If the small investor could buy his information from competent and disinterested sources, he might obtain better or more timely information than he does currently," said Mann. William Baumol expressed his skepticism that discount broker competition would reduce all research advisory services to the lowest common denominator. To Baumol, the willingness of investors to support many investment advisory services during a period of fixed rates, when they could obtain investment advice from securities brokers at no additional cost above the standard commission, suggested there was a strong demand for differentiated advisory services.

Summarizing the case against fixed New York Stock Exchange rates in a January 1969 brief filed with the SEC, the Justice Department argued that rate regulation should supersede competition only as a very last resort, implicitly in industries that actually had high economies of scale relative to consumer demand, such as public utilities, and was inappropriate for the securities brokerage industry because of the inherent deficiencies of the rate-regulatory process. Specifically, rate regulation was less effective than competition in compelling cost efficiency and innovation. Rate regulators tended to become overly protective of the industry they regulated. As Baumol observed, "For the regulator, it is the most difficult thing in the world to take the responsibility for some firm going out of existence; and so, as soon as competition threatens to become a reality, as soon as it threatens to do something for the consumer, which means somebody gets hurt, that is when the regulator is tempted to say, 'Stop. It is becoming destructive.' " And rate regulation would be particularly difficult in the heterogeneous securities industry, with hundreds of separate firms, where the SEC might have to assume the responsibilities of dictating levels of automation and controlling securities firm entry, exit, and merger to specify equitable fixed rates.

The Justice Department predicted that the elimination of fixed rates generally would lower commissions charged to investors and would "unbundle" the securities industry. This would enable investors to pay only for research and advisory services that they, in fact, used, and would reward cost efficient brokerage houses and the investment advisers whom investors chose in a competitive market. The elimination of higher-than-competitive-rate levels, claimed the Justice Department, also would greatly ameliorate the problems created by Rule 394, which prevented Exchange members from trading Exchange-listed securities competitively with third-market dealers. To minimize dislocations that might be caused by an abrupt elimination of fixed rates, the Department of Justice urged a gradual transition to a competitive system over a period of four years, beginning with a ban on fixed rates in transactions above $50,000. Simultaneously, the department urged that the SEC study the feasibility of increasing the number of Exchange members (a proposal that necessarily would decrease both the initial and annual costs of membership), abolishing Rule 394, and instituting a public insurance system along the lines of the Federal Deposit Insurance Act to protect customers from the effects of brokerage firm insolvency.

The New York Stock Exchange tacitly conceded that its existing fixed-commission-rate schedule could not be defended. In its initial appearance before the SEC commission-rate hearings, the Exchange announced that it would employ the services of the National Economic Research Associates (NERA) consulting firm to develop a new cost-based rate structure that could be termed "reasonable."[135] On January 22, 1969, just five days after the Justice Department filed its brief urging the SEC to "take steps leading to competitive rates on securities exchanges as quickly as possible," Exchange president Robert Haack addressed the Second Annual Institutional Investor Conference in New York City. Haack explained that the Exchange intended to pay NERA more than $400,000 to make, over the next twelve to eighteen months, "the most complete studies of commissions ever undertaken, leading to new proposals that will be put to the SEC." Frankly acknowledging the difficulties of designing reasonable fixed-commission-rate standards, Haack suggested that one solution might involve limiting fixed commission rates solely to execution and clearance of transactions and allowing investors to purchase separately investment research and advisory services. SEC chairman Manuel Cohen, addressing the same conference, expressed his skepticism that the Commission would wait twelve to eighteen months before insisting on additional changes in the New York Stock Exchange's commission-rate structure.[136]

Earlier, Cohen had lobbied effectively for congressional authorization of an Institutional Investor Study, funding the SEC to make a comprehensive investigation of the impact of banks, insurance companies, mutual funds, pension plans, and other institutions on the securities markets. As distinguished from the 1963 Special Study, the authorizing legislation significantly restricted the staff's independence, both stipulating that the Institutional Investor Study's report would directly reflect the views of the Commission and that the Commission would consult with various classes of institutional investors, members of the securities industry, representatives of other government agencies, and other interested persons, as well as "an advisory committee which it shall establish for the purpose of advising and consulting . . . on a regular basis on matters within the purview of [the] study." As later appointed, the Advisory Committee was dominated numerically by New York Stock Exchange, the NASD, and institutional investor executives, who were explicitly offered the opportunity "to spell out in the final report any irreconcilable differences they may have with its findings, conclusions, and recommendations." Even with these elaborate restraints, the Institutional Investor Study potentially was another means to focus attention on the New York Stock Exchange commission-rate structure.[137]

The SEC too long delayed a comprehensive investigation of the New York Stock Exchange's commission-rate structure and never during Cohen's chairmanship addressed the fundamental issues as effectively as did the Justice Department's Antitrust Division. However, David Ratner, Cohen's second executive assistant, fairly was to conclude that by the indirect maneuvers the latter part of his chairmanship, Cohen played "an important catalytic role in the process [that moved] the idea of competitive commission rates . . . from the unthinkable to the debatable to the inevitable."[138] By the end of Cohen's chairmanship, in February 1969, the abolition of fixed commission rates, although not yet ensured, had been elevated to the most prominent issue in SEC policy-making.

* * *

Historically, the breadth of the SEC's jurisdiction and the vagueness of pivotal provisions of the Commission's enabling statutes have contributed to the SEC's relative inattention to accounting and corporate governance. By requiring the same agency to regulate public utility holding companies, the investment company industry, all national securities markets, all interstate broker-dealers, as well as corporate disclosure, corporate governance, accounting and trust indenture requirements for all business firms above various statutes' minimum-size specifications, Congress created an extraordinarily broad mandate that all but ensured that significant portions of it would be largely ignored. To early SEC chairmen James Landis and William Douglas, this was a predictable result. As Landis argued in *The Administrative Process*, agencies will be led most efficiently by experts when their jurisdiction is narrow: "If the administrative process is to fill the need for expertness, obviously, as regulation increases, the number of our administrative authorities must increase."[139] Douglas, who rejected attempts by President Roosevelt to increase the SEC's jurisdiction, recalled telling Roosevelt, "Give me twice the amount of responsibility, and someone else will have to do the thinking. I won't be able to know all the facts or make good decisions."[140] History has amply corroborated the wisdom of such views. An SEC commissioner historically has required expertise in accounting, corporate and securities law, economics, investment banking, corporate governance, mutual fund management, the structure of the public utility industry, and litigation strategy, among other fields. In recent years, SEC commissioners also have confronted difficult questions about the automation of the securities industry, municipal finance, new investment forms, such as hedge funds or real estate investment trusts, and new securities exchanges, such as the options markets. In the postwar period, few who have been appointed to the Commission have had a strong grasp of the full range of issues that fall within the SEC's mandate. Only a few more have been able to develop broad expertise on the job. Lack of commissioner expertise has contributed to the SEC's passivity in such fields as accounting. Lacking commissioners with training or interest in the accounting field, the SEC's Office of Chief Accountant, consistently underfunded and understaffed, has not made studies of leading accounting problems, and has rarely proved able to attract outstanding theorists.

The SEC's history suggests that the breadth of the Commission's jurisdiction also has been disabling for political reasons. An agency like the SEC can sponsor only a few initiatives at one time. Securing Executive and Legislative Branch support, conducting empirical studies, presenting hearings, and negotiating with or confronting an industry are time-consuming and expensive activities. The very vagueness of the SEC's statutory mandates concerning accounting and corporate governance has afforded the Commission a justification to relegate these issues to a low priority and concentrate its political energies elsewhere.

During Manuel Cohen's chairmanship, the difficulties created by the SEC's broad mandate were illustrated by the Commission's limited response to the conglomerate-merger wave, a response that by March 1969 even Manuel Cohen, one month after the end of his chairmanship, conceded had been "inadequate." Cohen added, "There is no one to whom the blame should be put except the Commission."[141] The late 1960s' conglomerate-merger wave was one crisis too many for an SEC leadership focusing on mutual fund legislation, the securities exchanges' commission-rate structure, and the back-office problems of the securities brokerage houses. Although, in retrospect, Cohen would characterize the emergence of the conglomerates as "one of the very serious problems that is facing the American industrial capital structure . . . maybe so urgent that we cannot wait for a full-fledged study" and requiring the type of SEC remedies employed after the "analogous" 1920s' merger wave had developed the public utility holding companies,[142] Cohen's Commission neither studied the accounting or corporate finance aspects of the conglomerates nor initiated any significant reform proposal.

Given the economic significance of the 1960s' conglomerate-

merger wave, it is obvious, as Cohen put it, that this was an "inadequate" response. "In absolute terms," an FTC staff report concluded
in 1972, "there is no argument [that] the wave of merger activity
during the 1960s was the largest in American history."

Between 1962 and 1969, 22 percent of the companies included on
the *Fortune* 500 list of largest manufacturing corporations were acquired. In 1968 alone, twenty-six of the largest 500 manufacturing
firms were absorbed by other firms; in that one year, nearly 10
percent of all independent manufacturing corporations with $10
million or more in assets ceased to exist independently.[143]

Since over 80 percent of these acquisitions were conglomerate
mergers — that is, mergers between firms that neither competed nor
stood in a supplier-customer relationship — most of them could not
effectively be challenged under the prevailing antitrust laws. This
gap in the antitrust laws inspired the Justice Department's Antitrust Division and the Federal Trade Commission, as well as the
congressional committees with antitrust enforcement oversight, to
study the need for new merger legislation. Additional studies of the
antitrust laws and market concentration were conducted by a White
House task force on antitrust policy and President Johnson's Council of Economic Advisers.

Under these circumstances it clearly was not the responsibility of
the SEC to study the antitrust laws regulating conglomerate mergers. But other aspects of the 1960s' merger wave raised issues
specifically within the SEC's jurisdiction that were not effectively
addressed by the Commission either before the merger wave peaked
or after the period's antitrust-related studies and hearings focused
attention on them. Chief among these was whether generally accepted accounting principles, which, by statute, were subject to SEC
jurisdiction, artificially stimulated conglomerate mergers by permitting the exaggeration of earnings per share of consolidated firms.

Under the prevailing generally accepted accounting principles,
when one firm acquired another, the transaction could be treated as
a purchase. The assets of the acquired firm would be listed on the
acquiring firm's balance sheet either at their original cost minus
depreciation ("book value") or written up to their fair market value
at the time of the merger. The difference between the price an acquiring firm paid to buy the acquired firm and the aggregate value of
the acquired firm's assets was called goodwill. Since 1953, generally
accepted accounting principles had encouraged (but not required)
acquiring firms to write off a portion of the goodwill over a period of
years after the merger by deducting it from annual earnings.[144]

This made the purchase method of accounting for mergers unpopular with corporate managers. Whenever the purchase method was employed, the acquiring firm's earnings were reduced for a period of years by the expense of writing off goodwill. Since this expense was not a permissible tax deduction, purchase accounting might have deterred business combinations had the purchase method been the only method of accounting for a merger.

By contrast, the alternative "pooling" method of accounting for a merger permitted an acquiring firm to add together the assets of the two merging corporations as they were carried on financial records before the merger and not reflect the actual cost of the acquisition when it was in excess of book value. This suppression of the actual cost of the acquisition often permitted an acquiring firm to claim significant increases in earnings per share purely as a result of the accounting technique employed in the merger. For example, an acquiring firm could record the assets of an acquired firm at their book value, then shortly after the merger sell some or all of the acquired assets for their actual fair market value. This technique was employed in 1967 when Gulf & Western acquired Paramount Pictures for securities worth approximately $185 million at a time when the book value of Paramount's assets was approximately $100 million. Gulf & Western then generated approximately $20 million of "instant earnings" by selling at fair market value the television rights of Paramount's feature films, which had been depreciated to a trivial value on Paramount's books. This allowed Gulf & Western to claim that its earnings increased from $22,769,000 in 1966 to $46,109,000 in 1967. Had Gulf & Western placed a fair market value on the films it acquired from Paramount, its earnings would have increased between 1966 and 1967 not by $23 million, but rather by $3.7 million.

The same appearance of instant profits could be created when the two firms pooled their earnings while reducing the number of common stock shares, say, by paying for the acquisition in part with cash, debt securities, or preferred stock. This technique was employed by Ling-Temco-Vought. In 1967, LTV acquired Wilson & Company for $144 million of preferred stock and $81.5 million in cash, $80 million of which was financed by debt arrangements. Adding Wilson's $12 million earnings to LTV's other earnings appeared to instantly increase LTV's earnings per share by 31 percent, from $4.32 to $5.68. These and related opportunities for "creative" or "aggressive" accounting made pooling the most common method of accounting for mergers during the conglomerate-merger wave. One congressional staff study calculated that International Telephone and Telegraph, among the most active conglomerates of the period, would have suffered a 41 percent reduction in its 1968 net earnings had it been required to account for mergers it recorded on a pooling basis between 1964 and 1968 on the purchase basis instead.[145]

Because it was widely believed that the pooling method might artificially stimulate merger activity, encourage corporations to issue excessive debt or preferred stock securities, or mislead investors, the appropriateness of employing pooling was the leading accounting controversy of the 1960s. Pooling first became popular in the post–World War II period. In September 1950, the Committee on Accounting Procedure of the American Institute of Accountants, then the industry's accounting-principle-setting body, felt compelled to limit sharply the use of pooling. *Accounting Research Bulletin* No. 40 emphasized as an attribute of a pooling transaction that "all or substantially all of the equity interests in predecessor corporations continue." Three other factors, though not necessarily determinative, also were to be considered. These were similar size of the merging corporations, continuity of management, and similar or complementary business activities. *ARB* No. 40 suggested that pooling most clearly was permissible when similar-sized firms, in the same or related industries, consolidated while generally continuing the equity interests of both firms' common shareholders and the managerial functions of both firms' executives.

Seven years later the American Institute of Accountants' Committee on Accounting Procedure loosened the limitations imposed by *ARB* No. 40. In *Accounting Research Bulletin* No. 48, the committee no longer indicated "the presumption that a pooling of interests is involved would be strengthened if the activities of the businesses to be combined are either similar or complementary." Nor did *ARB* No. 48 consider relative size of the constituent firms to be determinative. Only when one firm was ten or twenty times the size of the other was there a "presumption that the transaction is a purchase rather than a pooling of interests."

Contrary to *ARB* No. 40's tight standard that "all or substantially all of the equity interests in predecessor corporations continue," *ARB* No. 48 stated that substantial proportionality of equity interest was a factor to be considered, but "any one factor might have varying degrees of significance in different cases." Similarly, the elimination of one of the constituent firms' management became a not "necessarily determinative" factor of "varying degrees of significance in different cases."[146]

By the early 1960s, it was widely recognized that *ARB* No. 48 did not impose effective limitations on the use of pooling. The Accounting Research Division of the American Institute of Certified Public Accountants (the new title of the American Institute of Accountants, usually called the AICPA) was sufficiently concerned that in March 1960 it hired University of Illinois professor Arthur Wyatt to study the matter. Wyatt's report, *A Critical Study of Accounting for Business Combinations,* ultimately published in 1963, concluded that *ARB* No. 48 had resulted in "the distinctions between those combinations deemed to be purchases and those deemed to be poolings [becoming] less clear than in previous periods." Since Wyatt believed it inappropriate for "the effect on earnings per share which will flow from the accounting for business combinations [to] influence the accounting for business combinations," he recommended the abolition of pooling whenever a business combination involved an exchange of assets or equities between independent parties.

The AICPA's response to Wyatt's study was equivocal. Maurice Moonitz, the institute's director of accounting research, in June 1963 agreed with Wyatt that "the general conclusion is unavoidable that accounting for business combinations has deteriorated in recent years so that a variety of practices can be described as 'accepted.'" But Moonitz, speaking for a committee of the AICPA's new standard-setting body, the Accounting Principles Board, reported disagreement with Wyatt's view that pooling should be discontinued: "The Committee feels that the distinction between poolings and purchases should be continued, but with such modifications as are necessary in the criteria relating to the two forms of business combinations to make the distinction rest on differences of substance and not of form."[147] "Such modifications," however, the APB initially did not make. Its next official word on the subject came in 1966. It then gave its opinion on how financial statements should be restated when pooling occurred, and mentioned in a footnote that Wyatt's *"Critical Study of Accounting for Business Combinations* has been published, and another research study on accounting for goodwill is in process. The Board plans to reconsider the entire subject of accounting for business combinations after the latter study is published."[148]

Two years later, the AICPA's study of goodwill "reached," in the words of its authors, George Catlett and Norman Olson of Arthur Andersen and Company, "the same conclusion [as Wyatt's]": pooling should not be permitted in most business combinations.[149] By then, the purchase versus pooling controversy had become a cause célèbre in the accounting and financial literature.[150] Accounting academic and practitioner fulminations against "dirty pooling" or "pooling-fooling," as the influential accounting gadfly Abraham Briloff memorably dubbed it,[151] had become so widespread that even news magazines like *Time* and *Newsweek* joined the denunciations of "Profits without Honor."[152] In 1969, an FTC staff report on corporate mergers branded pooling a "tool of deception" and made the recommendation "that the Securities and Exchange Commission immediately require pooling of interests to be eliminated as the normal mode of accounting for acquisitions involving the exchange of stock."[153] Corporate attorney A. A. Sommer, soon to be named an SEC commissioner by President Nixon, in an article surveying accounting developments during the 1960s castigated the Accounting Principles Board for five years of foot-dragging on the pooling versus purchase controversy after the publication of Wyatt's study. "During that five-year period billions of dollars of economic activity was accounted for in a manner," Sommer noted, "that *almost literally everyone* knew was an inadequate and sometimes downright misleading method of dealing with the transactions" (italics added).[154]

With several congressional committees holding hearings on conglomerate corporations, and under direct pressure from the FTC, accounting academics, several accounting practitioners, and the financial press, the Accounting Principles Board briefly considered abolishing pooling. In July 1969 the board's subject-area committee circulated a draft of an opinion prohibiting pooling. The draft opinion divided the profession. According to accounting historian Stephen Zeff, two of the "Big Eight" accounting firms soon communicated their opposition. The Corporate Reporting Committee of the Financial Executives Institute, the organization of accountants directly employed by business firms, not only made known its opposition to the abolition of pooling, but also sent an "action letter" to its members, urging them "to contact your outside auditors and request a meeting with the senior partners to discuss your views on the proposed opinion." The Accounting Principles Board was unable to muster the required two-thirds vote to abolish pooling.[155] Instead, in February 1970, the APB circulated a formal exposure draft of a proposed opinion which stated that pooling was acceptable when the size ratio of the acquiring and acquired firms was no greater than three to one.[156]

The Financial Executives Institute again swung into action. Columbia University accounting professor John Burton, later brought to the SEC to be its chief accountant, was hired by the Financial Executive Research Foundation to prepare a study of the exposure draft. Burton calculated that the three-to-one size criterion would have prohibited 90 percent of the mergers that employed pooling in 1967.[157] The chairman of the Financial Executives Institute's Corporate Reporting Committee sent a second letter to FEI members, urging them to communicate their opposition to the Accounting Principles Board February 1970 draft. In addition, a coalition of business leaders calling itself the Organization for Consistent Accounting Principles waged a separate letter-writing campaign to drum up opposition to the APB proposal, one of its letters going so far as to compare the Accounting Principles Board to a "junta" who had "arrogated to themselves the power to make new . . . rules under which business is required to operate."

These lobbying pressures were conspicuously effective. Approximately 860 letters were received by the APB, 90 percent of which opposed one or more aspects of its draft on business combinations. AICPA vice president Leonard Savoie reacted angrily to these lobbying efforts, insisting in a May address that the Accounting Principles Board's members "certainly have less bias than those in corporate management who oppose reform and favor nonaccountability."[158] But the APB was unable to achieve a two-thirds majority in favor of the three-to-one size criterion. In June 1970, the board circulated a second exposure draft opinion with the considerably less restrictive nine-to-one size criterion. Four of the Big Eight accounting firms — Arthur Andersen, Lybrand, Ross Bros. and Montgomery, Ernst and Ernst, and Haskins & Sells — opposed the APB's June 1970 draft opinion. Arthur Andersen hired antitrust counsel and indicated that it was contemplating bringing an antitrust action against the APB if the board adopted the nine-to-one size test. In August 1970, the APB formally promulgated Opinion No. 16, without any size test.[159]

Opinion No. 16 was harshly criticized. Six of the eighteen members of the Accounting Principles Board dissented from its promulgation, with three dissenters stating that they did not believe that the opinion, although "an improvement over present criteria," represented "a substantial response by the Accounting Principles Board to the overall problem." The other three dissenters stated that Opinion No. 16 was an inappropriate effort "to patch up some of the abuses of pooling. The real abuse is pooling itself. On that the only answer is to eliminate pooling."[160] Later, Homer Kripke, a leading law professor of accounting, would state, "Since pooling is still available if a deal is structured in the right fashion, APB Opinion No. 16 has not really settled anything."[161]

Dissatisfaction within the accounting profession was immediate and intense. At least three of the Big Eight accounting firms indicated skepticism that the APB could effectively promulgate accounting principles. One leading Big Eight firm — Touche, Ross — threatened to withdraw from the board. A second — Arthur Andersen and Company — again threatened to bring a lawsuit against the board. By December 1970, AICPA president Marshall Armstrong felt compelled to call a special conference to discuss the establishment of accounting principles. As a result of this conference the AICPA Board of Directors appointed a special committee led by former SEC commissioner Francis Wheat to review the operations of the APB. In 1972 the Wheat Committee recommended that the APB be abolished, and it was soon replaced by the Financial Accounting Standards Board.[162]

Throughout the entire two-decade period during which the pooling versus purchase controversy divided the accounting profession, the SEC at any time could have resolved the controversy by issuing a rule prohibiting or limiting the use of pooling. A review of the relevant memoranda on file with the SEC's Office of Chief Accountant makes plain that this option was never seriously considered by the Commission. Indeed, during the crucial 1969–1970 period, memoranda in the SEC's files strongly suggest that the private communications of the Commission's chief accountant, Andrew Barr, consistently undercut the efforts of reform-minded accountants on the Accounting Principles Board to negotiate a restrictive rule.

Barr preferred to leave the promulgation of accounting standards to the accounting profession, usually limiting the SEC's role in the setting of accounting standards to that of making recommendations to the APB. Even when Barr disagreed with an action of the board, he generally did not urge the SEC to employ its statutory powers to reverse the APB.[163]

Within the SEC, Barr defended this deferential approach as necessary to avoid another fiasco like the Accounting Principles Board Opinion No. 2. In December 1962, the APB issued, without prior consultation with the SEC, an opinion to deal with a novel tax incentive, the "investment credit," which had been enacted into law in October of that year. Four of the Big Eight accounting firms favored recognizing the credit in the year eligible assets had been acquired, the so-called flow-through method. The other four Big Eight firms favored recognizing the credit over the life of the asset, the so-called deferral method. By a two-thirds vote, the APB issued an opinion calling for the deferral method. Barr later wrote to SEC chairman William Casey, "I supported the Board position, believing it to be sound and that this was an opportunity to support one solution to a new accounting problem." After being importuned by the Treasury Department and business firms and accountants opposed to the APB opinion, the SEC reversed the APB in January 1963 with an Accounting Series Release that permitted use of either the flow-through or deferral method of accounting for the investment credit. In the undisputed view of AICPA vice president (and house historian) John Carey, "The prestige and authority of the Accounting Principles Board had been badly damaged in its first effort to advance the cause of comparability." Throughout the pooling versus purchase controversy, Barr frequently characterized his role as helping "effect a compromise that would be acceptable to all interested parties" and thus eliminating the need for SEC intervention.[164]

Barr was deeply influenced by a second consideration during the pooling controversy. Through 1970, few accounting concepts had been more fervently championed by the SEC than its opposition to the writing-up of assets above their original cost. Unjustified asset write-ups had been the most conspicuous accounting abuse of the public utility holding companies. Preventing similar write-ups and eliminating the goodwill produced by such write-ups historically had been among the paramount considerations in SEC accounting policy.

In many circumstances, Andrew Barr favored the pooling method of merger accounting when one firm used stock to acquire a second firm, because pooling avoided the writing-up of assets that might occur if the purchase method were employed. Barr wrote to Reed Storey, AICPA research director, in March 1969:

> In periods of high market price levels purchase accounting tends to introduce inflationary values into the balance sheet when the assets and intangibles of the acquired companies are valued at the market price of the stock issued. These amounts usually cannot reasonably be expected to be recovered from the earnings of the acquired companies. The financial abuses arising from such practices were an important consideration in the passage of the Securities Acts and the Public Utility Holding Company Act.[165]

At the same time, Barr, a scholarly and diligent civil servant, was well aware that the SEC's case-by-case application of *ARB* No. 48 had led to a "serious erosion" of standards. As early as January 1962, Barr delivered an address illustrating that the presumption in *Accounting Research Bulletin* No. 48 — that a merger should be accounted for as a purchase rather than a pooling transaction whenever one firm was more than ten or twenty times the size of the other — already had been "nickled and dimed away," as his successor John Burton subsequently would state.[166] After studying 153 recent mergers recorded as pooling transactions, Barr found that the owners of the acquired unit in 63 cases (41 percent) held less than 5 percent of the voting stock after the combination. In 102 of the 153 mergers (67 percent), the owners held less than 10 percent. Yet the SEC's first direct public response* to the principle-setting controversy did not come until June 1968, when the Commission issued a Securities Act Release warning that when firms merged employing pooling and compared the pooled earnings of the consolidated firms with the unpooled results of earlier years, the publication of "substantial percentage increases in sales, net income, and earnings per share obtained by such comparisons are misleading . . . comparisons in such cases should be made with financial data for the prior period restated on a combined [pooled] basis."[167]

Within the Commission, the SEC's June 1968 release was recognized as a small first step toward resolving the pooling versus purchase controversy. Later in 1968, Chairman Cohen publicly expressed alarm at the use of pooling to account for conglomerate mergers, stating in an October 26, 1968, address to the Financial Executives Institute:

> There is an urgent need for re-examination of the basic criteria established by the profession for determining the applicability of purchase or pooling accounting in a combination. These standards have been seriously eroded over the years . . . Where applicable accounting rules permit, the astute business manager still can increase a company's reported sales and earnings (if not apparent performance) by adding the sales and earnings of another company through merger or acquisition.[168]

Nearly simultaneously with Cohen's address, Chief Accountant Barr wrote a letter to the APB outlining what the SEC suggested were "acceptable criteria for pooling-of-interest accounting":

> The acquiring company should issue only unissued common shares or convertible preferred stock which is a common stock equivalent at issuance and has voting rights equal to those of the common stock into which it is convertible in exchange for the common shares or net assets of the company being acquired. Other types of securities, such as convertible debt and warrants, should not be used in a pooling transaction.
>
> The combination should be between viable corporate businesses and

---

* In 1966 and again in 1969, the SEC encouraged the APB to adopt Opinions Nos. 9 and 15, requiring that certain convertible securities and securities substantially equivalent to common stock be taken into account in calculating earnings per share. These opinions dealt with a tangential aspect of the pooling versus purchase controversy.

there should be a plan for continued operation of the businesses. The combination should be a tax-free reorganization.

As a practical matter, there should be a substantial size test with a minimum disparity of two to one between the combining enterprises.[169]

Even with an SEC chairman characterizing the pooling versus purchase controversy as "urgent" and the SEC's chief accountant able to describe a rule that would have resolved the controversy, the SEC did not act effectively. This, in part, was the consequence of the replacement of Cohen as chairman early in 1969 with Nixon's first appointee as chairman, Hamer Budge. In testimony prepared for Cohen to deliver in February 1969, he had intended to state that if the APB did not "promptly" solve the pooling problem, "the urgency of the situation may dictate rule-making by the Commission." But before Cohen could deliver this testimony, President Nixon accepted his resignation. Hamer Budge delivered the statement prepared for Cohen, but did not act on it.[170]

Approximately one year later, Budge testified to the Senate's Subcommittee on Antitrust and Monopoly that the APB soon would circulate a proposed draft of an opinion on business combinations that would include "very severe restrictions" encouraged by the SEC. Budge described some of these "restrictions," which bore a marked resemblance to Barr's suggestions to the APB in the fall of 1968. Notably, pooling was to be permitted only if the size ratio of the combining companies should be at least three to one.[171] Within three months, however, Budge made plain that the SEC had no intention of imposing such "very severe restrictions" on the APB. Responding to the lobbying efforts being waged by the Financial Executives Institute and others in opposition to the APB draft opinion, which the SEC had helped design, Budge informed the House Antitrust Subcommittee in May 1970:

> We are aware that there are strong objections to parts of this proposed opinion and that there is not unanimity of opinion on the proper recording of business combinations. The principal objections have been forcefully presented to the business world in releases of the Financial Executives Institute. This organization at first supported a 9-to-1 size test instead of the 3-to-1 test in the APB proposal but later reconsidered and it now takes the position that no size test should be imposed. The FEI also opposes mandatory amortization of intangibles. These views and those of all other interested parties must be considered. All concerned, I am sure, believe this to be one of the most important accounting problems today demanding a prompt solution, but it will be difficult to reach agreement on a definitive opinion.[172]

The following month, Budge repeated these remarks in an address to the American Society of Corporate Secretaries, adding that "some revisions may be made."[173] With the SEC thus refusing to impose the standards its own chief accountant earlier had suggested were appropriate, including the pivotal size test, the way was clear for the internally divided APB, in August 1970, to release its much-compromised Opinion No. 16, eliminating any size test and merely requiring that the combining companies be autonomous, employ voting common stock to effect the transaction, and for two years after the merger not plan to dispose of a significant part of the assets of the new combined firm. Although the SEC did secure from the board, in an accompanying APB Opinion No. 17 on intangible assets, a rule requiring that goodwill be written off over a period not exceeding forty years, there seems no plausible basis for believing that a Commission less reluctant to deal with accounting standards could not have issued a more effective rule several years earlier. As issued, APB Opinion No. 16 was little more restrictive than *ARB* No. 48 and almost as capable of being "seriously eroded" by case-by-case applications. A size test, by contrast, would have provided a workable and restrictive general rule.

During the 1969–1970 negotiations that culminated in the publication of APB Opinions Nos. 16 and 17, Barr's private communications to the board were notably different from the SEC's public statements. While Chairman Budge, at least until May 1970, publicly emphasized the SEC's intent to encourage "very severe restrictions" on pooling, Barr in private emphasized the SEC's intent to find a compromise rule satisfactory to all interested parties. The practical effect of Barr's private communications was to undercut the efforts of reform-minded members of the APB to achieve "very severe restrictions." It must be emphasized that at every step Barr moved with the approval of the SEC's five commissioners.

In August 1969 an APB subcommittee tentatively had voted to abolish pooling. Early in September, the SEC joined the Financial Executives Institute in opposing this reform, because "pooling of interests' accounting based on historical costs is valid and should be continued in appropriate circumstances." The SEC recommended that pooling be restricted and that " 'pooling of interests' accounting and 'purchase' should not be tolerated as alternative practices to attain a desired result."[174]

On October 8, 1969, the APB subcommittee again voted to proscribe all poolings. This time, Barr, though stating to the APB that he continued to believe "the pooling concept is valid in limited areas," encouraged the SEC to support the APB draft. "It is our opinion," he wrote to the Commission, "it will eliminate the flagrant abuses of pooling."[175]

When the full APB in December 1969 divided over its subcommittee's proposal to abolish all pooling, Barr telephoned the APB and stated that he expected the SEC to support a board opinion retaining pooling with a three-to-one size test.[176] At a January 20, 1970, meeting with an APB subcommittee, Barr went considerably further and stated "that while the Commission remained firm on mandatory amortization of acquired goodwill over a period not to exceed 40 years, the Commission would be prepared to withdraw its insistence on a size test if such action would assist the APB in hurdling the problem of attaining a two-thirds majority for exposure draft authorization or for ultimate adoption in an opinion."

SEC commissioner James Needham, also in attendance at the meeting, fully supported Barr. According to an SEC memorandum about the meeting, Needham stressed:

> If the APB desired to, or considered that it should, stand firm on the size test, or to abandon such test as a criterion for restricted pooling, the APB should be assured that their decision on this particular point would be supported by the Commission. Commissioner Needham expressly indicated that there was neither desire nor intent, on the part of the Commission, to negotiate with the APB, to get the APB to compromise its position on any facet of the draft opinion, or to tell the APB how the APB's draft opinions or final opinions should be written.[177]

Six months later, when the APB again divided over the size test, Barr repeated "that the Commission would support the position of eliminating the size test as long as the requirement for the mandatory amortization of goodwill was retained." In June 1970, what Barr "particularly emphasized" was that "the Commission desired a prompt resolution of this subject matter."[178]

At the time, the closest the SEC came to an official explanation of its passive approach toward the purchase versus pooling controversy was the conclusion of Cohen's October 1968 address to the Financial Executives Institute. Cohen conceded, "Many think we are taking too much time [to resolve the purchase versus pooling controversy]." But the SEC chairman did not see how the Commission could move any faster and hoped the profession itself would shoulder the burden of a "reasonably prompt solution . . . If you have followed our recent activities you know that we are not really looking for business. We have enough to keep us busy for some time . . . While I believe our sense of priorities here is sound, it should not be interpreted as a reflection of a lack of urgency or importance of a reasonably prompt solution of these problems."*

Although it was obviously true that the SEC's "sense of priorities" was the cause of the Commission's general inattention to the accounting aspects of the conglomerate-merger wave, this was not a satisfactory justification for the Commission's ineffectual oversight of accounting principles. In the years of Cohen's chairmanship, creative accounting plus debt leverage[180] gave the impression, as one FTC study put it, that the conglomerate was a "magic machine for generating money."[181] The "conglomerate mystique" was widely recognized as a stimulus to the feverish common stock speculation of the 1960s' "go-go" years, pushing Ling-Temco-Vought common stock, for one example, from $11 per share in 1964 to $136 in the 1968–1969 period. Inevitably, the high costs of buying "instant earnings" with fixed-interest debt securities and cumulative preferred stock caught up with LTV, and its common stock fell to $21 per share in March 1970, a decline of 85 percent during a period when the Dow Jones Industrial Average dropped 23 percent and Standard and Poor's Industrial Average 26 percent. LTV's experience was consistent with that of many other large conglomerates during this period. Between the stock market's 1968–1969 peak and March 1970, when the Dow Jones Average fell 23 percent, Litton common stock dropped 75 percent; Gulf & Western, 74 percent; Textron, 60 percent. Only ITT among the leading conglomerates outperformed the Dow Jones averages, declining only 16 percent. On average, the price of a sample of conglomerates dropped 56 percent between 1968 and mid-1970, compared with a drop in the average price of industrials of 37 percent. Because of their heavy leveraging, conglomerate bond prices fell 46 percent during the same period, or nearly six times the 8 percent decline of the Dow Jones Industrial Bond Average.†[182]

---

* William Cary offered a similar explanation for the SEC's "nonadversarial" relationship with the APB during his chairmanship. Cary noted that the SEC's chief accountant "was AICPA-oriented," the Office of Chief Accountant had a small staff, and there then did not appear to be "shocking problems" in the accounting field like those that became evident by the end of the 1960s.[179]

† Two economic studies concluded that investors, in fact, were not deceived by the pooling accounting technique. While these studies do suggest that the "rhetoric" of those who opposed pooling may have been somewhat overheated, they do not fully resolve the pooling controversy. It is difficult, given the stock price data quoted in the text, to believe that pooling did not contribute to artificial price run-ups in at least some instances. It also is difficult to believe that the rapid, wide price run-ups and declines of LTV, Litton, etc., did not persuade some investors to quit the market who might have remained in a market characterized by less extreme price oscillations.

The SEC's response to the conglomerate-merger wave was limited to two minor reforms, each of which was initiated by a member of Congress, rather than the Commission. In October 1965, Senator Harrison Williams proposed to protect "proud old companies" from "corporate raiders" by requiring that any shareholder or allied group of shareholders file a public statement with the SEC at least twenty days before making a cash tender offer that would result in the ownership of more than 5 percent of a class of stock of a firm subject to the 1934 Securities Exchange Act. The disclosure statement would remove the corporate raider's "cloak of secrecy," Williams explained, by describing the identity of the person making the tender offer, pre-existing shareholdings, the purpose of the tender offer, and the plans of the tenderer if he won control of the company. Senator Williams's melodramatic language aside, there was nothing particularly novel or far-reaching about his tender offer bill. When a person or corporation sought to gain control of a firm through a proxy election contest, comparable disclosures already were required by the 1934 Securities Exchange Act. By 1967, Great Britain, Canada, Australia, France, Germany, Italy, and the Netherlands had adopted rules regulating takeover bids.

The SEC followed a path of least resistance in helping Senator Williams refine his bill. The Commission made no study of possible abuses associated with takeover bids, the costs and benefits of tender offerer disclosure, or alternative remedial approaches. Nor did the Commission study the economic argument that it would be wise to minimize impediments to takeover bids since they theoretically tend to increase firm efficiency by reallocating control of productive resources from less profitable to more profitable managers. Instead, the SEC, in tandem with the New York Stock Exchange and various corporate representatives, suggested revisions to Senator Williams to transform his bill into a "neutral" disclosure statute that would give shareholders additional data with which to appraise a tender offer without "tipping the balance of regulation either in favor of management or in favor of the person making the takeover bid." This principally involved eliminating the requirement that a tender offerer file a statement twenty days in advance of the offer — which would have given the firm that was the "target" of the offer

Finally, it is difficult to believe that the opportunity to engage in pooling accounting did not motivate some firms' executives to engage in excessive debt leveraging. Nonetheless, these studies do suggest that the risks to investors of alternative accounting principles are reduced when the method of accounting is clearly disclosed.[183]

three extra weeks to plan defensive tactics or seek a friendlier suitor
— and requiring disclosures only from persons seeking 10 percent,
rather than 5 percent, of a class of stock. With these refinements the
Williams takeover bill was passed into law in July 1968.*

SEC chairman Cohen spoke or testified in favor of the Williams
takeover bill on several occasions in 1967 and 1968, emphasizing
the SEC's determination to avoid the raging policy controversy
about whether cash tender offers "are a *good* thing because they provide a method . . . of dislodging entrenched but incompetent management [or] a *bad* thing because they represent attempts by
disreputable people to obtain control of established companies." In
July 1968 testimony Cohen underlined the SEC's neutrality, stating
that "we do not wish to imply, however, that block acquisitions
should be encouraged or discouraged or that the Commission should
have power or responsibility to pass on the merits of a particular
acquisition or proposal."

It was precisely this policy that Cohen disowned eight months
later after leaving the Commission, when he no longer had the burden of husbanding the SEC's political resources or of speaking for
his relatively more conservative fellow commissioners. Testifying in
March 1969, he termed the Williams Act "obsolete" and its use of
disclosure to safeguard investors caught up in "mid-20th-century
industrial warfare" as "inadequate."† Cohen urged that the SEC be
empowered to set standards of conduct to regulate conglomerate
financial statements and debt-to-equity ratios "so that [the Com-
mission] does not have to rely on proving a fraud after the event,
which at best is a difficult problem." By the time of this testimony,
Richard Nixon was President and the SEC had been enjoined not to
pursue "heavy-handed bureaucratic regulatory schemes." The
Nixon SEC did not pursue Cohen's March 1969 proposals.[184]

The SEC again followed the path of least resistance in responding
to Senator Philip Hart's April 1965 inquiry about whether the securities laws should be amended to require financial disclosures by
conglomerate firms on a divisional basis.[185] The rapid increase in the
number of diversified or multiproduct-line firms during the 1960s
reduced the value of the securities laws' mandatory financial disclo-

---

* The Williams Act was modestly amended in December 1970, among other things,
reducing back to 5 percent the proportion of shares a tender offerer needed to seek to
trigger the act's filing requirement.
† Ironically, in spite of Senator Williams's original intention, studies of 137 contested
tender offers between 1972 and 1976 found that the success rate of unfriendly tender
offers "grew dramatically after Congress passed the Williams Act," apparently, in
part, because a federal disclosure statute made takeovers seem more respectable.

sures to investors and to antitrust enforcement agencies. In single-product firms, the securities laws' mandatory disclosures provided investors with operating results that could be compared with other firms' in the industry, thus giving investors a basis of appraising the competence of managerial performance. As corporations diversified, product-line data were lost.

Through 1965, the SEC usually required firms subject to the 1933 and 1934 securities laws to publish consolidated financial statements with accompanying description "insofar as practicable [of] the relative importance of each product or service or class of similar products or services which contributed 15 percent or more to the gross volume of business."[186] This requirement was sufficiently broad that financial data concerning entire industries disappeared from public scrutiny during the 1960s. A 1972 FTC staff report, for example, traced Gulf & Western's acquisition of ten firms with an aggregate asset value of $2.6 billion between 1965 and 1968, among them, the country's largest producer of cigars and the third-largest sugar refiner. "In 1965," the FTC reported, "one could obtain from public sources financial information for each of these companies. By 1970 all but [one] had effectively disappeared from public view." The FTC report further found that "in some industries, a number of the leading producers are controlled by large, diversified firms. In meatpacking, for instance, three of the four industry leaders [Armour, Wilson, and John Morrell] are no longer independent firms." Three diversified firms also accounted for a major portion of home appliance sales. Yet the loss of even a single industry leader could diminish the value of public financial data. As the FTC put it: "One cannot obtain a full understanding of the performance of the cigar industry, for example, if the profits of the leading firm are unknown."[187]

It was this phenomenon of information loss that prompted Senator Hart to write to the SEC in April 1965. Economics professor Joel Dirlam earlier had testified to Hart's Subcommittee on Antitrust and Monopoly:

> We are operating in almost complete ignorance in this area when we do not know even the sales of many of the major firms in different lines, let alone the profitability or losses incurred in these lines . . . the average investor . . . does not know what he is buying into when he purchases one of these large diversified firms. He has only the overall statements to go by. He judges then not the industry but the behavior of the firm itself, and he stakes his money on the management with a minimum of information.[188]

Dirlam's view was shared by many institutional investors and financial analysts. One executive of the Dreyfus Corporation wrote Senator Hart in May 1965 that without product-line data, investors had to proceed "on the basis of wholly inadequate information."[189] Later, a survey conducted by the Financial Analysts Federation would find that nearly two thirds of the research directors of firms in the securities industry indicated that product-line data, when available, improved their future earnings predictions in at least some cases.[190]

Nonetheless, Cohen's SEC responded hesitantly to Senator Hart's inquiry. Cohen reported that the SEC previously had refrained from requiring product-line data because of the technical difficulty of determining whether a multiproduct firm's financial results should be broken down "by divisions or companies, product lines or by industrial groupings" and the difficulty of allocating such common costs as overhead, research and development, and taxes among product lines. Cohen was doubtful that without precise rules concerning product-line definition and common cost allocation, product-line reporting would be "reliable or meaningful." His response also outlined the reasons that reporting corporations opposed product-line requirements, specifically noting the additional costs of obtaining product-line data, greater exposure to liabilities under the Securities Acts, and the more revealing disclosures that small firms would have to make in relation to large firms if a uniform percentage test (requiring disclosure of each product line responsible for 10 percent or more of sales) was applied.[191]

During the next three years, the SEC steered a middle course between investors and the antitrust agencies, which sought increased product-line data, and reporting corporations. In time, the Commission helped to fashion a rule that marginally increased disclosure to investors at a minimum cost to reporting corporations. Like its response to the Williams takeover bill, this action minimized political controversy in the short run but soon was characterized as "inadequate" by an official SEC report, among numerous other critics.

In addresses on May 19 and May 24, 1966, Chairman Cohen invited financial analysts and accountants to work with the Commission to develop conglomerate profit-and-loss statements on a divisional basis "so that a more complete financial picture of these complex companies can be made available."[192] After Cohen appeared before the Senate Antitrust and Monopoly Subcommittee in 1966 and testified before Senator Hart about the necessity and desirability of requiring conglomerate corporations to disclose product-line data,[193] the Financial Executives Institute indicated to the SEC that it would fund a major study of financial reporting by diversified companies to be headed by University of Illinois professor of accounting Robert Mautz. Although the FEI's members were exactly the same corporate officials who traditionally opposed product-line reporting, the *SEC Minutes* for September 30, 1966, stated that Chairman Cohen "assured the representatives of the FEI . . . of the Commission's support and cooperation in connection with the project."[194] The SEC met separately with the American Institute of Certified Public Accountants' Accounting Principles Board, which in September 1967 encouraged diversified firms to disclose voluntarily product-line data on a supplemental basis.[195] Cohen summarized the SEC's approach in a February 1967 address:

> The reluctance of some conglomerate or diversified companies to disclose the relative importance of the sources from which their earnings are derived has made it difficult, if not impossible, in many cases for investors to evaluate a company's performance and prospects in each of the various activities in which it is engaged and their effect on the future course of the enterprise as a whole. This removes or makes less effective an important internal control on management performance which was available when business structures were simpler; a division can be, and, indeed, has been operated inefficiently or at a loss for years without anyone outside the management being aware of it or of the extent of the drain on the results of other operations.

Although Cohen regarded this problem as serious, he concluded, "Again we are relying in the first instance on regulation by business and professional groups — in this case the Financial Executives Institute and the American Institute of Certified Public Accountants, as well as the individual companies themselves — to develop standards and to secure compliance with them."[196]

The SEC deviated only slightly from the standards subsequently recommended by the Financial Executives Institute. In 1968, Professor Mautz's study was published. While adopting the widely held belief of financial analysts that without "at least" knowledge of "the relative importance of the several industries engaged in by [a diversified] company . . . any forecast of its future prospects can scarcely be well-founded," Mautz concluded that management should be given "considerable discretion" to define product lines, allocate common costs, and price intracompany transfers. The Mautz report recommended that the SEC's prevailing requirement that product-line data be required only of each product or service contributing 15 percent or more of a company's gross revenue be retained.[197] In September 1968, Cohen's SEC proposed to amend its requirements for securities issues to specify that each product or service that contributed 10 percent or more to total sales disclose income. But, as the Mautz Report recommended, the SEC left to corporate management discretion to define product lines, allocate common costs, and price intracompany transfers. The SEC's proposal was adopted for securities issues in 1969 and for annual reports filed with the Commission in 1970. By its plain terms, the new product-line requirement failed to answer any of the technical problems whose resolution, Cohen had warned Senator Hart in 1965, were necessary to make product-line reporting "reliable or meaningful."[198]

Minimal as the Commission's reform was, two studies by Michigan State University's Daniel Collins found that the new standard "apparently does make a difference." Collins's 1975 study found that "investors were able to utilize these data to anticipate, to a large extent, changes in earnings which otherwise would have been 'unexpected' had they relied totally on consolidated data." Collins's 1976 study, however, added an important caveat: "Arbitrary allocations of joint costs [permissible under the SEC product-line disclosure rules] may limit the reliability and predictive usefulness of segment profitability data." In fact, the SEC's "flexible" line of business guidelines improved the accuracy of earnings forecasts based on product-line data by only 2 or 3 percent, Collins reported, compared with the "best" consolidated earnings formats.[199]

Few other studies of the SEC's product-line requirement were so generous in their assessments. In January 1969, a study by the staff of the Cabinet Committee on Price Stability found that the SEC's 10 percent rule "[fell] short of the degree of specificity required to provide the public with adequate information," explaining:

> Some conglomerate enterprises sell literally thousands of products falling into numerous "product classes," few of which constitute as much as 10 percent of total sales. Thus, the SEC standard would require complete reporting by the medium and large corporations whose output falls into only a few product classes, but the huge conglomerate would be required to make public the financial details of only a small share of its operations. For example, if the SEC 10 percent rule were interpreted to cover Census "industry categories," the 50 largest manufacturing companies would be required to provide financial information for only 14 percent of the industry categories in which they operated in 1963.

Both because the SEC's standard was considered "grossly inadequate" to protect investors and virtually meaningless for antitrust
enforcement, a Federal Trade Commission staff report later in 1969
joined the Cabinet Committee on Price Stability staff report in recommending divisional reporting for each corporate product line
with sales exceeding $25 million, under rules jointly framed by the
SEC and the FTC.[200]

In 1972, an FTC empirical study of nine conglomerate corporations found that a diversified firm under the SEC's reporting rules
could break down its earnings not by product line or division but by
generalized categories, such as "home products," which were "totally useless for evaluating the company in the markets in which it
operates."[201] The 1972 FTC report implied, according to economist
Frederic Scherer, who then was associated with the Federal Trade
Commission, "that many large corporations interpreted the SEC
rules in such a way as to report data of the least possible utility to
outsiders." Of the nine conglomerates studied, no loss was revealed
in any of the fifty-three product lines employed in 1971. Yet when
the FTC secured data on the nine firms' own 361 internal reporting divisions, seventy-nine (or one in eight) proved to be losing
money.[202]

Even the SEC subsequently did not disagree with attorney Dan
Goldwasser's assertion that the discretion afforded management to
define product lines and allocate common costs meant "the resulting reports were often a mockery."[203] The Commission's 1977 Advisory Committee on Corporate Disclosure reported "almost universal
dissatisfaction [among financial] analysts . . . with the level of seg-
mentation currently provided by registrants in SEC disclosure documents."*[204]

The SEC's response to the 1960s' conglomerate-merger wave revealed gaping weaknesses in the Commission's program to protect
investors, weaknesses that in some respects to this day have not been
repaired. The SEC's response suggested the inherent difficulty of
directing any federal regulatory agency under an ambiguous statutory mandate to alter to any measurable extent the practices of an
industry without effective support from either the Executive Branch
or Congress, if not both. The Commission's inadequate response to
the conglomerate-merger wave also powerfully suggested the need

---

* In 1976 and 1977 the Financial Accounting Standards Board and the SEC respectively promulgated rules to limit management's discretion in defining product lines
and allocating common costs.[205]

for Congress to oversee more effectively SEC regulation of accounting principles or empower the SEC to regulate accounting under a more explicit mandate. In the immediate aftermath of the go-go years, Congress did not do so. The Senate and House committees overseeing the SEC, like the Commission itself, concentrated on a long-overdue restructuring of the securities industry.

12

An Unfinished Agenda

The major regulatory problems in the securities industry have not by and large been the result of the ·SEC's lack of authority but rather of its unwillingness to use the powers it already has.

— *Senate "Securities*
Industry Study" (1973)

ONE OF THE most significant concepts in securities regulation is that of SEC supervision of industry self-regulation. SEC supervision of industry self-regulation is a thread that unites several aspects of the Commission's broad jurisdiction. There are obvious examples, such as SEC supervision of the securities exchanges and over-the-counter markets, as well as less immediately obvious examples, such as SEC supervision of accounting-standard-setting, new securities issues, and corporate governance. As articulated during the New Deal chairmanships of Landis, Douglas, and Frank, the necessity for SEC supervision of industry self-regulation stemmed from two quite distinct bases. First, the impracticality of direct SEC regulation of the several thousand broker-dealers and business corporations subject to its jurisdiction. Second, as well illustrated by the Commission's supervision of the geographic integration and simplification of the public utility holding companies, a preference for business, with its greater practical knowledge of its own affairs, to participate in the application of SEC rules and thus reduce the likelihood of unnecessary disruption or inefficiency.

Far from being a panacea, SEC supervision of industry self-regulation generally has been effective in its major applications only when the Commission has been willing to threaten or actually use its regulatory authority to create incentives for industrial self-regulation.

As a 1973 report of the Senate Subcommittee on Securities aptly stated:

> The inherent limitations in allowing an industry to regulate itself are well known: the natural lack of enthusiasm for regulation on the part of the group to be regulated, the temptation to use a facade of industry regulation as a shield to ward off more meaningful regulation, the tendency for businessmen to use collective action to advance their interests through the imposition of purely anticompetitive restraints as opposed to those justified by regulatory needs, and a resistance to changes in the regulatory pattern because of vested economic interests in its preservation.[1]

By the time of the Nixon-Ford presidential administration, deficiencies in several aspects of industrial self-regulation had become glaringly apparent. The 1963 SEC *Special Study* and 1968 commission-rate hearings documented that without a more assertive SEC, the New York Stock Exchange was unwilling to design a commission-rate structure related to transaction costs and that market forces alone were unable to evolve brokerage rates whose benefits directly redounded to investors. The 1967–1970 back-office crisis resulted in an unprecedented number of broker-dealer firm failures, some of which could have been avoided by more effective SEC or industry regulation of broker-dealer practices. After the 1969–1970 stock market crash it would be obvious, if it had not been earlier, that the laxity of accounting standards was not limited to the pooling versus purchase controversy. The 1970 Penn Central failure and the corporate bribery scandals of the mid-1970s would raise equally disturbing questions about the performance of corporate boards of directors.

The erratic character of President Nixon's SEC appointments profoundly influenced the Commission's response to each of these self-regulatory crises. Richard Nixon's clearest interest in the SEC during the first years of his presidency was to use his appointment powers for political purposes unrelated to the securities industry. Just as his October 1968 campaign letter criticizing the SEC for proposing "heavy-handed bureaucratic regulatory schemes" was an obvious appeal for Wall Street financial contributions, approximately half of Nixon's ten SEC appointments were made for predominantly political reasons. Embarrassment over the performance of Nixon's first SEC chairman, Hamer Budge, coupled with Nixon's determination after his third chairman, G. Bradford Cook, was implicated in the Watergate scandal to make SEC commissioner appointments strictly on merit, led to the appointment of several highly qualified men to be SEC commissioners. Ironically, given Nixon's initial indifference, at no time in SEC history, including the New Deal, was the Commission simultaneously served by five more able commissioners than it was during the 1973–1975 period, when Chairman Ray Garrett and Commissioners Philip Loomis, John Evans, A. A. Sommer, and Irving Pollack led the SEC.[2]

When Nixon began his presidency in January 1969, he had the statutory power to name the SEC's chairman, but there were no vacancies on the Commission. This meant, as a practical matter, that Nixon could have retained Manuel Cohen as chairman until the next vacancy on the Commission occurred or named one of the two Republican members of the Commission, Hamer Budge and Richard Smith, to be chairman. Not knowing Smith, Nixon in February 1969 abruptly dismissed Cohen and named Budge, a former colleague from the House of Representatives, to be chairman of the SEC.*

In 1964, Budge had been a controversial Johnson political appointee to the Commission.[3] A five-term congressman from Idaho, until he was defeated for re-election in 1960, Budge had served as a judge in Idaho until House Republican leader Charles Halleck persuaded Johnson to nominate Budge to the SEC. Lacking any experience in the securities industry, Budge, innately conservative, in June 1969 characterized his general approach to federal regulation with the observation "Just as an across-the-board statement, I feel the government should not tell people how to conduct their affairs."[4] Largely because of Budge's hostility to the use of federal regulatory power, Senator Lee Metcalf termed him "the worst possible choice" for the SEC when Budge was confirmed by the Senate in June 1964. During his four and a half years as a commissioner under Manuel Cohen, Budge was best remembered for his insistence that the SEC apply no more severe sanctions to small regional broker-dealers than to major New York City firms.

As chairman, Budge attempted to reverse the activism of the later Cohen years. Budge viewed the SEC as quasi-judicial in nature; he preferred that fundamental decisions concerning the securities in-

---

* Similar considerations led Nixon later in 1969 to select as a commissioner A. Sydney Herlong, a retired Democratic congressman from Florida who had campaigned for Nixon in 1968.

dustry be made by Congress, the federal courts, or the industry itself, and he favored limiting the commissioners' function largely to a review of staff initiatives.[5] To Budge's credit, he did rely on highly competent senior staff officials, notably General Counsel Philip Loomis, Trading and Markets Division director Irving Pollack, and Alan Levenson, whom Budge appointed to direct the Division of Corporate Finance. But Budge's restriction of the SEC to a quasi-judicial role early was recognized as impairing the SEC's ability to address securities industry policy issues.

President Nixon's Administrative Council on Executive Organization in 1971 would complain, "The SEC as a collegial body at times finds itself debating what is to be done while problems in the investment community continue to mount. Protracted proceedings and deliberations prevent it from keeping pace with change in the investment community." Other critics were more blunt. *Business Week*, in September 1969, reported concern on Wall Street "that [the] SEC may be grinding to a halt" because of "the men the President has chosen"; *The New York Times* ten months later added, "Among those who do keep informed, the blame for the near-paralysis of the Commission is assigned mainly to its present chairman, Hamer H. Budge." Similarly, *Time* magazine attributed to Budge "a penchant for delay."[6] Such views of Budge were not held by everyone. Several senior SEC officials during the Budge chairmanship, notably including Stanley Sporkin and chief economist Gene Finn, lauded Budge for his support of the Commission's program to deal with the back-office crisis and for his efforts to begin the unfixing of commission rates.

The most serious criticism of the Budge SEC was that its approach to the Commission's budget was self-defeating. During 1969, Budge's first year as chairman, 4706 securities registration statements were filed, nearly double the 1968 total. Simultaneously, the broker-dealer firms' back-office problems reached crisis proportions. The SEC's *Thirty-fifth Annual Report* emphasized, "In fiscal year 1969 . . . the Commission was so inundated with complaints [against broker-dealers] that at times it was unable to make a prompt reply to a complainant, much less an investigation of his charges." Despite the recommendations of some in Congress and fellow SEC commissioners Richard Smith and James Needham, Budge did not seek an adequate appropriation for the 1970 or 1971 fiscal years.[7] He reduced the effectiveness of the Division of Trading and Markets' enforcement staff by cutting back on travel money. The chairman took considerable pride in the fact that fees received by the SEC in 1969 exceeded the cost of funding the agency. But the average time for the SEC to process a security registration statement reached a median of 110 days in January 1970, five and a half times the statutory standard.[8]

By the second year of Budge's two-year chairmanship, the Commission was being assailed for its slow response to the broker-dealer firm back-office crisis, its failure to make decisions about the commission-rate issues, delays in publishing its *Institutional Investor Study*, the length of time required to process securities registration statements, slowness in completing studies of hedge funds and the Lockheed Corporation, its difficulty in retaining senior staff members, and its general passivity in supervising the securities industry's self-regulatory organizations.[9]

Budge himself seemed to have lost interest in the SEC chairmanship. Scarcely six months after having accepted the job, he had attempted to negotiate a job with Investors Diversified Services, the nation's largest complex of mutual funds. Embarrassed by Senator William Proxmire's accusation that it was a "gross conflict of interest" for an SEC chairman to negotiate for a job with a mutual fund while the SEC was lobbying for new legislation to regulate the mutual fund industry, Budge deferred his resignation for eighteen months.[10]

Before Budge left the SEC in January 1971, the Commission made considerable progress toward alleviating the broker-dealer firm back-office crisis, and secured enactment of three new securities laws, the Securities Investors Protection Act, the 1970 Investment Company Act Amendments, and the 1970 Williams Act Amendments. None of these accomplishments significantly lessened congressional frustration with Budge's leadership of the SEC. Near the conclusion of his tenure, House Commerce Subcommittee chairman John Moss and Senate Banking Subcommittee chairman Harrison Williams separately initiated major studies of the securities industry. Between 1971 and 1975, the SEC's supervision of stock market regulation was the subject of almost incessant congressional hearings and reports. Aided by former SEC officials David Ratner, Stephen Paradise, and, briefly, William Cary, congressional oversight of the SEC markedly influenced the SEC's subsequent decisions totally to unfix securities brokerage commissions and establish an electronically linked national securities market system, just as later congressional hearings would help inspire the SEC to take modest steps to reform corporate governance.

William Casey, Nixon's second SEC chairman, like Hamer Budge, was chosen primarily for political reasons. An attorney with little experience in the securities field, Casey was a law partner of former Republican Party national chairman Leonard Hall. In 1966 Casey had been an unsuccessful candidate for a Republican congressional nomination and in 1968 a major financial contributor to Republican candidates. Casey further supported Richard Nixon during 1969 as chairman of Citizens for the ABM and as one of the sponsors of a full-page advertisement in the *New York Times* defending the antiballistic missile when it was debated in Congress.* Casey was a man of diverse parts. During World War II, he had assisted David K. E. Bruce in coordinating the activities of the French Resistance and later was chief of OSS intelligence operations in the European theater. After the war, Casey amassed a fortune, principally as a tax attorney and self-styled "venture capitalist" investor and promoter of new enterprises. Author of several books, Casey served as chairman of the Board of Editors of the Institute for Business Planning, a subsidiary of Prentice-Hall, and lectured on tax law at New York University. He also participated in organizations as disparate as the International Rescue Committee, the Roosevelt Raceway, and the Brookings Institution's Advisory Committee on Presidential Selection Studies.[11]

Casey soon was subjected to intense congressional criticism. The Senate Banking Committee tentatively had agreed to report favorably on Casey's nomination to be SEC chairman on February 10, 1971, pending review of the litigation record of a plagiarism suit filed against Casey that had been settled out of court in 1960. But the Banking Committee learned that Casey had been the defendant in two other civil suits alleging violations of the securities laws, one settled in 1969 for $8000 of $10,000 sought, the second pending at the time of his nomination. The committee also learned that Casey's Senate testimony concerning the plagiarism suit inaccurately had given the impression that no plagiarism had occurred, though, in fact, Casey later acknowledged that an associate had plagiarized two and a half pages of a manuscript on employee benefit plans. By a 9–3 vote, the Banking Committee accepted Casey's explanation of each lawsuit and recommended Casey's confirmation, rejecting Senator Proxmire's view that Casey "had made less than a complete and accurate disclosure of his activities to Congress."[12]

Casey proved to be a decisive and able administrator. Rapidly concluding that neither the SEC nor industry self-regulation was working "as well as it should,"[13] Casey repaired several of the Com-

---

* In 1980, Casey served as the national chairman of Ronald Reagan's presidential campaign and the following year was chosen by Reagan to be director of the Central Intelligence Agency.

mission's obvious defects. With the aid of Commissioner Herlong, who until 1969 had been a member of the influential House Ways and Means Committee, Casey extracted from the White House Office of Management and Budget and Congress budget increases sufficient to expand the SEC staff from 1356 to 1814 between December 1971 and the 1974 fiscal year.[14] At Casey's insistence, General Counsel Philip Loomis was elevated to a commissionership in 1971, and the able John Burton was hired to be the Commission's chief accountant after Andrew Barr retired in 1972.[15]

Casey's chairmanship was dominated by two issues: the future of fixed commission rates and the development of a central securities market system. In the period between Budge's resignation in January 1971 and the beginning of Casey's chairmanship in mid-April, the SEC ordered the New York Stock Exchange to require competitive rates on all securities transactions in excess of $500,000. The SEC also recommended in its letter of transmittal accompanying the *Institutional Investor Study* as "a major goal and ideal of the securities markets . . . the creation of a strong central market system for securities of national importance, in which all buying and selling interest in these securities could participate and be represented under a competitive regime."[16] Subject to conflicting congressional and industry pressures concerning commission rates, the Casey SEC moved gingerly forward on this issue, eliminating fixed rates on orders above $300,000 in February 1972 and subsequently stating its intention to reduce the fixed-rate breakpoint to $100,000 by 1974.[17]

In sharp contrast, with the publication of the SEC's "Statement on the Future Structure of the Securities Markets" in February 1972, Casey became the first SEC chairman to address the mechanics of an electronically linked national securities market system. The "Future Structure Statement" represented a turning point in SEC history. The Commission assumed what Ray Garrett, later as chairman, termed "a new role in relation to our market system":

> Instead of being content to police a system developed and operated by the private sector, the Commission has undertaken a leading role in developing a new system. We have gone beyond criticism of specific aspects of a private system, where deemed necessary to ensure fairness and to protect small investors, to presuming to lay down a whole new pattern for the future.[18]

With the 1975 Securities Acts Amendments Congress endorsed the SEC's effort "to facilitate the establishment of a national market system." Significantly, while the 1975 amendments granted the SEC enabling powers, it left to the SEC the facilitation of the elements of the new securities market system. A 1975 Senate Banking Committee report explained:

> In the new regulatory environment created by this bill, self-regulation would be continued, but the SEC would be expected to play a much larger role than it has in the past to ensure that there is no gap between self-regulatory performance and regulatory need and, when appropriate, to provide leadership for the development of a more coherent and rational regulatory structure to correspond to and to police effectively the new national market system.[19]

Casey's chairmanship ended as controversially as it began. In August and September 1972, Senate and House subcommittees requested that the SEC provide copies of files it had compiled during the course of an investigation of alleged securities law violations by ITT. The congressional subcommittees were attempting to determine whether the SEC files contained documents substantiating allegations that ITT had tried to persuade the Nixon administration to settle an antitrust action by offering a financial contribution to the 1972 Republican National Convention. Subsequent congressional investigations revealed that after meeting with Nixon's counsel John Dean and former Attorney General John Mitchell, Casey persuaded the SEC to forward thirty-four cartons of ITT files to the Justice Department so that it could investigate a possible obstruction of justice. This effectively placed the files beyond the reach of Congress. Since Casey earlier had given Congressman Harley Staggers the impression that the SEC would consider a House subcommittee's request to see these files at the end of the Commission's ITT investigation, the abrupt transfer of the files to the Justice Department was condemned by Staggers and Congressman Moss as a serious affront [to Congress]."[20]

After Casey resigned his chairmanship in February 1973 to become Undersecretary of State, President Nixon nominated G. Bradford Cook to be the SEC chairman.* At thirty-five, Cook was the youngest man ever nominated to the position. As with Budge and Casey, Cook's nomination was more a reward for political services than a judgment on the merits. Cook's father, an influential Midwestern Republican fund-raiser, had been a senior official in Nixon's 1968

---

* Simultaneously Nixon nominated former Senate Banking Committee minority staff director John Evans to be an SEC commissioner. Evans, at one time an economics assistant to Utah senator Wallace Bennett, was nominated primarily as a result of Bennett's support. Unlike several other political nominees to the Commission, Evans, with seven years' experience on the Senate Banking Committee and economics training, was well prepared for service at the SEC.

and 1972 presidential campaigns. Still, Cook had considerable paper qualifications for the job. A 1962 graduate of the University of Nebraska Law School, Cook had been a partner in the Chicago law firm of Winston and Strawn, specializing in corporate and securities law, when, in 1971, Chairman Casey hired him to be the SEC's general counsel. As general counsel, Cook worked with Casey on the development of the SEC's 1972 "Future Structure Statement." When the SEC was reorganized in August 1972, Cook was named director of the Division of Market Regulation, becoming the senior staff official responsible for the SEC's two most important projects at the time, commission-rate regulation and the central securities market. During Cook's brief chairmanship, the SEC continued the Casey Commission's policies, most notably publishing the March 1973 "Policy Statement on the Structure of a Central Market System," amplifying the Casey SEC's February 1972 "Future Structure Statement."

Seventy-four days after beginning as SEC chairman, Cook resigned, the first SEC commissioner to be implicated in a scandal. During his confirmation hearings, Cook had testified that "I have had very few calls from the White House" and that these contacts with the White House had "all been innocuous, to say the least." Flatly contradicting this testimony, a mid-May 1973 criminal indictment, charging former Attorney General John Mitchell, former Secretary of Commerce Maurice Stans, and Robert Vesco with obstruction of justice, alleged that Stans "did cause" G. Bradford Cook to delete all references from a separate SEC injunction action alleging that Vesco had made a secret $200,000 cash contribution to the Committee to Re-Elect the President. The indictment also alleged that Stans caused Cook to request the SEC staff not to file publicly certain transcripts of testimony relating to the Vesco contribution.

Cook denied that the SEC's investigation of Vesco had been compromised and insisted that Commission senior officials, including Chairman Casey and Stanley Sporkin, had not objected to the deletion of the paragraph describing the Vesco campaign contribution. But Cook acknowledged that he had not "answer[ed] as candidly as I should have" when he testified at his confirmation hearings that he had had "very few calls from the White House." In Cook's own version of events, he had initiated discussion of the Vesco contribution with Maurice Stans during a November 13, 1972, hunting trip, approximately two weeks before the SEC's Vesco injunction case was filed. By then, Cook knew that Casey intended to leave the SEC and was actively campaigning for the chairmanship. Stans, Cook testified, two days later telephoned to ask "Why do you need that [the reference to the Vesco campaign contribution] in your complaint?" Cook then suggested to Sporkin that the reference be deleted, since it amounted to "pleading evidence." After the SEC's action against Vesco was filed on November 26, 1972, without reference to the campaign contribution, Stans informed Cook, "I will do whatever I can to see that you become chairman."

Within a few days after the criminal indictment against Mitchell, Stans, and Vesco was filed, Cook resigned, stating, "The web of circumstance that I find myself confronted with has made me feel that the effectiveness of the agency might be impaired." In an interview shortly after, the *Washington Star-News* reported Cook's concern that there soon would be calls for his impeachment had, in part, led to his conclusion that "it would be best for me to resign."[21]

Cook's resignation, less than three weeks after Nixon's two top White House associates, H. R. Haldeman and John Ehrlichman, resigned amid allegations that they had violated criminal laws during the Watergate scandal, moved Nixon, for the first time during his presidency, to nominate an SEC chairman purely on the basis of experience and ability. The selection of an SEC chairman became part of a broader Nixon campaign to save his presidency by demonstrating that his administration still could attract talented officials and effectively function despite Watergate.[22]

Early in the selection process, the SEC chairmanship was offered to Ray Garrett, Jr., a partner in the Chicago law firm of Gardner, Carton, Douglas, Children and Waud. Garrett, a conservative but essentially apolitical man, had been a member of the SEC staff between 1954 and 1958, for most of that period as director of the Division of Corporate Regulation. During his ensuing law firm career, Garrett had been a recognized leader of the national corporate and securities bar. In 1965, he had been selected chairman of the American Bar Association's Section on Corporation, Banking, and Business Law. Subsequently, Garrett chaired the Advisory Committee for the Corporate Department Financing Project of the American Bar Foundation and served as a consultant to Harvard Law School professor Louis Loss's American Law Institute Federal Securities Law Codification project.[23] For personal reasons, Garrett initially declined the SEC chairmanship and recommended instead a fellow leader of the corporate and securities bar, A. A. Sommer, Jr. Sommer, a partner in the Cleveland law firm of Calfee, Halter, Calfee, Griswold and Sommer, was a member of the Board of Governors of the NASD and a frequent lecturer and writer on securities, corporate, and accounting law. But he was not acceptable to the Nixon administration as an SEC chairman because he was a Democrat.[24] However, after A. Sydney Herlong's term as an SEC commissioner expired on June 30, 1973, Alexander Haig, then Nixon's chief of staff, persuaded Garrett to accept the SEC chairmanship, and Sommer agreed to succeed Herlong as a commissioner.

Senator Harrison Williams reflected the sentiments of many when he termed the nominations of Garrett and Sommer "a most refreshing breath of fresh air." The two new commissioners were sworn in together early in August 1973. Six months later, Nixon made his final SEC appointment. After Garrett, in the words of SEC commissioner John Evans, "laid his own position on the line" (that is, threatened to resign), Nixon nominated Irving Pollack to be a commissioner. Like his close friend Manuel Cohen, Pollack was a graduate of Brooklyn Law School and a career Commission staff attorney. Pollack was aptly described by *Time* as the "Maigret of the SEC" for his role in building up the SEC's headquarters enforcement staff while associate, and then full, director of the Commission's Division of Trading and Markets. Until the August 1972 Commission reorganization, Pollack also had supervised the SEC's market regulation staff, performing a key role in the Commission's initial efforts to unfix commission rates. In 1967 Pollack was awarded the SEC Distinguished Service Award for Outstanding Career Service, and in 1968 he was a corecipient of the Rockefeller Public Service Award in the field of law, legislation, and regulation.[25]

The cumulative effect of Nixon's declining political influence during the Watergate scandal and his appointment of five highly competent, but essentially apolitical, commissioners to serve during Garrett's 1973–1975 chairmanship was that the SEC gained an unusual degree of independence from the White House. This political independence was most vividly illustrated by the Garrett Commission's controversial program to require the disclosure of questionable or illegal corporate payments. The ensuing revelation by over 450 American business corporations that they had engaged in such practices as falsification of their accounting records or creation of slush funds to pay bribes to overseas or domestic political or commercial officials led to the enactment of the 1977 Foreign Corrupt Practices Act and precipitated broader SEC and congressional re-examinations of corporate governance.

Early during the Garrett chairmanship, the SEC decisively ended the decade-long debate on the necessity of fixed securities brokerage commission rates by ordering the abolition of all fixed rates on May 1, 1975. By the time the Garrett Commission acted, it was assumed that the abolition of fixed rates was inevitable. Had the SEC not acted, Congress was prepared to do so. But the Garrett Commission's decisive resolution of the issue, and its refusal to back down once the decision was made, bolstered congressional confidence in the SEC.

Under Garrett, the style of the New Deal and Cohen SEC was revived. As Garrett's close associate Harvey Pitt recalled, "He never forgot that he was once a member of the staff . . . every major appointment during his tenure came from within the agency." Discussion at the SEC table was uninhibited. Yet Garrett, even when his initial policy preferences on such pivotal issues as corporate questionable payment disclosure or commission rates did not prevail, vigorously defended Commission decisions in public.[26]

Roderick Hills, Gerald Ford's choice for SEC chairman after Garrett resigned in October 1975, was a less influential chairman than Garrett or Casey. Hills was an honors graduate of Stanford Law School, law clerk to Supreme Court Justice Stanley Reed, and a founding partner of a Los Angeles law firm. Subsequently, Hills had been a visiting professor at Harvard Law School during the 1969–1970 academic year and chairman of the board of the Republic Corporation between 1971 and 1975. Nonetheless, Hills began with the fundamental disadvantage of possessing little actual experience in the securities field. He was a labor law specialist whose appointments, first as counsel to President Ford in April 1975, then as SEC chairman six months later, were inspired by Ford's desire to give Hills meaningful assignments while Hills's wife served as Ford's Secretary of Housing and Urban Development. Having served as chairman of Ford's Task Force on Regulatory Reform, Hills evinced, during his eighteen months as the SEC's chairman, strong views on the need to "deregulate" the investment company industry. His chief contributions as SEC chairman would be the defense of the Commission's questionable payments disclosure program, supporting the initiation of an SEC Advisory Committee Study of its corporate disclosure program, and helping to initiate an SEC re-examination of corporate governance.[27]

*   *   *

The 1967–1970 broker-dealer firm back-office crisis was the most serious failure of securities industry self-regulation in the Commission's history, a collapse of industry regulatory controls so complete that it permitted, in the agency's retrospective view, "the most prolonged and severe crisis in the securities industry in forty years."[28]

The back-office crisis effectively occurred in two phases. During the period from 1967 to early 1969, as SEC chairman Budge testified, "brokerage firms [found] themselves in the paradox of being forced out of business by having too much business."[29] Average daily reported volume on the New York Stock Exchange grew by 265 percent between 1964 and 1968, from 4.89 million shares per average day in 1964 to 12.97 million shares in 1968, reaching a high of 14.9 million shares per average day during the month of December 1968.[30]

Back-office inefficiency in processing the increasing number of securities transactions increased concurrently.

> The operational crisis in the securities industry first reached major dimensions in August of 1967 [the SEC subsequently reported]. Newspaper reports of that period recall the feverish efforts of the Wall Street community to keep up with each day's business: Stock certificates and related documents were piled "halfway to the ceiling" in some offices; clerical personnel were working overtime, six and seven days a week, with some firms using a second or even a third shift to process each day's transactions.[31]

To alleviate the back-office paper crunch, the exchanges and the NASD shortened the trading day for a brief period in August 1967 and for about six weeks beginning in January 1968.[32]

These palliatives had little effect. Total complaints to the SEC concerning broker-dealers jumped from 3991 in the 1968 fiscal year to 12,494 in 1969, with nine out of ten complaints describing back-office problems, "particularly the failure to deliver customer funds and securities" in a timely manner.[33] In April 1968, the first month during which the New York Stock Exchange gathered relevant statistics, member firms' "fails" (that is, failure to deliver securities by the official settlement day) came to $2.67 billion, subsequently rising to $4.12 billion in December 1968. Throughout 1969 and 1970 the dollar value of fails declined, but as late as July 1969, SEC chairman Budge reported, "One out of every 8.4 transactions was a fail."[34]

The rising number of securities customer complaints and fails was symptomatic of an industrywide loss of control of record-keeping procedures. In the four-year period 1967–1970, the New York Stock Exchange would find it necessary to intervene directly in the affairs of nearly two hundred member organizations, over half of the Exchange member firms that dealt with the public, because of firms' operational deficiencies.[35]

The first broker-dealer firm liquidation related to the crisis occurred in May 1968, with the failure of the small NYSE firm of

Pickard & Company (3500 customers). Pickard had been a habitual violator of SEC and Exchange regulations since its admission to Exchange membership in 1963. In consenting to an SEC administration order in October 1968, Pickard admitted egregious violations of the securities laws, including misrepresenting its financial condition to lenders, who lost over $2 million as a result of the firm's liquidation, illegally selling unregistered stock, and manipulating the price of Rowland Products common stock. The initial paragraph of the Commission's findings in its October 1968 administrative proceeding also stated that Pickard had

> accepted orders for the purchase and sale of securities and effected securities transactions on behalf of customers when registrant's books and records were not current, contained numerous errors, and could not be relied upon accurately and promptly to reflect the securities or cash held for the accounts of customers; when it did not have the facilities and personnel necessary in order promptly to consummate customers' securities transactions and make delivery of securities and cash to such customers; and when it was not in compliance with the financial requirements imposed on members by the New York Stock Exchange.[36]

Similar findings were regularly reported during the second, or financial, phase of the back-office crisis, which roughly coincided with the stock market slump of 1969–1970. Between May 14, 1969, and May 26, 1970, the Dow Jones Industrial Average fell 35 percent, from a high of 968.85 to a low of 631.16,[37] precipitating a decline in New York Stock Exchange volume from a 1968 daily average of nearly 13 million shares to a 1969–1970 daily average of approximately 11 million shares.[38] The volume decline resulted in industrywide losses. For example, the average NYSE member firm reported a loss of 2.9 percent from securities business in 1969, compared with a profit of 9.9 percent in 1968. To cushion securities firm unprofitability, the SEC early in April 1970 approved an emergency $15 surcharge on all brokerage transactions of fewer than 1000 shares. Even with the surcharge, an SEC survey of seventy-two leading securities firms in May 1970 found that month's aggregate expenses exceeded aggregate income by nearly 11 percent.[39]

The securities industry's prolonged unprofitability, coupled with the financial losses created by the 1967–1968 back-office operations breakdown, set in motion the greatest rash of broker-dealer firm failures in Wall Street's history. Approximately 160 New York Stock Exchange member organizations went out of business in 1969 and 1970, about 80 merging with other firms, and the other 80, found a 1972 House of Representatives report, "quietly dissolved, self-liquidated, or retired from the securities business."[*][40] It was a period of "perpetual crisis" in New York Stock Exchange president Haack's view,[42] a period during which, subsequent SEC chairman William Casey opined, "firms and self-regulatory authorities were thrashing about in all directions fighting to avoid catastrophe," their problem comparable to that of Kutuzov, the Russian commander-in-chief in Tolstoy's *War and Peace,* who was "always in the midst of a series of shifting events and so he never can at any moment consider the whole import of an event that is occurring."[43]

The wave of brokerage house failures began in late October 1969 when the New York Stock Exchange appointed a liquidator for Gregory & Sons, a member firm. Ultimately, the Exchange had to expend $5.34 million of its Special Trust Fund to reimburse Gregory & Sons' customers during the firm's liquidation.[44] Two months later, the Exchange announced the liquidation of Amott, Baker & Company, subsequently expending $1.86 million of its Special Trust Fund, which was considered a sizable sum for a firm with only seven thousand customers.[45] In March 1970 the first major brokerage house failure occurred when McDonnell & Company collapsed. McDonnell & Company, journalist Chris Welles tersely wrote, was

> one of the largest and most respected houses on Wall Street, which only two years before had had $33 million in annual revenues, a net worth of $15 million, 26 branch offices throughout the United States and in France, membership on eight stock exchanges including three [seats] on the Big Board, 1500 employees including 350 salesmen, and close to 100,000 customers who made some 3500 trades daily.

The impression of McDonnell & Company as a future "Merrill Lynch" had been further bolstered in January 1969, when Lawrence O'Brien, long-time Kennedy family associate, then chairman of the Democratic National Committee, was hired to be the firm's president. Seven months later, O'Brien resigned. The firm's subsequent liquidation was reported to have cost nearly $19 million, with the New York Stock Exchange Special Trust Fund expending about $9

---

[*] Counting non–New York Stock Exchange securities firms, the total number of firms that went out of business during the 1969–1970 period was considerably greater. Securities firm failures continued at a high rate during the 1971–1973 period, with seventy-nine firms formally liquidating under the 1970 Securities Investor Protection Act through March 31, 1973.[41]

million, and the McDonnell family absorbing losses believed to be close to $10 million.[46]

After McDonnell & Company's collapse, the frequency of Exchange member firm failures accelerated. Less than two weeks later, Baerwald & De Boer was placed in liquidation; in April, Kleiner, Bell & Company; by June, four other firms: Meyerson & Company, Fusz-Schmelzle, Orvis Brothers, and Blair & Company. Of these failures, the most serious was that of Blair & Company, which, as recently as February 1969, had attempted to rescue the foundering Schwabacher & Company through a merger. The New York Stock Exchange set aside $26 million from the Special Trust Fund for Blair & Company, the most the Exchange was to expend directly on a liquidation. The following month, July 1970, the Exchange began its third major liquidation, soon allocating $21.8 million to protect the 70,000 customers of Dempsey-Tegeler & Company.[47] Weeks later, the Exchange supervised a fourth major firm failure, providing over $12 million in loan, purchase, and guarantee funds to enable forty-five of Hayden, Stone's branch offices (and most of its 65,000 customer accounts) to be absorbed by two other securities firms, Walston & Company and Cogan, Berlind, Weill & Levitt.[48] With its Special Trust Fund effectively depleted,[49] the Exchange refused to protect the customers of three small firms that also failed in August 1970: First Devonshire Corporation, Charles Plohn & Company, and Robinson & Company.[50]

It was then that the two most serious events of the back-office crisis occurred. In October 1970, Goodbody and Company, the nation's fifth-largest brokerage house, with nearly 250,000 customers, neared collapse and was hurriedly merged with Merrill Lynch, the nation's largest brokerage firm, after the Exchange arranged a $21 million bail-out of Goodbody's subordinated loans and guaranteed up to $30 million indemnification for lawsuits that might be filed against Goodbody.[51] Simultaneous with Goodbody's near bankruptcy, F. I. duPont, Glore Forgan, the second-largest member firm of the New York Stock Exchange, neared the precipice, surviving only after $79 million, according to one newspaper account, was advanced to the firm, principally by Electronics Data Systems' H. Ross Perot.[52]

The aggregate direct costs of the 1967–1970 back-office crisis were never fully calculated. New York Stock Exchange vice president Lee Arning testified in August 1971 that "the total cost of the Exchange's voluntary customer assistance program could exceed $130 million and if all authorized funds were to be used, reach $140 million."[53] Presumably greater aggregate losses were suffered by the partners, shareholders, and creditors of liquidated firms and by customers unable to make timely dispositions of their securities during periods when share certificates were unavailable because of back-office snafus or were formally frozen pending the completion of liquidation proceedings.

At least in retrospect, most agreed that the primary cause of the back-office crisis was incompetent broker-dealer firm management during the 1964–1968 securities volume surge. Securities firm managers almost invariably were sales-oriented, often far less concerned with the dreary task of administering back offices. There was no mystery about this. "The industry's problem," Exchange president Haack told *Business Week* in June 1968, "is its failure to gear total capacity of doing business to its capacity to produce business. Produce, produce, produce — and keep down the overhead — that has always been the rule."[54] The SEC's 1971 "Study of Unsafe and Unsound Practices of Brokers and Dealers," the definitive account of the crisis's pathology, highlighted the same criticism. "In the 1967–1970 period," concluded the study, "the securities industry concentrated its resources on sales, and paid insufficient attention to properly handling and processing the business brought in by its sales efforts."[55]

More charitable explanations of the crisis were not convincing. Donald Regan, then chairman of Merrill Lynch, Pierce, Fenner and Smith, conceded in 1971 that securities firm "managerial practices were slipshod and blindly optimistic" but urged a Senate Banking Subcommittee to conclude:

> Despite all the complicated overlays, the principal difficulty can be simply stated: A securities firm has high fixed costs, but wide variations in volume and revenues, a characteristic that has important implications for the industry's stability.
>
> The Ford Motor Company made 2,270,000 cars in 1970. It is quite certain that it will make around 2,350,000 cars this year, and around 2,450,000 next year. But what if sales in the fourth quarter of this year were suddenly to double and then triple and then dwindle by half? And what if Ford, in that erratically swinging situation, had to deliver every car that was ordered by the fifth day after the order was written? The prospect is enough to give nightmares to everyone within a 200-mile radius of Detroit.
>
> Yet the analogy is a close one. The securities firm has an obligation to settle trades on the fifth business day. It must also pay for a technical support system that can handle high volume, with capacity to handle more yet.

At the same time, the firm must stay profitable during prolonged periods of low volume — without, at the risk of its future, tearing down its capacity. Few businesses that I can think of confront such a managerial challenge.[56]

The challenge was real, but few other industries, presumably including the automobile industry, responded to it by accepting orders before they had the capability of processing them efficiently. Nor could it be a conventional practice in other industries to continue to promote new sales, open new branch offices, and hire new sales representatives while existing production facilities were in crisis. The uniqueness of the securities industry's managerial norms was well suggested by the experience of Jack Golsen, president of an Oklahoma manufacturing corporation, after he agreed to invest in the foundering Hayden, Stone firm in May 1970. Golsen quickly regretted his decision, explaining to *Fortune*'s Carol Loomis, "I went to one executive committee meeting, and I knew then I had a big bust on my hands. Those people were not for real. They knew nothing about budgeting and controlling costs. I said, 'You guys operate with a double standard. You would never underwrite a company run the way yours is.'" What particularly galled Golsen was Hayden, Stone's carelessness in resolving "short differences"; that is, securities that should be on hand, according to firm records, but cannot be found. In August 1969, Hayden, Stone had short differences of nearly $9 million. In the spring of 1970 about $7 million of differences were still unresolved. To manufacturer Golsen this was unbelievable. "In my business, if we are missing inventory, we stop everything and start looking for it. In Wall Street, if they are missing $7 million, they just accept it as a part of the game. I know of no other business in which that could possibly happen."[57]

Hayden, Stone's problems were typical of the industry. Between 1965 and 1968, NYSE member firms increased their total number of offices by 21 percent, from 3521 to 4278. The total number of registered sales representatives grew even more dramatically, increasing 55 percent, from 33,805 in 1965 to 52,466 in 1969.[58] Many broker-dealer firms did not adequately take into account the difficulties of a similar rapid expansion of back-office personnel. At the height of the stock market's volume surge, 1967–1968, Exchange member firms added a total of 25,000 employees to back offices, an increase of 20 percent in one year.

Most firms [explained Wilmer Wright, founder of a management consulting firm that made a study of the costs of back-office errors] would hire a new employee, sit him down by an experienced worker, and tell the worker to show the new employee how to perform the operation. Since the worker was not trained as an instructor and in many cases didn't really know the job he was supposed to be doing, the training period resulted in poor training and a net decrease in output of about 50 percent on the part of the experienced worker. In other words, for each new employee added, we temporarily reduced our total capacity by one-half employee.

Wright described the results: "The number of money errors in 1968 was five times the 1964 rate. Non-money errors increased at least three times as much."[59]

This increased error rate was the primary cause of the seven and a half–fold increase in New York Stock Exchange member firm losses from errors and bad debts between 1964 and 1969. During that period losses increased from 2.46 percent of net income before partners' compensation and taxes to 18.77 percent, with back-office loss of physical control of share certificates not only making industry-wide short stock differences, such as those at Hayden, Stone, but also making possible the theft of an officially estimated $100 to $400 million worth of securities.[60]

Several firms attempted to end back-office operational losses by abrupt conversion to computerized facilities, on some occasions with catastrophic results. "One of the main reasons for the failure of Goodbody & Company, the fifth-largest firm on the Street, was its overambitious efforts to automate," reported Regan of Merrill Lynch, the firm called in to rescue Goodbody through an eleventh-hour merger. "That ill-fated effort only succeeded in getting Goodbody in deeper trouble. It was trapped in the midst of change: efforts to automate failed, while manual procedure was deserted in anticipation of automation's success."[61] Similar "instant computerization" problems plagued several other New York Stock Exchange firm members forced to liquidate during the 1968–1970 period, notably including McDonnell & Company, Amott, Baker & Company, Schwabacher & Company, and Fusz-Schmelzle & Company, as well as Lehman Brothers (which narrowly survived collapse).[62]

The way in which securities firms financed their operations was yet another cause of the failure of many broker-dealers. Apart from the negligible $5000 initial net capital requirement of the SEC, and the NYSE requirement that member firms carrying customers' accounts maintain a net capital of at least $50,000, the principal mechanism for ensuring adequate capital structures in the securities industry were the so-called net capital rules issued by most stock exchanges and elsewhere enforced by the SEC. The Commission's Securities Exchange Act Rule 15c-3-1 and the New York

Stock Exchange's Rule 325 each then provided that no broker-dealer firm's aggregate indebtedness could exceed 2000 percent of its net capital at risk in the securities business (not counting fixed assets and the value of exchange memberships).[63]

There were striking differences between the net capital rules of the New York Stock Exchange and the SEC. The Exchange rule proved particularly ineffective in ensuring that Exchange members would have on hand sufficient liquid assets to meet their obligations during the back-office crisis. Rule 325 counted as capital subordinated loans or secured demand notes from customers or partners, which, as of 1970, made up 40 percent of the capital of all Exchange member partnerships and 34 percent of the capital of Exchange member corporations. Significantly, 25 percent of all Exchange member partnerships and nearly 10 percent of all Exchange member corporations had 70 percent or more of their total capital funds in some form of subordinated borrowing. Subordinated loans from customers or partners were a peculiarly evanescent form of capital, which, under Exchange Rule 325, could be withdrawn on as little as ninety days' notice, even if withdrawal would result in the financial collapse of a firm or a violation of the net capital rule.

As the 1969–1970 period's financial difficulties mounted, precisely this occurred at firms such as F. I. duPont, which had $12.7 million in excess net capital at the end of December 1970 but projected capital withdrawals of $24.8 million by August 1971. Secured demand notes, a form of debt capital used considerably less often, also proved unreliable. As was generally the case with subordinated loans, what usually by contract could be demanded were securities (technically held as collateral for the demand loans) whose value might rapidly shrink during a stock market plummet like that of 1969–1970. The failures respectively of Dempsey-Tegeler and Hayden, Stone became inevitable when the collateral value of their secured demand notes rapidly shrank early in 1970.[64]

The securities industry 1967–1970 back-office crisis powerfully suggested that there were limits to the extent to which investors and the SEC could rely on securities industry self-regulation. Consistently during the four-year crisis the SEC did not have reliable data on the seriousness of individual broker-dealer back-office or financial problems until it was too late for the Commission to prevent firm failures. Nor until it was too late did the SEC appreciate the weaknesses in New York Stock Exchange audit procedures or the extent to which the Exchange's unwarranted optimism endangered investors. According to the Commission's records, in the spring of 1968, the SEC and the Exchange instituted a campaign to inspect every major firm in the United States. Responsibility for inspection of New York Stock Exchange members rested with the Exchange. In July 1968, Irving Pollack, director of the SEC's Division of Trading and Markets, wrote Exchange president Robert Haack requesting that

> the Exchange would advise us of information developed in the course of an inspection or inquiry which indicates (1) problems with regard to the soundness of the financial condition or net capital position of any member organization or (2) possible misappropriation of customers' funds or securities, unregistered distribution, fraud, or other serious misconduct on the part of a member firm or an associated person.

The following month Haack refused, explaining, in part, "We doubt that the time of your staff should be occupied with possible duplication of worry, inquiry, and responsibility in the same such matters to which our staff is giving attention." In October 1968, Pollack renewed his request. The New York Stock Exchange again refused to share the results of individual firm inspections.[65]

During the summer of 1969, the SEC asked the NYSE, according. to Commissioner Hugh Owens, "for a report on its program for checking on the financial condition of member firms." A meeting was held in October 1969.

> Neither that meeting [explained Owens], nor a following one later in the month produced agreement as to an appropriate course of action. For example, our proposal for new financial reporting requirements, and the adoption of a financial questionnaire which would be used by the exchanges, was met with opposition. Among the objections raised were the following: the existing self-regulatory reporting programs were adequate; the Commission was already receiving enough data about exchange members; the report would be burdensome to firms.[66]

The SEC did review the financial records of some New York Stock Exchange firms experiencing financial difficulties in the fall of 1969.[67] During the course of this fall 1969 review, the SEC became aware, as Commission attorney Hurd Baruch put it, "that the Exchange was interpreting Rule 325 in a way which contravened the rule's fundamental nature as a test of liquidity [that is, readily available cash]." For example, in May 1969, the New York Stock Exchange, without notifying the SEC, had begun computing the net capital of member firms without deducting short stock differences. This was a highly significant revision. Had it not been made, the Commission apparently would have had earlier notification of the gravity of the financial crises both at F. I. duPont and Goodbody.[68] Several other changes also had been made by the New York Stock

Exchange in the interpretation and enforcement of its net capital rule, the Commission found, "to avoid placing a number of firms in violation."[69]

A practical consequence of the Exchange's numerous revisions in the enforcement and interpretation of its net capital rule was to delay the SEC's full understanding of the seriousness of member firm financial difficulties for several months. In April 1970, after the SEC's staff had made a "major inspection of the Exchange's administration of its net capital rule," the staff reported to the Commission: "We have found it difficult to gauge the extent of firms' financial problems because of the conflicting net capital computations made by the firms themselves and by the self-regulatory organizations."[70] This ignorance persisted. During the summer of 1970, Chairman Budge was requested by Congress to prepare a report on the financial condition of Exchange members. He asked the Exchange for information about the current status of member firms that might reasonably be expected to go into liquidation during the next six to twelve months, and inquired specifically about a list of firms that the SEC believed to be in financial difficulty. The Exchange responded on August 12, 1970, that only three of the listed firms could reasonably be expected to liquidate and that the Exchange expected all three would meet their obligations to customer accounts without Exchange assistance. The information proved inaccurate. Six days later, the Exchange suspended First Devonshire Corporation, a firm the Exchange had advised the SEC was not expected to liquidate. Only in mid-October, after the SEC inquired about Goodbody & Company, did the Exchange determine that this firm, too, was near collapse.[71]

Because the New York Stock Exchange assumed the primary responsibility for overseeing Exchange members' financial integrity, the Exchange, deservedly, received most of the after-the-crisis criticism for its inability to identify and prevent individual member firms' operational problems, resulting in the demise of as many as 160 member firms during the 1968–1970 period.

The SEC's use of administrative proceedings late in the crisis helped to minimize investor losses and to prevent an abrupt loss of investor confidence, which might have precipitated the securities industry equivalent to a "run on the bank." Like the securities industry, however, the SEC initially underestimated the late 1960s' volume surge and the problems it would create in broker-dealer firms. It also seriously miscalculated at first the ability of the New York Stock Exchange to ensure Exchange members' financial integrity. After World War II, SEC concern with Exchange member firms' operations and finances waned, in part because the Commission during the 1946–1961 period lacked the budget or staff regularly to inspect Exchange member firms; in larger part, because Exchange member firms' insolvencies were exceedingly rare.[72] Between 1938 and 1963 only one minor Exchange firm, DuPont, Homsey & Company, failed. The Exchange voluntarily paid $700,000 into a receivership in order to make whole all customers of DuPont, Homsey.[73] Impressed by the quality of Exchange oversight of member firms' operations and finances, the 1963 SEC *Special Study* ringingly endorsed Exchange self-regulation in this area: "The enforcement by the Exchange of its net capital rule should be the standard by which other aspects of its regulatory program are judged. The staff vigorously seeks out violations and they are processed swiftly and fairly."[74] The SEC's Division of Trading and Markets agreed. Describing a 1963 plan to oversee Exchange performance of self-regulatory functions, the division stated: "Areas such as enforcement of the Exchange's net capital rule, which the Exchange has shown itself to have handled with diligence and efficiency, will be left alone or given a very quick inspection."[75]

The New York Stock Exchange's response to the unanticipated failure of Ira Haupt and Company later in 1963 seemed to establish the wisdom of the SEC's policy of deferring to the Exchange on oversight of member firms' operations and finances. Soon after the Exchange learned, on November 19, 1963, that the well-respected Haupt firm was endangered because a major customer would be unable to meet margin calls on salad oil commodities contracts as a result of the celebrated Tino De Angelis "Salad Oil Swindle," the Exchange suspended Ira Haupt and Company and six days later announced that it would provide up to $12 million to protect the firm's 20,700 customer accounts during liquidation.[76]

In 1964 the Exchange created its Special Trust Fund, announcing that it would be provided with $10 million in cash and $15 million in lines of bank credit to ensure comparable protection in the event of future insolvencies. Thereafter, as Commissioner Owens later wrote Congress, the SEC generally acquiesced to Exchange leadership in regulation of member firms' operations and finances, assuming that

> self-regulation should be strongest in the area of financial responsibility, because firms trading with each other are highly interdependent and all have a direct self-interest in ensuring that a troubled firm does not pull the rest of them down with it. The industry generally has also been conscious of the need to prevent the financial difficulties of a

broker from causing losses to its customers, thereby undermining the public confidence upon which the markets rest.[77]

Through 1967, when the back-office crisis began, the SEC's deference to Exchange oversight of member firms' operations and finances seemed a reasonable policy, given the SEC's other regulatory responsibilities and limited budget. During the initial phases of the back-office crisis, the Commission continued to operate on the assumption that the Exchange effectively could regulate member firms' operations and finances. In 1966, the SEC received a markedly increased number of customer complaints about late-delivered funds and securities. In January 1967, the SEC wrote to the twelve firms about whom the greatest number of complaints was received to ask for an explanation and "whether there was anything the Commission could do to assist in this area." "In general," the SEC subsequently reported, "the firms indicated that their problems were of a 'business' and temporary nature, which they could handle. They not only opposed government intervention but expressed the view it would actually be harmful." Beyond receiving these written responses, the SEC did not further investigate these twelve firms at that time. It is worth emphasizing that four of these firms — F. I. du-Pont, Dempsey-Tegeler, Hayden, Stone, and Goodbody — subsequently failed.[78]

With "brokerage firm . . . operations backed up like the Long Island expressway in rush hour traffic," as one Exchange member firm officer informed the *Wall Street Journal* in August 1967,[79] the SEC met with Exchange and NASD officials on numerous occasions during the next fifteen months.[80] But it was not until the collapse of Pickard & Company in the spring of 1968 that the SEC made its first significant direct response to the back-office crisis. In April 1968 the SEC approved a New York Stock Exchange rule to begin collecting monthly fails data from member firms. In May, the SEC and Exchange initiated a campaign to inspect every major firm in the United States. According to the *National Journal*, "The investigations disclosed that back-office problems were worse than the SEC had suspected, and the agency invoked a seldom-used provision of the 1934 Act, threatening 40 to 50 firms with suspension of their registrations unless they cleaned up their paper backlogs." Various restrictions were placed on the operations of forty-seven Exchange member problem firms, including, a Senate subcommittee staff study explained, "no new sales offices, no increase in the number of registered representatives, no firm trading [that is, for member accounts], no solicitation of margin accounts, no underwriting, special [weekly] reporting, and restriction to a certain number of trades per day or week."[81] In June, the SEC helped persuade the Exchange to limit trading to a four-day week.[82]

These restrictions failed to avert the subsequent wave of insolvencies at some Exchange member firms, because they were put into effect too late to prevent substantial error losses. At the time, the SEC was aware that a crisis existed and that additional restrictions were necessary. On July 19, 1968 Chairman Cohen informed Exchange representatives at a meeting recorded in the Commission's *Minutes* that the NYSE's own statistics indicated that the situation was worsening. Cohen "stressed that additional measures were required." Eleven days later the SEC approved letters to the stock exchanges and the NASD, stating

> that it was imperative that the Exchanges and the NASD give immediate consideration to the following possible steps, among others: (1) prohibiting, for an indefinite period, all promotional and other advertising (whether in newspapers or on radio or television) designed to induce customers to engage in securities transactions; (2) prohibiting the opening of any new offices or employment of any new salesmen (some arrangement might be made to permit the replacement of salesmen leaving a firm, but the number of salesmen employed should be restricted to current levels); (3) prohibiting the publication or distribution of market letters and other sales literature, except to the extent that members had contractual obligations as investment advisers to furnish such material; and (4) prohibiting trading for firm accounts, and accounts of partners and other associated persons (including accounts in which such persons might have an interest, e.g., "hedge funds").

With New York Stock Exchange members enjoying record volume (and profits), its representatives resisted these and most other SEC proposals that might limit exchange volume. President Haack repeatedly insisted that "he would . . . advocate singling out o-t-c business for restriction." The SEC did not then insist on imposition of industrywide restrictions to reduce share volume, in part because of fear that they would precipitate an investor panic. Chairman Cohen's SEC instead emphasized private administrative proceedings, which could result in a firm's suspension, as a mechanism to impose restrictions on firms known to be in trouble. Only after firms subject to these proceedings had consented to remedial procedures (such as hiring outside auditors to resolve short differ-

ences) were the firms' violations of the securities laws publicly announced.[83]

Consistent with its enforcement strategy, the Commission
warned on July 29, 1968, "that it is a violation of applicable antifraud provisions for a broker-dealer to accept or execute any order for
the purchase or sale of a security if he does not have the personnel
and facilities to enable him to promptly execute and consummate
all of his securities transactions."[84] This warning, the SEC's enforcement actions, and the four-day trading week, which continued until
January 1969, did not fully succeed in immediately reducing the
operational crisis.

On November 4, 1968, Chairman Cohen opened an SEC meeting
with representatives of several exchanges by describing "an apparent increase in the gravity of back-office problems — as evidenced
by a growing number of complaints from members of the public and
from Congress about delayed deliveries of securities and delays in
providing customers with the proceeds of their sales of securities"
as well as "the enormous amounts of unlocated securities differences." Even at that late date some of the SEC's historic deference to
exchange regulation of member firms' financial integrity persisted.
The *Minutes* record that all participants at this SEC-industry meeting agreed "the problem was primarily the responsibility of the self-
regulatory agencies."[85]

The extent to which the SEC continued to defer to exchange regulation of member firms' operations and finances after the Commission became aware of the crisis was not fully defensible. As was
obvious in SEC oversight of NYSE self-regulation, at least since the
time of the Whitney scandal, Exchange regulators can be expected to
be reluctant to take steps that would put member firms out of business or would generally reduce member firms' income. It was exactly
these kinds of steps that were necessary throughout the crisis. In
retrospect, it is obvious that investors would have been better protected had the SEC, earlier in the crisis, conducted investigations of
broker-dealer firms' operations and imposed firm- or industrywide
trading restrictions. Salutary as was the Commission's back-office
enforcement program, it was a program that began too late to prevent the wave of broker-dealer firm failures during the 1969–1970
period.*

---

* SEC chairman Budge, who believed even more fervently than Manuel Cohen "in
the ability of the industry to solve its problems,"[86] was much criticized for limiting
SEC intervention during the climactic 1969–1970 period to securing assurances from
the NYSE that it would commit monies from its Special Trust Fund in the event that
specific firms failed, rather than insisting on the earliest possible knowledge of data

In the aftermath of the back-office crisis, several reforms were adopted. Most significantly, in December 1970, Congress enacted the Securities Investors Protection Act, creating the Securities Investor Protection Corporation (SIPC) to administer a fund providing $50,000 of insurance protection to each customer of virtually all broker-dealers registered with the SEC. Although SIPC was to be financed by assessments from its broker-dealer membership, the corporation, if given SEC approval, could borrow up to $1 billion from the United States Treasury, making SIPC a more reliable guarantor than the New York Stock Exchange Special Trust Fund, which technically was a discretionary fund and had run out of money during the summer of 1970. Besides creating the equivalent to a Federal Deposit Insurance Corporation for the securities industry, the Securities Investor Protection Act also sweepingly defined the SEC's powers to:

> (1) require any self-regulatory organization to adopt any specified alteration of or supplement to its rules, practices, and procedures with respect to the frequency and scope of inspections and examinations relating to the financial condition of members of such self-regulatory organization and the selection and qualification of examiners;
>
> (2) require any self-regulatory organization to furnish SIPC and the Commission with reports and records or copies thereof relating to the financial condition of members of such self-regulatory organization; and
>
> (3) require any self-regulatory organization to inspect or examine any members of such self-regulatory organization in relation to the financial condition of such members.[89]

Believing that "early warning signals were inadequate to foretell financial and operational difficulties in a reliable and timely manner,"[90] the SEC in July 1971 employed its rule-making authority to require almost all registered broker-dealers to give immediate notice, by telegram, whenever their net capital was insufficient or their books and records were not current.[91] A related rule, adopted three months later, required broker-dealers once every calendar quarter to exam-

---

on foundering member firms or control over programs to prevent operational crises from culminating in insolvencies.[87] The criticism was somewhat unfair. The decisive errors made by the SEC during the back-office emergency occurred during the chairmanship of Manuel Cohen, when the SEC allowed the crisis to get out of hand, not during the chairmanship of Hamer Budge. Budge, working closely with Trading and Markets Division director Pollack and associate director Sporkin, focused on the crisis to a much greater extent than had Cohen and was responsible for securing industry and Nixon administration support for the Securities Investors Protection Act of 1970.[88]

ine physically and count all securities in their possession, account for all other securities reflected in their books, and record all unresolved differences in their financial records within seven business days.[92] After four years of negotiations with the securities industry and interim reforms, the Commission in July 1975 adopted a uniform net capital rule, ending the power of the New York Stock Exchange and other exchanges to promulgate or create by interpretation less stringent net capital rules than those of the SEC.[93]

Combined, these statutory and rule revisions considerably lessened the likelihood of another back-office crisis. But they did not succeed in stemming a substantial reduction in individual trading on the securities exchanges. Between 1970 and 1975, the total number of individual owners of corporate stock and mutual funds sharply declined, from 30.85 million investors in 1970 to 25.27 million in 1975, the only reduction in the number of investors to occur during the 1952–1980 period. Individual investor aggregate trading volume also plummeted. In 1973, private investors bought and sold 20 percent less listed stock than they had in 1968. While individual investors in 1961 had accounted for 61 percent of the dollar value of nonmember trading volume on the New York Stock Exchange, by 1974 their share volume was less than 30 percent. Alarmed, Chairman G. Bradford Cook warned in April 1973 that "the individual investor already has acquired the status of an endangered species."

There were several causes of the small investors' flight, including discouragement after losses in the 1969–1970 market break, high bond interest rates, and the widespread belief that institutional investors received preferential treatment from brokers or inside information or had the power to manipulate stock prices. But virtually everyone agreed that the back-office crisis also had been a contributing cause of the individual investors' exodus. A 1973 report for the New York Stock Exchange based on 1234 interviews with small or potential investors, for example, found that three in ten small investors personally had experienced such back-office problems as lost or late-delivered securities; 57 percent agreed "if trading volume continues to increase, many brokerage firms will have the same bad paperwork foul-ups they had several years ago."[94]

*   *   *

The back-office crisis significantly influenced the ongoing policy debates on fixed commission rates and the structure of the securities markets. First affected were the commission-rate issues. Unexpectedly, in May 1969 New York Stock Exchange member firm Donaldson, Lufkin & Jenrette filed a registration statement with the

SEC preliminary to a sale of common stock to the public, abruptly bringing to a head a nearly decade-long debate within the Exchange on whether member firms could be publicly owned. The Exchange's opposition to public ownership of member firms was bound up with the Exchange's opposition to institutional membership. Mutual funds, insurance companies, and other institutional investors were barred from Exchange membership primarily by two provisions of the Exchange's constitution: the first prohibited public ownership of member firms; the second required the "primary purpose" of every member firm to be "the transaction of business as a broker or dealer in securities." For eight years, the Exchange had hesitated to repeal the prohibition of member firm public ownership because of its concern that repeal would prompt the Justice Department or an institutional investor to bring an antitrust suit challenging the "primary purpose" requirement. Such a suit, if successful, might have permitted institutions directly to own seats on the Exchange. Given the political realities of the period, the Exchange's concern was a realistic one. But when Donaldson, Lufkin announced that it had had to decline institutional business for lack of capital and argued that the public sale of common stock was the least expensive way an Exchange member could secure permanent capital to deal in large-block transactions and expand or computerize facilities, the Exchange had little choice but to remove its total prohibition of member firm public ownership.

By mid-1969, the Exchange could not persuasively rebut Donaldson, Lufkin's arguments that "the lack of access by Exchange members to permanent, public capital has begun to erode the Exchange's role as the nation's central auction market," and that "failure to invest in people and capital equipment contributed to periodic closings and shortened trading hours on the Exchange, reducing the access of investors to the central market."

On July 17, 1969, the New York Stock Exchange voted in principle "to support the concept of public ownership of equity securities issued by member corporations," subsequently reaffirming the proviso that any publicly owned member firm and any parent firm must be primarily engaged in business as brokers or dealers in securities. The New York Stock Exchange constitution officially was amended in March 1970. Within four years, Donaldson, Lufkin and fifteen other securities firms, including such leading Exchange firms as Merrill Lynch, E. F. Hutton, Bache & Company, Paine, Webber, Jackson & Curtis, Reynolds Securities, and Dean Witter were being publicly traded.[95]

The anticipated challenge to the New York Stock Exchange's prohibition of institutional members began four months before the new public ownership rule went into effect, continued to be intensely debated for close to six years, and was at last resolved by the 1975 Securities Acts Amendments. As early as January 1973, a book-length SEC release on the subject was able to state, with little risk of exaggeration, "We doubt whether any topic, and all of its concomitant ramifications, has been studied as intensively as this one, by so many different governmental bodies and individuals."[96] Complex though the institutional membership debate undeniably was, much of its intensity could be traced to two core issues. First, how much profit should broker-dealers be allowed to earn from the execution of institutional investor securities transactions? By the early 1970s, mutual funds, insurance companies, pension funds, and other institutional investors were generating 60 to 70 percent of nonmember trading volume on the New York Stock Exchange. Their primary motivation in seeking Exchange membership was to reduce the costs of securities transactions.[97] After the SEC, in 1973, decided to unfix commission rates, much of the pressure for institutional membership subsided.

But controversy did endure over the second issue framed by the institutional membership debate, that of defining the boundaries between stock exchange membership and other financial industries. Under the rules of the New York Stock Exchange (and most other exchanges), an Exchange member whose predominant business was securities brokerage or dealing could manage a mutual fund, pension fund, or generally otherwise engage in the business of institutional investors, but an insurance company, mutual fund, or pension fund whose predominant business was money management could not be a member of the Exchange. So self-serving a rule appeared unfair, as was recognized by several leaders of the Exchange itself, including Gustave Levy, who in January 1971 acknowledged, "Our Achilles' heel has always been that we have been in the money managing business and the money managers could not get into ours."[98]

The climactic institutional membership debate effectively began in November 1969, when the Justice Department filed comments with the SEC suggesting that the requirement in the New York Stock Exchange's proposed public ownership rule that a member firm's primary purpose "be the transaction of business as a broker or dealer in securities" was a violation of the antitrust laws. It was unlikely, claimed the department, that the primary purpose provision was exempted by the *Silver* decision, since it probably was not necessary "to achieve a legitimate goal of the Exchange Act."[99]

The SEC soon agreed with the Justice Department that two other restrictions in the Exchange's public ownership proposal were not "supported by a showing of self-regulatory purpose sufficient to outweigh their anticompetitive impact." The Commission asked the Exchange to remove from its rule proposal conditions barring an Exchange member from having as a customer any nonmember who acquired a 5 percent or greater participation in the member firm's profits and requiring that no more than 49 percent of a member corporation's voting stock be held by the public. But the SEC did not judge the permissibility of the primary purpose test before the Exchange public ownership rule became effective on March 26, 1970. Instead, it agreed with the Exchange to review the appropriateness of the requirement after it had had the benefit of an Exchange study of institutional membership, which, the SEC requested, "be completed no later than July 1, 1970."[100]

The New York Stock Exchange institutional membership study was never delivered to the SEC. But after the broker-dealer subsidiaries of the Investors Diversified Services (IDS), the nation's largest mutual fund complex, and of the Dreyfus Corporation applied for NYSE membership in January 1971, with IDS threatening to file an antitrust suit challenging the Exchange's primary purpose test if its application was rejected,[101] Exchange chairman Bernard Lasker and president Robert Haack announced the conclusion of the Exchange's Committee on Membership Qualifications: "that under appropriate conditions subject to self-regulatory practices, institutional membership is desirable on the New York Stock Exchange when coupled with competitive commission rates on trades at some amount to be determined."[102]

One month later the New York Stock Exchange Committee on Membership Qualifications withdrew its agreement in principle to recommend institutional membership. Former Exchange president William McChesney Martin, who earlier had been requested by the Board of Governors to prepare a comprehensive study of the New York Stock Exchange's constitution, rules, and procedures, persuaded the Membership Committee to defer resolution of the institutional membership controversy until after the publication of his report.[103]

The Martin Report, published early in August 1971, became the basis for renewed New York Stock Exchange opposition to institutional membership. With one significant exception, Martin endorsed the Exchange's one-sided "primary purpose" rule. Citing "the concentration of economic power which might result from institutional membership," the risk "that institutional membership could lead to a market dominated by dealers dealing for their own account," and the need "to facilitate regulation," Martin recommended that banks, trust companies, insurance companies, and other institutions be barred from Exchange membership, although he noted "that the purchase of 25 percent or less of the voting securities of a member corporation by an institution is not prohibited" by the Exchange's primary purpose rule. Since member firms had handled "reasonably well" the "unavoidable conflicts of interest [that] arise when money management and brokerage functions are combined within a single profit-making firm," Martin also endorsed allowing Exchange members to engage in all forms of money management, with the significant, but unexplained, exception of managing or advising mutual funds.[104]

After holding hearings on the future structure of the securities markets in October 1971, the SEC, in its February 1972 "Statement on the Future Structure of the Securities Markets" and its April 1972 "White Paper on Institutional Membership," adopted a position on institutional membership similar to that of the Martin Report. But the bases for the Commission's position were quite different from those in the Martin Report. The SEC's "White Paper" recognized that the institutional membership issue "first came to the fore" because of the Exchange's "rigid, fixed commission" schedule. By April 1972, however, the SEC had unfixed commission rates on transactions above $500,000, scheduled the breakpoint to drop to $300,000 with "further significant reductions in the breakpoint . . . highly probable in the not too distant future." To Chairman William Casey's SEC, there were substantial risks in affording institutional investors advantages in addition to lower, competitively determined commission rates. The confidence of small investors in the securities markets might further be undermined if institutions also were given the benefits of intramember commission rates and "the input of trading information received by the member both from other members and from activity on the floor." Moreover, the "White Paper" anticipated, the loss of institutional investor income immediately after the back-office crisis could "bring catastrophe to Wall Street."

Accordingly, the Commission concluded, "As a general rule . . . membership [in the securities markets] . . . should be open to those . . . who have the primary purpose of serving the public as brokers or market-makers." Adopting a recommendation of the New York Stock Exchange, the SEC defined "primary purpose" with the soon to be controversial "80–20" rule, which required a firm to do at least 80 percent of its commission business with unaffiliated customers in order to be eligible for membership on any exchange. The SEC concurred with the Martin Report that an exchange member should be allowed to engage in money management (including managing or advising mutual funds) as long as no more than 20 percent of its trading volume was executed on behalf of such affiliates, primarily because the Commission thought "it important that a portion of broker-dealer income be based on a more stable source than commission business." With a similar regard for lessening the securities industry's capital crisis, the SEC recommended abolition of the New York Stock Exchange "parent test," which prohibited a non-securities firm from establishing or acquiring a securities broker-dealer firm. As long as the parent corporation provided no more than 20 percent of the trading volume of the subsidiary securities firm, the SEC saw "no reason either of law or policy why this should not be permitted. The establishment of such a subsidiary doing a brokerage business for the public provides a useful source of permanent capital for the securities industry." On May 26, 1972, the SEC formally requested each national securities exchange to adopt a rule incorporating these restrictions on institutional membership no later than July 31, 1972.[105]

Substantial opposition to the SEC's recommended exchange rule regulating institutional membership began soon after the Commission's February 1972 "Future Structure Statement." More than any other exchange, the minuscule Philadelphia-Baltimore-Washington Stock Exchange, 43 percent of whose trading volume was derived from institutional members not in compliance with the SEC's recommended rule, was affected by the Commission's proposal. Facing the possibility of extinction, the Philadelphia Exchange refused to issue the SEC-recommended rule. On August 3, 1972, after it became apparent that several other exchanges also had not adopted the proposed rule, the SEC formally circulated for public comments its own institutional membership regulation, Rule 19b-2. With most New York Stock Exchange members and the Securities Industry Association (the successor to the Investment Bankers Association and the Association of Stock Exchange Firms) "wholeheartedly" favoring the SEC rule, the Philadelphia Exchange briefly shifted tactics at hearings the Commission held on proposed Rule 19b-2 and volunteered "not [to] seek appeal or enjoin" 19b-2 if the rule was phased in over a three-year period. To this, the SEC readily agreed, and on January 16, 1973, it officially promulgated Rule 19b-2, incorporating a three-year grace period. The rule was scheduled to become effective on March 15, 1973.

The SEC–Philadelphia Exchange compromise, however, soon broke down. Connecticut State treasurer Robert Berdon, trustee of more than $750 million in pension and other trust funds held on behalf of state employees, who had sought Philadelphia Exchange membership for Connecticut's brokerage affiliate to reduce securities commission costs, accused the Philadelphia Exchange of making a "secret deal" with the SEC. The Philadelphia Exchange then reversed its tactics and commenced a lawsuit in the Third Circuit Court of Appeals to prevent Rule 19b-2 from going into effect. The State of Connecticut soon joined the suit, and the Justice Department filed an *amicus* brief, each claiming that Rule 19b-2 was not permissible under the antitrust laws and included an arbitrary definition of "investing public" that did not "recognize that many institutional investors — such as mutual funds, and state welfare and pension funds — are actually serving a broad spectrum of the investing public even though their brokerage affiliates may only execute the parent's transactions." After briefly staying implementation of the rule, the Third Circuit Court of Appeals dismissed the lawsuit in September 1973 on the wholly procedural ground that a court of appeals lacked jurisdiction under the Securities Exchange Act to review directly an SEC rule, necessarily implying that appropriate judicial review should have begun in a federal district court. The Supreme Court declined to review the Third Circuit's procedural ruling in April 1974. The Philadelphia Exchange then filed an action in a federal district court but voluntarily agreed to the action's dismissal when it became obvious that the issue would be resolved by the 1975 Securities Acts Amendments.[106]

More effective opposition to the SEC's Rule 19b-2 emerged in Congress. Although both the Senate Securities and House Commerce and Finance subcommittees accepted the Commission's arguments in favor of barring institutions from exchange membership, neither subcommittee supported the SEC's 80–20 primary purpose test.

After the SEC's February 1972 "Future Structure Statement" was published, Senator Williams conducted hearings on the Commission's institutional membership proposal, pointedly identifying its one-sidedness when he stated to Chairman Casey:

> You seem to feel that when an institutional manager transacts business on behalf of hundreds or thousands of beneficial owners of a fund — a fund in which he himself has no beneficial interest — that is "private" business. But when a brokerage firm transacts business for the very same institution — or for a discretionary account or a hedge fund or for the firm's own account — that is "public" business. That does not at all square with my idea of what is "public" and what is "private."

Several subsequent congressional reports focused on the conflicts of interest inevitable when the same firm combined brokerage and money-management functions, one Senate Banking Committee report excoriating Rule 19b-2 as "a regretful chapter in the Commission's generally distinguished history." In 1975, as part of the Securities Acts Amendments, Congress directed the SEC to adopt a near-total ban on securities brokerage firms transacting business on behalf of affiliated institutional accounts, to become effective on May 1, 1978.*[107]

The practical effect of the Commission decision not to permit institutional memberships on the securities exchanges was to add to the already considerable pressures to unfix commission rates totally. In an address delivered in September 1969, Chairman Budge indicated that the SEC would await the results of a study prepared for the New York Stock Exchange by consultant economists for the National Economic Research Associates (NERA) "before resolving the basic question of whether there should be a minimum rate schedule. The Exchange has represented that the study will afford a basis for developing a fixed minimum commission rate which will achieve the desirable results of competition and do so without risking the adverse consequences to the securities markets it foresees from negotiated rates."[109] Under pressure from Exchange members, who were eager to secure a rate increase, the New York Stock Exchange's Board of Governors directed NERA to accelerate completion of its report.[110]

An initial NERA report was published in February 1970. Employing an approach analogous to that required in public utility rate-making, NERA proposed that securities brokerage commission rates be based directly on costs, including a return on equity of at least 15 percent (equal to the rate of return of the upper quadrile of industries) to compensate for the riskiness of the securities brokerage industry and ensure that new capital could be attracted. Specifically, NERA recommended retention of a fixed rate structure with rates on some small orders raised over 100 percent and rates on trades of three hundred or more shares reduced an average of 38 percent.[111] With six of every ten New York Stock Exchange member firms doing a public business having incurred losses on their securities commission business during 1969, the Exchange's Board of Gov-

---

* The concept of totally separating securities firm brokerage and money-management activities remained controversial after the 1975 act. In May 1978, at the Commission's request, Congress enacted legislation deferring for nine months the effective date of the section in the 1975 amendments directing the SEC to prohibit brokerage firms from executing transactions on behalf of affiliated institutional accounts.[108]

ernors immediately presented the NERA proposed rate changes to the SEC in mid-February 1970 without earlier approval by the Exchange's membership.[112]

Nonetheless, the NERA rate recommendations soon divided Wall Street, with a few firms, led by Merrill Lynch, vehemently opposed to raising rates on small orders, and other firms protesting that the proposed rate of return was insufficient "to attract new capital to a cyclical and risk-laden industry."[113] In March 1970, the NERA rate recommendations were withdrawn and the Exchange recommended instead an emergency surcharge of $15 or 50 percent of the applicable commission, whichever was less, on orders of 1000 shares or less. The SEC, agreeing "that immediate financial relief is required," permitted the surcharge to go into effect in April 1970, at first for a ninety-day period. In August 1970, it determined "to permit the continuation of the service charge until such time as circumstances warrant its termination." The SEC approved the surcharge, in part because of Commission concern that brokerage firms were terminating services to small investors. The SEC's release stated, "The Commission expressly predicates its non-objection to the interim increase in charges upon its expectation that the Exchange will take all steps necessary to assure that full brokerage services for small investors are restored and that transaction size and order limitations on such accounts imposed in the last year by the Exchange's membership will be removed."[114]

The New York Stock Exchange submitted a second proposal for a new commission-rate structure on June 30, 1970. The second proposal bore little resemblance to the original NERA recommendations and to some degree discarded the concept that commission rates should be based on actual costs plus a stipulated fair rate of return. No rates, in the new Exchange proposal, were to be reduced. Smaller increases, ranging from 25 to 50 percent, were to be permitted on orders of one hundred to four hundred shares. Given the findings of the original NERA report concerning the actual costs of large-share transactions, the Exchange's June 1970 proposal was ludicrous and quite clearly signified that the divided Board of Governors was incapable of forwarding a defensible proposal.

After holding hearings, the SEC concluded, in a release dated October 22, 1970, that the Exchange's June 1970 proposal was "not reasonable." In light of the $15 surcharge already in effect, and to keep small investors from bearing "an inordinate amount of [the] total commission increase sought by the Exchange," the Commission insisted that the rate increases for orders of one hundred to four hundred shares would have to be smaller. Without any explanation, the SEC then began the formal process of unfixing brokerage commission rates with its announcement that "the Commission is of the opinion that fixed charges for portions of orders in excess of $100,000 are neither necessary nor appropriate."[115] This would have eliminated fixed rates for orders that generated approximately 15 percent of all securities broker commission income.

Six weeks later, after Budge had announced his intent to resign, the SEC retreated from its conclusion that "fixed charges for portions of orders in excess of $100,000 are neither necessary nor appropriate." During what SEC attorney Hurd Baruch termed "an all-out [Exchange] . . . campaign of personal persuasion, legal action, and congressional pressure to get the Commission to back down and permit the continuance of the Exchange's complete prohibition on price competition among its members," Commissioner Richard Smith indicated at the Investment Bankers Association Annual Convention in early December 1970 that there was room for debate concerning the level at which negotiated rates would be introduced. This remained the SEC's position after Budge resigned, in January 1971. On February 10, 1971, the SEC indicated to the New York Stock Exchange that "the Commission will not object to the Exchange's commencing competitive rates on portions of orders above a level not higher than $500,000 rather than at the $100,000 figure mentioned in our October 22 letter."[116]

On April 5, 1971, fixed rates on orders above $500,000 were eliminated. This meant that only 5 percent of securities commission income was initially subject to competition. A 1971 Senate study found that "rates on the negotiated portions of these trades have been running approximately 50 percent below the previously fixed volume discount rate," but even New York Stock Exchange vice president Richard Howland conceded in September 1971 that "negotiated rates have apparently had little impact on the marketplace where member organizations execute orders of $500,000 or more." Total commission-rate revenues declined a mere 2 percent in the first five months of competitive rates above $500,000, equaling lost income of approximately $17 million.[117]

The SEC continued a hesitant approach toward unfixed commission rates during the chairmanships of William Casey and G. Bradford Cook. In March 1971, after Budge had resigned but before Casey had begun as SEC chairman, the SEC published its *Institutional Investor Study*, accompanied by a transmittal letter that stated: "The Commission regards noncompetitive, fixed minimum commission rates on securities transactions of institutional size as the source of a number of difficulties in the development of institu- ·

tional investing and the trading markets for equity securities. The clear conclusion from the Study Report is that competitive brokerage rates should be required at least on such transactions." But, after noting the SEC's February 1971 decision to require negotiated rates on securities transactions in excess of $500,000, the letter significantly added that "the Commission's subsequent steps in this and related areas must necessarily be guided to a considerable extent by its experience with the initial step."[118]

A similar "prudent gradualism" was pursued by the Casey Commission. Its February 1972 "Statement on the Future Structure of the Securities Markets" characterized as "a powerful argument against any precipitous movement to competitive commissions" the possibility of a "severe decline in the revenue of the securities industry if competitive rates were suddenly introduced on all institutional business," aggravating the injury wrought by "the industry's recent financial crisis." The statement also expressed concern that unfixing commission rates might result in small investors losing "the benefit of basic research now paid for by the minimum commission" or receiving recommendations of "unsuitable" securities. "Nevertheless," the statement announced, "we have determined that a reduction in the breakpoint to $300,000 should take effect in April 1972."[119] The following month Casey testified that the SEC anticipated reaching the $100,000 level for negotiated rates by the spring of 1974, with successive reductions in the breakpoint tentatively scheduled for April 1973 and April 1974.[120] This remained the SEC's policy until late March 1973, when Chairman Cook announced that, in light of the "serious financial situation in the brokerage community at this time," the Commission would not require an interim reduction in the negotiated rate level in April 1973, although it remained committed to lowering the breakpoint for negotiated rates to $100,000 by April 1974.[121]

It soon became obvious that the SEC's ad hoc approach to the commission-rate issues was no longer viable. With the SEC's January 1973 promulgation of Rule 19b-2, barring institutions from exchange membership, and congressional support for the ban on institutional membership, negotiated commission rates remained the single practical means for institutional investors to obtain reductions in the cost of securities transactions. Repeatedly, representatives of the Investors Diversified Services, the American Bankers Association, and the American Life Convention and Life Insurance Association of America testified in favor of competitive commission rates.[122]

Securities industry support for fixed rates simultaneously eroded.

NYSE president Robert Haack became the first major figure in the industry to state publicly his personal opposition to fixed commission rates, in a remarkable address entitled "Competition and the Future of the New York Stock Exchange," delivered on November 17, 1970.

In Haack's view, the New York Stock Exchange could no longer afford fixed rates. Haack had come to believe that fixed rates were responsible for the rapidly increasing diversion of business in New York Stock Exchange–listed securities to the regional exchanges and the over-the-counter third market.

> As recently as 1967 [Haack explained], the regional exchanges and the third market combined to account for just over 10 percent of all trading in our listed stocks. Today they account for almost 20 percent. Thus, in the past three years there has been a doubling in the share of off-board trading . . . The New York Stock Exchange, to put it crassly, no longer has the only game in town . . .
>
> Unless the New York Stock Exchange is willing to compete effectively with markets where commission fees are presently negotiated it faces a continued reduction in its share of overall trading, and at an accelerated pace. I submit it is not in the long-term interest of our members or the public to permit a continued erosion in the liquidity of our marketplace.

For not only did fixed rates jeopardize the role of the New York Stock Exchange as a central securities market; they also threatened the profitability of Exchange members. Regulatory lag, implied Haack, had been responsible, in part, for the large number of securities firms that sustained losses in 1969 and 1970. Similar losses were likely to recur as long as the industry remained subject to a commission schedule requiring SEC approval. "Better would it be," urged Haack, "for the industry to make its own competitive adjustments as economic conditions warrant, rather than to work on a new schedule as it has for almost eight years with still no end in sight."

Moreover, the back-office crisis had moved Haack to adopt implicitly the economist's traditional argument that a lack of price competition tended to foster managerial inefficiency.

> Although I have argued that negotiated rates would bring about a degree of destructive competition [Haack recalled, referring to his 1968 testimony before the SEC commission-rate hearings], I now ask myself whether fixed rates have not brought about that very same kind of self-destruction. I speak to the indiscreet excesses of the past several years which may have been precipitated in part by the um-

brella provided by the fixed minimum schedule. I inquire of myself as to whether overly zealous service type competition and inept management has not been fostered by fixed minimum rates.

Finally, Haack appreciated, long before the issue was decided by the SEC or Congress, that the introduction of negotiated rates would blunt much of the momentum for institutional membership. In the long run, the financial self-interest of Exchange members would be far better served, he suggested, if NYSE members accepted rate competition but held on to all commission business executed on the Exchange, rather than preserving fixed rates and allowing institutional members to execute 60 to 70 percent of nonmembers' transactions without employing an Exchange member as a broker or dealer.[123]

Haack emphasized in his November 1970 address that these were his individual views, not the views of the New York Stock Exchange's Board of Governors. Until May 1, 1975, when all securities brokerage commission rates were unfixed, a majority or near-majority of the Exchange's membership continued to favor fixed rates. But within one year of Haack's celebrated address, several other securities industry leaders publicly endorsed competitive rates, including Merrill Lynch's Donald Regan; Investment Bankers Association president Wheelock Whitney; Weeden and Company's Donald Weeden; Paine, Webber, Jackson & Curtis's James Davant; Salomon Brothers' William Salomon; Lehman Brothers' Andrew Sage; and, reversing his earlier position, Goldman, Sachs's Gustave Levy.[124] By the spring of 1973, Donald Feuerstein of Salomon Brothers could testify "that the great majority within the securities industry now believe that fully negotiated commission rates are either desirable or inevitable. The focus of the debate has thus shifted from whether fixed commission rates should be eliminated to how and when this should be done."[125]

Actions of the House and Senate Securities subcommittees and the Justice Department's Antitrust Division contributed to the impression that the abolition of all fixed securities commission rates was inevitable. David Ratner, who joined the Senate Securities Subcommittee staff in 1971, recalled how dramatically the dominant mood in Congress had changed during the three years he had been away from Washington. In 1968, when Ratner left the SEC, the Commission had begun its commission-rate hearings as a means of developing public support for unfixed commission rates but without certainty that the goal would be achieved, in part because few in Congress had addressed the issue. By 1971, the back-office crisis had focused attention on the securities industry, and many members of Congress were openly hostile to the New York Stock Exchange's long-advanced arguments that its fixed commission rates and its exclusionary membership and access rules were essential to the health of the securities industry. Instead, Ratner believed, in 1971 many in Congress would have insisted that the back-office crisis had occurred even though the Exchange had had fixed rates; now it was time to adopt rate competition to discipline broker-dealer firms and make them more efficient.[126] Commissioner James Needham, speaking in 1972, months before becoming New York Stock Exchange chairman, detected the same dramatic swing in congressional sentiment. "You've lost the battle for public opinion," he advised the securities industry, "and you've lost the battle in Washington, particularly in Congress . . . You've lost the battle on fixed commissions; it's that simple."[127]

As SEC chairmen Casey and Cook pursued a cautious, occasionally vacillating, course toward unfixing commission rates on large orders, the House Commerce and Finance and Senate Securities subcommittees became increasingly insistent that all commission rates be unfixed. In February 1972, the Senate Securities Subcommittee, with six senators publishing dissenting or additional views, put out its initial "Securities Industry Study," criticizing the SEC for its failure to publish "any discussion of what constitutes a 'reasonable' rate of commission" and the length of time involved in the SEC's commission-rate deliberations. The subcommittee's report memorably stated:

> Between the middle of 1968 and the present, the securities industry went through a complete boom-and-bust cycle, during which its members' ability to respond to economic pressures by adjustments in their rates was severely limited by the fixed-commission-rate schedule. The fact is that in a dynamic and volatile industry like securities, the length of a rate review proceeding almost guarantees that its conclusions will be obsolete by the time they are reached. And the SEC's inability to enumerate standards to be applied in future proceedings gives little cause for hope that they will be any more expeditious.

The Senate subcommittee majority accordingly concluded that both "the interests of the investing public" and "the long-term health of the securities industry itself" required that fully competitive rates be phased in over a period of two years or slightly longer, beginning with an immediate reduction in the breakpoint for negotiated rates to $100,000.[128]

Eight months later, the House Commerce and Finance Subcommittee concurred with the Senate Securities Subcommittee "that a competitive commission-rate system should be phased in without excessive delay."[129] On March 1, 1973, the House Subcommittee's chairman, John Moss, introduced legislation to eliminate fixed securities commission rates by February 1, 1975.[130] When SEC chairman Cook unexpectedly announced three weeks later that the SEC would not require a reduction in the breakpoint for negotiated rates in April 1973, as Chairman Casey had earlier stated it would, the Senate Securities Subcommittee responded by voting 3–2 to eliminate all fixed rates by April 30, 1974.[131]

Chairman Cook's unexpected announcement prompted a similar response from the Justice Department's Antitrust Division. In June 1972, Attorney General Richard Kleindienst had written the Senate Banking Committee that the department opposed legislation introduced by Senate Securities Subcommittee chairman Williams to require "that after December 1, 1973, no securities exchange shall maintain or enforce any rule fixing minimum commissions with respect to any portion of an order in excess of $100,000." Kleindienst explained: "As long as the Commission is moving reasonably along the road toward introducing competitive rates — by gradually lowering the breakpoint — we think the Commission should have flexibility in setting the timetable. There is little to be gained, as we view the matter, from setting an absolute deadline in the form of legislation."[132]

Six weeks after Cook's announcement, the Antitrust Division published a strikingly different recommendation, urging a federal district court to supersede the SEC and order the abolition of fixed minimum commission rates on July 1, 1974, or sixty days after the New York Stock Exchange exhausted its appellate remedies, whichever occurred later. "It is now clear," the Antitrust Division stated in its posttrial brief in the case of *Thill Securities Corporation* v. *New York Stock Exchange*, that "'prudent gradualism' can be carried to the point of mere delay and inertia which victimizes investors and creates false hopes in the more timid members of the industry that fixed commissions can be retained for yet another decade."*[133]

---

* Since the *Thill* case involved a broker-dealer's challenge to the New York Stock Exchange's antirebate rule, it was unlikely to lead to an injunction barring fixed commission rates. In 1974 and 1975, the Antitrust Division filed *amicus* briefs respectively with the Second Circuit Court of Appeals and the Supreme Court in the case of *Gordon* v. *New York Stock Exchange*,[134] which directly challenged the Exchange's fixed-commission-rate schedule as violative of the antitrust laws. Both courts rejected the division's arguments that securities commission rates should be

The abolition of all fixed commission rates was announced in an SEC release exactly five weeks and one day after the August 6, 1973, swearing-in of SEC chairman Ray Garrett and Commissioner A. A. Sommer. With roughly half of its member firms losing money during the first seven months of 1973 and aggregate pretax losses of $195 million on total securities activities sustained during that period, the New York Stock Exchange earlier had proposed an increase of 10 percent in commission charges on transactions up to $5000 and of 15 percent on transactions above $5000 up to $300,000. Hearings on the Exchange rate proposal were held in July 1973. Chairman Garrett, a highly conservative securities attorney, "entered the subject with the rather strong feeling that a practice that had lasted for almost two hundred years must be sound and should not be declared improper." It soon became apparent to Garrett that all four of the SEC's other commissioners disagreed with him. Within a month after his swearing-in, Garrett, too, became convinced "that fixed commission rates are doomed. The question is who will kill them and when and under what conditions."[135]

Garrett had been impressed with the argument that if fixed commission rates were doomed, it was preferable for the SEC rather than Congress or the Supreme Court to end them. The Commission, by maintaining control, could modify the steps leading to the abolition of fixed rates, if that became necessary, more ably than could a legislature or a court. Moreover, in the wake of the G. Bradford Cook scandal and the persistent criticism of the SEC's handling of the commission-rate issues, the prestige of the Commission was at stake. Under the circumstances, had the SEC not soon moved decisively, its historic reputation as "an outstanding example of the independent agency at its best" might have been permanently tarnished.

Additionally, Garrett concurred with the long-held view of many at the SEC that it was virtually impossible to design a "reasonable rate of return" for the securities industry. Eugene Rotberg testified during the *Thill* case that unlike a public utility commission, which typically sets a fair rate of return for a single firm with a natural monopoly, or at most a few firms, in the securities industry

> you have member firms who had anything from one branch office to 170 branch offices. You had firms with returns of capital from — in 1966, from minus 21 percent to plus 83 percent. Returns on profit margin, that is simply the ratio of profits to total commissions, which

---

subject to the antitrust laws. The Supreme Court's decision, however, was published in June 1975, after the SEC and Congress each had moved to end all fixed rates.

ranged from minus 24 percent to plus 50 percent. You had returns on total assets ranging from minus 1.7 to plus 23.6. You had gross income per partner in 1966 ranging from minus $259,000 per partner to plus $1,748,000 per general partner on gross income.

You had firms crossing through all of these ratios who were doing between 10 and 20 percent of their business in listed business to other firms doing 90 percent of their business [in] listed business. Some firms were primarily underwriters. Others were primarily institutional.

You had firms, some of whom took huge blocks and took tremendous risks in providing liquidity. Other firms did not bother at all and sold mutual funds and did listed business as it walked in off the street.[136]

On September 11, 1973, the SEC approved the New York Stock Exchange's requested commission-rate increase, but announced, "The Commission will act promptly to terminate the fixing of commission rates by national stock exchanges after April 30, 1975, if the stock exchanges do not, on their own initiative, adopt rule changes achieving that result in advance of that date." There were no dissenting votes. From that date until the actual abolition of all fixed rates on May 1, 1975, Garrett, "the reluctant dragon," personally led the SEC in resisting lobbying efforts of the New York Stock Exchange and the Securities Industry Association (SIA) to pressure the Commission to reverse or defer its decision totally to unfix commission rates.

After voluntarily lifting fixed rates on orders of $2000 or less in April 1974,[137] the NYSE steadfastly opposed the SEC's decision to abolish all fixed rates. Since a March 1, 1973, resolution of the Exchange's Board of Governors, the Exchange nominally had favored competitive commission rates, but only if the SEC or Congress simultaneously took steps "to maintain the flow of orders to the nation's auction markets" by eliminating third-market trading in securities listed on the New York Stock Exchange.[138] As long as the SEC refused to endorse this blatantly anticompetitive condition, the Exchange opposed unfixing commission rates. After the SEC circulated for comments proposed Rule 19b-3 to abolish fixed rates on May 1, 1975, Exchange chairman James Needham announced that the Exchange would consider bringing suit against the SEC if the rule was adopted without conditions precluding off-board trading by Exchange members in Exchange-listed stocks and the application of Exchange rules to third-market firms.[139]

SIA president Virgil Sherrill also lobbied to persuade the SEC not to enforce competitive rates. In January 1975 he offered a last-minute "compromise" plan to retain fixed rates on portions of transactions between $10,000 to $300,000.[140] The vehemence of the securities industry's opposition to rate competition was described by Commissioner John Evans in an address delivered two weeks before the May 1, 1975, date for the abolition of fixed rates.

> It has been predicted that competitive rates will destroy the New York Stock Exchange as well as the other exchanges in the country, create confusion and chaos in the markets for securities, destroy the greatest financial communications system the world has ever known, reduce the participation of small investors in our securities markets, bring about destructive competition and thus cause a high rate of failure among broker-dealers and concentrate the securities business in a handful of firms, lower the standards in the industry, weaken desirable surveillance mechanisms that protect public investors, reduce the depth and liquidity of our markets, eliminate public markets for many securities, destroy our capital-raising mechanism, and bring about the downfall of our free enterprise system.
>
> May 1, the day by which barriers to competitive rates must be removed, is sometimes referred to as "Mayday," a term used as an international distress signal. One witness at our recent 19b-3 hearings concerning whether to adopt a rule prohibiting exchanges from fixing minimum public commission rates repeated the Mayday reference and added, "I would like to carry this one step further. Mayday is a great holiday in Russia. And Russia has said there is no need to fight democracy. It will burn itself out. Well, Commissioners, you have the candle and the matches, and it will be a short fuse."[141]

In late November 1974, the securities industry lobby persuaded the House Rules Committee to bottle up for the duration of the Ninety-third Congress H.R. 5050, Congressman Moss's comprehensive Securities Acts Amendments bill, because of industry opposition to the provision mandating the unfixing of commission rates on May 1, 1975. Exchange chairman Needham insisted that "it would be a grave error [for the SEC] to disregard or denigrate a congressional decision to withhold such a mandate from the Commission."[142]

Chairman Garrett quickly rejected the significance of the "frantic, last-minute effort to kill H.R. 5050 . . . by a parade of horrors to scare the members of the Rules Committee, whose exposure to the bill is necessarily brief." In Garrett's view, the political calculus remained unchanged. At some time in 1975 either Congress or the Supreme Court would end fixed rates. It remained preferable that the SEC act first.[143] On January 23, 1975, the SEC formally adopted Rule 19b-3, ending, on May 1, 1975, all fixed commission rates charged nonmembers.[144] Days later the New York

Stock Exchange announced that it would not bring a suit contesting the rule.[145] By then it was obvious the suit would have been pointless. Congress soon also adopted legislation abolishing all fixed rates.[146]

After several years' experience with competitive rates, it now is obvious that May Day proved almost as beneficial for the New York Stock Exchange as it did for investors. Exactly as Haack anticipated in his November 1970 address, the unfixing of commission rates reversed the fragmentation in the trading of exchange-listed securities. Third-market volume rapidly shrank from 7.87 percent of total volume in Exchange-listed securities in 1972 to less than 3 percent early in 1978, when Weeden and Company, the largest third-market dealer, announced its decision to quit third-market operations. By September 1980, the New York Stock Exchange was responsible for 88 percent of the transactions in Exchange-listed securities. The regional markets maintained approximately 10 percent of the volume in Exchange-listed securities both before and after May Day; the third market, with a share of 2 percent, had almost disappeared.[147]

Simultaneously, commission-rate levels were substantially reduced. Between May 1, 1975, and the end of 1980, a study conducted by the SEC's Directorate of Economic and Policy Analysis calculated that commission charges computed as a percentage of the principal value of securities transactions declined 57 percent for institutional investors and 20 percent for individual investors. Even commission rates paid by individuals on orders of less than two hundred shares declined 6 percent during this period when computed on a percentage of principal basis.*[148]

The SEC estimated that in dollars-and-cents terms, investor savings for the year 1976 alone amounted to $485.3 million.[149] Further commission-rate savings could be anticipated with the emergence of discount brokers. Between 1976 and the fourth quarter of 1980, the market share of discount or no-frills brokers grew from less than 0.4 percent to 6.0 percent, with newspaper advertisements for dis-

---

* While it was true that the commission cost per average share of stock on individual orders under two hundred shares increased from 50.1 to 59.3 cents between April 1975 and the fourth quarter of 1980, there was no actual increase in investor costs. This apparent 18 percent increase, in fact, was less than one-third the 61.7 percent increase in the Consumer Price Index during that period. Moreover, between April 1975 and the final quarter of 1980, the value of an average share of stock also increased, with the result that the individual investor paid a commission of 1.91 percent of principal on orders of less than two hundred shares in the fourth quarter of 1980 as compared with a commission rate of 2.33 percent in April 1975.

count brokers regularly appearing in the financial press and promising rates 50 to 90 percent less than full-service brokerage houses.[150]

Yet the profitability of the securities industry was enhanced. As the Justice Department's economic witnesses had predicted at the SEC's 1968 commission-rate hearings, a reduction in securities transaction costs was likely to contribute to increased securities volume. Between 1974 and 1980, aggregate share volume on national securities exchanges more than tripled.*[151] While New York Stock Exchange member firms doing a public business in aggregate lost money in 1973 and barely broke even in 1974, the same firms earned average profits of 13.7, 14.2, 6.2, 7.7, 9.8, and 14.2 percent during the first six years that they were subject to negotiated rates.[152]

None of the adverse consequences that the NYSE in 1968 predicted would occur if commission rates were unfixed did occur. Nothing along the lines of "destructive competition" eventuated. Nor was there a wholesale desertion of Exchange memberships. As Demsetz prophesied, the cost of New York Stock Exchange seats did substantially decline.[153] But the number of member organizations on the New York Stock Exchange doing a public business only slightly decreased, from 422 in 1974 to 389 in 1980.[154] Similarly, although there were several much-publicized mergers in the securities industry during the late 1970s, aggregate concentration levels increased only marginally. In 1975, the top twenty-five broker-dealer firms generated 53 percent of the industry's gross revenues. By 1980, their share had grown to 61 percent. Between 1975 and 1980, the total revenues of the top four broker-dealer firms increased only from 21 to 24 percent. As the rapid growth of the discount brokers amply demonstrated, there were no significant barriers to entry into the securities industry. "Clearly, then," economists Seha Tinic and Richard West concluded a 1980 article, "the brokerage industry has not been one in which economies of scale have dictated that under competitive pricing, the largest four or five firms, or a particular group of firms, would grow inexorably at the expense of the rest.†[155]

---

* It should be borne in mind, however, that 1974 was a year of depressed share volume and that it is not clear how much of the 1974–1980 share volume increase can be attributed to reduced commission costs.

† However, by 1980 securities commissions, though still the largest revenue source for the securities industry, had declined as a percentage of aggregate revenues from a high of 55 percent in 1973 to 36 percent in 1980. While much of this decrease was attributable to an end-of-the-decade growth in securities firm interest revenues (in

Nor, in the first years of competitive commission rates, had persuasive evidence emerged that investors had been injured by the "unbundling" of research and brokerage services.[156] Instead, the coexistence of full-service brokerage firms offering investment research and advice, discount brokers offering brokerage but no investment research or advice, and investment advisers and publications offering only investment research and advice gave investors the opportunity to purchase only those investment services they actually desired. It may have been overstating matters to assert, as one finance professor did in 1978, that "May Day may have saved the NYSE as an institution."[157] But it was appropriate to conclude that the unfixing of securities industry commission rates generally benefited investors by reducing transaction costs, permitting discount brokers and unbundling brokerage services while simultaneously improving the overall health of the securities industry by contributing to an increase in share volume, and stimulating greater broker-dealer firm efficiency without significant increases in securities industry concentration levels.

* * *

With the total unfixing of brokerage commission rates in 1975, the restructuring of the securities markets by means of an electronically linked central market system became the SEC's predominant regulatory mission. It is likely to remain so for several more years.

The concept of a central securities market long antedated computer technology and traditionally has been the justification for the New York Stock Exchange's monopoly in securities listed on the NYSE.[158] By centralizing all buy and sell orders in a given security, investors theoretically should receive the best execution of their orders by a continuous matching of the highest-priced buy orders against the lowest-priced sell orders. With a regular volume of orders flowing to a single place of execution, a central market should be "orderly," without wide or abrupt price swings; "continuous," with minimum price variations between successive transactions; "liquid," that is, able immediately to process orders and have "depth" or the capacity to handle temporary imbalances in supply and demand caused by substantial volume without becoming disorderly.

The heart of the New York Stock Exchange's central market was

---

large part, a consequence of the end-of-the-decade higher interest rate levels), it also was clear that many securities firms during this period significantly increased their revenues from listed option transactions, commodity activities, money market funds, and other sources unrelated to the securities business.

its specialist system. Buy and sell orders, regardless of where in the country they originated, usually were communicated to the Exchange floor, where floor brokers would carry them to the post of the specialist who made a market in that security. If volume in a security was sufficiently active, the floor broker could execute the order by matching it against a reciprocal order of another floor broker standing in front of the specialist's post or against an agency order on the specialist's book. When buy and sell orders could not be matched, the Exchange specialist would function as a dealer, trading for his own account to ensure an orderly and continuous market. Alternatively, the floor broker could enter a limit order in the specialist's book to be executed at a specified price above, at, or below the current market.

During the late 1960s and early 1970s, four primary considerations led the SEC and Congress to conclude that the New York Stock Exchange specialist system was no longer capable of providing the best execution of all Exchange-listed securities transactions.

The first consideration was that NYSE specialists alone often were unable to perform adequately as a dealer offsetting large institutional buy and sell orders (popularly called block orders). Between the last quarter of 1964 and the third quarter of 1970, block trades of 10,000 or more shares grew from 2.1 to 14.8 percent of total New York Stock Exchange volume.* Data published in the SEC's 1971 *Institutional Investor Study* demonstrated that, on average, as the size of block trades increased, specialist dealer participation decreased. Increasingly, during this period, institutions executed large-block trades by making use of Exchange members who specialized in filling institutional orders off the Exchange floor. Popularly called "block positioners" or "block traders," these firms typically negotiated disposition of large-block trades with other institutions or broker-dealers through "upstairs" computer or telephone communication systems, going to the Exchange floor to "cross" the order formally only after its terms had been fully determined.

By the time the *Institutional Investor Study* was published in 1971, 35 percent of the volume in block trades of 10,000 or more shares in NYSE-listed shares was executed off the New York Stock Exchange floor, either in the regional markets or the over-the-counter market. In part, the growth in non-NYSE execution of block trades in Exchange-listed securities continued after the abolition of

---

* Block trading volume as a percentage of all trading volume continued to increase throughout the 1970s. In 1980, block trades of 10,000 or more shares were responsible for 29.2 percent of all New York Stock Exchange volume.

customer-directed give-ups and the institution of a volume discount because it remained possible for an institution to secure a lower commission rate off the NYSE by employing various reciprocal arrangements.[159]

A second reason faith waned that the New York Stock Exchange specialists alone could provide the best execution in Exchange-listed securities was the triumph of the belief within the SEC that market-maker competition was likely to provide better executions for investors than SEC and Exchange regulation of Exchange specialists.

The case for market-maker competition was persuasively urged by Donald Farrar, the director of the Institutional Investor Study, in a 1972 article published in the *Harvard Business Review*. Data published in the study's report had led Farrar to conclude that "specialists have a compelling economic reason for being unwilling to risk large amounts of their own capital in order to make deep markets in 'their' stocks." Specialists who best fulfilled their market-making responsibilities during the period covered by the study earned about a 29 percent return on high-volume stocks, but "those specialists who did not make deep markets and permitted great temporary price fluctuations in their stocks earned gross returns of 191 percent on high-volume stocks, while assuming far less risk on their more modest capital commitments."

"Regulation at best," argued Farrar, "can establish only minimal standards of performance. Once the system is working, regulation tends to be more effective in punishing misconduct than in motivating participants to take steps to improve the system's performance." On the contrary, Farrar wrote:

> There is every reason to believe, however, that competition between market-makers in a single marketplace would provide the needed inducement for dealers to place their capital on the line. Market-making can be very remunerative, especially for dealers who participate in a large volume of trading. Under a competitive regime, any dealer whose quotes and depth are not competitive would simply forfeit to others the opportunity to participate in all, or at least part, of that volume.[160]

The back-office crisis provided a third basis for doubting that the specialist system was capable of providing the best execution of all NYSE-listed securities transactions. In the aftermath of the crisis, several private industry and congressional studies concurred with the SEC's "Study of Unsafe and Unsound Practices of Brokers and Dealers" that "the methods of handling securities certificates in effecting deliveries and transfers are positively archaic."[161] A typical individual investor buy order during the 1960s required a brokerage firm to use approximately thirty-three different documents to execute and record the transaction. Virtually all of the steps in executing an order were manual.[162]

The length and complexity of the securities order, clearance, transfer, and settlement process convinced many, as James Stone wrote in *One Way for Wall Street*, that "the portable stock certificates may be the single greatest villain of the back-office story."[163] In February 1971, SEC commissioner Richard Smith termed "the rapid, systematic elimination of the stock certificate . . . the only final solution" to the securities industry's paperwork problems.[164] However, after the SEC held a conference on the stock certificate four months later,[165] the Commission published a report describing obstacles to a rapid abolition of stock certificates; principally, the need for extensive statutory law changes, the necessity for industrywide acceptance of an alternative approach, and "the psychological feeling of . . . many investors [who] do not feel that they actually own their securities until they have them in their physical possession."[166] Instead of seeking a rapid abolition of share certificates, the SEC sought, and ultimately was granted from Congress as part of the 1975 Securities Acts Amendments additional authority "to facilitate the establishment of a national system for the prompt and accurate clearance and settlement of transactions in securities." The amendments specifically found that "new data processing and communications techniques" and "the linking of all clearance and settlement facilities and the development of uniform standards and procedures for clearance and settlement will reduce unnecessary costs and increase the protection of investors."[167]

The automation and linkage of securities clearance and settlement facilities suggested a more comprehensive reform. A 1969 study conducted for the American Stock Exchange by the North American Rockwell Information Systems Company estimated that errors in the securities order process cost brokerage firms approximately $100 million per year. By automating securities-ordering via a nationwide computer network linking brokers to market-makers to clearance and settlement facilities, error costs could be reduced; and further savings could be achieved by the elimination of floor brokers and the integration of transaction reporting, quotation, record-keeping, and regulatory organizations.[168] In 1977, SRI International estimated that the cost savings from the creation of an electronically linked central securities market would come to more than $130 million a year.[169]

The final primary reason for doubting that the New York Stock Exchange specialist system could provide the best execution of all NYSE-listed securities transactions was the design and successful implementation of the NASDAQ over-the-counter quotation system in February 1971.

Before NASDAQ began operations, quotations in over-the-counter securities had been reported in daily "pink sheets" published by the National Quotation Bureau, listing bid and asked prices of each dealer in each stock for the previous trading day. To obtain up-to-the-minute competitive quotations, a stockbroker or dealer had to telephone one or more dealers in an over-the-counter security; the time and difficulty involved in telephoning over-the-counter dealers frequently discouraged brokers or dealers placing orders from engaging in rigorous comparative shopping.[170]

NASDAQ dramatically improved the quality of the over-the-counter securities market. At the heart of the NASDAQ system was the Central Processing Complex, located in Trumbull, Connecticut. The complex consisted of two Univac 1108 computers, either of which was capable of handling the full load of NASDAQ traffic. The computers were connected by high-speed trunk lines, regional concentrator centers, and 20,000 miles of leased telephone lines to desktop terminals located throughout the country. Each terminal consisted of a specially designed keyboard and a cathode-ray tube screen capable of instantaneous display of data. Initially, NASDAQ provided three levels of service. In the NASDAQ Level 1 service, brokers or dealers could view a representative quotation for any NASDAQ security. On Level 2, brokers or dealers could view the current bid and ask prices of each market-maker for any NASDAQ security available. Level 3 service allowed NASDAQ market-makers instantaneously to insert new quotations into the system.

NASDAQ Levels 2 and 3 service revolutionized the O-T-C market. At the touch of a few buttons, a broker or dealer could instantly see the competitive quotations of all market-makers in a given security. Newspapers could be supplied with volume data concerning each over-the-counter security for the first time. Investors could obtain current quotations.[171] Most significantly, the simultaneous availability of rival market-makers' quotations narrowed price spreads. Several economic studies corroborated this result. One calculated that between 1970 and 1972, the mean market spread for a sample of over-the-counter securities fell from 0.4871 to 0.4028.[172] In part because of the NASDAQ competitive market-maker system and because an increased number of newspapers began publishing over-the-counter quotations, a number of firms whose securities were traded over the counter did not seek an exchange listing at the earliest possible opportunity. As of December 1980, approximately a thousand securities eligible for trading on the American Stock Exchange and approximately five hundred eligible for listing on the New York Stock Exchange remained solely traded in the NASDAQ system.[173] Between 1974 and 1979, NASDAQ volume as a percentage of New York Stock Exchange volume grew from 32 to 44 percent. Spreads on 85 percent of NASDAQ securities further narrowed after NASDAQ, on July 7, 1980, began making available to newspapers the best-bid and best-offer prices of NASDAQ securities, rather than the arguably misleading "median" or "representative" quotations previously published. Between July 7 and the end of September 1980, NASDAQ volume was 57.5 percent of New York Stock Exchange volume (expressed on a share basis). By the week ending June 12, 1981, NASDAQ volume had reached 63 percent of NYSE volume and was nearly six times greater than volume on the American Stock Exchange.[174]

Nonetheless, NASDAQ initially had been designed to have a minimal impact on O-T-C market-makers and NASD members who held seats on the New York Stock Exchange. A memorandum prepared by the SEC's Division of Trading and Markets in December 1970 explained that because NASD "believed that the system would not get off the ground unless enough firms were willing to accept it," NASDAQ planned "to be primarily a quotations system designed to relieve the growing and unmanageable demand by retail firms (and their customers) for informational quotations." A number of other technically feasible functions had not been incorporated because of fear of broker-dealer firm resistance. The SEC's memorandum specifically described the assumptions underlying the first NASDAQ design:

> (2) All system input was to emanate from market-makers. In other words, unlike exchange floors, there was to be no possibility within the system for direct meeting of retail orders originating from non-market-making firms.
>
> (3) Although technically feasible, the NASDAQ system itself was not to provide for negotiation and execution of transactions between retail traders and market-makers.
>
> (4) While the system would provide an input capability for market-makers to report volume, such reporting was to take place only after the close of business each day and was to be publicly disclosed in aggregates and through newspaper release. From this it follows that NASDAQ would not contain a built-in capability for a real time "tape."[175]

The most notorious political limitation on the initial NASDAQ system was the decision of the NASD Board of Governors not to include in the system over-the-counter quotations in securities listed on the New York or American Stock exchanges, so-called third-market quotations.[176] An August 22, 1968, memorandum prepared by the NASD justified this decision on the ground, among others, that without the financial support of Exchange members "it is unlikely that the NASDAQ system would ever become operational" and that "Exchange members cannot be expected to deliberately bring into being a quotations system which might undo the efforts of the Exchange to achieve a viable market, with depth, in listed securities." That is to say, the NASD assumed that New York Stock Exchange members would boycott the NASDAQ system if it facilitated third-market competition with Exchange specialists in Exchange-listed securities. After repeated protests by the SEC's Division of Trading and Markets, the NASD agreed in late 1968 that third-market quotations would be included in the NASDAQ system. NASD president Gordon Macklin subsequently explained that the relevant "by-law was adopted in late 1968 primarily because the Board of Governors believed that the Commission would disapprove it should it not include listed securities."

As the NASDAQ system neared implementation in October 1970, both American Stock Exchange president Ralph Saul and New York Stock Exchange president Robert Haack formally requested that the SEC bar inclusion of exchange-listed securities in the NASDAQ system until the SEC held a full hearing on the issue. At the time, sixteen of the twenty-three members of the NASD Board of Governors were members of New York Stock Exchange firms. On October 22, 1970, Macklin wrote SEC chairman Budge on behalf of the NASD board also requesting that third-market quotations not be included initially in the NASDAQ system, citing, among other arguments, "the possible effect on exchange markets."

Nearly simultaneously, Irving Pollack of the Division of Trading and Markets prepared the draft of a letter for SEC approval, rejecting Saul's request that listed securities not be included in the NASDAQ system. Pollack's letter explained that the exchanges had had nearly two years to comment on the relevant by-law and that he could "see no basis for the Commission interposing any objection to inclusion of listed securities in that system if the securities and their market-makers meet the appropriate regulatory standards adopted by the NASD."

Unexpectedly, the Budge SEC overruled Pollack on October 22,

1970, and permitted exclusion of third-market quotations from the NASDAQ system.

Third-market dealers Donald Weeden and M. A. Schapiro soon wrote the NASD, the SEC, and Congressman Emanuel Celler, chairman of the House Antitrust and Monopoly Subcommittee, protesting the NASD's "last-minute decision to exclude third-market securities from the NASDAQ system." Within weeks, Shumate and Company, a small Dallas, Texas, over-the-counter firm, filed a class action against the NASD, alleging that the decision to exclude listed securities violated the antitrust laws.

Given the SEC's 1965 report on Rule 394 and the earlier efforts of the Commission to require inclusion of third-market quotations, Shumate's suit had a reasonable probability of success. In March 1971, the NASD Board of Governors announced a compromise resolution of the issue. Adopting a suggestion earlier made by Donald Weeden, the board voted to include a controlled group of thirty-six exchange-listed securities in the NASDAQ system on a test basis for 90 to 180 days. In September 1971 the NASD board voted to continue the test, significantly expanding the number of securities by adding any listed issue for which two or more third-market firms were registered as market-maker, provided the security had at least 100,000 shares and met other specified requirements.

The results of the NASD test were published in April 1972. Focusing on eighty-four securities quoted in the NASDAQ system and dually traded on an exchange and over the counter, the NASD summarized its statistical evidence as showing that

> investors able to deal directly with third-market-makers realize significant savings over the cost of executing trades on exchanges . . . No deleterious effects on the general market structure have been observed following inclusion of exchange-listed issues in NASDAQ. The NASDAQ third-market-makers handle blocks with no more disturbance to prices, and sometimes less, than occurs on the NYSE . . . Moreover, the high degree of competition between NASDAQ and exchange quotations has had a small but significant effect in reducing dealer spreads for issues included in NASDAQ.

Specifically, the NASD found that approximately one third of the time third-market quotations in Exchange-listed securities were better for investors than those offered on the New York Stock Exchange.*

* SEC staff studies conducted in 1965 and 1969 reached similar results. The larger 1969 study compared matched sets of third-market and New York Stock Exchange quotations and found that in 45 percent of 492 purchase transactions and 42 percent

Third-market volume in the Exchange-listed securities included in the test increased to 11.7 percent of NYSE volume. As Donald Farrar had predicted, with increased competition among market-makers had come narrower price quotations. New York Stock Exchange quotation spreads had narrowed 5 percent on the Exchange-listed securities included in the NASDAQ system from the beginning of the NASD's test and 6.5 percent for Exchange-listed securities added to the test in September 1971.

The NASD's Board of Governors unanimously voted permanently to include Exchange-listed securities in the NASDAQ system on May 9, 1972. Thereafter, New York Stock Exchange Rule 394, which generally barred Exchange members from buying or selling Exchange-listed securities from over-the-counter dealers, became the principal cap on growth of the NASDAQ system. As former SEC attorney Thomas Russo and Assistant Professor William Wang wrote, in a 1972 law review article: "If Rule 394 were eliminated, NASDAQ might gradually supplant the New York Stock Exchange. If it were to survive, the Exchange would certainly be forced to adopt technological innovations it should have implemented long ago."[178]

Taking into account each of the four primary considerations that inspired the movement to create an electronically linked central securities market, it was possible by the early 1970s to envision the contours of a new national securities market system. Employing computer technology, all securities market-makers — the Exchange specialists, the over-the-counter dealers, the Exchange block positioners — could be linked by a composite transaction- and quotation-reporting system. Removal of Rule 394 and other barriers to market-maker competition would give the market greater "depth," since the capital of more market-makers would be available to handle temporary imbalances in supply and demand. If each Exchange specialist's limit-order book was replaced with a system-wide limit-order book, investors would have a more effective guarantee of best order execution. The fragmentation of the securities market into numerous unconnected market centers could be prevented either by technology that automatically matched and executed best bids and offers or by a "best execution" rule that prevented any broker from executing a transaction when a better price was available elsewhere in the system. Price spreads would be kept close by competing market-makers and by centralizing volume within the electronic market. Market orders would be executed by

---

of 465 sales transactions, investors received the same or better prices in the third market.[177]

brokers or dealers through NASDAQ-type desk consoles. The brokers or dealers would match buy or sell orders against the system-wide limit-order book or against the entries of other brokers and dealers. Simultaneously, the central computer facility could record the transaction on a systemwide transaction tape and arrange securities clearance and settlement. Eventually, a central computer could replace entirely the exchange's floor brokers and back-office personnel and reduce reliance on exchange specialists. Hardwood exchange floors could be superseded by brokerage firm desk consoles and a central computer facility in a nationwide "exchange without walls."[179]

In the broadest sense, three general types of benefits could be expected from such an electronic market. First, the automation and linking of securities execution, clearance, transfer, and settlement would lower transaction costs and reduce the risks of a second back-office crisis. Second, elimination of barriers to market-maker competition, such as the New York Stock Exchange's off-board trading rules, and the facilitation of market-maker competition through a composite quotation system, automatic routing of orders to the best market, and a composite limit-order book, would further reduce transaction costs, particularly in heavily traded securities. Third, and the least analyzed though potentially a highly significant source of savings, would be the replacement of pricing of securities in one-eighth points (necessitated by the practicalities of shouting orders on a stock exchange floor) with a decimal system (by which securities could be priced in one-hundredth points, for example, $27.01, $27.02, and so on). Conversion to a decimal system of securities trading would be practicable only when transactions were effected by broker-dealers through desktop terminal devices. Narrower price spreads would be immediately possible if trading were conducted in differentials as small as one cent.

It is worth emphasizing that the value of these benefits is open to reasonable debate. SEC chairman Harold Williams, for one prominent example, believed that other steps taken by the securities industry (such as automatic order routing) had substantially reduced the risk of a second back-office crisis and that the $100 to $200 million that could be saved in lower execution, clearance, transfer, and settlement was "inconsequential," "between one and two cents a share." Further, Williams believed that the economic benefits of increased market-maker competition were unlikely to be great enough to justify any significant risk of disrupting existing securities markets by implementing a new market system. By contrast, Congress in enacting the 1975 Securities Acts Amendments required that the SEC facilitate creation of a national securities market system because it believed that the benefits of an electronic market would outweigh the costs and risks of implementation. To minimize these costs and risks, Congress left to the SEC broad discretion in facilitating the technology employed in the new markets and in timing its implementation. In enacting the 1975 amendments, Congress was most concerned about preventing the type of error losses associated with the 1967–1970 back-office crisis and narrowing price spreads by enhancing market-maker competition. Arguably, when the value of decimal trading is added to these savings, the congressional decision was a wise one.[180]

As will be shown, there were difficult technical problems and policy decisions involved in converting a system of unaffiliated securities exchanges and over-the-counter markets into a nationwide electronic securities system. The major obstacles, however, were political. There was virtually no incentive for the New York Stock Exchange and the specialists and other floor members who dominated its governance to help create a central market system that could reduce NYSE floor members' profits by removing their monopoly in listed securities trading and increasing the effectiveness of market-maker competition. Similarly, there was no incentive for *any* securities exchange to support a central market system that would increase the proportion of listed security orders that could be executed "upstairs" by broker-dealer firms that were exchange members. To the regional exchanges in particular the threat posed by an efficient central market system was acute. Much or all of their order flow might be more efficiently handled by market-makers in major broker-dealer firms like Merrill Lynch. The exchanges also were threatened by NASDAQ and other potential developers of central market computer technology, who could argue that construction and administration of an electronic market should be granted to those most experienced in employing computer facilities. Under these circumstances, it never was realistic to assume that industry-wide cooperation rapidly could lead to a cost-efficient central market system. Implementation of the new marketplace aptly could be compared to a nineteenth-century frontier land-grab, with the New York Stock Exchange floor members trying to retain — and the regional exchanges, over-the-counter dealers, and major broker-dealer firms trying to secure — the most desirable flow of orders in the securities industry. The New York Stock Exchange could not be expected, Professor James Lorie perceptively stated, "to take the leadership in the euthanasia of the floor community."[181] The NYSE, however, could be expected fervently to oppose initiatives that so fundamentally threatened its survival and profitability.

The SEC's role in facilitating the creation of the central electronic market, thus, was pivotal. Only the SEC had the authority and expertise to prod or compel the New York Stock Exchange and the other exchanges to accept change, referee alternative proposals, and prevent industry initiatives from excluding competition or unnecessarily raising transaction costs. From the outset, it was predictable that progress toward creation of a central market system substantially would turn on how effectively the SEC moved the securities industry to implement technology that would reduce investor costs.*

The SEC's first formal statement concerning the need to create a national securities market system appeared in the transmittal letter accompanying the publication of its *Institutional Investor Study* in March 1971. Disclaiming any intent to mandate or describe in detail the future structure of the securities markets, the SEC stated that its "objective" would be "to see a strong central market system created to which all investors have access, in which all qualified broker-dealers and existing market institutions may participate in accordance with their respective capabilities, and which is controlled not only by appropriate regulation but also by the forces of competition."[183]

Five months later the New York Stock Exchange joined the issue, with the publication of William McChesney Martin's eagerly awaited report on the securities markets. Martin, writing as an independent unpaid adviser of the New York Stock Exchange Board of Governors, began with the undocumented assertion that "competition between markets has not been beneficial because it has depended upon unequal regulation which, among other things, has not required full disclosure and equal responsibility of participants." Without considering whether market-maker competition ever could be beneficial, Martin then proceeded to outline a national market system almost entirely opposite to that proposed by the SEC, one in

---

* Congress, in enacting the 1975 Securities Acts Amendments, underlined its expectation that the SEC initially would work to stimulate securities industry efforts to design an electronic market by causing the rescission of Exchange rules that restricted market-maker competition. A Senate report preceding enactment, for example, stated, "The first order of priority in creating a national market system is to break down the unnecessary regulatory restrictions which now impede contact between brokers and market-makers and which restrain competition among markets and market makers."[182]

which the New York Stock Exchange's monopolistic position in trading listed securities largely would be preserved. Martin recommended that the New York Stock Exchange, the American Stock Exchange, and the regional exchanges be integrated to provide a single, national auction market for each security qualified for listing. All over-the-counter trading in exchange-listed securities thereafter would be prohibited, because, wrote Martin, again without factual corroboration, "there is no doubt that the growth of the third market presents a danger to the maintenance of fair and disclosed pricing and to the regulatory system." To improve the performance of the much-criticized specialists, Martin proposed raising minimum capital requirements and allocating new securities only to those specialists who best met clearly defined performance criteria. Martin's report did not make clear whether he meant that the regional exchanges would continue to provide competitive markets for securities listed on the New York Stock Exchange. Alternatively, he may have meant that there should be one specialist for each listed security and no regional exchange competition along the lines of the proposal made by the New York Stock Exchange in 1940 (when Martin was its president) to ban all multiple trading of New York Stock Exchange–listed securities. Martin did state, "The New York Stock Exchange has, to some extent, all of the characteristics prescribed above for the proposed national exchange system."[184]

The New York Stock Exchange and a committee of fifty-two broker-dealer firms soon endorsed the basic conclusions of the Martin Report.[185] Among others in the securities industry, reported the *New York Post*'s Carol Mathews, "the 26-page report was met with hoots of laughter and private expression of disbelief." Nineteen economists, ranging from the University of Chicago's Milton Friedman to MIT's Paul Samuelson, signed a petition endorsing the recommendations of the SEC in its *Institutional Investor Study* transmittal letter and stating: "Acceptance of the recommendations of the Martin Report would help to re-establish the eroding monopoly power of the New York Stock Exchange and to subject that power primarily to regulation by the monopolist." In his covering letter James Lorie added, "This is a little like having the rabbits guard the lettuce." Elsewhere, Samuelson characterized the Martin Report as a "grievous disappointment." Former SEC Institutional Investor Study director Donald Farrar similarly termed it a "great leap backward." *Business Week* accurately concluded: "The Martin Report has lost Wall Street a chance to bring about reform on its own."[186]

Three weeks after the publication of the report, Chairman William Casey announced that the Commission would hold hearings on the future structure of the securities markets.[187] These hearings culminated in the SEC's February 1972 "Statement on the Future Structure of the Securities Markets," which was most significant for its rejection of the Martin Report's proposal to abolish the third market and its reaffirmation of the SEC's commitment to market-maker competition.

> The central market system we look toward . . . [explained the statement] would entail, among other things, the following elements: 1. Implementation of a nationwide disclosure or market information system to make universally available price and volume in all markets and quotations from all market makers. 2. Elimination of artificial impediments, created by exchange rules or otherwise, to dealing in the best available market. 3. Establishment of terms and conditions upon which any qualified broker-dealer can attain access to all exchanges . . . [and] 4. Integration of third-market firms into the central market system . . .

The SEC intended to enhance

> the competition which now takes place among the separate exchange markets and between all of them and the third market [while] centralizing all buying and selling interest and maximizing market-maker capability . . . so that securities can be bought and sold at reasonably continuous and stable prices, and to ensure that each investor will receive the best possible execution of his order, regardless of where it originates.[188]

After receiving the report of the Advisory Committee on a Central Market System, appointed by the Casey SEC,[189] Cook's SEC outlined some of the concrete steps necessary to create a nationwide electronic market system in its March 1973 "Policy Statement on the Structure of a Central Market System." Three broad projects were envisioned. First, creation of a systemwide communications system. Second, since "the most important objective of the system is to foster the development of strong competition among its participants," the statement called for the elimination of unjustifiable impediments to market-maker competition. Specifically the statement noted that "restrictions such as Rule 394, regardless of their past appropriateness, are incompatible with a central market system and will have to be rescinded by the time the quotation system is in operation." Finally, the statement anticipated creation of a systemwide specialist limit-order book and, apparently also an electronic execution system. The statement was vague about details of the systemwide limit-order book and execution system, providing little or no discussion of such questions as the technology to be employed, how the systemwide limit-order book and execution system would be linked to the systemwide communications network, and whether NASDAQ's facilities could or should be employed to bring the central securities market on line most rapidly. To ensure that public orders would receive preferential treatment, the SEC's 1973 statement did underline the Commission's "commitment to the preservation of an auction-agency market rather than a purely 'dealer market' for listed securities."*[190]

Shortly before the 1973 "Central Market Policy Statement" was published, SEC chairman-designate Cook predicted, "In my judgment, all of the major elements of this system . . . can and should be in operation no later than two years from now."[191] Nearly a decade later full implementation of an electronic securities market has not been achieved. There were several reasons for the central market system's slow progress.

Before the 1975 Securities Acts Amendments explicitly provided the SEC with authority to "facilitate the establishment of a national market system for securities," the Commission's authority to require that the securities industry implement composite tape and quotation systems and other elements of the new electronic market was open to reasonable legal question. Even when the SEC arguably possessed the necessary authority, the threat of protracted litigation often persuaded the Commission to attempt to negotiate industry acceptance of an SEC initiative rather than proceed by fiat. These efforts at persuasion often also proved to be protracted.[192]

Between 1972 and 1977, the SEC relied on three successive industry advisory groups to help design a central market system.† This reliance was almost entirely misplaced. Although the individuals advising the SEC were highly competent, all worked on a part-time basis, with little or no staff. Like the securities industry itself, each advisory group reflected highly conflicting viewpoints. None of the advisory groups proved able to resolve the most controversial questions concerning the electronic market. Nor did the SEC provide effective guidance to the industry in its efforts to develop the most

---

* This was both a critical and a debatable principle. If the aim of a central market system was to maximize dealer competition, while preserving an auction-agency market, it would have been preferable to require that dealer and public orders receive equal treatment. To create an incentive for dealer competition, all dealers making an identical bid or offer might be placed in a "time queue" within a computer system, with dealers receiving business on a time and price priority basis. To some degree this incentive for competition will be dissipated if dealers surrender their place in the queue whenever an identically priced public bid or offer is made.

† The final group, the National Market Advisory Board, was required by the 1975 Securities Acts Amendments.

controversial components of the central market system, a system-wide linkage and order-routing system and a systemwide limit-order book.* The SEC's 1972 "Future Structure" and 1973 "Central Market" statements focused on the development of composite last-sale and quotation systems. Neither statement attempted to describe the specifications of the computer system that would bring about systemwide order execution or how the execution system would be linked to the composite tape and quotations system. The lack of a blueprint or meaningful guidelines contributed to industry deadlocks and risked unnecessarily raising investor transaction costs. Merrill Lynch president William Schreyer testified in September 1979:

> Despite torrents of words and showers of papers on the subject, no one in any position of authority has yet defined what a national market is . . . Without consensus, there is no way that the industry can construct facilities necessary to build one. It is somewhat like building a house where the architect, the plumber, the carpenter and the electrician each has his own conception of what the house should look like and performs his tasks without regard to what the others are doing.[193]

But the primary reason no central securities market yet exists is quite different. The SEC during the 1977–1981 chairmanship of Harold Williams ceased to treat as "the most important objective of the system . . . the development of strong competition among its participants." The goal of maximum market-maker competition was subordinated to the more conservative objective of avoiding disruptions in securities trading while implementing a central market system. Williams memorably defended the SEC's slow progress in 1979 by stating, "I am not about to be the person to come back to Congress and say I am sorry I implemented your program and it blew [up]. The capital markets of this country are too important."[194]

The conservative approach of Chairman Williams stemmed primarily from three bases. First, his philosophical belief that industry should "maintain the initiative in design and implementation of the system," because the SEC was "not well suited by experience or disposition" to serve as "a planner for industry." Williams stated,

---

* This is not to suggest that the SEC should have dictated the precise details of the technology to be employed. It is, however, to suggest that the Commission, for example, could have scheduled the removal of NYSE Rule 394 and other anticompetitive rules to create incentives for the securities industry to implement the technology of an electronic market by a specified date. Similarly, the SEC could have defined the minimum characteristics of a national market system (e.g., all bids and orders should be able to interact, with best bid always able to meet best offer) and left it to the securities industry to design the appropriate technology by specified dates.

"If a transition to a fully automated trading system is to be developed, it should occur as a result of economic forces and acceptance by investors rather than by Commission mandate."[195] The difficulty with such an approach was that the securities industry was too divided to design a cost-efficient system without firm SEC guidance. The SEC's historical experience with regulation of the securities markets and the mandate of the 1975 amendments both suggested that the Commission needed to perform a more activist role than Williams was prepared to do.

Williams also was skeptical of the wisdom of increasing market-maker competition. In his view, the best prices for investors were most likely to result when orders interacted on a single exchange floor. He doubted that allowing major securities firms like Merrill Lynch to internalize execution of orders would narrow price spreads throughout the national market system. Rather, like the New York Stock Exchange, Williams believed increased market-maker competition would fragment the securities markets and loosen price spreads.

Finally, Williams believed it was essential to bring on line any new automated system gradually, preferably after controlled experiments. As he once put it, attempting to implement a new market system during a trading volume surge would be like trying to change the wheels on a moving locomotive. In a 1981 interview, Williams recalled how difficult it had been for some business firms to computerize payroll services, obviously a far simpler operation than automating the securities industry. The dismal experience of the broker-dealer firms that attempted "instant computerization" of their back-office operations during the 1967–1970 crisis also may be cited in support of Williams's cautious approach.

Nonetheless, considerable evidence exists that the Williams SEC took risk avoidance too far. Consistently the Commission seemed badly divided on national market system decisions. Repeatedly SEC efforts to enhance market-maker competition were deferred or withdrawn without publication of convincing explanations. Moreover, there were potential costs to investors in the Williams SEC's cautious approach. The House Subcommittee on Oversight and Investigations in 1980 wrote of the SEC's lack of leadership in facilitating a national market system:

> The danger . . . is that the Commission will be led by the strongest, most articulate and persistent voices in the industry rather than its own independent assessment of the systems and rules necessary . . . The danger is that a system may evolve which makes superficial

changes in competition, links some markets and in other ways appears to improve the process of buying and selling securities, but fails to fulfill the fundamental purposes of assuring that the securities markets provide the best price to investors in the most efficient way possible.[196]

Sustained Congressional criticism spurred the Williams SEC during its last year to perform a more forceful role in supervising the implementation of a central market. But arguably its failure to require rescission of the NYSE off-floor trading restrictions and require the securities industry to develop a central limit-order book, employing time and price priorities, delayed implementation of a cost-efficient electronic securities market.

The SEC's efforts to facilitate creation of a central electronic market initially focused on implementation of a systemwide communications network. Before the SEC's effort to create a composite transaction-reporting system, the only transaction (or last-sale price) reporting of exchange-listed securities was provided by New York Stock Exchange and American Stock Exchange ticker tapes and electronic displays, which gave a continuous report of transactions executed on the floor of the two New York City exchanges. Off-board trading in New York Stock Exchange–listed securities effected by regional exchange or third-market market-makers was not reported on the New York Stock Exchange tape.[197] Thus, the SEC's attempt to create a composite transaction tape essentially was a proposal to increase the visibility of regional exchange specialists and over-the-counter dealers who made markets in NYSE-listed securities by including reports of their transactions on the same tape that reported transactions executed on the New York Stock Exchange. This alone was a modest first step toward integrating all market-makers into a central electronic market, unlikely to cause a significant diversion of trading from the Exchange to other markets. But the design of the composite tape was significant because it provided the initial test for determining which securities and market-makers would be included in the central securities market and began to resolve the problem of who would control the central market's machinery.

For four years, New York Stock Exchange "foot-dragging," as former SEC commissioner Sommer put it, delayed implementation of a composite tape.[198] In late 1971, after the SEC's *Institutional Investor Study* transmittal letter and the Martin Report each recommended creation of a consolidated transaction report system, the New York Stock Exchange requested representatives of the other exchanges and the NASD to join it and form a task force to study the issue. In February 1972, representatives of the regional exchanges reported to the SEC that, although all members of the task force agreed that a consolidated tape could become operational in three to six months, discussions had ground to a halt because of disagreements between the regional stock exchanges on the one hand and the NYSE and Amex on the other. SEC attorneys Lloyd Feller and George Simon later wrote: "The NYSE and Amex did not want to proceed with the consolidated tape until all other central market system issues had been resolved," and "the NYSE was only willing to consider reporting of regional and third-market transactions on the Amex tape."[199]

In an effort to break the deadlock, the SEC in March 1972 proposed for comment Rule 17a-15, which required each exchange and the NASD to file on or before June 15, 1972, a plan with the Commission for the dissemination of transaction reports in listed securities.[200] Significantly, the proposed rule stated that "vendors," not the exchanges, would provide consolidated transaction reporting. This approach was consistent with the subsequent recommendation of the SEC's Advisory Committee on Market Disclosure that the central processor or service bureau assembling the consolidated transaction tape "should be a 'neutral' body (i.e., not under control or domination of any particular market center)."[201]

In their comments on proposed Rule 17a-15, the New York and American stock exchanges sharply questioned the SEC's authority to issue the rule or deprive them of their right to derive income from the dissemination of last-sale data. The two exchanges proposed an alternative to a rule requiring vendor administration of the consolidated tape; they suggested that the system be administered by their jointly owned subsidiary, the Securities Industry Automation Corporation (SIAC).[202] This would permit the NYSE and Amex to retain income from last-sale data while making feasible retransmission by commercial vendors on a fee basis. The SEC agreed, both because of Commission uncertainty about its statutory authority[203] and because, as subsequent SEC chairman Ray Garrett explained, an SIAC system "will be compatible with ticker and cathode ray tube equipment presently found in most brokerage offices [and] is not expected to increase the costs of broker-dealers who now subscribe to either of the present New York or Amex tapes."[204] In August 1972, the SEC revised and in November 1972 adopted Rule 17a-15.[205]

Only one plan was submitted for administration of a consolidated tape. This plan did achieve the SEC's paramount objective of reporting regional exchange and third-market trading in New York Stock

Exchange—listed securities over the same tape that reported NYSE trading. But practical control of the consolidated tape and certain reporting advantages were reserved for the New York and American stock exchanges. The joint plan, submitted in March 1972 by those two exchanges, the NASD, and three regional exchanges envisioned the creation of the Consolidated Tape Association (CTA). The CTA would administer the SIAC consolidated tape. On Network A of the SIAC tape would be reported all trading in New York Stock Exchange—listed securities, regardless of the market where the transaction was executed. This was the SEC's key concern. On Network B would be reported all trading in Amex securities and in regional exchange securities that met eligibility requirements. The Consolidated Tape Association was to be dominated by the New York and American stock exchanges, each of which had two votes, to one vote each for the NASD and the three regional exchanges. In addition, no proposed amendment to the CTA plan could be made if it was opposed by any participant that provided SIAC with 51 percent or more of the last-sale prices reported over either Network A or Network B. This meant not only that the New York and American stock exchanges had half of CTA's eight votes, but each exchange also had a veto power over amendments.

The plan was initially designed to permit termination of daily reporting at 3:30 P.M. (thus permitting Eastern evening newspapers easily to publish closing New York Stock Exchange prices but preventing all Pacific Coast Exchange closing transactions from being reported). The plan defined eligible securities to ensure that all NYSE and Amex securities, but only some regional exchange securities, would be reported over the consolidated tape.[206]

The NYSE and Amex domination of the Consolidated Tape Association, selection of their wholly owned subsidiary, SIAC, to process transaction reports, and the reporting disadvantages of the regional exchanges provoked congressional and regional exchange criticism of the plan.[207] Unyielding, the New York Stock Exchange renewed its argument that implementation of the consolidated tape should be deferred until all participating exchanges and over-the-counter dealers were subject to uniform rules regulating manipulation, short sales, and market-maker responsibilities.[208] The SEC rejected the Exchange's "equal regulation" argument, but after fourteen months of negotiation was able to secure only minor, largely technical, revisions in the March 1973 plan.[209] The plan was declared effective in May 1974. Operations on Network A of the consolidated tape began in June 1975. The system became fully operational on April 30, 1976.[210]

The more significant component of the central market communications network was the composite quotations system. "Such a system," wrote the SEC's Advisory Committee on Market Disclosure in November 1972, is "the cornerstone on which a central market system will be built."[211] Unlike the composite last-sale reporting tape, the composite quotations system provided the basis for a significant potential diversion of securities trading from the New York and American stock exchanges to the regional exchanges and the third market. The SEC's 1973 "Policy Statement on the Structure of a Central Market System" explained:

> The progress we anticipate toward implementation of composite . . .
> quotation systems should serve not only to facilitate but in most
> cases to require that a broker execute an order wherever the best price
> is obtainable. For one thing, a broker will be able to check all the
> quotations of all market-makers and specialists in a particular secu-
> rity promptly and simultaneously . . . Thus it appears that within the
> near future brokers will be able, in many cases for the first time, to
> look beyond their own market centers to satisfy their basic agency
> duty to their customers.[212]

In March 1972, simultaneous with the circulation of the first draft of its proposed composite transaction rule, the SEC circulated for comment proposed Rule 17a-14, requiring every exchange and the NASD to make available to vendors specialist and over-the-counter dealer quotations in exchange-listed securities "on a current and continuing basis."[213] One practical consequence of the proposed rule would have been to allow NASDAQ to disseminate New York Stock Exchange quotations. Subsequently, NASD president Macklin estimated that, though NASDAQ initially cost about $25 million to construct, it could be expanded to provide quotations in all listed securities for about $1.5 million. Because NASDAQ could provide a listed-securities quotation service more rapidly and less expensively than the New York Stock Exchange or independent vendors, Macklin urged the SEC to award NASDAQ an exclusive franchise, arguing, "Wouldn't it make sense to have a single quotation system, a single stock ticker, a single clearing entity, and a single self-regulator?"[214] At no time was the SEC officially willing to mandate that NASDAQ alone be enfranchised to disseminate listed-securities quotations. Instead, the Commission consistently favored its free-market vendor rule approach to allow the most efficient quotations services, whichever they might be, to secure broker-dealer firm business.

Until the month before enactment of the 1975 Securities Acts

Amendments, the New York Stock Exchange steadfastly refused to participate in any composite quotations system that included over-the-counter dealer quotations in Exchange-listed securities or to recognize the SEC's power to adopt Rule 17a-14.

The principal concern of the New York Stock Exchange was that a composite quotations system would enable Exchange member firms to act as upstairs market-makers rather than routing their orders to the Exchange floor, and thus might lead to the "demise" of the New York Stock Exchange.[215] Since the SEC at that time was committed to enhancing market-maker competition, the Exchange's view, no matter how dramatically expressed, was unable to forestall the Commission.

In August 1974, the SEC published a revised version of Rule 17a-14, permitting the exchanges and the NASD to file a plan to implement a composite quotations system.[216] The revised proposal specified, however, that independent vendors would be permitted to disseminate composite quotations. As, in fact, came to be the case, the revised proposal envisioned that the securities exchanges and the NASD would have responsibility for collection of quotation information through an organization such as SIAC, and independent quotation services would be permitted to disseminate the composite quotations to broker-dealer firms and other subscribers.

Both the New York and American stock exchanges indicated that they would refuse to file a plan to implement a composite quotations system. The New York Stock Exchange's comment letter on the proposed rule stated that "proposed Rule 17a-14 is beyond the authority of the Commission under the existing provisions of the Securities Exchange Act of 1934," it "would deprive the Exchange of property in violation of the due process provisions of the Constitution of the United States," and was "premature [since] the proposed Rule appears designed to require the creation of an entity that would be an integral component of an as-yet undefined central market system."[217]

In March 1975, the SEC, pursuant to Section 19(b) of the 1934 Securities Exchange Act, formally requested each registered exchange to eliminate rules or practices restricting dissemination of quotation information.[218] Consideration of Rule 17a-14 was deferred. By then it was generally assumed within the Commission that the SEC might have to go to court to create a composite quotations system including third-market dealers and that the SEC's authority to eliminate restrictive exchange rules under Section 19(b) was clear, though its authority under Section 17(a) to issue the vendor rule was open to serious question. Acquiescing in the New York

Stock Exchange's effort to exclude third-market dealers from the central market's quotations system, by contrast, would have frustrated what the SEC earlier had termed "the most important objective" of its central market initiative: "[fostering] the development of strong competition among its participants." Moreover, the Commission's attempts to negotiate a mutually acceptable composite quotations system with the New York Stock Exchange did not appear to be succeeding.

The following month the New York Stock Exchange agreed in principle to the dissemination of its quotations.[219] By then, passage of the 1975 Securities Acts Amendments was inevitable. On June 4, 1975, the amendments gave the SEC explicit statutory authority to implement a composite quotations system. The Senate Banking Committee report on the relevant provisions pointedly noted both "the SEC's basic role . . . to remove burdens on competition which would unjustifiably hinder the market's natural economic evolution" and the need for the SEC to "assume a special oversight and regulatory role" in supervising the creation of a composite quotations system.[220]

Employing the authority granted by the 1975 amendments, the SEC laboriously fashioned, over the next two and a half years, Rule 11A c1-1, which was to ensure that the exchanges and over-the-counter dealers provided reliable quotations to independent vendors. As adopted in January 1978, the rule required each registered exchange and the NASD during trading hours continuously to make available to quotation vendors the highest bid and lowest offer communicated on an exchange floor or by a third-market dealer, including the number of shares covered by the bid or offer. The rule facilitated efforts by composite quotation services like GTE Information Systems, Instinet, and NASDAQ to provide broker-dealers with desktop cathode-ray displays of competitive quotations in listed securities similar to the quotations in over-the-counter securities that NASDAQ had begun disseminating in 1971.*[221]

* As adopted in 1978, the quote rule obliged market-makers to execute orders up to the published quote size at the quote price. The SEC explained: "Thus, for the first time, relatively reliable and comprehensive information as to prices and sizes of quotations for all reported securities from all markets, whether on exchanges or over-the-counter, will be made available to market professionals and the public." The "firm" quote requirement proved controversial. Writing about the time the rule first went into effect, Milton Cohen noted a likely consequence of the rule: "Since all quotations must be firm, no market-maker (or institution) can be expected to show in the quotation system the full size that he might be willing to buy or sell if every quotation did not have to be firm. Thus in an increasingly institutionalized market the published quotations may be of limited significance with respect to the very

With the implementation of a composite quotations system in listed securities, a "cornerstone" of a central securities market, in fact, was in place. But ensuring that investors would receive the best execution of their orders required several other steps, at least including: elimination of unjustifiable restraints on market-maker competition, electronic linkage of brokers to the markets with the best prices, electronic linkage of the securities markets themselves, and development of a systemwide limit-order book. Through early 1981, the SEC, however, had neither completed the removal of unjustifiable restraints on market-marker competition nor fully defined the characteristics of a nationwide electronic order routing and limit-order system.

The most significant restraint on market-maker competition, New York Stock Exchange Rule 394, effectively barred an Exchange member from executing a trade off the floor through an over-the-counter dealer. After SEC staff attorney Eugene Rotberg prepared a detailed study of Rule 394 in 1965, the Commission's general counsel, Philip Loomis, and its Trading and Markets Division director, Irving Pollack, had supported Rotberg's recommendation that the rule be eliminated. Instead, the SEC negotiated with the Exchange a

---

substantial part of total volume made up of institutional blocks." SEC experience with the "firm" quote rule through early 1981 resulted in discovery of other problems:

> While certain regional exchange specialists do actively compete for order flow by disseminating competitive quotations in a limited number of actively traded (exchange-listed) stocks, regional exchanges (and their specialists), by and large, prefer to continue to use other methods to compete with the primary exchanges for order flow. These methods include reductions in charges for execution or clearing services and guarantees (either to individual retail brokerage firms or on individual orders) against transactions occurring on the primary exchanges at equal or superior prices. Even where regional exchanges have elected to compete on the basis of machine-displayed quotations, that competition has not, for the most part, had any significant effects on order flow patterns. First, retail brokerage firms continue to route most of their customer orders directly to the primary exchanges irrespective of the displayed quotations of other market centers. Second, specialists on the primary exchanges often provide brokers and dealers on the floors of those exchanges with executions which match superior displayed quotations from the regional exchanges, thereby lessening the extent to which regional exchange specialists are able to attract order flow . . . by disseminating competitive quotations.

To reduce the cost impact on regional exchange specialists and third-market-makers, the SEC in February 1981 proposed a rule permitting them under most circumstances to disseminate quotations on a voluntary basis in exchange-listed securities, rather than requiring them to enter quotes in the composite quotations system in all Exchange-listed securities they traded.[222]

procedurally cumbersome compromise, NYSE Rule 394(b), which permitted an Exchange member to trade with an over-the-counter dealer, but only after twice contacting the Exchange specialist to see if the specialist could offer an equal or better price and reporting to an Exchange floor governor. As interpreted and enforced by the New York Stock Exchange, Rule 394(b) almost totally prevented Exchange members from executing trades over the counter. In the fifty-four-month period from January 1969 to June 1973, for example, exactly sixty-four transactions were executed in whole or in part off the New York Stock Exchange floor under Rule 394(b). Of the more than fifteen billion shares traded over the New York Stock Exchange between 1969 and 1972, fewer than one million (or 0.00005 percent) were executed under the rule.[223]

The anticompetitive nature of Rule 394(b) was repeatedly criticized by the SEC. Implicitly in its 1971 *Institutional Investor Study* transmittal letter and its 1972 "Statement on the Future Structure of the Securities Markets," and explicitly in its 1973 "Policy Statement on the Structure of a Central Market System," the SEC indicated its intention to eliminate Rule 394 as part of its program to implement a competitive central market system.[224]

In opposition, after the 1971 Martin Report urged the abolition of third-market trading to "enhance the depth and liquidity of the central public auction market," New York Stock Exchange chairman James Needham waged a three-year lobbying campaign to convince Congress that "the major problem facing the industry today is one of fragmentation." Needham predicted that if fixed commission rates were ended and Rule 394 rescinded, the incentives for New York Stock Exchange membership effectively would cease. Major broker-dealer firms like Merrill Lynch would attempt to execute most trades in-house; the New York Stock Exchange's central auction market would "fragment" into numerous unconnected market centers. Investors, particularly small investors, would be harmed by less close prices, since each market-maker would have less volume than the New York Stock Exchange previously had.[225]

Arguably, this was an Exchange worst-case scenario, as unlikely to prove accurate as its 1968 predictions concerning the economic effects of abolishing fixed commission rates. The SEC favored competitive market-makers. Indeed, it said that "the most important objective of the [central market] system is to foster the development of strong competition among its members," precisely because empirical data consistently showed that effective market-maker competition aided investors by closing price spreads. It was unclear that the risks associated with "fragmentation" of the securities market would be significant when a central market system was operational. The composite quotations system and SEC best-execution rules could prevent a broker-dealer firm from internalizing an order except when the price in-house equaled the best price available from any other market-maker. Since it was anticipated that only a relatively small percentage of orders could be executed at the best prices within even the largest broker-dealer firm, the SEC's "Central Market System Policy Statement" predicted, "It would be most difficult for a responsible broker to avoid doing much of its business on exchanges . . . so long as the market-makers on those exchanges remain competitive."[226]

Although the 1975 Securities Acts Amendments in some respects were ambiguous, it is clear that Congress supported the SEC's intention to preserve third-market trading and eliminate Rule 394. The Senate Subcommittee on Securities' 1973 "Security Industry Study" report recommended amendment of New York Stock Exchange Rule 394 to permit Exchange members to deal with third-market-makers without prior permission of the Exchange and retention of competitive market-makers (including those in the over-the-counter third market) "to make simultaneous competing markets in each security within the new central system."[227] Rather than expressly require the removal of Rule 394, Senator Harrison Williams's 1973 National Securities Market System bill, as introduced, placed on the SEC, explained Williams in his official summary of the bill, "the affirmative obligation 'to remove burdens on competition not reasonably necessary to the achievement of the purposes' of the Exchange Act."[228]

In 1974, Senator Williams also introduced legislation to give the SEC discretionary power until a national market system had been created or April 30, 1978, whichever was earlier, to confine trading in listed securities to registered stock exchanges, that is, abolish third-market trading of exchange-listed securities. Williams explained that his rationale for introducing this bill was to grant the SEC a "fail-safe" power in the event that the abolition of fixed commission rates led to a severe disruption of exchange trading. Williams stated:

> The New York Stock Exchange, in particular, argues that the elimination of fixed rates will remove the primary incentive for firms to belong to stock exchanges. With that incentive gone, so the argument runs, firms will leave the exchanges, execute their orders in the third market or in their back offices, and thereby erode the strength of the auction market and the protections it provides public investors.
> I do not share the New York Stock Exchange's fears, but I think we

can all agree that no one can predict with absolute certainty what will happen once fixed rates are abolished. The New York Stock Exchange may be right, and that is the point of S.3126. Focusing on the period between the end of price-fixing and the establishment of a national market system, the bill would direct the SEC, if it finds that trading away from stock exchanges — that is, in the third market — is causing serious harm to the fairness or orderliness of the auction markets, to require broker-dealers to confine their trading in listed securities to the exchanges.[229]

As ultimately passed in April 1975, the Senate Securities Acts Amendments bill contained provisions charging the SEC with an affirmative obligation to eliminate anticompetitive restraints, such as Rule 394, if they could not be justified by the purposes of the 1934 Securities Exchange Act, and granting it the fail-safe power to confine trading in listed securities to exchange floors, but only if lesser steps failed to correct any adverse effect on the fairness and orderliness of the market for listed securities caused by third-market trading. The Senate Banking Committee's report on the bill emphasized, "The Committee has carefully evaluated all arguments that have been presented in support of abolishing the third market and found them unpersuasive." The SEC's power to abolish third-market trading was to be exercised only if "serious disruptions" in exchange trading occurred and the Commission found "no exchange rule whatsoever unreasonably restricted competition among dealers generally or between any class of dealers and registered specialists."[230]

The House of Representatives adopted an even more emphatic position in favor of abolishing Rule 394. As passed by the House of Representatives in April 1975, its version of the Securities Acts Amendments bill contained a provision that would have required the New York Stock Exchange to rescind Rule 394.[231] The House-passed bill also contained a fail-safe provision authorizing the SEC to limit trading in listed securities to the exchanges, but only after a hearing found that investors could not be protected nor fair and orderly markets maintained through any other lawful means.[232]

The SEC supported the Senate's more flexible approach to abolishing Rule 394[233] and, in essence, it was enacted in the 1975 Securities Acts Amendments. Subsection 11A(c)(4)(A) required the SEC to review Rule 394 and all other rules "which limit or condition the ability of members to effect transactions in securities otherwise than on such exchanges." Within ninety days of the enactment of the 1975 law, the SEC was required to report to Congress the results of its review and commence a proceeding "to amend any such rule imposing a burden on competition which does not appear to the Commission to be necessary or appropriate in furtherance of the purposes of this title." The amendment proceeding itself was to be completed "within ninety days of the date of publication of notice of its commencement." Compromise fail-safe provisions also were adopted, with the conference report reiterating "that they are provisions which may only be used as regulatory powers of last resort."[234]

Otherwise, the 1975 Securities Acts Amendments gave the SEC little explicit direction concerning the ultimate character of the central securities market. The SEC was granted enabling powers to "facilitate the establishment of a national market system for securities" in accordance with the fact findings and objectives of Subsection 11A(a)(1) of the amendments. That subsection implicitly endorsed granting the SEC discretion to supervise creation of a central market consistent with the SEC's 1972 and 1973 statements concerning a future central market. Subsection 11A(a)(1) stated in its entirety:

> The Congress finds that—
> (A) The securities markets are an important national asset which must be preserved and strengthened.
> (B) New data processing and communications techniques create the opportunity for more efficient and effective market operations.
> (C) It is in the public interest and appropriate for the protection of investors and the maintenance of fair and orderly markets to assure—
> (i) economically efficient execution of securities transactions;
> (ii) fair competition among brokers and dealers, among exchange markets, and between exchange markets and markets other than exchange markets;
> (iii) the availability to brokers, dealers, and investors of information with respect to quotations for and transactions in securities;
> (iv) the practicability of brokers executing investors' orders in the best market; and
> (v) an opportunity, consistent with the provisions of clauses (i) and (iv) of this subparagraph, for investors' orders to be executed without the participation of a dealer.
> (D) The linking of all markets for qualified securities through communication and data processing facilities will foster efficiency, enhance competition, increase the information available to brokers, dealers, and investors, facilitate the offsetting of investors' orders, and contribute to best execution of such orders.

Milton Cohen, among others, has observed that "the five Congressional objectives [in Subsection 11A(a)(1)(C)] are themselves partially conflicting rather than totally harmonious, in the sense that maximum achievement of any one of them may be inconsistent with maximum achievement of one or more of the others." In a related footnote, Cohen explained, "For example, maximum opportunity for investors' orders to be executed without the participation of a dealer [that is, the preservation of securities markets like the New York Stock Exchange] may not be achievable along with maximum competition among brokers and dealers or among exchange markets." As a matter of abstract logic, Cohen obviously is correct. Thus, it is important to emphasize that in providing a legislative history of this subsection, the congressional conference report again underlined the significance of eliminating Rule 394, stating, "It is the intent of the conferees that the national market system evolve through the interplay of competitive forces as unnecessary regulatory restrictions are removed."[235]

The 1975 amendments also required the SEC to establish a fifteen-member National Market Advisory Board (NMAB), a majority of whose members would be persons associated with broker-dealer firms. The board represented a near-total defeat of an earlier Securities Industry Association proposal to remove authority from the SEC to supervise creation of a central market and vest it in a securities industry–dominated Federal Capital Markets Board. Wholly advisory, the NMAB was authorized to "study and make recommendations to the Commission as to the steps it finds appropriate to facilitate the establishment of a national market system." The SEC retained all pertinent regulatory powers.*[236]

Given the plain language of Subsection 11A(c)(4)(A), the legislative history of the 1975 Securities Acts Amendments, and the SEC's statements of intent in 1971, 1972, and 1973, the Congress that enacted the 1975 securities law must have assumed that the SEC soon would require the NYSE to rescind Rule 394 and permit Exchange members to trade with third-market dealers unless the Commission identified new and significant events that neither it nor the Congress earlier had considered. The New York Stock Exchange's campaign to abolish third-market trading clearly had failed. Although the SEC was vested with the power to limit or abolish third-market trading, the convoluted restrictions on its use and the legislative history of the fail-safe provision made it obvious that Congress did not expect the SEC to use this power unless the quality of exchange trading dramatically deteriorated.

---

* In addition, the 1975 Securities Acts Amendments contained provisions regulating municipal securities, institutional investor disclosure, and, as earlier noted, securities clearance, transfer, and settlement facilities.

That the SEC under these circumstances did not proceed to abolish Rule 394 was one of the most significant policy reversals in the agency's history.

As required by the 1975 amendments, the SEC within ninety days forwarded to Congress its report on exchange rules "which limit or condition the ability of members to effect transactions in securities otherwise than on such exchanges." The SEC concluded "that off-board trading rules of exchanges [including Rule 394] impose burdens on competition, and that the Commission is not now prepared to conclude that these burdens are necessary or appropriate in furtherance of the purposes of the Act." The requisite hearing to abrogate or amend Rule 394 was commenced.[237]

The importance of the SEC's Rule 394 proceeding was widely understood. "I doubt," Commissioner Sommer began an address in October 1975, "if anyone would dispute me if I suggest that at the moment the most critical problem confronting the SEC and the industry . . . is the fate of Rule 394."[238] At issue, quite simply, was how rapidly the SEC would dissolve the long-standing barriers between competitive securities market-makers and create incentives for the securities industry to fashion a nationwide electronic market.

The SEC's December 1975 report on Rule 394 again affirmed that Rule 394 and similar rules "cannot be permitted to remain in effect" because of "a number of significant benefits . . . increased competition among market-makers can yield . . . to the markets."

But the report waffled on the question of when Rule 394 would be wholly repealed. The SEC (with Commissioner Evans dissenting in part) announced that it would issue a rule, to be fully effective on January 2, 1977, prohibiting exchanges from barring members *acting as agents* from trading in the third markets. This meant that an exchange member could direct a customer's order to a nonexchange member who acted as a third-market dealer, but an exchange member could not itself act as a competitive market-maker and execute the order off an exchange. The Commission recognized that this agency rule alone was unlikely to have much impact. In the SEC's official factual finding, "the Commission is not now prepared to conclude that a major reallocation of order flow . . . will necessarily occur."

The SEC's December 1975 report on Rule 394 suggested that the Commission also intended to permit Exchange members to act as over-the-counter market-makers but wanted to defer issuance of the necessary rule until the securities industry's self-regulatory organizations had an opportunity to develop more of the central securities market's systems. The report noted that concern had been expressed at its Rule 394 proceeding that allowing major Exchange members to act as competitive market-makers might lead to "overreaching." That is, broker-dealer firms acting as dealers might execute transactions for their brokerage customers at prices less favorable than the customers would have obtained had the firms acted as brokers and directed the transactions to a securities exchange floor for execution. The SEC's December 1975 report also took note of the concern that when orders were internalized in Exchange member firms, the securities markets might fragment into a series of unconnected market centers, each with less ability to provide depth (close prices when large volumes created temporary supply and demand disparities) or narrow price spreads. The report expressed skepticism that any of these adverse consequences would occur, but noted that if overreaching or the problems associated with fragmentation did materialize, the SEC could adopt a best-execution rule "requiring the prices at which transactions with . . . customers are effected to be no less favorable than those which the firm knew or ought to have known could have been obtained for these customers had the firm been acting in an agency capacity." Accordingly, the SEC concluded that permitting Exchange members to act as over-the-counter dealers was "more likely to improve the securities markets than injure them." The Commission announced that no later than March 1, 1977, it would reconsider its decision not to permit Exchange members to act as over-the-counter market-makers. By that time, the Commission suggested, the risks associated with overreaching and fragmentation of the market could be minimized by implementation of the composite quotations system, an electronic limit-order book, and new rules defining best execution. Additionally, the SEC's report stated, delay until 1977 would permit the National Market Advisory Board to offer its advice on the issue.[239]

The SEC's decision to defer full repeal of Rule 394 was criticized by a 1976 House Commerce Subcommittee report for creating an additional incentive for the securities industry to seek delays in completing the electronic market.[240] But in other respects, the SEC's December 1975 Rule 394 report seemed to be a cautious first step leading toward full rescission of the rule.

The approach of the SEC during Harold Williams's chairmanship was more enigmatic. By the time Williams began as SEC chairman in April 1977, it was obvious to the Commission that its partial rescission of Rule 394 "appears to have had little impact on the historical patterns of market selection by exchange members acting as brokers," as an SEC release subsequently stated.[241] In February

1977, the National Market Advisory Board had tentatively concluded that the purposes of the 1975 Securities Acts Amendments "do not justify exchanges maintaining such restrictions generally and indefinitely." A subsequent NMAB statement urged the SEC to repeal fully off-board trading restrictions once a composite quotations system, more equal regulation of exchange specialists and off-board market-makers, and new limit-order and best-execution rules were implemented. The NMAB anticipated that all of these recommended prerequisites to removal of off-board trading restrictions could "be accomplished without significant delay."*[242]

In June 1977, the SEC proposed its long-anticipated Rule 19c-2 to rescind fully the New York Stock Exchange's off-board trading restrictions. (The enduring restrictions in Rule 394, by then, had been renumbered Exchange Rule 390.)

The SEC's June 1977 release dismissed as unlikely the possibility that removal of Rule 390 would lead to "a significant increase in fragmentation" of the securities markets. But even if it did, the SEC did not perceive why "the adverse effects of any such increase would not be prevented or ameliorated as a natural consequence of competitive forces in the market place. Finally, if competitive forces alone . . . are insufficient to combat those effects," the SEC was confident that new regulations "would presumably be adequate to address that problem.[244]

In the next four years, the SEC's faith in either marketplace competition or its own rule-making initiatives to ameliorate the risks associated with full rescission of the New York Stock Exchange's off-board trading rules waned perceptibly. The policy shift was so

---

* In a related development, under SEC pressure, the New York and American stock exchanges rescinded their "New York City" rules. These rules had prohibited securities listed on either New York City exchange from being traded on the other. Through 1979, the rescission of the New York City rules had virtually no practical effect. The New York Stock Exchange's 1980 *Fact Book* indicated that Amex trading of NYSE-listed securities climbed to a trivial 0.02 percent of total NYSE share volume in 1977, then declined to 0.00 percent in 1979.[243]

The SEC did not then require rescission of New York Stock Exchange Rule 113, which in relevant part prohibits an Exchange specialist from accepting orders in a specialty stock directly from an institutional investor. The rule prevents specialists from directly competing with "upstairs" firms for institutional transactions. Rule 113 also is consistent with the historic division of securities trading: the upstairs firms do not engage in market-making in securities handled by Exchange specialists, and Exchange specialists usually do not deal directly with customers. Investors, by contrast, probably would benefit from the end of this market division if there were greater competition at the market-making level. To fully achieve this result it would be necessary to rescind NYSE Rule 113 as well as Rule 390.

poorly explained that it can be understood only as a consequence of divisions within the SEC caused by the 1977 appointments of Chairman Harold Williams and Commissioner Roberta Karmel.*

The policy change was announced officially in January 1978, when a Commission release stated that further consideration of its proposed Rule 19c-2 to abolish all New York Stock Exchange off-board trading restrictions would be deferred until the agency could evaluate securities industry and stock exchanges responses to several other central market initiatives. This approach seemed to contradict the SEC's release of just six months before, which suggested that the Commission was prepared to require rescission of Exchange Rule 390 without further delay.

The SEC's January 1978 release offered little explanation of the agency's policy reversal, other than the observation that "many commentators in the Commission's proceedings with respect to off-board trading restrictions have made clear their belief that the risks they perceive as being associated with removal of these restrictions would diminish to the extent of meaningful progress toward implementation of a national market system." If, as the SEC had found just six months earlier, there were clear benefits to a competitive market-maker system, this explanation alone was hardly convincing. But more objectionable still was that the SEC rested a decision of this magnitude on a few general sentences without presenting any supporting evidence.

Obviously, the inability of the SEC to explain clearly its deferral of further consideration of proposed Rule 19c-2 was a consequence of divisions among the five commissioners. There may also have been real uncertainty in the minds of some or all of the commissioners as to the ultimate disposition of Rule 19c-2.

---

* At the time of the June 1977 release, the SEC had four commissioners, two of whom (Evans and Pollack) favored removal of Rule 390. By January 1978, Roberta Karmel had begun her term, creating a three (Karmel, Loomis, and Williams)-to-two (Evans and Pollack) majority in opposition to full rescission of Rule 390.

Before and after the June 1977 release, the NYSE orchestrated a lobbying campaign against the SEC's proposal to require full rescission of Rule 390. Among others who voiced opposition to the removal of Rule 390 were officials of nineteen of the twenty-two largest securities firms, executives of many corporations listed on the NYSE, such as Rubbermaid's Donald Noble, New York mayoral candidate Ed Koch, the AFL union that represented 1800 NYSE clerical employees, Congressmen Edward Boland, James Florio, and Jack Kemp, and Senators Howard Baker, Jacob Javits, Daniel Moynihan, and Robert Packwood. In an interview, SEC chairman Harold Williams, who was skeptical of the wisdom of rescinding Rule 390 when he arrived at the Commission in April 1977, doubted that the NYSE lobbying campaign affected the vote of any of the five SEC commissioners on this issue.[245]

The SEC's January 1978 release also stated:

> While the Commission has not yet concluded whether adoption of proposed Rule 19c-2 at this time must be deemed necessary or appropriate to conform exchange rules to the requirements of the Act or otherwise in furtherance of the Act's purposes, the Commission does not wish its determination to defer consideration of proposed Rule 19c-2 at this time to be perceived as indicating that the Commission is willing to postpone removal of off-board trading restrictions indefinitely or until further progress has been made toward implementation of any particular additional element of a national market system. To the contrary, the Commission has repeatedly expressed the view that the present restrictions must ultimately be eliminated, and remains concerned that retention of those restrictions, in addition to impeding competition, may retard achievement of a national market system.[246]

The impression conveyed by the January 1978 release — that the SEC subsequently would adopt Rule 19c-2 — turned out to be an erroneous one. Late in 1978, the SEC approved changes in the American Stock Exchange's domestic and foreign listing requirements that increased the number of issuers eligible to list securities on the Amex. The practical effect of the Commission's action was to permit the extension of the American Stock Exchange's off-board trading restrictions to a new group of securities that previously had been traded in the competitive over-the-counter market. Commissioners Evans and Pollack sharply dissented, because they believed the SEC's approval of the new Amex listing requirement would result in "the curtailment or elimination of intense inter-dealer competition in the O-T-C market with little possibility of inter-market competition between the Amex and the O-T-C markets." Evans and Pollack pointedly noted that it would have been possible for the SEC to approve the lowering of Amex listing requirements on condition that the Amex not apply its off-board trading restrictions to securities that chose to list on the Amex under the new, lower standards.[247]

The Evans and Pollack dissent inspired the SEC, in April 1979, to propose Rule 19c-3, prohibiting all off-board restrictions on securities listed on an exchange after April 26, 1979.[248] The proposal also was consonant with Chairman Williams's belief that it was preferable to engage in controlled experiments before approving major actions concerning the national securities market system, such as the prohibition of all off-board trading restrictions. However, in June 1980, before the SEC voted to approve Rule 19c-3, Williams insisted that Evans and Pollack agree to withdraw Rule 19c-2.[249] Again, there was no published statement that persuasively explained why the SEC had reversed its repeatedly stated intention to eliminate all off-board trading restrictions.

The Williams SEC's lack of interest in the benefits of market-maker competition also deserved explanation. Quite contrary to the New York Stock Exchange's worst-case prediction — that trading on the Exchange would fragment after fixed commission rates were abolished — between 1976 and 1980 the Exchange's share of trading in Exchange-listed securities increased from about 85 to 88 percent of all volume in exchange-listed securities. Third-market trading steadily declined. Even given this circumstance, the Williams SEC exhibited little or no interest in enhancing third-market competition. The objective of increasing "strong competition" among market-makers, which the SEC repeatedly affirmed was its "most important objective" in the five years preceding the Williams chairmanship, was subordinated during his chairmanship to concern about "risks" that, as late as June 1977, the agency had found insubstantial or outweighed by the benefits of a competitive system.

The Williams SEC off-board trading rule policy reversal was severely criticized by a House Commerce Subcommittee in August 1980. Calling the SEC's record on this issue "dismal," the subcommittee concluded:

> The Commission has clearly lost sight of its responsibility to eliminate anticompetitive rules and practices that cannot be justified in light of the purposes of the [1975] Act. And it has lost sight of the relationship between the nurturing of competition among market-makers and the development of a national market system.

Continued Subcommittee chairman Bob Eckhardt in an accompanying transmittal letter, "The Commission has approached its task of shepherding the development of a national market with timidity and apparent purposelessness. Because of the Commission's failure to utilize its extensive authority, the statute, many years in the drafting, is being eroded away by agency inaction."[250]

The caution and vacillation of the SEC during the 1975–1981 period also influenced the character and time of implementation of the central computer and electronic technology necessary to complete a national securities market system. By the mid-1970s, the SEC had a clear choice. On the one hand, the Commission could facilitate development of an electronic securities market in which brokers and dealers could view all available quotations (including limit orders) in a given security on a desktop screen and directly execute orders or make offers and bids by pressing keys on a computer console. This model of a national market system popularly was known as a "hard CLOB" (that is, a Composite Limit-Order Book, which could automatically execute orders) approach, and throughout the late 1970s was most nearly approximated by an experiment on the Cincinnati Stock Exchange.

The Cincinnati hard CLOB system allowed brokers or dealers in their offices throughout the country or market-makers on an exchange floor to enter bids and offers through computer terminals. The system was updated instantly as each bid or offer was made. When like-priced bids and offers were entered into the system, an execution automatically occurred, based on a strict first-come, first-serve basis (that is the bidder or offeror making the first order at the appropriate price received the business — so-called price and time priority), with the significant exception that all public investors' orders were given priority over market-makers' orders. The system itself made no pricing decisions, but it did allow a broker or dealer the opportunity either to accept an outstanding bid or offer by making a reciprocal offer or bid or to try for a better price by entering a new offer or bid.

When a transaction was executed, the execution was instantly displayed to the buyer and the seller on their respective video screen terminals. Subsequently, the buyer and the seller would each receive a paper documenting the transaction. A report simultaneously would be made to the consolidated tape, and a record be preserved for audit purposes. The system also could trigger the necessary entries to clear and settle the transaction.

The advantages of a Cincinnati-type hard CLOB system were numerous and significant.

The system provided an efficient composite quotations system that was integrated with the equipment necessary to make bids and offers or execute transactions.

The system could eliminate the problems associated with lack of firmness of quotes, ensure best execution of customers' orders, and route orders to the best market.

The system provided strict price and time priority, which was essential if public investors' orders were to be executed at the most favorable price existing at the time. Strict price and time priority also eliminated the advantages of being on the floor of the exchange and effectively placed stock market specialists, floor traders, and all other brokers and dealers, wherever physically located, on an equal competitive footing. As the University of Chicago's James Lorie testified:

> Price and time priority correspond to most notions of equity, but more importantly price and time priority are extremely important in enhanc-

ing competition. Price and time priority provide the only certain and completely impersonal mechanism for ensuring that the broker-dealer with the best "deal" will get the business. Price and time priority eliminate the advantages of size, location, historical relationships, or personality. The terms of the transaction are all that matter.[251]

In addition, during the late 1970s, a Cincinnati hard CLOB system possessed the potential of being less costly to operate than existing securities markets because the existing markets were more reliant on manual operations and more complicated communications systems. In 1978, Donald Weeden, who had invested in the Cincinnati experiment, estimated that the annual cost of handling limit orders alone could be cut from $50 million to $500,000.

Finally, if all bids and offers were entered into the system, the problems associated with SEC or self-regulatory organization market surveillance would have been eased, since the system would preserve a complete record of all bids, offers, and transactions.

The Cincinnati hard CLOB approach, if it were used for all securities trading, could create the near-equivalent in the securities industry to what economists call "perfect competition."* All brokers and dealers would have an equal opportunity to vie for profit, with equal access to a nationwide computer system and equal information. For investors this would mean that all bids and offers in the computer system could interact, with best bid always able to meet best offer, and with the greatest possible competition among market-makers.

Politically, however, achieving acceptance of a Cincinnati-type hard CLOB would be difficult. A hard CLOB system inevitably would lead to more effective market-maker competition at the expense of the existing securities exchanges. At the very least, a hard CLOB system would make floor brokers and physical exchange floors unnecessary. In place of floor brokers congregating at specialists' posts to shout orders in an "auditory crowd," there would be brokers and dealers in their offices throughout the country, creating the equivalent of a "visual crowd" as they communicated bids and offers via computer consoles and visual displays. Although the Cincinnati system does not preclude the existence of specialists, it would reduce their commission income by withdrawing from them the exclusive franchise to run a specialist book. Such a book would be unnecessary once a composite quotations system provided a visual display of all bids and offers (including those below or above the

---

* The system, in theory, could be taken further. Ultimately it may be possible for institutional investors, or conceivably all investors, to enter bids or offers directly, without a broker.

market prices that previously would have been recorded in a specialist's book). Whether or not specialists continued to exist probably would turn on whether or not it was considered desirable to create new means to compensate market-makers for observing an affirmative obligation to preserve price continuity in specific securities. Without specialists, it was unclear whether securities prices would be less close or have less depth. Competing dealers presumably would keep price spreads narrow by buying or selling for their own accounts whenever profit opportunities developed.

Because of the threat to their existence, other securities exchanges opposed the Cincinnati hard CLOB system. Specifically, other securities exchanges complained that the Cincinnati system would permit a sizable share of orders to be executed by broker-dealers in-house and would end the use of floor brokers to negotiate market prices. Neither "advantage" of auction markets need be discarded to the detriment of public investors. As earlier noted, a best-execution rule could prohibit broker-dealer firms from internalizing order flow unless they gave investors prices at least equal to the best prices available elsewhere in the market system. In a hard CLOB system requiring all orders to be entered into the system, it was unlikely that many orders would be internalized. Moreover, in a computer age, the floor brokers' function was an anachronism. Brokers and dealers in their offices could perform an equivalent function less expensively, and with fewer errors, by punching keys on a computer console. But a hard CLOB system did threaten the economic interests of the exchanges and their floor members. Thus, the exchanges generally agreed with the Pacific Coast Exchange that "the Cincinnati system is not an appropriate design for the national system."[252]

As an alternative to a hard CLOB system, most exchanges favored a national market system that preserved the exchange floors' central role. Beginning in April 1978, the American, Boston, Midwest, New York, Pacific, and Philadelphia stock exchanges began operating the Intermarket Trading System (ITS). ITS was essentially a communications system allowing specialists and floor brokers on one exchange floor to transmit buy or sell orders to market-makers on another exchange floor. If a specialist or floor broker saw a better price on the composite quotations system available on another exchange, the ITS system allowed him to transmit a "commitment to trade" to the appropriate market-maker on that exchange. The market-maker there would either accept the commitment or he could decline. If there was no response to the initial commitment to trade, the commitment would automatically expire after a designated time period.

There were important differences between a hard CLOB system and ITS. Brokers and dealers could utilize a Cincinnati-type system from their offices. The ITS system required orders first to be routed to an exchange and then allowed only specialists and floor brokers to have access to the ITS computer consoles. A hard CLOB system permitted automatic execution of orders. ITS allowed market-makers to reject orders even when they earlier had published quotations indicating that they would transact business at the order price. Alternatively, specialists could increase their bid to match better offers in the system. This discouraged competitive quotations, because the New York Stock Exchange specialist could discourage an NYSE member from trading elsewhere by matching an off-the-floor quotation. A hard CLOB system automatically matched highest bids and lowest offers. As originally designed, ITS was a discretionary system, and could not guarantee that investors would receive best-order execution. A Cincinnati-type system would have one systemwide limit-order book against which all brokers and dealers could execute orders. As originally envisioned, the ITS system would permit separate specialists' limit-order books on each exchange.[253]

Nonetheless, the SEC did not facilitate the implementation of a national securities market employing a systemwide hard CLOB approach. During the 1973–1981 period, the Commission did not proceed in a consistent fashion nor did it issue a clear statement of objectives for the national securities market. The result has been unnecessarily long delays in the implementation of the system's central execution facilities. And possibly the assurance that the technology that the SEC ultimately does facilitate will be neither the least expensive for investors nor the most efficient for the securities industry.

After the publication of its 1973 "Central Market Policy Statement," the SEC relied on an industry advisory group to propose the design of a national market system. In March 1974, the Commission appointed Alexander Yearley to chair a twelve-person Advisory Committee on the Implementation of a Central Market System. Yearley's committee included SEC Market Regulation Division director Lee Pickard, New York Stock Exchange specialist Donald Stone, Lazard Frères' Felix Rohatyn, the Harvard Business School's M. Colyer Crum, and eight broker-dealer firm, institutional investor, and securities issuer representatives. After thirteen months of meetings, the committee issued a report that ducked most of the significant questions about implementation of an electronic order-execution system. The Yearley Committee report anticipated that "when a consolidated transaction reporting system, a composite quotation system, and a consolidated limit-order book are in operation and some form of centralized goverance exists to insure that all participants are subject to equitable regulation, the Committee believes that a basic central market system will be in existence." But the committee ignored "the cost and technological considerations of its recommendations." Of the most significant central market system controversy, Yearley's committee "concluded that, while a consolidated limit-order book is essential to a national central market system, the design and characteristics of a limit-order book will be decided by future developments which cannot now be predicted."[254]

The failure of the Yearley Committee to propose "the design and characteristics of a limit order book" moved the SEC to address the issue directly. In December 1975, as part of its release discussing off-board trading restrictions, the Commission announced "the steps it intends to take in the immediate future to provide . . . comprehensive limit-order protection." The SEC began with the premise that an investor giving a limit order (an order to be executed at a specified price above or below the then prevailing market prices) would be assured fair treatment only if his or her order could interact with all orders in the system rather than just with the orders arriving at the specialist's post where his or her limit order happened to be recorded. The Commission believed "that the answer to the problem of providing adequate protection for public limit orders is not to maintain existing rules which perforce provide only imperfect protection and have certain undesirable anticompetitive effects, but rather to use the advanced technology now available to provide for a computerized limit-order repository or composite book."

Accordingly, the SEC announced that it planned to propose a rule requiring the submission of plans for the design, construction, and operation of a composite limit-order book. Although the Commission "ha[d] not made any final determination as to the characteristics which each plan should include . . . for purposes of securing meaningful discussion," the agency proposed a list of nine "minimum specified" characteristics of a composite book. Notably, these proposed characteristics required a single systemwide book with price and time priority, except that public orders at a particular price would have priority over orders entered for the accounts of brokers and dealers. Initially limit orders were to be entered only by existing specialists and third-market dealers, not by securities brokers. In March 1976 the SEC formally requested public comments on its proposed characteristics for a composite limit-order book.[255]

By August 1976, *Securities Week* reported the SEC had received sixteen CLOB proposals, including separate proposals from Merrill Lynch, the Justice Department, the Cincinnati Stock Exchange, and Junius Peake, Morris Mendelson, and R. T. Williams, calling for a composite limit-order book with price and time priority and automatic execution capacity—so-called hard CLOB proposals.[256] Of these, the most widely discussed hard CLOB proposal was that of securities industry consultants Peake and Williams and University of Pennsylvania economics professor Mendelson. Peake, Mendelson, and Williams urged that existing exchanges be replaced by a National Book System similar in its mechanics to the hard CLOB system later developed by the Cincinnati Stock Exchange.

The Peake-Mendelson-Williams proposal discussed, among other topics, the advantages of designing the entire system as a coherent whole, rather than evolving a national market created in stages:

> If a National System should be implemented in stages, starting with a consolidated book with no execution capability, and evolving to an ultimate national system, the process will be time-consuming [between ten and fifteen years will probably be required between initial planning and ultimate realization] and complex. [At each stage of implementation, a workable system has to be developed and implemented, only to be scrapped later.] That will be costly.
>
> It seems to us that a system that both provides for an electronic book, with execution capability, a tape, and on-line inquiry, will cost less, largely because the same communications facilities are used to display information, accept orders and record executions.

The Peake-Mendelson-Williams submission concluded by urging the SEC to fund a simulation of a hard CLOB system, to develop precise design criteria, and to study a series of specific related issues, such as the cost savings that could be achieved in a hard CLOB system.[257]

The approach of the SEC during the chairmanship of Roderick Hills (1975–1977) was strikingly different. The SEC itself did not study the technological problems involved in implementing a national securities market system or the costs and benefits of such a system. Instead, after its initial forceful December 1975 and March 1976 releases, the Hills SEC largely deferred to the congressionally required National Market Advisory Board, which deliberated and issued reports between September 1975 and December 1977. The fifteen members of the NMAB intentionally were selected to represent a variety of viewpoints and included both New York Stock Exchange specialist Donald Stone and hard CLOB advocates Donald Weeden and James Lorie, as well as Bache & Company's John Leslie (who served as the NMAB's chairman) and former SEC senior staff members Milton Cohen and Ralph Saul. Although the quality of the

NMAB's several reports was technically superior to those of the Yearley Committee, the NMAB proved equally indecisive. Its December 1977 "Report on Establishment of a National Market System" disclosed that factions of its membership favored four different initial facilities to establish a central market system, including a Cincinnati-type hard CLOB system and an ITS-type market linkage system. The December 1977 NMAB report acknowledged that the board could not agree on what steps the SEC next ought to take to develop a central market system.[258]

With the NMAB deadlocked, pressure again mounted on the SEC to assume a more active role in facilitating creation of an electronic order execution system.[259] Early in his chairmanship, Harold Williams repeatedly indicated that "the Commission is not completely satisfied with the rate of progress toward achievement of a national market system." Williams understood that, "in part, progress has been impeded by the inability of the self-regulatory organizations and other elements of the securities industry to overcome parochial interests and settle on a common course of action." But though conceding that "the Commission must play a more active role in guiding the development [of a national market system]," the new chairman added, "I believe it highly preferable that the development of the national market system be essentially an industry undertaking — not one to be solved by government fiat."[260]

In January 1978, the Williams SEC issued the first of two significant statements on the development of a national market system. Responding to congressional criticism of the SEC's lack of leadership, the January 1978 statement began by stressing that implementation of the national market system must be "accelerated . . . if the idea of a national market system is to progress beyond the theoretical stage and become a functioning reality."

The substance of the January 1978 release's discussion of limit-order protection, however, amounted to a terse, contradictory statement that left in doubt the Commission's objectives in facilitating a national market system. On the one hand, the SEC urged the securities exchanges and the NASD to submit a plan, no later than September 30, 1978, for the design, construction, and operation of a composite limit-order book (which the SEC now called a "central limit order file"). The SEC reaffirmed its intention to require strict price and time priority and seemed to go further than its earlier CLOB releases in suggesting that brokers, as well as specialists and other market-makers, should be allowed to enter directly, alter, or withdraw limit orders. The SEC's January 1978 release threatened that if the securities exchanges or the NASD was unable to submit an appropriate plan, "the Commission intends to commence rulemaking to consider the manner and timing of compulsory development of a central file [including the question of whether that task should be assigned principally to a single self-regulatory organization]." The Commission's reaffirmation of the principle of price and time priority and its threat to compel development of a single systemwide limit-order book suggested to some observers that the SEC would insist on creation of a hard CLOB system.[261]

On the other hand, other language in the SEC's January 1978 release suggested that the SEC would not require the securities exchanges and the NASD to implement a hard CLOB system against their will. The SEC stated in its January 1978 release:

> A second alternative would be the creation of an electronic market system in which all orders, whether from public investors or from market-makers, would be entered into a computer-based system and would be executed automatically in that system on the basis of strict time and price priority. This type of proposal has been advanced with considerable conviction by responsible persons and, if perfected, would appear to have the potential for significant efficiencies in securities trading. Such a system, however, would have an impact upon existing market institutions which could properly be viewed as a fundamental change in the manner in which securities trading is now conducted, and it is difficult to foresee, and to provide against, the problems and difficulties which might arise. Consequently, the Commission has not espoused these proposals. In addition, the Commission believes that if a change of this magnitude is to be made, it probably should occur as a result of evolutionary forces in the markets rather than by Commission mandate.[262]

Only in the aftermath of its January 1978 release did the Williams SEC fully make clear that it would not compel the securities exchanges to participate in a composite limit-order book employing price and time priority. Instead, the SEC largely relied on the very securities exchanges most threatened by a hard CLOB to design an intermarket limit-order system.

The New York Stock Exchange and most regional exchanges vehemently opposed the language in the SEC's January 1978 release, calling for a central limit-order file employing price and time priority primarily on the ground that such a system "would eventually lead to the elimination of exchange trading floors by inexorably forcing all trading into a fully automated trading system." As an alternative, the New York and Midwest stock exchanges urged the SEC to allow the existing exchanges to modify the ITS system to provide limit-order protection. In the view of these exchanges, investors could be protected from nonexecution of limit orders at superior prices even if each exchange had a separate specialist book.

This would require brokers and dealers (including specialists), before executing an order, to use the ITS system to check the contents of relevant specialists' books on other exchanges. Brokers and dealers (including specialists) generally would be prohibited from executing any order to buy or sell a security at a price inferior to the price of any limit order displayed by the ITS system. Thus, investors with limit orders theoretically would be provided with "price" but not "time" priority.[263]

In March 1979, the Williams SEC, in its second significant release on the development of a national market system, agreed to give the New York and regional exchanges an opportunity to modify the ITS system to provide limit-order protection. After extensive citation of the arguments made by the New York and Midwest stock exchanges, the Williams SEC abandoned its commitment to price and time priority because "the Commission recognizes the possibility that introduction of a system based upon the absolute time priority concept could have a radical and potentially disruptive impact on the trading process as it exists today."[264]

Quite aside from the merits of the decision, this was not a responsible way for the SEC to resolve so important an issue. The SEC neither before its January 1978 release nor before its March 1979 release made an independent study of the extent to which a hard CLOB system could achieve "significant efficiencies in securities trading." Neither statement adequately addressed the background of the issue, discussed to what extent the SEC could minimize "problems and difficulties" or "potentially disruptive impact," or explained why employment of the existing exchange floors and an ITS system, however modified, was preferable to a hard CLOB system.

Nor was it realistic for the SEC to rely on "evolutionary forces in the markets" to determine the future structure of the securities industry. The endurance of Rule 390 prevented market forces from producing a more efficient central market system. Moreover, Congress had enacted the 1975 Securities Acts Amendments, which endorsed the SEC's decisions to unfix commission rates and facilitate implementation of a central market because it was generally recognized that the market power of the New York Stock Exchange long had frustrated competition from effectively operating. It was not realistic to assume that the New York Stock Exchange or any other actor in the securities industry voluntarily would adopt a plan that threatened its economic interest. Just as in the case of fixed commission rates, investors required the active efforts of the SEC if they were to be fully protected. This did not mean that the SEC had to proceed by fiat or recklessly. It did mean the Commission had the responsibility to study practical alternatives, help facilitate evolution of the alternatives that best protected investors, and remove such impediments to market-maker competition as Rule 390.

In the two years after the Commission's March 1979 release, there was little progress toward the implementation of any system of limit-order protection. In May 1979, the SEC proposed a rule requiring that all limit orders collected by exchange specialists or third-market dealers and disseminated over the ITS system receive inter-market price protection against executions at inferior prices.[265] Consistent with this proposal, the New York Stock Exchange proposed a Limit Order Information System (LOIS), explaining in 1979: "The new facility will produce a total display of limit orders entered from all Participants, at various price levels. When a broker-dealer on any of the Participant exchanges contemplates a trade below the bid or above the offer, he will be able to request a LOIS display that will show him, in advance, the limit orders he must protect."[266] In July 1981, the BNA Securities Regulation and Law Report reported, "Implementation of the system has been delayed, however, as a result of concerns raised by the regional exchanges. They asserted that LOIS as proposed was unworkable, because it would have required specialists continuously to update their limit-order displays and would have required block traders to enter numerous commitments to trade in order to execute each block."[267] Through July 1981, the SEC had not adopted its May 1979 or any other proposed rule requiring limit-order protection.[268]

Other actions taken by the SEC during the 1977–1981 period furthered the drift toward a New York Stock Exchange–dominated central market system.

Soon after its January 1978 "Statement on Development of a National Market System," the SEC approved on a short-term basis both the Intermarket Trading System plan, initially proposed by the NYSE and four other exchanges, and the Cincinnati Stock Exchange's hard CLOB experiment. In September 1979 the SEC approved three-year extensions of both plans.[269]

Other than Merrill Lynch and Moseley, Hallgarten, Estabrook and Weeden, almost no New York Stock Exchange firms made use of the Cincinnati hard CLOB system through May 1981. The volume of trading was so slight that the SEC found "it difficult . . . to evaluate the effects of trading in an electronic facility of this type." The SEC acknowledged that the Cincinnati hard CLOB system "offers a unique opportunity to study whether an automated trading facility can link various types of exchange-based and upstairs broker-dealers in differing geographic locations."[270] But the Commission did not take steps, such as requiring price and time priority and eliminating Rule 390, that would have created incentives for securities firms to participate in the Cincinnati experiment and produce a meaningful test of the feasibility of an automatic order execution system.[271]

While the Cincinnati hard CLOB system foundered for want of broker-dealer firm participation, the SEC approved steps to enhance the ITS system. They may eventually result in a modified ITS system that will be recognized by the SEC as *the* national market system.

The Williams SEC, which had not required a hard CLOB system in its January 1979 release, announced that it would "encourage and, if necessary, mandate the prompt development of comprehensive market linkage and order routing systems to permit the efficient transmission of orders (i) among the various markets for qualified securities . . . and (ii) from brokers and dealers to all qualified markets."

Automated routing of orders from brokers directly to specialists' posts predated the Commission's 1978 release. In 1976, the New York Stock Exchange had begun operating its Designated Order Turnabout (DOT) system to permit member firms to reduce their costs (by avoiding the expense of floor brokerage) and improve their efficiency in handling small orders (that is, market orders up to 299 shares; limit orders up to 500 shares). By 1979, DOT orders accounted for some 10 percent of all reported NYSE share volume.[272] "Some regional exchanges," a 1980 House Commerce Subcommittee report explained, "compete with the New York system by offering even more streamlined alternative systems. For example, the computerized system of the Philadelphia Stock Exchange automatically executes small orders and guarantees that they are executed at the better price on the Philadelphia or the New York Stock Exchange. Similarly, the Pacific Stock Exchange recently installed a system which provides automatic execution for small orders at the highest bid or lowest offer of any markets that participates in the Intermarket Trading System."[273] In 1981, the NASD commenced pilot operations of an enhanced NASDAQ system, known as the Computer Assisted Execution System (CAES). CAES enabled broker-dealer firms to route buy and sell orders for automatic execution by any authorized o-t-c market-maker disseminating quotations through the NASDAQ system. Broker-dealer firms could route market orders or limit orders and could designate a particular market-maker to which the order would be routed or enter an "undesignated" order, which would be routed to the market-maker with the best quotation, determined by price and time priorities.[274]

The most significant national market system initiative of the Williams SEC culminated in an April 1981 order requiring the securities exchanges participating in the ITS system* and the NASD to implement, by March 1, 1982, an "automated interface" between the ITS and NASDAQ systems, including a broker to market-maker order routing system and automatic execution capability.[276] The initial significance of the ITS-NASDAQ linkage and order routing system is that brokers or dealers will be able to route orders automatically to the exchange specialist or over-the-counter market-maker with the best price in a Rule 19c-3 security. An August 1981 SEC monitoring report found that without an automated interface it was rarely economical for a broker manually to route a small order to an over-the-counter market-maker in a 19c-3 security even when the O-T-C market-maker had a superior price. For this reason, relatively few over-the-counter firms had attempted to provide competitive market-making in 19c-3 securities.[277]

Once the ITS-NASDAQ linkage is in effect, the SEC will have the opportunity to study whether or not competition between over-the-counter dealers and exchange specialists in 19c-3 securities on balance benefits investors by narrowing price spreads or disserves investors by fragmenting the securities markets.† If the SEC

---

* Relatedly, in February 1981, the Williams SEC approved a manual interface of the Cincinnati Stock Exchange to the ITS trading system.[275]

† To minimize the possible abuses associated with the upstairs broker-dealer firms internalizing order flow, the SEC also may adopt (or cause the exchanges and the NASD to adopt) one of several different types of best-execution rules. Under one approach, an upstairs market-maker could execute a trade in-house only if its price quotation was *superior* to those offered by all other market-makers. This type of best-execution rule probably would result in relatively little internalization and probably discourage some securities firms from engaging in upstairs market-making. A rule of this type would permit an exchange specialist to claim a broker-dealer firm's orders whenever the specialist matched the broker-dealer firm's quotation. Since specialists would not be subject to a comparable rule, such a rule might be unfair to over-the-counter market-makers.

A second type of best-execution rule would permit internalization of orders whenever the upstairs market-maker's quotation *equaled* the best quotation elsewhere available. This type of rule probably would lead to a much greater amount of upstairs market-making. However, this type of rule also has greater potential to fragment the securities markets. The pivotal question concerning such a best-execution rule is whether it would lead to better prices for investors and greater market depth because of increased market-maker competition or whether it would be a disservice to investors by loosening price spreads and decreasing depth.

A third approach to best-execution regulation would require upstairs market-makers to "hold out" orders they intend to execute in-house for a period of time to allow other market-makers to secure the order by making, depending on how the rule was drawn, either an equal or better bid or offer. This type of rule would enable the specialists to secure some of the order flow that otherwise would be internalized in broker-dealer firms. Among other questions raised by such a rule is the extent to which it would discourage broker-dealer firms from engaging in upstairs market-

concludes that this market-maker competition, on balance, is beneficial to investors, it will inevitably face again the issue of whether to rescind NYSE Rule 390. It can be argued that the linkage of the ITS and NASDAQ systems according to the SEC's April 1981 order and the full rescission of NYSE Rule 390 essentially would create a national securities market. This, at any rate, seemed to be the goal toward which the SEC, in the 1977–1981 period, was moving. In addition to the ITS-NASDAQ linkage, the Williams SEC also encouraged reduction of the response time necessary to execute a transaction over ITS and to prevent "trade-throughs," that is, executions of an order in one ITS market center when another market center offered a better price.[278]

It seems clear that if NYSE Rule 390 remains in effect, the ITS system can hardly be considered a national securities market. In all securities listed on the NYSE before April 26, 1979, NYSE specialists would be subject to the competition only of regional exchange specialists also trading these securities. Data published in the SEC's February 1981 "Monitoring Report on the Operation of the Intermarket Trading System" well suggested how trivial would be the impact of regional exchange specialists trading in these securities through the ITS system. The report found, "In terms of share volume, the ITS accounted for 3.1% of total NYSE volume in [871] ITS stocks during November 1980." Because New York Stock Exchange response time remained over forty seconds, the system apparently often was by-passed during hectic trading. Price spreads were unaffected by the system. The New York Stock Exchange dominated ITS trading, participating in about 90 percent of all ITS trades.[279] Whether regional exchange specialists may be more effective competitors after the ITS system is enhanced remains to be seen. Similarly, if Rule 390 is removed, whether or not the ITS system as enhanced and linked to NASDAQ effectively could provide a competitive securities market trading environment also is not yet clear.

It is not premature, however, to question the wisdom of the SEC's 1978–1981 decisions facilitating the national market system. To an unwarranted degree the SEC seems to have been concerned with preserving existing institutions and jobs. Electronic technology has been approved, but as with the ITS, it often has been superimposed on exchange-floor operations rather than used to replace them. Delays in implementing the system have been granted frequently. SEC decisions often have not been adequately explained. What makes

---

making. Again, there also is a question of fairness involved. Should upstairs market-makers be required to hold out some of their order flow if exchange specialists do not?

the Commission's performance so troublesome is that on this project it clearly had the responsibility to be "the investor's representative." After enacting the 1975 securities law, Congress was unlikely to devote extended attention to the securities industry for some time. No investors' organization exists that effectively can countervail the efforts of the Securities Industry Association and the New York Stock Exchange. Given this reality, an SEC more firmly in control of implementing the national securities market system would have served investors far better.

* * *

The 1970s witnessed the most significant consideration of corporate governance reform since the New Deal period. For close to a decade, such fundamental questions as the legitimacy of the giant business corporation, the functions of the corporate board of directors, and the appropriate legal duties of corporate officers and directors were debated, first in public interest proxy contests and the technical literature, later before congressional and SEC hearings.

The role of the SEC in the corporate governance debate was a peculiar one. Given the Commission's authority to supervise corporate proxy elections, the SEC was the federal agency with statutory responsibility to study the need for corporate governance reform. Yet the SEC's authority to regulate corporate proxy elections long had been treated by the agency as tangential to the Commission's primary responsibilities: stock market regulation, corporate disclosure, and antifraud litigation. Historically, the SEC had approached the regulation of proxy elections largely as a matter of adequate disclosure in required proxy literature, regarding other aspects of corporate governance as matters for state law.

The persistence of the belief that corporate governance regulation was a peripheral concern or a matter of adequate disclosure contributed to the SEC's paradoxical response to the corporate governance debate. On the one hand, the Commission's campaign to require disclosure of corporate bribes paid overseas and within the United States was the chief factor in sustaining public interest in the mechanics of corporate governance. On the other hand, the SEC's response to the corporate governance debate per se was strikingly limited. During the successive chairmanships of Ray Garrett, Roderick Hills, and Harold Williams, the SEC progressed from viewing the corporate bribery cases largely as a disclosure problem to support of legislative and New York Stock Exchange reforms of corporate auditing to necessitating protracted hearings generally reexamining corporate governance. At no time, however, did the Commission systematically study corporate governance, as it often earlier had the securities markets or investment companies. No SEC special study of corporate governance investigated such fundamental questions as how it was possible for so much fraud and falsification of corporate records to have occurred despite existing SEC and state laws. Or how the giant corporation, in fact, was governed. Or whether it would be appropriate to replace or augment the corporate board of directors with new mechanisms to ensure accountability. To its credit, the SEC did vigorously enforce the securities laws and lobby for reforms in the corporate auditing process. But it never seriously considered the possibility that postwar changes in the structure of the giant corporation or the problems suggested by the 1970s' corporate fraud and bribery cases necessitated a major reworking of state and federal corporate governance law.

On no other topic of comparable significance has the SEC proceeded with such indifference to the technical literature or to empirical study. As Columbia Law School professor John Coffee has written:

> We cannot "constitutionalize the corporation" until we understand it . . . Although lawyers as a group are frequently inattentive to developments in allied social sciences, the field of corporation law presents an egregious example of cultural lag. Dominated by centuries-old fiduciary concepts borrowed from the law of agency and the law of trusts, corporate law has not considered to any significant degree the relevance of the social sciences.[280]

Specifically, the SEC during the 1970s proceeded as if much of the postwar generation of economics, business school, and psychology literature bearing on the governance of the giant corporation did not exist. Although provocative works by Oliver Williamson, Alfred Chandler, John Kenneth Galbraith, and Christopher Stone suggested that the strictures of state corporation statutes were all but irrelevant to the way in which the modern corporation was governed, the SEC's contribution to the 1970s' corporate governance debate was to propose modest reforms and ignore the fundamental questions.

The 1970s' corporate governance debate effectively began with the efforts of public interest shareholder groups to employ the SEC's proxy rules to publicize their opposition to corporate Vietnam War, environmental, occupational safety, and employment policies. Among the most important of the early public interest proxy campaigns was the 1968 effort of the Medical Committee for Human Rights to petition Dow Chemical Company not to manufacture napalm for "[use] on or against human beings" and the much-publicized efforts of Campaign GM, beginning in February 1970, to persuade the nation's largest business corporation to adopt "socially responsible" policies on mass transportation, air pollution, auto safety, and minority employment. Reflecting related concerns, the National Resources Defense Council in 1971 filed a petition requesting the SEC to adopt new rules that would require corporate registrants to disclose detailed information about their environmental and equal employment practices. Each of these public interest proxy campaigns could claim some success in "raising consciousness" about important policy issues, but none focused on the mechanics of corporate governance as distinct from specific corporate policies.[281]

Other events, however, did. The SEC's 1971 *Institutional Investor Study* found that 213 selected bank trust departments, mutual funds, insurance companies, and pension funds held in aggregate over 50 percent of the common stock of several firms, including Xerox, Gulf Oil, and Ford, and nearly 50 percent of several other major business corporations, including IBM, Eastman Kodak, and Sears. By the end of 1978, institutional investors owned 36.3 percent of all common and preferred stock outstanding. Since institutional investors traditionally followed the "Wall Street Rule" and either voted for incumbent management or sold their stock, the institutionalization of corporate voting stockholdings raised obvious questions about the extent to which shareholder voting, even in theory, could be expected to be a mechanism for ensuring honest and efficient corporate management.[282]

At approximately the same time, a series of major corporate bankruptcies and fraud cases strongly suggested deficiencies in the performance of corporate boards of directors.[283] Most significant was the failure of the Penn Central, which at the time of its bankruptcy in June 1970 was the nation's largest railroad company and sixth-largest industrial corporation. In the two years before the Penn Central's collapse, its directors had approved dividend payments of over $100 million while the railroad's debts soared and its working capital deteriorated. The passivity and ignorance of the Penn Central's board prompted nearly universal criticism. As outside director E. Clayton Gengras recounted in oft-quoted words: "The board was definitely responsible for the trouble. They took their fees and they didn't do anything. Over a period of years, people just sat there. That poor man from the University of Pennsylvania [the university's president, Gaylord Harnwell], he never opened his mouth. They didn't know the factual picture and they didn't try to find out." After an exhaustive study, a staff report of the House Banking and Currency Committee agreed: "It is not so much what they [Penn Central's Board of Directors] did, but what they did not do that helped cause the Railroad's decline."[284]

Subsequently financial press and academic literature emphasized that the somnolent Penn Central Board of Directors had been typical of most giant corporations' boards in the postwar period. As *Dun's* magazine stated in an editorial entitled "Is the Board of Directors Obsolete?": "The sad case of Penn Central is worth mentioning, not because it is unique, but because it is not. Many another U.S. corporation has gotten into trouble because its directors did not do what they were supposed to do — that is, keep a warily inquiring eye on management, and ask the right questions at the right time."[285]

The most influential academic study, by Harvard Business School professor Myles Mace,[286] began with the premise that the board's statutory legal duty "to manage the business and affairs of every corporation" was a myth. After conducting several hundred interviews with corporate executives and directors, Mace concluded that the modern large or medium-sized firm's board of directors had ceased to function as a meaningful check on the corporation's chief executive officer.

Directors did not establish the basic objectives, corporate strategies, and broad policies in most large and medium-sized companies, Mace found. Full-time employee executives did. As the senior partner of a well-known consulting group reported to Mace, "I don't know of a single board that I've ever heard of that really digs into the strategy of the business, or sets targets for growth and holds management accountable for the results."

Nor did the board select the corporation's chief executive officers. "What is perhaps the most common definition of a function of the board of directors — namely, to select the president — was found to be the greatest myth," Mace wrote. "The board of directors in most companies . . . except in a crisis, does not select the president. The president usually chooses the man who succeeds him to that position, and the board complies with the legal amenities in endorsing and voting his election."

Typically, directors did not even ask discerning questions. It was considered "discourteous" or a breach of "corporate manners" for directors to "challenge" the corporation's chief executive officers.

Mace and others offered several explanations for the board's quiescence. Of paramount significance was the fact that corporate presidents usually controlled the selection of members of the board of directors.[287] This was a consequence of state judicial decisions that permitted incumbent corporate management to use corporate funds to pay the proxy election campaign expenses of their directorial candidates while requiring all other shareholders to bear the costs of proxy solicitations for opposition nominees, with·reimbursement possible only if the opposition candidates won control of the board.[288] As the number of shareholders in giant corporations and the costs of proxy elections increased, the nomination of directors by anyone other than incumbent management became virtually impossible. In 1974, for example, the SEC supervised the proxy solicitations of 6615 corporations. Management ran unopposed in 6600 companies, or 99.8 percent. In 6606 companies, or 99.9 percent, management's entire slate was elected.[289]

Consistently, corporate chief executives employed their control to select board members who would not "rock the boat." As one corporate president explained to Mace, "What would you do if you were president? You control the company and you control the board. You want to perpetuate this control. You certainly don't want anyone on your board who even slightly might be a challenge or a question to your tenure."[290] In the early 1970s, law professor Melvin Eisenberg characterized as "the most striking element" of the board's composition "the degree to which the typical board includes persons who are economically or psychologically dependent upon or tied to the corporation's executives, particularly its chief executive." Eisenberg cited several studies which found that approximately half of the largest industrial corporations' directors were firm executives. The unlikelihood of a corporate employee effectively monitoring the performance of senior executives was patent.[291]

Outside directors were little more likely to perform an adversarial role. A sizable proportion were retired corporate executives or investment bankers, commercial bankers, attorneys, customers, or suppliers dependent on the good will of senior corporate executives.[292] In other instances, James Nance, chairman of a Cleveland investment firm, believed: "Memberships often overlapped through friendships. There was a tendency for executives to say to one another, 'You be on my board and I'll be on yours.' "[293] Nor was there an expectation among corporate outside directors that they were hired to perform a rigorous monitoring role. A majority of those interviewed by Professor Mace expressed the judgment that the prestige of outside directors was a critical element among the qualifications desired for directorship. One stated: "You've got to have the names of outside directors who look impressive in the annual report. They are, after all, nothing more or less than ornaments on the corporate Christmas tree."[294]

Moreover, few boards of directors met frequently enough to perform a useful role. A 1970 survey of 474 industrial corporations by the management-consulting firm of Heidrick & Struggles found that about half these firms' boards of directors met for eighteen hours or less each year; few boards met for thirty-six hours or more annually. Significantly, Heidrick & Struggles also found that only 17.2 percent of the firms surveyed sent directors manufacturing data prior to the meeting, only 21.3 percent sent marketing data, only 5.7 percent sent an agenda, and 11 percent sent no information at all.[295] The infrequency of board meetings, lack of effective questioning by directors, and paucity of information available to them often resulted in boards' not being aware of adverse events until a crisis had become unavoidable. As management theorist Peter Drucker observed, the board "was always the last group to hear of trouble in the great business catastrophes of the century."[296] Reaching the same conclusion after a study of the work of Professor Oliver Williamson, John Coffee likened the board of directors to a "seventeenth-century monarch—holding absolute power in theory, but cut off from access to information and thereby manipulated by the ministers who are its nominal servants."[297]

No series of events better illustrated the deficiencies of the corporate board of directors than the SEC questionable payments cases.

The Commission's corporate bribery program indirectly was inspired by a 1972 Common Cause lawsuit against the Finance Committee of President Nixon's Committee to Re-Elect the President. Before April 7, 1972, when the Federal Election Campaign Act of 1971 went into effect, individual contributions to political candidates to finance primary campaigns did not have to be disclosed. Common Cause, aware that Nixon's Finance Committee had raised over $22 million by that date, brought suit in a federal district court to require disclosure of the names of the contributors, arguing that most of the money actually would be used to finance Nixon's general election and therefore did have to be disclosed under the law in effect. Five days before the 1972 election, the committee agreed to make available the origins of $6 million in contributions it had received before March 10, 1972. Then, in September 1973, as part of a final settlement of the Common Cause lawsuit, the committee made public information about another $11.4 million in contributions it had received between March 10 and April 7, 1972. Among the latter disclosures was a list of twenty-nine contributors, kept by Nixon's personal secretary, Rosemary Woods. Two of the contributors were firms that had made illegal campaign contributions.

Soon after its formation in late May 1973, the Watergate Special Prosecution Force began an investigation into illegal corporate campaign contributions made during the 1972 presidential election. In July 1973, Special Prosecutor Archibald Cox announced a so-called amnesty program. Corporate officers who came forward voluntarily and admitted illegal political contributions, stated Cox, would find "their voluntary acknowledgment . . . considered as a mitigating circumstance in deciding what charges to bring." American Airlines confessed to a one-count violation in October 1973 and received a $5000 fine. During the next two months, Minnesota Mining and Manufacturing, Goodyear, Braniff, Gulf Oil, Ashland Oil, Phillips Petroleum, and Carnation also made voluntary disclosures. Twelve other firms later were indicted by the Watergate special prosecutor. Subsequently, the special prosecutor brought additional charges against Gulf Oil and Ashland Oil as a result of their failure to make full disclosure during initial investigations.

The use of "slush funds" created by fictitious or unrecorded transactions to finance illegal corporate campaign contributions early attracted the interest of the SEC's Enforcement Division.* By their nature, such slush funds require falsification both of corporate internal financial records and the financial statements filed with the SEC. In addition, the moving of funds outside the normal record-keeping process presented the opportunity for outright theft of corporate assets. Arrangements were made for the SEC to have access to the information gathered by the Watergate Special Prosecution Force and initiate its own "management fraud" program.[300]

---

* No history of the Securities and Exchange Commission would be complete without noting the competence and ingenuity of the Commission's Enforcement Division under its second director, Stanley Sporkin. Sporkin played a major role in initiating the SEC's questionable payments program and in directing the Commission's attention to such related problems as domestic commercial bribery and misuse of executive perquisites. Each of these controversial programs not only illustrated the political integrity of the division, but also its doctrinal ingenuity. Under Sporkin, and his predecessor as division director, Irving Pollack, the SEC began frequent use of ancillary relief[298] (e.g., disgorgement of insider trading profits to defrauded investors or appointment of special directors) and significantly increased enforcement proceedings against attorneys and accountants who helped prepare fraudulent securities disclosure documents.[299] The latter cases were meant to ensure that private attorneys and accountants performed a meaningful role in voluntary compliance with the securities laws. Pollack and Sporkin also presided over the SEC enforcement program when it commenced each of its most publicized "big cases" during the late 1960s and 1970s: Texas Gulf Sulphur, Robert Vesco's looting of IOS, National Student Marketing, Arnholdt Smith's misuse of funds of the United States National Bank of San Diego, Stirling Homex, and the SEC investigations of Bert Lance, G. William Miller, and New York City's finances. Sporkin's contributions to the SEC's enforcement program were repeatedly recognized. He was awarded the Commission's Distinguished Service Award in 1971, the National Civil Service League Special Achievement Award in 1976, the Rockefeller Public Service Award in 1978, and awards for distinguished service both from President Carter and President Reagan.

The Commission's first action was brought in April 1974, against American Ship Building Company and its chief executive officer, George Steinbrenner. The complaint alleged that the company and Steinbrenner had violated the 1934 Securities Exchange Act by failing to record or disclose illegal contributions made since 1970. On October 4, 1974, American Ship Building and Steinbrenner agreed to settle the SEC's action by a consent decree. The chief consequence of the consent decree was the appointment of a special review committee, composed of three independent, outside directors. The committee's charge was to prepare a report on American Ship Building's illegal contributions and determine whether other corporate funds had been used for purposes other than those recorded on the corporation's books.[301]

A similar enforcement approach was employed by the SEC in twelve other cases filed through May 1976. After identifying evidence of falsification of corporate books and records, the Commission in each case agreed to a consent decree requiring the corporate defendant to establish an independent special review committee to conduct a full investigation of the irregularities alleged in the SEC's complaint. The special review committees usually hired independent accountants and legal counsel and submitted reports to the corporation's full board of directors. In all cases the SEC reserved the right to reopen its own investigation if it was dissatisfied with the actions the corporate defendant took pursuant to the consent decree.[302]

This special committee procedure proved to be the key to the SEC's program on questionable payments. Enforcement Division director Stanley Sporkin knew that if he frequently went to trial in questionable payments cases, it would drain the resources of his division, minimizing the number of questionable payments cases the SEC could pursue. But he also knew how much a guilty corporate executive would prefer a single special committee report to a protracted trial, and a summary voluntary disclosure of his firm's illegal payoffs to a special committee report. By insisting that the special committee reports be painstakingly assembled and highly detailed, Sporkin created a powerful incentive for firms to make voluntary disclosures to the SEC.

By mid-1975, the number of SEC questionable payments investigations had increased so rapidly that the full Commission concluded it could no longer afford to deal on a case-by-case basis with determining what specific disclosures each firm publicly would be required to make. In testimony before the House Subcommittee on

International Economic Policy, delivered in July and September 1975, Commissioner Philip Loomis outlined an SEC "voluntary disclosure" program. As refined over the following six months, the program allowed a firm that had made questionable or illegal payments to avoid an SEC enforcement action by conducting its own investigation of the payments. Such an investigation was typically supervised by the company's nonemployee directors, with the assistance of the firm's accounting firm and, if necessary, independent outside counsel. At the conclusion of the investigation, a complete report had to be submitted to the full board of directors. Material information compiled during the investigation had to be publicly disclosed in a filing with the SEC.

In September 1975, Cities Service Company became the first firm to file with the SEC a voluntary disclosure of its overseas bribery and record falsification.[303] Over the next eighteen months, voluntary disclosures of questionable payments by major American firms were made on a near-daily basis. Ultimately close to four hundred firms voluntarily admitted having bribed foreign or American political or commercial officials or making illegal American campaign contributions. Another sixty-two firms' questionable payments would be proven in SEC enforcement actions.[304]

Putting aside the much-debated question of the morality of overseas corporate bribery, the paramount significance of these cases was well defined in an SEC report published in May 1976:

> The almost universal characteristic of the cases reviewed . . . has been the apparent frustration of our system of corporate accountability . . . Millions of dollars of funds have been inaccurately recorded in corporate books and records to facilitate the making of questionable payments. Such falsification of records has been known to corporate employees and often to top management, but often has been concealed from outside auditors and counsel and outside directors.

Indeed, a close reading of the SEC's summary of the first ninety-five disclosures of questionable corporate payments revealed that in nearly half of the cases, some member of corporate management "had knowledge of, approved of, or participated" in the payment. But apparently in few, if any, cases were nonemployee members of the board informed that the firm they nominally directed was paying bribes.[305]

The classic study of the "frustration of our system of corporate accountability" was the 298-page report on the Gulf Oil Corporation, prepared for its Board of Directors by a special committee headed by John J. McCloy. After ten months of investigation by thirty-two attorneys and accountants, the committee alleged that Gulf had made $12.6 million in foreign and domestic payments over a fifteen-year period. Among the payments were more than $4 million in illegal campaign contributions to U.S. politicians, including President Richard Nixon, Senator Henry Jackson, Senator Hugh Scott, Senator Hubert Humphrey, Congressman Wilbur Mills, and more than a dozen other members of Congress, as well as state political officials in Texas, Kansas, Louisiana, and Pennsylvania.

Gulf's illicit course of action apparently began in 1959, when William K. Whiteford, the firm's chairman and chief executive officer, concluded that he would get no effective support from the State Department in connection with Gulf's overseas expansion unless he could develop a "more conducive political atmosphere." Whiteford dispatched an assistant comptroller to Nassau to launder funds, which were then returned to Gulf's Pittsburgh headquarters and later sent to Washington or abroad for pay-out. Whiteford and his two successors as chairman directly or through Gulf's Washington lobbyist, Claude G. Wild, supervised payments delivered by nineteen Gulf executives. They also supervised fraudulent accounting by another twenty or so executives, the creation or employment of three phony corporations in the Bahamas to launder funds, and the banishment of at least one squeamish vice president — all without the knowledge of outside directors on the board or senior executives reputed to be "boy scouts," and without effective challenge by the company's general counsel, Royce Savage, a former federal district court judge, who allegedly knew of some of the payoffs.[306]

The Gulf Oil pattern of a dominant corporate chief executive officer violating laws without the supervision or knowledge of outside corporate directors consistently was found in other companies that were required to provide detailed information about their questionable payments. The complex program of disguised corporate contributions at American Ship Building was organized by George Steinbrenner, who persuaded several senior executives to accept "bonuses," which they passed on as political contributions. He also persuaded other executives to record the "bonuses" falsely in the company's books. At Northrop, Chairman Thomas V. Jones and Vice President James Allen, without the knowledge of the board, administered a slush fund to stimulate jet sales in Europe. At Minnesota Mining and Manufacturing, the chairman and financial vice president ordered the insurance department to pay out $509,000 for imaginary insurance; the money was actually used for political contributions. This transaction was later "verified" by the outside auditor, Haskins & Sells.[307]

In the aftermath of the questionable-payment disclosures, several proposals to reform corporate governance were widely debated, among them former SEC chairman William Cary's March 1974 proposal to enact federal "minimum standards" for state corporate law. Cary's proposal was motivated by his belief not only that state legislatures had long relaxed the statutory corporate law requirements in order to increase incorporation fees, but that in Delaware, the state where a plurality of large firms were incorporated, the judiciary had rendered decisions "on the basis of a desire to foster incorporations in Delaware." With uncharacteristic heat, Cary wrote, "The first step is to escape from the present predicament in which a pygmy among the fifty states prescribes, interprets, and indeed denigrates national corporate policy as an incentive to encourage incorporation within its borders, thereby increasing its revenues." To remove the incentive to incorporate in Delaware or other "chartermongering" states, Cary proposed enactment of a federal statute that would establish standards of officer and director conduct for all firms above a minimum size. If adopted, Cary's proposal would have permitted shareholder suits against corporate directors who approved any transaction legally "unfair" to their firm or otherwise failed to observe their fiduciary duties.[308]

The previous year, one of Cary's colleagues at Columbia Law School, Harvey Goldschmid, offered a widely noted proposal to restructure boards of directors so that each could provide "a meaningful, independent" review of corporate management. Goldschmid proposed that the board be composed entirely of nonemployee (or outside) directors, who would be adequately paid to devote "weeks or months instead of hours" to the review and approval of operating executive decisions. Adopting a recommendation earlier made by former Supreme Court Justice Arthur Goldberg, Goldschmid urged that the board have access to important operating and financial data and be aided by its own independent staff. Goldschmid also urged that shareholders be given some opportunity to nominate director candidates directly.*[309]

---

* From a different perspective, University of Southern California Law School professor Christopher Stone recommended that a federal agency appoint "general public directors" to serve on the boards of the largest industrial and financial firms. Stone recommended that when a corporation repeatedly violated the law, the federal courts additionally appoint "special public directors" to prevent further delinquency.[310]

The most far-reaching proposal was advanced in 1976 by Ralph Nader and two of his associates.* Nader recommended the federal incorporation of all industrial, retail, and transportation firms with sales of $250 million or more that employed ten thousand or more persons. Under a proposed new federal statute, each of the firms would be led by full-time directors. To ensure the board's independence from the operating management it reviewed, each federally chartered firm's directors could be nominated only by shareholders unaffiliated with the firm's operating executives. The most controversial aspect of the Nader proposal was the attempt to ensure board concern for chartered corporations' chief impacts on employees, shareholders, and neighboring communities. Each firm was to be led by nine directors, who would have both a general duty to see that the corporation was profitably administered as well as a specific oversight responsibility, such as "employee welfare," "consumer protection," or "management efficiency." The Nader federal chartering proposal, like its TNEC precursors, also was intended to be an omnibus bill, with other sections addressed to antitrust law, corporate disclosure, and employee rights.[311]

Congressional hearings were held in 1976 and 1977 on the need for a new federal corporate law.[312] A 1976 petition signed by eighty corporate law professors argued, "With public concern about various kinds of corporate impropriety running at a high level, there is a particular urgency at this time for the Congress to consider some form of federal intervention in this area, whether through the means of a federal chartering statute, through federal 'minimum standards' for state corporation laws, or some other mechanism."[313] For similar reasons, Stanley Sporkin of the SEC's Enforcement Division recommended a new federal corporate law in 1977.[314]

The SEC's commissioners, however, at no point during the 1970s supported federal legislation that would have changed to any degree the duties or structure of boards of directors.

The initial response of the Garrett SEC to the questionable-payment revelations was to view them strictly as an issue of adequate corporate disclosure. The SEC first addressed the issue in a March 1974 release, publishing the Division of Corporate Finance's view that conviction under the federal statute proscribing corporate campaign contributions must be disclosed to shareholders. But in cases in which no formal proceeding had been commenced, the Corporate Finance Division averred that "management is usually in the best position to inquire into, to examine and weigh the facts and

* One of whom was the author.

circumstances, and to determine whether disclosure is necessary."[315] This position was implicitly abandoned by the full SEC the following month, when it endorsed the Enforcement Division's action against American Ship Building, which required the disclosure of illegal campaign contributions that had not yet been the subject of a formal proceeding.[316] In the view of Sporkin, any transaction that required the falsification of corporate books and records was a material event because of what it revealed about the integrity of corporate management.[317] By contrast, Commissioner Sommer and others at the SEC believed that so absolute a view "[lost] sight of the most fundamental question, what is really important to investors?" Sommer argued that the SEC's disclosure rules should not "become in effect a substitute for the enforcement of other substantive laws" but should require publication of a fact only when it conveyed to investors important information about a business corporation.[318]

In the 1975–1976 period, Sporkin and Sommer engaged in a protracted debate about whether the SEC should issue guidelines delineating when firms should reveal questionable payments. Sporkin disparaged the proposed guidelines as "a road map to fraud." Sommer publicly termed the lack of guidelines a "terrible failure" of the SEC. The issue was finally resolved in May 1976, when the SEC published nineteen pages of vague guidelines.[319]

By the time of Roderick Hills's chairmanship, it was no longer possible for the SEC to view the bribery revelations strictly as a problem of corporate disclosure. With the Commission's voluntary disclosure program in full stride, revelations of corporate bribery had become a matter of public and congressional concern.

In several speeches and in congressional testimony, Hills acknowledged that "there should be little question that there is a profound and pressing need to seek ways to raise the levels of conduct of corporate management." Hills implicitly conceded that the essence of the criticism of corporate boards made by Myles Mace, Harvey Goldschmid, Nader, and others was persuasive. The SEC chairman stated, for example, in a November 8, 1976, address:

> Let's see if we can agree on what's wrong with management now.
> Too many boards are dominated by inside directors . . .
> Compensation for directors is often set at a figure so low that no real work is expected.
> Information provided boards in too many cases is the product of management; outside directors feel no responsibility to make independent inquiry.
> Inside directors control the vote too often on salaries, on merger proposals, tender offers, on management succession, and the filling of

board vacancies — all subjects where the stockholders' interest may be different than that of management.

Thus, many companies limp along under poor management until economic setbacks are so severe that a large perceptive investor bids for stock control recognizing that the corporate assets can produce better profits.

Stockholder democracy in many cases therefore means nothing more than the right to sell stock.

What is missing on too many boards — in short — is a truly independent character that has the practical capacity to monitor and change management.[320]

Yet Hills opposed federal legislation that would directly address the boards' deficiencies. "The point is," Hills had testified in June 1976, "we do not need new Federal behavioral standards. Rather, we need a more effective reporting system so that directors will be aware of conduct that is clearly incorrect by existing standards."[321] Hills made no attempt to explain how "a more effective reporting system" alone could improve corporate management if, as he himself stated, boards of directors were "dominated by inside directors" and lacked "a truly independent character." Nor did Hills personally, or the SEC during his chairmanship, publish an analysis of proposals as minimalist as those of former chairman William Cary, or initiate any independent factual study of why so many boards of directors had functioned poorly.

Instead, the Hills SEC focused its attention on two "limited purpose" reforms. On May 11, 1976, Hills requested that the New York Stock Exchange consider amending its listing requirements so that each listed company had to "maintain an audit committee composed of independent directors with full access to all information and regular private meetings with outside auditors." In 1977 the New York Stock Exchange made the change. This was a salutary, though modest, reform. For thirty-five years, the SEC periodically had encouraged business corporations to form board of director audit committees. By the time he wrote the New York Stock Exchange, according to Hills, almost 90 percent of the nation's largest corporations already had independent audit committees. A 1980 SEC survey of twelve hundred business corporations whose securities were publicly traded found that the typical audit committee met 2.7 times per year and limited its functions to approval of the selection of the firm's outside auditor and review of audit plans and results. No one could seriously argue that any committee that met so infrequently and had such narrow functions was a substitution for an effective and independent corporate board of directors.[322]

The Hills SEC also lobbied for a reform in corporate record-keeping. In its May 1976 "Report on Questionable and Illegal Corporate Payments and Practices," the Commission recommended enactment of legislation prohibiting the falsification of corporate accounting records and requiring management to maintain a system of internal accounting controls to ensure that corporate transactions were executed in accordance with management's authorization. Congress enacted the SEC's record-keeping proposals as a part of the 1977 Foreign Corrupt Practices Act. Again, this was a salutary reform. But as Professor John Coffee of Columbia Law School wrote, "Limiting SEC reform efforts to accounting controls does not make sense from a policy perspective."[323] Honest internal corporate financial records alone could not ensure that the board of directors would be independent, meet often enough to play an effective role, be adequately informed, require management to function efficiently, or proscribe wasteful or unfair corporate transactions.*

With the election of a Democratic President in 1976, it would have been reasonable to assume that the SEC would take a less restricted look at the need for corporate governance reform. As a presidential candidate, Jimmy Carter in August 1976 had endorsed Professor Cary's proposal for a new federal statute to set minimum standards for corporate law.[326] But Carter's 1977 appointments of SEC chairman Harold Williams and SEC commissioner Roberta Karmel halted whatever momentum statutory corporate governance reform might have had within the SEC.

Like Roderick Hills's pronouncements, Harold Williams's speeches on the subject echoed many of the arguments made by critics of corporate boards of directors. In a much-noted address, "Corporate Accountability," delivered in January 1978, Williams outlined a proposal for an "ideal" board of directors that could function as "a countervailing force":

> It must be recognized that there are some people who do not belong on boards, members of management, outside counsel, investment bankers, commercial bankers and others who might realistically be thought of as suppliers hired by management. Some of these, as individuals, can and do make excellent directors. Yet all must be excluded unless a mechanism can be designed whereby they establish their

---

* Hills also ably defended the SEC Enforcement Division's questionable-payment program when it was attacked by Ford administration Commerce Secretary Elliot Richardson for being based "on tenuous legal grounds" and being a policy of "continued zeal or militancy."[324] Several efforts were made by the Ford administration to remove jurisdiction over questionable-payment sanctions from the SEC. Each was rejected by Congress.[325]

ability to function on a basis independent of their management-related role.

On Williams's ideal board, management would not be represented except by the chief executive officer, and the chief executive would be barred from serving as chairman of the board.

Williams vigorously defended this pattern of corporate governance:

> Many boards of directors, although by no means all, cannot truly be said to exercise the accountability function. The board itself is a mini-society, with all the forces of cooption and cooperation, desire for compatibility, and distaste for divisiveness, which characterize any group. Moreover, the board environment is not particularly conducive to nurturing challenge when the majority of directors are beholden — as employees, suppliers of goods or services, or due to other conflicting roles — to the chairman and chief executive. Even friendship itself often inhibits vigorous directorship, although a strong independent director, asking hard questions, in my judgment performs an act of true friendship. Dissenting directors are, however, rare, and for some reasons, they often seem to have short tenure. Thus, the board, in effect, often insulates management rather than holding it accountable.[327]

But in flat contradiction of at least the spirit of his boardroom criticism, Williams opposed federal corporate governance legislation, "even," he said in November 1980, "to implement the ideal board which I have suggested." His contradictory stance could best be understood in terms of his philosophical preference for private initiatives and his distrust of federal legislation. As Williams testified, federal corporate governance legislation "is likely to hamper seriously the ability of corporations to deliver the economic results necessary to assure our social and political future [and] highly likely to stimulate still more comprehensive legislation."[328]

During Williams's chairmanship, the SEC did hold protracted hearings, re-examining "rules relating to shareholder communications, shareholder participation in the corporate electoral process, and corporate governance generally."* [329] In 1978 it adopted a rule

---

* The structure of the hearings was highly unusual for the SEC. Usually when the Commission considered the need for a new regulatory or legislative initiative, it would request its staff to prepare a study and, if necessary, propose a rule. A hearing then would be held on the rule proposal. By contrast, the SEC corporate governance hearings were preceded by a literature survey but no factual investigation. Hearings were held on some thirty-two questions concerning corporate governance. An SEC release explained, "The Commission specifically requests public comment on the desirability of federal legislation such as a bill establishing minimum

requiring registered firms to disclose additional information on the independence of its directors, whether the firms had audit, nominating, and compensation committees, and whether an incumbent director had attended fewer than 75 percent of a firm's board meetings during the past fiscal year. A subsequent rule, adopted in 1979, required modest changes in the form of corporate proxies. But the emphasis throughout Williams's chairmanship was on exhorting business executives voluntarily to reform their boards.[330]

The practical consequence of the Hills-Williams opposition to federal legislation was that at the end of the 1970s the typical large firm's board of directors was little more independent than it had been at the beginning of the decade. Both men had agreed that operating executive domination of the board was the principal impediment to an effective directorate. According to the SEC's own staff study of twelve hundred major firms during the 1978–1979 period, 65 percent of these firms' directors either were corporate employees or had another relationship with the firm (such as being its attorney or investment banker), "which potentially could interfere with the exercise of independent judgment."[331] Professor Myles Mace's reconsideration of the operations of the corporate board approximately a decade after publishing his influential book similarly led him

> to the conclusion that boards of directors operate pretty much as they did ten years ago. Most boards today do not establish objectives, ask discerning questions, or measure the performance of CEOs on the basis of any formal criteria. The hundreds of thousands of stockholders of large widely held companies continue to be unorganized and unorganizable, and CEOs continue to control board functions through the proxy process. There are few exceptions."[332]

There were, to be sure, specific companies that did restructure their boards to give outside directors a more effective and independent role. Litigation, especially under Sections 10(b) and 14(a) of the

---

federal standards of corporate conduct and shareholder rights. Based upon the results of this proceeding, the Commission will give careful consideration to the advisability of recommending such legislation to Congress." Instead, after the hearings, Chairman Williams directed Barbara Lucas, the Corporate Finance Division staff attorney in charge, to defer consideration of any new legislation. Shortly after, Lucas and Corporate Finance Division director Richard Rowe left the SEC. Michael Klein and John Olson, two Washington, D.C., corporate attorneys who supported Williams's approach to corporate governance, not unreasonably characterized the basic purpose of Williams's corporate governance speeches and hearings as "soothing" the votaries of reform. Williams, Klein and Olson wrote, was in fact "a sheep dressed in wolf's clothing."

1934 act, presumably did contribute to directors having a heightened awareness of their legal duties. Undoubtedly the board audit committees initiated during the 1970s, and the exhortations of Hills and Williams, made contributions as well. But with full recognition of each of these, it still is a fair conclusion that in the history of the SEC no series of scandals comparable to the failure of the Penn Central and corporate bribery revelations prompted so limited a Commission response.

* * *

By contrast, the Commission's supervision of accounting-principles standard-setting improved during the 1970s.

Throughout the century, comparability has been the Holy Grail of accounting reformers. If firms were to apply the same accounting principles over time and all firms in each industry were to apply the same principles, the readers of financial statements would be able to compare the performance of a firm with its performance in previous periods and with competitive firms. Arguably, uniform (that is, comparable) accounting principles can help ensure the most efficient allocation of investor resources and the most accurate appraisal of a given firm's management.

The failure of the American Institute of Certified Public Accountants' (AICPA) two successive accounting-principles organizations, the Committee on Accounting Procedures (1938–1959) and the Accounting Principles Board (1959–1973), to limit sufficiently the employment of alternative generally accepted accounting principles was the primary cause of each organization's demise.[333] By the early 1970s, as the Accounting Principles Board neared collapse, the prevailing cynicism about the board's inability to reduce the number of alternative generally accepted accounting principles perhaps was most tellingly conveyed by a *New Yorker* cartoon that showed a corporate executive introducing his company's accountant with a wink and the words, "In examining our books, Mr. Matthews promises to use generally accepted accounting principles, *if you know what I mean*" (italics added).[334]

Staff reports of the Federal Trade Commission (1969) and the House Judiciary Antitrust Subcommittee (1971) documented, in the words of the FTC report, that

> on a number of key issues, "generally accepted accounting principles" permit a range of reporting choices that can materially alter reported company operating results. There need be no consistency in the treatment of depreciation charges, inventory evaluation, the expensing of research and development, and other factors. The specific method of reporting selected by management may be changed from one period to

another. It may be said categorically that accounting statements often are neither consistent over time nor comparable among firms.[335]

Admiral Hyman Rickover would find himself so "astounded by some of the creative accounting' that enables a contractor to report a wide range of profit figures for a given situation" that he would lead the lobbying efforts to create the federal government's Cost Accounting Standards Board "to step in and establish a standard-setting organization [for government contracts] where the accounting profession was unwilling or unable to do the job."[336]

Commentators offered several explanations for the Accounting Principles Board's failure to narrow the different generally accepted accounting principles that were used.[337] The board was unable to develop a code of basic accounting principles. Instead, it focused on ad hoc firefighting, frequently issuing opinions, Columbia professor John Burton noted in 1971, that closed "the number of loopholes which exist for misleading reporting [only] after they have been exploited."[338]

APB opinions were not binding. Under the relevant rule of the AICPA, firms could employ as "generally accepted accounting principles" those which had "substantial authoritative support," including "principles that differ from opinions of the Accounting Principles Board." Since the "substantial authoritative support" test could be satisfied if some leading firms employed a principle or if the principle was sufficiently supported in the accounting literature, "there is at present," reported an AICPA special report in 1964, "no means of assuring either that [the APB's opinions] will be universally followed or that departures from them will be disclosed by independent auditors."[339]

Corporate management, not the accountant who certified a firm's financial reports, selected which generally accepted accounting principles would be employed. Given management's interest in the publication of favorable reports, this was, A. A. Sommer argued, "the most egregious conflict of interest of them all." It was, accounting professor Charles Horngren claimed, analogous to "having the baseball batter calling the balls and the strikes." In 1970, Professor Homer Kripke of New York University Law School would insist, "There can be no general progress in accounting until the accountant puts his own integrity on the line unmistakably by certifying that the principles used are those that *he* (not his client) deems appropriate on the facts."[340]

Precisely because corporate management possessed the power to select generally accepted accounting principles and the related power to hire and fire outside auditors, there was widespread skepticism that the APB's members, most of whom were practitioners associated with leading firms, possessed sufficient independence to engage in standard-setting. "It is the doubts cast on the disinterestedness of a part-time board which troubles its critics the most," stated the AICPA's 1972 *Wheat Report.*

> They assert that Board members having a continuing affiliation with their firms or companies must inevitably find their loyalties divided . . . The proponents of a part-time board must confront this dilemma. The more importance they attach to the continuing professional contacts of Board members, the more difficult it is for them to argue that such men maintain undivided loyalty to the Board.[341]

Finally, as well illustrated by the pooling versus purchase accounting controversy described in Chapter 11, "the buffeting the [APB] took in its attempt to resolve difficult issues," wrote its onetime research director, Maurice Moonitz, "led it, in later years, to avoid them and concentrate instead on compiling a record by issuing opinions on less controversial topics." *The Wheat Report* calculated that two APB statements respectively required 133 and 98 months to complete; two controversial APB opinions, 128 and 96 months from the initial research studies to final publication.[342] Equally important, when the APB did issue opinions on controversial topics, they often were elaborate compromises permitting alternative generally accepted accounting principles; they did not designate a single principle that would ensure the comparability of firm financial statements.

Professor Kripke, Professor Robert Chatov, and Senator Max Baucus of Montana, who earlier had served as SEC chairman Hamer Budge's legal assistant, considered such failings at standard-setting so fundamental that they recommended that the SEC directly promulgate accounting principles.[343] This, the Commission during the Budge and Casey chairmanships never seriously considered. The SEC tacitly delegated all responsibility for remedying the loss of confidence to the AICPA's Wheat Committee.[344] The Commission's *Minutes* for October 28, 1971, indicate that the SEC determined not even to state a public position on such questions formulated by the Wheat Committee as "Should the primary responsibility for establishing accounting standards reside in a governmental body or a nongovernmental body?"

The Wheat Committee published its report in March 1972. To

broaden support for private accounting-principles standard-setting, the report recommended the creation of the Financial Accounting Foundation. The foundation was to have nine trustees, all appointed by the AICPA Board of Directors, a minority of whom would be chosen from names submitted by the Financial Executives Institute, the National Association of Accountants, the Financial Analysts Federation, and the American Accounting Association. The principal duty of the Financial Accounting Foundation was to appoint the seven members of a new accounting-principles standard-setting body, the Financial Accounting Standards Board (FASB). A key distinction between the FASB and the APB was that the new board would be made up of full-time members who would "have no other business affiliations." The authority of the FASB was to be strengthened by a new AICPA rule making it unethical for a member to "express an opinion that financial statements are presented in conformity with generally accepted accounting principles if such statements contain any departure from an accounting principle promulgated by [the APB or FASB] which has a material effect on the statements taken as a whole, unless the member can demonstrate that due to unusual circumstances the financial statements would otherwise have been misleading."[345] The apparent commitment of the AICPA to establishing a basic conceptual framework for accounting-principles standard-setting was underlined by the appointment of a separate committee, chaired by Robert Trueblood, to prepare a report on the objectives of financial statements. Within two months, the SEC officially endorsed the Wheat Committee's recommendations. The FASB soon afterward began operations. In December 1973, the SEC issued Accounting Series Release No. 150. ASR No. 150 required registrants to prepare financial statements in accordance with SEC rules, regulations, or other official releases when the Commission had taken a position on a specific issue. Otherwise, only financial statements prepared in accordance with the "principles, standards, and practices promulgated by the FASB" would be acceptable to the SEC; "those contrary to such FASB promulgations" would be deemed lacking "substantial authoritative support."[346]

At the same time as Casey's SEC pled formal obeisance to the FASB, the SEC took steps to improve its supervision of the board's standard-setting. More than any earlier SEC chairman, William Casey emphasized the importance of accounting-principles standard-setting. "I believe," Casey informed the New York Stock Exchange Board of Directors in January 1973, "the public has lost more money through the use of permissible variations in accounting to exaggerate earnings and growth and to obscure declining performance than through the whole catalogue of things which we have made impermissible." Although it was always Casey's "personal preference to keep the formulation of accounting principles . . . in the hands of the profession," he pointedly informed the AICPA in October 1972:

> As I look back at the record and the progress in improving accounting standards to deal with the growing complexity of business and the proliferating requirements of users of financial statements, I find myself virtually forced to the view that the Commission should exercise more vigorous oversight and undertake to force the pace at which the profession meets the multiplicity of demands made upon it and generates reports which are more comparable, more revealing and more meaningful.[347]

Casey's most significant step toward improving SEC oversight of private accounting-principles standard-setting was to hire Columbia Business School professor John Burton to be the SEC's chief accountant after Andrew Barr retired in 1972. Burton believed the SEC should be a "creative irritant" in the accounting-principles standard-setting process, like "the sand in the oyster." In retrospect, Burton would state: "In the financial reporting environment as it exists today, substantial change will not occur in the absence of SEC stimulation. If there is to be innovation, the Securities and Exchange Commission must be a principal source." From the start, Burton's job, as SEC commissioner James Needham put it in April 1972, was to "play the gadfly role," dispelling the notion that "a cozy relationship exists between the accountants and the SEC." Burton arrived at the SEC with strong qualifications for such a role. By temperament, he was a reformer. As A. A. Sommer put it, Burton was a man who "threw off sparks." After a career combining practice at the Big Eight accounting firm Arthur Young and Company and a decade's teaching and writing at Columbia, Burton began at the SEC with established views on a long list of accounting controversies. SEC chairman Garrett, in addition, attributed to Burton the "Law of Anticipatory Multiplication": "It holds," Garrett explained, "that all changes seem several times more significant and more threatening when viewed in prospect than in retrospect."[348]

Nonetheless, during the four years that Burton served as chief accountant, the Commission's contribution to the task of reducing alternative generally accepted accounting principles was modest. The SEC did somewhat reduce the availability of the pooling method of recording a merger by issuing Accounting Series Releases that prohibited pooling when a transaction was contingent on a third party's purchase of any of the common stock employed or when a firm reacquired its own stock during the two years before a merger for use in effecting the merger.[349] Burton also notably (though unsuccessfully) pressed for a major reform of accounting for retail land sales.[350]

Despite these and other "creative irritations," the FASB, in the words of Sommer, "got off to a distressingly slow start."[351] In October 1976, the House Commerce Subcommittee on Oversight and Investigations, chaired by Congressman John Moss, reported:

> The FASB has accomplished virtually nothing toward resolving fundamental accounting problems plaguing the profession. These include the plethora of optional "generally accepted" accounting principles (GAAPs), the ambiguities inherent in many of those principles, and the manifestations of private accountants' lack of independence with respect to their corporate clients.[352]

The following year, a staff report of the Senate Governmental Affairs Subcommittee on Reports, Accounting, and Management, chaired by Senator Lee Metcalf, revived the proposal that "the Federal Government should directly establish financial accounting standards for publicly owned corporations."[353] Although the SEC continued to oppose assuming responsibility for the direct promulgation of accounting principles, by 1980 it reported that it, too, was "concerned with the FASB's rate of progress in moving toward more concrete positions [in its conceptual framework project]. Almost all of the planned phases of the project have experienced delays. Of equal importance, certain fundamental issues have not yet been addressed."[354]

Nonetheless, between 1972 and 1976, Burton played a significant role in improving the usefulness of corporate financial statements to investors by initiating reforms of the SEC's corporate disclosure rules. Several of the Burton-initiated reforms were designed to reduce the likelihood that firm managements would change accounting principles to create the appearance of increased earnings. A controversial Accounting Series Release adopted in September 1975 required that "when a business enterprise changes an accounting principle . . . in the first [subsequent quarterly financial report], a letter from the registrant's independent accountants shall be filed as an exhibit indicating whether or not the change is to an alternative principle which in his judgment is preferable under the circumstances."[355] A related rule required any firms that changed accountants to disclose whether there had been a material disagreement with the first accountant.* [356]

Other Burton initiatives substantially altered the assumptions underlying SEC disclosure policy. To invoke one of Homer Kripke's more inspired phrases, Burton helped end "the myth of the informed layman." Burton, following Kripke's influential analysis, believed that the SEC best protected investors when it required disclosure documents most likely to be read by sophisticated investors and professional analysts through whom information would be filtered down to less sophisticated investors and their brokers. Accordingly, Burton championed the policy of "differential disclosure," recognizing the "need for two kinds of disclosures and footnotes associated with financial statements: that which is necessary for general purpose financial statements prepared in conformity with generally accepted accounting principles and aimed at the stockholder without clout, if you will, and that which is aimed primarily at the professional analyst."[358] During Burton's tenure as chief accountant, the Commission ended its insistence that corporate financial statements reflect only historical cost data; it issued Accounting Series Releases No. 151 and 190, which respectively encouraged, and then required, supplemental disclosure of the current replacement cost of certain specified assets whose value was likely to be markedly affected by inflation.[359] The SEC also encouraged more detailed disclosure by firms of unusual risks and uncertainties in financial reporting.[360]

The most important SEC disclosure policy reform initiated when Burton was chief accountant concerned earnings forecasts. For over three decades, the SEC had generally prohibited the publication of predictions of a firm's future economic performance on the grounds that such projections were not "facts," were inherently unreliable, would be given undue credence by investors, and would be susceptible to improper manipulation by unscrupulous corporate managers. The most often-quoted explanation of the SEC's traditional policy barring earnings forecasts was published by Harry Heller, long a senior SEC staff attorney, in a 1961 law review article:

> As early as 1904 Veblen expressed the view that the value of an investment basically is a function of future earning power . . .

---

* There were several other Burton initiatives, notably those in ASRs 147, 149, and 177, involving lease disclosure, tax disclosure, and interim financial reporting. Burton also initiated a rule proposal requiring firms to disclose an estimate of the effect on net income of the use of specific accounting principles as compared to alternative accounting principles. In 1978 the SEC withdrew this rule proposal.[357]

The question will be raised, if the determination of future earnings is the prime task confronting the investor, why not require or permit a direct prediction of such earnings? The answer to this is that the Securities Act, like the hero of "Dragnet," is interested exclusively in facts. Conjectures and speculations as to the future are left by the Act to the investor on the theory that he is as competent as anyone to predict the future from the given facts. Since an expert can speak with authority only as to subjects upon which he has professional knowledge and since no engineering course or other professional training has ever been known to qualify anyone as a clairvoyant, attempts by companies to predict future earnings on their own or on the authority of experts have almost invariably been held by the Commission to be misleading because they suggest to the investor a competence and authority which in fact does not exist.[361]

By the early 1970s, the SEC's policy on this matter was being severely criticized. The most influential critic was Professor Homer Kripke. In a 1970 law review article entitled "The SEC, the Accountants, Some Myths and Some Realities," he dismissed the SEC's traditional policy as "nonsense." Noting that virtually all corporations used

projections of future sales and revenues and capital needs as the basis for making very important decisions as to borrowing, building new plants, establishing new branches, ordering materials, hiring and training labor, etc. [Kripke argued that] the management . . . certainly is in a better position than the public to forecast where the company is going.

By prohibiting disclosure of earnings projections in SEC filings, the Commission had perpetuated a totally inequitable form of differential disclosure.

The professionals get management projections informally through press conferences, speeches to analysts' societies, or press releases, and these projections form the basis for professional judgments. Under its present system the SEC precludes the giving of this information equally to all investors through the documents filed with it.

Nor did Kripke believe the danger of management exaggeration of future earnings prospects posed a major problem. If there was a rational basis for a forecast and if managerial "good faith" was required, "the SEC staff would have no difficulty dealing with unreasoned or unduly optimistic projections of promotional companies, any more than it did in the early 1930s or even today with unsound estimates of mineral resources." Kripke concluded:

> The importance of this point on projections cannot be overestimated. If there is any hope that the public or even the professionals can make an informed investment judgment, it must start from a crystallization of all of the plethora of information into a projection for the future. The management is in the best position to make the initial estimate; on the basis of it the professional or investor could then make his own modifications. No other single change could add as much meaning to the unmanageable and unfocused flood of facts in present Commission documents.[362]

Soon after beginning his chairmanship, William Casey initiated a review of the SEC's policy barring the publication of earnings projections.[363] Impressed by the British practice of including forecasts in public documents, Casey's SEC held hearings on the earnings forecast issue in November and December 1972. Three months later an SEC statement announced that thenceforth firms would be permitted to publish earnings projections in documents filed with the Commission. Echoing the equity arguments that the SEC had propounded in such leading 10b-5 cases as *Cady, Roberts* and *Texas Gulf Sulphur*, the Commission's 1973 "Statement on the Disclosure of Projections of Future Economic Performance" explained:

> Information gathered at the hearings reinforced the Commission's own observation that management's assessment of a company's future performance is information of significant importance to the investor, that such assessment should be able to be understood in light of the assumptions made, and that such information should be available, if at all, on an equitable basis to all investors.[364]

After a time-consuming false start, the SEC in 1979 adopted a "safe harbor" rule to encourage firms voluntarily to project such "forward-looking" information as forecasts of future income, earnings, capital expenditures, dividends, and managerial plans for future operations. Firms publishing any forward-looking statement would not be considered by the SEC to have violated the securities fraud laws "unless it was shown that such statement was made or reaffirmed without a reasonable basis or was disclosed other than in good faith."[365]

The SEC's 1979 rule left unanswered an important question about earnings projections: Should they be permissive or mandatory? The SEC's Advisory Committee on Corporate Disclosure in 1977, citing four reasons, had concluded that a voluntary projection disclosure program was more appropriate than a mandatory program. First, a period of experimentation with a voluntary system was desirable before a mandatory rule was adopted. Second, "all public companies should not be required to sustain the expense and other burdens that may be associated with a program for the public disclosure of projections. In some instances, companies might reasonably find that the burdens of projection disclosure would outweigh any corresponding benefits." Third, there was what Sommer called the "biggest headache," the concern of corporations publishing a projection that they would be liable for inaccurate projections. In part, this concern stemmed from the fact that a federal district court in a private damages action could hold that a corporation violated the securities laws by publishing an inaccurate projection even if it met the SEC's safe harbor rule's requirements of "good faith" and a "rational basis." One district court, in the aberrant 1974 *Beecher* v. *Able* decision, held that a firm would violate the securities statutes if its projections were not based on facts that made the realization "highly probable." Had this standard been followed by other courts, it would, according to corporate law professor Ted Fiflis, have "practically [outlawed] forward-looking data for all but a few situations." Finally, the Advisory Committee observed, "Many companies would find it difficult, if not impossible, to prepare reasonable projections due to a lack of operating history, general economic factors, or industry conditions."[366]

The Advisory Committee's chairman, A. A. Sommer, among others, was not convinced by the committee's published arguments. He elsewhere wrote:

> Lurking in the Advisory Committe's conclusion that issuers should be encouraged to publish soft information is a strange and troubling anomaly. The Committee's recommendation appears to be premised on the conclusion that such information is important to investors, important enough that issuers should be pressed to disclose it. Yet the Committee recoiled from making such disclosure mandatory. With respect to information demonstrably less important to decision-making than forecasts, for example, compensation to top officers, the Commission had not refrained from laying down a flat requirement of disclosure. The Committee equivocated, and the Commission continues to equivocate, with respect to "soft" information. Eventually the Commission will have to face up to this inconsistency and the consequences of recognizing the materiality of such information.[367]

If, as is apparently the case, relatively few firms have voluntarily published earnings forecasts, and informal communication of forecasts to professional analysts continues, at times through the process euphemistically known as "guiding,"[368] a respectable case can be made for a mandatory projection program. Only a mandatory rule would permit all investors to have access to projections at the same time. Only a mandatory rule would provide investors with a basis for useful comparative firm evaluations. A mandatory rule would end the apparent unwillingness of the vast majority of firms to publish projections. A mandatory projection program, if effected through amendments to the securities laws, would provide a truly safe "safe harbor" rule and end the risk of such decisions as *Beecher* v. *Able*.[369]

* * *

It is appropriate to conclude with a last look at the SEC's corporate disclosure program. During the first four decades of the Commission's history, no aspect of the SEC's work was more strongly supported by affected industries than corporate disclosure; no program was less controversial. Even the critics of the SEC's mandated disclosure program paid homage to its popularity. Professor George Stigler, for example, in 1964 wrote:

> It is doubtful whether any other type of public regulation of economic activity has been so widely admired as the regulation of the securities markets by the Securities and Exchange Commission. The purpose of this regulation is to increase the portion of truth in the world and to prevent or punish fraud, and who can defend ignorance or fraud? The Commission has led a scandal-free life as federal regulatory bodies go. It has been essentially a "technical" body, and has enjoyed the friendship, or at least avoided the enmity, of both political parties.[370]

In a similar vein, Professor Kripke conceded fifteen years later, "The Commission's approach to the content of disclosure has been accepted, with comparatively few exceptions . . . by the practicing professionals — accountants, lawyers, investment bankers."[371]

The administrative technique, popularized by the SEC, of regulating by mandated disclosure rather than by more direct government controls has had a profound influence on post–World War II legislation. The 1957 Civil Rights Act, the various air, water, and toxic substances pollution statutes, the Occupational Safety and Health Act, the Equal Employment Opportunity Act, the Truth in Lending Act, the Employee Retirement Income Security Act, and innumerable other federal statutes have employed the concept of mandatory disclosure.[372]

During the postwar period, the SEC's mandated disclosure program could be justified on the basis of three types of evidence. First, several SEC and academic studies demonstrated that at least during the early decades of the Commission's existence, the mandatory disclosure provisions of the 1933 Securities Act had led to a reduction in underwriter costs, a savings to investors that seemed to exceed the direct costs of registering a security with the SEC.[373] These data suggested that the 1933 and 1934 Securities Acts' disclosure provisions may have performed a significant role in preventing management conflicts of interest and self-favoritism. A 1969 SEC study explained:

> The registration process has sometimes been referred to as a house-cleaning: one of its most valuable consequences is the elimination of conflicts of interest and questionable business practices which, exposed to public view, have what Justice Frankfurter once termed "a shrinking quality." Many illustrations could be given; one representative example is provided by a paragraph from a recent '33 Act registration statement:
>
> "From time to time during the past three years, certain officers, directors, and stockholders received loan accommodation from (name of company), without interest, all of which loans were repaid by September 30, 1968. This practice has been discontinued and such loans will not be made in the future."[374]

A second category of evidence suggested that the securities laws had reduced, though not eliminated, securities fraud. The most persuasive compendium of such evidence was summarized in Chapter 10. Part III of the SEC's 1963 *Special Study* found that 99 of 107 SEC fraud actions in an eighteen-month period "involved issuers that were not subject to the continuous reporting requirements of the [1934] Exchange Act," powerfully suggesting the deterrent value of both securities laws' mandated disclosure requirements.

Finally, it was widely believed by those who participated in the securities markets that the SEC's disclosure programs had had some influence in increasing "investor confidence" in the securities markets, especially during the first two decades after World War II.[375] While this was opinion evidence, not subject to objective corroboration, the convictions of stock exchange officials, corporate issuers, and institutional investors that the SEC's mandatory disclosure program had helped increase the number of securities investors and the aggregate amount of securities investment were entitled to some weight.*

---

* Such evidence indicated that a persuasive case could have been made for the retention of some form of mandated disclosure program. But such evidence did not clearly suggest what specific data corporations should be compelled to disclose. Nor did the general case for a mandated corporate disclosure program address the question of which data should be disclosed by different types of corporations. Nor did the general case for mandated corporate disclosure at all address the issue of whether corporate disclosure should be decreased as the costs of disclosure rose.

Nevertheless, beginning in the 1960s, economic research on the investment process raised fundamental questions about the usefulness of the SEC's corporate disclosure program. Several studies appeared to corroborate the "efficient market" hypothesis, which, in its "semistrong form," posited that securities prices rapidly reflected all public information about the underlying security. Thus, efforts to acquire and analyze public data concerning firms could not be expected to yield superior investment results. The most dramatic corroboration of this theory appeared in several studies which documented that the professional investors who managed mutual funds did not outperform randomly selected investment portfolios. This suggested that the competition among mutual funds, other institutional investors, and sophisticated investors was so acute that, at least with respect to those securities followed by such investors, an efficient market did, in fact, function. For securities law, the crucial implication of the efficient market hypothesis was that securities prices theoretically would be the same regardless of whether most investors ever received or read mandatory corporate prospectuses and reports. All that was necessary was that a "sufficient" number of investors act on available public data.[376]

Similar fundamental questions were raised by what was called the "portfolio" theory. This theory suggested that since investment risk could be substantially reduced by diversification of an investment portfolio, the value of data concerning any individual security's risks or potential rewards was substantially reduced.[377]

Two libertarian economists, the University of Chicago's George Stigler and the University of Rochester's George Benston, attempted to corroborate a more sweeping hypothesis: that there was no value whatsoever to the mandatory disclosures required by the 1933 and 1934 Securities Acts. In 1964, Stigler published a study comparing the performance of a sample of new-issue stock prices during the years 1923–1928 (before the enactment of the 1933 Securities Act) and 1949–1955 (after enactment). Finding no significant differences in new-issue prices relative to market prices in the two periods, Stigler concluded that "the SEC registration requirements had no important effect on the quality of new securities sold to the public." Data errors in Stigler's research and some highly debatable inferences he drew from his study "substantially invalidated" Stigler's conclusion, in the words of Wharton School professor Morris Mendelson and the opinion of others.[378]

Professor Benston's numerous articles concerning the SEC's mandatory disclosure program presented a more detailed critique. Of most significance was a 1973 Benston article entitled "Required Disclosure and the Stock Market: An Evaluation of the Securities Exchange Act of 1934." In this article, Benston combined historical and empirical research to attempt to demonstrate "that the disclosure requirements of the Securities Exchange Act of 1934 had no measurable positive effect on the securities traded on the NYSE. There appears to have been little basis for the legislation and no evidence that it was needed or desirable."

Benston propounded several arguments to justify his conclusion. He argued that the 1934 act's mandatory disclosures were not necessary for securities traded on the New York Stock Exchange:

> Prior to the passage of the Securities Exchange Act, corporations could disclose what they wished to their current and potential stockholders and, if they were listed on the New York Stock Exchange (NYSE), American, Chicago (Midwest), or other regional exchanges, had to submit balance sheets and income statements to the Exchange . . .
>
> One could . . . argue that the disclosure policy followed by corporations in the absence of legislation is in the best interests of their stockholders. If management believed that the marginal revenue to the stockholders as a group from disclosure would exceed the marginal cost of preparing and supplying the information, they would disclose their financial and other data.

Next, Benston suggested that the 1934 Securities Exchange Act did not deter much securities fraud. His argument was that little fraud existed before the law was enacted. He wrote:

> A search of the available literature, including the Senate and House hearings on the proposed securities legislation, fails to reveal much evidence of fraud in the preparation or dissemination of financial statements prior to 1934. For example, Wiley Rich, the author of a comprehensive survey of the legal responsibilities of accountants, states that "an extensive search has revealed not a single American case in which a public accountant has been held liable in a crime for fraud."

Echoing the efficient market hypothesis, Benston then published the results of a study to illustrate that the financial data published in the disclosure documents required by the 1934 act "on average" were not "timely or relevant" when published. A second study purported to demonstrate that the mandated disclosure of corporate sales figures "were of no apparent value to investors."[379]

Several economists have criticized the appropriateness of Benston's studies, the quality of his research designs, and his analysis of his empirical findings.[380] The economists, however, generally ignored the rather glaring deficiencies of Benston's historical research. In particular, Benston's suggestion that there was little securities fraud before 1934 was ludicrous. His "search of the available literature" apparently did not lead him to read of a single enforcement action brought by any of the forty-seven states that enacted blue sky securities regulation laws between 1911 and 1933. Yet in the year 1932, the State of New York alone secured injunctions against 1522 persons and firms and instituted 146 criminal prosecutions.* [381]

But the cumulative significance of economic theories such as the "efficient market hypothesis" and "portfolio theory" and the Stigler and Benston critiques did prompt the SEC, during the chairmanship of Roderick Hills, to appoint A. A. Sommer to chair an Advisory Committee on Corporate Disclosure. Joining Sommer on the committee were John Burton, securities attorneys Arthur Fleischer, Alan Levenson, and Martin Lipton; accountants Ray Groves and Frank Weston; investment analysts Deborah Kelly, Robert Malin, and David Norr; public interest representative Elliot Weiss; financial executive Victor Brown; investment manager Warren Buffet; economics professor William Beaver; law professor Homer Kripke; business school professor Roger Murray, and business school dean Harold Williams, who was to succeed Hills as SEC chairman.

The principal achievement of the Sommer Committee was to publish a rationale for a mandatory corporate disclosure system that took into account the recent economics literature. With only Professor Kripke publishing a dissent, a majority of the committee members concurred in the statement: "The disclosure system established by the Congress in the Securities Act of 1933 and the Securities Exchange Act of 1934, as implemented and developed by the Securities and Exchange Commission . . . is sound and does not need radical reform or renovation."

The Sommer Committee's majority began with the premise that "reliable and timely information sufficient to the needs of those who have the responsibility for the allocation of investment [capital] resources is essential to the efficient allocation of resources in any economy."

Could sufficient data be compiled in the absence of a mandatory

---

* Benston also did not analyze the significance of the Post Office Department's pre–1934 securities fraud enforcement actions, common law securities fraud civil cases, or even such notorious events as the Pecora hearings' revelations of the material factual omissions in the National City Company's Peruvian bond sales.

disclosure system? "It has been suggested," the committee's report noted,

> that this [information] can be assured through market forces. Essentially the argument is this. At the present time, securities markets are characterized by the presence of a large number of professionals who are constantly seeking out information from corporations . . . These analysts have an interest in securing reliable information on a timely basis and, it is agreed, it is often in the interest of issuers to provide that information to them. The latter's interest derives, it is said, from a desire to have a good market for the company's securities, the necessities of tapping the public market for financing, the benefits of a corporate image that reflects integrity and honesty in dealing with the public, and the awareness that a failure of disclosure or misrepresentations would have an adverse effect upon all of these desired benefits.

The report offered four grounds for doubting that market forces alone would result in the publication of sufficient, reliable, and timely data. First, "very often there are significant motives for at least temporary concealment of adverse information on the part of corporate executives. Often a sizable part of management's total compensation, such as benefits from stock options or stock bonus plans, depends upon the price levels of the company's securities." Second, the actual experiences of many financial analysts led them to believe that in the absence of requirements imposed by federal law they would be seriously handicapped in securing corporate data.

> They frequently cited as an example their difficulties prior to 1969, when the Commission first mandated segmented disclosure, in securing useful information with respect to the various constituent parts of a conglomerate business . . . They cite too the difficulties that they have experienced in many cases in securing from management estimates with respect to earnings, information concerning management's plans (especially capital spending plans) and objectives, and similar types of information which are regarded by virtually all classes of investors as useful to their decision-making.

Third, even if analyst interest could prompt disclosure of adequate firm data, the vast majority of publicly traded securities were not followed by analysts. Finally, securities analysts sought information for themselves and their customers: "They do not regard themselves as surrogates for the universe of investors and hence do not feel under obligation to disseminate widely information which they secure."

This last point underlined a key deficiency of reliance on market forces to bring into the market sufficient, reliable, timely information. Such a system likely would subvert small investors' confidence in the securities markets. If the informational advantages of professional investors were enhanced, probably fewer unsophisticated investors would feel confident that they had a fair or equal opportunity to profit in the securities markets.

Nor did the Sommer Committee report express the belief that the efficient market hypothesis, even if valid, remedied these market imperfections. It stated:

> The efficient market hypothesis, as commonly articulated, is indifferent to the quantity and quality of information that is available to investors. The market price of a security reflects true information and false information with equal efficiency . . . Thus, a fraudulent income statement, not known to be false, will be reflected in the market price of the security to the same extent as a true one.

Admittedly, much of the information published in mandatory corporate documents was redundant and at best confirmed information that earlier had been disseminated by other media. But the report concluded that the mandatory system still played a pivotal role in ensuring the initial corporate disclosure through whatever means and in ensuring the accuracy of the data disclosed.

> The Committee recognizes that the portion of the corporate disclosure system administered by the Securities and Exchange Commission satisfies *directly* the needs of only a small proportion of the users of company-originated information in investment decision-making. Most investors, particularly those customarily referred to as individual investors, secure their information from a host of sources that present, format, summarize, and simplify in varying degrees and ways in an effort to secure the favor and patronage of various classes of users. These privately operated sources of information are extremely important parts of the total disclosure system, for they provide accessibility, both from the dissemination standpoint and the understandability standpoint.
>
> These sources of information are the beneficiaries of the Commission disclosure system and without that system their activities would be severely hampered. Much of the information that they disseminate they secure from Commission filings. Further, the mandatory disclosure system, with its possible penalties not only for misstatements and omissions in filed material but in other corporate disclosures as well, provides a high degree of assurance that all information furnished by corporations, privately and publicly, outside filings as well as in them, will be responsible and accurate.[382]

The report was vulnerable to the criticism that it did not effectively analyze the costs and benefits of specific corporate disclosure items. As Kripke stated in his dissent, "The Committee never went beyond the conclusion that some mandatory disclosure was needed, to the question 'How much?'"[383] The report also was not notably successful in resolving the difficult question of how the SEC should respond to the greater proportionate cost burden of small firms. Although the committee sympathized with the small firms' plight, it did not effectively address the question of whether the SEC should reduce small firm mandatory disclosure requirements, given historical data indicating that a large number of securities fraud violations were proven against small firms not subject to the SEC's mandatory disclosure system.[384] But, that said, the Advisory Committee on Corporate Disclosure did provide an articulate defense for mandatory corporate disclosure.

*   *   *

As the Commission neared completion of its first half-century, its reputation as "an outstanding example of the independent commission at its best" remained intact. Although the wisdom of specific policies of the SEC reasonably could be doubted, the overall value of the agency reasonably could not be. In reducing securities fraud and unfairness through its corporate disclosure and enforcement programs, restructuring the public utility industry, and eliminating anticompetitive practices in the stock markets, the SEC had made signal contributions to the nation's financial system. Its history well illustrated the usefulness of a well-administered federal regulatory agency. By dint of the Commission's vigilance, Wall Street, indeed, has been transformed.

Notes

IN THE INTEREST of brevity, a few self-explanatory abbreviated references have been employed. For example, the House Interstate and Foreign Commerce Committee is referred to as the House Commerce Committee. Similarly, the Senate Banking and Currency Committee is referred to as the Senate Banking Committee; the BNA *Securities Regulation and Law Report* is called the BNA *Securities Reporter*. Notes on magazine articles often do not cite the author and title of an article, but merely the magazine, date, and page numbers.

I studied several collections of papers in researching this book. In most instances the citation specifies the physical location of the collection. In addition, let me note that the Franklin Delano Roosevelt papers are stored in Hyde Park, New York. The Carter Glass papers are stored at the University of Virginia, Charlottesville, Virginia. The John Fitzgerald Kennedy Library is in Boston, Massachusetts.

The documents that the Securities and Exchange Commission made available to me were held in several different places within the Commission. The *SEC Minutes* were held by the Commission's Office of the Secretary. The papers of SEC commissioners who served between 1934 and 1963 were held by the SEC Records Section under the supervision of Nathan Harrison. Throughout the notes, these papers are identified by commissioner and container number (e.g., Kennedy SEC Commissioner Files, Container No. 1). When I began my research, there were two collections of Manuel Cohen papers. In the SEC library were approximately 170 bound volumes of Cohen's papers concerning securities legislation. These papers are cited in the notes by volume and item number. The balance of Cohen's papers, approximately twenty-five boxes of materials, were held by the law firm of Wilmer, Cutler & Pickering.

These papers are identified in the notes as Cohen SEC Papers. They
were organized by topic but not otherwise identified. At my suggestion, the SEC, which earlier had declined to accept Cohen's non-
securities legislation–related papers, decided to accept them and
also store them in the Commission library. The firm of Wilmer,
Cutler & Pickering graciously donated them. Cohen's papers were
the most comprehensive and useful of all the collections I employed
in preparing this history.

The speeches of SEC officials and certain other documents are
cited as "on file with the SEC." This means they are in the SEC
library. All other SEC documents used are identified by their holder.
For example, certain accounting-related materials are noted as being
"on file with the Office of the Chief Accountant."

In requesting access to SEC papers, I usually wrote the SEC's
General Counsel. At no time did I make a formal Freedom of Information Act request. In a letter responding to my last document
request, Mr. George Fitzsimmons, Secretary to the Commission,
informed me:

> As you know, the Commission has granted you access to materials
> you have heretofore requested without imposing any condition upon
> access, the material requested in the past being of strictly historical
> interest. However, you now seek access to materials concerning is-
> sues of current interest. Because of this the Commission must be
> sensitive to the Freedom of Information Act which generally requires
> that when an agency makes available a record to one member of the
> public it must make the record equally available to all. *Department of
> the Air Force* v. *Rose*, 425 U.S. 352 (1976).

CHAPTER 1: After the Crash

1. "Stock Exchange Practices" Hearings before the Senate Banking Committee, 72nd and 73rd Congs. (1932–1934) (hereinafter, Stock Exchange
Practices Hearings).

2. "Stock Exchange Practices Report," Senate Report No. 1455, 73rd
Cong., 2nd Sess. (1934) (hereinafter "Stock Exchange Practices Report") p. 7;
"Federal Supervision of Traffic in Investment Securities in Interstate Com-
merce," House Report No. 85, 73rd Cong., 1st Sess. (1933), p. 2; and Samuel
Morison, *The Oxford History of the American People*, vol. 3 (New York:
New American Library, 1972), p. 286.

3. A number of works earlier described this period, among them John
Kenneth Galbraith, *The Great Crash*, 3rd ed. (Boston: Houghton Mifflin,
1972); Robert Sobel, *The Great Bull Market* (New York: W. W. Norton,
1968); Herbert Hoover, *Memoirs: The Great Depression* (New York, Macmillan, 1952); John Brooks, *Once in Golconda* (New York: Harper & Row,

1969); Arthur Schlesinger, Jr., *The Crisis of the Old Order* (Boston: Houghton Mifflin, 1957); Frederick Lewis Allen, *Only Yesterday* (New York: Harper & Row, 1931); Twentieth Century Fund, *Stock Market Control* (New York, Appleton-Century, 1934); and John T. Flynn, *Security Speculation* (New York: Harcourt, Brace, 1934).

4. Hoover, *Memoirs: The Great Depression*, pp. 5–14.

5. Herbert Hoover, *Memoirs: The Cabinet and the Presidency* (New York: Macmillan, 1952), pp. 203–204; and Schlesinger, *The Crisis of the Old Order*, p. 88.

6. Hoover, *Memoirs: The Cabinet and the Presidency*, p. 204; and Hoover, *Memoirs: The Great Depression*, pp. 19–20.

7. Hoover, *Memoirs: The Great Depression*, p. 16. The Federal Reserve Board's two February statements are excerpted in Galbraith, *The Great Crash*, pp. 38–39.

8. William Starr Myers and Walter H. Newton, *The Hoover Administration* (New York: Scribner's, 1936), p. 14.

9. Galbraith, *The Great Crash*, pp. 40–43.

10. Ibid., pp. 42–43; and Myers and Newton, *The Hoover Administration*, p. 15.

11. Myers and Newton, *The Hoover Administration*, p. 15–16.

12. Hoover, *Memoirs: The Great Depression*, p. 9.

13. Myers and Newton, *The Hoover Administration*, p. 23.

14. Hoover, *Memoirs: The Great Depression*, pp. 43–45. For a tongue-in-cheek account of these "do-no-business" conferences, see Galbraith, *The Great Crash*, pp. 142–146. *New York Times* accounts appeared on Nov. 23, 1929, pp. 1 and 4, Nov. 24, 1929, I, p. 2, and Nov. 25, 1929, p. 1.

15. Hoover, *Memoirs: The Great Depression*, pp. 30–31.

16. Ray Lyman Wilbur and Arthur Mastick Hyde, *The Hoover Policies* (New York: Scribner's, 1937), p. 347; and Hoover, *Memoirs: The Great Depression*, p. 126.

17. *Congressional Record*, 71st Cong., 1st Sess., Nov. 1, 1929, p. 5063; and Myers and Newton, *The Hoover Administration*, p. 21.

18. The six bills were, in chronological order, H.R. 5060, 71st Cong., 1st Sess. (Nov. 11, 1929), H.R. 5412, 71st Cong., 1st Sess. (Nov. 21, 1929); H.R. 5658, 71st Cong., 2nd Sess. (Dec. 2, 1929); H.R. 6122, 71st Cong., 2nd Sess. (Dec. 3, 1929); H.R. 6985, 71st Cong., 2nd Sess. (Dec. 9, 1929); and S. 2846, 71st Cong., 2nd Sess. (Jan. 6, 1930).

19. Compare the 147-point drop in *New York Times* Average of 50 stocks between September 3, 1929, and November 13, 1929, with the 81-point gain between Nov. 13 and Apr. 10, 1930.

20. William Starr Myers, ed., *The State Papers and Other Public Writings of Herbert Hoover*, vol. 1 (Garden City, N.Y.: Doubleday, Doran, 1934), p. 154.

21. Hoover, *Memoirs: The Great Depression*, p. 57.

22. Allen, *Only Yesterday*, p. 283.

23. Hoover, *Memoirs: The Great Depression*, p. 58.

24. Allen, *Only Yesterday*, p. 284.

25. *New York Times*, June 17, 1930, p. 1, and June 23, 1930, p. 4.

26. See, e.g., H.R. 12171, 71st Cong., 2nd Sess. (May 5, 1930), discussed in the *Congressional Record*, May 6, 1930, pp. 8456–8457, and June 19, 1930, pp. 11228–11229.

27. Carter Glass, *An Adventure in Constructive Finance* (Garden City, New York: Doubleday, Page, 1927), p. 2; Carter Glass, "The Federal Reserve System Grossly Misused," *Review of Reviews*, September 1928, pp. 257–258; Rixey Smith and Norman Beasley, *Carter Glass: A Biography* (New York: Longmans, Green, 1939); James E. Palmer, *Carter Glass: Unreconstructed Rebel* (Roanoke, Va.: The Institute of American Biography, 1938); and James T. Patterson, *Congressional Conservatism and the New Deal* (Lexington: University of Kentucky Press, 1967), pp. 13–21.

28. Hoover, *Memoirs: The Great Depression*, p. 121.

29. S. 4723, 71st Cong., 2nd Sess. (1930).

30. *Congressional Record*, 71st Cong., 2nd Sess., June 16, 1930, pp. 10874–10879. On background of State Department system, see Vincent Carosso, *Investment Banking in America* (Cambridge: Harvard University Press, 1970), pp. 248–249.

31. Senate Doc. No. 187, 71st Cong., 2nd Sess. (1930).

32. *Congressional Record*, 71st Cong., 2nd Sess., June 25, 1930, p. 11647; and *Congressional Record*, 71st Cong., 3rd Sess., Feb. 26, 1931, p. 6103. See also David Saul Levin, "Regulating the Securities Industry: The Evolution of a Government Policy," Ph.D. dissertation, Columbia University, 1969, pp. 68–70.

33. *New York Times*, Oct. 15, 1930, p. 1, and Oct. 16, 1930, p. 25; and Myers and Newton, *The Hoover Administration*, pp. 51–52.

34. Hoover, *Memoirs: The Great Depression*, p. 17.

35. *New York Times*, May 27, 1931, p. 39, June 6, 1931, p. 26, and July 1, 1931, p. 44.

36. *New York Times*, Sept. 24, 1931, p. 1.

37. Whitney's Hartford speech was reprinted in Stock Exchange Practices Hearings, 72nd Cong., pp. 187–193.

38. Each of the following bills was presented on Dec. 8, 9, or 10 of the 1st Sess. of the 72nd Cong.: H.R. 4, H.R. 5, H.R. 348, H.R. 4604, H.R. 4638, H.R. 4639, H.R. 4642, S. 127, S. 1309, and S. 1311.

39. S. 1309 and S. 1311.

40. S. 127.

41. *New York Times*, Oct. 1, 1931, p. 15.

42. A brief biography of Senator Johnson appears in the *Dictionary of American Biography*, Supplement Three (New York: Scribner's, 1973), pp. 393–398.

43. The text of Senate Resolution 19 appears on pp. 1–2 of "Sale of Foreign Bonds or Securities in the United States," Hearings before the Committee on Finance, U.S. Senate, 72nd Cong., 1st Sess. (1931–1932) (hereinafter referred to as Foreign Bond Hearings). See also, *Congressional Record*, 72nd Cong., 1st Sess., Dec. 9, 1931, p. 213, and Dec. 10, 1931, p. 271.

44. *Congressional Record*, 72nd Cong., 1st Sess., March 15, 1932, p. 6052.

45. "Stock Exchange Practices Report," p. 89.

46. Bureau of the Census, *Historical Statistics of the United States: Colonial Times to 1970*, vol. 2, p. 1006, tables concerning corporate securities issues and state and government issues.

47. Henry Doyle, "Investors' Losses in South America," *Current History*, February 1932, pp. 720–721; Foreign Bonds Hearings, pp. 324–327 and 395; *Congressional Record*, 72nd Cong., 1st Sess., March 15, 1932, p. 6057.

48. Foreign Bond Hearings, pp. 615–616, 621–622, 852, 1273–1274, and 1356.

49. Ibid., p. 743; and *Congressional Record*, 72nd Cong., 1st Sess., March 15, 1932, pp. 6054–6055 and 6057.

50. Foreign Bond Hearings, pp. 1279–1280 and 1772–1773; *Congressional Record*, 72nd Cong., 1st Sess., March 15, 1932, p. 6060.

51. Foreign Bond Hearings, pp. 1953 and 1971.

52. Ibid., pp. 1295, 1297, 1309, 1362–1365, 1500, and 1772–1773.

53. Ibid., pp. 1911 and 1903. The Department of Commerce also was criticized. See Ibid., pp. 727 and 748. But see also pp. 1620–1621.

54. Mellon quoted in Hoover, *Memoirs: The Great Depression*, p. 30. Economic conditions in 1932 are described in Bureau of Census, *Historical Statistics of the United States: Colonial Times to 1970*, vol. 1, pp. 135, 235, 228; and vol. 2, pp. 666 and 1006. See also Brooks, *Once in Golconda*, p. 137; and Frederick Lewis Allen, *The Lords of Creation* (New York: Harper & Brothers, 1935), pp. 416–418.

55. Hoover, *Memoirs: The Great Depression*, p. 126; and Levin, "Regulating the Securities Industry," pp. 116–117.

56. *New York Times*, Feb. 19, 1932, pp. 1 and 2; "Short-Selling of Securities," Hearings before the House Judiciary Committee, 72nd Cong., 1st Sess. (1932) (hereinafter Short-Sale Hearings), p. 121; *Business Week*, March 2, 1932, p. 7; and *Wall Street Journal*, Feb. 26, 1932, p. 1.

57. Hoover's warning was reprinted in Wilbur and Hyde, *The Hoover Policies*, p. 344.

58. *New York Times*, Apr. 28, 1949, p. 31; and *The National Cyclopedia of American Biography*, vol. 17 (New York: James White, 1958), p. 57.

59. Hoover, *Memoirs: The Great Depression*, p. 127; Wilbur and Hyde, *The Hoover Policies*, pp. 345–346; and *New York Times*, Feb. 27, 1932, p. 2.

60. Hoover, *Memoirs: The Great Depression*, p. 127; *New York Times*, Feb. 27, 1932, p. 2, Feb. 28, 1929, II, p. 1, Feb. 29, 1932, p. 2, March 2, 1932, p. 1, March 4, 1932, p. 2, and March 5, 1932, pp. 1 and 5; *Washington Post*, March 4, 1932, p. 4; *Barron's*, March 7, 1932, p. 16; Brooks, *Once in Golconda*, pp. 137–140; and John T. Flynn, "Wall Street Medicine," *Collier's*, Nov. 11, 1933, pp. 12–13.

61. *New York Times*, March 2, 1932, p. 1.

62. *New York Times*, March 4, 1932, p. 2, March 5, 1932, p. 1, and March 6, 1932, p. 2.

63. *New York Times*, March 8, 1932, p. 32, March 10, 1932, p. 31, March 12, 1932, p. 21, and Apr. 5, 1932, p. 18.

64. Levin, "Regulating the Securities Industry," pp. 125–128; Ralph De Bedts, *The New Deal's SEC* (New York: Columbia University Press, 1964), p. 18.

65. *New York Times*, Apr. 9, 1932, pp. 1–2, and Apr. 11, 1932, p. 1.

66. Gilbert Fite, *Peter Norbeck: Prairie Statesman* (Columbia: University of Missouri Press, 1948); John T. Flynn, "The Marines Land in Wall Street," *Harper's Monthly* magazine, July 1934, pp. 148–149; and Flynn, "Wall Street Medicine," *Collier's*, Nov. 11, 1933, pp. 12–13.

67. Fite, *Peter Norbeck*, pp. 173–174; and *New York Times*, Apr. 5, 1932, p. 18.

68. Stock Exchange Practices Hearings, 72nd Cong., pp. 1–106, especially pp. 16, 18, 32, and 43–44; and *New York Times*, Apr. 14, 1932, p. 33.

69. Stock Exchange Practices Hearings, 72nd Cong., pp. 107–288, especially pp. 111, 134, 145, 171–179, 219, 225, 253, and 277–279.

70. *New York Times*, Apr. 21, 1932, pp. 1 and 16, and Apr. 26, 1932, p. 2.

71. Levin, "Regulating the Securities Industry," p. 136.

72. *New York Times*, Apr. 22, 1932, p. 2.

73. *New York Times*, Apr. 26, 1932, p. 1; and *Commercial and Financial Chronicle*, Apr. 30, 1932, p. 3196.

74. Stock Exchange Practices Hearings, 72nd Cong., p. 307.

75. *New York Times*, Apr. 26, 1932, p. 1, and Apr. 27, 1932, p. 1; and Stock Exchange Practices Hearings, 72nd Cong., pp. 444–464.

76. *New York Times*, Apr. 28, 1932, p. 3.

77. Levin, "Regulating the Securities Industry," pp. 150–151.

78. Stock Exchange Practices Hearings, 72nd Cong., pp. 466–476, 493–494, and 518.

79. Ibid., pp. 627–653.

80. Ibid., pp. 677, 680, 685, and 689.

81. Ibid., pp. 985–987.

82. Ibid., pp. 712–749.

83. Levin, "Regulating the Securities Industry," pp. 172–173; and *New York Times*, June 18, 1932, p. 1.

84. *New York Times*, June 25, 1932, p. 19.

85. Fite, *Peter Norbeck*, pp. 178–179.

86. Myers, *The State Papers of Herbert Hoover*, vol. 2, p. 403.

87. *The Public Papers and Addresses of Franklin D. Roosevelt*, vol. 1 (New York: Random House, 1938), p. 653.

88. Kirk H. Porter and Donald Bruce Johnson, *National Party Platforms 1840–1968* (Urbana: University of Illinois Press, 1970), pp. 332–333.

89. *The Public Papers and Addresses of Franklin D. Roosevelt*, vol. 1, pp. 669–684.

90. Ibid., pp. 737–738 and 755.

91. *New York Times*, Nov. 18, 1932, p. 27.

92. Levin, "Regulating the Securities Industry," p. 190.

93. *New York Times*, Jan. 11, 1933, p. 3.

94. *New York Times*, Jan. 18, 1933, p. 3, and Jan. 19, 1933, pp. 1 and 6; and *Commercial and Financial Chronicle*, Jan. 28, 1933, pp. 586–588.

95. Levin, "Regulating the Securities Industry," p. 196.

96. *New York Times*, Jan. 25, 1933, p. 23, and May 21, 1933, VIII, p. 2; *Newsweek*, June 10, 1933, p. 16; Levin, "Regulating the Securities Industry," pp. 196–198; William Leuchtenburg, *Franklin D. Roosevelt and the New Deal* (New York: Harper & Row, 1963), p. 59; and De Bedts, *The New Deal's SEC*, p. 41.

97. *New York Times*, January 25, 1933, p. 23.

98. Levin, "Regulating the Securities Industry," p. 198.

99. Stock Exchange Practices Hearings, 72nd Cong., pp. 1401–1404, 1408–1409, 1434–1435, 1440, 1443–1444, 1454, 1460–1461, 1473–1474, 1483, 1489–1490, 1515–1516, 1529–1530, 1532, 1615–1617, 1620–1626, 1660–1661, and 1666; "Stock Exchange Practices Report," pp. 360–362; Ferdinand Pecora, *Wall Street Under Oath* (New York: Simon & Schuster, 1939), pp. 224–233; and Forrest McDonald, *Insull* (Chicago: University of Chicago Press, 1962), pp. 274–315.

100. See Carosso, *Investment Banking in America*, pp. 84–85, 97–98, and 271–281.

101. Pecora, *Wall Street Under Oath*, pp. 71–92; Allen, *The Lords of Creation*, pp. 311–315; Brooks, *Once in Golconda*, p. 101, Stock Exchange Practices Hearings, 72nd Cong., pp. 1774–1775 and 2028–2030; Bruce Barton, "Is There Anything Here That Other Men Couldn't Do?," *American* magazine, Feb. 1923, pp. 16 and 128–135; Bruce Barton, *The Man Nobody Knows* (Indianapolis: Bobbs-Merrill, 1924); Edmund Wilson, "Sunshine Charley," *New Republic*, June 28, 1933, pp. 59 and 177–178; and Charles Mitchell, "Sound Inflation," *Magazine of Wall Street*, June 9, 1917, pp. 295–296.

102. "Stock Exchange Practices Report," pp. 206–208.

103. Pecora, *Wall Street Under Oath*, pp. 127–129.

104. "Stock Exchange Practices Report," pp. 107–109.

105. Mitchell defense of salary quoted in George Thomas Washington and V. Henry Rothschild, *Compensating the Corporate Executive*, vol. 2 (New York: Ronald Press, 1962), p. 890. See also *Gallin* v. *National City Bank*, 281 N.Y. Supp. 795 (1935).

106. Stock Exchange Practices Hearings, 72nd Cong., pp. 1811–1814.

107. *New York Times*, Feb. 25, 1933, p. 1.

108. *New York Times*, Feb. 27, 1933, p. 1, and Feb. 28, 1933, p. 1.

109. Stock Exchange Practices Hearings, 72nd Cong., p. 1779.

110. "Stock Exchange Practices Report," pp. 126–131; Stock Exchange Practices Hearings, 72nd Cong., pp. 2058, 2061, and 2068–2069; and Pecora, *Wall Street Under Oath*, pp. 100–102.

111. "Stock Exchange Practices Report," pp. 168–171; Stock Exchange Practices Hearings, 72nd Cong., pp. 2000–2001 and 2022; and Pecora, *Wall Street Under Oath*, pp. 110–111.

112. "Stock Exchange Practices Report," pp. 214–215.

113. *Literary Digest*, March 11, 1933, pp. 11–12; and Leuchtenburg, *Franklin D. Roosevelt and the New Deal*, p. 22.

114. *The Public Papers and Addresses of Franklin D. Roosevelt*, vol. 2, p. 12.

115. Ibid., pp. 64–65.

116. *New York Times*, March 14, 1933, p. 1.

117. Ibid., p. 1.

118. *New York Times*, March 15, 1933, p. 9, and March 18, 1933, p. 1.

119. *Newsweek*, Apr. 1, 1933, p. 23.

120. Wayne Flynt, *Duncan Upshaw Fletcher, Dixie's Reluctant Progressive* (Tallahassee: Florida State University Press, 1971), p. 169.

121. Ibid., pp. 50 and 170; and De Bedts, *The New Deal's SEC*, pp. 41–42.

122. *New York Times*, May 6, 1933, p. 1; *New Republic*, June 7, 1933, p. 98; and Ernest K. Lindley, *The Roosevelt Revolution* (New York: Viking Press, 1933), pp. 138–143.

123. William Harbaugh, *Lawyer's Lawyer: The Life of John W. Davis* (New York: Oxford University Press, 1973), p. 318.

124. Levin, "Regulating the Securities Industry," p. 232.

125. Harbaugh, *Lawyer's Lawyer*, p. 322.

126. Ibid., p. 322; and *New York Times*, March 31, 1933, p. 1. See also Brooks, *Once in Golconda*, pp. 182–183.

127. The text of Senate Resolution 56 appears in Stock Exchange Practices Hearings, 73rd Cong., pp. 1–2.

128. New York Times, Apr. 5, 1933, p. 7.

129. Stock Exchange Practices Hearings, 73rd Cong., pp. 3, 4, 18, 76, and 189.

130. New York Times, May 24, 1933, p. 1; *Literary Digest,* June 10, 1933, p. 3; *New Republic,* June 7, 1933, p. 98; *Newsweek,* June 3, 1933, p. 1; *Time,* June 5, 1933, pp. 51–56; Lindley, *The Roosevelt Revolution,* pp. 138–143; Pecora, *Wall Street Under Oath,* pp. 4–5; and Levin, "Regulating the Securities Industry," p. 231.

131. Edwin P. Hoyt, *The House of Morgan* (New York: Dodd, Mead, 1966), pp. 333–395; *Dictionary of American Biography,* Supplement Three (New York: Scribner's, 1973), pp. 537–538; *New York Times,* March 13, 1943, pp. 1 and 7; and Brooks, *Once in Golconda,* pp. 43–49.

132. Stock Exchange Practices Hearings, 73rd Cong., pp. 29–32, 166–167, and 406; Pecora, *Wall Street Under Oath,* pp. 6–19 and 36–40; and Carosso, *Investment Banking in America,* p. 256.

133. Stock Exchange Practices Hearings, 73rd Cong., pp. 3–6.

134. Harbaugh, *Lawyer's Lawyer,* p. 324.

135. Pecora, *Wall Street Under Oath,* p. 5; and Stock Exchange Practices Hearings, 73rd Cong., pp. 3–6.

136. Stock Exchange Practices Hearings, 73rd Cong., pp. 22, 42–44, 47–49, 53, 72–74, 80, and 879; "Stock Exchange Practices Report," pp. 329–331; *New York Times,* May 24, 1933, p. 1, and June 2, 1933, p. 1; and Harbaugh, *Lawyer's Lawyer,* pp. 327–330. See also Brooks, *Once in Golconda,* p. 191.

137. Stock Exchange Practices Hearings, 73rd Cong., pp. 138–140, 143, 153–155, 172–175, 190–191, 220–221, 370–373, 824, and 826–827; "Stock Exchange Practices Report," pp. 101–105; Pecora, *Wall Street Under Oath,* pp. 27–35; and *New York Times,* May 25, 1933, pp. 14–15.

138. Stock Exchange Practices Hearings, 73rd Cong., pp. 307–323, 328–329, 332–334, 339, 364, 370–373, 378–383, 412, 444–455, 468, and 491–497; Flynn, *Security Speculation,* pp. 155–157; Pecora, *Wall Street Under Oath,* pp. 21–25; and Note, "High Finance in the 'Twenties: The United Corporation," 37 *Columbia Law Review,* pp. 785–815 (1937).

139. New York Times, May 27, 1933, p. 12; *New York Herald Tribune,* May 26, 1933, p. 21; *Literary Digest,* June 10, 1933, pp. 4–5, and *Business Week,* June 7, 1933, p. 32.

140. New York Times, May 26, 1933, p. 1; and *New Republic,* June 7, 1933, p. 98.

141. Senate Resolution No. 93, *Congressional Record,* 73rd Cong., 1st Sess., June 8, 1933, p. 5233.

142. The Public Papers and Addresses of Franklin D. Roosevelt, vol. 2, pp. 213–214.

CHAPTER 2: Frankfurter's Turn

1. Adolf A. Berle, "High Finance: Master or Servant." 23 *Yale Review,* p. 43 (1933).

2. Raymond Moley, *After Seven Years* (New York: Harper & Row, 1939), pp. 23–24 and 370–371; and Raymond Moley, *The First New Deal* (New York: Harcourt, Brace & World, 1966), p. 225.

3. Moley, *The First New Deal*, pp. 306 and 314.

4. Raymond Moley, "An N.R.A. for Finance," *Today* magazine, Dec. 30, 1933, p. 13.

5. R. G. Tugwell, *The Brains Trust* (New York: Viking Press, 1968), pp. 277–278 and 525–528; and R. G. Tugwell, *The Industrial Discipline and the Governmental Arts* (New York: Columbia University Press, 1933), pp. 203–207. See also Bernard Sternsher, *Rexford Tugwell and the New Deal* (New Brunswick: Rutgers University Press, 1964); and Ellis Hawley, *The New Deal and the Problem of Monopoly* (Princeton: Princeton University Press, 1966), especially pp. 43–46.

6. Adolf A. Berle, *Navigating the Rapids* (New York: Harcourt Brace Jovanovich, 1973), p. 47. See, generally, pp. 45–48, 55, and 58–59.

7. Besides statements in Chapter 2, see also Berle, *Navigating the Rapids*, pp. 53–55; and Tugwell, *The Brains Trust*, pp. 409–410 and 473–474.

8. Louis D. Brandeis, *Other People's Money* (New York: Frederick A. Stokes, 1914).

9. A classic study of these statutes appears in Justice Brandeis's dissent in *Liggett Co.* v. *Lee*, 288 U.S. 517 (1933). See, also, Adolf Berle and Gardiner Means, *The Modern Corporation and Private Property*, revised edition (New York: Harcourt, Brace & World, 1968), pp. 119–128; and Ralph Nader, Mark Green, and Joel Seligman, *Taming the Giant Corporation* (New York: W. W. Norton, 1976), pp. 33–61.

10. Berle and Means, *The Modern Corporation and Private Property*, pp. 131–132 and 142.

11. See Ibid., pp. 143–146; William Z. Ripley, *Main Street and Wall Street* (Boston: Little, Brown, 1927), pp. 46–54; James Bonbright, "The Dangers of Shares Without Par Value," 24 *Columbia Law Review*, p. 449 (1924); and Adolf Berle, "Problems of No-Par Stock," 25 *Columbia Law Review*, p. 43 (1925).

12. Bonbright, "The Dangers of Shares Without Par Value," 24 *Columbia Law Review*, pp. 452–453; Ripley, *Main Street and Wall Street*, pp. 192–193; Nader, Green, and Seligman, *Taming the Giant Corporation*, pp. 45–46; and Vincent Carosso, *Investment Banking in America* (Cambridge: Harvard University Press, 1970), pp. 76–77.

13. Adolf Berle, "Corporations and the Public Investor," 20 *American Economic Review*, p. 62 (1930); Note, "High Finance in the Twenties: The United Corporation (II)." 37 *Columbia Law Review*, pp. 968–969 (1937); and Berle and Means, *The Modern Corporation and Private Property*, pp. 133–135 and 160–163. Pre-emptive rights were judicially created in the case of *Gray* v. *Portland Bank*, 3 Massachusetts 363 (1807). The Delaware provision that made them discretionary was *Del. Laws* 1927, c. 85, Sec. 5.

14. Adolf Berle, "Investors and the Revised Delaware Corporation Act," 29 *Columbia Law Review*, pp. 570–573 (1929); Berle and Means, *The Modern Corporation and Private Property*, pp. 164–167; and Note, "High Finance in the Twenties: The United Corporation (II)," 37 *Columbia Law Review*, pp. 974–976.

15. Berle, "Investors and the Revised Delaware Corporation Act," 29

Columbia Law Review, pp. 565–567; and Berle and Means, *The Modern Corporation and Private Property*, pp. 167–169.

   16. Berle, "Corporations and the Public Investor," 20 *American Economic Review*, p. 65.

   17. Louis Loss and Edward Cowett, *Blue Sky Law* (Boston: Little, Brown, 1958), pp. 7–10; Michael Parrish, *Securities Regulation and the New Deal* (New Haven: Yale University Press, 1970), pp. 6–7; Edward Willett, "The Securities Act of 1933," Ph.D. dissertation, Princeton University, 1939, pp. 58–62; David Saul Levin, "Regulating the Securities Industry," Ph.D. dissertation, Columbia University, 1969, pp. 25–27; and Carosso, *Investment Banking in America*, pp. 163 and 189. The Kansas statute may be found in *Kansas Laws 1911*, Chapter 133.

   18. See discussion in Loss and Cowett, *Blue Sky Law*, pp. 10–13.

   19. Louis Loss, *Securities Regulation* (Boston: Little, Brown, 1961), p. 30; and Loss and Cowett, *Blue Sky Law*, p. 17.

   20. Parrish, *Securities Regulation and the New Deal*, p. 29; Department of Commerce, "A Study of the Economic and Legal Aspects of the Proposed Federal Securities Act," appearing in "Federal Securities Act" Hearings, House Commerce Committee, 73rd Cong., 1st Sess. [1933] (hereinafter, "A Study of the Economic and Legal Aspects of the Proposed Federal Securities Act"), p. 100; and testimony of Robert Healy, "Federal Securities Act" Hearings, pp. 228–230.

   21. Parrish, *Securities Regulation and the New Deal*, pp. 21–28; and Carosso, *Investment Banking in America*, pp. 165–173.

   22. Loss, *Securities Regulation*, pp. 32–33, 64–67, and 106–107; Parrish, *Securities Regulation and the New Deal*, pp. 29–30; Forrest Ashby, *The Economic Effects of Blue Sky Laws* (Philadelphia: University of Pennsylvania, 1926), pp. 46–47; and "A Study of the Economic and Legal Aspects of the Proposed Federal Securities Act," p. 96.

   23. Parrish, *Securities Regulation and the New Deal*, pp. 28–29; Homer Cherrington, *The Investor and the Securities Act* (Washington, D.C.: American Council on Public Affairs, 1942), p. 56; and Ashby, *The Economic Effects of Blue Sky Laws*, pp. 43–45. See also Loss, *Securities Regulation*, pp. 105–106.

   24. Compare testimony of William Breed, Counsel, Investment Bankers Association, in "Federal Securities Act" Hearings, House Commerce Committee, 73rd Cong., 1st Sess. (1933), p. 166, with Cherrington, *The Investor and the Securities Act*, p. 52.

   25. The requirements as of 1930 are set out in J. Edward Meeker, *The Work of the Stock Exchange* (New York: Ronald Press, 1930), pp. 549–567.

   26. The English Companies Act in effect in 1933 may be found in 19 and 20 George V c. 23. Among others, President Roosevelt stated: "The Securities Act was modeled on the British Companies Act," *Roosevelt Press Conferences*, vol. 2, pp. 347–348. Similar statements were made by James Landis in "The Legislative History of the Securities Act of 1933," 28 *George Washington Law Review*, p. 34 (1959).

   27. Ripley, *Main Street and Wall Street*, p. 210. See also pp. 213–214.

   28. Berle quoted in Rudolph Weissman, *The New Wall Street* (New York: Harper & Brothers, 1939), p. 111.

   29. "Stock Exchange Practices Report," Senate Report No. 1455, 73rd

Cong., 2nd Sess. (1934) (hereinafter, "Stock Exchange Practices Report"), pp. 68–70. See also Ripley, *Main Street and Wall Street*, pp. 213–214.

30. "Stock Exchange Practices Report," pp. 70–73; and Parrish, *Securities Regulation and the New Deal*, pp. 39–40.

31. Twentieth Century Fund, *The Security Markets* (New York: Twentieth Century Fund, 1935), pp. 590–591. See also Meeker, *The Work of the Stock Exchange*, pp. 560–561.

32. In 1926, George O. May declared the practice of having audits "had become almost universal." May quoted in David Hawkins, "The Development of Modern Financial Reporting Practices Among American Manufacturing Corporations," 37 *Business History Review*, p. 156 (1963). A more conservative estimate of 85 percent of the companies that are listed on the exchanges in New York was offered by Col. A. H. Carter, President, New York State Society of Certified Public Accountants, in testimony at "Securities Act" Hearings, Senate Banking Committee, 73rd Cong., 1st Sess. (1933), pp. 56 and 60.

33. Hawkins, "The Development of Modern Financial Reporting Practices Among American Manufacturing Corporations," 37 *Business History Review*, pp. 135–162; Frank P. Smith, "Accounting Requirements of Stock Exchanges 1933," 17 *Accounting Review*, pp. 145–148 (1937); Ripley, *Main Street and Wall Street*, pp. 156–208; Twentieth Century Fund, *The Security Markets*, pp. 579–609; and Parrish, *Securities Regulation and the New Deal*, pp. 40–41.

34. Robert Healy, chief counsel, FTC, "Federal Securities Act" Hearings, House Commerce Committee, 73rd Cong., 1st Sess. (1933), p. 231.

35. Hoxsey speech quoted in Twentieth Century Fund, *The Security Markets*, pp. 587–588, n. 2.

36. Hawkins, "The Development of Modern Financial Reporting Practices Among American Manufacturing Corporations," 37 *Business History Review*, p. 161.

37. Ibid., p. 161.

38. Testimony of Robert Healy, "Federal Securities Act" Hearings, House Commerce Committee, 73rd Cong., 1st Sess. (1933), p. 232; and Berle and Means, *The Modern Corporation and Private Property*, pp. 135–138; both describing Section 31 of the Delaware General Corporation Law as revised in March 1929.

39. Twentieth Century Fund, *The Security Markets*, p. 581.

40. Report of the Capital Issues Committee to the House Committee on Ways and Means, 65th Cong., 3rd Sess., House Doc. No. 1485 (Dec. 2, 1918); Report of the Capital Issues Committee to the House Committee on Ways and Means, 65th Cong., 3rd Sess., House Doc. No. 1836 (Feb. 28, 1919); and Woodbury Willoughby, *The Capital Issues Committee and War Finance Corporation* (Baltimore: Johns Hopkins University Press, 1934). See also Loss, *Securities Regulation*, pp. 112–116; and Carosso, *Investment Banking in America*, pp. 230–234 and 354.

41. See passage from Wilson's Aug. 8, 1919, Message to Congress quoted in "Federal Securities Act" Hearings, House Commerce Committee, 73rd Cong., 1st Sess. (1933), p. 91.

42. See discussion in Loss, *Securities Regulation*, pp. 116–117, especially n. 14; and Willett, "The Securities Act of 1933," pp. 75–80.

43. The Dennison bill was the subject of extensive hearings in the 67th Congress. See House Commerce Committee Hearings on H.R. 7215. See discussion in Willett, "The Securities Act of 1933," pp. 79–80; Cherrington, *The Investor and the Securities Act*, pp. 47–51; and "A Study of the Economic and Legal Aspects of the Proposed Federal Securities Act," pp. 101–102.

44. Telegram to Hon. Franklin D. Roosevelt, Roosevelt Papers, PPF 1333.

45. Parrish, *Securities Regulation and the New Deal*, pp. 45–46; Carosso, *Investment Banking in America*, pp. 354–355; Cherrington, *The Investor and the Securities Act*, p. 43; "A Study of the Economic and Legal Aspects of the Proposed Federal Securities Act," p. 103; and Huston Thompson, "Regulation of the Sale of Securities in Interstate Commerce," 9 *American Bar Association Journal*, p. 157 (1923).

46. Letters to Franklin D. Roosevelt, from Thompson, June 11, 1932, and July 7, 1932. Huston Thompson Papers, Container No. 3, Library of Congress.

47. Letter to Thompson from Norris, April 8, 1933, Huston Thompson Papers, Container No. 3, Library of Congress; and Huston Thompson Diary, April 21, 1933, Huston Thompson Papers, Container No. 1, Library of Congress.

48. Thompson letter to Roosevelt, November 25, 1932, Roosevelt Papers, PPF 1333.

49. Berle, *Navigating the Rapids*, pp. 77–78; and Moley, *After Seven Years*, p. 176.

50. Moley, *After Seven Years*, pp. 83–84 and 165–166; and Moley, *The First New Deal*, p. 232.

51. Moley, *After Seven Years*, pp. 176–177; Moley, *The First New Deal*, pp. 308–309; Frank Freidel, *Franklin D. Roosevelt: Launching the New Deal* (Boston: Little, Brown, 1973), pp. 77 and 341–343; and "The Legend of Landis," *Fortune*, Aug. 1934, p. 118.

52. A copy dated Apr. 2 may be found in the Felix Frankfurter Papers, Reel 7, Microfilm collection, Harvard Law School.

53. Moley, *After Seven Years*, p. 177.

54. Ibid., p. 177; Moley, *The First New Deal*, p. 310; Freidel, *Franklin D. Roosevelt: Launching the New Deal*, p. 342; "The Legend of Landis," *Fortune*, Aug. 1934, p. 118; and Parrish, *Securities Regulation and the New Deal*, pp. 44–47.

55. Moley, *After Seven Years*, pp. 165–166; and Moley, *The First New Deal*, p. 232

56. Huston Thompson Diary, March 13, 1933, Huston Thompson Papers, Container No. 1, Library of Congress. See also background paper prepared by Thompson, Miller, and Butler, "A Study of the Economic and Legal Aspects of the Proposed Federal Securities Act," pp. 87–111; and Parrish, *Securities Regulation and the New Deal*, pp. 44–51.

57. Huston Thompson Diary, March 19 and 20, 1933, Huston Thompson Papers, Container No. 1, Library of Congress.

58. Ibid., March 21, 1933; and *New York Times*, March 24, 1933, p. 11.

59. Huston Thompson Diary, March 19, 1933, Huston Thompson Papers, Container No. 1, Library of Congress.

60. Ibid.; Moley, *The First New Deal*, p. 311; and Moley, *After Seven Years*, pp. 177–178.

61. The changes requested and made are described in a letter to Franklin D. Roosevelt from Huston Thompson, March 28, 1933, Roosevelt Papers, OF 242, and in Huston Thompson Diary, March 20, 1933, Huston Thompson Papers, Container No. 1, Library of Congress. See also Parrish, *Securities Regulation and the New Deal*, pp. 46–47.

62. *Congressional Record*, 73rd Cong., 1st Sess., March 29, 1933, pp. 937 and 954. The accompanying message was reprinted in innumerable sources, including "Federal Securities Act" Hearings, House Commerce Committee, 73rd Cong., 1st Sess. (1933), p. 1.

63. *New York Times*, March 31, 1933, p. 1.

64. *Wall Street Journal*, March 31, 1933, p. 1.

65. *Barron's*, April 3, 1933, p. 10.

66. The text of the Thompson bill, H.R. 4314, as originally submitted appears in "Federal Securities Act" Hearings, House Commerce Committee, 73rd Cong., 1st Sess. (1933), pp. 1–9. An accompanying analysis of the bill, made by Thompson, Miller, and Butler, appears at pp. 107–111. In addition, the testimony of Thompson, Miller, and Butler amplifies their analysis of the bill; see pp. 130 and 133, where Butler explains why there is no prior approval of securities, and Thompson testimony, pp. 53 and 57–58, regarding the revocation provision. On p. 213, Thompson states that he was authorized by President Roosevelt to say that "the President is in favor of revocation as expressed in Section Six, Page 12, House bill No. 4314; that he did not attempt to or intend his message to Congress to convey any more than the general statement regarding the bill." Two useful analyses of Thompson's bill are Landis, "The Legislative History of the Securities Act of 1933," 28 *George Washington Law Review*, pp. 30–33, and Parrish, *Securities Regulation and the New Deal*, pp. 47–51.

67. Dwight Dorrough, *Mr. Sam* (New York: Random House, 1962); Alfred Steinberg, *Sam Rayburn: A Biography* (New York: Hawthorne Books, 1975); and Raymond Moley, *Masters of Politics* (New York: Funk & Wagnalls, 1949), pp. 242–249. For a brief description of the regulation of railroad securities by the ICC, see Loss, *Securities Regulation*, pp. 118–119.

68. Remark of the chairman (Rayburn) on p. 43, "Federal Securities Act" Hearings, House Commerce Committee, 73rd Cong., 1st Sess. (1933).

69. Ibid., pp. 9–87, 116–146, and 209–228. On amount of "worthless or undesirable securities," see pp. 80 and 91; on failure of blue sky laws, see especially pp. 10 and 40.

70. Only near the conclusion of the second day of hearings did Rayburn announce arrangements to permit representatives of the investment bankers to testify more than briefly; Ibid., pp. 146–147. By that time Rayburn already had begun to lose faith in the bill; see his questions at pp. 133–137.

71. See Ibid., pp. 166–170, 178–181, 225–228, and 243–248; and Memorandum of Alexander I. Henderson and Arthur H. Dean, written to Rayburn, April 4, 1933, on H.R. 4314 (Thompson's bill), a copy of which may be found in a volume of legislative materials assembled by James Landis, "The Legislative Genesis of the 1933 Securities Act," in the Harvard Law School Library.

72. "Federal Securities Act" Hearings, House Commerce Committee, 73rd Cong., 1st Sess. (1933), p. 135.

73. *New York Times*, April 6, 1933, p. 3; Moley, *After Seven Years*, pp.

178–179; Freidel, *Franklin D. Roosevelt: Launching the New Deal*, pp. 346–347; and Parrish, *Securities Regulation and The New Deal*, pp. 56–57.

74. Moley, *The First New Deal*, p. 312; and Moley, *After Seven Years*, pp. 178–179.

75. See especially Thompson Diary quoted in Parrish, *Securities Regulation and the New Deal*, p. 57, n. 23; and *New York Times*, April 6, 1933, p. 3.

76. Letter to Landis from Frankfurter, March 23, 1933, Frankfurter Papers, Reel 7, Harvard Law School.

77. Frankfurter recommendation of Flexner quoted in Parrish, *Securities Regulation and the New Deal*, pp. 62–63.

78. Moley, *The First New Deal*, p. 312; Moley, *After Seven Years*, p. 179; and Frankfurter Diary, May 8, 1933, Frankfurter Papers, Container No. 1, Library of Congress.

79. Frankfurter Apr. 4 wire quoted in Liva Baker, *Felix Frankfurter* (New York: Coward, McCann, 1969), p. 155.

80. Huston Thompson Diary, May 5, 1933, Huston Thompson Papers, Container No. 1, Library of Congress.

81. Joseph Lash, *From the Diaries of Felix Frankfurter* (New York: W. W. Norton, 1975), pp. 44–47.

82. Frankfurter letter to Moley dated Nov. 16, 1935, Frankfurter Papers, Reel 4, Harvard Law School.

83. Felix Frankfurter and J. Forrester Davison, *Cases and Other Materials on Administrative Law* (New York: Commerce Clearing House, 1932), p. vii.

84. Act of July 2, 1890, Ch. 647, 26 *Stat.* 209.

85. The famous "rule of reason" decision was *Standard Oil Co. of New Jersey* v. *United States*, 221 U.S. 1 (1911).

86. Act of October 15, 1914, Ch. 322, 38 *Stat.* 730. The most significant loophole appeared in the merger provision — Section 7 — which originally restrained mergers effected by stock purchases, but was ineffective against asset acquisitions. Section 7 was amended in 1950 to cover asset acquisitions.

87. Felix Frankfurter, *The Public and Its Government* (New Haven: Yale University Press, 1930), p. 161.

88. Frankfurter letter to Douglas quoted in Parrish, *Securities Regulation and the New Deal*, p. 61.

89. Letter to Walter Lippmann quoted in Lash, *From the Diaries of Felix Frankfurter*, p. 53.

90. Frankfurter, *The Public and Its Government*, p. 152.

91. Frankfurter letter to Henry Stimson, quoted in Lash, *From the Diaries of Felix Frankfurter*, p. 53.

92. Frankfurter, *The Public and Its Government*, p. 144.

93. Frankfurter letter to Lippmann dated Apr. 17, 1933, Frankfurter Papers, Container No. 78, Library of Congress.

94. *The Reminiscences of James Landis* (Columbia University Oral History Research Office, 1964) (hereinafter, Landis, *Oral History*), pp. 1–146; "The Legend of Landis," *Fortune*, August 1934, pp. 44–47 and 118–120; and Donald Ritchie, *James M. Landis* (Cambridge: Harvard University Press, 1980).

95. James Landis, *The Administrative Process* (New Haven: Yale University Press, 1938), pp. 5, 12, 16, 19, 23–24, 30–31, 51, 62, 66–70, 75, 99, 116–119, 122, 142, and 155; and "Crucial Issues in Administrative Law," 53 *Harvard Law Review,* pp. 1077–1078 (1940). See also Landis, "Significance of Administrative Commissions in the Growth of the Law," 12 *Indiana Law Journal,* pp. 474–477 (1937).

96. Landis, "The Legislative History of the Securities Act of 1933," 28 *George Washington Law Review,* p. 34; William O. Douglas, *Go East, Young Man* (New York: Dell, 1974), p. 369; Parrish, *Securities Regulation and the New Deal,* p. 59; Frankfurter Diary, May 8, 1933, Frankfurter Papers, Container No. 1, Library of Congress.

97. Joseph Alsop and Robert Kintner, *Men Around the President* (New York: Doubleday, Doran, 1939), pp. 54–61; Parrish, *Securities Regulation and the New Deal,* pp. 59–60; and Hawley, *The New Deal and the Problem of Monopoly,* pp. 284–285.

98. Letter to Frankfurter from Cohen, Jan. 1, 1934, Frankfurter Papers, Container No. 115, Library of Congress; and letter to Frankfurter from Corcoran, Dec. 11, 1933, Frankfurter Papers, Container No. 116, Library of Congress.

99. Moley, *After Seven Years,* p. 181; but see somewhat different account in Moley, *The First New Deal,* p. 312. Frankfurter's own account appears in the May 8 entry in his diary; Frankfurter Papers, Container No. 1, Library of Congress.

100. Landis, "The Legislative History of the Securities Act of 1933," 28 *George Washington Law Review,* pp. 34–35; Landis, *Oral History,* pp. 159–161.

101. Landis, "The Legislative History of the Securities Act of 1933," 28 *George Washington Law Review,* pp. 36–37; and Landis, *Oral History,* pp. 161–162.

102. Huston Thompson Diary, April 7, 11, and 21, and May 5, 1933, Huston Thompson Papers, Container No. 1, Library of Congress.

103. Landis, "The Legislative History of the Securities Act of 1933," 28 *George Washington Law Review,* pp. 36–38; Landis, *Oral History,* pp. 161–164; and Ritchie, *James M. Landis,* p. 47.

104. Frankfurter telegram to Roosevelt dated Apr. 14, 1933, Felix Frankfurter Papers, Reel 7, Harvard Law School.

105. Frankfurter Apr. 17 letter to Roosevelt, Roosevelt Papers, PPF 140.

106. Frankfurter telegram to Cohen, April 14, 1933, and Frankfurter telegram to Moley, April 14, 1933, both Frankfurter Papers, Reel 7, Harvard Law School.

107. Landis, "The Legislative History of the Securities Act of 1933," 28 *George Washington Law Review,* pp. 37–38; and Parrish, *Securities Regulation and the New Deal,* pp. 64–65.

108. Letter to Manuel Cohen from James Landis, Cohen SEC Papers, vol. 41, item 7.

109. Landis, "The Legislative History of the Securities Act of 1933," 28 *George Washington Law Review,* pp. 38–41; Landis, *Oral History,* pp. 164–167; Parrish, *Securities Regulation and the New Deal,* pp. 66–68; Moley, *The First New Deal,* pp. 312–313; and Moley, *After Seven Years,* p. 181.

110. *Congressional Record,* 73rd Cong., 1st Sess., May 3, 1933, p. 2838.

111. *Congressional Record*, 73rd Cong., 1st Sess., May 4, 1933, p. 2907. See also Landis, "The Legislative History of the Securities Act of 1933," 28 *George Washington Law Review*, p. 41.

112. *Congressional Record*, 73rd Cong., 1st Sess., May 5, 1933, pp. 2910–2954; Rayburn's conclusion, p. 2919; Congressman Greenwood, pp. 2913–2914; enactment, p. 2954; and *New York Times*, May 6, 1933, p. 1.

113. Letter to Landis from Cohen, May 5, 1933, Landis Papers, Container No. 4, Library of Congress. See also Landis, "The Legislative History of the Securities Act of 1933," 28 *George Washington Law Review*, p. 41.

114. Thompson testimony, "Securities Act" Hearings, Senate Banking Committee, 73rd Cong., 1st Sess. (1933), especially, pp. 98, 103–105, and 115–116. For list of changes made in Senate on Thompson bill, see Levin, "Regulating the Securities Industry," pp. 279–281.

115. *Congressional Record*, 73rd Cong., 1st Sess., May 8, 1933 p. 2978.

116. A detailed comparison of the House and Senate drafts appears in Landis, "Legislative Genesis of the 1933 Act."

117. "Securities Act" Hearings, Senate Banking Committee, 73rd Cong., 1st Sess. (1933), p. 145.

118. *Congressional Record*, 73rd Cong., 1st Sess., May 20, 1933, p. 3801.

119. Night letter, Frankfurter to Moley, Apr. 27, 1933, Frankfurter Papers, Reel 7, Harvard Law School.

120. Moley's view described in letter to Landis from Cohen, May 5, 1933, Landis Papers, Container No. 4, Library of Congress.

121. Moley acknowledged as much in his memoirs, *After Seven Years*, p. 181; and *The First New Deal*, p. 312. An interesting contemporaneous account of Moley's attitude appears in the Apr. 17, 1933 entry in the diary of James P. Warburg, *The Reminiscences of James P. Warburg* (Columbia University Oral History, 1952), p. 476. Warburg wrote, "I told Moley that I heard rather unpleasant reports concerning the new securities bill whereupon Moley flew off the handle and said that he was sick and tired of the yawping from interested parties in New York, that he had put the matter in Frankfurter's hands and must rely on Frankfurter to produce a good bill."

122. Telegram, Frankfurter Papers, Reel 7, Harvard Law School.

123. Moley, *The First New Deal*, p. 313.

124. Ibid., p. 313; Undated day letter from Frankfurter to Robinson, and Robinson letter to Frankfurter, May 9, 1933, both in Frankfurter Papers, Reel 7, Harvard Law School.

125. Undated day letter to Corcoran from Frankfurter, Frankfurter Papers, Reel 7, Harvard Law School.

126. *Congressional Record*, 73rd Cong., 1st Sess., May 8, 1933, pp. 2978–3000.

127. Letter to Louis Howe from Herbert Feis, Office of the Economic Adviser, Department of State, May 10, 1933, Roosevelt Papers, OF 100-B. A detailed discussion of Title II appears in Parrish, *Securities Regulation and the New Deal*, pp. 73–107.

128. Roosevelt letter to Senator Johnson, May 20, 1933, Roosevelt Papers, OF 242.

129. Robinson letter to Frankfurter, May 9, 1933, Frankfurter Papers, Reel 7, Harvard Law School.

130. Landis, "The Legislative History of the Securities Act of 1933," 28 *George Washington Law Review*, pp. 43–49; Landis, *Oral History*, pp. 169–

172; Parrish, *Securities Regulation and the New Deal*, p. 70; Levin, "Regulating the Securities Industry," pp. 286–292; Frankfurter letter to Moley, May 16, 1933, Frankfurter Papers, Reel 7, Harvard Law School; and Statement of Conferees, *Congressional Record*, 73rd Cong., 1st Sess., May 22, 1933, pp. 3900–3903.

131. Parrish, *Securities Regulation and the New Deal*, pp. 90–96.

132. Note, "High Finance in the Twenties (III)," 37 *Columbia Law Review*, pp. 1161–1170.

133. Fortune, Aug. 1933, pp. 53–55 and 106–111.

134. New Republic, Apr. 26, 1933, p. 309.

135. Moley, *The First New Deal*, p. 314.

136. Adolf A. Berle, "High Finance: Master or Servant," 23 *Yale Review*, p. 42.

137. William O. Douglas, "Protecting the Investor," 23 *Yale Review*, pp. 528–530 (1933). See also William O. Douglas and George Bates, "The Federal Securities Act of 1933," 43 *Yale Law Journal*, p. 171 (1933).

CHAPTER 3: "A Perfect Institution"

1. Whitney quoted in Joseph Alsop and Richard Kintner, "The Battle of the Market Place," *Saturday Evening Post*, June 11, 1938, p. 9.

2. SEC Press Release, Nov. 23, 1937, reprinted in William O. Douglas, *Democracy and Finance* (New Haven: Yale University Press, 1940), pp. 65 and 70.

3. "Stock Exchange Practices Report," Senate Report No. 1455, Senate Banking Committee, 73rd Cong., 2nd Sess. (1934) (hereinafter, "Stock Exchange Practices Report"), pp. 5–6; Twentieth Century Fund, *Stock Market Control* (New York: Appleton-Century, 1934), pp. 18–19; and John T. Flynn, *Security Speculation* (New York: Harcourt, Brace, 1934), p. 28.

4. J. Edward Meeker, *The Work of the Stock Exchange*, revised edition (New York: Ronald Press, 1930), pp. 443–444 and 63; and Flynn, *Security Speculation*, pp. 24–26.

5. "Stock Exchange Practices Report," pp. 23–25 and 47–50; Flynn, *Security Speculation*, pp. 68–69 and 229–242; Testimony of Richard Whitney, "National Securities Exchanges" Hearings, House Commerce Committee, 73rd Cong., 2nd Sess. (1934), (hereinafter, House Stock Exchange Practices Hearings), pp. 216–217; and Raymond Vernon, *The Regulation of Stock Exchange Members* (New York: Columbia University Press, 1941), pp. 58–96.

6. "Stock Exchange Practices Report," pp. 19–20 and 23; Flynn, *Security Speculation*, pp. 62–66 and 242–243; and House Stock Exchange Practices Hearings, p. 124.

7. "Stock Exchange Practices Report," p. 23; Flynn, *Security Speculation*, pp. 66 and 68; and Robert Sobel, *NYSE* (New York: Weybright & Talley, 1975), pp. 18–20.

8. Matthew Josephson, "Groton, Harvard, Wall Street," *New Yorker*, Apr. 2, 1932, pp. 19–22; *Literary Digest*, Apr. 23, 1932, pp. 42–43; and John Brooks, *Once in Golconda* (New York: Harper & Row, 1969), pp. 124–128, 130–132, and 142–143.

9. Whitney letter to Roosevelt, Apr. 14, 1933, in James Landis, *Legislative History of the 1934 Securities Exchange Act*, vol. 8 (Cambridge: Harvard Law Library, n.d.) and *New York Times*, Apr. 6, 1933, p. 3.

10. Vernon, *Regulation of Stock Exchange Members*, p. 18, and *New York Times*, Aug. 3, 1933, p. 1.

11. Letter to Duncan Fletcher from Roosevelt, March 26, 1934, Roosevelt Papers, OF 34.

12. *Literary Digest*, July 1, 1933, p. 6. In 1938 Mitchell settled a subsequent civil suit brought by the Internal Revenue Service. See Ferdinand Pecora, *Wall Street Under Oath* (New York: Simon & Schuster, 1939), p. 196.

13. Arthur Dean, "The Federal Securities Act: I," *Fortune*, Aug. 1933, pp. 104 and 106.

14. *New York Times*, Oct. 31, 1933, p. 29.

15. Letter to Roosevelt from R. C. Leffingwell, Jan. 4, 1934, Roosevelt Papers, PPF 886.

16. *Roosevelt Press Conferences*, vol. 2, Oct. 18, 1933, pp. 347–348, and Dec. 6, 1933, p. 514.

17. Pecora's account appears in Pecora, *Wall Street Under Oath*, pp. 131–187.

18. Letter to Felix Frankfurter from Thomas Corcoran, Sept. 8, 1933, Frankfurter Papers, Reel 10, Harvard Law School; and Michael Parrish, *Securities Regulation and the New Deal* (New Haven: Yale University Press, 1970), p. 187.

19. Letter to Roosevelt from Wallace, Sept. 2, 1933, Roosevelt Papers, OF 396.

20. David Saul Levin, "Regulating the Securities Industry: The Evolution of a Government Policy," Ph.D. dissertation, Columbia University, 1969, p. 326.

21. Ibid., p. 329.

22. *The Reminiscences of James Landis* (Columbia University Oral History Research Office, 1964) (hereinafter, Landis, *Oral History*), p. 177.

23. On early appointments, see letter to Roosevelt from Frankfurter, May 29, 1933, Frankfurter Papers, Container No. 97, Library of Congress; Frankfurter Memorandum for Roosevelt, June 24, 1933, Roosevelt Papers, OF 100B; Telegram to President from Frankfurter, June 10, 1933, Roosevelt Papers, PPF 140; Letter to President from Frankfurter, July 6, 1933, Roosevelt Papers, PPF 140; Day letter to Roosevelt from Frankfurter, July 14, 1933, Frankfurter Papers, Container No. 92, Library of Congress; and Telegram to President from Frankfurter, Sept. 26, 1933, Roosevelt Papers, PPF 140. On early approval of forms and registration statement, see Note to Missy Le Hand from Roosevelt, July 7, 1933, Roosevelt Papers, OF 100; Letter to Ray Stevens from Roosevelt, July 28, 1933, Roosevelt Papers, OF 100B; Letter to Frankfurter from Elwin Davis, July 8, 1933, Frankfurter Papers, Container No. 135, Library of Congress; Letter to Davis from Frankfurter, July 14, 1935, Frankfurter Papers, Container No. 135, Library of Congress; and Letter to Frankfurter from Davis, July 24, 1933, Frankfurter Papers, Container No. 135, Library of Congress.

24. Letter to Roosevelt from Frankfurter, July 6, 1933, Roosevelt Papers, PPF 140.

25. Letter to the President from Frankfurter, Oct. 1, 1933, Roosevelt Papers, Felix Frankfurter PSF.

26. Letter to Henry Stimson from Felix Frankfurter, December 19, 1933, Frankfurter Papers, Reel 25, Harvard Law Library.

27. Letter to Felix Frankfurter from Sam Rayburn, May 26, 1933, Frankfurter Papers, Reel 10, Harvard Law Library.

28. Letter to Roosevelt from Charles March, Roosevelt Papers, OF 100; Letter to Roosevelt from Ray Stevens, Sept. 21, 1933, Roosevelt Papers, OF 100; and Telegram to Roosevelt from Frankfurter, September 26, 1933, Roosevelt Papers, PPF 140.

29. Landis, *Oral History* p. 177.

30. Landis address to New York State Accountants reprinted in *Commercial and Finance Chronicle,* Nov. 4, 1933, p. 3243.

31. *New York Times,* Dec. 3, 1933, p. 1, and Oct. 11, 1933, p. 33; and Jesse Jones, *Fifty Billion Dollars* (New York: Macmillan, 1951), p. 31.

32. Letter to the President from Henry Bruere, Oct. 27, 1933, Landis, *Legislative History of the 1934 Securities Exchange Act,* vol. 8.

33. Henry Bruere Memorandum, Oct. 29, 1933, Roosevelt Papers, OF 213.

34. Letter to the President from Bruere, Nov. 18, 1933, Roosevelt Papers, OF 21.

35. Letter to Roosevelt from Daniel Roper, Nov. 25, 1933, Roosevelt Papers, OF 242.

36. Letter to Landis from Roosevelt, Nov. 14, 1933, Landis Papers, Container No. 149, Library of Congress.

37. See, e.g., Arthur Schlesinger, Jr., *The Coming of the New Deal* (Boston: Houghton Mifflin, 1958), p. 425; and Letter to Roosevelt from Daniel Roper, Nov. 25, 1933, Roosevelt Papers, OF 242.

38. *New York Times,* May 18, 1933, p. 7.

39. *New York Times,* Oct. 7, 1933, p. 30.

40. Letter to Roosevelt from Roper, Feb. 2, 1934, Roosevelt Papers, OF 242. The majority report was signed by Dickinson and Richardson, since Landis and Dean withdrew from the final deliberations of the committee because of their leading public roles in the debate. Berle dissented. The full "Report to Secretary of Commerce of Committee on Stock Exchange Regulation" also is in the Roosevelt Papers, OF 242.

41. Memorandum included in Landis, *The Legislative History of the 1934 Securities Exchange Act,* vol. 8.

42. Memorandum included in Ibid., vol. 2.

43. Letter to Roosevelt from Landis, Nov. 24, 1933, Roosevelt Papers, OF 100.

44. Levin, "Regulating the Securities Industry," pp. 338–339; and *New York Times,* Dec. 5, 1933, p. 35.

45. Letter to President from Landis, December 4, 1933, Landis Papers, Box 9, File 5, Harvard Law School. On background of meeting, see also Landis, *Oral History,* pp. 197–198. Landis later admitted, "The Securities Act of 1933 in its original form did hamper the normal flow of capital into enterprise." But this "was due less to the provisions of the original act than to their misinterpretation, deliberate to a great degree, by widely publicized utterances of persons prominent in the financial world together with their

lawyers." James Landis, "The Legislative History of the Securities Act of 1933," 28 *George Washington Law Review* p. 40, n. 18 (1959).

46. *New York Times,* Dec. 7, 1933, p. 2, and Dec. 14, 1933, p. 35.

47. *Wall Street Journal,* Dec. 13, 1933, p. 1. Privately Landis also wrote Rayburn the same day, volunteering to be "at your service in this matter." Letter to Rayburn from Landis, Dec. 13, 1933, Landis Papers, Box 9, File 2, Harvard Law School.

48. Much of Stokes work can be found in Landis, *The Legislative History of the 1934 Securities Exchange Act,* vol. 2. See, also, Levin, "Regulating the Securities Industry," pp. 347–348.

49. Raymond Moley, *After Seven Years* (New York: Harper & Row, 1939), p. 284. See, also, Raymond Moley, *The First New Deal* (New York: Harcourt, Brace & World, 1966), p. 517.

50. *New York Times,* Dec. 3, 1933, p. 1.

51. Landis, *Legislative History of the 1934 Securities Exchange Act,* vol. 2.

52. The Dickinson report was reprinted in several periodicals, including *Commercial and Financial Chronicle,* Feb. 10, 1934, pp. 925–930.

53. *New York Times,* Feb. 4, 1934, p. 5.

54. Donald A. Ritchie, "The Legislative Impact of the Pecora Investigation," *Capital Studies,* Fall 1977, vol. 5, p. 97; and Landis, *Legislative History of the 1934 Securities Exchange Act,* vol. 2.

55. *Congressional Record,* 73rd Cong., 2nd Sess., Feb. 9, 1934, p. 2264, and Feb. 10, 1934, p. 2356.

56. *New York Times,* Feb. 10, 1934, p. 1; *Nation,* Feb. 28, 1934, p. 250; and *Newsweek,* Feb. 17, 1934, p. 26.

57. See Roosevelt letter to Rayburn, March 26, 1934, reprinted in Report No. 1383, House of Representatives, 73rd Cong., 2nd Sess. (1934), p. 2.

58. *Congressional Record,* 73rd Cong., 2nd Sess., Feb. 9, 1934, pp. 2264–2272, and Feb. 10, 1934, p. 2378.

59. *New York Times,* Feb. 10, 1934, p. 1.

60. A copy of the bill appears on pp. 1–15 in House Stock Exchange Practices Hearings. Corcoran's testimony concerning margin loans appear in those Hearings on p. 94; concerning segregation provisions at pp. 123–124 and 130–131, and concerning proxies on p. 140. Regarding segregation, see also Parrish, *Securities Regulation and the New Deal,* p. 119. Corcoran in the House hearings on p. 134, and Pecora, *Wall Street Under Oath,* p. 269, among others, referred to the insider-trading sections as "anti-Wiggin" provisions.

61. *Roosevelt Press Conferences,* vol. 3, Feb. 28, 1934, pp. 210–211. The Senate Banking Committee stated, "The cure for our corporate ailments, circumvention of the law, investment-trust and holding-company abuses, and interlocking directorates may lie in a national incorporation act," on p. 391, "Stock Exchange Practices Report." The Twentieth Century Fund recommendation appeared in *Stock Market Control,* pp. 170–173; Dickinson's report stated "that, perhaps, the most effective way to deal with certain evils connected with manipulaton of stock by directors and officers, issue of stock to insiders for inadequate consideration, incomplete publicity of corporate accounts and similar problems is by the requirement of federal incorporation for corporations engaged in interstate commerce"; *Commerce and*

Financial Chronicle, Feb. 10, 1934, p. 926. The New York Stock Exchange's preference for a federal corporate law was expressed on numerous occasions; House Stock Exchange Practices Hearings, pp. 9, 163, 480, and 782, and "Stock Exchange Practices" Hearings, Senate Banking Committee, 73rd Cong., 2nd Sess. (1934) (hereinafter, Senate Stock Exchange Practices Hearings), pp. 6536, 6538, and 6939–6940.

62. Pecora prepared two contemporaneous accounts of the American Commercial pool. One appeared in the *Congressional Record*, 73rd Cong., 2nd Sess., May 7, 1934, pp. 8169–8174, the other in the "Stock Exchange Practices Report," pp. 55–69. See also pp. 189–203, and Levin, "Regulating the Securities Industry," pp. 369–370.

63. Ferdinand Pecora, "Wall Street Under the Flag," *Collier's*, March 30, 1935, p. 12.

64. Letter to Berle from Roosevelt, August 15, 1934 reprinted in Adolf Berle, *Navigating the Rapids* (New York: Harcourt Brace Jovanovich, 1973), pp. 103–104.

65. *New York Times*, Oct. 17, 1933, p. 31, Oct. 19, 1933, p. 12, and Oct. 31, 1933, p. 29; Alsop and Kintner, "The Battle of the Market Place," *Saturday Evening Post*, June 11, 1938, p. 9; and Pecora, "Wall Street Under the Flag," *Collier's*, March 30, 1935, pp. 12–13.

66. *New York Times*, Oct. 26, 1933, p. 29.

67. The rules are described in *New York Times*, Feb. 14, 1934, pp. 29 and 31.

68. Letter to Roosevelt from Whitney, February 8, 1934, Roosevelt Papers, PPF 1275.

69. Whitney's lobbying efforts are described in *New York Times*, Feb. 15, 1934, p. 27, Feb. 17, 1934, p. 21, and March 12, 1934, p. 1; Senate Stock Exchange Practices Hearings, pp. 7281–7286; *Commercial and Financial Chronicle*, March 31, 1934, p. 2170, and Apr. 14, 1934, p. 2501; *Congressional Record*, 73rd Cong., 2nd Sess., Apr. 30, 1934, pp. 7689, 7693–7697, May 2, 1934, pp. 7925 and 7934–7935, May 4, 1934, p. 8097, May 7, 1934, pp. 8196–8197; *Newsweek*, May 19, 1934, p. 27; Statement of the Board of Directors, U.S. Chamber of Commerce, March 3, 1934; and Statement of the Standard Tobacco Company, both in Carter Glass Papers, Box No. 329; "SEC," *Fortune*, June 1940, p. 123; and Letter to Roosevelt from Herbert Lehman, March 24, 1934, quoted in Ralph De Bedts, *The New Deal's SEC* (New York: Columbia University Press, 1964), p. 67.

70. House Stock Exchange Practices Hearings, pp. 152–155, 160, 186–187, 209, 211–212, and 214–215; and Senate Stock Exchange Practices Hearings, p. 6584.

71. House Stock Exchange Practices Hearings, pp. 237–238, 240, and 246.

72. Ibid., pp. 889–890.

73. Ibid., pp. 252, 272, 278–279, and 298.

74. Dean Witter, Ibid., p. 402; the Chamber of Commerce, Ibid., p. 440; The National Association of Manufacturers, Senate Stock Exchange Practices Hearings, pp. 7241–7243; The Investment Bankers Association, House Stock Exchange Practices Hearings, p. 595; The New York Curb Exchange, Ibid., p. 368; Lehman Brothers, Ibid., pp. 465–466; 18 other investment houses, p. 359; and Archibald Roosevelt, *Newsweek*, March 17, 1934, p. 30.

75. Alsop and Kintner, "The Battle of the Market Place," *Saturday Evening Post*, June 11, 1938, pp. 9 and 74–75; and "SEC," *Fortune*, June 1940, pp. 120 and 123.

76. House Stock Exchange Practices Hearings, pp. 312–315.

77. Ibid., pp. 508–511 and 543.

78. Senate Stock Exchange Practices Hearings, p. 6937.

79. Letter to Frankfurter from Landis, March 6, 1934, Frankfurter Papers, Container No. 117, Library of Congress.

80. *New York Times*, Feb. 28, 1934, pp. 1 and 2.

81. House Stock Exchange Practices Hearings, p. 395.

82. *New York Times*, March 6, 1934, p. 1.

83. *New York Times*, March 8, 1934, p. 1.

84. *New York Times*, March 9, 1934, p. 1.

85. Levin, "Regulating the Securities Industry," pp. 377–378; Parrish, *Securities Regulation and the New Deal*, pp. 121–122 and 124–127; *New York Times*, March 14, 1934, p. 27; Ritchie, "The Legislative Impact of the Pecora Investigation," *Capital Studies*, Fall 1977, vol. 5, p. 98.

86. The final compromise bill was introduced into the House on March 19, 1934; see *Congressional Record*, 73rd Cong., 2nd Sess., p. 4876. It next appears in House Stock Exchange Practices Hearings, pp. 625–644.

87. Landis memorandum concerning amendments to the 1933 Securities Act, March 9, 1934, Roosevelt Papers, OF 242; *Commercial and Financial Chronicle*, Apr. 21, 1934, pp. 2674–2675; Parrish, *Securities Regulation and the New Deal*, pp. 195–197; and Levin, "Regulating the Securities Industry," p. 398–400. See also Letter to Frankfurter from Landis, March 6, 1934, Frankfurter Papers, Container No. 117, Library of Congress.

88. House Stock Exchange Practices Hearings, pp. 701–704.

89. Ibid., p. 809.

90. Ibid., p. 845.

91. *New York Times*, Apr. 3, 1934, p. 1.

92. *The Press Conferences of President Roosevelt*, vol. 3, March 23, 1934, p. 256.

93. *New York Times*, March 14, 1934, p. 27.

94. A copy of the letter to Fletcher appears in Senate Stock Exchange Practices Hearings, pp. 7577–7578.

95. Testimony of Evans Clark, House Stock Exchange Practices Hearings, pp. 775–776; and letter to Fletcher from Bernheim, March 24, 1934, reprinted in *Congressional Record*, 73rd Cong., 2nd Sess., May 4, 1934, p. 8180.

96. House Stock Exchange Practices Hearings, p. 723.

97. Letter to Roosevelt from Whitney, April 12, 1934, Roosevelt Papers, OF 34.

98. Desvernine submitted a revised bill and accompanying memorandum, which can be found in Landis Papers, Container No. 150, Library of Congress.

99. Letter to Rayburn from Paul Shields, March 22, 1934, Roosevelt Papers, OF 34.

100. *New York Times*, Apr. 3, 1934, p. 4.

101. *New York Times*, May 7, 1934, p. 1.

102. Letter to Frankfurter from Corcoran, April 22, 1934, Frankfurter Papers, Container No. 116, Library of Congress; "SEC," *Fortune*, June 1940,

p. 120; House Stock Exchange Practices Hearings, pp. 759–770; *Congressional Record*, 73rd Cong., 2nd Sess., May 2, 1934, p. 7944; and Schlesinger, *The Coming of the New Deal*, pp. 457–459.

103. *New York Times*, Apr. 10, 1934, p. 1; and Apr. 15, 1934, II, p. 11; Senate Stock Exchange Practices Hearings, p. 7555; *Wall Street Journal*, April 10, 1934, p. 1; Parrish, *Securities Regulation and the New Deal*, pp. 133–136; and Levin, "Regulating the Securities Industry," pp. 389–391. See also Glass view of FTC members, *Congressional Record*, 73rd Cong., 2nd Sess., May 7, 1934, p. 8286.

104. *New York Times*, Apr. 12, 1934, p. 19.

105. House Report No. 1383, 73rd Cong., 2nd Sess. (1934), pp. 7–9. See also Parrish, *Securities Regulation and the New Deal*, pp. 137–138; and Levin, "Regulating the Securities Industry," pp. 391–394.

106. *Congressional Record*, 73rd Cong., 2nd Sess., Apr. 30, 1934, pp. 7693–7696, and May 4, 1934, p. 8116.

107. *Congressional Record*, 73rd Cong., 2nd Sess., May 12, 1934, pp. 8667–8669 and 8710.

108. Ibid., May 12, 1934, pp. 8711–8713.

109. Ibid., May 12, 1934, p. 8714; and *New York Times*, May 13, 1934, p. 1.

110. *New York Times*, May 16, 1934, p. 1, May 17, 1934, pp. 1 and 24, May 20, 1934, IV, p. 1, and May 26, 1934, p. 25; *Commercial and Financial Chronicle*, May 19, 1934, pp. 3360–3361; *Newsweek*, May 26, 1934, p. 24; *Roosevelt Press Conferences*, vol. 3, May 16, 1934, pp. 348–350; and Landis memorandum, "Reasons for Making the Federal Trade Commission the Administrative Agency for Securities Exchange Legislation," Carter Glass Papers, Box No. 316.

111. House Report No. 1838, 73rd Cong., 2nd Sess. (1934); and *Congressional Record*, 73rd Cong., 2nd Sess., June 1, 1934, pp. 10185 and 10269.

112. Donald Ritchie, *James M. Landis* (Cambridge: Harvard University Press, 1980), p. 59. See also *New York Times*, June 7, 1934, p. 7.

CHAPTER 4: Moley's Man

1. Corcoran testimony at "National Securities Exchanges" Hearings, House Commerce Committee, 73rd Cong., 2nd Sess. (1934) (hereinafter, House Stock Exchange Practices Hearings), p. 149.

2. *New York Times*, May 27, 1934, p. 1.

3. *Newsweek*, June 9, 1934, p. 28; see also *Newsweek*, May 12, 1934, p. 15, for a more tentative prediction.

4. *Time*, June 11, 1934, p. 62.

5. *Business Week*, June 9, 1934, pp. 9–10.

6. *Fortune*, Aug. 1934, pp. 44–47 and 118–120.

7. Corcoran letter to Frankfurter, addressed "Dear Horn and Tails," April 22, 1934, Frankfurter Papers, Container No. 116, Library of Congress.

8. Felix Frankfurter letter to Roosevelt, May 23, 1934, reprinted in Max Freedman, annotator, *Roosevelt and Frankfurter: Their Correspondence, 1928–1945* (Boston: Little, Brown, 1967), pp. 220–221.

9. House Stock Exchange Practices Hearings, pp. 906–909.

10. See, e.g., Securities Act of 1933 Releases Nos. 54 and 66 (1933).

11. Securities Act of 1933 Releases Nos. 26, 30, 32, 37, 58, 59, 60, 61, 62, 63, 72, 76, 90, 94, 103, 113, 130, 137, 139, 140, 141, 144, 156, 170, 171, and 187.

12. "The Legend of Landis," *Fortune*, Aug. 1934, pp. 44–47 and 118–120, was the basis for a number of subsequent newspaper accounts. On overwork, see also Felix Frankfurter letter to James Landis, March 17, 1934, Frankfurter Papers, Container No. 117, Library of Congress.

13. Thomas Corcoran letter to Felix Frankfurter, May 11, 1934, Frankfurter Papers, Container No. 116, Library of Congress.

14. Ibid.

15. James MacGregor Burns, *Roosevelt: The Lion and the Fox* (New York: Harcourt, Brace & World, 1956), pp. 183–208.

16. Arthur Schlesinger, Jr., *The Coming of the New Deal* (Boston: Houghton Mifflin, 1958), p. 503.

17. *The Public Papers and Addresses of Franklin D. Roosevelt*, vol. 3 (New York: Random House, 1938), pp. 439 and 438.

18. Raymond Moley, "And Now Give Us Good Men," *Today*, May 19, 1934, p. 12.

19. Raymond Moley, *The First New Deal* (New York: Harcourt, Brace & World, 1966), pp. 517–520; and Moley, *After Seven Years* (New York: Harper & Row, 1939), pp. 286–290.

20. Richard Whalen, *The Founding Father: The Story of Joseph P. Kennedy* (New York: New American Library, 1964), pp. 3–161; David Koskoff, *Joseph P. Kennedy: A Life and Times* (Englewood Cliffs, N.J.: Prentice-Hall, 1974), pp. 42–69; Moley, *The First New Deal*, pp. 379–382; Joseph P. Kennedy, *I'm for Roosevelt* (New York: Reynal & Hitchcock, 1936), pp. 7–8, 14–15, and 106–107; "Mr. Kennedy, the Chairman," *Fortune*, Sept. 1937, pp. 56–59 and 138–144; and Joseph P. Kennedy, "Big Business, What Now?," *Saturday Evening Post*, Jan. 16, 1937, pp. 10–11 and 78–82.

21. *Roosevelt Press Conferences*, vol. 3, June 29, 1934, p. 436.

22. Harold Ickes, *The Secret Diary of Harold Ickes: The First Thousand Days* (New York: Simon & Schuster, 1953), p. 173.

23. *New York Times*, June 28, 1934, p. 1.

24. *New York Times*, July 2, 1934, p. 29.

25. Whalen, *The Founding Father*, pp. 139–140; Moley, *After Seven Years*, pp. 287–288; Moley, *The First New Deal*, p. 519; and Koskoff, *Joseph P. Kennedy: A Life and Times*, p. 57.

26. *The Remiscences of James Landis* (Columbia University Oral History Research Office, 1964) (hereinafter, Landis, *Oral History*), pp. 191–193.

27. *New Republic*, July 11, 1934, p. 220.

28. *New Republic*, July 11, 1934, p. 236, and July 18, 1934, p. 265.

29. Frank quoted in Koskoff, *Joseph P. Kennedy: A Life and Times*, p. 59.

30. Theodore Knappen, "The Rulers of the Stock Market," *Magazine of Wall Street*, July 21, 1934, p. 329.

31. Moley, *After Seven Years*, p. 289.

32. Kennedy, *I'm For Roosevelt*, p. 97; *SEC Minutes*, Oct. 24, 1934, Oct. 26, 1934, Oct. 30, 1934, Dec. 10, 1934, and Jan. 1, 1935.

33. Whalen, *The Founding Father*, p. 388.

34. Letter to Frankfurter from Kennedy, July 31, 1934, Frankfurter Papers, Reel 10, Harvard Law School; and Landis memorandum concerning appointment of Ben Cohen to be SEC general counsel, Frankfurter Papers, Container No. 182, Library of Congress.

35. Joseph P. Kennedy telegrams to Frankfurter, Apr. 11 and 12, 1935, SEC Commissioners Files, Container No. 1.

36. Ferdinand Pecora, "Wall Street Under the Flag," *Collier's*, March 30, 1935, p. 60; *New York Times*, Dec. 21, 1934, p. 43, Jan. 15, 1935, p. 27, and Jan. 17, 1935, p. 32; and *Commercial and Financial Chronicle*, Sept. 22, 1934, pp. 1787–1788, and July 21, 1934, p. 362.

37. Ralph De Bedts, *The New Deal's SEC* (New York: Columbia University Press, 1964), pp. 92–94 and 103–104; M. L. Ramsay, *Pyramids of Power* (New York: Bobbs-Merrill, 1937), pp. 174–175; William O. Douglas, *Go East, Young Man* (New York: Dell, 1974), p. 266; and Chester Lane, *Oral History* (Columbia University, 1957), p. 239.

38. Douglas, *Go East, Young Man*, p. 266; De Bedts, *The New Deal's SEC*, pp. 92 and 102–103; and Knappen, "The Rulers of the Stock Market," *Magazine of Wall Street*, July 21, 1934, pp. 331 and 368.

39. Whalen, *The Founding Father*, pp. 156–157; and Ickes, *The Secret Diary of Harold Ickes: The First Thousand Days*; pp. 203, 206, 351, and 692.

40. Besides Krock articles noted throughout this chapter, see Arthur Krock, *Memoirs* (New York: Funk & Wagnalls, 1968), pp. 330–331.

41. All may be found in Kennedy's Sept. 1935 correspondence file, SEC Commissioners Files, Container No. 1.

42. *Congressional Record*, 73rd Cong., 2nd Sess., June 13, 1934, p. 11328; Landis letter to Roosevelt, June 14, 1934, Roosevelt Papers, OF 1060; *New York Times*, Jan. 10, 1935, p. 2, Jan. 11, 1935, p. 36, Jan. 12, 1935, p. 2, Jan. 13, 1935, II, p. 15, and Jan. 18, 1935, p. 3; and *Commercial and Financial Chronicle*, Jan. 12, 1935, p. 235.

43. *Commercial and Financial Chronicle*, July 27, 1934, p. 362; and *SEC Minutes*, July 16 and 17, 1934.

44. *SEC Minutes*, July 16, 1934; Whalen, *The Founding Father*, p. 150; *New York Times*, July 17, 1934, p. 29; and Burns Telegram to Frankfurter, May 10, 1935, Frankfurter Papers, Reel 10, Harvard Law School.

45. Landis memorandum concerning appointment of Ben Cohen to be SEC general counsel, Frankfurter Papers, Container No. 182, Library of Congress. See also Donald Ritchie, *James M. Landis* (Cambridge: Harvard University Press, 1980), pp. 59–60 and 63–64.

46. Landis, *Oral History*, pp. 232–233; Douglas, *Go East, Young Man*, pp. 258–259; and Letter to Landis from Douglas, July 12, 1934, Douglas Papers, Container No. 6, Library of Congress.

47. *SEC Minutes*, Nov. 7, 1934, July 1, 1935, and July 20, 1935. Clark, after agreeing to serve as an SEC trial examiner, later withdrew.

48. SEC *First Annual Report*, p. 38.

49. SEC *First Annual Report*, pp. 6–7.

50. Koskoff, *Joseph P. Kennedy: A Life and Times*, p. 62; Whalen, *The Founding Father*, p. 150; and *New York Times*, Sept. 18, 1934, p. 33.

51. Kennedy, *I'm for Roosevelt*, pp. 98–100; Joseph P. Kennedy, "Regulation of Security Exchanges," *Vital Speeches of the Day*, Dec. 17, 1934, pp. 187–191.

52. *Newsweek*, Aug. 4, 1934, p. 27.

53. The text of Kennedy's address was reprinted in *New York Times*, July 26, 1934, p. 13.

54. SEC *First Annual Report,* pp. 20–21; *Commercial and Financial Chronicle,* July 28, 1934, p. 522; *New York Times,* July 19, 1934, p. 27, July 21, 1934, p. 17, July 27, 1934, p. 23, Aug. 8, 1934, p. 29, Aug. 10, 1934, p. 28, Aug. 17, 1934, p. 23, Sept. 11, 1934, p. 29, Sept. 12, 1934, p. 40, Sept. 13, 1934, p. 13, and Sept. 14, 1934, p. 35; *SEC Minutes,* Nov. 27, 1934, and Nov. 28, 1934; and John J. Burns address to investment dinner of Financial Advertisers Association, Sept. 10, 1935, p. 4, on file at Harvard Law School.

55. Kennedy, *I'm For Roosevelt,* pp. 99–100.

56. Literary Digest, Sept. 29, 1934, p. 34; and *New York Times,* Sept. 19, 1934, p. 27. See Matthew Josephson's melodramatic and apparently inaccurate account of the visit in *Infidel in the Temple* (New York: Knopf, 1967), p. 308.

57. See, e.g., Whitney statements in *Commercial and Financial Chronicle,* July 28, 1934, p. 522, and Feb. 2, 1935, p. 719; *Literary Digest,* Nov. 24, 1934, p. 40; and *New York Times,* Feb. 8, 1935, p. 7.

58. New York Times, July 4, 1934, p. 25, and Jan. 20, 1935, IX, p. 2.

59. SEC Minutes, Oct. 1, 1934 (Kansas City Board of Trade), Oct. 5, 1934 (New York Mining Exchange), Oct. 16, 1934 (Los Angeles Curb Exchange), Nov. 22, 1934 (California Stock Exchange), June 21, 1935 (Merger of two Seattle Exchanges), July 29, 1935 (Pacific Stock Exchange), and Aug. 5, 1935 (Louisville Stock Exchange); *New York Times,* July 1, 1935, p. 31 (Boston Curb Exchange, Hartford Stock Exchange, and Philippine Stock Exchange). See also 1934 Securities Exchange Act Releases Nos. 62 (1934), 78 (1934), and 183 (1935); and Joseph P. Kennedy, "Shielding the Sheep," *Saturday Evening Post,* Jan. 18, 1936, pp. 64–68. The New York Produce Exchange's discontinuance of securities operations is described in 1934 Securities Exchange Act Release No. 76 (1935). The termination of unlisted trading on the Baltimore Stock Exchange is described in *SEC Minutes,* July 17, 1935.

60. SEC *First Annual Report,* p. 31.

61. Kennedy, "Shielding the Sheep," *Saturday Evening Post,* Jan. 18, 1936, pp. 64–68; and Joseph Alsop and Robert Kintner, "The Battle of the Market Place," *Saturday Evening Post,* June 11, 1938, p. 76.

62. SEC Minutes, Aug. 11, 1934, and Sept. 27, 1934; 1934 Securities Exchange Act Releases Nos. 5 and 18 (both 1934); and *New York Times,* Aug. 14, 1934, pp. 1 and 30, and Sept. 15, 1934, p. 21.

63. SEC Minutes, Aug. 28, 1934.

64. 1934 Securities Exchange Act Release No. 66 (1934); and *SEC Minutes,* Nov. 28, 1934, Dec. 5, 1934, Dec. 11, 1934, Dec. 12, 1934, Dec. 17, 1934, and Dec. 18, 1934.

65. SEC *First Annual Report,* pp. 17 and 24.

66. Felix Frankfurter letter to Roosevelt, November 21, 1934, Frankfurter Papers, Container No. 97, Library of Congress.

67. Compare 1933 Securities Act Release No. 224 (1934) with Release No. 299 (1935).

68. Kennedy, "Regulation of Security Exchanges," *Vital Speeches of the Day,* Dec. 17, 1934, p. 189.

69. SEC Minutes, Dec. 5, 1934.

70. New York Times, Dec. 9, 1934, IV, p. 1.

71. See, e.g., *SEC Minutes,* Dec. 12, 1934, Jan. 4, 1935, Jan. 10, 1935, Jan. 11, 1935, and Jan. 12, 1935.

72. *New York Times*, Jan. 14, 1935, p. 1; *Commercial and Financial Chronicle*, Jan. 19, 1935, p. 382; and 1933 Act Release No. 276 (1935).

73. Ritchie, *James M. Landis*, p. 66.

74. Address of Joseph P. Kennedy at Union League Club of Chicago, Feb. 8, 1935, on file at the SEC.

75. Kennedy address to the American Arbitration Association, March 19, 1935, reprinted in full in 1933 Securities Act Release No. 317 (1935).

76. *SEC Minutes*, February 1, 1935.

77. 1933 Securities Act Release No. 308 (1935).

78. *SEC Minutes*, July 18, 1935.

79. *New York Times*, March 8, 1935, p. 1; and 1933 Securities Act Release No. 322 (1935).

80. *SEC Minutes*, Feb. 28, 1935.

81. Paul R. Gourrich, "Investment Banking Methods prior to and since the Securities Act of 1933," 4 *Law and Contemporary Problems*, p. 69 (1937).

82. Ibid., p. 69. See also Louis Loss, *Securities Regulation* (Boston: Little, Brown, 1961), pp. 370–373; and Vincent Carosso, *Investment Banking in America* (Cambridge: Harvard University Press, 1970), pp. 395–396.

83. 1933 Securities Act Release No. 389 (1935).

84. 1933 Securities Act Release No. 328 (1935).

85. Kennedy, March 19, 1935, speech, quoted in 1933 Securities Act Release No. 317 (1935).

86. 1933 Securities Act Releases No. 381, 458, and 470 (1935); and R. W. Goldschmidt, "Registration under the Securities Act of 1933," 4 *Law and Contemporary Problems*, p. 28 (1937).

87. *New York Times*, March 8, 1935, p. 20.

88. *New Republic*, Oct. 9, 1935, p. 244.

89. *Time*, July 22, 1935, p. 41. See also March 22, 1937, p. 63.

90. *New York Times*, July 19, 1934, p. 27, and July 21, 1934, p. 17.

91. *Business Week*, Aug. 11, 1934, p. 27.

92. Kennedy quoted in Whalen, *The Founding Father*, p. 176.

93. *SEC Minutes*, Oct. 31, 1934, Nov. 1, 1934, and Nov. 8, 1934; 1933 Securities Act Release No. 254 (1934); and *Nation*, June 19, 1935, pp. 706–708.

94. *SEC Minutes*, Dec. 5, 1934.

95. *SEC Minutes*, Dec. 11, 1934.

96. *SEC Minutes*, Dec. 18, 1934. Some sense of the intensity of this controversy is suggested by the fact that this was the only issue during Kennedy's term in which the *Minutes* quoted individual commissioners' views rather than merely reciting the nature of the motion and the final vote.

97. "Report on the Government of Securities Exchanges," House of Representatives Document No. 85, 74th Cong., 1st Sess. (1935).

98. *New York Times*, Feb. 7, 1935, p. 29; and Alsop and Kintner, "The Battle of the Market Place," *Saturday Evening Post*, June 11, 1938, pp. 76–77. See also *New York Times*, Feb. 9, 1935, p. 21.

99. *New York Times*, Jan. 29, 1935, p. 29, and Feb. 6, 1935, p. 29.

100. *New York Times*, Feb. 8, 1935, p. 7.

101. *New York Times*, March 19, 1935, p. 31, and March 21, 1935, p. 33; and 1934 Securities Exchange Act Release No. 131 (1935).

102. *New York Times*, Feb. 26, 1935, p. 27.

103. *New York Times*, March 5, 1933, p. 33; and De Bedts, *The New Deal's SEC*, pp. 146–147.

104. *New York Times*, March 8, 1933, p. 31.

105. *New York Times*, March 23, 1935, p. 23; Apr. 6, 1935, p. 1, and Apr. 9, 1935, p. 31.

106. Robert Sobel, *NYSE* (New York: Weybright & Talley, 1975), p. 10; and *Newsweek*, Apr. 13, 1935, p. 28.

107. *New York Times*, Apr. 14, 1935, IV, p. 8.

108. *New York Times*, May 14, 1935, p. 29, and May 15, 1935, p. 31; De Bedts, *The New Deal's SEC*, p. 148; and *Business Week*, May 18, 1935, pp. 20–21.

109. The rules themselves are reprinted in an Appendix to the SEC *First Annual Report*, pp. 40–44. See also p. 13 of the *First Annual Report;* and *SEC Minutes*, Oct. 2, 1934, Jan. 3, 1935, Apr. 12, 1935, Apr. 15, 1935, Apr. 16, 1935, and May 22, 1935. On limitations of the rules, see references to SEC, "Special Study of Security Markets," H.R. Doc. No. 95, 88th Cong., 1st Sess. (1963), cited in Walter Werner, "Adventure in Social Control of Finance: The National Market System for Securities," 75 *Columbia Law Review*, p. 1262, n. 119 (1975).

110. Kennedy, *I'm for Roosevelt*, p. 97.

111. Whalen, *The Founding Father*, pp. 174–175.

112. *The Public Papers and Addresses of Franklin D. Roosevelt*, vol. 4, p. 220.

113. *New York Times*, June 2, 1935, III, p. 1.

114. *New York Times*, June 13, 1935, p. 39.

115. SEC *First Annual Report*, p. 32; and *Jones* v. *SEC*, 298 U.S. 1 (1936).

116. Felix Frankfurter letter to Jerome Frank, June 10, 1935, Frankfurter Papers, Container No. 55, Library of Congress.

117. *New York Times*, July 10, 1935, p. 7; and Memorandum to Missy Le Hand (for Roosevelt) from Kennedy, July 15, 1935, Douglas SEC Commissioner Files.

118. *Wall Street Journal*, Aug. 24, 1935, p. 1; *New York Times*, Aug. 24, 1935, p. 3; Douglas, *Go East, Young Man*, p. 267; Ramsay, *Pyramids of Power*, pp. 200–203; and Freedman, *Roosevelt and Frankfurter: Their Correspondence, 1928–1945*, pp. 283–285.

119. Kennedy draft of resignation letter to Roosevelt, Aug. 1935, Frankfurter Papers, Container No. 98, Library of Congress.

120. Kennedy letter to Roosevelt, Sept. 6, 1935, Roosevelt Papers, PPF 207.

CHAPTER 5: James Landis and the Administrative Process

1. *Time*, June 11, 1934, p. 62.

2. Corcoran letter to Frankfurter, May 11, 1934, Frankfurter Papers, Container No. 116, Library of Congress.

3. *New York Times*, Sept. 24, 1935, p. 37.

4. *Business Week*, Sept. 28, 1935, p. 23.

5. *Business Week*, Oct. 19, 1935, p. 14.

6. *New York Times*, Sept. 24, 1935, p. 35.

7. *New Republic*, Oct. 9, 1935, p. 244.

8. James M. Landis, *The Administrative Process* (New Haven: Yale University Press, 1938), pp. 2, 10, 12, and 14–16.

9. Landis letter to Arthur Hays Sulzberger, July 3, 1936, SEC Commissioners Files, Container No. 1.

10. William O. Douglas, *Go East, Young Man* (New York: Dell, 1974), pp. 265–266.

11. "Utility Corporations," Summary Report of the Federal Trade Commission to the Senate of the United States, 70th Cong., 1st Sess., Doc. No. 92 (hereinafter, FTC *Utility Corporations Report*), part 72-A, pp. 38–39, 46–49, and part 73-A, pp. 32–33 and 57.

12. See, e.g., Ibid., part 72-A, pp. 118–126.

13. *SEC Twenty-fifth Annual Report*, pp. XVII–XVIII.

14. FTC *Utility Corporations Report*, part 72-A, p. 75.

15. Ibid., pp. 136–154.

16. Twentieth Century Fund, *Electric Power and Government Policy* (New York: Twentieth Century Fund, 1948), pp. 35–36.

17. FTC *Utility Corporations Report*, part 72-A, pp. 298–303 and 845.

18. Ibid., part 73-A, p. 64.

19. Ibid., part 72-A, pp. 496–512.

20. Ibid., part 72-A, pp. 512–515.

21. "Report of National Power Policy Committee," 74th Cong., 1st Sess. (1935), House Doc. No. 137, pp. 8–12. On the background of the committee, see Michael Parrish, *Securities Regulation and the New Deal* (New Haven: Yale University Press, 1970), pp. 153–159.

22. Wheeler quoted in Parrish, *Securities Regulation and the New Deal*, p. 157.

23. The legislative history of the act often has been told before. See, e.g., Ellis Hawley, *The New Deal and the Problem of Monopoly* (Princeton: Princeton University Press, 1966), pp. 325–337; Parrish, *Securities Regulation and the New Deal*, pp. 145–178; Arthur Schlesinger, Jr., *The Politics of Upheaval* (Boston: Houghton Mifflin, 1960), pp. 302–324; Ralph De Bedts, *The New Deal's SEC* (New York: Columbia University Press, 1964), pp. 112–143; and Philip J. Funigiello, *Toward a National Power Policy* (Pittsburgh: University of Pittsburgh Press, 1973), pp. 3–121.

24. Edison Electric Institute, pamphlet, "Federal Domination of Local Business," a copy of which may be found in Landis Papers, Box 11, File 10, Harvard Law School.

25. *New York Times*, Oct. 9, 1935, p. 39.

26. William Harbaugh, *Lawyer's Lawyer* (New York: Oxford University Press, 1973), p. 371; and *New York Times*, Aug. 26, 1935, p. 13.

27. *New York Times*, Nov. 20, 1935, p. 19.

28. *New York Times*, Sept. 13, 1935, p. 9.

29. Landis letters to Sam Rayburn, Oct. 21, 1935, Dr. Virgil Jordan, Dec. 9, 1935, Mrs. Helen Reid, Sept. 30, 1935, Mr. John Flynn, Nov. 27, 1935, and Mr. Edward Allen Pierce, Oct. 7, 1935, all in SEC Commissioners Files, Container No. 1.

30. *New York Times*, Sept. 25, 1935, p. 35, and Sept. 26, 1935, p. 33.

31. CBS radio broadcast, September 28, 1935, reprinted in Public Utility Holding Company Act Release No. 3 (1935).

32. Interview with Roger Foster, July 24, 1980, Washington, D.C.; Harbaugh, *Lawyer's Lawyer*, pp. 367–370; *New Republic*, Oct. 30, 1935, pp. 333–335, and Nov. 20, 1935, pp. 35–37; *New York Times*, Sept. 28, 1935, p. 1, and Sept. 29, 1935, p. 1. The ultimate decision was *In Re: American States Public Service Co.*, 12 F. Supp. 667 (D. Maryland, 1935).

33. *New Republic*, Nov. 20, 1935, p. 35.

34. Landis speech, September 28, 1935, reprinted in Public Utility Holding Company Act Release No. 3 (1935).

35. Cohen remark recalled by Milton Katz, interview, Oct. 6, 1979, Cambridge, Mass.

36. *New York Times*, Nov. 9, 1935, p. 4.

37. Parrish, *Securities Regulation and the New Deal*, pp. 219–220; and Douglas, *Go East, Young Man*, pp. 277–278.

38. Statistics appearing in SEC *Third Annual Report*, p. 49; SEC *Second Annual Report*, pp. 37 and 52; and *New York Times*, Dec. 2, 1935, p. 1.

39. SEC enforcement policy in *SEC Minutes*, Oct. 7, 1935, and *New York Times*, Dec. 2, 1935, p. 1.

40. Public Utility Holding Company Act Releases Nos. 31 and 35 (1935).

41. *New York Times*, May 19, 1937, p. 18.

42. *The Reminiscences of James Landis* (Columbia University Oral History Research Office, 1964) (hereinafter, Landis, *Oral History*), pp. 220–224; *New York Times*, Nov. 27, 1935, p. 1; and *SEC Minutes*, Nov. 26, 1935.

43. FTC *Utility Corporations Report*, part 72-A, pp. 56, 84–92, 169–170, 215, 258–265, 322–323, 335–336, 363–365, 394–395, 405–407, 427, 462–466, 476, 486–487, 510–516, 599–621, and 844. See also House Report No. 827, 73rd Cong., 2nd Sess. (1934), part 3, pp. 437–468.

44. *New York Times*, July 1, 1936, p. 35, and Nov. 13, 1936, p. 33.

45. *New York Times*, Dec. 12, 1935, p. 1, Dec. 13, 1935, p. 5, and Oct. 28, 1936, p. 36. The subsequent history of the proceeding is described in SEC *Second Annual Report*, p. 142.

46. Landis, *Oral History*, pp. 220–224; and *New York Times*, Dec. 12, 1935, p. 6. See also De Bedts, *The New Deal's SEC*, pp. 175–176.

47. De Bedts, *The New Deal's SEC*, pp. 175–176. See also *SEC Minutes*, Nov. 21, 1935, and Landis address to the Twenty-fifth Annual Convention of the Investment Bankers Association of America, Dec. 4, 1936, pp. 9–10, on file with SEC Library.

48. *SEC v. Electric Bond and Share*, 18 F. Supp. 131 (S.D.N.Y., 1937).

49. *New York Times*, February 10, 1937, p. 33.

50. Public Utility Holding Company Act Release No. 574 (1937).

51. *New York Times*, June 2, 1937, p. 15.

52. *Burco v. Whitworth*, 81 F. 2d 721 (4th Cir. 1936).

53. See data in SEC *Third Annual Report*, pp. 29–31.

54. See *SEC Minutes*, March 28, 1936, (service contracts); *SEC Minutes*, Aug. 8, 1936, and Public Utility Holding Company Act Releases Nos. 229 (1936) and 349 (1936) (uniform system of accounts); *SEC Minutes*, July 26, 1937, and Public Utility Holding Company Act Release No. 759 (1937) (proxy rules); and *SEC Minutes*, Sept. 10, 1937 (annual report form).

55. *Electric Bond and Share Co. v. SEC*, 303 U.S. 419 (1938).

56. Landis letter to E. A. Pierce, Oct. 7, 1935, SEC Commissioners Files, Container No. 1.

57. Louis Loss, *Securities Regulation* (Boston: Little, Brown, 1961), pp. 1132–1133; and SEC "Report on Trading in Unlisted Securities Upon Exchanges" (1936), pp. 1–3.

58. Milton Katz interview, Oct. 6, 1979, Cambridge, Mass.; and *New York Times*, Oct. 5, 1937, p. 35.

59. SEC, "Report on Trading in Unlisted Securities Upon Exchanges," pp. 4–6; SEC *Second Annual Report*, p. 116; *Business Week*, May 16, 1936, pp. 37–38; *New York Times*, May 20, 1936, p. 33; and James Landis testimony, "Trading in Unlisted Securities Upon Exchanges" Hearings, Senate Banking Committee, 74th Cong., 2nd Sess. (1936) (hereinafter, Senate Unlisted Trading Hearings), pp. 1–15 and 19–46.

60. Senate Unlisted Trading Hearings, pp. 3–5.

61. SEC, "Report on Trading in Unlisted Securities Upon Exchanges," pp. 8, 12–13, and 15.

62. James Landis, Address Before the National Association of State Security Commissioners, Nov. 12, 1934, p. 5, on file with the SEC.

63. SEC, "Report on Trading in Unlisted Securities Upon Exchanges," p. 12.

64. Ibid., pp. 15–16; and *New York Times*, Jan. 1, 1936, p. 41. See also Parrish, *Securities Regulation and the New Deal*, pp. 213–214; and Landis letters to Manuel Cohen, Cohen SEC Papers, vol. 32, item 25, and vol. 33, item 6.

65. Joseph P. Kennedy address to American Arbitration Association, March 19, 1935, reprinted in 1933 Securities Act Release No. 317 (1935), p. 7.

66. *New York Times*, Feb. 9, 1935, p. 21.

67. SEC, *Report on the Feasibility and Advisability of the Complete Segregation of the Functions of Dealer and Broker (1936)*, pp. 65–77; SEC *Second Annual Report*, p. 21; Loss, *Securities Regulation*, pp. 1150–1151 and 1277–1282; Rudolph Weissman, *The New Wall Street* (New York: Harper & Brothers, 1939), p. 175; William Taft Lesh, "Federal Regulation of Over-the-Counter Brokers and Dealers in Securities," 59 *Harvard Law Review*, pp. 1237–1243 (1946); *Time*, July 22, 1935, pp. 42–43; and *New York Times*, March 1, 1936, IV, p. 7.

68. SEC *Second Annual Report*, p. 19; SEC, "Report on Trading in Unlisted Securities Upon Exchanges," pp. 17–21; and Loss, *Securities Regulation*, pp. 1150–1151.

69. James Landis addresss before the New England Council, Boston, Mass., Nov. 22, 1935, on file with SEC.

70. 1934 Securities Exchange Act Release No. 451 (1935). See also Releases Nos. 211 (1935), 368 (1935), and 775 (1936).

71. House of Representatives Report No. 2601, 74th Cong., 2nd Sess. (1936); SEC, "Report on Trading in Unlisted Securities Upon Exchanges," p. 20; and *New York Times*, Feb. 12, 1936, p. 31, Feb. 13, 1936, p. 33, Feb. 15, 1936, pp. 21 and 26, Feb. 26, 1936, p. 31, Feb. 29, 1936, p. 23, March 8, 1936, III, p. 1, and March 13, 1936, p. 33.

72. Testimony of Oliver Troster and John D. Rocamora, Senate Unlisted Trading Hearings, pp. 58–72.

73. *New York Times*, Apr. 25, 1936, p. 23; May 22, 1936, p. 33, May 26, 1936, p. 35, and May 27, 1936, p. 35.

74. *New York Times*, March 8, 1936, III, p. 1.

75. *New Republic*, Jan. 8, 1936, p. 253, and July 8, 1936, pp. 260–262.

76. *SEC Minutes*, Dec. 14, 1936, Jan. 16, 1937, May 10, 1937, and June 29, 1937; *New York Times*, May 21, 1936, p. 39, and Oct. 5, 1937, pp. 35 and 42; Parrish, *Securities Regulation and the New Deal*, p. 210; and Donald Ritchie, *James M. Landis* (Cambridge: Harvard University Press, 1980), pp. 73–74. The Simpson-Ballinger report, entitled *Studies on the Feasibility and Advisability of the Complete Segregation of the Functions of Dealer and Broker*, is on file at the SEC.

77. SEC, *Report on the Feasibility and Advisability of the Complete Segregation of the Functions of Dealer and Broker*, pp. 16–17, 101–102, and 108–113. As promised in the report, the SEC did continue to study the segregation issue. See Raymond Vernon, *The Regulation of Stock Exchange Members* (New York: Columbia University Press, 1941), pp. 69–96.

78. *New Republic*, July 8, 1936, p. 261.

79. Lowenthal letter to Frankfurter quoted in Parrish, *Securities Regulation and the New Deal*, p. 210.

80. Landis letter to Bliven, July 3, 1936, SEC Commissioners Files, Container No. 1.

81. James Landis letter to Felix Frankfurter, July 6, 1936, SEC Commissioners Files, Container No. 1; and *Literary Digest*, July 4, 1936, p. 38.

82. *SEC Minutes*, Nov. 18, 1936; and *New York Times*, Nov. 19, 1936, p. 39.

83. *New York Times*, Nov. 20, 1936, p. 35, and Jan. 4, 1937, p. 37.

84. *New York Times*, Jan. 4, 1937, p. 37.

85. The New York Stock Exchange accepted two minor changes: 1934 Securities Exchange Act Releases Nos. 1074 and 1117 (1936); and *New York Times*, Apr. 7, 1937, p. 40.

86. *New York Times*, Aug. 18, 1937, pp. 1 and 31. See also *New York Times*, Apr. 28, 1937, p. 31, and July 5, 1937, p. 23.

87. *New York Times*, Sept. 15, 1937, p. 33.

88. The last attempt to negotiate such a rule during Landis's term was reflected in the *SEC Minutes*, Sept. 13, 1937.

89. Landis, *The Administrative Process*, pp. 108–109; James Landis, "Enforcement Activities" memo, May 1936, Frankfurter Papers, Container No. 74, Library of Congress; and Landis letter to Senator Fletcher, March 6, 1936, SEC Commissioners Files, Container No. 1.

90. 1934 Securities Exchange Act Releases Nos. 437 (1935) and 1358 (1937); Landis, *Oral History*, pp. 229–230; *Literary Digest*, Dec. 26, 1936, p. 37; and *Newsweek*, Dec. 21, 1935, pp. 36–37.

91. See, e.g., *The Literary Digest*, Dec. 26, 1936, p. 37; and *Newsweek*, Dec. 21, 1935, pp. 36–37.

92. *Jones v. SEC*, 298 U.S. 1 (1936).

93. Landis, *The Administrative Process*, pp. 136–140; Robert Kintner, "The SEC Dictatorship," *American Mercury*, June 1936, pp. 180–187; *New York Times*, April 8, 1936, p. 22; and Roland Redmond, "The Securities Exchange Act of 1934: An Experiment in Administrative Law," 47 *Yale Law Journal*, pp. 622 and 635–646 (1938); and *The Public Papers and Addresses of Franklin D. Roosevelt*, vol. 5, p. 679.

94. Kenneth Culp Davis, *Handbook on Administrative Law* (St. Paul,

Minn.: West Publishing, 1951), pp. 6–9; George Warren, ed., *The Federal Administrative Procedure Act and the Administrative Agencies* (New York: New York University School of Law, 1947), pp. 10–13; Jerome Frank, *If Men Were Angels* (New York: Harper & Brothers, 1942), pp. 18–32, 51–52, 141–146, 163, 179, and 184–185; SEC *Twelfth Annual Report*, pp. 128–129; James Landis, "Crucial Issues in Administrative Law," 53 *Harvard Law Review*, p. 1102 (1940); Note, "The Federal Administrative Procedure Act," 56 *Yale Law Journal*, pp. 670–674 and 703, n. 203 (1947); "Administrative Procedure in Government Agencies" (The Acheson Committee Final Report), Senate Doc. No. 8, 77th Cong., 1st Sess. (1941), especially pp. 7–24; S. 915 and H.R. 6324 (The Walter-Logan bill), 76th Cong., 1st Sess. (1939); "Comments of the SEC on Enrolled Bill H.R. 6324," and letter to Henry Ashhurst from Jerome Frank, May 6, 1940, Frank SEC Commissioner Files, Container No. 26; Memo on the Administrative Law Bill, July 22, 1939, Eicher SEC Commissioner Files, Container No. 33; and letter to James Landis from Sam Rayburn, May 14, 1940, Landis Papers, Container No. 27, Library of Congress.

95. Landis letter to Roosevelt, Dec. 20, 1935, Roosevelt Papers, OF 1060.

96. Landis letter to Roosevelt, May 4, 1936, Landis Papers, Container No. 13, Library of Congress.

97. Landis letter to Roosevelt, Jan. 13, 1937, Landis Papers, Container No. 13, Library of Congress; Ritchie, *James M. Landis*, p. 75; and *New York Times*, Jan. 12, 1937, p. 25, May 22, 1937, p. 21, and May 25, 1937, p. 41.

98. 1934 Securities Exchange Act Releases Nos. 640 (1936), 713 (1936), 735 (1936), 1189 (1937), and 1196 (1937); *New York Times*, Apr. 14, 1937, p. 37, Apr. 16, 1937, p. 33, May 12, 1937, p. 33, May 26, 1937, p. 37, June 4, 1937, p. 35, June 22, 1937, p. 33, and Aug. 22, 1937, III, p. 5.

99. Douglas, *Go East, Young Man*, p. 281.

100. See, e.g., William O. Douglas, *Democracy and Finance* (New Haven: Yale University Press, 1940).

101. *New Republic*, Jan. 20, 1937, p. 357; and *Nation*, Jan. 23, 1937, pp. 86–87.

102. See, e.g., Public Utility Holding Company Act Releases Nos. 486 (1936) and 521 (1937).

103. Douglas, *Go East, Young Man*, pp. 258–281.

104. Landis, *Oral History*, pp. 302–303; Milton Katz interview, Oct. 6, 1979, Cambridge, Mass.; and Landis address before the Fourth Annual Woman's Congress, March 10, 1937, on file at the SEC. The extent of Douglas's involvement in the court-packing campaign is suggested by Douglas correspondence on the subject in Douglas Papers, Container No. 21, Library of Congress.

105. Douglas, *Go East, Young Man*, p. 281. See also letter to Douglas from Adolf Berle, Sept. 23, 1937, Douglas Papers, Container No. 24, Library of Congress.

106. Landis letter to Roosevelt, Sept. 11, 1937, Roosevelt Papers, OF 1060 and PPF 4858.

107. *New York Times*, Sept. 16, 1937, p. 24. See also, e.g., *New York Herald Tribune*, Jan. 12, 1937, p. 16; and *New Republic*, Jan. 27, 1937, p. 384.

108. *New York Times*, Sept. 23, 1937, p. 45.

CHAPTER 6: The Man Who Got Things Done

1. On Douglas background, see William O. Douglas, *Go East, Young Man* (New York, Dell, 1974); William O. Douglas, *Democracy and Finance* (New Haven: Yale University Press, 1940); William O. Douglas, "Foreward," 28 *George Washington Law Review*, pp. 1–5 (1959); Ralph De Bedts, *The New Deal's SEC* (New York: Columbia University Press, 1964), especially pp. 152–159; Michael Parrish, *Securities Regulation and the New Deal* (New Haven: Yale University Press, 1970), especially pp. 179–186; Chester Lane, *Oral History Memoir* (Columbia University Oral History Research Office, 1957), especially, pp. 330–331, 343–344, and 413; Douglas Papers, especially biographical materials in Containers Nos. 6, 10, 13, 16, and 24, Library of Congress; John T. Flynn, "Washing Wall Street's Face," *Collier's*, Jan. 29, 1938, pp. 12–13 and 25; Max Lerner, "Wall Street's New Mentor," *Nation*, Oct. 23, 1937, pp. 429–432; Transcript of Douglas's press conference, Sept. 22, 1937, Douglas Papers, Container No. 21, Library of Congress; Memorandum to the President from Douglas, Feb. 24, 1938, Roosevelt Papers, OF 1060; Frankfurter-Douglas correspondence dated Dec. 8, 1933, Jan. 16, 1934, and Feb. 19, 1934, Douglas Papers, Container No. 6, Library of Congress; Letter to Willis Ballinger from Douglas, Douglas Papers, Container No. 10, Library of Congress; and Interview with Abe Fortas, Dec. 28, 1979, Washington, D.C.

2. The political backdrop of the Douglas chairmanship (Sept. 1937–Apr. 1939) is described in James MacGregor Burns, *Roosevelt: The Lion and the Fox* (New York: Harcourt, Brace & World, 1956), pp. 291–380; William E. Leuchtenburg, *Franklin D. Roosevelt and the New Deal* (New York: Harper & Row, 1963), pp. 231–274; and Ellis Hawley, *The New Deal and the Problem of Monopoly* (Princeton: Princeton University Press, 1966), pp. 380–419, among other New Deal histories. The economic background is described in Kenneth Roose, *The Economics of Recession and Revival* (New Haven: Yale University Press, 1954), pp. 20–55; and Charles Kindleberger, *The World in Depression* (Berkeley: University of California Press, 1973), pp. 271–277.

3. *Literary Digest*, Nov. 6, 1937, p. 33.

4. Excerpt reprinted in *New York Times*, Oct. 15, 1937, pp. 1 and 12.

5. See, e.g., *New York Times*, Sept. 26, 1937, III, p. 1, and Oct. 24, 1937, III, p. 1; *Magazine of Wall Street*, Oct. 23, 1937, pp. 76–77 and 120; and *Newsweek*, Oct. 25, 1937, p. 28.

6. Interview with Abe Fortas, Dec. 28, 1979, Washington, D.C.

7. *New York Times*, Oct. 26, 1937, p. 22.

8. *New York Times*, Oct. 27, 1937, p. 12.

9. *SEC Minutes*, Oct. 18, 1937; and *New York Times*, Oct. 15, 1937, p. 12.

10. *New York Times*, Dec. 11, 1937, p. 25. On Hanes, see *Time*, Dec. 20, 1937, p. 53; *Business Week*, Dec. 18, 1937, p. 18; Douglas, *Go East, Young Man*, p. 267; Parrish, *Securities Regulation and the New Deal*, p. 199; Memorandum to Frank from Hanes, April 15, 1938, Frank Papers, Box 28, File No. 290, Yale; and *New Republic*, Dec. 15, 1937, p. 169.

11. See, e.g., John Brooks, *Once in Golconda* (New York: Harper & Row, 1969), pp. 230–287; John Kenneth Galbraith, *The Great Crash*, third edition (Boston: Houghton Mifflin, 1972), pp. 164–172; Ferdinand Lundberg,

America's Sixty Families (New York: Vanguard Press, 1938), pp. 522–533; and Robert Sobel, *NYSE* (New York: Weybright & Talley, 1975), pp. 30–65.

12. Joseph Alsop and Robert Kintner, "The Battle of the Market Place", *Saturday Evening Post*, June 11, 1938, p. 78 and June 25, 1938, p. 10; "Wall Street Itself", *Fortune*, June 1937, p. 160; *Business Week*, June 18, 1938, p. 22; Rudolph Weissman, *The New Wall Street* (New York: Harper & Brothers, 1939), p. 283; Lane, *Oral History Memoir*, pp. 330–331; Fred Rodell, "Douglas Over the Stock Exchange," *Fortune*, Feb. 1938, pp. 120–122; Memorandum to Douglas from Milton Katz, Oct. 11, 1937, Douglas SEC Commissioner Files; and Douglas press conference, Sept. 22, 1937, Douglas Papers, Container No. 21, Library of Congress.

13. Alsop and Kintner, "The Battle of the Market Place," *Saturday Evening Post*, June 25, 1938, pp. 78–80; and De Bedts, *The New Deal's SEC*, pp. 160–163.

14. Memorandum to Douglas from New York regional office, October 15, 1937, Douglas SEC Commissioner Files.

15. Douglas Nov. 23 press release reprinted in Douglas, *Democracy and Finance*, pp. 63–73.

16. *New York Times*, Nov. 30, 1937, p. 12.

17. *New York Times*'s belief reprinted in Rodell, "Douglas Over the Stock Exchange," *Fortune*, Feb. 1938, p. 120.

18. Sobel, *NYSE*, pp. 37–38; *New York Times*, Dec. 11, 1937, p. 25, and Dec. 15, 1937, p. 39; and *Time*, Aug. 15, 1938, pp. 44 and 46.

19. Ganson Purcell memorandum entitled "Problems of Organization and Administration of the New York Stock Exchange," undated, Douglas SEC Commissioner Files.

20. 1934 Securities Exchange Act Release No. 1548 (1938) and *New York Times*, Jan. 25, 1938, p. 1. Fourteen months later the rule was modified, see 1934 Securities Exchange Act Release No. 2039 (1939).

21. The Conway report, reprinted in *New York Times*, Jan. 28, 1938, pp. 1 and 36.

22. *New York Times*, Feb. 2, 1938, p. 27.

23. *New York Times*, Feb. 1, 1938, p. 25, and Feb. 24, 1938, p. 29; Alsop and Kintner, "The Battle of the Market Place," *Saturday Evening Post*, June 25, 1938, pp. 81–82; and Sobel, *NYSE*, pp. 42–45.

24. SEC, *In the Matter of Richard Whitney, et al.*, vol. 1 (1938), pp. 1 and 51; Douglas, *Go East, Young Man*, p. 289; Alsop and Kintner, "The Battle of the Market Place," *Saturday Evening Post*, June 25, 1938, p. 82; *New York Times*, March 9, 1938, p. 1; Lane, *Oral History Memoir*, pp. 330–331; Douglas and John W. Hanes memoranda regarding events of March 7 and 8, 1938, Douglas SEC Commissioner Files; and *SEC Minutes*, March 8, 1938.

25. *New York Times*, March 10, 1938, p. 1.

26. *New York Times*, March 11, 1938, pp. 1 and 4, March 12, 1938, pp. 1 and 18, March 15, 1938, pp. 1 and 12, March 17, 1938, pp. 22, and March 18, 1938, p. 29; and SEC, *In the Matter of Richard Whitney*, vol. 1, pp. 1–3 and 53–55.

27. Douglas, *Go East, Young Man*, pp. 289–290.

28. Ibid., p. 200; Telegram to Thomas E. Dewey from William O. Douglas, March 22, 1938, Douglas SEC Commissioner Files; and I. F. Stone, "Questions on the Whitney Case," *Nation*, Jan. 14, 1939, pp. 55–58.

29. *SEC Minutes,* April 1–6, 1938.

30. Securities Exchange Act Release No. 1640 (1938); and SEC, *In the Matter of Richard Whitney,* vol. 1, pp. 2–3.

31. The findings were assembled in SEC, *In the Matter of Richard Whitney.*

32. Morgan's view on leisure class quoted in Arthur Schlesinger, Jr., *The Coming of the New Deal* (Boston: Houghton Mifflin, 1958), p. 479.

33. Alsop and Kintner, "The Battle of the Market Place," *Saturday Evening Post,* June 25, 1938, p. 82.

34. Letter to Brien McMahon from Chester Lane, Nov. 29, 1938, Douglas SEC Commissioner Files.

35. Douglas, *Go East, Young Man,* pp. 302–303.

36. Letter to William McChesney Martin, Jr., from Douglas, Nov. 1, 1938, Douglas SEC Commissioner Files.

37. Letter to Douglas from Robert Hutchins, Jan. 26, 1939, Douglas Papers, Container No. 30, Library of Congress.

38. Letter to John Hanes from Jerome Frank, Nov. 7, 1938, Frank Papers, Box 28, File No. 290, Yale.

39. Memorandum entitled "Possible alternative courses of action by SEC re: the Whitney case in the light of the recent white-wash," Dec. 18, 1938, Douglas SEC Commissioner Files.

40. Letter to Attorney General Frank Murphy from Jerome Frank, March 15, 1939, Frank Papers, Box 34, File No. 508, Yale.

41. *SEC Minutes,* Dec. 22, 1938. See also letter to William McChesney Martin, Jr., from Douglas, Dec. 27, 1938, Douglas SEC Commissioner Files.

42. Interview with Milton Katz, Oct. 6, 1979, Cambridge, Mass.; and Memorandum to Douglas from Paul Gourrich Oct. 31, 1938, Douglas SEC Commissioner Files.

43. Interview with Milton Katz, Oct. 6, 1979, Cambridge, Mass.

44. *New York Times,* March 18, 1938, p. 29.

45. *SEC Minutes,* February 9, 1938.

46. Press release dated March 19, 1938, Douglas SEC Commissioner File.

47. *New York Times,* Apr. 12, 1938, p. 33; Sobel, *NYSE,* p. 55; and *Fortune,* Aug. 1938, p. 48.

48. See, e.g., *Fortune,* Aug. 1938, pp. 47–48 and 85–86; *Time,* Aug. 15, 1938, pp. 40–47; John T. Flynn, "Lamb of Wall Street," *Collier's,* July 30, 1938, pp. 11 and 41–42; *Business Week,* July 9, 1938, pp. 13–14; and *New York Times,* May 14, 1938, p. 2, July 1, 1938, p. 25, and July 2, 1938, p. 17.

49. Douglas address reprinted in Douglas, *Democracy and Finance,* pp. 79–91.

50. *SEC Minutes,* May 17 and 19, 1938; and "Memorandum of conference between representatives of the Commission and representatives of the New York Stock Exchange at the Hotel Powhatan, May 18, 1938," Douglas SEC Commissioner Files.

51. *SEC Minutes,* March 18, 1938, July 19, 1938, July 28, 1938, Aug. 5, 1938, Oct. 20, 1938, and Nov. 22, 1938. See also *New York Times,* July 23, 1938, p. 17, July 24, 1938, p. 3, and Dec. 23, 1938, p. 27; Memorandum to the Commission from Ganson Purcell re: Broker-Dealer segregation experiment proposed by New York Stock Exchange Committee on floor procedure, July 27, 1938, Douglas SEC Commissioner Files; and Memorandum of NYSE conference, August 25, 1938, Douglas SEC Commissioner Files.

52. Exchange reforms discussed and reprinted in part II of the SEC's *In the Matter of Richard Whitney.*

53. SEC *Fifth Annual Report*, p. 44; and *Sixth Annual Report*, pp. 82–87. See also SEC *Tenth Annual Report*, pp. 38–39; and several memoranda regarding protection of customers' funds in Frank SEC Commissioner Files, Containers Nos. 26 and 29.

54. Alsop and Kintner, "The Battle of the Market Place," *Saturday Evening Post*, June 25, 1938, p. 10.

55. *Electric Bond and Share* v. *SEC*, 303 U.S. 419 (1938).

56. Interview with Abe Fortas, Dec. 28, 1979, Washington, D.C.

57. *New York Times*, Nov. 9, 1937, pp. 33 and 37.

58. Douglas address, "A Call for Leadership," reprinted in Douglas, *Democracy and Finance*, pp. 128–133.

59. *New York Times*, Apr. 5, 1938, p. 43. At the time the Supreme Court's decision was handed down, only 44 percent of the industry had been registered; *New York Times*, March 30, 1938, p. 20.

60. *New York Times*, May 11, 1938, p. 10.

61. Memorandum to Judge Healy from Chairman Douglas, Apr. 26, 1938, Douglas SEC Commissioner Files.

62. Letter to William Douglas from C. E. Groesbeck and J. F. Fogarty, Douglas SEC Commissioner Files.

63. Groesbeck meeting with Frank described in Memorandum from Jerome Frank to the Securities and Exchange Commission, May 16, 1938, Douglas SEC Commissioner Files.

64. Letter to Groesbeck and Fogarty, May 17, 1938, reprinted in *SEC Minutes*, May 17, 1938.

65. Douglas speech reprinted in Douglas, *Democracy and Finance*, pp. 143–162.

66. SEC *Fifth Annual Report*, p. 70; and *New York Times*, Aug. 5, 1938, p. 21.

67. *New York Times*, Dec. 2, 1938, p. 35; and *Business Week*, Dec. 10, 1938, p. 20.

68. Parrish, *Securities Regulation and the New Deal*, p. 226.

69. Telephone interviews with Abe Fortas, June 4, 1980, Robert O'Brien, May 29, 1980, and Roger Foster, May 30, 1980; Letter to Thomas Corcoran from Jerome Frank, April 1, 1939, Frank Papers, Box No. 24, File No. 127, Yale; Letter to the author from Robert O'Brien, Sept. 10, 1980; Letters to Douglas from Smith, April 11, 1939, to Frank from Healy, Dec. 5, 1938, to Smith from Douglas, Apr. 4, 1939, from Eicher and Frank, Apr. 1, 1939, to Healy from Frank, Dec. 27, 1938, to the Commission from Douglas, Apr. 12, 1939, and to Frank from Smith, May 9, 1939, all in Frank Papers, Container No. 37, File 644, Yale; and Memorandum to Healy from Frank, Nov. 22, 1938, Purcell SEC Commissioner Files, Container No. 50.

70. SEC *Tenth Annual Report*, pp. 87–91,115–140, and 268–278; Public Utility Holding Company Act Release No. 1946 (1940); and Letter to the author from Robert O'Brien, Sept. 10, 1980.

71. Landis address before the New England Council, Boston, Mass., Nov. 22, 1935, p. 4, on file with the SEC.

72. A. A. Berle, "Action to Avoid Another 1929," *American Bankers Association Journal*, July 1933, pp. 16–18.

73. Vincent Carosso, *Investment Banking in America* (Cambridge: Har-

vard University Press, 1970), pp. 384–389; and B. Howell Griswold testimony, "Regulation of Over-the-Counter Markets" Hearings, Senate Banking Committee, 75th Cong., 3rd Sess. (1938) (hereinafter, "Regulation of Over-the-Counter Markets" Hearings), pp. 36–41.

74. *SEC Minutes,* April 8, 1935. See also *Minutes,* May 6, 1935, May 24, 1935, and June 3, 1935.

75. Memorandum to the SEC from Paul Gourrich, June 12, 1935, Landis Papers, Box 6, File 10, Harvard Law School.

76. *SEC Minutes,* June 3, 1935, Sept. 23, 1935, Nov. 15, 1935, Jan. 29, 1936, and June 29, 1936; and *New York Times,* Sept. 30, 1935, p. 25, and Oct. 14, 1935, p. 27.

77. Carosso, *Investment Banking in America,* pp. 389–390.

78. Mathews testimony at "Regulation of Over-the-Counter Markets" Hearings, pp. 15–16.

79. Douglas attitude recalled by Abe Fortas, interviewed, Washington, D.C., Dec. 28, 1979.

80. Testimony of George Mathews, at "Regulation of Over-the-Counter Markets" Hearings, p. 7.

81. *New York Times,* Dec. 21, 1937, p. 35; and *SEC Minutes,* Oct. 11, 1937.

82. Douglas, *Democracy and Finance,* p. 82.

83. Douglas Hartford address quoted in Weissman, *The New Wall Street,* pp. 186–188, and *New York Times,* Jan. 8, 1938, p. 21.

84. Original Maloney bill reprinted in "Regulation of Over-the-Counter Markets" Hearings, pp. 1–6.

85. Memorandum for Chairman Douglas from Roosevelt, Feb. 1, 1938, Roosevelt Papers, OF 1060.

86. *New York Times,* Jan. 23, 1938, III, p. 1.

87. See Subsection 15A(n) of act as adopted. Draftsman Milton Katz explained the significance of this subsection to me in an interview on Oct. 6, 1979, in Cambridge, Mass. See also Louis Loss, *Securities Regulation* (Boston: Little, Brown, 1961) pp. 1369–1370.

88. "Regulation of Over-the-Counter Markets" Hearings, pp. 63–76; and House Report No. 2307, 75th Cong., 3rd Sess. (1938), pp. 1–2.

89. *New York Times,* Feb. 26, 1938, p. 19.

90. *New York Times,* March 2, 1938, p. 29; and Section 15A(m) of the Maloney Act.

91. *New York Times,* March 11, 1938, p. 27.

92. Letter to William Douglas from Felix Frankfurter, Jan. 16, 1934, Douglas Papers, Container No. 6, Library of Congress.

93. Memorandum to Roosevelt from Douglas, May 19, 1938, Douglas SEC Commissioner Files.

94. *SEC Minutes,* Apr. 22, 1935, and Apr. 29, 1938.

95. Griswold testimony at "Regulation of Over-the-Counter Markets" Hearings, p. 38.

96. Letter to the author, July 29, 1980.

97. Robert T. Swaine, " 'Democratization' of Corporate Reorganizations," 38 *Columbia Law Review,* especially pp. 257–259 (1938). See also E. Merrick Dodd, "The Securities and Exchange Commission's Reform Program for Bankruptcy Reorganizations," 38 *Columbia Law Review,* p. 225

(1938). Swaine, it might be noted, was Douglas's superior at Cravath, de-Gersdorff, Swaine and Wood. See Douglas, *Go East, Young Man,* pp. 151–156.

98. A copy of the Lea Committee bill and related hearings appear in "To Amend the Securities Act of 1933," Hearings, House Commerce Committee, 75th Cong., 1st Sess. (1937). See also Dodd, "The Securities and Exchange Commission's Reform Program for Bankruptcy Reorganizations," 38 *Columbia Law Review,* pp. 245–255; and Swaine, " 'Democratization' of Corporate Reorganizations," 38 *Columbia Law Review,* pp. 260–262.

99. Sabath testified against the Lea bill in "To amend the Securities Act of 1933," Hearings, House Commerce Committee, 75th Cong., 1st Sess. (1937), pp. 307–320. The testimony of Congressman West appears at p. 561. The chronicle of Sabath's opposition to the Lea bill is reflected in: Memorandum entitled "Interview between Mr. Bolard and Mr. Comer," Jan. 10, 1935, Douglas Papers, Container No. 13, Library of Congress; Letter to A. J. Sabath from Abe Fortas, Apr. 8, 1935, Douglas Papers, Container No. 13, Library of Congress; "Memorandum to Mr. Douglas," from Abe Fortas, Oct. 7, 1935, Douglas Papers, Container No. 12, Library of Congress; "Memorandum to the Commission," from Protective Committee Study, Feb. 20, 1936, Douglas Papers, Container No. 13, Library of Congress; and Letter to Marvin McIntyre (Secretary to President Roosevelt), Apr. 7, 1937, Douglas Papers, Container No. 20, Library of Congress.

100. The Chandler Bankruptcy Revision Act appears in 52 *Stat.* 840. Its legislative history is discussed in: House Report No. 1409, 75th Cong., 1st Sess. (1937); Senate Reports Nos. 1916 and 2073, 75th Cong., 3rd Sess. (1938); "Revision of the Bankruptcy Act" Hearings, House Judiciary Committee, 76th Cong., 1st Sess. (1939), especially pp. 1–8 and 162–197; "Revision of the National Bankruptcy Act" Hearings, Senate Judiciary Subcommittee, 75th Cong., 2nd Sess. (1937–1938), especially pp. 1–16; and Edward Altman, *Corporate Bankruptcy in America* (Lexington, Mass.: D. C. Heath, 1971), pp. 5–19. See also Dodd, "The Securities and Exchange Commission's Reform Program for Bankruptcy Proceedings," 38 *Columbia Law Review,* pp. 223–245; SEC *Fifth Annual Report,* pp. 7–9 and 14–15; and Loss, *Securities Regulation,* pp. 754–763. The text quoted part I of the SEC's *Protective Committee Study Report,* pp. 868–869 and 897–903. Roosevelt supported the Douglas draft of Chap. X in a letter to Hatton Summers, chairman of the House Judiciary Committee, May 24, 1937, Douglas Papers, Container No. 20, Library of Congress.

101. Memorandum to SEC from Douglas, Nov. 27, 1934, Douglas Papers, Container No. 12, Library of Congress. That Douglas did not originally contemplate such a study is obvious from Memorandum to James Landis from Douglas, July 17, 1934, Douglas Papers, Container No. 12, Library of Congress.

102. Letter to Arthur L. Corbin from William O. Douglas, March 12, 1937, Douglas Papers, Container No. 23, Library of Congress. In the letter Douglas acknowledged, "he [Levi] did so much work I felt a little guilty afterwards in not mentioning his name in the report."

103. The legislative history of the Trust Indenture Act was assembled from "Regulation of Sale of Securities" Hearings, Senate Banking Committee, 75th Cong., 1st Sess. (1937), especially pp. 15–42, 87–88, and 185–195;

"Trust Indentures" Hearings, House Commerce Committee, 75th Cong., 3rd Sess. (1938), especially pp. 16–43 and 72–75; "Trust Indentures" Hearings, House Commerce Committee, 76th Cong., 1st Sess. (1939), especially pp. 35–56; "Trust Indenture Act" Hearings, Senate Banking Committee, 76th Cong., 1st Sess. (1939), especially pp. 17–71 and 99–123; Letter from R. G. Page to President of the Member Addressed, American Bankers Association, Aug. 26, 1936, Douglas SEC Commissioner Files; Letter to Senator Robert F. Wagner from Franklin D. Roosevelt, May 24, 1937, Douglas Papers, Container No. 20, Library of Congress; *SEC Minutes*, March 7 and 8, 1938, Memorandum to Mr. Burke and Mr. McKellar from Chairman Douglas, Dec. 28, 1938, Douglas SEC Commissioner Files; and *New York Times*, May 3, 1939, p. 35. The Trust Indenture Act itself may be found at 53 *Stat.* 1149–1178. See also Loss, *Securities Regulation*, pp. 726–753.

104. Douglas, *Go East, Young Man*, pp. 274–276.

105. Memorandum for Mr. Bane from Edward T. McCormick, Nov. 9, 1937, Douglas SEC Commissioner Files.

106. Landis quoted in Robert Chatov, *Corporate Financial Reporting* (New York: Free Press, 1975), pp. 114 and 117.

107. Carman Blough, "The Relationship of the Securities and Exchange Commission to the Accountant," 63 *Journal of Accountancy*, pp. 23–39 (1937).

108. A transcript of that press conference, September 22, 1937, may be found in Douglas Papers, Container No. 21, Library of Congress.

109. Address reprinted in 13 *The Accounting Review*, pp. 1–9 (1938). Douglas associates himself with this address in *Go East, Young Man*, p. 275.

110. Douglas, *Go East, Young Man* p. 275.

111. George C. Mathews, "Accounting in the Regulation of Security Sales," 13 *Accounting Review* p. 226 (1938).

112. SEC Minutes, Feb. 12, 1938, March 25, 1938, and April 13, 1938.

113. Maurice Kaplan and Daniel Reaugh, "Accounting, Reports to Stockholders and the SEC," 48 *Yale Law Journal*, pp. 965 and 978 (1939).

114. See, e.g., "Hearings on a Comparative Print Showing Proposed Changes in the Securities Act of 1933 and the Securities Exchange Act of 1934," House Commerce Committee, 78th Cong., 1st Sess. (1942), p. 1386; and Report of Special Study of Securities Markets of the Securities and Exchange Commission, House Doc. No. 95, 88th Cong., 1st Sess. (1963), part 3.

115. SEC Statistical Series Release No. 133 (1938). See also "Trust Indentures" Hearings, House Commerce Committee, 76th Cong., 1st Sess. (1939), pp. 48–50; and TNEC Monograph No. 17, "Problems of Small Business" (1941). On securities issue costs and the structure of investment banking, generally, during this period, see Carosso, *Investment Banking in America*, pp. 393–430.

116. TNEC Monograph No. 17, "Problems of Small Business," p. 227.

117. Letter to Marriner Eccles from Douglas, Aug. 10, 1938, Douglas Papers, Container No. 30, Library of Congress.

118. See ibid.

119. Memorandum to the President from Douglas, March 1, 1938, Douglas Papers, Container No. 32, Library of Congress.

120. Ibid. A copy of the Industrial Finance Act of 1938 was attached to a memorandum to the Secretary of the Treasury from Douglas, March 17, 1938, Douglas Papers, Container No. 31, Library of Congress. The concept also was discussed with members of Congress. On March 8, 1938, Senator Claude Pepper delivered a nationwide CBS radio address urging federal industrial banks; the address was written by the SEC's David Ginsburg. On June 3, 1938, a memo to Douglas from Ginsburg indicated that Congressman Jerry Voorhis introduced the SEC's industrial finance bill and it was denominated H.R. 10789. See Douglas Papers, Container No. 32, Library of Congress. During that session, Senator Pepper (S. 3430 and 3630), Senator Vandenberg (S. 3640), Congressman Mead (H.R. 9814), and Congressman Koppelman (H.R. 9291) introduced similar bills. During Jerome Frank's chairmanship, SEC attorneys drafted a bill introduced by Senator Mead, S. 2343, 76th Cong., 1st Sess., to have the RFC guarantee loans to small business. Roosevelt supported the bill; see Purcell SEC Commissioner Files, Container No. 43.

121. Letter to Roosevelt from Douglas, March 26, 1938, Douglas Papers, Container No. 31, Library of Congress.

122. John Morton Blum, *From the Morgenthau Diaries* (Boston: Houghton Mifflin, 1959), pp. 415–416.

123. Memorandum to the President from Wayne Taylor, Apr. 4, 1938, Douglas Papers, Container No. 31, Library of Congress; and Letter to Wayne Taylor from Douglas, Apr. 2, 1938, Douglas Papers, Container No. 31, Library of Congress.

124. Letter to Congressman James Mead from Douglas, January 17, 1938, Douglas SEC Commissioner Files.

125. Letter to Henry Wallace from Douglas, Apr. 11, 1938, Douglas Papers, Container No. 31, Library of Congress.

126. 52 *Stat.* 212–213.

127. The Public Papers and Addresses of Franklin D. Roosevelt (1938), pp. 221–233. That Roosevelt's direction to the SEC was meant to appease the small-business community was made obvious by his remarks at an Apr. 15 press conference; see *Roosevelt Press Conferences,* vol. 11, p. 315.

128. SEC Minutes, Apr. 14, 1938, Apr. 15, 1938, and Apr. 19, 1938. See also *New York Times,* Apr. 16, 1938, p. 22.

129. Memorandum to the President from Frank, Apr. 10, 1941, Roosevelt Papers, OF 1060.

130. TNEC Monograph No. 17, "Problems of Small Business," pp. 227–229 and 242–243.

131. Statement of SEC Commissioner Pike, Feb. 25, 1941, reprinted in TNEC, *Final Report,* Senate Doc. No. 35, 77th Cong., 1st Sess. (1941) pp. 479–485.

132. New York Times, May 25, 1938, p. 6, and March 1, 1939, p. 14.

133. Testimony of William Green, "Federal Licensing of Corporations" Hearings, Senate Judiciary Subcommittee, 75th Cong., 1st Sess. (1937), pp. 87–89. But see also *New York Times,* Oct. 13, 1938, p. 2, for evidence that minority of AFL opposed Green on this issue.

134. Letter to Frankfurter from Douglas, Dec. 8, 1933, Douglas Papers, Container No. 6, Library of Congress.

135. Letter to Frankfurter from Douglas, February 19, 1934, Douglas Papers, Container No. 6, Library of Congress.

136. William O. Douglas, "Directors Who Do Not Direct," 47 *Harvard Law Review,* pp. 1305–1334 (1934).

137. Douglas related address on directors reprinted in Douglas, *Democracy and Finance,* pp. 46–55.

138. Memorandum to the President from Douglas, Feb. 18, 1938, Douglas SEC Commissioner Files. A draft of the proposed Federal Corporation Registration Act may be found in Memorandum to Douglas from Chester Lane, Feb. 15, 1938, Douglas SEC Commissioner Files.

139. *Congressional Record,* 74th Cong., 1st Sess., Aug. 5, 1935, p. 12452. See also "Federal Licensing of Corporations" Hearings, Senate Judiciary Subcommittee, 75th Cong., 1st Sess. (1937); and *Congressional Record,* 74th Cong., 1st Sess., Aug. 6, 1935, pp. 12551–12556.

140. Harold Ickes, *The Secret Diary of Harold Ickes,* vol. 2 (New York: Simon & Schuster, 1954), pp. 19–20.

141. *Congressional Record,* 75th Cong., 1st Sess., Jan. 12, 1937, pp. 178–179.

142. Ickes, *The Secret Diary,* vol. 2, pp. 263 and 283–287; *New York Times,* Dec. 31, 1937, p. 1, and Jan. 2, 1938, p. 1; and Hawley, *The New Deal and the Problem of Monopoly,* pp. 391–395.

143. *Congressional Record,* 75th Cong., 2nd Sess., Nov. 30, 1937, pp. 494–498; and *New York Times,* Dec. 1, 1937, p. 1.

144. Hawley, *The New Deal and the Problem of Monopoly,* pp. 388–419; Burns, *Roosevelt: The Lion and the Fox,* pp. 319–328; Leuchtenburg, *Franklin D. Roosevelt and the New Deal,* pp. 246–259; and Joseph Alsop and Robert Kintner, "We Shall Make America Over," *Saturday Evening Post,* Nov. 19, 1938, pp. 14–15 and 85–92.

145. *New York Times,* Apr. 23, 1938, p. 1.

146. *The Public Papers and Addresses of Franklin D. Roosevelt* (1938), pp. 305–320.

147. Hawley, *The New Deal and the Problem of Monopoly,* pp. 411–419. See also David Lynch, *The Concentration of Economic Power* (New York: Columbia University Press, 1946), p. 27.

148. Public Resolution No. 113, 75th Cong., 3rd Sess. (1938). On legislative history, see Lynch, *The Concentration of Economic Power,* pp. 25–34 and 52–53.

149. Dwight Macdonald, "The Monopoly Committee: A Study in Frustration," *American Scholar,* vol. 8, pp. 295–308 (1939).

150. TNEC, *Final Report,* pp. 681–684. See also pp. 24–29.

151. SEC, *Protective Committee Study,* part 7, pp. 412–413.

152. *SEC Minutes,* Dec. 30, 1938, and Feb. 1, 1939. See also Memorandum to Jerome Frank from Thomas Lynch, March 24, 1939, Douglas SEC Commissioner Files.

153. The end of Douglas's chairmanship is described in Douglas, *Go East, Young Man,* pp. 459–465; Arthur Krock, *Memoirs* (New York: Funk & Wagnalls, 1968), pp. 176–177; Letter to Roosevelt from Douglas, Apr. 12, 1939, Douglas SEC Commissioner Files; SEC Press Release, March 15, 1939, with respect to the Hancock Committee, Roosevelt Papers, OF 1060; Douglas Press Conference, March 15, 1939, Douglas Papers, Container No. 21, Library of Congress; and *New York Times,* March 15, 1939, p. 37, March 16, 1939, p. 35, March 21, 1939, pp. 1 and 33, March 26, 1939, IV, p. 3, and March 29, 1939, p. 22.

CHAPTER 7: The End of the New Deal

1. J. Sinclair Armstrong, "Congress and the Securities and Exchange Commission," 45 *Virginia Law Review,* pp. 798–799 (1959).

2. Memorandum to Jerome Frank from Ganson Purcell, Apr. 11, 1939, Purcell SEC Commissioner Files, Container No. 39.

3. Jerome Frank, "In Time of War Prepare for Peace," Address, April 8, 1940, on file with SEC; Memoranda concerning SEC wartime role, Purcell SEC Commissioner Files, Container Nos. 37, 41, and 50; Eicher SEC Commissioner Files, Container No. 33; Frank Papers, Box No. 37, File No. 606, Yale; and Frank SEC Commissioner Files, Container Nos. 30 and 31.

4. SEC *Ninth Annual Report,* p. 3; *Tenth Annual Report,* pp. 209–210; *Eleventh Annual Report,* pp. 94–95; and *New York Times,* March 1, 1942, p. 27.

5. Jerome Frank background described in Walter Volkomer, *The Passionate Liberal: The Political and Legal Ideas of Jerome Frank* (The Hague: Martinus Nijhoff, 1970), especially pp. 1–19; Arthur Schlesinger, Jr., *The Coming of the New Deal* (Boston: Houghton Mifflin, 1958), pp. 40–84; William O. Douglas, *Go East, Young Man* (New York, Dell, 1974), pp. 267 and 397; Jerome Frank, *Reminiscences* (Columbia University Oral History, 1950); Chester Lane, *Oral History Memoir* (Columbia University Oral History, 1957) (hereinafter, Lane, *Oral History*), pp. 341–342, 389–390, and 414–419; William O. Douglas and Richard Rovere, "Jerome Frank, 1889–1957," The Association of the Bar of the City of New York (1957); Felix Frankfurter, William O. Douglas, and Thurman Arnold, "Jerome Frank," 24 *University of Chicago Law Review,* pp. 625–642 (1957); Charles E. Clark, "Jerome N. Frank," 66 *Yale Law Journal,* pp. 817–818 (1957); *Time,* March 11, 1940, pp. 71–77; *Fortune,* June 1940, pp. 135–139; Memorandum to the President from William O. Douglas, Dec. 7, 1937, Frank SEC Commissioner Files, Container No. 32; Letter to Frank from Roosevelt, April 24, 1941, Roosevelt Papers, OF 1060; Frank correspondence with Douglas, Frank Papers, Container No. 11, File No. 72, Yale; Address of Jerome Frank, Buffalo, N.Y., May 29, 1938, on file with SEC; and Jerome Frank press conference, May 18, 1939, Frank SEC Commissioner Files, Container No. 29.

6. Most notably in the *North American* case, Holding Company Act Release No. 1427 (1939). See letter to Douglas from Frank, Jan. 12, 1939, Frank Papers, Container No. 25, File No. 166, Yale; and Michael Parrish, *Securities Regulation and the New Deal* (New Haven: Yale University Press, 1970), pp. 223–224.

7. Memorandum of telephone conversation with the President, April 19, 1939, Frank Papers, Container No. 37, File No. 606, Yale; Letter to Corcoran from Frank, Apr. 1, 1939, Frank Papers, Container No. 24, File No. 127, Yale; and *New York Times,* March 22, 1939, p. 33, Apr. 22, 1939, p. 23, and May 19, 1939, p. 33.

8. Memorandum re: Securities and Exchange Commission, May 24, 1940, Roosevelt Papers, OF 1060; Lane, *Oral History,* pp. 414–419; and SEC Press Release, Oct. 24, 1940, concerning Smith.

9. Memorandum to the President from Frank, June 13, 1939, Roosevelt Papers, PSF: Frank.

10. Memorandum to the President from Frank, March 17, 1941, Roosevelt Papers, OF 1060. See also *New York Times,* March 21, 1941, p. 29.

11. SEC *Tenth Annual Report,* p. 115, n. 56; and Robert Ritchie, *Integration of Public Utility Holding Companies* (Ann Arbor: University of Michigan Law School, 1954), pp. 21–23.

12. Vincent Carosso, *Investment Banking in America* (Cambridge: Harvard University Press, 1970), p. 431.

13. "An examination of the proposal of the SEC staff for compulsory competitive bidding in the sale of certain public utility securities," Investment Bankers Association (Jan. 18, 1941) (hereinafter, IBA Examination).

14. 118 F. Supp. 621 (S.D.N.Y. 1953).

15. "The Problem of Maintaining Arm's Length Bargaining and Competitive Conditions in the Sale and Distribution of Securities of Registered Public Utility Holding Companies and Their Subsidiaries," Report of the Public Utilities Division, SEC (Dec. 18, 1940) (hereinafter, "Public Utilities Division Report"), pp. 9–12.

16. "Public Utilities Division Report," pp. 36–37.

17. 1 *SEC* 891 (1936).

18. Holding Company Act Release No. 2676 (1941), pp. 6–7. See aso IBA Examination, p. 25, regarding use of compulsory bidding by the RFC and the United States Treasury.

19. Holding Company Act Release No. 1380 (1938), and No. 2676 (1941), pp. 10–11; and "Public Utilities Division Report," pp. 3–9.

20. 6 *SEC* 457 (1939).

21. "Public Utilities Division Report," especially pp. 22–23.

22. Ibid., p. 23; IBA Examination; Carosso, *Investment Banking in America,* pp. 431–443; *Business Week,* Jan. 25, 1941, p. 50; and *Time,* Feb. 17, 1941, pp. 80–82.

23. *Time,* Feb. 17, 1941, pp. 80–82; *New York Times,* Feb. 2, 1941, III, p. 1, and Feb. 7, 1941, p. 29; and telephone interview with Robert O'Brien, May 29, 1980.

24. Robert O'Brien telephone interview, May 29, 1980; and *New York Times,* May 1, 1941, p. 33.

25. Holding Company Act Release No. 2676 (1941).

26. SEC *Tenth Annual Report,* pp. 105–107; SEC *Fifteenth Annual Report,* pp. 88–90; Carosso, *Investment Banking in America,* pp. 452–454; Donald J. Emblem, *Competitive Bidding for Corporate Securities* (Canton, N.Y.: Plaindealer Press, 1944); Sidney Robbins, "Competitive Bidding in Sale of Securities," *Harvard Business Review* pp. 646–664, (1949); John Falvey, "Competitive Bidding Proves Out," *Public Utilities Fortnightly,* Nov. 22, 1951, pp. 703–709; Louis Ederington, "Negotiated versus Competitive Underwritings of Corporate Bonds," 31 *Journal of Finance,* pp. 17–28 (1976); Richard Edelman, "Underwriters' Commissions on Utility Securities from 1970 to 1976," *Public Utilities Fortnightly,* March 3, 1977, pp. 43–45; Irwin Friend, et al., *Investment Banking and the New Issues Market* (New York: World Publishing, 1967), pp. 385–393; Edward Dyl and Michael Joehnk, "Competitive versus negotiated underwriting of public utility debt," 7 *Bell Journal of Economics,* pp. 680–689 (1976); Charles Christenson, *Strategic Aspects of Competitive Bidding* (Boston: Harvard University Graduate School of Business Administration, 1961), pp. 16–17; and Frank Fabozzi and Gregory Li Calzi, "Negotiated versus Competitive Underwriting of Corporate Bonds, 1974–1976," *Quarterly Review of Economics and Business,* Aug. 1978, pp. 109–117.

27. Michael Joehnk and David S. Kidwell, "Comparative Costs of Competitive and Negotiated Underwritings in the State and Local Bond Market," 34 *Journal of Finance*, pp. 725–731 (1979); and Eric Sorensen, "The Impact of Underwriting Method and Bidder Competition Upon Corporate Bond Interest Cost," 34 *Journal of Finance*, pp. 863–869 (1979). Ederington has concurring views; see "Bidding for Securities: The Effect on the Issuer's Interest Costs," 51 *Journal of Business*, pp. 673–686 (1978).

28. Tamar Frankel, *The Regulation of Money Managers*, vol. 1 (Boston: Little, Brown, 1978), pp. 21–28; and Louis Loss, *Securities Regulation* (Boston: Little, Brown, 1961), pp. 1392–1417. See also SEC *Seventh Annual Report*, pp. 29–35.

29. SEC *Seventh Annual Report*, p. 2.

30. Hugh Bullock, *The Story of Investment Companies* (New York: Columbia University Press, 1959), p. 14; John Kenneth Galbraith, *The Great Crash*, third edition (Boston: Houghton Mifflin, 1972), p. 51; "Stock Exchange Practices," Report of the Senate Banking Committee, Report No. 1455, 73rd Cong., 2nd Sess. (1934) (hereinafter, "Stock Exchange Practices Report"), pp. 333–359; and SEC, *Investment Trusts and Investment Companies*, I, pp. 1–2 and 36, II, pp. 363 and 386–387, and III, pp. 1–4 and 879.

31. SEC, *Investment Trusts and Investment Companies*, III, pp. 40–43.

32. "Investment Trusts and Investment Companies" Hearings, Senate Banking Subcommittee, 76th Cong., 3rd Sess. (1940) (hereinafter, Senate Hearings on S. 3580), p. 34; SEC, *Investment Trusts and Investment Companies*, I, p. 4, and III, pp. 44–47. Flynn's article was succeeded by others, all of which were republished in his book *Investment Trusts Gone Wrong* (New York: New Republic, 1931).

33. "Stock Exchange Practices Report," pp. 333–359.

34. "Investment Trust Study," August 7, 1935, Landis Papers, Container No. 6, Files 10–11, Harvard Law School.

35. Interview with Harry Heller, May 20, 1980, Washington, D.C.; and SEC, *Investment Trusts and Investment Companies*, II, pp. 27–38, and III, p. 48.

36. *Investment Trusts and Investment Companies*, III, pp. 34, 879, 943, 1598–1603, and 1665–1667; "Stock Exchange Practices Report," pp. 334–359; Ferdinand Pecora, *Wall Street Under Oath* (New York: Simon & Schuster, 1939), pp. 206–214; Flynn, *Investment Trusts Gone Wrong*, pp. 56–58; and Bullock, *The Story of Investment Companies*, pp. 19–20.

37. SEC, *Investment Trusts and Investment Companies*, II, p. 276.

38. Ibid., III, pp. 18–26, 1021–1031, 1052–1072, 1316–1335, and 1411–1522.

39. Senate Hearings on S. 3580, pp. 399–405 and 1049; Alfred Jaretzki, "The Investment Company Act of 1940," 26 *Washington University Law Quarterly*, p. 308 (1941); and *New York Times*, March 12, 1940, p. 33.

40. *New York Times*, March 16, 1940, p. 14.

41. Senate Hearings on S. 3580, pp. 1–32.

42. Ibid., p. 132.

43. Jaretzki, "The Investment Company Act of 1940," 26 *Washington University Law Quarterly*, p. 309; *Business Week*, May 4, 1940, p. 45; and Bullock, *The Story of Investment Companies*, p. 77.

44. Taft, quoted in Jerome Frank, *If Men Were Angels* (New York: Harper & Brothers, 1942), p. 149.

45. Senate Hearings on S. 3580, p. 326.

46. Ibid., pp. 326, 345, 401, and 1109; Jaretzki, 26 *Washington University Law Quarterly*, p. 311; and Harry Heller interview, May 20, 1980, Washington, D.C.

47. Senate Hearings on S. 3580, p. 345.

48. Ibid., pp. 1052–1059.

49. Ibid., pp. 1105–1109; and "Investment Trusts and Investment Companies" Hearings, House Commerce Subcommittee, 76th Cong., 3rd Sess. (1940), pp. 62–63, 71–75, and 95–100.

50. Public Law 768, 54 *Stat.* Chapter 686, 76th Cong., 3rd Sess. (1940). See discussion, Senate Hearings on S. 3580, pp. 1109–1117; Jaretzki, 26 *Washington University Law Quarterly*, pp. 312–347; and J. Woodrow Thomas, "The Investment Company Act of 1940," 9 *George Washington Law Review*, pp. 918–946 (1941).

51. "Investment Trusts and Investment Companies" Hearings, House Commerce Subcommittee, 76th Cong., 3rd Sess. (1940), p. 75.

52. SEC *Tenth Annual Report*, p. 158.

53. Senate Report No. 1775, 76th Cong., 3rd Sess., p. 2. See similar statements in Jaretzki, 26 *Washington University Law Quarterly*, pp. 310–311.

54. *The Public Papers and Addresses of Franklin D. Roosevelt* (1940), pp. 334–336.

55. William Cary, "Federalism and Corporate Law," 83 *Yale Law Journal*, pp. 700–703 (1974).

56. *New York Times*, Feb. 24, 1939, p. 27, March 15, 1939, p. 31, and March 16, 1939, p. 35.

57. SEC *Second Annual Report*, table following p. 116, and *Seventh Annual Report*, pp. 288–295; Robert Sobel, *NYSE*, (New York: Weybright & Talley, 1975), pp. 126–127; "Hearings on a Comparative Print Showing Proposed Changes in the Securities Act of 1933," House Commerce Committee, 77th Cong., 1st Sess. (1941) (hereinafter, House Hearings on a Comparative Print), p. 99; and *Fortune*, Dec. 1942, p. 128.

58. Memorandum, "Conference with William McChesney Martin," Sept. 15, 1939, Frank SEC Commissioner Files, Container No. 30.

59. *New York Times*, Dec. 8, 1939, p. 17; and Jerome Frank memorandum "Conferences with Martin et al.," July 14 and 16, 1939, Frank SEC Commissioner Files, Container No. 26.

60. Frank memorandum "Conferences with Martin et al.," July 14 and 16, 1939, Frank SEC Commissioner Files, Container No. 26; and Letter to William McChesney Martin, Jr., Sept. 3, 1939, Frank SEC Commissioner Files, Container No. 26.

61. Securities Exchange Act Release No. 3033 (1941), pp. 3–4; SEC, "Summary of Findings and Conclusions to Be Contained in Report to the Commission by the Trading and Exchange Division on the Problem of Multiple Exchange Trading" (Oct. 22, 1940) (hereinafter, "SEC, October Report on Multiple Trading"), pp. 1–5; and SEC Trading and Exchange Division, "The Problem of Multiple Trading on Securities Exchanges" (Nov. 20, 1940) (hereinafter, SEC, "Final Report on Multiple Trading"), pp. 35–43 and Appendix A.

62. Memorandum, "Conference with William McChesney Martin," Sept. 15, 1939, Frank SEC Commissioner Files, Container No. 30. See also

draft of Frank letter to Martin, Sept. 3, 1939, Frank SEC Commissioner Files, Container No. 26.

63. "Memorandum of a conversation between Chairman James M. Landis, Mr. W. H. Jackson, and Mr. Roland Redmond, on Tuesday, October 27, 1936 at 9:30 A.M.," Douglas SEC Commissioner Files.

64. SEC, "Final Report on Multiple Trading," pp. 13 and 63.

65. SEC, "October Report on Multiple Trading," pp. 5, 7, and 11; SEC, "Final Report on Multiple Trading," pp. 2–4; Memorandum to the Commission from Commissioner Healy, Nov. 25, 1940, Frank SEC Commissioner Files, Container No. 29; and *New York Times*, March 30, 1940, p. 23, Apr. 23, 1940, p. 33, and May 9, 1940, p. 35.

66. SEC, "Final Report on Multiple Trading," p. 3. See also *New York Times*, July 13, 1940, p. 17.

67. SEC, "Final Report on Multiple Trading," pp. 3–4 and Appendix C.

68. Ibid., Appendix C; and *New York Times*, Aug. 31, 1940, p. 17.

69. SEC, "October Report on Multiple Trading," pp. 1 and 11.

70. Securities Exchange Act Release No. 3033 (1941), p. 5.

71. *New York Times*, Dec. 28, 1940, p. 21.

72. *New York Times*, March 6, 1941, p. 31.

73. March 1941 memorandum regarding Martin, Eicher SEC Commissioner Files, Container No. 33; Letter to Sam Rayburn from Frank, March 7, 1941, Frank Papers, Container No. 37, File No. 587, Yale; and *New York Times*, March 7, 1941, p. 29.

74. *Fortune*, Dec. 1942, p. 162.

75. *New York Times*, June 26, 1941, p. 33; Sobel, *NYSE*, pp. 104–121 and 147; *Business Week*, May 10, 1941, pp. 62–63; and House Hearings on a Comparative Print, pp. 102–105.

76. Securities Exchange Act Releases Nos. 3033 and 3053 (1941).

77. *New York Times*, Oct. 28, 1941, p. 35.

78. *New York Times*, Feb. 24, 1939, p. 27, and March 4, 1939, p. 21.

79. Chamber of Commerce: *New York Times*, May 5, 1939, p. 6; Investment Bankers Association: *New York Times*, May 16, 1939, p. 33; NAM: *New York Times*, Jan. 3, 1940, p. 28; New York Curb Exchange: *New York Times*, March 22, 1940, p. 31; The American Bar Association: House Hearings on a Comparative Print, pp. 704–719; and Senator Taft: *New York Times*, Feb. 4, 1940, p. 3.

80. "Statement by Clarence Lea, Chairman, Interstate and Foreign Commerce Committee, House of Representatives," June 14, 1940, Purcell SEC Commissioner Files, Container No. 41. That the SEC was taken by surprise was publicly stated on several occasions, including Eicher address, "The Amendments, A Lesson in Round Table," Dec. 4, 1941, on file with SEC.

81. Memorandum to the President from Jerome Frank, June 12, 1940, Frank SEC Commissioner Files, Container No. 32; and Letter to Sam Rayburn from Frank, Frank SEC Commissioner Files, Container No. 30.

82. Ibid.; and SEC Press Releases, June 19, 20, and 21, 1940, including correspondence among Frank, Lea, and the Investment Bankers Association.

83. Memorandum to the Chairman from Edwin A. Sheridan, "Twenty-Day Waiting Period," Sept. 28, 1939, Eicher SEC Commissioner Files, Container No. 34; Letter to Frank from John Starkweather, Jan. 15, 1940, Frank

SEC Commissioner Files, Container No. 30; *New York Times*, June 26, 1940, p. 33, June 27, 1940, p. 5, and July 10, 1940, p. 27. See also Frank–Lauchlin Currie correspondence, July 9, 10, and 13, 1940, Roosevelt Papers, OF 1060; Loss Papers, Harvard Law School; and Frank SEC Commissioner Files, Container No. 32.

84. House Hearings on a Comparative Print, p. 4; "Report on the Conferences with the Securities and Exchange Commission and Its Staff," by the Investment Bankers Association, et al., July 30, 1941; and SEC Staff "Report on Proposals for Amendments to the Securities Act of 1933 and the Securities Exchange Act of 1934" (July 7, 1941), Loss Papers, Harvard Law School.

85. House Hearings on a Comparative Print, pp. 1027–1031.

86. *New York Times*, March 6, 1941, p. 31.

87. Investment Bankers Association, July 30 Report on Conferences with SEC, p. xiv; *New York Times*, Nov. 17, 1940, III, p. 1, and Jan. 2, 1941, p. 48; and Sobel, *NYSE*, pp. 94–97.

88. *New York Times*, Dec. 5, 1941, p. 1; and House Hearings on a Comparative Print, pp. 1186–1187.

89. SEC *Eleventh Annual Report*, p. 4. The small-issue exemption had been initially sought during the 1940–1941 negotiations among the SEC and financial community's representatives. See SEC July 7 Staff Report, pp. 41–42.

90. Eicher memorandum for the President, Apr. 14, 1941, Frank SEC Commissioner Files, Container No. 32.

91. James Rowe, "Memorandum for the President: SEC," Dec. 19, 1941, Roosevelt Papers, OF 1060-a; and Roosevelt correspondence with Landis, Douglas, and Frank, Dec. 1941, Roosevelt Papers, OF 1060-a.

92. Memorandum to the President from the SEC, Jan. 3, 1942, Roosevelt Papers, OF 1060.

93. Securities Exchange Act Release No. 2887 (1942); SEC Records Section File 67A3613 #1054 20/88-2-1 (re: earlier staff proposals); and Memoranda to the Commission from Milton Freeman, October 1942, Purcell SEC Commissioner Files, Container No. 45.

94. "Securities and Exchange Commission Proxy Rules" Hearings, House Commerce Committee, 78th Cong., 1st Sess. (1943); *Business Week*, Dec. 26, 1942, p. 66; *Washington Post*, Feb. 18, 1943, p. 8; *Nation's Business*, Apr. 1943, p. 66; *Congressional Record*, 78th Cong., 1st Sess., Feb. 16, 1943, pp. 1075–1076, and Feb. 19, 1943, pp. A721–A722; and Milton Freeman interview, May 19, 1980, Washington, D.C.

95. Memorandum to the President from Purcell, June 5, 1943, Purcell SEC Commissioner Files, Container No. 38; *New York Times*, Jan. 3, 1944, p. 25; *Philadelphia Record*, June 17, 1943, p. 28; and *Roosevelt Press Conferences*, vol. 22, pp. 164 and 169 (Oct. 19, 1943).

96. SEC Trading and Exchanges Division, "Report on Floor Trading" (Jan. 15, 1945); Securities Exchange Act Release No. 3727 (1945); Chairman's Memorandum of Conference with Emil Schram, June 22, 1945, Purcell SEC Commissioner Files, Container No. 44. Louis Kohlmeier, *The Regulators* (New York: Harper & Row, 1969), pp. 41–42; Telephone interview with Raymond Vernon, Sept. 22, 1980; *SEC Minutes*, Aug. 8 and 22, 1945; and *Report of Special Study of Securities Markets of the Securities and Exchange Commission* to the House Commerce Committee, House Doc. No. 95, 88th Cong., 1st Sess. (1963), II, pp. 231–232.

97. The Trading and Exchange Division 1946 Report, dated July 12, 1946, is in Hanrahan SEC Commissioner Files, Container No. 66.

98. Gale Eugene Peterson, "President Harry S. Truman and the Independent Regulatory Agencies," Ph.D. dissertation, University of Maryland, 1973, p. 231; *Commercial and Financial Chronicle*, March 28, 1946, p. 1631; and interview with Milton Freeman, May 19, 1980, Washington, D.C.

CHAPTER 8: The Public Utility Holding Company Act Commission

1. Gale Eugene Peterson, "President Harry S. Truman and the Independent Regulatory Commissions," Ph.D. dissertation, University of Maryland, 1973, pp. 221 and 226–227; and *Staff Report on the Securities and Exchange Commission*, prepared for the Committee on Independent Regulatory Commissions, Sept. 1948 (hereinafter, *Hoover Staff Report on the SEC*), p. III-3. By contrast, as a United States senator Truman had supported the purposes of the securities and public utility holding company acts; see Alonzo Hamby, *Beyond the New Deal: Harry S. Truman and American Liberalism* (New York: Columbia University Press, 1973), pp. 43–47 and 249–252; Alfred Steinberg, *The Man from Missouri* (New York: Putnam's, 1962), pp. 144–149; and Peterson, "President Harry S. Truman and the Independent Regulatory Commissions," pp. 228–229.

2. Bernard Schwartz, *The Professor and the Commissions* (New York: Knopf, 1959), p. 42; and Louis Kohlmeier, *The Regulators* (New York: Harper & Row, 1969), pp. 34 and 237.

3. Peterson, "President Harry S. Truman and the Independent Regulatory Commissions," p. 232; and *Hoover Staff Report on the SEC*, pp. III-5 and IV-11.

4. Peterson, "President Harry S. Truman and the Independent Regulatory Commissions," pp. 229–230 and 371–373; SEC *Twelfth Annual Report*, pp. 126–127; *Thirteenth Annual Report*, p. 138; *Fourteenth Annual Report*, p. 124; *Fifteenth Annual Report*, pp. 193–195; and *Sixteenth Annual Report*, pp. 167–168.

5. See, e.g., Hamby, *Beyond the New Deal: Harry S. Truman and American Liberalism*, pp. 55–59, 71–72, 79, 82, 90, 133–134, 161, 213, 335–338, and 344; Steinberg, *The Man from Missouri*, p. 301; and Peterson, "President Harry S. Truman and the Independent Regulatory Commissions," pp. 17–18, 48, and 257.

6. Hamby, *Beyond the New Deal: President Harry S. Truman and American Liberalism*, pp. 338–339 and 460–466; Jules Abels, *The Truman Scandals* (Chicago: Henry Regnery, 1956); William Manchester, *The Glory and the Dream* (New York: Bantam Books, 1974), pp. 602–606; and *New Republic*, March 26, 1951, pp. 5–6.

7. Peterson, "President Harry S. Truman and the Independent Regulatory Commissions," pp. 231–232; *Time*, Aug. 5, 1946, p. 79; and *Commercial and Financial Chronicle*, July 25, 1946, p. 484.

8. *SEC Minutes*, July 23, 1946.

9. Telephone interview with Robert Millonzi, August 15, 1980; and Peterson, "President Harry S. Truman and the Independent Regulatory Commissions," p. 558.

10. SEC Minutes, July 23, 1946; Peterson, "President Harry S. Truman and the Independent Regulatory Commissions," p. 231; Robert Sobel, *Inside Wall Street* (New York; W. W. Norton, 1977), p. 171; *New York Times,* July 3, 1946, p. 33; and interview with Roger Foster, July 24, 1980, Washington, D.C.

11. Interview with Donald Cook, Sept. 16, 1980, New York; Peterson, "President Harry S. Truman and the Independent Regulatory Commissions," p. 370; *Forbes,* Feb. 15, 1950, pp. 14–16; *New York Times,* May 25, 1950, p. 1, and July 29, 1950, p. 18; McDonald biography in Caffrey SEC Commissioner Files, Container No. 53; and Address of Harry S. McDonald to the Investment Bankers Association, Dec. 4–9, 1949, on file with the SEC.

12. Truman formally assumed this power with respect to the SEC through a reorganization plan forwarded to Congress on March 13, 1950, 15 F.R. 3175, 64 *Stat.* 1265.

13. Interview with Donald Cook, Sept. 16, 1980, New York; Peterson, "President Harry S. Truman and the Independent Regulatory Commissions," pp. 554–555 and 557; *Time,* March 10, 1952, p. 89; and *Business Week,* Jan. 19, 1952, pp. 27–28.

14. Congressional Record, 82nd Cong., 2nd Sess., Feb. 25, 1952, pp. 1317–1319.

15. Memorandum to Chairman Demmler from William Timbers, Jan. 27, 1954, Demmler SEC Commissioner Files, Container No. 110.

16. New York Herald Tribune, Aug. 20, 1951, p. 1; *Time,* Aug. 27, 1951, p. 91, and *New York Times,* Aug. 23, 1951, p. 35. The SEC immediately responded, in an Aug. 20, 1951, press release, that the charge was "literally fantastic."

17. "Study of the Securities and Exchange Commission," House Commerce Committee, House Report No. 2508, 82nd Cong., 2nd Sess. (1952).

18. 1933 Securities Act Release No. 3465 (1953).

19. Task Force Report on Regulatory Commissions (Appendix N), Prepared for the Commission on Organization of the Executive Branch of Government (Jan. 1949), pp. 144 and 146; and *Hoover Staff Report on the SEC,* pp. II-14 and II-21. The same point also was made by James Landis, "Report on Regulatory Agencies to the President-Elect" (Dec. 1960), pp. 46–47.

20. Landis, "Report on Regulatory Agencies to the President-Elect," p. 47.

21. Chairman Hanrahan estimated "that he devoted nearly three fourths of his work day to the public utility financing issues." Peterson, "President Harry S. Truman and the Independent Regulatory Commissions," p. 232. Louis Loss, SEC associate general counsel during this period, once related to the author "that you could not get a seat at the table unless you had a public utility issue."

22. Emery Troxel, *Economics of Public Utilities* (New York: Rinehart, 1947), pp. 172 and 187–188; Clair Wilcox, *Public Policies Toward Business* (Homewood, Ill.: Richard D. Irwin, 1966), p. 366; Ronald Finlayson, "The Public Utility Holding Company Under Federal Regulation," *Journal of Business* Supplement (July 1946), p. 11; Note, "Section 11(b) of the Holding Company Act: Fifteen Years in Retrospect," 59 *Yale Law Journal,* p. 1088 (1950); and William Anderson, "Public Utility Holding Companies: The

Death Sentence and the Future," 23 *Journal of Land and Public Utility Economics*, pp. 253–254 (1947).

23. Section 10(b) of H.R. 5423, 74th Cong., 1st Sess. (1935).

24. *In the Matter of American Water Works and Electric Company*, 2 *SEC* 972 (1937); and interviews with Milton Cohen, Aug. 4, 1980, Chicago, and Roger Foster, July 24, 1980, Washington, D.C. See also Finlayson, "The Public Utility Holding Company Under Federal Regulation," *Journal of Business* Supplement, pp. 19–20.

25. *In the Matter of Columbia Gas and Electric Corp.*, 8 *SEC* pp. 460 and 463 (1941).

26. SEC *Eighteenth Annual Report*, p. 136. Long before the Supreme Court upheld the SEC's interpretations of Section 11, the results were anticipated. See, e.g., *New York Times*, Apr. 2, 1946, p. 35, Apr. 7, 1946, III, p. 1, and Dec. 1, 1946, III, p. 1.

27. Learned Hand remark quoted in Milton Freeman, "A Private Practitioner's View of the Development of the Securities and Exchange Commission," 28 *George Washington Law Review*, p. 23 (1959).

28. SEC *Sixth Annual Report*, pp. 11–16, and *Ninth Annual Report*, p. 24.

29. Roger Foster, Book Review, 8 *Stanford Law Review*, p. 313 (1956); and Roger Foster interview, July 24, 1980, Washington, D.C.

30. "The Public Utility Holding Company Act of 1935," Report of the SEC to the Senate Subcommittee on Monopoly, 82nd Cong., 2nd Sess. (1952) (hereinafter, "SEC 1952 Senate Report"), p. 6.

31. See *Standard Oil Co.* v. *United States*, 221 U.S. pp. 77–82 (1911); *United States* v. *American Tobacco*, 221 U.S. pp. 187–188 (1911); and *United States* v. *Union Pacific R.R. Co.*, 226 U.S. pp. 96–98 (1912).

32. Internal Revenue Code of Feb. 10, 1939, Supplement R, Sections 371–373; and 1942 amendments, 56 *Stat.* Ch. 619, p. 960, Section 1808 (f). The significance of these tax provisions is noted in "SEC 1952 Senate Report," pp. 6–7.

33. *In the Matter of Columbia Gas and Electric Corp.*, 8 *SEC* pp. 460–463 (1941); and *In the Matter of United Gas Improvement Company*, 9 *SEC* pp. 77–83 (1941). Discussion of the doctrinal shift from *American Water Works* to *Columbia Gas* and *UGI* appears in Robert Ritchie, *Integration of Public Utility Holding Companies* (Ann Arbor: University of Michigan Law School, 1954), pp. 25–33.

34. *In the Matter of United Gas Improvement Company*, 9 *SEC* pp. 69–73 (1941); and *In the Matter of North American Company*, 11 *SEC* pp. 218–220 (1942). See also *In the Matter of United Gas Improvement Company*, Holding Company Release No. 2500 (1941); and 11 *SEC* pp. 346–347 (1942); *In the Matter of Engineers Public Service Co.*, 12 *SEC* 41 (1942); Ritchie, *Integration of Public Utility Holding Companies*, pp. 230–292; Troxel, *Economics of Public Utilities*, pp. 181–183; and Note, 59 *Yale Law Journal*, pp. 1096–1097.

35. *In the Matter of United Gas Improvement Company*, 9 *SEC* p. 65 (1941); *In the Matter of Engineers Public Service Company*, 9 *SEC* p. 774 (1941); and *In the Matter of the North American Company*, 11 *SEC* p. 206 (1942).

36. *In the Matter of Engineers Public Service Company*, 9 *SEC* pp. 775–

787 (1941); SEC *Seventh Annual Report*, p. 77; and Ritchie, *Integration of Public Utility Holding Companies*, pp. 191–193.

37. The key cases were *In the Matter of North American Company*, 11 *SEC* pp. 208–215 (1942); and *In the Matter of Engineers Public Service Company*, 12 *SEC* pp. 57–61 and 65–71 (1942).

38. See *In the Matter of Electric Bond and Share*, Holding Company Release No. 3750 (1942), pp. 69–73; and *In the Matter of Commonwealth and Southern Corporation*, 11 *SEC* pp. 152–164 (1942). A succinct discussion of the SEC's interpretation of the "unduly or unnecessarily complicated" clause appears in Note, 59 *Yale Law Journal*, pp. 1105–1106. A detailed discussion of the related "unfairly or inequitably distributes voting power clause" appears in Leo Leary, " 'Fair and Equitable' Distribution of Voting Power Under the Public Utility Holding Company Act of 1935," 52 *Michigan Law Review*, pp. 71–110 (1953).

39. Ritchie, *Integration of Public Utility Holding Companies*, pp. 220–229, and Ernest Abrams, "Ten Years of the Public Utility Act of 1935," *Public Utilities Fortnightly*, Nov. 8, 1945, p. 619, summarize the principal instances of this practice; *In the Matter of Middle West Corporation*, 15 *SEC* 309 (1944); *In the Matter of Columbia Gas & Electric Corporation*, 17 *SEC* 494 (1944); *In the Matter of American Gas & Electric Corporation*, Holding Company Act Release No. 6333 (1945); and *In the Matter of Commonwealth & Southern Corporation*, Holding Company Act Release No. 7615 (1947).

40. Milton Cohen interview, Aug. 4, 1980, Chicago. Operating company ownership of both gas and electric properties was criticized by the SEC in *In the Matter of North American Company*, 18 *SEC* pp. 615–621 (1945).

41. See, e.g., financial analysts' statements reprinted in Robert Blair-Smith and Leonard Helfenstein, "A Death Sentence or A New Lease on Life," 94 *University of Pennsylvania Law Review*, pp. 198–201 (1946); and "SEC 1952 Senate Report," pp. 19–20.

42. Senate Report No. 621, 74th Cong., 1st Sess. (1935), pp. 14–17. The SEC's principal investment value decisions are analyzed in E. Merrick Dodd, "The Relative Rights of Preferred and Common Shareholders in Recapitalization Plans Under the Holding Company Act," 57 *Harvard Law Review*, pp. 295–327 (1944). The investment value theory was approved by the Supreme Court in *Otis & Company* v. *SEC*, 323 U.S. 624 (1945). See also *SEC* v. *Central Illinois Corp.*, 338 U.S., pp. 155–159 (1949); *Niagara Hudson Power Corp.* v. Leventritt 340 U.S. 336 (1951); Victor Brudney, "The Investment-Value Doctrine and Corporate Readjustments," 72 *Harvard Law Review*, p. 645 (1959); and Note, 59 *Yale Law Journal*, pp. 1106–1110.

43. *In the Matter of United Gas Improvement Company*, Holding Company Act Releases Nos. 4011 (1942) and 4173 (1943) quoting p. 24; Milton Cohen interview, Aug. 4, 1980, and Roger Foster interview, July 24, 1980, Washington, D.C.

44. SEC *Tenth Annual Report*, p. 97.

45. Standard and Poor's, quoted in Ibid., p. 97.

46. Foster, Book Review, 8 *Stanford Law Review*, pp. 313–314.

47. Weiner point of view described in Ibid., p. 313, and, in similar words by Milton Cohen, in interview, Aug. 4, 1980, Chicago.

48. SEC *Ninth Annual Report*, p. 24.

49. SEC *Thirteenth Annual Report,* p. 225.

50. *North American Company* v. *SEC,* 327 U.S. 686 (1946); and *American Power & Light* v. *SEC,* 329 U.S. 90 (1946).

51. SEC *Thirteenth Annual Report,* p. 225; and *Fourteenth Annual Report,* p. 57.

52. "SEC 1952 Senate Report," p. 17.

53. See, e.g., SEC *Fifteenth Annual Report,* pp. 82–85.

54. SEC *Eighteenth Annual Report,* pp. 83–86; and "SEC 1952 Senate Report," pp. 8–9.

55. SEC *Twenty-fifth Annual Report,* pp. XXV–XXVII.

56. SEC *Twenty-seventh Annual Report,* pp. 100–101; *In the Matter of Electric Bond and Share Company,* Holding Company Act Release No. 14326 (1960); and 9 *SEC* 981–985 (1941).

57. The reorganization of Electric Bond and Share is described in: 9 *SEC* 978 (1941); 11 *SEC* 1146 (1942); 29 *SEC* 52 and 624 (1949); 32 *SEC* 487 (1951); and 35 *SEC* 46 (1953); SEC *Fifteenth Annual Report,* pp. 99–102; "SEC 1952 Senate Report," pp. 9–16; and William Zentz, "The Economic Effects of Forced Geographic Integration of Electric Utility Holding Companies," Ph.D. dissertation, University of Michigan, 1952, pp. 124–144. American's dissolution was responsible for the creation of ten utilities: Central Arizona Power (21 *SEC* 260 (1945)); Florida Power & Light (30 *SEC* 155 (1949)); Kansas Gas & Electric (Holding Company Act Releases Nos. 9150 and 9205 (1949)); Minnesota Power & Light (13 *SEC* 57 (1943), 19 *SEC* 376 (1945), 30 *SEC* 155 (1949)); Nebraska Power (30 *SEC* p. 167, Note 13); New Mexico Electric Service Co. (21 *SEC* 471 (1945)); Pacific Power & Light (25 *SEC* 618 (1947) and 30 *SEC* 818 (1950)); Portland Gas & Coke (35 *SEC* 46 (1953)); Texas Utilities (18 *SEC* 686 (1945), 19 *SEC* 129 (1945), and 30 *SEC* 155 (1949)); and Texas Public Utilities (Holding Company Act Release No. 7456 (1947)). Electric Power and Light's dissolution into Utah Power & Light, United Gas, Middle South, and Idaho Power is described in SEC *Tenth Annual Report,* p. 122; 29 *SEC* 52 (1949); and 29 *SEC* 624 (1949). The dissolution of National Power and Light resulted in Birmingham Electric (Holding Company Act Release No. 6796 (1946)); Carolina Power (Holding Company Release No. 6796 (1946) and 14 *SEC* 910 (1943)); Houston Lighting & Power (13 *SEC* 199 (1943)); Memphis Generating (Holding Company Act Release No. 6229 (1945)); and Pennsylvania Power & Light (Holding Company Act Release No. 6747 (1946)).

58. Holding Company Act Releases Nos. 6639 (1946), 20633 (1976), and 21433 (1980). See also Zentz, "The Effects of Forced Geographic Integration," pp. 106–110 and 118–119.

59. 21 *SEC* 575 (1945); Ritchie, *Integration of Public Utility Holding Companies,* pp. 77–90; Zentz, "The Effects of Forced Geographic Integration," pp. 101–124; and Milton Cohen interview, August 4, 1980, Chicago.

60. SEC *Fourth Annual Report,* pp. 7–8, and *Fifteenth Annual Report,* p. 115. The 50 percent figure assumes that United controlled Commonwealth and Southern, separately listed as a holding company system with $1.2 billion of assets.

61. The transformation of Electric Bond and Share is described in the text. The United Corporation at the outset of its reorganization was described in SEC *Fifteenth Annual Report,* pp. 115–116; 13 *SEC* 854 (1943); and Holding Company Act Release No. 13088 (1956). The dissolution of

United largely was effected through the disintegration of its four principal sub-holding companies: United Gas Improvement, Columbia Gas and Electric, Niagara Hudson, and the Public Service Company of New Jersey. In addition, United indirectly controlled the Commonwealth and Southern Corporation. The dissolution of these five holding company systems are described respectively in the following source notes. *United Gas Improvement Company:* SEC *Tenth Annual Report,* pp. 257, 261, and 266; *Eleventh Annual Report,* pp. A-28–A-29; *Fifteenth Annual Report;* pp. 117–118; *Eighteenth Annual Report,* p. 105; 9 *SEC* 52 (1941); 9 *SEC* 818 (1941); 11 *SEC* 338 (1942); 12 *SEC* 1080 (1943); 15 *SEC* 131 (1943); 27 *SEC* 248 (1947); 32 *SEC* 290 (1951); 32 *SEC* 440 (1951); 33 *SEC* 729 (1952); and Zentz, "The Economic Effects of Forced Geographic Integration," pp. 260–271. *Columbia Gas and Electric: Tenth Annual Report,* p. 259; *Twelfth Annual Report,* p. 171; *Thirteenth Annual Report,* p. 178; *Fifteenth Annual Report,* pp. 116–117; 17 *SEC* 494 (1944); Zentz, "The Economic Effects of Forced Geographic Integration," pp. 202–210; and Ritchie, *Integration of Public Utility Holding Companies,* pp. 99–103. *Niagara Hudson and Public Service Company of New Jersey:* 29 *SEC* 773 (1949); and 27 *SEC* 682 (1948). *Commonwealth and Southern:* Zentz, "The Economic Effects of Forced Geographic Integration," pp. 210–228. The SEC's disintegration of the nonbankrupt Insull interests largely was effected through its reorganization of the Middle West Corporation. This is described in: 15 *SEC* 309 (1944); SEC *Seventh Annual Report,* p. 80; *Tenth Annual Report,* pp. 132–133; *Eleventh Annual Report,* pp. 52–54; *Twelfth Annual Report,* pp. 64–65; *Thirteenth Annual Report,* p. 82; *Fifteenth Annual Report,* pp. 107–108; *Sixteenth Annual Report,* pp. 77–78; Ritchie, *Integration of Public Utility Holding Companies,* pp. 64–77; and Zentz, "The Economic Effects of Forced Geographic Integration," pp. 156–177.

62. Zentz, "The Economic Effects of Forced Geographic Integration," especially pp. 19–39b, 57–66, 126–132, 217–218, and 296–308.

63. Ibid., pp. 32–39b and 302–308.

64. Twentieth Century Fund, *Electric Power and Government Policy* (New York: Twentieth Century Fund, 1948), pp. 35–36 and 313–319; Paul Garfield and Wallace Lovejoy, *Public Utility Economics* (Englewood Cliffs, N.J.: Prentice-Hall, 1964), p. 444; Donald Cook and Herbert Cohn, "Capital Structures of Electric Utilities Under the Public Utility Holding Company Act," 45 *Virginia Law Review,* p. 981 (1959); and Roger L. Miller, "Government Regulation of Corporate Financing with Particular Reference to the Authority of the Securities and Exchange Commission Under the Public Utility Holding Company Act," Ph.D dissertation, University of Illinois, 1966, pp. 110–161, 231–233, and 244–245. Jerome Frank's decisions were crucial to the evolution of this policy. See especially his dissent in *In the Matter of the North American Company,* 4 *SEC* 462 (1939); and his opinion in *In the Matter of Consumers Power Company,* 6 *SEC* 450 (1939). See also *In the Matter of El Paso Electric Company* 8 SEC pp. 383–393 (1941).

65. SEC *Fifteenth Annual Report,* pp. 86–87 and *Seventeenth Annual Report,* pp. 66–67; and Cook and Cohn, "Capital Structures of Electrical Utilities Under the Public Utility Holding Company Act," 45 *Virginia Law Review,* pp. 992–993.

66. SEC *Sixth Annual Report,* pp. 38–39; *Seventh Annual Report,* pp. 103–104; *Tenth Annual Report,* pp. 100–102; *Seventeenth Annual Report,*

p. 67; Address of Richard McEntire before the National Association of Railroad and Utilities Commissioners, July 17, 1947, on file with the SEC. See also Troxel, *Economics of Public Utilities,* pp. 161–162; Twentieth Century Fund, *Electric Power and Government Policy,* pp. 309–311; Cook and Cohn, "Capital Structures of Electrical Utilities Under the Public Utility Holding Company Act," 45 *Virginia Law Review,* pp. 993–994; and Miller, "Government Regulation of Corporate Financing," pp. 229–231.

67. SEC *Sixth Annual Report,* pp. 41–42; *Ninth Annual Report,* pp. 24–25; *Twelfth Annual Report,* pp. 76–77, and *Seventeenth Annual Report,* p. 68. The SEC protective provision policies were described in the 1951 Commission Report to the SEC Subcommittee of the House Commerce Committee, McDonald SEC Commissioner Files, Container No. 74, pp. 100–108; and Miller, "Government Regulation of Corporate Financing," pp. 185–223.

68. Identical data appear in SEC *Seventeenth Annual Report,* pp. 69–72; and "SEC 1952 Senate Report" pp. 19–23.

69. "SEC 1952 Senate Report," pp. 17–18.

70. Cook and Cohn, "Capital Structures of Electric Utilities Under the Public Utility Holding Company Act," 45 *Virginia Law Review,* pp. 997–1005. See also Miller, "Government Regulation of Corporate Financing," pp. 161–185.

71. *In the Matter of the North American Company,* 18 *SEC* p. 621 (1945). The SEC also was criticized for failing to publish studies of the most efficient size, type, and location of individual public utility companies as some argued was required by Section 30 of the act. See, e.g., address by Donald Cook, July 17, 1952, on file with the SEC.

CHAPTER 9: The Budget Bureau's SEC

1. Arthur Dean, Book Review, 50 *Michigan Law Review,* p. 1396 (1952). A minority of conservatives disagreed; see a representative article by Leslie Gould, "SEC A Good Idea Gone Wrong," *American Mercury,* July 1953, pp. 51–56.

2. The Eisenhower budget-cutting efforts are described in Dwight D. Eisenhower, *Mandate for Change* (Garden City, N.Y.: Doubleday, 1963), pp. 33, 64, 121, 127–130, and 296–297; and Dwight D. Eisenhower, *Waging Peace* (Garden City, N.Y.: Doubleday, 1965), p. 218; Sherman Adams, *Firsthand Report* (New York: Harper & Brothers, 1961), p. 154; and Herbert S. Parmet, *Eisenhower and the American Crusades* (New York: Macmillan, 1972), p. 218. See also Emmet John Hughes, *The Ordeal of Power* (New York: Atheneum, 1963), pp. 138–139 and 235–236; and William Cary, *Politics and the Regulatory Agencies* (New York: McGraw-Hill, 1967), pp. 6–7 and 11–12.

3. SEC *Eighteenth Annual Report,* pp. 194–196; SEC *Fifteenth Annual Report,* p. xiv; Rossbach Letter, *New York Times,* Apr. 22, 1954, p. 28; Testimony of Richard McEntire, "Independent Offices Appropriation Bill for 1954" Hearings, House Committee on Appropriations, 83rd Cong., 1st Sess. (1953), p. 515, "Securities and Exchange Commission Confidential Memorandum re: 1953 Appropriation Cut," Cook SEC Commissioner

Files, Container No. 83; and "Study of the Securities and Exchange Commission," Report of the House Commerce Committee, House Report No. 2508, 82nd Cong., 2nd Sess. (1952), pp. 1–4.

4. *New York Times*, Apr. 11, 1953, p. 21.

5. Demmler Letter to Leverett Saltonstall, July 13, 1953, Demmler SEC Commissioner Files, Container No. 109; Demmler Letter to Joseph Dodge, Nov. 17, 1953, Demler SEC Commissioner Files, Container No. 109; SEC *Twenty-second Annual Report*, p. 223; and SEC *Twenty-first Annual Report*, p. 121.

6. *New York Times*, Feb. 11, 1955, p. 32; SEC *Thirty-fifth Annual Report*, p. 199; Philip Loomis, "Enforcement Problems Under the Federal Securities Laws," 14 *Business Lawyer*, p. 680, n. 29 (1959); Interview with Philip Loomis, Sept. 19, 1980, Washington, D.C.; and *SEC Minutes*, Sept. 23, 1953, and Feb. 16, 1954.

7. Demmler background assembled from interview with Ralph Demmler, August 24, 1980, Pittsburgh; Interview with Irving Pollock, July 25, 1980, Washington, D.C.; Interview with Roger Foster, July 24, 1980, Washington, D.C.; Interview with Byron Woodside, July 22, 1980, Washington, D.C.; Ralph Demmler confirmation hearings, Senate Banking Committee, 83rd Cong., 1st Sess. (June 11, 1953) (hereinafter, Demmler confirmation hearings); Addresses of Ralph Demmler, Sept. 24, 1953, Dec. 2, 1953, and Jan. 13, 1954, on file with the SEC; and Ralph Demmler press release, July 16, 1953, Demmler SEC Commissioner Files, Container No. 114.

8. Address of Ralph Demmler, Sept. 24, 1953, on file with the SEC, pp. 8–9; and Edwin Dale, "Broad Changes Are Under Way at SEC," *Finance*, Nov. 15, 1953, p. 66. See also *SEC Minutes*, Oct. 8, 1953, where the SEC officially declined Judge Weinfeld's request to participate as *amicus curiae* in a Chapter XI proceeding.

9. See Demmler Letter to Congressman Bennett on pp. 160–161, "Amendments to Securities Act of 1933" Hearings, House Commerce Committee, 84th Cong. (1955–1956).

10. See, e.g., SEC *Twentieth Annual Report*, pp. 3–8; and Address of Ralph Demmler, Jan. 13, 1954, on file with the SEC.

11. SEC 1954 amendments to proxy rules described in 1934 Securities Exchange Act Release No. 4979 (1954); *SEC Minutes*, August 7, 1953, Jan. 26, 1954, Feb. 19, 1954, March 2, 1954, and March 11, 1954; SEC *Twenty-second Annual Report*, pp. 102–103, and *Twenty-third Annual Report*, pp. 76–77; 1934 Securities Exchange Act Release No. 3638 (1945); *Peck* v. *Greyhound Corp.*, 97 F. Supp. 679 (S.D.N.Y. 1951); *SEC* v. *Transamerica Corp.*, 163 F.2d 511, 517 (3d Cir. 1947); *Medical Committee for Human Rights* v. *SEC*, 432 F.2d 659, 681 (D.C. Cir. 1970); Louis Loss, *Securities Regulation* (Boston: Little, Brown, 1961), pp. 900–915; and Thomas Clusserath, "The Amended Stockholder Proposal Rule: A Decade Later," 40 *Notre Dame Lawyer*, p. 13 (1964).

12. Demmler quoted in Dale, "Broad Changes Are Under Way at SEC," *Finance*, Nov. 15, 1953, p. 66.

13. Interview with Ralph Demmler, Aug. 24, 1980, Pittsburgh.

14. Public Law 577, 68 *Stat.* 683. The principal practice legitimated in the 1954 amendments had been widely used at least as early as 1946. See Address by James Caffrey, Sept. 27, 1946, on file with the SEC.

15. Demmler confirmation hearing, p. 7; and Address of Ralph Demmler,

Sept. 24, 1953, pp. 3–4, on file with the SEC. See also *New Republic*, Sept. 14, 1953, p. 5.

16. Memorandum from William Cary to the Commission, Oct. 15, 1962, Cary SEC Commissioner Files, Container No. 197.

17. *New York Times*, Oct. 30, 1953, p. 35.

18. *Report of Special Study of Securities Markets of the Securities and Exchange Commission* to the House Commerce Committee, House Doc. No. 95, 88th Cong., 1st Sess. (1963) (hereinafter, SEC, *Special Study*), II, pp. 229–237.

19. "Stock Market Study Report," Senate Banking Committee, Senate Report No. 376, 84th Cong., 1st Sess. (1955) (hereinafter, "Senate Stock Market Report"), pp. 1–7.

20. Memorandum to Byron Woodside from Harold Patterson, May 27, 1955, Cohen SEC Papers, XI, File No. 14; "Stock Market Study" Hearings, Senate Banking Committee, 84th Cong., 1st Sess. (1955) (hereinafter, Senate Stock Market Hearings), pp. 324–329; "Amendments to Securities Act of 1933" Hearings, House Commerce Committee, 84th Cong. (1955–1956), pp. 3–6, 80, 272, 300, and 575; SEC, *Special Study*, I, p. 307; and Hillel Black, *The Watchdogs of Wall Street* (New York: William Morrow, 1962), pp. 20–49.

21. See, e.g., *Business Week*, Nov. 10, 1956, pp. 145–150; "Senate Stock Market Report," pp. 10–11; SEC *Seventeenth Annual Report*, pp. 159–160; and William Timbers and Irving Pollack, "Extradition from Canada to the United States for Securities Fraud: Frustration of the National Policies of Both Countries," 24 *Fordham Law Review*, p. 301 (1955).

22. Senate Stock Market Hearings, pp. 132–153; Robert Sobel, *NYSE* (New York: Weybright & Talley, 1975), p. 223; John Brooks, *The Seven Fat Years* (New York: Harper & Brothers, 1958), pp. 193–203; and *Time*, March 15, 1954, pp. 95–96.

23. *Time*, July 16, 1956, p. 82.

24. Senate Stock Market Hearings, pp. 928–931 and 966.

25. "Senate Stock Market Report," pp. 13 and 4.

26. "Amendments to Securities Act of 1933" Hearings, House Commerce Committee, 84th Cong. (1955–1956), see especially pp. 1–16, 160–161, 714, and 719.

27. Hearings on the nomination of Harold Patterson, Senate Banking Subcommittee, 84th Cong., 1st Sess. (1955); Hearings on the nomination of Harold Patterson, Senate Banking Committee, 84th Cong., 1st Sess. (1955); *New York Times*, July 28, 1955, p. 47, Aug. 3, 1955, p. 11, and Aug. 30, 1955, p. 18.

28. Adams, *Firsthand Report*, p. 312; and Hughes, *The Ordeal of Power*, p. 152.

29. Aaron Wildavsky, *Dixon-Yates: A Study in Power Politics* (New Haven: Yale University Press, 1962); "Power Policy: Dixon-Yates Contract" Hearings, Senate Subcommittee on Antitrust and Monopoly, 84th Cong., 1st Sess. (1955), especially pp. 1–2, 773–777, and 1260–1293; Jason Finkle, *The President Makes a Decision: A Study of Dixon-Yates* (Ann Arbor: University of Michigan Press, 1960); In the Matter of Mississippi Valley Generating Company, 36 *SEC* pp. 159–194 (1955); SEC *Twenty-second Annual Report*, pp. 19–21; Eisenhower, *Mandate for Change*, pp. 376–385; and interview with Ralph Demmler, Aug. 24, 1980, Pittsburgh.

30. Finkle, *The President Makes a Decision,* p. 193.

31. *Congressional Record,* 84th Cong., 2nd Sess., Aug. 13, 1956, p. A6439.

32. "Independent Regulatory Commissions," Report of the Special Sub-committee on Legislative Oversight, House Report No. 2711, 85th Cong., 2nd Sess. (1959), pp. 1–3 and 41–50; Bernard Schwartz, *The Professor and the Commissions* (New York: Knopf, 1959), pp. 6–7 and 228–234; Eisenhower, *Waging Peace,* pp. 311–316; and Adams, *Firsthand Report,* pp. 435–451.

33. Letter to Congressman Klein from G. Keith Funston, June 4, 1956, Armstrong SEC Commissioner Files, Container No. 132.

34. Gadsby quoted in *Fortune,* Nov. 1958, p. 226; and Booz Allen & Hamilton, "Survey of Organization and Operations, Securities and Exchange Commission" (Oct. 31, 1960) (hereinafter Booz Allen & Hamilton, "Survey of SEC Operations"), on file with the SEC.

35. SEC *Twenty-seventh Annual Report,* p. 197. Compare with 1945 employment, SEC *Eleventh Annual Report,* p. 94.

36. SEC, *Special Study,* I, pp. 21–23 and 36; SEC *Twenty-seventh Annual Report,* pp. 5–6, 27, and 201. See also Booz Allen & Hamilton, "Survey of SEC Operations," Exhibit I; and Robert Sobel, *Amex* (New York: Weybright & Talley, 1972), p. 231.

37. SEC, *Special Study,* I, p. 245.

38. Ibid., I, p. 487. See also I, pp. 550–551.

39. Richard Phalon quoted in Black, *The Watchdogs of Wall Street,* p. 73.

40. *Time,* Aug. 1, 1960, p. 60.

41. Compare SEC *Twenty-first Annual Report,* p. 8, with *Twenty-seventh Annual Report,* p. 27.

42. James Landis, "Report on the Regulatory Agencies to the President-elect," (Dec. 1960), p. 45.

43. Edward Gadsby, "Historical Development of the SEC — The Government View," 28 *George Washington Law Review,* pp. 16–17 (1959).

44. Interview with Ralph Demmler, Aug. 24, 1980, Pittsburgh; J. Sinclair Armstrong, "The Role of the Securities and Exchange Commission in Proxy Contests of Listed Companies," 11 *Business Lawyer,* p. 122 (1955); Booz Allen & Hamilton, "Survey of SEC Operations," Exhibit I; *New York Times,* July 10, 1955, p. 22; and address of J. Sinclair Armstrong, Nov. 13, 1956, on file with the SEC.

45. See, e.g., *New York Times,* Jan. 5, 1958, III, p. 1, and Jan. 12, 1959, p. 42. Windels also was an inspiration for Black's book, *The Watchdogs of Wall Street.*

46. *New York Times,* May 6, 1959, p. 57, and May 10, 1959, III, p. I.

47. Memorandum to Chairman Cary from Philip Loomis, Jan. 30, 1962, Cary SEC Commissioner Files, Container No. 202.

48. SEC, *Special Study,* IV, pp. 711–722.

49. Cary testimony, "Securities Markets Investigation" Hearings, House Commerce Committee, 87th Cong., 1st Sess. (1961), p. 5.

50. Booz Allen & Hamilton, "Survey of SEC Operations," pp. 128–129.

51. SEC, *Special Study,* I, pp. 275–280.

52. Addresses of William Cary, Nov. 28, 1962, and Dec. 2, 1963, on file with the SEC.

53. SEC "Staff Report on Organization, Management, and Regulation of

Conduct of Members of the American Stock Exchange" (Jan. 3, 1962) (hereinafter, SEC "Staff Report on American Stock Exchange"), pp. 8–10.

54. Ibid., pp. 11–13 and 15.

55. Ibid., p. 15.

56. Ibid., p. 55.

57. Ibid., pp. 17–18.

58. Memorandum to William Cary from Philip Loomis, Jan. 30, 1962, Cary SEC Commissioner Files, Container No. 202.

59. Remarks of J. Sinclair Armstrong, "The Role of the American Stock Exchange," June 19, 1956, on file with the SEC.

60. The Crowell-Collier distribution and Gilligan, Will are described in "Independent Regulatory Commissions," Report of the Special House Subcommittee on Legislative Oversight, House Report No. 2711, 85th Cong., 2nd Sess. (1959), pp. 50–53; SEC "Staff Report on the American Stock Exchange," pp. 23–46; *Gilligan, Will & Co.* v. *SEC*, 267 F.2d, 461 (2d Circuit 1959); 1934 Securities Exchange Act Releases Nos. 5562 (1957), 5686 (1958), and 5689 (1958); and *New York Times*, Feb. 22, 1957, p. 30.

61. SEC, *Special Study*, IV, p. 582.

62. Two extended popular accounts of the Re scandal have been published: Frank Cormier, *Wall Street's Shady Side* (Washington, D.C.: Public Affairs Press, 1962), pp. 37–38; and Sobel, *Amex.* My account was derived from the following government documents: Brief of the Division of Trading and Exchanges before the SEC, *In the Matter of Re, Re and Sagarese* (Apr. 28, 1961); SEC Orders, *In the Matter of Re, Re and Sagarese* (May 12, 1960 and Aug. 24, 1960); *U.S.* v. *Re*, 336 F.2d 306 (2d Cir. 1964); 1934 Securities Exchange Act Release No. 6551 (1961); SEC Litigation Releases No. 2689 (1963) and No. 2741 (1963); SEC "Staff Report on the American Stock Exchange," pp. 52–53; Memorandum to Cary from Loomis, Jan. 30, 1962, Cary SEC Commissioner Files, Container No. 202; *Re, Re and Sagarese*, 41 *SEC* 230 (1962); SEC *Special Study*, IV, pp. 577–579 and 583; and "Securities Markets Investigation" Hearings, House Commerce Subcommittee, 87th Cong., 1st Sess. (1961), pp. 123–133.

63. Memorandum to William Cary from Philip Loomis, Jan. 30, 1962, Cary SEC Commissioner Files, Container No. 202.

CHAPTER 10: Revitalization Under Cary

1. James Landis and his SEC–related recommendations can be found in James M. Landis, "Report on Regulatory Agencies to the President-Elect," (Dec. 1960), especially, pp. 1–7, 11–13, 18, 35–36, 45–48, 66–72, and 81–83; "Regulatory Agencies of Our Government," Presidential Message, Apr. 13, 1961, House Doc. No. 135, 87th Cong., 1st Sess. (1961); Donald Ritchie, *James M. Landis* (Cambridge: Harvard University Press, 1980), pp. 176–185; William Cary, *Politics and the Regulatory Agencies* (New York: McGraw-Hill, 1967), pp. 7–26 and 36–37; *New York Times*, Nov. 11, 1960, pp. 1 and 20; Memorandum for Ralph Dungan from James Landis, Aug. 10, 1961, Kennedy Library, White House Staff Papers, James Landis, Box 14, Folder "SEC Memoranda"; SEC *Twenty-eighth Annual Report*, p. 166; "Special Message to the Congress: Transmitting Reorganization Plan I of 1961,"

Public Papers of John F. Kennedy (1961), p. 324; and Public Law No. 592, 76 *Stat.* 394–395, 87th Cong., 2nd Sess. (1962). See also *Wall Street Journal,* Jan. 5, 1961, p. 16.

2. Arthur Schlesinger, Jr., *A Thousand Days* (Boston: Houghton Mifflin, 1965), pp. 707–713; and Theodore Sorenson, *Kennedy* (New York: Harper & Row, 1965), pp. 339–353. See also James MacGregor Burns, *The Deadlock of Democracy* (Englewood Cliffs, N.J.: Prentice-Hall, 1963), pp. 309–315.

3. Cary, *Politics and the Regulatory Agencies,* p. 7; and Interview with William Cary, October 28–29, 1980, New York City.

4. Cary, *Politics and the Regulatory Agencies,* p. 69.

5. Cary's background was assembled from interview with William Cary, Oct. 28–29, 1980, New York City; Memorandum to the Commission from William Cary, re: Lunch with G. Keith Funston, Oct. 15, 1962, Cary SEC Commissioner Files, Container No. 197; Cary, *Politics and the Regulatory Agencies;* William Cary, "Self-Regulation in the Securities Industry," 49 *American Bar Association Journal,* pp. 244–247 (1963); William Cary, "Corporate Standards and Legal Rules," 50 *California Law Review,* pp. 408–420 (1962); William Cary, "Pressure Groups and the Revenue Code: A Requiem in Honor of the Departing Uniformity of the Tax Laws," 68 *Harvard Law Review,* p. 745 (1955); "Resolution of the Faculty" and "Writings of William Cary," 79 *Columbia Law Review,* pp. 609–617 (1979); *Newsweek,* Dec. 10, 1962, p. 69; and John Brooks, *The Go-Go Years* (New York: Weybright & Talley, 1973), pp. 82–87. The later article by Cary, "Federalism and Corporate Law: Reflections Upon Delaware," appears in 83 *Yale Law Journal* 663 (1974).

6. Interview with William Cary, Oct. 28–29, 1980, New York City.

7. Weiner prepared highly detailed memoranda concerning the Investment Company, Public Utility, Securities, and Securities Exchange acts, which may be found in Cary SEC Commissioner Files, Container No. 205. See also Cary, *Politics and the Regulatory Agencies,* pp. 70–71. Goldsmith's analysis can be found in a letter to Cary, May 15, 1961, in Cary SEC Commissioner Papers, Container No. 181. Schneider's function was explained in an interview with Cary, Oct. 28–29, 1980, New York. See also Carl Schneider, "Reform of the Federal Securities Laws," 115 *Univeristy of Pennsylvania Law Review,* p. 1023 (1967).

8. "Securities Markets Investigation" Hearings, House Commerce Subcommittee, 87th Cong., 1st Sess. (1961); *Public Law* 87–196, 75 *Stat.* 465 (1961); and Cary, *Politics and the Regulatory Agencies,* p. 71.

9. "Securities Markets Investigation" Hearings, House Commerce Subcommittee, 87th Cong., 1st Sess. (1961), p. 32.

10. Telephone interview with David Silver, March 9, 1981. Milton Cohen had a similar recollection in a telephone interview, March 11, 1981.

11. Telephone interview with Milton Cohen, March 11, 1981.

12. Memorandum to the Commission from William Cary, re: Lunch with G. Keith Funston, Oct. 15, 1962, Cary SEC Commissioner Files, Container No. 197; Cary, *Politics and the Regulatory Agencies,* pp. 19 and 71–78; William Cary, "The Special Study of Securities Markets of the Securities and Exchange Commission," 62 *Michigan Law Review,* p. 557 (1964); and *Forbes,* June 15, 1962, p. 41.

13. Telephone interview with David Silver, March 9, 1981.

14. Telephone interview with Milton Cohen, March 11, 1981.

15. "Report of Special Study of Securities Markets of the Securities and Exchange Commission" to the House Commerce Committee, House Doc. No. 95, 88th Cong., 1st Sess. (1963) (hereinafter, SEC, *Special Study*), I, p. v, and IV, pp. 693–728. See also Richard Jennings, "Self-Regulation in the Securities Industry: The Role of the Securities and Exchange Commission," 29 *Law and Contemporary Problems*, p. 663 (1964).

16. SEC, *Special Study*, I, p. 16, and IV, pp. 646–682.

17. Ibid., I, pp. 118–119.

18. Ibid., I, pp. 112–115.

19. Ibid., I, p. 111.

20. Ibid., I, p. 95.

21. Ibid., I, pp. 83–92. See also George Stigler, "Public Regulation of the Securities Markets," 37 *Journal of Business* pp. 117–120 (1964); and Irwin Friend and Edward Herman, "The SEC Through a Glass Darkly," 37 *Journal of Business*, pp. 382–387 (1964).

22. Ames quoted in SEC, *Special Study*, I, p. 47.

23. Ibid., II, pp. 329–346, 349, and 428.

24. Ibid., II, pp. 296, 316, and 321–323.

25. Ibid., II, pp. 311–316 and 953–955.

26. Ibid., II, pp. 316–321.

27. Ibid., II, pp. 302–311.

28. Ibid., II, pp. 323 and 349–351; and interviews with Eugene Rotberg, Feb. 26, 1981, Washington, D.C.; Ralph Saul, March 5, 1981, Philadelphia; David Silver, March 9, 1981 (telephone); and Milton Cohen, March 11, 1981 (telephone).

29. Cary, "Self-Regulation in the Securities Industry," 49 *American Bar Association Journal*, p. 245.

30. 1934 Securities Exchange Act Release No. 6551 (1961); *In the Matter of Re, Re and Sagarese*, 41 *SEC* 230 (1962); *SEC Minutes*, May 9, 1961, May 12, 1961, and May 19, 1961; SEC "Staff Report on Organization, Management and Regulation of Conduct of Members of the American Stock Exchange" (hereinafter, SEC *American Stock Exchange Report*) (Jan. 3, 1962), p. 1, n. 1; and interview with William Cary, October 28–29, 1980, New York City.

31. Cary, *Politics and the Regulatory Agencies*, p. 72.

32. Ibid., pp. 72–73; interview with William Cary, October 28–29, New York City; interview with Philip Loomis, Sept. 9, 1980, Washington, D.C.; SEC, *Special Study*, IV, p. 579; Address of Edwin Etherington, "A Report on the American Stock Exchange: What Ought to Be Done, Can Be Done," March 26, 1963, in Cary SEC Commissioner Files, Container No. 197; and Gustave Levy remark on p. 14 of transcript of SEC "Conference Relating to American Stock Exchange," Feb. 5, 1962, on file in Cary SEC Commissioner Files, Container No. 198.

33. *SEC Minutes*, Dec. 19–21, 1961, Jan. 4, 8, 10, 16, and 22, 1962; SEC *American Stock Exchange Report*, especially pp. 53–54; SEC "Conference Relating to the American Stock Exchange," Feb. 5, 1962, on file in Cary SEC Commissioner Files, Container No. 198; SEC, *Special Study*, IV, pp. 577–583; "Investor Protection" Hearings, House Commerce Committee, 88th Cong., 1st Sess. (1963) (hereinafter, House "Investor Protection" Hearings), pp. 417–436 and 597–598; Special Committee for Study of American Stock Exchange (the Levy Committee) Reports, December 21, 1961, January

30, 1962, and Feb. 15, 1962; Edwin Etherington addresses, Sept. 19, 1962, and March 26, 1963, on file in Cary SEC Commissioner Files, Container No. 197; Brooks, *The Go-Go Years,* pp. 51–53; and *Newsweek,* Jan. 22, 1962, p. 66.

34. The recommendations are contained in the Special Committee for Study of American Stock Exchange's three reports dated Dec. 21, 1961, Jan. 30, 1962, and Feb. 15, 1962. Their acceptance by the Amex membership is discussed in SEC, *Special Study,* IV, pp. 577–583; and House "Investor Protection" Hearings, pp. 417–436.

35. SEC, *Special Study,* IV, p. 579; House "Investor Protection" Hearings, pp. 422 and 597–599; and Edwin Etherington Address, Sept. 19, 1962, on file in Cary SEC Commissioner Files, Container No. 197.

36. SEC, *American Stock Exchange Report,* pp. 47–52; *SEC Minutes,* May 10, 1962; SEC, *Special Study,* IV, pp. 582–583; and House "Investor Protection" Hearings, pp. 436 and 599.

37. SEC, *Special Study,* IV, p. 582; and House "Investor Protection" Hearings, p. 423.

38. Brooks, *The Go-Go Years,* p. 53.

39. Cohen, Saul, Robbins background derived from Interview with William Cary, Oct. 28–29, 1980, New York City; *Newsweek,* Nov. 6, 1961, p. 75; and *Time,* Aug. 26, 1966, p. 68.

40. The 175 recommendations of the Special Study are reprinted in SEC, *Special Study,* V. The text quotes V, p. 66.

41. Cary, *Politics and the Regulatory Agencies,* pp. 99 and 111–112; and *New York Times,* Feb. 9, 1964, III, p. 1.

42. *Public Papers of Lyndon Johnson* (1963–1964), pp. 263 and 267.

43. Memoranda to the chairman of the Commission from Arthur Fleischer, dated Sept. 10, 1962, Jan. 24, 1963, Jan. 31, 1963, and Apr. 1, 1963, Cary SEC Commissioner Files, Container No. 179; Memorandum to the Commission from Walter North, May 14, 1963, Cohen SEC Papers, vol. 32, item 10; Cary transmittal letter, Apr. 3, 1963, SEC, *Special Study,* I, pp. III–IX; Cary transmittal letter, Aug. 8, 1963, SEC, *Special Study,* V, p. 17; and Special Market Study Releases No. 25 (Apr. 30, 1963) and No. 33 (July 23, 1963).

44. Letter to the President of the Senate and to the Speaker of the House of Representatives from William Cary, June 3, 1963, Cary SEC Commissioner Files, Container No. 204.

45. Cary, *Politics and the Regulatory Agencies,* p. 98.

46. Ibid., pp. 98 and 69.

47. Memorandum to the Commission from Milton Cohen, Dec. 12, 1962, Cohen SEC Papers, vol. 40, item 31E.

48. Investment Bankers Association, Memorandum to the Board of Governors, January 7, 1963, Cary SEC Commissioner Files, Container No. 183.

49. *SEC Minutes,* Apr. 24, 1963, May 14, 1963, and May 22, 1963; Memorandum to the Chairman from Douglas North, "Changes Made As a Result of Discussions with Industry," Nov. 27, 1963, Cary SEC Commissioner Files, Container No. 200; and Cary, *Politics and the Regulatory Agencies,* pp. 95–96.

50. "SEC Legislation, 1963" Hearings, Senate Banking Committee, 88th Cong., 1st Sess. (1963) (hereinafter, Senate Hearings on S. 1642); New York Stock Exchange endorsement, pp. 137–140; American Stock Exchange en-

dorsement, pp. 142–143; Midwest Stock Exchange, p. 161; NASD, pp. 65–69; the Association of Stock Exchange Firms, pp. 75–77; the Investment Bankers Association, pp. 80–83 and 281–285; and Chamber of Commerce qualified endorsement, pp. 277–278. Other organizations supported the bill as well. The American Bar Association endorsement appears in a letter to William Cary from the ABA's secretary, Gibson Gayle, July 2, 1964, Cary SEC Commissioner Files, Container No. 201. The Mutual Fund Plan Association endorsement appeared in a letter to Manuel Cohen from James Landis, the association's counsel, June 26, 1963, Cohen SEC Papers, vol. 47, item 32. The "blunting" of the National Association of Manufacturers' opposition is described in Cary, *Politics and the Regulatory Agencies*, p. 95. Javits and Etherington remarks appear in the above cited Senate Hearings on pp. 2–3 and 143, respectively.

51. See SEC *Twenty-ninth Annual Report*, p. 4, n. 2. The bills were denominated S. 1642, H.R. 6789, and H.R. 6793, 88th Cong., 1st Sess.

52. The history of earlier efforts to enact the Frear-Fulbright bill appears in Louis Loss, *Securities Regulation* (Boston: Little, Brown, 1961) pp. 1149–1164; SEC, "Proposal to Safeguard Investors in Unregistered Securities," House Doc. No. 672, 79th Cong., 2nd Sess. (1946); Report of the SEC on S. 2054, 84th Cong., 2nd Sess. (1956); and SEC, *Special Study*, III, pp. 1–17.

53. *SEC Minutes*, March 9, 1962; Memorandum to the Chairman from Arthur Fleischer, March 7, 1962, Cohen SEC Papers, vol. 40, item 31m; and Cary, *Politics and the Regulatory Agencies*, p. 98.

54. SEC, *Special Study*, III, pp. 10 and 9. Regarding unlisted securities cases involving fraud, see also Senate Hearings on S. 1642, 88th Cong., 1st Sess., pp. 288–307.

55. Testimony concerning costs appears in House "Investor Protection" Hearings, p. 78. Testimony concerning insurance securities price dispersion appears in the same House Hearings, pp. 90–95. The George Stigler article quoted appears in *Journal of Political Economy*, pp. 213–225 (1961).

56. The bill as introduced appears on pp. 313–351 of Senate Hearings on S.1642. The compromises were explained in Memorandum to the Chairman from Douglas North, Nov. 27, 1963, Cary SEC Commissioner Files, Container No. 200; SEC Memorandum with Respect to Modification of S. 1642 Proposed by the IBA, June 25, 1963, Cary SEC Commissioner Files, Container No. 183; Proposed IBA Position on the Legislative Proposals of the SEC, June 6, 1963, Cary SEC Commissioner Files, Container No. 202; Cary, *Politics and the Regulatory Agencies*, pp. 96–97; Cary testimony at Senate Hearings on S.1642, pp. 14–17; and *Wall Street Journal*, March 26, 1964, p. 2.

57. House Report No. 1418, 88th Cong., 2nd Sess. (1964), p. 11; and Cary, *Politics and the Regulatory Agencies*, pp. 118–119.

58. Memorandum to the Chairman from Douglas North, Nov. 27, 1963, Cary SEC Commissioner Files, Container No. 200; "Memorandum of the SEC on the provisions of H.R. 6789 that would require membership in a registered securities association," Jan. 1964, Cary SEC Commissioner Files, Container No. 200; Cary testimony, Senate Hearings on S.1642, pp. 40–49; and Cary, *Politics and the Regulatory Agencies*, p. 97.

59. S. 1642, as enacted by the Senate, appears at pp. 54–64 in House "Investor Protection" Hearings. The William-Javits banking amendment is Section 3(e) at p. 56. The legislative process is described in Senate Hearings on S.1642, pp. 1–4, 171–179, and 248–251; House "Investor Protection" Hearings, pp. 1356–1371; *Congressional Record*, 88th Cong., 1st Sess., July 30, 1963, p. 13722; Comptroller of the Currency Press Release, June 5, 1963, Cohen SEC Papers, vol. 41, item 20; and *New York Times*, July 10, 1963, p. 43, July 17, 1963, p. 37, and July 31, 1963, p. 33. Cary's account appears in his *Politics and the Regulatory Agencies*, pp. 99–104.

60. Cary, *Politics and the Regulatory Agencies*, p. 106. A similar view was held by subcommittee chairman Harley Staggers. See *Congressional Record*, 88th Cong., 2nd Sess., Aug. 5, 1964, p. 18182.

61. Oren Harris background assembled from House "Investor Protection" Hearings, pp. 268–269, 274, 740–742, 791–792, 890, 917, 1132, and 1293; *New York Times*, Nov. 21, 1963, p. 55; and Bernard Schwartz, *The Professor and the Commissions* (New York: Knopf, 1959), pp. 8–15, 96, and 215.

62. Interview with William Cary, Oct. 28–29, 1980, New York City; and interview with Philip Loomis, Sept. 19, 1980, Washington, D.C.

63. House "Investor Protection" Hearings, pp. 21 and 26–27; Memorandum to the Commission from Cary, June 19, 1963, Cohen SEC Papers, vol. 33, item 32; and *New York Times*, July 17, 1963, p. 37.

64. See letter to Stevenson from Cary and related materials reprinted in House "Investor Protection" Hearings, pp. 291–293.

65. Senate Hearings on S.1642, pp. 228–241, 267–271, and 275–277; House "Investor Protection" Hearings, pp. 741 and 1001; and *New York Times*, July 17, 1963, p. 42.

66. House "Investor Protection" Hearings, pp. 82–95, 119–122, 175–178, 304–311, 741, 785–789, 893–916, 1001, 1057–1059, 1203–1215, 1271–1283, and 1293; Cary, *Politics and the Regulatory Agencies*, pp. 113–117; Loss, *Securities Regulation*, pp. 1241–1255; *SEC Minutes*, Aug. 26, 1963; and Letter to Harvey Combs, Commissioner, Insurance Department, Arkansas, from William Cary, September 18, 1963, Cohen SEC Papers, vol. 43, item 12. The ultimate compromise is found in Section 12(g)(2)(G) of the 1964 act. See also House Report No. 1418, 88th Cong., 2nd Sess. (1964), pp. 9–11; and *New York Times*, Feb. 20, 1964, p. 39, and March 20, 1964, p. 45.

67. *New York Times*, Oct. 9, 1963, p. 42; Memorandum to the Commission, et al., from Cary, Oct. 14, 1963, Cohen SEC Papers, vol. 35, item 7; and Cary, *Politics and the Regulatory Agencies*, pp. 106–107. Harris was irritated by the newspaper criticism; see House "Investor Protection" Hearings, p. 265.

68. Harris's use of the hearings to allow the insurance industry ample opportunity to be heard is found on p. 822 of House "Investor Protection" Hearings; the state securities commissioners' opposition appears on pp. 733–742 and 783–784. See also Harris comments at p. 289; Cary, *Politics and the Regulatory Agencies*, pp. 107–110; and *SEC Minutes*, Jan. 8, 1964.

69. *New York Times*, Nov. 17, 1963, III, p. 1, Nov. 29, 1963, p. 36, and Jan. 19, 1964, IV, p. 12. Cary, in his memoirs, speculated that the *Times*'s lobbying made little difference: "What is a critical story in a New York paper to an Arkansas congressman?" See *Politics and the Regulatory Agencies*, p. 106.

70. *Public Papers of Lyndon B. Johnson* (1963–1964), pp. 263 and 267; and *New York Times*, Jan. 22, 1964, p. 50, and Feb. 9, 1964, III, p. 1.

71. House "Investor Protection" Hearings, p. 822.

72. Compare *New York Times*, article Jan. 19, 1964, p. 50 (before Johnson's January 21 endorsement of the bill), in which Harris refused to discuss his plans for the securities bill with the *Wall Street Journal*, Jan. 23, 1964, p. 5, the day after Johnson's endorsement, which reported "several signs during the hearing yesterday of the lawmakers' intent to get moving on the bill" and *New York Times*, Feb. 9, 1964, III, p. 1 reporting, "According to talk on Capitol Hill, it was, in fact, the President's endorsement of the legislation that caused Representative Oren Harris . . . to decide that the legislation had been studied long enough."

73. House Report No. 1418, 88th Cong., 2nd Sess. (1964), pp. 8–13; *New York Times*, Feb. 20, 1964, p. 39 (concerning insurance exemption); House "Investor Protection" Hearings, p. 274 (concerning farm cooperatives); and *SEC Minutes*, March 20, 1964, Apr. 28 and 30, 1964 (concerning Insurance Securities, Incorporated, role in compromise concerning compulsory membership in broker-dealer firms. On this issue, see also Cary, *Politics and the Regulatory Agencies*, pp. 109–110). On Harris's control of process, see also *New York Times*, Apr. 30, 1964, p. 47, and May 8, 1964, p. 43.

74. Memorandum to the files re: meeting with Congressman Oren Harris on H.R. 6789, June 3, 1964, Cary SEC Commissioner Files, Container No. 201; Cary, *Politics and the Regulatory Agencies*, pp. 119–120; and comparison of House Commerce Committee version of the revised Section 12(i) of the 1934 Securities Exchange Act reprinted in House Report No. 1418, 88th Cong., 2nd Sess. (1964), pp. 53–54, with that section as ultimately enacted.

75. Cary, *Politics and the Regulatory Agencies*, pp. 4 and 118; and Interview with William Cary, Oct. 28–29, 1980, New York City.

76. House Report No. 1418, 88th Cong., 2nd Sess. (1964) p. 8.

77. The Special Study's recommendations were printed in a summary volume V.

78. A convenient summary of results through Aug. 20, 1964, may be found in a letter to Oren Harris from William Cary, August 20, 1964, reprinted in *Congressional Record*, 88th Cong., 2nd Sess., Aug. 21, 1964, pp. 20776–20778. See also *SEC Minutes*, July 22, 1963, Oct. 10 and 29, 1963; and Memoranda to the Commission from Walter Werner, dated Sept. 20, 1963, Cary SEC Commissioners Files, Container No. 182, and Oct. 14, 1963, Cary Commissioner Files, Container No. 199. The new entrance requirements were criticized in the aftermath of the 1960s' "back-office" crisis. See House Commerce Committee Report, "Securities Industry Study," House Report No. 92-1519, 92nd Cong., 2nd Sess. (1972), pp. 19–24; and "Review of SEC Records of the Demise of Selected Broker-Dealers," House Commerce Special Subcommittee on Investigations Staff Study, Subcommittee print, 92nd Cong., 1st Sess. (1971), pp. 5–8, 18–26, and 110–118.

79. SEC, *Special Study*, IV, pp. 504–577; and Memorandum to the Commission from Ralph Saul, "New York Stock Exchange Organization," Apr. 27, 1964, Cary SEC Commissioner Files, Container No. 197.

80. William Cary memorandum "Meeting with Mr. G. Keith Funston in my office today," Jan. 8, 1964, Cary SEC Commissioner Files, Container No. 197; Memorandum to the Commission from Ralph Saul, "New York Stock Exchange Organization," Apr. 27, 1964, Cary SEC Commissioner Files, Container No. 197; *SEC Minutes*, Apr. 29, 1964 and July 15, 1965; *Business Week*, June 20, 1964, p. 120; and interview with Ralph Saul, March 5, 1981, Philadelphia.

81. The Martin Report was reprinted in BNA *Securities Reporter* No. 114; August 11, 1971, pp. E1–E7. The ensuing changes are described in BNA *Securities Reporter*, No. 133, Jan. 5, 1972, pp. A15–A17; and Chris Welles, *The Last Days of the Club* (New York: Dutton, 1975), pp. 103–104.

82. SEC, *Special Study*, II, pp. 203–242. See also "Memorandum prepared by the Division of Trading and Markets in reply to Chairman Staggers's letter dated December 2, 1963," Cary SEC Commissioner Files, Container No. 186, which on p. 5 described floor-trader activity in 25 securities immediately after it was learned President Kennedy had been assassinated on November 22, 1963: "Many of the floor traders' sales came immediately after the news of the assassination but before the public reacted."

83. 40 *SEC* 907 (1961).

84. Memorandum to the Commission from Byron Woodside, "Floor Trading," March 24, 1964, Cary SEC Commissioner Files, Container No. 180.

85. Memorandum to the Commission from Saul, "Floor Trading on the New York and American Stock Exchanges," Feb. 28, 1964, Cary SEC Commissioner Files, Container No. 180.

86. The "Segregation Report" was quoted in SEC, *Special Study*, II, p. 220.

87. Extracts from the testimony of several floor traders can be found in Cary SEC Commissioner Files, Container No. 180.

88. SEC, Special Market Study Release No. 33 (July 23, 1963), p. 3.

89. Interview with William Cary, Oct. 28–29, 1980, New York City. See also Letter to Cary from Milton Cohen, March 10, 1964, Cary SEC Commissioner Files, Container No. 180.

90. *SEC Minutes*, Oct. 29, 1963, and Nov. 6, 1963.

91. A Feb. 1964 version of the report, entitled "New York Stock Exchange Study of Floor Trading" appears in Cary SEC Commissioner Files, Container No. 180. This is the modified version of the report. The Cresap firm's understanding of its role appears on pp. I-2–I-3.

92. Memoranda to the Commission from Ralph Saul, dated Feb. 28, 1964, and March 24, 1964, Cary SEC Commissioner Files, Container No. 180; *SEC Minutes*, March 13, 1964; Interview with William Cary, Oct. 28–29, 1980, New York City; and *New York Times*, Apr. 6, 1964, p. 45, and Apr. 12, 1964, III, p. 1.

93. *SEC Minutes*, Feb. 13, 1964, Feb. 19, 1964, March 26, 1964, and May 14, 1964.

94. *SEC Minutes*, Feb. 20, 1964, March 13, 1964, and March 17, 1964.

95. Interview with William Cary, Oct. 28–29, 1980, New York City.

96. *New York Times*, Apr. 6, 1964, p. 45, and Apr. 12, 1964, III, p. 1.

97. 1934 Securities Exchange Act Release No. 7290 (1964), p. 10.

98. Telephone interview with David Silver, July 7, 1981; *SEC Minutes*, March 13, 1964; 1934 Securities Exchange Act Release No. 7290 (1964); Memorandum to the Commission from Ralph Saul, "Floor Trading," March 24, 1964, Cary SEC Commissioner Files, Container No. 180; and *New York Times*, March 23, 1964, p. 45.

99. Memorandum to Members and Allied Members from Funston, "Discussions with the SEC on Floor Trading," March 14, 1964, Cary SEC Commissioner Files, Container No. 180.

100. Letter to Ralph Saul from Funston, March 20, 1964, Cary SEC Commission Files, Container No. 180.

101. Cary, *Politics and the Regulatory Agencies*, pp. 16–18; and *New York Times*, March 23, 1964, p. 45, and March 26, 1964, p. 49.

102. Telephone interview with David Silver, July 7, 1981; *SEC Minutes*, March 26, 1964; and *Newsweek*, June 22, 1964, p. 63.

103. *SEC Minutes*, March 31, 1964, and May 25, 1964; 1934 Securities Exchange Act Releases Nos. 7290 (1964) and 7330 (1964); and Memorandum to the Commission from Ralph Saul, "Floor Trading," March 31, 1964, Cary SEC Commissioner Files, Container No. 180.

104. Loss, *Securities Regulation*, p. 3237.

105. Interview with Ralph Saul, March 5, 1981, Philadelphia.

106. SEC, *Special Study*, II, pp. 101–106 and 223–225; and Cresap, McCormick, and Paget, "New York Stock Exchange Study of Floor Trading," p. V–4. See also Richard Jennings and Harold Marsh, *Securities Regulation*, fourth edition (Mineola, N.Y.: Foundation Press, 1977), pp. 615–616.

107. Branch of Trading and Special Studies, Division of Trading and Markets, "Report on Floor Trading on the NYSE under Commission Rule 11a–1," (May 1965) on file in SEC Library. The New York Stock Exchange's unwillingness to enforce effectively the 1964 floor-trading rule proved to be a persistent problem. The SEC's May 19, 1967 *Minutes*, for example, reported that the Trading and Markets Division Staff "had concluded that the Exchange was not enforcing the new floor-trading rules effectively despite numerous and repeated violations by members."

108. Interview with William Cary, Oct. 28–29, 1980, New York City.

109. Interview with William Cary, Oct. 28–29, 1980, New York City; Sidney Robbins, *The Securities Markets* (New York: Free Press, 1966), pp. 202–204; interview with Walter Werner, Oct. 28, 1980, New York City; and *Newsweek*, June 22, 1964, p. 63.

110. *Fortune*, May 1964, p. 149.

111. SEC, *American Stock Exchange Report*, p. 23.

112. Regarding the historical controversy concerning specialists, see Chap. 3 and Chap. 5. See also, Nicholas Wolfson, Richard Phillips, and Thomas Russo, *Regulation of Brokers, Dealers and Securities Markets* (Boston: Warren, Gorham & Lamont, 1977), pp. 11-2–11-19; and Raymond Vernon, *The Regulation of Stock Exchange Members* (New York: Columbia University Press, 1941), pp. 69–96.

113. Brief of the Division of Trading and Exchanges before the SEC, *In the Matter of Re, Re and Sagarese* (April 28, 1961).

114. SEC, *American Stock Exchange Report*, pp. 23–39.

115. SEC, *Special Study*, II, 110–114 and 120–121.

116. SEC, "Memorandum prepared by the Division of Trading and Markets in reply to Chairman Staggers' letter dated December 2, 1963," Cary SEC Commissioner Files, Container No. 186.

117. SEC, *Special Study*, II, p. 167.

118. Ibid., especially pp. 106–110.

119. Letter to the author, September 22, 1981.

120. SEC, *Report on the Feasibility and Advisability of the Complete Segregation of the Functions of Dealer and Broker* (1936), p. 41.

121. SEC, *Special Study*, II, pp. 62–63. Compare G. Keith Funston "Letter of Comment, *Harvard Business Review*, Sept.–Oct. 1962, pp. 7–12, with Funston statement quoted in *Special Study*, II, pp. 955–956. Regarding end of specialist competition in 1967, see John Christian Knorr, "An Appraisal of the Securities and Exchange Commission's Regulation of the New York Stock Exchange Specialist," D.B.A. dissertation, Arizona State University, 1975, p. 21.

122. SEC, *Special Study*, II, pp. 837–841.

123. Ibid., II, pp. 848, 857–858, 865, and 899. See II, pp. 870–904, generally.

124. Ibid., II, pp. 939–940.

125. Ibid., II, pp. 959–961.

126. Ibid., II, p. 951.

127. SEC, *Special Study*, II, pp. 90–92, 366, and 379.

128. NYSE data summarized in *Securities Week*, Feb. 23, 1976, pp. 1–2.

129. SEC, *Special Study*, II, pp. 68 and 371–372.

130. Vernon, *The Regulation of Stock Exchange Members*, pp. 91–93.

131. SEC, *Special Study*, II, p. 160.

132. Ibid., II, pp. 146–150 and 160–161.

133. Ibid., II, pp. 74–78.

134. Ibid., II, pp. 101–106.

135. Ibid., pp. 105–106 and 355–356.

136. Robbins, *The Securities Markets*, pp. 199–200.

137. "Securities Industry Study" Hearings, Senate Banking Subcommittee, 92nd Cong., 2nd Sess. (1972), IV, pp. 22–28.

138. SEC, *Special Study*, II, pp. 167–171.

139. Interview with William Cary, October 28–29, 1980, New York City. See similar proposals in *Harvard Business Review*, May–June 1962, p. 145; and *Financial Analysts Journal*, Nov.–Dec. 1969, pp. 104A–104D.

140. The SEC-Exchange specialist rule negotiations are discussed in "Securities Industry Study" Hearings, Senate Banking Subcommittee, 92nd Cong., 2nd Sess. (1972), IV, pp. 1–21; "Securities Industry Study Report" of the Senate Banking Subcommittee, Senate Doc. No. 93–13, 93rd Cong., 1st Sess. (1973), pp. 201–204; 1934 Securities Exchange Act Releases Nos. 7432 and 7465 (1964); Nicholas Wolfson and Thomas Russo, "The Stock Exchange Specialist: An Economic and Legal Analysis," 1970 *Duke Law Journal*, pp. 707–746; and *Business Week*, Oct. 3, 1964, pp. 120 and 124.

141. The 1970 SEC staff investigation is summarized in "Securities Industry Study" Hearings, Senate Banking Subcommittee, 92nd Cong., 2nd Sess. (1972), IV, pp. 34–35 and 38–46. See also Commissioner Loomis's comments on pp. 57–73; and Knorr, "An Appraisal of the Securities and Exchange Commission's Regulation of the New York Stock Exchange Specialist," a statistical analysis of the SEC's 1964 specialist rule.

142. SEC, *Institutional Investor Study*, House Doc. No. 92–64, 92nd Cong., 1st Sess. (1971), I, p. XXV; and SEC "Statement on the Future Structure of the Securities Market," Feb. 2, 1972, p. 11.

143. 283 *Mass.* 358 (1933).

144. William Cary, "Corporate Standards and Legal Rules," Walter Perry Johnson Lecture, Berkeley, California, March 24, 1962, Cary SEC Commissioner Files, Container No. 186.

145. 40 *SEC* 907 (1961).

146. Louis Loss, "The American Law Institute's Federal Securities Code Project," 25 *Business Lawyer*, p. 34 (1969).

147. 1934 Securities Exchange Act Release No. 3230 (1942); *In the Matter of the Ward La France Trucking Corporation*, 1934 Securities Exchange Act Release No. 3445 (1943); Loss, *Securities Regulation*, pp. 1448–1474, see especially pp. 1455–1456; and remarks of Milton Freeman, reprinted in 22 *Business Lawyer*, pp. 921 923 (1967).

148. Cary, *Politics and the Regulatory Agencies*, p. 84; and Interview with William Cary, October 28–29, 1980, New York City.

149. 377 U.S. 426 (1964).

150. *Annual Report of the Director of the Administrative Office of the United States Courts* (1961), p. 239, (1963), p. 199, and (1970), pp. 232–233; Loss, *Securities Regulation*, p. 1449; and Alan Bromberg, *Securities Law: Fraud SEC Rule 10b-5* (Colorado Springs: Shepard's, Inc., 1967).

151. *Public Papers of Lyndon Johnson* (1963–1964), pp. 993, 1132, and 1150–1151.

152. Interview with William Cary, Oct. 28–29, 1980, New York City; Cary, *Politics and the Regulatory Agencies*, pp. 19 and 63; and *Wall Street Journal*, May 14, 1964, p. 1.

153. Lyndon Johnson, *The Vantage Point* (New York: Holt, Rinehart & Winston, 1971), especially, pp. 27–30 and 69–81.

154. *New York Times*, June 6, 1964, p. 27, June 9, 1964, p. 34, June 21, 1964, p. 48, and June 22, 1964, p. 38; and *Nation*, June 22, 1964, p. 613.

155. *Public Papers of Lyndon Johnson* (1963–1964), p. 993.

156. SEC *Thirtieth Annual Report*, p. 160; *Thirty-first Annual Report*, p. 156; *Thirty-second Annual Report*, p. 149; *Thirty-third Annual Report*, p. 148; *Thirty-fourth Annual Report*, p. 171; and *Thirty-fifth Annual Report*, p. 181.

CHAPTER 11: The Midlife Crisis of the SEC

1. William Cary, *Politics and the Regulatory Agencies* (New York: McGraw-Hill, 1967), p. 7.

2. Telephone interview with Leonard Leiman, March 20, 1981.

3. SEC *Thirty-fourth Annual Report*, pp. xvii and 11–12; *Thirty-fifth Annual Report*, pp. 32, 76, and 187; and SEC, *Institutional Investor Study*, House Doc. No. 92-64, 92nd Cong., 1st Sess. (1971) (hereinafter, SEC, *Institutional Investor Study*), pp. 2160–2161.

4. SEC, *Institutional Investor Study*, pp. 58–62, 119, 1389, and 2167–2168; "Report of Special Study of Securities Markets of the Securities and Exchange Commission" to the House Commerce Committee, House Doc. No. 95, 88th Cong., 1st Sess. (1963) (hereinafter, SEC, *Special Study*), II, pp. 6 and 837–870; and Raymond Goldsmith, *Institutional Investors and Corporate Stock: A Background Study* (New York: Columbia University Press, 1973). See also Robert Soldofsky, *Institutional Holdings of Common Stock*: 1900–2000 (University of Michigan Bureau of Business Research, 1971).

5. SEC, *Institutional Investor Study*, pp. 1537–1541, 1622–1630, 1819–1824, 1959–1961, and 2167; Lawrence Shepard, *The Securities Brokerage Industry* (Lexington, Mass.: Lexington Books, 1975), p. 27; and Chris Welles, *The Last Days of the Club* (New York: Dutton, 1975), pp. 53–60.

6. SEC *Institutional Investor Study,* pp. 1630–1633; SEC *Thirty-fourth Annual Report,* pp. xix and 15–16; and *Thirty-seventh Annual Report,* pp. 8–10; *SEC Minutes,* Jan. 31, 1964, and Sept. 10, 1964; and Robert Sobel, *NYSE* (New York: Weybright & Talley, 1975), pp. 330–354.

7. SEC *Thirty-fifth Annual Report,* pp. 18 and 193; Address of SEC commissioner Hugh Owens, Oct. 20, 1967, reprinted in "Investment Company Act Amendments of 1967" Hearings, House Commerce Subcommittee, 90th Cong., 1st Sess. (1967) (hereinafter, House 1967 Mutual Fund Hearings), pp. 740–744; John Brooks, *The Go-Go Years* (New York: Weybright & Talley, 1973), pp. 127–149 and 266–285; Robert Sobel, *The Last Bull Market* (New York: W. W. Norton, 1980), pp. 107, 188–192, and 204–205; Peter Wyckoff, *Wall Street and the Stock Markets* (New York: Chilton Book, 1972), pp. 115, 124, and 127–128; and *Business Week,* Jan. 18, 1969, pp. 108–114.

8. Cohen background assembled from Manuel Cohen, "The SEC and Proxy Contests," 20 *Federal Bar Journal,* p. 91 (1960); "Broker-Dealer Selling Practice Standards: The Importance of Administrative Adjudication in Their Development," 29 *Law and Contemporary Problems,* p. 691 (1964); Book Review, "Cary's Politics and the Regulatory Agencies," 35 *University of Chicago Law Review,* p. 399 (1968); Addresses dated March 10, 1964; Aug. 11, 1964, and Dec. 1, 1964, on file with the SEC; Arthur Mathews and Michael Klein, "Manuel F. Cohen in Perspective: Manny — We Miss Your Sparkle!" 46 *George Washington Law Review,* p. 719 (1978); *Business Week,* July 18, 1964, pp. 26–27; Leonard Leiman, David Ratner, and Meyer Eisenberg, "Manuel F. Cohen: In Memoriam," 46 *George Washington Law Review,* p. 711 (1978); Interviews with Leonard Leiman, March 20, 1981 (telephone), David Ratner, Feb. 12, 1981 (telephone), Meyer Eisenberg, March 2, 1981, Washington, D.C., Philip Loomis, March 4, 1981, Washington, D.C. and Arthur Mathews, March 4, 1981, Washington, D.C.; *Washington Post,* June 18, 1977, p. D3; *New York Times,* July 11, 1964, pp. 1 and 20; *Time,* July 17, 1964, p. 74; *Wall Street Journal,* July 13, 1964, p. 5; and William Cary Memorandum to the White House, "Appointment of SEC Commissioner," July 6, 1961, White House Central Subject File, Box 179, File FG 281, John Fitzgerald Kennedy Library.

9. Cohen quoted in *Institutional Investor,* Feb. 1969, pp. 75 and 149.

10. Manuel F. Cohen and George Stigler, *Can Regulatory Agencies Protect Consumers?* (Washington, D.C.: American Enterprise Institute, 1971), pp. 39–40.

11. Cohen response to Nixon quoted in *Washington Post,* Oct. 9, 1968, p. D7.

12. Cohen quoted in *Institutional Investor,* Feb. 1969, p. 149.

13. For a succinct summary of the leading cases of this period, see Mathews and Klein, "Manuel F. Cohen in Perspective," 46 *George Washington Law Review,* pp. 724–732. The text was largely based on interviews with Stanley Sporkin, March 2, 1981, Washington, D.C.; Ralph Saul, March 5, 1981, Philadelphia; Ira Pearce, telephone interview, March 20, 1981 (Pearce supplied data on number of cases initiated by reading an Enforcement Division computer tabulation); Philip Loomis, March 4, 1981, Washington, D.C.; Meyer Eisenberg, March 2, 1981, Washington, D.C.; and Arthur Mathews, March 4, 1981, Washington, D.C. The work of Jaegerman and Callahan also was noted in *Fortune,* June 1940, p. 128; and Hillel Black,

The Watchdogs of Wall Street (New York: William Morrow, 1962). The Merrill Lynch consent decree appears at 43 *SEC* 933 (1968). See also 44 *SEC* 633 (1971).

14. "Report of the Securities and Exchange Commission on the Public Policy Implications of Investment Company Growth," House of Representatives Report No. 2337, 89th Cong., 2nd Sess. (1966) (hereinafter, SEC *1966 Investment Company Report*) p. VII; Irwin Friend, Marshall Blume, and Jean Crockett, *Mutual Funds and Other Institutional Investors* (New York: McGraw-Hill, 1970), pp. 11–16, quoting Investment Company Institute data at p. 15; Brooks, *The Go-Go Years,* pp. 128–149; and Sobel, *The Last Bull Market,* pp. 150–159.

15. SEC 1966 *Investment Company Report,* pp. 311–324; Sobel, *The Last Bull Market,* pp. 156–159; and 1934 Securities Exchange Act Releases Nos. 7816 (1966) and 8083 (1967).

16. See Carol J. Loomis, "The SEC Has a Little List," *Fortune,* Jan. 1967, p. 154. See also *New York Times,* May 16, 1966, p. 1, May 17, 1966, p. 1, and May 18, 1966, p. 1.

17. SEC *Twenty-seventh Annual Report,* pp. 3–4; and SEC 1966 *Investment Company Report,* pp. 132–137.

18. Gadsby address quoted in Joseph Weiner memorandum, "The Administration of the Investment Company Act," Dec. 21, 1961, Cary SEC Commissioner Files, Container No. 205.

19. Ibid.; and SEC 1966 *Investment Company Report,* pp. 201–209.

20. Wharton School of Finance and Commerce, "A Study of Mutual Funds," House Report No. 2274, 87th Cong., 2nd Sess. (1962) (hereinafter, *Wharton Mutual Fund Study*), pp. 16–21 and 345–347; and Friend, Blume, and Crockett, *Mutual Funds and Other Institutional Investors,* pp. 17–18.

21. "Mutual Fund Legislation of 1967" Hearings, Senate Banking Committee, 90th Cong., 1st Sess. (1967) (hereinafter, 1967 Senate Mutual Fund Hearings) pp. 803–805.

22. *Wharton Mutual Fund Study,* pp. 3 and 6–9; and 1967 House Mutual Fund Hearings, p. 696.

23. Griswold quoted in SEC 1966 *Investment Company Report,* pp. 94–95.

24. Ibid., pp. 95–104 and 121–123; and *Wharton Mutual Fund Study,* pp. 28–30 and 480–525.

25. *Wharton Mutual Fund Study,* pp. 30–32 and 469–471; and SEC 1966 *Investment Company Report,* pp. 208–209.

26. SEC, *Special Study,* IV, pp. 96 and 109–110. See also 1967 Senate Mutual Fund Hearings, pp. 177–184.

27. Interview with William Cary, October 28–29, 1980, New York City.

28. *SEC Minutes,* June 28, 1962; Memorandum to the Commission from Coker, June 19, 1962, Cohen SEC Papers, vol. 103c–III, item 61; and undated Coker draft memorandum, Cohen SEC Papers, vol. 103c–III, item 58. See also Allan Conwill address, Oct. 25, 1962, on file with the SEC.

29. Memorandum to the Commission, July 23, 1962, Cohen SEC Papers, vol. 103c–III, item 65; and telephone interview with Jack Whitney, March 20, 1981.

30. Cary letter of transmittal reprinted both in the *Wharton Mutual Fund Study* and in Investment Company Act Release No. 3530 (1962).

31. Cohen SEC Papers, vol. 103c–IV, item No. 4.

32. SEC, *Special Study*, IV, pp. 169–212. See also SEC 1966 *Investment Company Report*, pp. 57–58 and 223–247.

33. SEC 1966 *Investment Company Report*, p. VIII.

34. Leon Levy and Sidney Robbins, "Has the SEC Forgotten its Economics?," *Columbia Journal of World Business*, May–June 1967, p. 7.

35. Walter Werner, "Protecting the Mutual Fund Investor: the SEC Reports on the SEC," 68 *Columbia Law Review*, p. 2 (1968).

36. Testimony of Paul Samuelson at 1967 Senate Mutual Fund Hearings, pp. 347–355, and at "Investment Company Amendments Act of 1969" Hearings, Senate Banking Committee, 91st Cong., 1st Sess. (1969) (hereinafter, 1969 Senate Mutual Fund Hearings), p. 55; Cohen and Stigler, *Can Regulatory Agencies Protect Consumers*, p. 8; the Department of Justice, 1967 House Mutual Fund Hearings, pp. 20–22, and Summary of Statements of Department of Justice, Henry Wallich, and Donald Farrar, SEC staff report, "Mutual Fund Distribution and Section 22(d) of the Investment Company Act of 1940" (Aug. 1974), pp. 69–73; Statement of Irwin Friend, 1967 Senate Mutual Fund Hearings, p. 685; Letter from Gardner Ackley, Chairman of the Council of Economic Advisers, Aug. 1, 1967, 1967 Senate Mutual Fund Hearings, p. 957; and SEC staff report, "The Potential Economic Impact of a Repeal of Section 22(d) of the Investment Company Act of 1940" (1972), excerpted in BNA *Securities Reporter*, No. 177, Nov. 15, 1972, part 2. See also related Justice Department antitrust action, *U.S.* v. *NASD, et al.*, 374 F. Supp. 95, especially p. 107 (1973); *aff'd*, 422 U.S. 694 (1975).

37. *Investment Company Institute* v. *Camp*, 401 U.S. 617 (1971); Investment Company Act Release No. 4538 (1966); and Tamar Frankel, *The Regulation of Money Managers* (Boston: Little, Brown, 1978), I, pp. 58–66.

38. SEC 1966 *Investment Company Report*, p. 59; SEC staff report, "The Potential Economic Impact of a Repeal of Section 22(d) of the Investment Company Act of 1940," BNA *Securities Reporter*, No. 177, Nov. 15, 1972, part 2, pp. 21–23; and Frankel, *The Regulation of Money Managers*, IV, pp. 105–108.

39. Senate 1967 Mutual Fund Hearings, p. 685. See also Friend, Blume, and Crockett, *Mutual Funds and Other Institutional Investors*, pp. 105–106.

40. SEC 1966 *Investment Company Report*, pp. 218–223; SEC staff report, "The Potential Economic Impact of a Repeal of Section 22(d) of the Investment Company Act of 1940" (1972); SEC staff report, "Mutual Fund Distribution and Section 22(d) of the Investment Company Act of 1940" (1974); 1967 Senate Mutual Fund Hearings, pp. 151–155; and Frankel, *The Regulation of Money Managers*, IV, pp. 41–105.

41. 1967 Senate Mutual Fund Hearings, p. 25.

42. Memorandum to Chairman Cohen from Philip Loomis, July 8, 1966, Cohen SEC Papers, vol. 103c-VI, item 56; and Memorandum to the chairman from Richard Phillips, July 27, 1966, Cohen SEC Papers, vol. 103c-VI, item 58. See also Memorandum to Manuel Cohen from Richard Phillips, Oct. 20, 1965, Cohen SEC Papers, vol. 103c-V, item 37.

43. Compare Cohen testimony, 1967 House Mutual Fund Hearings, p. 702, with Samuelson testimony, 1967 Senate Mutual Fund Hearings, pp. 347–351.

44. SEC 1966 *Investment Company Report*, pp. 222–223.

45. 1967 Senate Mutual Fund Hearings, p. 153; and Address of Manuel Cohen, May 1, 1967, on file with the SEC, p. 12.

46. 1969 Senate Mutual Fund Hearings, pp. 18–19.

47. See *Wall Street Journal*, Dec. 26, 1968, p. 6; and Interviews with Philip Loomis, March 4, 1981, Washington, D.C., and David Ratner, Feb. 12, 1981 (telephone).

48. Senate Report No. 91–184, 91st Cong., 1st Sess. (1969), p. 8.

49. SEC staff report, "The Potential Economic Impact of a Repeal of Section 22(d) of the Investment Company Act of 1940" (1972); SEC staff report, "Mutual Fund Distribution and Section 22(d) of the Investment Company Act of 1940" (Aug. 1974); and Investment Company Act Release No. 8570 (1974). See Frankel, *The Regulation of Money Managers*, IV, pp. 97–111, for subsequent developments.

50. SEC 1966 *Investment Company Report*, pp. 209–215. On the reason 5 percent limit was selected the report was silent, p. 223, but see discussion by David Ratner, "Regulation of the Compensation of Securities Dealers," 55 *Cornell Law Review*, pp. 376–377 (1969).

51. SEC 1966 *Investment Company Report*, pp. 143–149.

52. The economic theory of the firm is summarized in Richard Posner and Kenneth Scott, eds., *Economics of Corporation Law and Securities Regulation* (Boston: Little, Brown, 1980), pp. 2–6. See *Wharton Mutual Fund Study*, pp. 494–495. Pomerantz testimony appears in 1967 Senate Mutual Fund Hearings, pp. 704–709. See also testimony of Richard Jennings, 1967 Senate Mutual Fund Hearings, p. 721.

53. The text of the bill, S. 1659, appears in 1967 Senate Mutual Fund Hearings, pp. 897–956.

54. Landis, See SEC *Special Study*, IV, pp. 179–185; Demmler, 1967 Senate Mutual Fund Hearings, pp. 186 and 221–232; and *Barron's*, Aug. 7, 1967, p. 1. Gadsby, see William O. Douglas, *Go East, Young Man* (New York: Dell, 1974), p. 315; and Robbins, "Has the SEC Forgotten Its Economics?," *Columbia Journal of World Business*, May–June 1967, pp. 7–19.

55. Testimony of ICI, NASD, and New York Stock Exchange, 1967 Senate Mutual Fund Hearings, pp. 186–336, 549–604, and 733–740; IBA Statement regarding the SEC report on investment companies, Jan. 10, 1967, Cohen SEC Papers, vol. 105, item 22a; NASD special report to NASD members, May 1967, "Summary of the NASD Study Measuring the Impact on the Securities Business of SEC Mutual Fund Recommendations"; SEC Memorandum of Conference with ICI, Jan. 10, 1967, Cohen SEC Papers, vol. 105, item 21d; and *U.S. News and World Report*, May 15, 1967, pp. 118–120, and Sept. 18, 1967, pp. 80–82.

56. *New York Times*, Dec. 7, 1966, p. 65, and June 5, 1967, p. 40. Compare with identical criticism by ICI chairman Francis Williams, *U.S. News and World Report*, Sept. 18, 1967, p. 81.

57. Justice Department, 1967 House Mutual Fund Hearings, pp. 20–22; Council of Economic Advisers, 1967 Senate Mutual Fund Hearings, p. 957; Samuelson, 1967 Senate Mutual Fund Hearings, pp. 347–355; Friend, 1967 Senate Mutual Fund Hearings, pp. 682–689; Pomerantz, 1967 Senate Mutual Fund Hearings, pp. 704–709; and Jennings, 1967 Senate Mutual Fund Hearings, pp. 719–722. But see statement of fifteen law professors and one economics professor, May 23, 1967, unequivocally supporting the SEC bill, Cohen SEC Papers, vol. 110, item 14.

58. See letters to Sparkman from the New York Stock Exchange, June 15, 1967, the American Stock Exchange, June 15, 1967, NASD, June 16, 1967, and ICI, June 15, 1967, Cohen SEC Papers, vol. 111, items 5, 12, 13, and 14.

59. The text of the bill as passed appears in 1969 Senate Mutual Fund Hearings, pp. 215–287. See also SEC *Thirty-fourth Annual Report*, pp. 4–6.

60. 1969 Mutual Fund Hearings, pp. 215–287; SEC *Thirty-third Annual Report*, p. 2, and SEC *Thirty-sixth Annual Report*, p. 16.

61. See, e.g., *Washington Post*, Sept. 11, 1968, p. D7, and Sept. 15, 1968, p. F1.

62. Ibid.; and Letter to Manuel Cohen from Stuckey, Aug. 14, 1968, Cohen SEC Papers, vol. 122, item 59.

63. *Congressional Record*, 90th Cong., 2nd Sess., Oct. 3, 1968, pp. S11923–11924; *Congressional Record*, 90th Cong., 2nd Sess., Oct. 11, 1968, p. S12582; and *Business Week*, Feb. 15, 1969, p. 110.

64. Analysis of 1970 act assembled from *Public Law* 91–547, 84 *Stat.* 1413; *Investment Company Institute* v. *Camp*, 401 U.S. 617 (1971) (re: Glass-Steagall Act prohibition of bank collective investment accounts); SEC *Thirty-seventh Annual Report*, pp. 14–15 (advisory fee breach of duty standard equal to earlier reasonableness standard); Frankel, *The Regulation of Money Managers*, IV, pp. 101–105 (for description of NASD adoption of sales load limits); and Gerard Manges, "The Investment Company Amendments Act of 1970: An Analysis and Appraisal After Two Years," 14 *Boston College Industrial and Commercial Law Review*, pp. 387–436 (1973).

65. SEC staff report, "Mutual Fund Distribution and Section 22(d) of the Investment Company Act of 1940" (Aug. 1974), pp. 69–71; and 1969 House Mutual Fund Hearings, pp. 135–136.

66. Testimony of Paul Samuelson, "Stock Exchange Commission Rates" Hearings, Senate Banking Subcommittee, 92nd Cong., 2nd Sess. (1972), p. 142.

67. Shepard, *The Securities Brokerage Industry*, p. 38.

68. Louis Kohlmeier, *The Regulators* (New York: Harper & Row, 1969), pp. 240–241 and 305.

69. SEC *Thirty-second Annual Report*, pp. 2–3; see also SEC, *Special Study*, II, pp. 181–186, 202, and 325–327.

70. *SEC Minutes*, Nov. 23, 1964. See also Werner, "Protecting the Mutual Fund Investor . . ." 68 *Columbia Law Review*, p. 46, n. 239; and Sidney Robbins, *The Securities Markets* (New York: Free Press, 1966), p. 177.

71. Cohen Dec. 1, 1964, address, on file with the SEC.

72. *SEC Minutes*, Apr. 6, 1965.

73. *SEC Minutes*, June 21, 1965, and July 14, 1965; and Cohen address, Nov. 30, 1965, on file with the SEC.

74. "Memorandum of conference with New York Stock Exchange Committee on Costs and Revenues," Oct. 29, 1965, Cohen SEC Papers, vol. 103C-V, item 42.

75. *Gordon* v. *New York Stock Exchange*, 422 U.S. pp. 664–667 (1975); and Justice Department brief *In the Matter of Commission Rate Structure of Registered National Securities Exchanges*, Hearings before the SEC (1969), p. 24. See also Abe Fortas, "The Frontier Between the Antitrust Law and the Securities Markets," 61 *Illinois Bar Journal*, p. 25 (1972); Louis Loss, *Securities Regulation* (Boston: Little, Brown, 1969), pp. 3156–3157;

and Thomas Linden, "A Reconciliation of Antitrust Law With Securities Regulation: The Judicial Approach," 45 *George Washington Law Review*, p. 179 (1977).

76. *Silver* v. *New York Stock Exchange*, 373 U.S. 341 (1963).

77. SEC, *Special Study*, V, p. 14.

78. His letter to Senator Robertson appears in the *Congressional Record*, 89th Cong., 1st Sess., Aug. 2, 1965, pp. 19019–19022. Other Cohen statements on the subject appear in speeches dated March 10, 1964, and Nov. 30, 1965, on file with the SEC.

79. Cellar and Hart views are quoted in Robbins, *The Securities Markets*, pp. 278–279. See subsequent rejections of antitrust immunity, "Securities Industry Study Report," House Commerce Subcommittee, House Report No. 92–1519, 92nd Cong., 2nd Sess. (1972), pp. 155–168; and "Securities Industry Study Report," Senate Banking Subcommittee, Senate Doc. No. 93–13, 93rd Cong., 1st Sess. (1973) (hereinafter, 1973 Senate "Securities Industry Study Report"), pp. 19–21.

80. 250 F. Supp. 562 (N.D. Ill. 1966), *affirmed*, 371 F.2d 409 (7th Cir. 1967), *certiorari denied* 389 U.S. 954 (1967). On other antitrust challenges of the period, see Loss, *Securities Regulation*, pp. 3163–3170. The specific commission-rate issue in *Kaplan* ultimately was addressed by the Supreme Court in *Gordon* v. *New York Stock Exchange*, 422 U.S. 659 (1975).

81. Cohen address to Investment Bankers Association, dated Nov. 29, 1967, on file with the SEC.

82. The single most useful document concerning Rule 394 was a 211-page SEC staff study prepared in 1965. The study was made public as a result of a freedom of information suit, *M. A. Schapiro* v. *SEC*, 339 F.Supp. 467 (D.D.C. 1972), and published, with certain omissions, in BNA *Securities Reporter* No. 132, Dec. 22, 1971, pp. D1–D49. An unexpurgated copy may be found among Manuel Cohen's chairmanship papers at the SEC. On this subject, generally, see also M. A. Schapiro, "Rule 394: The Story of a Privileged Monopoly" (Nov. 7, 1968), published by M. A. Schapiro & Co., Inc., New York, N.Y., also on file in the Cohen SEC Papers; Note, "NYSE Rules and the Antitrust Laws: Rule 394 . . ." 45 *St. John's Law Review*, p. 812 (1971); and the staff memoranda in the Cohen SEC Papers on NYSE Rule 394.

83. Quoting *Edison Electric Illuminating Company of Boston*, 1 *SEC* p. 913 (1936). See also SEC, *Special Study*, II, p. 958; and SEC 1965 staff report on Rule 394, pp. 76–89.

84. 1934 Securities Exchange Act Release No. 3033 (1941).

85. SEC, *Special Study*, II, pp. 958 and 961.

86. *SEC Minutes*, Dec. 14, 1965; "Memorandum of Conference" with Schapiro, Nov. 12, 1965, Cohen SEC Papers; and Schapiro, "Rule 394: The Story of a Privileged Monopoly," pp. 10–11 and 28.

87. See especially Celler press release, Dec. 11, 1968, Cohen SEC Papers, summarizing Celler's long involvement with the issue.

88. *SEC Minutes*, March 24, 1965; and Memorandum to the Commission from Ralph Saul, Dec. 16, 1964, Cohen SEC Papers.

89. *SEC Minutes*, Feb. 19, 1965, and March 1, 1965.

90. I directly quoted or paraphrased the SEC's 1965 Report on Rule 394, pp. 4–7, 198–201, and 107–210. Merrill Lynch's suggestions are included not in the report, but in a Memorandum to the Chairman from Eugene

Rotberg, "Conference with Merrill Lynch re Rule 394," Aug. 20, 1965, Cohen SEC Papers.

91. Memorandum, "Conference with New York Stock Exchange re Commission Rate Structure and Rule 394," Nov. 24, 1965, Cohen SEC Papers.

92. Funston remarks quoted in Loomis, "The SEC Has a Little List," *Fortune*, Jan. 1967, p. 113.

93. Memorandum to the Commission from Irving Pollack, "Rate Structure and Rule 394," Dec. 8, 1965, Cohen SEC Papers.

94. See Note, "Informal Bargaining Process: An Analysis of the SEC's Regulation of the New York Stock Exchange," 80 *Yale Law Journal*, p. 822 (1971); and *M. A. Schapiro* v. *SEC*, 339 F.Supp. 467 (D.D.C. 1972).

95. Cohen Dec. 22, 1965, letter included in Cohen SEC Papers.

96. SEC-Exchange negotiations on Rule 394 are described in *SEC Minutes*, March 10, 1966, March 24, 1966, May 11, 1966, June 23, 1966, July 13, 1966, and July 19, 1966; and Letter to Manuel Cohen from Keith Funston, Sept. 15, 1966, Cohen SEC Papers.

97. 1934 Securities Exchange Act Releases Nos. 7954 and 7981 (1966); Loss, *Securities Regulation*, pp. 3168–3170; and Note, "Informal Bargaining Process," 80 *Yale Law Journal*, p. 823.

98. Memorandum to Irving Pollack from Norman Poser, "Rule 394(b)," Nov. 29, 1966; Memorandum to the Commission from Irving Pollack, "Rule 394," Dec. 2, 1966; Memorandum to the Commission from Irving Pollack, "Rule 394(b)," March 29, 1967; Letter to Keith Funston from Manuel Cohen, Aug. 23, 1967; Letter to Manuel Cohen from Robert Haack, Oct. 3, 1967; and Memorandum to the Commission from the Division of Trading and Markets, "Rule 394(b)," Oct. 26, 1967, all memoranda in Cohen SEC Papers; and *SEC Minutes*, Apr. 3, 1967. See also Weeden and Company advertisement, *Wall Street Journal*, Nov. 27, 1967, p. 10.

99. The institutional membership controversy is described in *SEC Minutes*, June 25, 1965, and Aug. 30, 1965; SEC, *Institutional Investor Study*, pp. 2298–2311; 1973 Senate "Securities Industry Study Report," pp. 71–73; Welles, *The Last Days of the Club*, pp. 81–83; and Robbins, *The Securities Markets*, pp. 276–277.

100. SEC, *Institutional Investor Study*, pp. 2183–2184 and 2192. See also *Business Week*, Jan. 14, 1967, pp. 125–128; and Welles, *The Last Days of the Club*, pp. 74–79.

101. 1934 Securities Exchange Act Release No. 8239 (1968).

102. Paul Samuelson testimony, SEC Commission Rate Hearings (1968), Oct. 30, 1968.

103. SEC 1966 *Investment Company Report*, pp. 169–187. See also *In the Matter of Delaware Management Company*, 1934 Securities Exchange Act Release No. 8128 (1967).

104. Memorandum to the Commission from Irving Pollack, "Rate Structure and Rule 394," Dec. 8, 1965, Cohen SEC Papers.

105. Letter to G. Keith Funston from Manuel Cohen, Dec. 22, 1965, Cohen SEC Papers. See related discussion, *SEC Minutes*, March 24, 1966.

106. Staff memorandum described in *SEC Minutes*, Apr. 26, 1966.

107. *SEC Minutes*, May 19, 1966.

108. Pollack letter reprinted in 1969 House Mutual Fund Hearings, pp. 216–218.

109. *SEC Minutes*, October 19, 1966.

110. Manuel Cohen address, November 29, 1966, on file with the SEC. See also SEC 1966 *Investment Company Report*, pp. 184–187.

111. Memorandum to David Ratner from Robert Block, March 17, 1967, Cohen SEC Papers, vol. 167, item 48.

112. Letter to "Manny" from "Gene," dated in pencil "6/67," Cohen SEC Papers, vol. 110, item 24.

113. Quoted in memorandum to the Commission from Irving Pollack, "Give-up and Reciprocal Practices — Recommended Regulatory Action," dated in pencil "11/20/67," item 2a, Cohen SEC Papers.

114. *SEC Minutes*, July 6, 1967.

115. Included in two memoranda to the Commission, both dated November 20, 1967, concerning give-ups, denominated items "2a" and "3," Cohen SEC Papers.

116. *SEC Minutes*, Dec. 4, 1967.

117. The proposal was widely reprinted, including as an attachment to 1934 Securities Exchange Act Release No. 8239 (1968).

118. Memorandum to the Commission from Eugene Rotberg, re: "New York Stock Exchange Rate Structure Proposals Meeting with Robert Haack and Bob Bishop," Jan. 11, 1968, Cohen SEC Papers.

119. *SEC Minutes*, Jan. 12, 1968.

120. 1934 Securities Exchange Act Release No. 8239 (1968); David Ratner, "The SEC: Portrait of the Agency as a Thirty-Seven Year Old," 45 *St. John's Law Review*, p. 592 (1971); Leiman and Ratner, "Manuel F. Cohen: In Memoriam," 46 *George Washington Law Review*, pp. 713 and 715; Eugene Rotberg, unpublished article, "Competition and the Securities Markets," and transcript of remarks of 1969 Institutional Investors public forum, both on file with Eugene Rotberg, Washington, D.C.; and interviews with Eugene Rotberg, Feb. 26, 1981, Washington, D.C.; Meyer Eisenberg, March 2, 1981, Washington, D.C., Philip Loomis, March 4, 1981, Washington, D.C., David Ratner, Feb. 12, 1981 (telephone), and Richard Smith, March 20, 1981 (telephone). See also p. 7 of Ray Garrett address, Nov. 29, 1973, on file with the SEC; and SEC Memorandum of Conference with Robert Haack and Gustave Levy, Sept. 29, 1967, on file with the SEC Secretary.

121. Paul Samuelson testimony, "Stock Exchange Commission Rates" Hearings, Senate Banking Subcommittee, 92nd Cong., 2nd Sess. (1972), p. 142.

122. 1934 Securities Exchange Act Release No. 8239 (1968).

123. Welles, *The Last Days of the Club*, pp. 88–89.

124. The comments of the United States Department of Justice on SEC Release No. 8239, Apr. 1, 1968, Cohen SEC Papers.

125. Ratner, "The SEC: Portrait of the Agency as a Thirty-Seven Year Old," 45 *St. John's Law Review*, p. 593.

126. Cohen and Stigler, *Can Regulatory Agencies Protect Consumers*, p. 36.

127. The letter is reprinted in 1934 Securities Exchange Act Release No. 8324 (1968); the Address before the American Pension Conference is on file with the SEC.

128. Exchange proposals described in letter to Manuel Cohen from Robert Haack, Aug. 8, 1968, CCH *Securities Report*, Paragraph 77,585. See also *Wall Street Journal*, June 28, 196, p. 3.

129. See, e.g., 1934 Securities Exchange Act Release No. 10867 (1974).

130. Letter to Manuel Cohen from Robert Haack, Aug. 8, 1968, CCH *Securities Report*, Paragraph 77,585; 1934 Securities Exchange Act Release No. 8399 (1968); and Memorandum to the Commission from Eugene Rotberg, June 6, 1968, Cohen SEC Papers. On the effect of the Exchange's Dec. 1968 interim rate changes, see SEC, *Institutional Investor Study*, pp. 2199–2208. The $150 million saving was frequently noted, see, e.g., SEC *Thirty-fourth Annual Report*, p. 2.

131. A full transcript of the hearings and the Exchange and Justice Department comments, analyses, and briefs are available at the SEC library. Other libraries, including that at Harvard Law School, also have copies of the hearings' transcript. The New York Stock Exchange commission-rate debate spawned an extensive secondary literature. Particularly useful works include Richard West and Seha Tinic, *The Economics of the Stock Market* (New York: Praeger, 1971); William Baxter, "NYSE Fixed Commission Rates: A Private Cartel Goes Public," 22 *Stanford Law Review,* p. 675 (1970); and Alfred Kahn, *The Economics of Regulation* (New York: John Wiley, 1971), vol. 2, pp. 193–209. For the lay reader, Welles, *The Last Days of the Club,* is an especially successful effort to reduce this highly technical debate to nontechnical terms. In the notes to Chap. 12, relevant additional primary sources are cited, of which the SEC's 1971 *Institutional Investor Study,* and the House and Senate 1971–1974 hearings and reports, are the most significant. Three other sources are particularly useful: Harold Demsetz, "The Cost of Transacting," 82 *Quarterly Journal of Economics,* p. 33 (1968), completed shortly before the hearings began and relied on by both the Exchange and the Justice Department; the Supreme Court decision *Gordon* v. *New York Stock Exchange,* 422 U.S. 659 (1975); and Irwin Friend and Marshall Blume, "The Consequences of Competitive Commissions on the New York Stock Exchange," reprinted in "Stock Exchange Commission Rate" Hearings, Senate Banking Subcommittee, 92nd Cong., 2nd Sess. (1972), pp. 259–401. A summary of the views of the five economists presented by the Justice Department may be found in the Antitrust Division's "Memorandum of the United States Department of Justice on the Fixed Commission Rate Structure" (Jan. 1969), a brief filed with the SEC commission rate hearings (hereinafter, Justice Department 1969 brief). On 1970 Exchange firm personnel lay-offs, see Donald Regan, *A View From the Street* (New York: New American Library, 1972), pp. 109–110.

132. Besides the transcript of the first day of the SEC's commission rate hearings, this passage relied on an interview with Rotberg, Feb. 26, 1981, Washington, D.C., and the *New York Daily News,* July 8, 1968, p. 42.

133. Besides Samuelson's testimony at the SEC commission rate hearings, this passage relies on Shepard, *The Securities Brokerage Industry,* p. 17; Justice Department 1969 brief, p. 101; Friend and Blume, "The Consequences of Competitive Commissions on the New York Stock Exchange," reprinted in "Stock Exchange Commission Rate Hearings," Hearings, Senate Banking Subcommittee, 92nd Cong., 2nd Sess. (1972), p. 270; and *Forbes,* June 15, 1968, p. 31.

134. See citations and discussion in Kahn, *The Economics of Regulation,* vol. 2, p. 206.

135. Exchange testimony summarized in Memorandum to the Commission from Division of Trading and Markets Office of Policy Research, "New York Stock Exchange Commission Rate Proposal," Oct. 1, 1970, p. 4.

136. Robert Haack January 22, 1969, Address on file in Cohen SEC Papers. Cohen's remarks are quoted in *New York Times*, Jan. 23, 1969, p. 65.

137. SEC, *Institutional Investor Study*, pp. 1–22; *SEC Minutes*, Nov. 27, 1968; Cohen SEC Papers, vol. 163, item 15; and interviews with Richard Smith, March 20, 1981 (telephone), and Meyer Eisenberg, March 2, 1981, Washington, D.C.

138. Ratner, "Manuel Cohen: In Memoriam," 46 *George Washington Law Review*, p. 715.

139. James Landis, *The Administrative Process* (New Haven: Yale University Press, 1938), p. 24.

140. William Douglas, *Go East, Young Man* (New York: Dell, 1974), p. 308.

141. Testimony of Manuel Cohen, "Securities Markets Agencies" Hearings, House Commerce Subcommittee, 91st Cong., 1st Sess. (1969), p. 278.

142. Ibid., pp. 277–278 and 290–294. See also Cohen address, Oct. 26, 1968, to the Financial Executives Institute, on file with the SEC.

143. Federal Trade Commission, "Staff Report on Conglomerate Merger Performance" (1972), especially pp. 1–30; FTC Report on Mergers and Acquisitions (Oct. 1973), pp. 143–156; FTC press release (March 18, 1968), quoted in Joel Davidow, "Conglomerate Concentration and Section Seven: The Limitations of the Anti-Merger Act," 68 *Columbia Law Review*, p. 1234 (1968); "Investigation of Conglomerate Corporations" Hearings, House Judiciary Antitrust Subcommittee, 91st Cong. (1969), I, p. 2; and "Investigation of Conglomerate Corporations," staff report of the House Judiciary Antitrust Subcommittee, 92nd Cong., 1st Sess. (1971), pp. 1–7. See also Robert Chatov, *Corporate Financial Reporting* (New York: Free Press, 1975), pp. 201–202.

144. See discussion in Arthur Wyatt, *A Critical Study of Accounting for Business Combinations* (AICPA, Accounting Research Study No. 5, 1963), pp. 58–60; and *Accounting Research Bulletin* No. 43.

145. Chatov, *Corporate Financial Reporting*, pp. 207–222; "Investigation of Conglomerate Corporations," House Judiciary Antitrust Subcommittee staff study, 92nd Cong., 1st Sess. (1971), pp. 402–403 and 411–417; FTC staff report, "Economic Report on Corporate Mergers," Appendix to part 8 of "Economic Concentration" Hearings, Senate Judiciary Antitrust Subcommittee, 91st Cong., 1st Sess. (1969) (hereinafter FTC 1969 "Economic Report on Corporate Mergers"), pp. 119–138; and Abraham Brilloff, *Unaccountable Accounting* (New York: Harper & Row, 1972), pp. 59–87.

146. Wyatt, *A Critical Study of Accounting for Business Combinations*; *Accounting Research Bulletins*, Nos. 40 and 48; Samuel Sapienza, "Distinguishing Between Purchase and Pooling," *Journal of Accountancy*, June 1961, pp. 35–40.

147. Moonitz preface to Wyatt, *A Critical Study of Accounting for Business Combinations*, pp. xi–xiii.

148. APB Opinion No. 10, Note 6.

149. George Catlett and Norman Olson, *Accounting for Goodwill* (AICPA, Accounting Research Study No. 10, 1968), p. 105.

150. See, e.g., sources cited in Stephen Zeff, *Forging Accounting Principles in Five Countries* (Champaign, Ill.: Stipes Publishing, 1972), pp. 212–216; and Chatov, *Corporate Financial Reporting*, pp. 214–222.

151. Abraham Brilloff, "Dirty Pooling," 42 *Accounting Review,* p. 489 (1967). Other articles followed. See, generally, Brilloff, *Unaccountable Accounting,* pp. 59–107.

152. Time, Apr. 11, 1969, p. 96, and March 9, 1970, p. 62; and *Newsweek,* Apr. 7, 1969, p. 66, and July 13, 1970, p. 42.

153. FTC 1969 "Economic Report on Corporate Mergers," pp. 23 and 119–134.

154. A. A. Sommer, "Survey of Accounting Developments in the 60s: What's Ahead in the 70s," 26 *Business Lawyer,* p. 221 (1970).

155. Zeff, *Forging Accounting Principles in Five Countries,* pp. 213–214.

156. Included as an Appendix to John Burton, *Accounting for Business Combinations* (New York: Financial Executives Research Foundation, 1970).

157. Ibid., p. 82.

158. Savoie quoted in Zeff, *Forging Accounting Principles in Five Countries,* p. 215. See also Note, "Accounting for Business Combinations: A Critique of APB Opinion Number 16," 23 *Stanford Law Review,* p. 347 (1971).

159. Zeff, *Forging Accounting Principles in Five Countries,* pp. 212–216; Chatov, *Corporate Financial Reporting,* pp. 221–222; Organization for Consistent Accounting Principles Letter, July 15, 1970, on file with the SEC's Office of Chief Accountant, and Memorandum, July 23, 1970, Re: Conference to Discuss Possible Legal Implications of the Size-Test in the Proposed APB Opinion, on file with the SEC's Office of Chief Accountant.

160. Dissents of Broeker, Burger, and Weston; and Davidson, Horngren, and Seidman.

161. Kripke quoted in Ted Fiflis and Homer Kripke, *Accounting for Business Lawyers,* second edition (St. Paul, Minn.: West Publishing, 1977), p. 615.

162. Memorandum to the Commission from the chief accountant, "Subject: AICPA Study Group" (Wheat Committee), Oct. 12, 1971, on file with the SEC Office of Chief Accountant; and Zeff, *Forging Accounting Principles in Five Countries,* pp. 224–227. See also view of Samuel Gunther quoted in Brilloff, *Unaccountable Accounting,* pp. 99–100.

163. Andrew Barr addresses dated Jan. 18, 1962, Nov. 18, 1967, Jan. 24, 1969, and Apr. 23, 1969, on file with the SEC. Barr's case-by-case approach in this area also was explained in an article by Barr, "Accounting Aspects of Business Combinations," 34 *Accounting Review,* p. 175 (1959), and in a telephone interview March 19, 1981. On SEC response to pooling controversy generally, see also Chatov, *Corporate Financial Reporting,* pp. 218–222, and Zeff, *Forging Accounting Principles in Five Countries,* pp. 213–216.

164. Memorandum to Chairman Casey from Andrew Barr, May 18, 1971, p. 6, on file with the SEC Office of Chief Accountant; Letter to Dean Eiteman from Andrew Barr, Aug. 13, 1970, on file with the SEC Office of Chief Accountant; John Carey, *The Rise of the Accounting Profession* (New York: AICPA, 1970), pp. 98–105; Zeff, *Forging Accounting Principles in Five Countries,* pp. 178–180; and Gary John Previts, "The SEC and Its Chief Accountants," *Journal of Accountancy,* August 1978, p. 88.

165. Memorandum to the Commission from the chief accountant, "Subject: Accounting for Goodwill," Feb. 24, 1969, and letter to Reed Storey from Andrew Barr, March 19, 1969, both on file with the SEC Office of Chief Accountant.

166. Interview with John Burton, Feb. 13, 1981, New York City.

167. 1933 Securities Act Release No. 4910 (1968).

168. Cohen Oct. 26, 1968, speech on file with the SEC.

169. Quoting Address of Andrew Barr, Apr. 23, 1969, on file with the SEC.

170. Testimony of Hamer Budge, "Securities Markets Agencies" Hearings, House Commerce Subcommittee, 91st Cong., 1st Sess. (1969), pp. 17–19.

171. Testimony of Hamer Budge before the Senate Subcommittee on Antitrust and Monopoly, Feb. 18, 1970, reprinted in BNA *Securities Reporter*, No. 38, Feb. 18, 1970, pp. X18–X21.

172. Testimony of Hamer Budge, "Investigation of Conglomerate Corporations" Hearings, House Judiciary Antitrust Subcommittee, 91st Cong., 2nd Sess. (1970), p. 75.

173. Budge address, June 12, 1970, on file with the SEC.

174. Letter to Mr. George Watt, Chairman, Business Combinations and Goodwill Subcommittee, APB, from Eugene Minahan, Chairman, FEI Subcommittee on Business Combinations, Sept. 5, 1969; Letter to participants in the June 17 Symposium on Accounting for Business Combinations from Richard Lytle, APB administrative director, Sept. 17, 1969; and Memorandum to the Commission from Andrew Barr, Oct. 17, 1969. All documents on file with the SEC Office of Chief Accountant.

175. Memorandum to the Commission from Andrew Barr, Oct. 17, 1969, and "Position Paper of the Chief Accountant of the SEC on APB Draft Opinion of October 8, 1969," both on file with the SEC Office of Chief Accountant.

176. Memorandum to Chairman Budge, et al., from Andrew Barr, "Subject: Progress Report from the Accounting Principles Board," Dec. 8, 1969, on file with the SEC Office of Chief Accountant.

177. Mervyn Williams, SEC staff accountant, Memorandum for files, "Subject: APB Draft Opinion of January 9, 1970, on Business Combinations and Intangible Assets," Jan. 20, 1970, on file with the SEC Office of Chief Accountant.

178. Harry Stahl, SEC representative, Memorandum, "Re: Conference with members of the Accounting Principles Board concerning the proposed APB Opinion: Business Combinations and Intangible Assets," June 22, 1970, on file with the SEC Office of Chief Accountant.

179. Interview with William Cary, Oct. 28–29, 1980, New York City.

180. See, e.g., "Investigation of Conglomerate Corporations," House Judiciary Antitrust Subcommittee staff report, 92nd Cong., 1st Sess. (1971), pp. 393–403.

181. FTC, "Conglomerate Merger Performance: An Empirical Analysis of Nine Corporations (Nov. 1972), p. 133.

182. Ibid., pp. 133–134; 1969 FTC, "Economic Report on Corporate Mergers," p. 104; Statement by Joel Dean, "Economic Concentration" Hearings, Senate Judiciary Antitrust Subcommittee, 91st Cong., 2nd Sess. (1970), p. 5254; and studies summarized in Dennis Mueller, "The Effects of Conglomerate Mergers," 1 *Journal of Banking and Finance*, pp. 322–323 (1977).

183. James Lorie and Paul Halpern, "Conglomerates: The Rhetoric and the Evidence," 13 *Journal of Law and Economics,* pp. 157–163 and 165–166 (1970); and Hai Hong, Robert Kaplan, and Gershon Mandelker, "Pooling vs. Purchase: The Effects of Accounting for Mergers on Stock Prices," 53 *Accounting Review,* p. 31 (1978). See citations to studies investigating other alternative accounting principles in George Benston, *Corporate Financial Disclosure in the UK and USA* (Lexington, Mass.: Lexington Books, 1976), pp. 110–114.

184. The history of the Williams Act was assembled from *Public Laws* 90–439 (July 29, 1968) and 91–567 (Dec. 22, 1970); *Congressional Record,* 89th Cong., 1st Sess., Oct. 22, 1965, pp. 28257–28260; 89th Cong., 2nd Sess., Aug. 11, 1966, pp. 19003–19006; and 90th Cong., 1st Sess., Jan. 18, 1967, pp. S.443–S.448; Manuel Cohen Address, Apr. 14, 1967, on file with the SEC; Testimony of Manuel Cohen, "Takeover Bids" Hearings, House Commerce Subcommittee, 90th Cong., 2nd Sess. (1968), pp. 10–15; Testimony of Manuel Cohen, "Securities Markets Agencies" Hearings, House Commerce Subcommittee, 91st Cong., 1st Sess. (1969), pp. 277–278 and 290–294; Loss, *Securities Regulation,* pp. 3658–3669; and James Jordan and David Woodward, "An Appraisal of Disclosure Requirements in Contests for Control Under the Williams Act," 46 *George Washington Law Review,* p. 837 (1978).

185. "Economic Concentration" Hearings, Senate Antitrust and Monopoly Subcommittee, 89th Cong., 1st Sess. (1965) (hereinafter, Economic Concentration Hearings), pp. 1069–1071.

186. Ibid., p. 1070.

187. FTC, "Conglomerate Merger Performance: An Empirical Analysis of Nine Corporations," pp. 129–131.

188. Economic Concentration Hearings, pp. 769–770.

189. Ibid., p. 1071.

190. Summarized in Daniel Collins, "SEC Line-of-Business Reporting and Earnings Forecasts," 4 *Journal of Business Research,* p. 117 (1976).

191. Cohen's response to Hart appears in Economic Concentration Hearings, pp. 1069–1071.

192. Cohen May 19 and 24, 1966, Addresses, on file with the SEC.

193. Economic Concentration Hearings, pp. 1981–1997.

194. *SEC Minutes,* Sept. 30, 1966.

195. Address by Manuel Cohen, Oct. 26, 1968, on file with the SEC. The APB's statement encouraging voluntary disclosure appears in *Journal of Accountancy,* Oct. 1967, pp. 51–52.

196. Cohen Address dated Feb. 16, 1967, quoting p. 4, on file with the SEC.

197. Robert Mautz, *Financial Reporting by Diversified Companies* (New York: Financial Executives Research Foundation, 1968), pp. 126–127 and 157–158.

198. 1933 Securities Act Releases Nos. 4922 (1968), 4949 (1969), 4988 (1969), 4996–4998 (1969).

199. Daniel Collins, "SEC Product-Line Reporting and Market Efficiency," 2 *Journal of Financial Economics,* pp. 125–164 (1975); and "SEC Line-of-Business Reporting and Earnings Forecasts," 4 *Journal of Business Research,* pp. 117–130 (1976). See also Richard Simonds and Daniel Collins, "Line of Business Reporting and Security Prices . . . " 9 *Bell Journal of Economics,* pp. 646–658 (1978), and related rejoinder by Bertram Horwitz and Richard Kolodny, 9 *Bell Journal of Economics,* pp. 659–663 (1978).

200. FTC 1969 "Economic Report on Corporate Mergers," pp. 20–22 and 139–141.

201. FTC, "Conglomerate Merger Performance: An Empirical Analysis of Nine Corporations," pp. 170–172. See also "Investigation of Conglomerate Corporations," House Judiciary Antitrust Subcommittee staff report, 92nd Cong., 1st Sess. (1971), pp. 434–435.

202. Frederic Scherer, "Segmental Financial Reporting: Needs and Trade-Offs," in Harvey Goldschmid, editor, *Business Disclosure: Government's Need to Know* (New York: McGraw-Hill, 1979), p. 15–19.

203. Dan Goldwasser, "Reporting for Segments of a Business Enterprise," 33 *Business Lawyer,* p. 2483 (1978).

204. "Report of the Advisory Committee on Corporate Disclosure to the Securities and Exchange Commission," House Committee Print 95-29, 95th Cong., 1st Sess. (1977), I, pp. 380–390.

205. FASB Statement No. 14 (1976), and SEC Accounting Series Release No. 236 (1977).

CHAPTER 12: An Unfinished Agenda

1. "Securities Industry Study," Report of the Senate Subcommittee on Securities, Senate Doc. No. 93-13, 93rd Cong., 1st Sess. (1973) (hereinafter, 1973 Senate "Securities Industry Study"), p. 145.

2. See *Study on Federal Regulation,* Senate Committee on Government Operations, 95th Cong., 1st Sess. (1977), Committee Print, "The Regulatory Appointments Process," pp. 7–10.

3. See, e.g. *New York Times,* June 6, 1964, p. 27, June 21, 1964, p. 48, June 22, 1964, p. 38, and June 27, 1964, p. 28.

4. *The Institutional Investor,* June 1969, p. 33.

5. Ibid., pp. 29–33; *New York Times,* June 1, 1970, pp. 1 and 54; *National Journal,* Feb. 20, 1971, pp. 373–388; and *Time,* Aug. 8, 1969, pp. 69–70.

6. "A New Regulatory Framework," Report on Selected Independent Regulatory Agencies by the President's Advisory Council on Executive Organization (1971), reprinted in BNA *Securities Reporter,* No. 89, Feb. 17, 1971, quoting p. F7; *Business Week,* Sept. 6, 1969, p. 27; *New York Times,* June 1, 1970, p. 54; and *Time,* Aug. 8, 1969, p. 69.

7. *National Journal,* Feb. 20, 1971, pp. 377, 380, and 387–388; *Business Week,* Sept. 6, 1969, p. 28; BNA *Securities Reporter,* No. 40, March 4, 1970, p. A12; "Securities Industry Study," House Report No. 92-1519, House Commerce Subcommittee, 92nd Cong., 2nd Sess. (1972) (hereinafter, House "Securities Industry Study"), pp. 169–170; SEC *Thirty-fifth Annual Report,* pp. 1–2 and 181, *Thirty-sixth Annual Report,* pp. 29 and 209, and *Thirty-seventh Annual Report,* p. 214.

8. The SEC's response to the back-office crisis may also have been affected by insufficient personnel. See, e.g., House "Securities Industry Study," p. 11; and "Study of the Securities Industry" Hearings, House Commerce Subcommittee, 92nd Cong., 1st Sess. (1971) (hereinafter, House Securities Industry Hearings) I, p. 6.

9. See especially *New York Times*, June 1, 1970, pp. 1 and 54; and *National Journal*, Feb. 20, 1971, pp. 373–388.

10. BNA *Securities Reporter*, No. 8, July 23, 1969, p. A6; and *New York Times*, Aug. 5, 1969, p. 41, June 1, 1970, p. 54, Nov. 14, 1970, pp. 1 and 45, and Dec. 16, 1970, p. 69.

11. "Nomination of William J. Casey," Senate Report No. 92–4, 92nd Cong., 1st Sess. (1971); SEC *Thirty-seventh Annual Report*, p. vii; *National Journal*, Feb. 20, 1971, p. 379; and *Business Week*, Feb. 6, 1971, p. 18, and Oct. 16, 1971, p. 71.

12. "Nomination of William J. Casey," Senate Report No. 92–4, 92nd Cong., 1st Sess. (1971), p. 5.

13. *National Journal*, Feb. 20, 1971, p. 375; and House Securities Industry Hearings, pp. 1714–1715.

14. SEC *Thirty-eighth Annual Report*, pp. 135–136, and *Fortieth Annual Report*, p. 138. But see also House "Securities Industry Study," pp. 169–170.

15. See also discussion of SEC reorganization, SEC *Thirty-eighth Annual Report*, p. 133; BNA *Securities Reporter*, No. 163, Aug. 2, 1972, pp. A11–A13, and No. 164, Aug. 9, 1972, pp. A10–A11.

16. 1934 Securities Exchange Act Release No. 9079 (1971); and SEC, *Institutional Investor Study Report*, House Doc. No. 92–64, 92nd Cong., 1st Sess. (1971) (hereinafter, SEC, *Institutional Investor Study*), I, pp. xxiii–xxv.

17. SEC, "Statement on the Future Structure of the Securities Markets" (Feb. 2, 1972) (hereinafter, "Future Structure Statement"), pp. 14–17 and 24; and Testimony of William Casey, "Stock Exchange Commission Rate" Hearings, Senate Securities Subcommittee, 92nd Cong., 2nd Sess. (1972), p. 19.

18. Address of Ray Garrett, "The State of the SEC," erroneously dated March 1, 1973, on file with the SEC, quoting p. 17.

19. Senate Report No. 94–75, 94th Cong., 1st Sess. (1975), p. 2.

20. Relevant congressional testimony and correspondence concerning Casey and the ITT files is excerpted in BNA *Securities Reporter*, No. 175, Nov. 1, 1972, pp. A5–A8 and D1–D3, No. 182, Dec. 20, 1972, pp. A13–A17, and No. 209, July 4, 1973, pp. A12–A13.

21. Testimony of G. Bradford .Cook, "Legislative Oversight of SEC: Agency Independence and the ITT Case" Hearings, House Interstate Commerce Special Subcommittee, 93rd Cong., 1st Sess. (1973), pp. 1–41; *New York Times*, May 17, 1973, p. 1, and May 26, 1973, p. 10 (quoting *Washington Star-News* article noted in text); *Juris Doctor*, June–July 1973, pp. 18–20; and BNA *Securities Reporter*, No. 190, Feb. 21, 1973, pp. A9–A10, and No. 202, May 16, 1973, pp. AA1–AA2.

22. See, e.g., *New York Times*, July 9, 1973, p. 24.

23. Interview with A. A. Sommer, March 2, 1981, Washington, D.C.; BNA *Securities Reporter*, No. 213, Aug. 1, 1973, pp. A14–A15; "Ray Garrett, Jr.," Memorial Service, March 7, 1980 (printed by the SEC); *Fortune*, Nov. 1974, pp. 139–141 and 242–253; *Newsweek*, July 16, 1973, pp. 65–66; *Business Week*, July 14, 1973, pp. 28–29; and SEC *Thirty-ninth Annual Report*, p. ix.

24. Interview with A. A. Sommer, March 2, 1981, Washington, D.C.; and SEC *Fortieth Annual Report*, p. x.

25. *Time*, Feb. 11, 1974, p. 103; SEC *Fortieth Annual Report*, p. x–xi; and

Remarks of John Evans, "Ray Garrett, Jr.," Memorial Service, March 7, 1980.

26. Interview with Theodore Levine, March 3, 1981, Washington, D.C.; Interview with Ed Herlihy, Feb. 25, 1981, Washington, D.C.; and "Ray Garrett, Jr.," Memorial Service, March 7, 1980.

27. SEC *Forty-first Annual Report*, p. ix; and BNA *Securities Reporter*, No. 322, Oct. 8, 1975, pp.AA1–AA6; No. 338, Feb. 4, 1976, pp. A1–A2 and F1–F5; No. 348, Apr. 14, 1976, p. A14; and No. 357, June 16, 1976, pp. AA1–AA9.

28. SEC, "Study of Unsafe and Unsound Practices of Brokers and Dealers," House Doc. No. 92–231, 92nd Cong., 1st Sess. (Dec. 1971) (hereinafter, SEC, "Study of Unsafe and Unsound Practices"), p. 1.

29. "Securities Markets Agencies" Hearings, House Commerce Subcommittee, 91st Cong., 1st Sess. (1969), (hereinafter, House Securities Market Agencies Hearings), p. 8.

30. House "Securities Industry Study," p. 3; Hurd Baruch, *Wall Street: Security Risk* (Washington, D.C.: Acropolis Books, 1971), p. 86; and SEC *Thirty-fifth Annual Report*, p. 1.

31. SEC, "Study of Unsafe and Unsound Practices," p. 219.

32. Ibid., p. 222.

33. SEC *Thirty-fifth Annual Report*, p. 2.

34. Baruch, *Wall Street: Security Risk*, pp. 101–103; SEC *Thirty-fifth Annual Report*, p. 2; SEC, "Study of Unsafe and Unsound Practices," pp. 53 and 95–107; and Address of Hamer Budge, Sept. 4, 1969, on file with the SEC. Late-delivered securities were hardly a novel problem for the security industry or the SEC. See SEC "Report of Special Study of Securities Market," House Doc. No. 95, 88th Cong., 1st Sess. (1963) (hereinafter, SEC, *Special Study*), I, pp. 416–428.

35. Testimony of Lee Arning, vice president, New York Stock Exchange, House Securities Industry Hearings, I, p. 8.

36. 1934 Securities Exchange Act Release No. 8433 (1968); "Securities Industry Study" Hearings, Senate Subcommittee on Securities, 92nd Cong., 2nd Sess. (1972), IV, pp. 223–224; "Review of SEC Records of the Demise of Selected Broker-Dealers," Staff Study for the Special Subcommittee on Investigations, House Commerce Committee, 92nd Cong., 1st Sess. (1971) (hereinafter, House Subcommittee, "Demise Review"), pp. 136–140; Baruch, *Wall Street: Security Risk*, pp. 190–191 and 203; and Chris Welles, *The Last Days of the Club*, (New York: Dutton, 1975), pp. 165–167.

37. Peter Wyckoff, *Wall Street and the Stock Market* (Philadelphia: Chilton Book, 1972), pp. 130 and 134.

38. House "Securities Industry Study," p. 9; and House Subcommittee, "Demise Review," p. 3.

39. House Subcommittee, "Demise Review," p. 3; "Securities Industry Study" Report of the Senate Banking Committee, 92nd Cong., 2nd Sess. (1972) (hereinafter, 1972 Senate "Securities Industry Study"), pp. 7–8; "Federal Broker-Dealer Insurance Corporation" Hearings, Senate Banking Subcommittee on Securities, 91st Cong., 2nd Sess. (1970) (hereinafter, Senate SIPC Hearings), p. I; and Baruch, *Wall Street: Security Risk*, pp. 147–149. On SEC approval of emergency surcharge, see 1934 Securities Exchange Act Release No. 8860 (1970). The broker-dealer firms' figures on losses in their commission business should be read skeptically. At the time, methods for

allocating firm fixed costs among their various business activities (e.g., underwriting and brokerage commissions) were the subject of some controversy.

40. House "Securities Industry Study," p. 10. See similar estimates, House Subcommittee, "Demise Review," p. 7; and Testimony of Lee Arning, vice president, New York Stock Exchange, House Securities Industry Hearings, I, p. 8.

41. Securities Investor Protection Corporation (hereinafter, SIPC); *Second Annual Report*, p. 2.

42. *Newsweek*, Oct. 12, 1970, p. 87.

43. SEC, "Study of Unsafe and Unsound Practices," pp. 1–2.

44. Baruch, *Wall Street: Security Risk*, pp. 191–192; and House Subcommittee, "Demise Review," pp. 101–102.

45. Baruch, *Wall Street: Security Risk*, p. 192; and House Subcommittee, "Demise Review," pp. 50–51.

46. Welles, *The Last Days of the Club*, pp. 172–209; Baruch, *Wall Street: Security Risk*, pp. 193–196; and House Subcommittee, "Demise Review," pp. 122–127.

47. Exchange member firm failures, March–July 1971, summarized in Baruch, *Wall Street: Security Risk*, pp. 196–211. Regarding Dempsey-Tegeler & Company, see also Welles, *The Last Days of the Club*, pp. 209–241. Regarding Baerwald-De Boer, see House Subcommittee, "Demise Review," p. 57.

48. Baruch, *Wall Street: Security Risk*, pp. 223–227; House Subcommittee, "Demise Review," pp. 103–110; and *Fortune*, Dec. 1970, p. 63, and Jan. 1971, pp. 114–116 and 154–159.

49. See Baruch, *Wall Street: Security Risk*, pp. 212–217.

50. Ibid., pp. 216–223.

51. Ibid., pp. 231–240.

52. Ibid., pp. 241–248; "Securities Industry Study" Hearings, Senate Subcommittee on Securities, 92nd Cong., 1st Sess. (1972), IV, pp. 263–265; testimony of Wallace LaTour, Senate SIPC Hearings, pp. 38–45; and House Subcommittee, "Demise Review," pp. 76–82.

53. Testimony of Lee Arning, vice president, New York Stock Exchange, House Securities Industry Hearings, I, p. 8. On expense to investors, see Baruch, *Wall Street: Security Risk*, p. 15; Testimony of Philip Loomis, "Securities Investor Protection" Hearings, House Commerce Subcommittee, 91st Cong., 2nd Sess. (1970) (hereinafter, House SIPC Hearings), p. 228; and House Subcommittee, "Demise Review," p. 4.

54. *Business Week*, June 29, 1968, p. 104.

55. SEC, "Study of Unsafe and Unsound Practices," pp. 95–122.

56. Regan testimony, "Securities Industry Study" Hearings, Senate Banking Subcommittee, 92nd Cong., 1st Sess. (1971), II, pp. 2–3.

57. *Fortune*, Jan. 1971, pp. 114–116 and 154–159, quoting p. 154.

58. The New York Stock Exchange's data are summarized in Donald Regan, *A View from the Street* (New York: New American Library, 1972), p. 94.

59. Wright address quoted in SEC, "Study of Unsafe and Unsound Practices," p. 117. See also Welles, *The Last Days of the Club*, p. 170.

60. SEC, "Study of Unsafe and Unsound Practices," pp. 98–105 and 145–150.

61. Regan, *A View from the Street*, p. 105.

62. Baruch, *Wall Street: Security Risk*, pp. 106–110, 112, 192, and 199; Welles, *The Last Days of the Club*, pp. 172–209; and SEC, "Study of Unsafe and Unsound Practices," pp. 120–121.

63. House Subcommittee, "Demise Review," pp. 26–29.

64. Ibid., p. 29; SEC, "Study of Unsafe and Unsound Practices," pp. 49–94; Baruch, *Wall Street: Security Risk*, pp. 177–188 and 154–170; and Hugh Sowards and James Mofsky, "The Securities Investor Protection Act of 1970," 26 *Business Lawyer*, pp. 1272–1273 (1971).

65. Excerpts from Pollack-Haack correspondence reprinted in "Securities Industry Study" Hearings, Senate Subcommittee on Securities, 92nd Cong., 2nd Sess. (1972), IV, pp. 226–227.

66. Hugh Owens letter to Harley Staggers, reprinted in full in SEC, "Study of Unsafe and Unsound Practices," pp. 249–256, quoting p. 253.

67. Ibid., pp. 253–254; and Baruch, *Wall Street: Security Risk*, p. 185.

68. SEC, "Study of Unsafe and Unsound Practices," p. 103; House Subcommittee, "Securities Industry Study," p. 94; and Baruch, *Wall Street: Security Risk*, pp. 185 and 180.

69. "Securities Industry Study" Hearings, Senate Subcommittee on Securities, 92nd Cong., 2nd Sess. (1972), IV, p. 243; 1973 Senate "Securities Industry Study," pp. 30–31; and Welles, *The Last Days of the Club*, pp. 196–198.

70. Staff memorandum quoted in Senate 1973 "Security Industry Study," p. 30. That the inspection occurred in January is noted by Baruch, *Wall Street: Security Risk*, p. 185. There were several similar SEC statements respecting its lack of knowledge. See, e.g., "Securities Industry Study," Hearings, Senate Subcommittee on Securities, 92nd Cong., 2nd Sess. (1972), IV, pp. 232–234; and Senate SIPC Hearings, p. 266.

71. "Securities Industry Study" Hearings, Senate Subcommittee on Securities, 92nd Cong., 2nd Sess. (1972), IV, p. 235. See, relatedly, BNA *Securities Reporter*, No. 59, July 15, 1970, p. A4; House "Securities Industry Study," pp. 95–96; and Baruch, *Wall Street: Security Risk*, p. 185.

72. SEC *Special Study*, I, pp. 87 and 400; and "Securities Industry Study" Hearings, Senate Subcommittee on Securities, 92nd Cong., 2nd Sess. (1972), IV, pp. 220–221.

73. Louis Loss, *Securities Regulation* (Boston: Little, Brown, 1969) pp. 3197–3198. See, relatedly, Senate SIPC Hearings, p. 176.

74. SEC, *Special Study*, IV, p. 527.

75. "Securities Industry Study" Hearings, Senate Subcommittee on Securities, 92nd Cong., 2nd Sess. (1972), IV, p. 220. See also IV, p. 329.

76. Testimony of Keith Funston, "Investor Protection" Hearings, House Commerce Subcommittee, 88th Cong., 1st Sess. (1964), pp. 1072–1079; "Securities Industry Study" Hearings, Senate Subcommittee on Securities, 92nd Cong., 2nd Sess. (1972), IV, p. 221; SEC "Study of Unsafe and Unsound Practices," p. 207; and BNA *Securities Reporter*, No. 85, Jan. 20, 1971, pp. B1–B2.

77. Hugh Owens letter to Harley Staggers, reprinted in SEC, "Study of Unsafe and Unsound Practices," quoting, p. 250.

78. Ibid., pp. 220–221 and 251.

79. *Wall Street Journal*, Aug. 4, 1967 article reprinted in House Securities Markets Agencies Hearings, pp. 87–89.

80. SEC, "Study of Unsafe and Unsound Practices," pp. 251–252 and 226–227.

81. Ibid., p. 227; "Securities Industry Study" Hearings, Senate Subcommittee on Securities, 92nd Cong., 2nd Sess. (1972), IV, p. 225; and *National Journal*, Feb. 20, 1971, p. 381.

82. Wyckoff, *Wall Street and the Stock Market*, p. 130.

83. Telephone interview with Stanley Sporkin, Sept. 22, 1981; *SEC Minutes*, July 17, 1968, July 19, 1968, July 26, 1968, and July 30, 1968; Baruch, *Wall Street: Security Risk*, pp. 130–136; SEC, "Study of Unsafe and Unsound Practices," pp. 227–230; and House Securities Industry Hearings, p. 118.

84. 1934 Securities Exchange Act Release No. 8363 (1968).

85. *SEC Minutes*, Nov. 4, 1968. See also *SEC Minutes*, Dec. 27, 1968, Dec. 31, 1968, and Jan. 3, 1969.

86. Testimony of Hamer Budge, House Securities Markets Agencies Hearings, p. 9.

87. "Securities Industry Study" Hearings, Senate Subcommittee on Securities, 92nd Cong., 2nd Sess. (1972), IV, pp. 230–231; and Welles, *The Last Days of the Club*, pp. 162–163 and 229–231. See also, SEC, "Study of Unsafe and Unsound Practices," pp. 207–209.

88. Statement of Congressman John Moss, *Congressional Record*, 91st Cong., 2nd Sess., Dec. 1, 1970, p. 39350; House SIPC Hearings, pp. 344–345 and 352–353; Senate SIPC Hearings, pp. 241–242 and 258; and BNA *Securities Reporter*, No. 54, June 10, 1970, p. A6, No. 55, June 17, 1970, pp. 1 and A1, No. 59, July 15, 1970, pp. A1–A4, and No. 60, July 22, 1970, pp. A2–A4.

89. Public Law 91–598, 84 *Stat.* 1636–1657. The text directly quotes Subsection 9(f). See, relatedly, Subsection 7(d). The legislative history of the act appears in: Senate SIPC Hearings; House SIPC Hearings; Senate Report No. 91–1218; and House Reports 91–1613 and 91–1788. See also Baruch, *Wall Street: Security Risk*, pp. 64–80; David Greenberg, "An Analysis of the Securities Investor Protection Act of 1970," 16 *Howard Law Journal*, p. 907 (1971); and Sowards and Mofsky, "The Securities Investor Protection Act of 1970," 26 *Business Lawyer*, p. 1271. That the New York Stock Exchange Special Trust Fund was discretionary and ran out of money was made obvious by its failure to protect the customers of the Charles Plohn, First Devonshire, and Robinson firms, during the summer of 1970. See, e.g., *Newsweek*, Oct. 12, 1970, pp. 87–88, 90, and 95.

90. SEC, "Study of Unsafe and Unsound Practices," p. 2. On auditing deficiencies generally, see pp. 151–161; House Study of the Securities Industries Hearings, pp. 1080–1081 and 1091–1108; and Welles, *The Last Days of the Club*, pp. 161–162.

91. 1934 Securities Exchange Act Release No. 9268 (1971).

92. 1934 Securities Exchange Act Release No. 9376 (1971).

93. 1934 Securities Exchange Act Release No. 11497 (1975).

94. James Lorie, "Public Policy for American Capital Markets," submitted to the Secretary and Deputy Secretary of the United States Treasury Department (1974), p. 5; Address of G. Bradford Cook, Apr. 25, 1973, on file with the SEC; Address of Ray Garrett, March 22, 1974, on file with the SEC; James Sargent, "The SEC and the Individual Investor: Restoring His Confidence in the Market," 60 *Virginia Law Review*, p. 553 (1974); Charles

Rolo, "The Case of the Vanishing Investor," *New York Times* magazine, June 9, 1974, pp. 14–15, 47–48, 52–54, and 58–60; *Dun's*, March 1970, p. 124, "Securities Exchange Act Amendment of 1973" Hearings, House Commerce Subcommittee, 93rd Cong., 1st Sess. (1973), pp. 678–685; New York Stock Exchange, "Shareownership 1980" (1981); and New York Stock Exchange, "Marketing Securities to the Small Investor" (June 1973), pp. 40 and 47.

95. Regan, *A View from the Street*, pp. 130–133; SEC *Thirty-seventh Annual Report*, pp. 6–8; SEC, "Study of Unsafe and Unsound Practices," p. 80; 1934 Securities Exchange Act Release No. 8717 (1969); Sargent, "The SEC and the Institutional Investor," 60 *Virginia Law Review*, pp. 566–567; *Fortune*, Aug. 1, 1969, pp. 88–90, 137–138, and 157–159; and BNA *Securities Reporter*, No. 1, June 4, 1969, pp. A1–A2 and X12–X13, No. 8, July 23, 1969, p. X6, No. 38, Feb. 18, 1970, pp. X1–X2, and No. 44, Apr. 1, 1970, pp. A11–A12.

96. 1934 Securities Exchange Act Release No. 9950 (1973), p. 36. See SEC, *Institutional Investor Study*, IV, pp. 2296–2311 and 2321–2322, for earlier SEC discussion of issues involved.

97. See, e.g., Justice Department statement in House Securities Industry Study Hearings, VII, p. 3142; and testimony of American Bankers Association officials before "Fixed Rates and Institutional Membership" Hearings, Senate Subcommittee on Securities, 93rd Cong., 1st Sess. (1973), p. 284.

98. See, e.g., 1973 Senate "Securities Industry Study," pp. 68 and 84 (quoting Gustave Levy); 1972 Senate "Securities Industry Study," pp. 60–69; House "Securities Industry Study," p. 153; and Regan, *A View from the Street*, pp. 183–184.

99. Submission to SEC, reprinted in BNA *Securities Reporter*, No. 25, Nov. 19, 1969, pp. X37–X42.

100. 1972 Senate "Securities Industry Study," pp. 61–64; and BNA *Securities Reporter*, No. 40, March 4, 1970, pp. A5–A8 and A15, and No. 42, March 18, 1970, p. A1.

101. BNA *Securities Reporter*, No. 25, Nov. 19, 1969, p. A3, No. 85, Jan. 20, 1971, pp. A1–A3, and No. 86, Jan. 27, 1971, pp. A1–A2; and Welles, *The Last Days of the Club*, p. 94.

102. Committee announcement quoted in BNA *Securities Reporter*, No. 86, Jan. 27, 1971, pp. A1–A2.

103. BNA *Securities Reporter*, No. 91, March 3, 1971, pp. A10–A11; and *Business Week*, Feb. 27, 1971, p. 44.

104. The Martin Report reprinted in BNA *Securities Reporter*, No. 114, Aug. 11, 1971, pp. E1–E7, text quotes p. E5. Robert Haack, officially speaking on behalf of the Exchange, essentially adopted Martin's position at the SEC's Oct. 1971 hearings on the Future Structure of the Securities Markets; BNA *Securities Reporter*, No. 124, Oct. 27, 1971, pp. A1–A2. Earlier in October the Exchange rejected the IDS membership application; BNA *Securities Reporter*, No. 121, Oct. 6, 1971, p. A7.

105. The SEC "Statement on the Future Structure of the Securities Markets" (Feb. 2, 1972) was published as a pamphlet; pp. 20–24 discuss the institutional membership issue. The "White Paper on Institutional Membership" (Apr. 20, 1972) was presented by Chairman Casey in testimony to

the Senate Subcommittee on Securities and reprinted in BNA *Securities Reporter*, No. 149, Apr. 26, 1972, pp. I1–I7. See also 1934 Securities Exchange Act Release No. 9950, p. 34; and SEC *Thirty-ninth Annual Report*, pp. 8–9.

106. BNA *Securities Reporter*, No. 142, March 8, 1972, pp. A4–A5 and E1–E5, No. 163, Aug. 2, 1972, pp. A9–A10, No. 164, Aug. 9, 1972, pp. A3–A4 and D1–D3, No. 172, Oct. 11, 1972, pp. A5–A7; No. 179, Nov. 29, 1972, pp. A1–A3, G1, and H1, No. 180, Dec. 6, 1972, pp. A1–A2 and E1–E2, No. 189, Feb. 14, 1973, p. A1, No. 190, Feb. 21, 1973, pp. A5–A6, No. 193, March 14, 1973, pp. AA1–AA2 and G1, No. 194, March 21, 1973, pp. A1–A2, No. 195, March 28, 1973, pp. A4–A6 and D1, No. 221, Oct. 3, 1973, pp. D1–D17, and No. 338, Feb. 4, 1976, p. E1, n.3; and SEC *Thirty-ninth Annual Report*, pp. 8–9, and *Fortieth Annual Report*, p. 6.

107. See especially House "Securities Industry Study," pp. 148–149; 1973 Senate "Securities Industry Study," pp. 8–9 and 64–87; House Report No. 94–123, 94th Cong., 1st Sess. (1975), p. 57; and Senate Report No. 94–75, 94th Cong., 1st Sess. (1975), pp. 65–67. Several congressional hearings focused on the issue. The text quotes Apr. 1972 Senate Subcommittee Hearings excerpted in BNA *Securities Reporter*, No. 149, Apr. 26, 1972, pp. A8–A12. The SEC's 80–20 test also was criticized by Nixon-Ford Justice Department (BNA *Securities Reporter*, No. 171, Oct. 4, 1972, pp. I1–I7) and Treasury Department (BNA *Securities Reporter*, No. 238, Feb. 6, 1974, pp. A2–A3; and Lorie, "Public Policy for American Capital Markets," pp. 7–8) as well as by representatives of the insurance industry (BNA *Securities Reporter*, No. 171, Oct. 4, 1972, p. A19) and banking industry ("Fixed Rates and Institutional Membership" Hearings, Senate Subcommittee on Securities, 93rd Cong., 1st Sess. (1973), pp. 283–285). In Feb. and March 1973, the New York Stock Exchange ceased to support the 80–20 test; see Senate "Fixed Rates and Institutional Membership" Hearings, pp. 437–438 and 465. The relevant section of the 1975 Securities Acts Amendments appears in 89 *Stat.* pp. 110–111.

108. BNA *Securities Reporter*, No. 395, March 23, 1977, pp. H1–H28, No. 438, Feb. 1, 1978, pp. A10–A11, No. 441, Feb. 22, 1978, pp. A2–A3, No. 443, March 8, 1978, pp. A1–A2, No. 445, March 22, 1978, pp. A1–A2, No. 453, May 17, 1978, pp. A14–A15, No. 454, May 24, 1978, p. A20, and No. 455, May 31, 1978, p. A11; and SEC *Forty-fourth Annual Report*, pp. 5–6, *Forty-fifth Annual Report*, pp. 6–7; and "Securities Act Amendments of 1975-Oversight" Hearings, House Commerce Committee, 95th Cong., 1st Sess. (1977), pp. 661–892.

109. Address of Hamer Budge, Sept. 4, 1969, on file with the SEC.

110. Memorandum to the Commission from Division of Trading and Markets, Office of Policy Research, "New York Stock Exchange Commission Rate Proposal," Oct. 1, 1970, p. 4.

111. National Economic Research Associates, "Reasonable Public Rates for Brokerage Commissions" (Feb. 1970).

112. Letter from .Robert Haack to Exchange members, Feb. 12, 1970, reprinted in BNA *Securities Reporter*, No. 38, Feb. 18, 1970, pp. X2–X4. The 1969 loss figures were reprinted in BNA *Securities Reporter*, No. 59, July 15, 1970, p. A18, and later independently corroborated by the SEC in its *Institutional Investor Study*, pp. 2214–2215.

113. Regan, *A View from the Street*, pp. 114–116; 1972 Senate "Securi-

ties Industry Study," p. 55; and BNA *Securities Reporter*, No. 57, July 1, 1970, pp. A1–A2.

114. 1934 Securities Exchange Act Releases Nos. 8860, 8923, and 8969 (all, 1970); BNA *Securities Reporter*, No. 66, Sept. 2, 1970, pp. F1–F3; and Regan, *A View from the Street*, pp. 120–121.

115. 1934 Securities Exchange Act Release No. 9007 (1970); SEC *Thirty-sixth Annual Report*, p. 6; 1972 Senate "Securities Industry Study," pp. 54–55; and Welles, *The Last Days of the Club*, p. 93.

116. Baruch, *Wall Street: Security Risk*, pp. 294–295; 1972 Senate "Securities Industry Study," p. 55; BNA *Securities Reporter*, No. 79, Dec. 2, 1970, p. AA1 (quoting Smith); and No. 96, Apr. 7, 1971, p. M1; 1934 Securities Exchange Act Releases Nos. 9079 and 9096 (1971); and Welles, *The Last Days of the Club*, p. 93.

117. House "Securities Industry Study," p. 134; 1972 Senate "Securities Industry Study," p. 55 (summarizing 1971 study); and Testimony of Richard Howland, "Securities Industry Study" Hearings, Senate Securities Subcommittee, 92nd Cong., 1st Sess. (1971), I, pp. 121–122. An estimate of the reduced cost per share on institutional Large-block trades appears in "Securities Exchange Act Amendments of 1973" Hearings, House Commerce Subcommittee, 93rd Cong., 1st Sess. (1973), p. 665.

118. SEC, *Institutional Investor Study*, I, p. vii.

119. SEC, "Future Structure Statement," pp. 14–18.

120. Testimony of William Casey, "Stock Exchange Commission Rates" Hearings, Senate Securities Subcommittee, 92nd Cong., 2nd Sess. (1972), p. 19.

121. BNA *Securities Reporter*, No. 195, March 28, 1973, pp. A15–A16. See also discussion in Justice Department brief in case of *Thill Securities Corporation* v. *New York Stock Exchange* reprinted in "National Securities Marker System Act of 1973" Hearings, Senate Subcommittee on Securities, 93rd Cong., 1st Sess. (1973), pp. 292–293.

122. See, e.g., 1972 Senate "Securities Industry Study," p. 56.

123. Haack November 1970 Address reprinted in BNA *Securities Reporter*, No. 77, Nov. 18, 1970, pp. J1–J3. A sense of how unpopular Haack's address was with some Exchange members is conveyed by Lewis Lapham, "The Coming Wounds of Wall Street," *Harper's*, May 1971, p. 52.

124. 1972 Senate "Securities Industry Study," p. 56.

125. "Fixed Rates and Institutional Membership" Hearings, Senate Securities Subcommittee, 93rd Cong., 1st Sess. (1973), p. 303.

126. Telephone interview with David Ratner, Feb. 12, 1981.

127. Needham quoted in 1973 Senate "Securities Industry Study," p. 63.

128. 1972 Senate "Securities Industry Study," pp. 53–60, quoting p. 59. See also 1973 Senate "Securities Industry Study," pp. 5–7 and 43–63; and BNA *Securities Reporter*, No. 139, Feb. 16, 1972, p. A11.

129. House "Securities Industry Study," pp. 131–132.

130. BNA *Securities Reporter*, No. 192, March 7, 1973, p. A1.

131. BNA *Securities Reporter*, No. 196, Apr. 4, 1973, p. A3, and No. 197, Apr. 11, 1973, pp. A10–A11. But see BNA *Securities Reporter*, No. 202, May 16, 1973, p. AA2 (full Senate committee refused to accept deadline).

132. Kleindienst June 1972 letter to Senate printed in "Stock Exchange Commission Rates" Hearings, Senate Subcommittee on Securities, 92nd Cong., 2nd Sess. (1972), pp. 525–527.

133. The department's brief in the *Thill* case was reprinted in "National Securities Market System Act of 1973" Hearings, Senate Subcommittee on Securities, 93rd Cong., 1st Sess. (1973), beginning at p. 207. The text quotes p. 414. See discussion, generally, pp. 410–419.

134. 498 F.2d 1303 (2d Cir. 1974), *aff'd* 422 U.S. 659 (1975).

135. 1934 Securities Exchange Act Release No. 10383 (1973); Letter to James Needham from Ray Garrett, Dec. 14, 1973, reprinted in BNA *Securities Reporter*, No. 232, Dec. 14, 1973, pp. M1–M3; Addresses of Ray Garrett, Feb. 12, 1974, quoting p. 4, and Dec. 4, 1974, quoting p. 5, on file at the SEC; Interview with John Evans, March 3, 1981, Washington, D.C.; and Interview with A. A. Sommer, March 2, 1981, Washington, D.C. A detailed discussion of the economic background behind the New York Stock Exchange's 1973 rate increase proposal and a similar proposal considered in 1974 appears in New York Stock Exchange, "The Crisis of Member Firm Profitability and the Need for a Securities Commission Rate Increase," a report submitted to the SEC, Sept. 3, 1974.

136. Rotberg testimony quoted in Justice Department brief, reprinted in "National Securities Marker System Act of 1973" Hearings, Senate Subcommittee on Securities, 93rd Cong., 1st Sess. (1973), p. 258.

137. BNA *Securities Reporter*, No. 239, Feb. 13, 1974, pp. A4–A5, and No. 243, March 13, 1974, p. A7.

138. Testimony of James Needham, "Fixed Rates and Institutional Membership" Hearings, Senate Subcommittee on Securities, 93rd Cong., 1st Sess. (1973), pp. 436–437 and 464–465; BNA *Securities Reporter*, No. 274, Oct. 23, 1974, p. A2, and No. 281, Dec. 11, 1974, pp. E1–E3.

139. BNA *Securities Reporter*, No. 286, Jan. 22, 1975, pp. A3–A4; and *Business Week*, Dec. 14, 1974, p. 68.

140. BNA *Securities Reporter*, No. 282, Dec. 18, 1974, pp. AA3–AA4, and No. 286, Jan. 22, 1975, pp. A2–A3; and Interview with A. A. Sommer, March 2, 1981, Washington, D.C.

141. John Evans address dated Apr. 15, 1975, on file with the SEC.

142. BNA *Securities Reporter*, No. 281, Dec. 11, 1974, pp. AA1–AA2, and No. 282, Dec. 18, 1974, pp. AA1–AA3.

143. Address of Ray Garrett, Dec. 4, 1974, on file with the SEC, quoting p. 4. See also *Wall Street Letter*, Dec. 23, 1974, pp. 4–5.

144. 1934 Securities Exchange Act Release No. 11203 (1975).

145. BNA *Securities Reporter*, No. 289, Feb. 12, 1975, p. A1.

146. Public Law 94-29, 89 *Stat.* pp. 107–108.

147. Leroy Verschuur, "The Securities Acts Amendments of 1975: A Move Toward Competition," Ph.D. dissertation, University of Nebraska 1978, p. 22 and 24; Lawrence Goldberg and Lawrence White, eds., *The Deregulation of the Banking and Securities Industries* (Lexington, Mass.: Lexington Books, 1979), p. 159; SEC, *Monthly Statistical Review*, Oct. 1980, p. 13; and New York Stock Exchange, *Fact Book* (1980), p. 15.

148. SEC staff report, "The Securities Industry in 1980," pp. 83–85, 92–94, and Appendices F1 and F2.

149. SEC, "Fifth Report to Congress on the Effect of the Absence of Fixed Rates of Commissions" (May 26, 1977), p. iii.

150. Ibid., p. 48; SEC staff report, "The Securities Industry in 1980," pp. 85–86 and 102; *New York Times*, March 4, 1979, III, p. 1, and June 1, 1980, III, p. 1; and representative ads, e.g., *New York Times*, Jan. 28, 1979, p. F9.

151. SEC staff report, "The Securities Industry in 1980," Appendix A-2.
152. Ibid., p. 27.
153. New York Stock Exchange, *Fact Book* (1980), p. 74; and *Fact Book* (1981), p. 53.
154. New York Stock Exchange, *Fact Book* (1981), p. 53.
155. SEC staff report, "The Securities Industry in 1980," pp. 79–80 and 90; SEC staff report, "The Securities Industry in 1978," pp. 53–57; and Seha Tinic and Richard West, "The Securities Industry under negotiated brokerage commissions: changes in the structure and performance of New York Stock Exchange member firms", 11 *Bell Journal of Economics*, pp. 29–41 (1980). A brief discussion of diversification in the securities industry appears in SEC staff report, "The Securities Industry in 1980," pp. 77–79.
156. See, e.g., Tinic and West, "The Securities Industry under negotiated brokerage commissions," pp. 39–40. A *San Francisco Chronicle* survey of thirty-six institutional investors, conducted in Sept. 1981, similarly found that "almost all of the institutions thought the quality of equity research had improved over the past three years. This was, they said, the result of the reduction in the number of analysts doing research, with the marginal analysts the ones squeezed out." *San Francisco Chronicle*, Sept. 16, 1981, p. 29.
157. Michael Keenan, "The Scope of Deregulation in the Securities Industry" in Goldberg and White, *The Deregulation of the Banking and Securities Industries*, p. 123.
158. See, e.g., 1973 Senate "Securities Industry Study," pp. 106–135.
159. SEC, *Institutional Investor Study*, Chaps. 11 and 12, especially pp. 1541, 1587–1607, 1842–1843, and 1936, and Part VIII, pp. 87–90 and 98; and 1973 Senate "Securities Industry Study," pp. 107–109. 1980 block trading data from SEC, "The Securities Industry in 1980," pp. 4–5 and Appendix A3.
160. The position of the Institutional Investor Study is stated in vol. 1, p. xxv. Farrar's argument appears in the *Harvard Business Review*, Sept. 1972, pp. 114–115. An argument similar to that made by Farrar appears in James Stone, *One Way for Wall Street* (Boston: Little, Brown, 1975), pp. 48–49. On specialists' income, see also BNA *Securities Reporter* No. 341, Feb. 25, 1976, pp. A1–A3.
161. The leading studies are summarized in SEC, "Study of Unsafe and Unsound Practices," pp. 35–39 and 165–203; House "Securities Industry Study," pp. 59–77; and 1972 Senate "Securities Industry Study," pp. 2–3 and 11–27. The full text of the leading studies plus detailed testimony concerning the stock certificate–clearance settlement issues appears in six congressional hearings held between 1971 and 1973. They were: "Securities Industry Study" Hearings, Senate Securities Subcommittee, 92nd Cong., 1st Sess. (1971), II, pp. 63–455; House Securities Industry Hearings, pp. 1315–1638 and 1833–2889; "Clearance and Settlement of Securities Transactions" Hearings, Senate Securities Subcommittee, 92nd Cong., 2nd Sess. (1972); "Securities Processing Act" Hearings, House Commerce Subcommittee, 92nd Cong., 2nd Sess. (1972); "Regulation of Clearing Agencies and Transfer Agents" Hearings, Senate Securities Subcommittee, 93rd Cong., 1st Sess. (1973); and "Securities Exchange Act Amendments of 1973" Hearings, House Commerce Subcommittee, 93rd Cong., 1st Sess. (1973), pp. 1778–1992.
162. House "Securities Industry Study," pp. 59–60.

163. Stone, *One Way for Wall Street*, p. 34.

164. Address of Richard Smith, quoted in BNA *Securities Reporter*, No. 88, Feb. 10, 1971, p. A10.

165. Summarized in 1934 Securities Exchange Act Release No. 9240 (1971).

166. SEC "Study of Unsafe and Unsound Practices," pp. 194–197.

167. The SEC's initial legislative proposal appears in BNA *Securities Reporter*, No. 144, March 22, 1972, pp. G1, H1–H3 and I1–I3. The relevant language of the 1975 amendments appears at 89 *Stat.* pp. 141–146. See also 1973 Senate "Securities Industry Study," pp. 40–42.

168. SEC, "Study of Unsafe and Unsound Practices," pp. 176–178 (describing Rockwell study noted in text), 191–192, and 196; and House "Securities Industry Study," p. 71.

169. SRI cost estimate described in *Securities Week*, July 25, 1977, pp. 1–2, and in testimony of Junius Peake, "Progress Toward the Development of a National Market System" Hearings, House Commerce Subcommittees, 96th Cong., 1st Sess. (1979) (hereinafter, House Progress Toward the Development of a National Market System Hearings), p. 107. On cost savings, see these hearings, also at pp. 76–77, 102, and 128–129.

170. Welles, *The Last Days of the Club*, pp. 284–287, and 1973 Senate "Securities Industry Study," p. 90.

171. NASD, "Three Issues in the Development of a Central Securities Market System" (Washington, D.C., 1976), pp. 20–23; 1934 Securities Exchange Act Release No. 8440 (1968); and NASDAQ sales brochure undated, supplied by SEC Division of Market Regulation from NASDAQ file.

172. James Hamilton, "Marketplace Organization and Marketability: NASDAQ, the Stock Exchange and the National Market System," 33 *Journal of Finance*, p. 487 (1978), cites the earlier studies. The findings in Hamilton's study are paraphrased in the text.

173. *NASDAQ News*, Dec. 1980, p. 2.

174. Ibid., pp. 1–3; NASD *Fact Book* (1979), pp. 29 and 32; New York Stock Exchange, *Fact Book* (1980), p. 63; address of John Evans, Oct. 11, 1981, on file with the SEC; and *New York Times*, June 14, 1981, pp. F11, F16, and F17.

175. Memorandum to the Commission from the Division of Trading and Markets, "Division Memorandum of October 5, 1970, relating to the procedures for compilation of volume data for securities quoted on the NASDAQ system," Dec. 2, 1970, forwarded by the SEC's Division of Market Regulation from its NASDAQ file.

176. A detailed account of the NASDAQ–third-market quotation controversy appears in "Securities Industry Study" Hearings, Senate Subcommittee on Securities, 92nd Cong., 2nd Sess. (1972), III, pp. 1–17. My account also relied on documents supplied to me by the SEC's Division of Market Regulation from its NASDAQ file; most significantly: Letter to the SEC from Ralph Saul, Oct. 9, 1970; Letter to Hamer Budge from Robert Haack, Oct. 13, 1970; undated draft of Letter to Ralph Saul from Irving Pollack (never sent); Letter to Hamer Budge from Gordon Macklin, Oct. 22, 1970; Excerpt from *SEC Minutes*, Oct. 22, 1970; Letter to the commissioners from Donald Weeden, Dec. 15, 1970; Memorandum to the Commission from the Division of Trading and Markcts, "Suit filed against the NASD by Shumate and Company," Jan. 7, 1971; Letter to Emmanuel Celler from M. A. Schapiro, Feb. 19, 1971; NASD press releases, March 15, 1971, and Sept. 21, 1971; and NASD "The NASDAQ–third market Study" (Apr. 1972). The SEC's NASDAQ file also contained the results of two limited studies of the effect of NASDAQ quotations on NYSE spreads, conducted respectively by the Commission's Helen Steiner (dated May 19, 1971) and Weeden and Company (June 8, 1971). Both produced evidence that NASDAQ's third market quotations apparently led to closer NYSE specialists' spreads. Similar results appear in Irwin Friend and Marshall Blume, "The Consequences of Competitive Commissions on the New York Stock Exchange," in "Stock Exchange Commission Rate" Hearings, Senate Subcommittee on Securities, 92nd Cong., 2nd Sess. (1972), pp. 352–354.

177. SEC, "Rules of National Securities Exchanges Which Limit or Condition the Ability of Members to Effect Transactions Otherwise Than on Such Exchanges" (1975), pp. D2–D7.

178. Thomas Russo and William Wang, "The Structure of the Securities Market — Past and Future," 41 *Fordham Law Review*, p. 39 (1972).

179. Several commentators attempted to do so. See, e.g., Wheelock Whitney prediction quoted in Baruch, *Wall Street: Security Risk*, p. 289; Donald Weeden remarks summarized in BNA *Securities Reporter*, No. 76, Nov. 11, 1970, pp. A4–A5; Ralph Saul remarks summarized in BNA *Securities Reporter*, No. 81, Dec. 16, 1970, pp. A18–A19; House "Securities Industry Study," pp. 117–130; 1972 Senate "Securities Industry Study," pp. 33–51; and Morris Mendelson, "Nostalgia vs. the Computer," 4 *Securities Law Review*, p. 503 (1972), for representative statements of the period.

180. See testimony at House Progress Toward the Development of a National Market System Hearings, pp. 76–77, 92, 101–102, and 481. My characterization of Williams's view was based, in part, on an interview, Nov. 7, 1981, Philadelphia, Pennsylvania. On decimal trading, see Junius Peake, Morris Mendelson, and R. T. Williams, "The National Book System," submission to the SEC, April 30, 1976, Reference File No. S7–619 (hereinafter, Peake-Mendelson-Williams, "National Book System"), p. 27.

181. Testimony at House Progress Toward the Development of a National Market System Hearings, p. 82.

182. Senate Report No. 94-75, 94th Cong., 1st Sess. (1975), pp. 12–13.

183. SEC, *Institutional Investor Study*, I, pp. xxii–xxv.

184. The Martin Report reprinted in BNA *Securities Reporter*, No. 114, Aug. 11, 1971, pp. E1–E7.

185. 1973 "Securities Industry Study," pp. 95–96; "Securities Industry Study" Hearings, Senate Subcommittee on Securities, 92nd Cong., 2nd Sess. (1972), VIII, pp. 4095–4110; and House Securities Industry Hearings, pp. 2902–2917.

186. Statements by Mathews, nineteen economists, Lorie, and Samuelson reprinted in House Securities Industry Hearings, pp. 3246, 2892–2893, and 3249; Donald Farrar, "Wall Street's Proposed 'Great Leap Backward,'" *Financial Analyst Journal*, Sept.–Oct. 1971, pp. 14–16 and 59–62; and *Business Week* article, Aug. 14, 1971, reprinted in "Securities Industry Study" Hearings, Senate Securities Subcommittee, 92nd Cong., 1st Sess. (1971), I, p. 93.

187. 1934 Securities Exchange Act Release No. 9315 (1971). The hearings are described in the SEC's *Thirty-eighth Annual Report,* p. 7; and BNA *Securities Reporter,* No. 122, Oct. 13, 1971, pp. A1–A3, No. 123, Oct. 20, 1971, pp. A1–A8.

188. SEC, "Future Structure Statement," quoting pp. 7–9.

189. Reprinted in BNA *Securities Reporter,* No. 192, March 7, 1973, pp. I1–I7. Two other advisory committees were named by Casey; see BNA *Securities Reporter,* No. 146, Apr. 5, 1972, p. A3.

190. SEC, "Policy Statement on the Structure of a Central Market System," quoting or paraphrasing pp. 8, 18, 21–25, 48, 57–58, and 63–64.

191. Address of G. Bradford Cook, Feb. 23, 1973, on file with the SEC.

192. See, e.g., Senate Report No. 93–865, 93rd Cong., 2nd Sess. (1974), pp. 5–8.

193. House Progress Toward the Development of a National Market System Hearings, pp. 68 and 74. The GAO agreed. See GAO, "Improvements Needed in the Securities and Exchange Commission's Efforts to Establish a National Market System," p. i.

194. Interview with Harold Williams, Nov. 7, 1981, Philadelphia, Pennsylvania; and Williams 1979 testimony quoted in House Committee Print 96–IFC 56, 96th Cong., 2nd Sess. (1980), p. 2. Milton Cohen, whose views were similar to those of Harold Williams, published a detailed explanation of the reasons for a "modest" evolutionary approach, "The National Market System — A Modest Proposal," 46 *George Washington Law Review,* p. 743 (1978).

195. See addresses of Harold Williams, Nov. 30, 1979, pp. 7–9, and Dec. 4, 1980, pp. 19–20, and transcript of press conference with Williams, Sept. 15, 1980, p. 5, all on file at the SEC.

196. House Committee Print No. 96-IFC 56, 96th Cong., 2nd Sess. (1980), p. 12.

197. 1973 Senate "Securities Industry Study," p. 96; Senate Report No. 93–865, 93rd Cong., 2nd Sess. (1974), pp. 5–8; and Welles, *The Last Days of the Club,* pp. 303–309.

198. Interview with A. A. Sommer, March 2, 1981, Washington, D.C. Commissioner Evans had a similar recollection in an interview, March 3, 1981, Washington, D.C.

199. Lloyd Feller and George Simon, "The National Market System in Perspective: A selective outline of significant events" (Unpublished, on file with the SEC's Division of Market Regulation, dated May 15, 1978) p. 26. The New York Stock Exchange published a similar account of events; see Letter to Ray Garrett from James Needham, Aug. 10, 1973, reprinted in "National Securities Market System Act of 1973" Hearings, Senate Subcommittee on Securities, 93rd Cong., 1st Sess. (1973), p. 122.

200. 1934 Securities Exchange Act Release No. 9530 (1972).

201. Advisory Committee Report reprinted in BNA *Securities Reporter,* No. 161, July 19, 1972, pp. E1–E2.

202. Feller and Simon, "The National Market System in Perspective," pp. 26–27.

203. Interview with A. A. Sommer, March 2, 1981, Washington, D.C.; and 1973 Senate "Securities Industry Study," pp. 99–100.

204. Address of Ray Garrett, Jan. 15, 1974, on file with the SEC.

205. 1934 Securities Exchange Act Releases Nos. 9731 and 9850 (1972).

206. CTA plan reprinted in BNA *Securities Reporter*, No. 192, March 7, 1973, pp. J1–J10.

207. See, e.g., BNA *Securities Reporter*, No. 193, March 14, 1973, p. A9; No. 199, April 25, 1973, pp. A9–A11; and No. 258, June 26, 1974, Special Supplement, pp. 7–10.

208. New York Stock Exchange, "Equal or Uniform Regulation and a Consolidated Tape System for Listed Securities (Sept. 20, 1973) pp. 19–20; and Address of Ray Garrett, Jan. 15, 1974, on file with the SEC.

209. Address of Ray Garrett, Jan. 15, 1974, on file with the SEC; 1934 Securities Exchange Act Release No. 10218 (1973); BNA *Securities Reporter*, No. 216, Aug. 22, 1973, pp. A1–A4; "National Securities Market System Act of 1973" Hearings, Senate Subcommittee on Securities, 93rd Cong., 1st Sess. (1973), pp. 121–135; 1934 Securities Exchange Act Release No. 10671 (1974); BNA *Securities Reporter*, No. 250, May 1, 1974, pp. A6–A9 and I1–I12; and 1934 Securities Exchange Act Release No. 10787 (1974).

210. BNA *Securities Reporter*, No. 307, June 18, 1975, pp. A13–A14. For subsequent developments concerning the tape, see 1934 Securities Exchange Act Releases Nos. 16589–16590, 16802, and 17368 (all 1980).

211. "Advisory Committee Report" was reprinted in BNA *Securities Reporter*, No. 178, Nov. 22, 1972, pp. H1–H3.

212. SEC, "Policy Statement on the Structure of a Central Market System," quoting p. 48.

213. 1934 Securities Exchange Act Release No. 9529 (1972).

214. Macklin quoted in BNA *Securities Reporter*, No. 270, Sept. 25, 1974, pp. A5–A6. See also BNA *Securities Reporter*, No. 201, May 9, 1973, p. A10, and No. 258, June 26, 1974, Special Supplement, p. 10; Commissioner Evans remarks quoted in *Wall Street Letter*, May 27, 1974, p. 1; and Welles, *The Last Days of the Club*, pp. 309–313.

215. Memorandum to NYSE Board of Directors from William Freund, "Proposal on Competing Quotations" (Sept. 25, 1972); and 1973 Senate "Securities Industry Study," p. 101.

216. 1934 Securities Exchange Act Release No. 10969 (1974).

217. Their comment letters are quoted in BNA *Securities Reporter* No. 283, Jan. 1, 1975, pp. A14–A16.

218. 1934 Securities Exchange Act Release No. 11288 (1975).

219. BNA *Securities Reporter*, No. 297, April 9, 1975, p. A7; and 1934 Securities Exchange Act Release No. 11406 (1975).

220. The Act added Sections 11A(6) and 11(c)(1) to the Securities Exchange Act; see 89 *Stat.* 112–116; and Senate Report No. 94–75, 94th Cong., 1st Sess., pp. 9–12.

221. 1934 Securities Exchange Act Releases Nos. 12670 (1976), 13626 (1977), and 14415 (1978). On final adoption, see also BNA *Securities Reporter*, No. 434, Jan. 4, 1978, pp. A10–A11. In July 1978, the SEC agreed that SIAC could collect and disseminate quotations to vendors subject to the administration of a Consolidated Quotation Association similar to the Consolidated Tape Association. 1934 Securities Exchange Act Release No. 15009.

222. Cohen, "The National Market System," 46 *George Washington Law Review*, p. 765; and 1934 Securities Exchange Act Release No. 17583 (1981). See also 1934 Securities Exchange Act Release No. 16590 (1980).

223. "Securities Exchange Act Amendments of 1973" Hearings, House Commerce Subcommittee, 93rd Cong., 1st Sess. (1973), p. 1037; and New York Stock Exchange *Fact Book* (1980), p. 67. Updated figures appear in 1934 Securities Exchange Act Release No. 11628 (1975).

224. SEC, *Institutional Investor Study*, I, p. xxiv–xxv; SEC, "Statement on the Future Structure of the Securities Market," pp. 7–12; and SEC, "Policy Statement on the Structure of a Central Market System," p. 48.

225. See, e.g., Needham address, Dec. 1, 1972, reprinted in BNA *Securities Reporter*, No. 180, Dec. 6, 1972, pp. I1–I3; BNA *Securities Reporter*, No. 181, Dec. 13, 1972, pp. A7–A8, and No. 187, Jan. 31, 1973, p. A11; "National Securities Market System Act of 1973" Hearings, Senate Subcommittee on Securities, 93rd Cong., 1st Sess. (1973), pp. 165–171; "Securities Exchange Act Amendments of 1973" Hearings, House Commerce Subcommittee, 93rd Cong., 1st Sess. (1973), pp. 1056–1062; and "SEC Authority Over Third Market Trading" Hearings, Senate Subcommittee on Securities, 93rd Cong., 2nd Sess. (1974), pp. 1–3.

226. SEC "Central Market Statement," quoting p. 58.

227. 1973 Senate "Securities Industry Study," pp. 105 and 125–126.

228. Williams explanation reprinted in BNA *Securities Reporter*, No. 221, Oct. 3, 1973, p. E1.

229. "SEC Authority Over Third-Market Trading" Hearings, Senate Subcommittee on Securities, 93rd Cong., 2nd Sess. (1974), quoting pp. 1–2. See also p. 6–11 (Senator Hart opposition), pp. 17–21 (SEC opposition), pp. 35–39 (Treasury Department opposition), pp. 41–46 (Justice Department opposition), pp. 65–67 (SIA support), and pp. 79–82 (NYSE support).

230. Senate Report No. 94–75, 94th Cong., 1st Sess. (1975), pp. 20–22 and 72–73.

231. House Report No. 94–229, 94th Cong., 1st Sess. (1975), p. 94; and House Report No. 94–123, 94th Cong., 1st Sess. (1975), p. 94.

232. House Report No. 94–229, 94th Cong., 1st Sess. (1975), p. 96.

233. Interview with John Evans, March 3, 1981, Washington, D.C. See also *Securities Week*, May 12, 1975, p. 2, May 19, 1975, pp. 2b–3, and June 30, 1975, pp. 1–2.

234. House Report No. 94–229, 94th Cong., 1st Sess. (1975), p. 95.

235. Ibid., p. 92; and Cohen, "The National Market System . . ." 46 *George Washington Law Review*, p. 749.

236. Section 11A(d) of the 1975 act, 89 *Stat.* pp. 116–117. See also BNA *Securities Reporter*, No. 230, Dec. 5, 1973, pp. A7–A8, No. 245, March 27, 1974, p. A13, No. 293, March 12, 1975, pp. G1–G2, and No. 295, March 26, 1975, pp. A12–A16; and *Securities Week*, Apr. 21, 1975, pp. 1–2.

237. SEC, "Rules of National Securities Exchanges Which Limit or Condition the Ability of Members to Effect Transactions Otherwise Than on Such Exchanges" (Sept. 2, 1975), quoting p. 1. The report, but not the accompanying appendices, was republished in 1934 Securities Exchange Act Release No. 11628 (1975).

238. Address of A. A. Sommer, Oct. 10, 1975, on file with the SEC. Similar statements were voiced by Exchange Chairman Needham. See *Newsweek*, Nov. 3, 1975, p. 84.

239. 1934 Securities Exchange Act Release No. 11942 (1975). Useful discussion of the "overreaching," "internalization," "fragmentation," and related issues also appears in the SEC's Sept. 1975 report "Rules of National

Securities Exchanges Which Limit or Condition the Ability of Members to Effect Transactions Otherwise Than on Such Exchanges." See also 1934 Securities Exchange Act Releases Nos. 13662 (1977) and 16888 (1980); and Cohen, "The National Market System," 46 *George Washington Law Review*, pp. 754–757. Regarding the dangers of overreaching see also SEC, "A Monitoring Report on the Operation and Effects of Rule 19c–3 under the Securities Exchange Act of 1934" (1981), especially pp. 25–27 and 33–35. It suggests that the risks to investors of overreaching are slight.

240. "Federal Regulation and Regulatory Reform," House Commerce Subcommittee Report, House Doc. No. 95–134, 95th Cong., 1st Sess. (1976), pp. 24–29. See also *Securities Week*, Dec. 29, 1975, pp. 1–2.

241. 1934 Securities Exchange Act Release No. 13662, reprinted in BNA *Securities Reporter*, No. 409, June 29, 1977, quoting p. E4.

242. Ibid., pp. E2–E3.

243. Ibid., pp. E5–E6; and New York Stock Exchange *Fact Book* (1980), p. 15.

244. 1934 Securities Exchange Act Release No. 13662, reprinted in BNA *Securities Reporter*, No. 409, June 29, 1977, quoting pp. E7–E9.

245. Interview with Harold Williams, Nov. 7, 1981, Philadelphia, Pennsylvania; and *Securities Week*, June 6, 1977, pp. 2–2b, Aug. 22, 1977, pp. 1 and 5, Aug. 29, 1977, pp. 5–6, Nov. 7, 1977, p. 13, Nov. 14, 1977, p. 15, and Nov. 21, 1977, p. 9.

246. 1934 Securities Exchange Act Release No. 14416 (1978), reprinted in BNA *Securities Reporter*, No. 438, Feb. 1, 1978, quoting E7. See also Senator Williams's letter, BNA *Securities Reporter*, No. 421, Sept. 28, 1977, pp. G1–G3; and BNA *Securities Reporter*, No. 431, Dec. 7, 1977, pp. A1–A2.

247. 1934 Securities Exchange Act Release No. 15376 (1978). See also *Wall Street Letter*, Oct. 9, 1978, pp. 1 and 7–8.

248. 1934 Securities Exchange Act Release No. 15769 (1979).

249. Interview with Harold Williams, Nov. 7, 1981, Philadelphia, Pennsylvania; and 1934 Securities Exchange Act Releases Nos. 16888 and 16889 (1980). Through August 1981, the SEC believed that there had been too little trading under Rule 19c-3 to draw any significant conclusions about the Rule. 1934 Securities Exchange Act Release No. 18062 (1981).

250. House Committee Print 96-IFC 56, 96th Cong., 2nd Sess. (1980), pp. III-V and 13–20, quoting pp. III and 15.

251. House Progress Toward the Development of a National Market System Hearings, p. 85.

252. Cincinnati hard CLOB system described in House Progress Toward the Development of a National Market System Hearings, especially pp. 6–7, 85, 93, 132–150, 250–251, 277–285, and 475; House Committee Print 96-IFC 56, 96th Cong., 2nd Sess. (1980), p. 28; SEC, "A Monitoring Report on the Operation of the Cincinnati Stock Exchange National Securities Trading System" (1981); and BNA *Securities Reporter*, No. 458, June 21, 1978, pp. A10–A14, No. 461, July 12, 1978, pp. A2–A3, and No. 472, Oct. 4, 1978, p. A4.

253. The Intermarket Trading System (ITS) described in House Progress Toward the Development of a National Market System Hearings, pp. 6–7, 70–88, 132–150, and 250–251; House Committee Print 96-IFC 56, 96th Cong., 2nd Sess. (1980), p. 21; SEC, "A Monitoring Report on the Operation of the Intermarket Trading System" (1981), pp. 5–9; Feller and Simon, "The

National Market Trading System in Perspective," pp. 41–56; and BNA *Securities Reporter*, No. 432, Dec. 14, 1977, pp. A6–A7, No. 449, Apr. 9, 1978, pp. A7–A8, and No. 478, Nov. 15, 1978, pp. A1 and A5.

254. SEC, "Reports of the Advisory Committee on the Implementation of a Central Market System" (September 12, 1975), quoting pp. 26, 6 and 15. The inability of the Yearley Committee to resolve the key central market issues was frequently noted in the securities industry trade journals at that time. See, e.g., *Wall Street Letter*, Aug. 26, 1974, p. 2, and Nov. 4, 1974, p. 3.

255. 1934 Securities Exchange Act Release No. 11942 (1975) reprinted in BNA *Securities Reporter*, No. 333, Dec. 24, 1975, pp. F18–F21; and 1934 Securities Exchange Act Release No. 12159 (1976), reprinted in BNA *Securities Reporter*, No. 343, March 10, 1976, pp. E1–E4.

256. *Securities Week*, Aug. 16, 1976, Special Supplement. Merrill Lynch honed its recommendations over the next three years. See *Securities Week*, July 19, 1977, Special Issue; and House Progress Toward the Development of a National Market System Hearings, pp. 68–79.

257. The Peake-Mendelson-Williams proposal for a National Book System was made to the SEC in a letter dated Apr. 30, 1976, which may be found in SEC Reference File No. S7-619. The proposal was amplified in a series of subsequent letters, articles, and testimony. See especially letters to NMAB from Peake, Mendelson, and Williams, June 10, 1976, July 12, 1976, July 13, 1976, Aug. 11, 1976, Aug. 20, 1976, and Nov. 4, 1976, on file with Junius Peake; and House Progress Toward the Development of a National Market System Hearings, pp. 109–150. See also, generally, *Proposals for a Securities Market Law for Canada* (1979), vol. III, pp. 124–130, 1020–1036, and 1086–1105.

258. 1934 Securities Exchange Act Release No. 11623 (1975); and "NMAB Report to SEC on Establishment of a National Market System," reprinted in BNA *Securities Reporter*, No. 432, Dec. 14, 1977, pp. I1–I6. See also Cohen, "The National Market System," 46 *George Washington Law Review*, p. 743; and *Securities Week*, Nov. 21, 1977, p. 2a.

259. See, e.g., House Progress Toward the Development of a National Market System Hearings, p. 2.

260. "Securities Acts Amendments of 1975 — Oversight" Hearings, House Commerce Subcommittee, 95th Cong., 1st Sess. (1977), p. 515; and Address of Harold Williams, Jan. 28, 1978, on file with the SEC.

261. See, e.g., *Wall Street Letter*, Jan. 30, 1978, pp. 1 and 9–10.

262. 1934 Securities Exchange Act Release No. 14416, reprinted in BNA *Securities Reporter*, No. 438, Feb. 1, 1978, pp. E1–E10.

263. 1934 Securities Exchange Act Release No. 15671 (1979), reprinted in BNA *Securities Reporter*, No. 496, March 28, 1979, p. E4; House Progress Toward the Development of a National Securities Market Hearings, pp. 419–421; and letter to Mr. George Fitzsimmons, secretary, Securities and Exchange Commission, from James E. Buck, secretary, New York Stock Exchange, May 31, 1978, on file with the New York Stock Exchange.

264. 1934 Securities Exchange Act Release No. 15671, reprinted in BNA *Securities Reporter*, No. 496, March 28, 1979, quoting p. E4.

265. 1934 Securities Exchange Act Release No. 15770 (1979).

266. NYSE descriptions of LOIS appear in House Progress Toward the Development of a National Market Hearings, pp. 183–186 and 407–412.

267. BNA *Securities Reporter*, No. 613, July 22, 1981, p. B11.

268. But see 1934 Securities Exchange Act Release No. 17704 (1981); and 1934 Securities Exchange Act Release No. 17744 (1981), reprinted in BNA *Securities Reporter* No. 600, Apr. 22, 1981, p. G5.

269. SEC *Forty-fourth Annual Report*, pp. 2–3; and BNA *Securities Reporter*, No. 521, Sept. 26, 1979, p. A15.

270. 1934 Securities Exchange Act Release No. 15671 (1979); BNA *Securities Reporter*, No. 496, March 28, 1979, pp. E6–E7; BNA *Securities Reporter*, No. 604, May 20, 1981, pp. A5–A6; and SEC, "A Monitoring Report on the Operation of the Cincinnati Stock Exchange National Securities Trading System" (1981).

271. House Progress Toward the Development of a National Securities Market Hearings, pp. 282–285. See also Chairman Williams's testimony at pp. 475–476.

272. House Progress Toward the Development of a National Market System Hearings, pp. 143 and 191–193.

273. House Committee Print 96-IFC 56, 96th Cong., 2nd Sess. (1980), p. 9. See also discussion in Cohen, "A National Market System," 46 *George Washington Law Review*, pp. 766–768; and House Progress Toward the Development of a National Market System Hearings, p. 70.

274. SEC, "Monitoring Report on the Operations and Effects of Rule 19c-3 . . ." pp. 38–41.

275. SEC, "A Monitoring Report on the Operation of the Intermarket Trading System," p. 4.

276. 1934 Securities Exchange Act Release No. 17744 (1981), reprinted in BNA *Securities Reporter*, No. 600, Apr. 22, 1981, pp. G1–G11. For the background of this order, see 1934 Securities Exchange Act Release No. 14416 (1978), reprinted in BNA *Securities Reporter*, No. 438, Feb. 1, 1978, pp. E5–E6; 1934 Securities Exchange Act Release No. 14885 (1978); 1934 Securities Exchange Act Release No. 17516 (1981); and House Committee Print 96-IFC 56, 96th Cong., 2nd Sess. (1980), pp. 31–32 and 42–43.

277. SEC, "A Monitoring Report on the Operation and Effects of Rule 19c-3 . . ." pp. 11–12 and 17.

278. 1934 Securities Exchange Act Release No. 17704 (1981); House Committee Print 96-IFC 56, pp. 22–27; and SEC, "A Monitoring Report on the Operation of the Intermarket Trading System," pp. 23 and 35–36.

279. SEC, "A Monitoring Report on the Operation of the Intermarket Trading System," pp. 5–6, 10–12, 15, 38, and 45; and *Wall Street Journal*, May 5, 1980, pp. 1 and 30.

280. John Coffee, "Beyond the Shut-Eyed Sentry: Toward a Theoretical View of Corporate Misconduct and an Effective Legal Response," 63 *Virginia Law Review*, pp. 1109–1110 (1977).

281. See, e.g., *Medical Committee for Human Rights* v. *SEC*, 432 F.2d 659 (Ct. of Ap., D.C. Cir., 1970), *vacated and dismissed as moot*, 401 U.S. 403 (1972); Donald E. Schwartz, "The Public-Interest Proxy Campaign: Reflections on Campaign GM," 69 *Michigan Law Review*, p. 421 (1971); and description of NROC petition and ensuing litigation, in SEC "Staff Report on Corporate Accountability," printed for use by the Senate Banking Committee, 96th Cong., 2nd Sess. (1980) (hereinafter, SEC "Staff Report on Corporate Accountability"), pp. 251–259. See also Donald Schwartz and Elliot Weiss, "An Assessment of the SEC Shareholder Proposal Rule," 65 *Georgetown Law Journal*, p. 635 (1977).

282. SEC, *Institutional Investor Study*, III, pp. 1364–1373; and SEC, "Staff Report on Corporate Accountability," pp. 381 and 392–398. See, generally, Melvin Eisenberg, *The Structure of the Corporation* (Boston: Little, Brown, 1976), pp. 53–63; and "Voting Rights in Major Corporations," Staff Report of the Subcommittee on Reports, Accounting and Management, Senate Committee on Governmental Affairs, 95th Cong., 1st Sess. (1978), especially pp. 565–799.

283. These included Robert Vesco's looting of IOS Ltd, SEC *Thirty-ninth Annual Report*, pp. 22–23; the Equity Funding Fraud, SEC *Forty-first Annual Report*, pp. 32–33, and *Fortune*, Aug. 1973, pp. 81–85 and 120–132; the National Student Marketing case, SEC *Forty-second Annual Report*, pp. 42–43, *Forty-third Annual Report*, pp. 59–60, and *Forty-fourth Annual Report*, pp. 35–36; C. Arnholdt Smith's misuse of funds of the United States National Bank of San Diego, SEC, *Fortieth Annual Report*, p. 20; the Stirling Homex case, SEC, *Forty-first Annual Report*, pp. 35–36; and the bankruptcy of W. T. Grant, *New York Times*, Feb. 13, 1976, p. 1.

284. Joseph Daughen and Peter Binzen, *The Wreck of the Penn Central* (Boston: Little, Brown, 1971), quoting pp. 303 and 336; "The Penn Central Failure and the Role of Financial Institutions," Staff report of the House Banking Committee, Committee Print, 92nd Cong., 1st Sess. (1972), quoting p. 149; and Daniel J. Schwartz, "Penn Central: A Case Study of Outside Director Responsibility Under the Federal Securities Laws," 45 *UMKC Law Review*, p. 1 (1977).

285. *Dun's*, Aug. 1970, p. 72. See similar articles in *Business Week*, July 4, 1970, pp. 76–78, and May 22, 1977, pp. 50–58.

286. Myles Mace, *Directors: Myth and Reality* (Cambridge: Harvard University Press, 1971), especially pp. 3, 43, 52, and 70.

287. Ibid., pp. 94–101.

288. See citations and discussion in Joel Seligman, "The Securities and Exchange Commission and Corporate Democracy," 3 *Dayton Law Review*, p. 1 (1978); and Eisenberg, *The Structure of the Corporation*, pp. 97–127.

289. Seligman, "The Securities and Exchange Commission and Corporate Democracy," 3 *Dayton Law Review*, pp. 9–10.

290. Mace, *Directors: Myth and Reality*, p. 99.

291. Eisenberg, *The Structure of the Corporation*, pp. 144–145.

292. Mace, *Directors: Myth and Reality*, pp. 87–91.

293. Nance quoted in *Business Week*, May 22, 1971, p. 51.

294. Mace, *Directors: Myth and Reality*, pp. 87–91, quoting p. 90.

295. Heidrick & Struggles survey described in Eisenberg, *The Structure of the Corporation*, pp. 141–143.

296. Peter Drucker observation quoted in Coffee, "Beyond the Shut-Eyed Sentry . . ." 63 *Virginia Law Review*, p. 1134.

297. Ibid., p. 1143.

298. *SEC* v. *Texas Gulf Sulphur*, 446 F.2d 1301 (2d Cir., 1971); Comment, "Equitable Remedies in SEC Enforcement Actions," 123 *University of Pennsylvania Law Review*, p. 1188 (1975); Stanley Sporkin, "SEC Developments in Litigation and the Molding of Remedies," 29 *Business Lawyer*, p. 121, Special Issue (1974); John Ellsworth, "Disgorgement in Securities Fraud Actions Brought by the SEC," 1977 *Duke Law Journal*, p. 641; and Comment, "Court-appointed Directors: Ancillary Relief in Federal Securi-

ties Law Enforcement Actions," 64 *Georgetown Law Journal*, p. 737 (1976).

299. *SEC* v. *National Student Marketing Corp.* Fed. Sec. L. Rep. CCH Paragraph 93,360 (D.D.C. 1972); *Wall Street Journal*, Feb. 15, 1972, p. 1; *SEC* v. *National Student Marketing Corp.*, 360 Fed. Supp. 284 (D.D.C. 1973); Lewis Lowenfels, "Expanding Public Responsibilities of Securities Lawyers: An Analysis of the New Trend in Standard of Care and Priorities of Duties," 74 *Columbia Law Review*, p. 412 (1974); and Stuart Margolis, "Sanctions Against Accountants for Violations of the Securities Laws: A Reappraisal," 4 *Delaware Journal of Corporate Law*, p. 399 (1979). See also Monroe Freedman, "A Civil Libertarian Looks at Securities Regulation," 30 *Ohio State Law Journal*, p. 280 (1974), for a critical view of this development.

300. *Watergate Special Prosecution Force Reports* (1975), pp. 71–77; and (1977), pp. 8–12; Joel Seligman, "Crimes in the Suites," *MBA* magazine, June 1976, p. 28; Address of Ray Garrett, June 27, 1975, on file with the SEC; Ronald Kane and Samuel Butler, "Improper Corporate Payments: The Second Half of Watergate," 8 *Loyola University* (Chicago) *Law Review*, pp. 6–8 (1976); and Edward Herlihy and Theodore Levine, "Corporate Crisis: The Overseas Payment Problem," 8 *Law and Policy in International Business*, especially pp. 554–558 and 573–576 (1976). See, generally, Coffee, "Beyond the Shut-Eyed Sentry," 63 *Virginia Law Review*, pp. 1099–1278.

301. Kane and Butler, "Improper Corporate Payments . . ." 8 *Loyola Law Review*, pp. 9–11.

302. SEC, "Report on Questionable and Illegal Corporate Payments and Practices," submitted to the Senate Banking Committee, 94th Cong., 2nd Sess. (1976) (hereinafter, SEC, "Report on Questionable and Illegal Corporate Payments and Practices"), pp. 4–5.

303. Testimony of Philip Loomis, "The Activities of American Multinational Corporations Abroad" Hearings, House Subcommittee on International Economic Policy, 94th Cong., 1st Sess. (1975), pp. 63–64 and 180–185; SEC, "Report on Questionable and Illegal Corporate Payments and Practices," pp. 6–13; Interview with A. A. Sommer, March 2, 1981, Washington, D.C.; Interview with Stanley Sporkin, March 2, 1981, Washington, D.C.; and Herlihy and Levine, "Corporate Crisis: The Overseas Payment Problem," 8 *Law and Policy in International Business*, pp. 584–594. Certain aspects of the program were criticized in "SEC Voluntary Compliance Program on Corporate Disclosure," Staff Study of the House Commerce Subcommittee on Oversight and Investigations (May 20, 1976).

304. SEC, "Report on Questionable and Illegal Corporate Payments and Practices" (First seven months' data); SEC *Forty-fourth Annual Report*, p. 27; and lists of SEC voluntary questionable payments disclosures and management fraud litigation to unspecified date in 1981 by the SEC Office of Public Affairs.

305. SEC, "Report on Questionable and Illegal Corporate Payments and Practices," quoting p. a. See especially Exhibit A. See also Coffee, "Beyond the Shut-Eyed Sentry," 63 *Virginia Law Review*, p. 1128.

306. "Report of the Special Review Committee of the Board of Directors of Gulf Oil Corporation" (Dec. 30, 1975). I earlier summarized this report in "Crime in the Suites," *MBA* magazine, June 1976, pp. 28–29.

307. Seligman, "Crime in the Suites," *MBA*, June 1976, p. 31, based on study of American Ship Building, Northrop, and Minnesota Mining and

Manufacturing special review committee reports and other disclosure documents filed with the SEC.

308. William Cary, "Federalism and Corporate Law: Reflections Upon Delaware," 83 *Yale Law Journal*, p. 663 (1974).

309. Harvey Goldschmid, "The Greening of the Board Room: Reflections on Corporate Responsibility," 10 *Columbia Journal of Law and Social Problems*, pp. 17–28 especially pp. 24–28 (1973). Regarding Justice Goldberg's proposal, see SEC, "Staff Report on Corporate Accountability," pp. 572–574; and Eisenberg, *The Structure of the Corporation*, pp. 154–156.

310. Christopher Stone, *Where the Law Ends* (New York: Harper & Row, 1975), pp. 134–183. Settlement of SEC enforcement actions during the mid-1970s regularly required the appointment of independent directors. See citations and discussion, Coffee "Beyond the Shut-Eyed Sentry," 63 *Virginia Law Review*, pp. 1248–1249.

311. Ralph Nader, Mark Green, and Joel Seligman, *Taming the Giant Corporation* (New York: W. W. Norton, 1976), especially pp. 118–131 and 240. Regarding TNEC precursors, see Chap. 6. See also Donald Schwartz, "Symposium: Federal Chartering of Corporations: An Introduction," 61 *Georgetown Law Journal*, p. 71 (1972).

312. "Corporate Rights and Responsibilities" Hearings, Senate Commerce Committee, 94th Cong., 2nd Sess. (1976); and "The Role of the Shareholder in the Corporate World" Hearings, Senate Judiciary Subcommittee on Citizens and Shareholder Rights and Remedies, 95th Cong., 1st Sess. (1977). See SEC, "Staff Report on Corporate Accountability," pp. 722–734, for discussion of subsequent events.

313. Law professor petition reprinted in "Corporate Rights and Responsibilities" Hearings, Senate Commerce Committee, 94th Cong., 2nd Sess. (1976), pp. 344–346.

314. Stanley Sporkin, "A Bill of Rights for Investors," address reprinted in BNA *Securities Reporter*, No. 402, May 11, 1977, pp. G1–G2.

315. 1933 Securities Act Release No. 5466 (1974).

316. See discussion in A. A. Sommer Address, April 2, 1976, pp. 10–11, on file with the SEC.

317. Interview with Stanley Sporkin, March 2, 1981, Washington, D.C.; Interview with A. A. Sommer, March 2, 1981, Washington, D.C.; and Interview with John Evans, March 3, 1981, Washington, D.C.

318. Addresses of A. A. Sommer, Dec. 8, 1975, and Apr. 2, 1976, on file with the SEC.

319. SEC, "Report on Questionable and Illegal Corporate Payments and Practices," pp. 13–32.

320. Hills testimony at "Corporate Rights and Responsibilities" Hearings, Senate Commerce Committee, 94th Cong., 2nd Sess. (1976), pp. 301–308; Addresses of Roderick Hills, June 21, 1976, June 30, 1976, and Nov. 8, 1976, on file with the SEC.

321. Hills testimony at "Corporate Rights and Responsibilities" Hearings, Senate Commerce Committee, 94th Cong., 2nd Sess. (1976), quoting p. 303.

322. Addresses of Roderick Hills, June 21, 1976, and June 30, 1976, on file with the SEC; 1934 Securities Exchange Act Release No. 13346 (1977); SEC, "Staff Report on Corporate Accountability," pp. 478, 486–506, 607–608, 618, and 635–637; Michael Riley Marget, "The Audit Committee," 3

Journal of Corporation Law, p. 400 (1978); and Edward Greene and Bernard Falk, "The Audit Committee: A Measured Contribution to Corporate Governance," 34 Business Lawyer, p. 1229 (1979). See also Eisenberg, The Structure of the Corporation, pp. 205–209.

323. SEC, "Report on Questionable and Illegal Corporate Payments and Practices," pp. 57–69; Public Law 95–213, 91 Stat. 1494–1500; Conference Report on "Foreign Corrupt Practices Act of 1977" reprinted in BNA Securities Reporter, No. 432, Dec. 14, 1977, pp. H1–H4; Coffee, "Beyond the Shut-Eyed Sentry," 63 Virginia Law Review, quoting p. 1270; Daniel Goelzer, "The Accounting Provisions of the Foreign Corrupt Practices Act," 5 Journal of Corporation Law, p. 1 (1979); and "A Guide to the New Section 13(b)(2) Accounting Requirements of the Securities Exchange Act of 1934," 34 Business Law, p. 307 (1978). The SEC already possessed the authority to implement similar requirements by rule. See 1934 Securities Exchange Act Release No. 13185 (1977).

324. BNA Securities Reporter, No. 358, June 23, 1976, pp. A17–A18.

325. "Corporate Rights and Responsibilities" Hearings, Senate Commerce Committee, 94th Cong., 2nd Sess. (1976), pp. 308–309; White House Doc. reprinted in BNA Securities Reporter, No. 365, Aug. 11, 1976, pp. F1–F7; and Ralph Nader and Joel Seligman, "Curbing Corporate Bribery," Washington Post, June 13, 1976, pp. C1 and C3.

326. Excerpt from transcript of Carter remarks at Public Citizen Forum, Washington, D.C., Aug. 9, 1976, reprinted in Statement of Michael Pertschuk before the SEC "Re-examination of Corporate Governance" Hearings, Sept. 29, 1977.

327. Address of Harold Williams, Jan. 18, 1978, on file with the SEC.

328. Statement of Harold Williams before the Subcommittee on Securities of the Senate Banking Committee in connection with Hearings on S. 2567, Nov. 19, 1980, quoting pp. 2–3.

329. 1934 Securities Exchange Act Releases Nos. 13482 and 13901 (1977); Interview with Barbara Lucas, March 5, 1981, Washington, D.C., and Michael Klein and John Olson, "Harold Williams: Adieu to a First-Rate SEC Chairman," Legal Times of Washington, Feb. 16, 1981, pp. 13–17. After the hearings the SEC issued its 1980 "Staff Report on Corporate Accountability."

330. 1934 Securities Exchange Act Releases Nos. 15384 (1978) and 16356 (1979). See also SEC "Staff Report on Corporate Accountability," pp. 70–72.

331. SEC "Staff Report on Corporate Accountability," pp. 432–433 and 598.

332. Myles Mace, "Directors: Myth and Reality — Ten Years Later," 32 Rutgers Law Review, quoting p. 297 (1979).

333. See, e.g., John Carey, The Rise of the Accounting Profession: To Responsibility and Authority, 1937–1969 (New York: AICPA, 1970), pp. 56–95; Stephen Zeff, Forging Accounting Principles in Five Countries (Champaign, Ill.: Stipes Publishing Company, 1971), pp. 134–173; and Robert Chatov, Corporate Financial Reporting (New York: Free Press, 1975), pp. 133–231.

334. Described by Congressman John Moss in his testimony before "Accounting and Auditing Practices and Procedures" Hearings, Senate Governmental Affairs Subcommittee on Reports, Accounting and Management, 95th Cong., 1st Sess. (1977), p. 13.

335. Staff report of the Federal Trade Commission, "Economic Report on Corporate Mergers," printed in "Economic Concentration" Hearings, Senate Judiciary Subcommittee on Antitrust and Monopoly, 91st Cong., 1st Sess. (1969), part 8A, pp. 120–138; and "Investigation of Conglomerate Corporations," Staff Report of the House Judiciary Antitrust Subcommittee, 92nd Cong., 1st Sess. (1971), pp. 411–417. See, also, "The Accounting Establishment," Staff Study prepared by the Senate Government Operations Subcommittee on Reports, Accounting and Management, Senate Doc. No. 95–34, 95th Cong., 1st Sess. (1977) (hereinafter, "The Accounting Establishment"), p. 134.

336. Admiral Rickover testimony reprinted in "The Accounting Establishment," pp. 1711–1728, quoting pp. 1712–1713.

337. The most frequently cited commentaries included: Report of the AICPA Study on Establishment of Accounting Principles, *Establishing Financial Accounting Principles* (1972) (hereinafter, *The Wheat Report*); "Federal Regulation and Regulatory Reform," Report by the House Commerce Subcommittee on Oversight and Investigations, House Doc. No. 95–134, 95th Cong., 1st Sess. (1976) (hereinafter, House Commerce Subcommittee Report, "Federal Regulation and Regulatory Reform"), pp. 31–42; the Senate Governmental Operations Subcommittee staff study, "The Accounting Establishment"; "The Role of the American Accounting Association in the Developing of Accounting Principles," *Accounting Review*, July 1971, pp. 609–616; the books of Abraham Brilloff; Eisenberg, *The Structure of the Corporation*, pp. 186–211; Chatov, *Corporate Financial Reporting*, pp. 195–231; and Homer Kripke, "The SEC, the Accountants, Some Myths and Some Realities," 45 *New York University Law Review*, pp. 1175–1188 (1970).

338. Burton quoted in Chatov, *Corporate Financial Reporting*, p. 229.

339. *The Wheat Report*, pp. 39–43, quoting AICPA special report quoted in text at p. 40; House Commerce Subcommittee report, "Federal Regulation and Regulatory Reform," p. 32; and Eisenberg, *The Structure of the Corporation*, pp. 188–195.

340. A. A. Sommer, "Survey of Accounting Developments in the 60s; What's Ahead in the 70s," 26 *Business Lawyer* quoting p. 212 (1970); Charles Horngren quoted in Eisenberg, *The Structure of the Corporation*, p. 188; and Kripke, "The SEC, the Accountants . . ." 45 *New York University Law Review*, quoting p. 1186.

341. *The Wheat Report*, quoting, p. 61.

342. Ibid., p. 36; and Moonitz quoted in House Commerce Subcommittee Report, "Federal Regulation and Regulatory Reform," p. 32.

343. Kripke, "The SEC, the Accountants . . ." 45 *New York University Law Review*, p. 1187; Chatov, *Corporate Financial Reporting*, pp. 293–297; and Testimony of Max Backus, "Accounting and Auditing Practices and Procedures" Hearings, Senate Governmental Affairs Subcommittee on Reports, Accounting, and Management, 95th Cong., 1st Sess. (1977), pp. 1752–1754. *The Wheat Report*, pp. 22–24, explains why it rejected this recommendation.

344. *SEC Minutes*, Oct. 28, 1971; Memorandum to the Commission from the chief accountant, "Subject: AICPA Study Group [Wheat Committee] on Accounting Principles Public Hearing in New York City on Novem-

ber 3–4, 1971" Oct. 12, 1971 (with attachments), on file with the SEC Office of Chief Accountant; Interview with A. A. Sommer, March 2, 1981, Washington, D.C.; and Interview with John Burton, Feb. 13, 1981, New York City.

345. The Wheat Report, see especially pp. 2, 8–11, 43, and 83. The AICPA ethical rule noted in the text was adopted later in 1972, AICPA, Code of Professional Ethics, Rule 203. Critical views of the FASB appear in "The Accounting Establishment," pp. 130–172; and Chatov, *Corporate Financial Reporting*, pp. 232–249.

346. Letter to AICPA from the SEC, May 4, 1972, quoted in John Burton address, May 10–11, 1973, on file with the SEC. See also William Casey Address, May 19, 1972, on file with the SEC. The SEC's Accounting Series Release No. 150 later was unsuccessfully attacked in a lawsuit brought by Arthur Andersen & Company. See BNA *Securities Reporter*, No. 448, April 12, 1978, pp. D1–D2.

347. Addresses of William Casey, Oct. 2, 1972, on file with the SEC, and Jan. 4, 1973, quoted in Chatov, *Corporate Financial Reporting*, p. 257.

348. John Burton, "The SEC and Financial Reporting: The Sand in the Oyster," in A. Rashad Abdel-Khalik, ed., *Government Regulation of Accounting and Information* (University of Florida Accounting Series No. 11, 1980), quoting pp. 74–75; *Business Week*, Apr. 8, 1972, p. 21; Gary John Previts, "The SEC and Its Chief Accountants . . ." *Journal of Accountancy*, Aug. 1978, pp. 89–90; Interview with A. A. Sommer, March 2, 1981, Washington, D.C., and Address of Ray Garrett, Jan. 6, 1975, on file with the SEC.

349. Accounting Series Releases Nos. 130 (1972), 135 (1973), 146 (1973), and 146A (1974). See also Chatov, *Corporate Financial Reporting*, pp. 259–260.

350. Letter to Committee on Land Development Companies, AICPA, from John Burton, Nov. 10, 1972, reprinted in BNA *Securities Reporter*, No. 178, Nov. 22, 1972, p. E1; and BNA *Securities Reporter*, No. 184, Jan. 10, 1973, p. A14.

351. Interview with A. A. Sommer, March 2, 1981, Washington, D.C.; address of A. A. Sommer, March 17, 1976, on file with the SEC; and Remarks of A. A. Sommer, quoted in "Corporate Responsibility in the Financial Accounting and Disclosure Areas," 34 *Business Lawyer*, p. 2002 (1979).

352. House Commerce Subcommittee Report, "Federal Regulation and Regulatory Reform," pp. 32–33.

353. "The Accounting Establishment," p. 21. The staff's recommendation was not endorsed by the subcommittee. See "Improving the Accountability of Publicly Owned Corporations and Their Auditors," Senate Governmental Affairs Subcommittee on Reports, Accounting, and Management, 95th Cong., 1st Sess. (1977), p. 10.

354. SEC report, "The Accounting Profession and the Commission's Oversight Role" (1980), p. 55.

355. Accounting Series Release No. 177 (1975). See SEC "Report to Congress on the Accounting Profession and the Commission's Oversight Role," published as a Committee Print, Senate Committee on Governmental Affairs, Subcommittee on Governmental Efficiency and the District of Columbia, 95th Cong., 2nd Sess. (1978) (hereinafter, SEC 1978 Report on the Accounting Profession), pp. 275–276.

356. Accounting Series Release No. 165 (1974); 1933 Securities Act Release No. 5701 (1976); and SEC 1978 Report on the Accounting Profession, p. 277.

357. SEC 1978 Report on the Accounting Profession, pp. 282–284.

358. John Burton, "Elephants, Flexibility and the Financial Accounting Standards Board," 29 *Business Lawyer,* quoting p. 152 (1974). See also Homer Kripke, "The Myth of the Informed Layman," 28 *Business Lawyer,* p. 631 (1973); and Kripke, "The SEC, the Accountants . . ." 45 *New York University Law Review,* pp. 1164–1170.

359. For later related events, see 1933 Securities Act Release No. 5696 (1976); FASB Statement No. 33 (1979); and Accounting Series Release No. 271 (1979).

360. Accounting Series Release No. 166 (1974).

361. Harry Heller, "Disclosure Requirements Under Federal Securities Regulation," 16 *Business Lawyer,* quoting pp. 304 and 307 (1961); and "Report of the Advisory Committee on Corporate Disclosure to the SEC," published as House Committee Print No. 95–30, House Commerce Committee, 95th Cong., 1st Sess. (1977) (hereinafter, Sommer Advisory Committee Report), II, pp. A266–A273. The literature on this subject generally has ignored an important exception to the SEC's historic opposition to earnings forecasts, the SEC's use of its own earnings forecasts in approving Section 11(e) plans under the Public Utility Holding Company Act. See, e.g., *In the Matter of Niagara Hudson Power Corporation,* 29 *SEC* 773, 797–807 (1949).

362. Kripke, "The SEC, the Accountants . . ." 45 *New York University Law Review,* quoting pp. 1198–1199. On the extent of internal forecasting, see also *Fortune,* Jan. 1973, pp. 43–45.

363. For Casey's view of earnings forecasts see, e.g., Address of William Casey, May 19, 1972, on file with the SEC. See also Address of John Burton, Apr. 2, 1973, on file with the SEC; and 1933 Securities Act Release No. 5276 (1972), a rule proposed to require first-time securities issuers that had not conducted business operations for at least three years to publish "a budget of anticipated cash expenditures and resources."

364. 1933 Securities Act Release No. 5362 (1973).

365. 1933 Securities Act Release No. 6084 (1979). The long, tortuous process by which the SEC evolved this rule may be reconstructed from: 1933 Securities Act Release No. 5581 (1975); BNA *Securities Reporter,* No. 320, Sept. 24, 1975, pp. D1–D4; 1933 Securities Act Release No. 5699 (1976); Sommer Advisory Committee Report, II, pp. A276–A408, and I, pp. D14–D16 and 347–379; and 1933 Securities Act Releases Nos. 5992 and 5993 (1978). See also Item 11 of SEC Regulation S-K, requiring corporate management in 1933 and 1934 act filings to "describe any known trends or uncertainties . . . which the registrant reasonably expects will have a material favorable or unfavorable impact on net sales or revenues or income from continuing operations."

366. Sommer Advisory Committee Report, I, p. D16. Sommer characterized concern about liability as "the biggest headache" in an interview, March 2, 1981, Washington, D.C. *Beecher* v. *Able* (S.D.N.Y. 1974), 374 F. Supp. 341, and the general liability issue are analyzed in Ted Fiflis, "Soft Information: The SEC's Former Exogenous Zone," 26 *U.C.L.A. Law Review,* pp. 114–146 (1978).

367. A. A. Sommer, "Report of the Advisory Committee on Corporate Disclosure to the Securities and Exchange Commission: Foreword," 26 *U.C.L.A. Law Review*, pp. 54–55 (1978).

368. See, e.g., letter from Walter Kissinger, *New York Times*, July 19, 1981, p. F2.

369. See discussion in Sommer Advisory Committee Report, II, pp. A318–A320. See also the Conference Board, "Public Disclosure of Corporate Earnings Forecasts" (Report No. 804, 1981).

370. George Stigler, "Public Regulation of the Securities Markets," 37 *Journal of Business*, quoting p. 117 (1964).

371. Homer Kripke, *The SEC and Corporate Disclosure: Regulation in Search of a Purpose* (New York: Harcourt Brace Jovanovich, 1979), p. 21.

372. See additional examples in Russell Stevenson, "The SEC and the New Disclosure," 62 *Cornell Law Review*, p. 50 (1976).

373. See, e.g., Morris Mendelson, "Economics and the Assessment of Disclosure Requirements," 1 *Journal of Comparative Corporate Law and Securities Regulation*, pp. 58–59 (1978); Paul Gourrich, "Investment Banking Methods prior to and since the Securities Act of 1933," 4 *Law and Contemporary Problems*, p. 69 (1937); Loss, *Securities Regulation*, pp. 370–373; and Vincent Carosso, *Investment Banking in America* (Cambridge: Harvard University Press, 1970), pp. 395–396.

374. SEC, "Disclosure to Investors: A Reappraisal of Federal Administrative Policies Under the '33 and '34 Acts" (1969), p. 51.

375. See, e.g., summary of these officials' testimony in favor of the 1964 Securities Acts Amendments, Chap. 10.

376. Descriptions of the theory and the relevant studies appear in James Lorie and Mary Hamilton, *The Stock Market: Theories and Evidence* (Homewood, Ill.: Richard Irwin, 1973), pp. 70–110; William Beaver, *Financial Reporting: An Accounting Revolution* (Englewood Cliffs, N.J.: Prentice-Hall, 1981), pp. 142–180; and Kripke, *The SEC and Corporate Disclosure*, especially pp. 309–311.

377. See citations and discussion in Beaver, *Financial Reporting*, pp. 22–39; Kripke, *The SEC and Corporate Disclosure*, pp. 88–95; and Lorie and Hamilton, *The Stock Market*, pp. 171–197.

378. Stigler, "Public Regulation of the Securities Markets," 37 *Journal of Business*, pp. 120–124; Mendelson, "Economics and the Assessment of Disclosure Requirements," 1 *Journal of Comparative Corporate Law and Securities Regulation*, quoting p. 57; and Irwin Friend and Edward Herman, "The SEC Through a Glass Darkly," 37 *Journal of Business*, p. 382 (1964).

379. George Benston, "Required Disclosure and the Stock Market: An Evaluation of the Securities Exchange Act of 1934," 63 *American Economic Review*, p. 132 (1973).

380. See Irwin Friend and Randolph Westerfield, "Required Disclosure and the Stock Market," 65 *American Economic Review*, p. 467 (1975); and citations in Beaver, *Financial Reporting*, pp. 197–200.

381. See discussion and citations in Chap. 1 and Chap. 2.

382. Sommer Advisory Committee Report, I, pp. 1–3 and I–XLIX, quoting pp. 2, II, XVIII–XIX, XXVIII, XXI–XXII, XLV, and XXXIII–XXXIV.

383. Ibid., pp. D49–D56, quoting p. D50.

384. Ibid., pp. 511–523.

Index